THE POLITICS OF DECOLONIAL INVESTIGATIONS

ON DECOLONIALITY a series edited by
Walter D. Mignolo and Catherine E. Walsh

On Decoloniality interconnects a diverse array of perspectives from the lived experiences of coloniality and decolonial thought/praxis in different local histories from across the globe. The series is concerned with coloniality's global logic and scope and with the myriad of decolonial responses and engagements that contest coloniality/modernity's totalizing violences, claims, and frame, opening toward an otherwise of being, thinking, sensing, knowing, and living; that is, of re-existences and worlds-making. Aimed at a broad audience, from scholars, students, and artists to journalists, activists, and socially engaged intellectuals, On Decoloniality invites a wide range of participants to join one of the fastest-growing debates in the humanities and social sciences that attends to the lived concerns of dignity, life, and the survival of the planet.

WALTER D. MIGNOLO

THE POLITICS OF DECOLONIAL INVESTIGATIONS

DUKE UNIVERSITY PRESS   DURHAM AND LONDON   2021

Printed in the United States of America on acid-free paper ∞
Designed by Aimee C. Harrison
Typeset in Portrait Text Regular and ITC Avant Garde Gothic by
Westchester Publishing Services

Library of Congress Cataloging-in-Publication Data
Names: Mignolo, Walter, author.
Title: The politics of decolonial investigations / Walter D. Mignolo.
Description: Durham : Duke University Press, 2021. | Series:
On decoloniality | Includes bibliographical references and index. |
Identifiers: LCCN 2020042286 (print)
LCCN 2020042287 (ebook)
ISBN 9781478001140 (hardcover)
ISBN 9781478002574 (ebook)
ISBN 9781478001492 (paperback)
Subjects: LCSH: Decolonization. | Postcolonialism. | Racism—Political
aspects. | Knowledge, Theory of—Political aspects. | Civilization,
Western. | Civilization, Modern.
Classification: LCC JV51 (ebook) | LCC JV51 .M5445 2021 (print) |
DDC 325/.3—dc23
LC record available at https://lccn.loc.gov/ 2020042286

Cover art: Zorikto Dorzhiev, *Sea*, 2009. Oil on canvas,
80 cm × 135 cm. Courtesy of Khankhalaev Gallery.

To the memory of Nieves y Mingo,

mi madre y mi padre,

who moved from the countryside to a nearby small town, Corral de Bustos, when I was seven,

so I could go to school.

Contents

Part IV Geopolitics of Knowing, the Question of the Human,
and the Third Nomos of the Earth

Preface

I

The manuscript for this book was forwarded to Duke University Press in March of 2020. The pandemic was reaching the US. Europe was reporting alarming statistics, while China, South Korea, and Taiwan were reporting their successful management of the events, whether unavoidable, carelessly managed, or planned (and by whom?). I received the copyedited manuscript at the beginning of October 2020. The US had been reporting alarming statistics for several months: infections, deaths, unemployment. Congress and the Federal Reserve took action with a broad array of programs to limit the economic damage from the pandemic, including lending trillions of dollars to support households, employers, financial markets, and state and local governments. The statistics around the planet were disconcerting. Under the circumstances, in reading a manuscript that was finished before the shock—whatever the causes, the reasons, and the origination—something arose in my consciousness that has been in my thoughts for a while: that we, on the planet, are experiencing a change of era, and no longer an epoch of changes. I couldn't at that point do too much with the manuscript, other than acknowledging that the cycle of Westernization of the planet was decisively over. The agony will last for a few decades, and it will not be pretty. Multipolarity in the interstate system is displacing unipolar Westernization; pluriversality is displacing the Western universality of knowing and sensing. This is the main argument of the book. It remains valid to me. The pandemic only accelerated a process that is irreversible and provided more evidence that the long-lasting consequences of coloniality are no longer hidden under the rhetoric of modernity, development, progress, growth, "more is better," and "bigger is virtuous."

The era that is closing I have dated 1500–2000. It is the era of Westernization of the planet, political and economic unilaterality, and epistemic and aesthetic universality. It is exploding, and out of the debris three trajectories are defining the change of era: de-Westernization and decoloniality provoked the counterreformation, that is, re-Westernization. The change of era invades and, like a whirlwind, eats into domestic and interstate politics and economics, with cultural corollaries across the board in the spheres of knowing and sensing: from research and teaching institutions (e.g., universities and museums) to the philosophical thinking that emerges from the trenches of everyday life-forming manifested in people's organizing to stop extractivism, agrobusiness, state abuses, uses and misuses of the pandemic, etc. The change of era is the overall frame of the book that I render in chapter 14 as the third nomos of the Earth. The sense of the change of epoch or era "floats," so to speak, over the other chapters. Hence, the book floats in the borderlands of the closing era of changes and the opening change of era.

This book is published by a university press. It is a scholarly book. Decolonial critical minds fear that the decolonial is surrendering to academia. Some critics even consider that Duke University is not a proper place to make decolonial claims. I respect those critics. Everyone is entitled to her or his own opinion. I am not apologizing for it. Being able to interact with undergraduate and graduate students around these ideas at Duke—but also in many universities and museums in the US, Latin America, western Europe, South Africa, Taiwan, China, and Hong Kong—is not something that shall be rejected. Many others are like me. Universities and museums, think tanks composed by actors who have been through the university, and millions of people in the world, yesterday and today, have been through state and private pedagogical institutions, from primary school to graduate and professional schools. There is strong opposition in both universities and museums to thinking decolonially; it is also olympically ignored in the mass media.

An increasing number of professionals today (in law, medicine, engineering, design, computing) are becoming aware of the *coloniality of knowledge and sensing*, realizing how it has affected epistemology (the principles and assumptions that regulate knowing) and aesthetics (the principles and assumptions that regulate taste and subjectivity) over the past five hundred years. From 1500 to 1800, Christian theology (Catholic and Protestant) regulated both knowing and sensing. From 1800 to 2000, epistemology and aesthetics mutated into secular management, although theology never went away. The year 1800 could be taken as the year of the first drastic intramural overturning of the modern/colonial era. Theology and hegemony and dominance split into three secular trajectories: conservatism (e.g., the secularization of theological beliefs), liberalism (the bourgeois system of ideas regulating politics, economy, epistemology, and aesthetics), and socialism/communism (e.g., the dissenting trajectory emerging from the theological wreckages). These three trajectories remained, with modulations. Since 1970, there has been an "evolutionary drift": neoliberalism and globalism emerged out of liberalism, but liberalism persisted; conservatism mutated into fundamentalist nationalism (e.g., the alt-right, neofascism); and socialism/communism has had to be reconsidered after the collapse of the Soviet Union and the mutations of China after Mao Zedong.

This is a brief scheme of the constitution and closing of the era of changes (e.g., the formation of Western civilization and the Westernization of the planet). De-Westernization and decoloniality cannot ignore Westernization, but they do not have to obey it anymore. And both trajectories are founded on disobedience and delinking. The change of era can no longer be captured by adding the prefix "post-." The post- prefix is valid within re-Westernization, the counterreformation that intends to maintain the privileges built over five hundred years of Westernization, but it is meaningless for de-Westernization and decoloniality. The prefix "de-" takes the field, breaking up Western universality and totality into multiple temporalities, knowledges, and praxes of living. Neither trajectory has precedence within the era of changes (1500–1800). But because Westernization cannot be ignored, not having precedence doesn't mean that both trajectories start *ab ovo*. The de- prefix means that you disobey and delink from a belief in unipolarity and universality; you take what you need to restitute that which has been destituted and that is relevant to the arising of *multipolarity* in the interstate relations and *pluriversality*. Multipolarity is the goal of de-Westernization in the interstate system and the global order; pluriversality in the spheres of knowing, sensing, understanding, believing, and being in the world is the goal of decoloniality in the hands of the emerging global political society.[1] Decoloniality is not a state-led task; it cannot be. The nation-state and the capitalist economy are today entrenched all over the planet. De-Westernization, however, can only be advanced by a strong state that is economically and financially solid. That is why China is leading the way in this trajectory. The current tendencies in China, Russia, India, and Turkey to mutate the nation-state into the civilization-state are revealing signs of restituting what has been destituted. I am not saying that civilization-states will be "better" than nation-states. I am just saying that most likely they will be.

As in my previous books, my love of jazz improvisations and blues movements guides the prose and the argument. There is a set of concepts that shepherds the melody. To start with the concepts in the title, politics and decolonial investigations: gnoseological and aesthesic *reconstitutions* confront head on the epistemic and aesthetic *constitutions/destitutions*, not to replace or supersede them but to reduce both of them to their own regional and deserved sphere.[2] The reader is advised to uncouple *aesthesis* from *aesthetics*. While aesthetics has been circumscribed to the sphere of fine arts, and also transposed to refer to other areas of experience involving "taste" (e.g., having good taste in food, wine, clothes, cars, furniture, etc.) and "beauty" (e.g., aesthetic surgery, fashion design, an attractive—as in pleasing to the senses—woman or a handsome man), I use "aesthesis" in its original meaning to refer to sensing and emotioning and, therefore, inseparable from knowing and believing. Epistemology and aesthetics are two key concepts of the rhetoric of modernity separated from each other: the first refers to knowledge and the second to taste and beauty. I am shifting that relationship in this book. Aesthesis is in all and everything we do, including, of course, living and thinking. The triad constitution/destitution/reconstitution ran parallel to modernity/coloniality/decoloniality and to domination/exploitation/conflict, the latter singling out the triple energy that holds together the colonial matrix of power, or CMP (see introduction, section III), and provokes the making of and the responses to colonial and imperial differences. In their turn, colonial and imperial differences created the conditions of border dwelling and border thinking—briefly, of being in the world, which I highlight with the work of Gloria Anzaldúa (see introduction, section III.3.6). To weave and make these concepts work to reveal, on the one hand, the *hidden underlying history* of the CMP and, on the other, the events, discourses, dates, names, images, maps, etc., in the *visible surface of thematic histories* requires a certain freedom to let the argument flow with the movements of the CMP and the gnoseological and aesthesic reconstitutions of the destituted. The flow and freedom of movement of improvisation in jazz and blues provide liberating energies to delink from the linearity of English composition. Besides, I came of intellectual age in the 1960s reading the great Argentine and Latin American essayists who were thinking and writing before the social sciences' regulations of thinking were introduced with the packaging and the promises of development and modernization.

II

The Politics of Decolonial Investigations continues the archeology of Western civilization that I began with *The Darker Side of the Renaissance: Literacy, Territoriality, and Colonization* (1995). Two archeological sites are the European Renaissance (fourteenth to seventeenth centuries) and the *colonial revolution*, better known as the discovery and colonization of the New World.[3] The two archeological sites of Western civilization are only one of the three Greek branches. One branch spread to the caliphate of Damascus and Baghdad; a second branch spread to Orthodox Christianity, which reached Moscow and the Slavic area; and the third one nourished Muslim philosophers from Central Asia (Ibn Sina), Western Asia (Al-Ghazali), and Maghreb (Ibn Rushd). Civilizations come out of narrative interpretations of signs of the past taken for historical facts that already carried the tag of their meaning in the present. "Western civilization" was not a tag pegged to thoughts and deeds in ancient Greece and Rome. Greece and Rome became the fountains of Western civilization during the European Renaissance at the intersection of Western Christianity after the Crusades and the loss of Jerusalem. The conquest and colonization of the New World (the colonial revolution) emboldened Western Christian theologians, men of letters and monarchs in the Iberian Peninsula and Italy, to rebuild themselves after their defeat in the Crusades.

The excavation I venture is within neither epistemic territory (existing knowledges and ways of knowing) nor aesthetic territory (regulation of taste, evaluation of genius, and ranking of human activities), but the destituted exteriorities (see introduction, section III.2) in the name of constituting (introduction, section III.1) and promoting Western civilization. Exteriorities are not ontic outsides but locations created in the constitution of the inside. What is ontic outside is out of reach and control, but exteriority is invented to be able to control and manage the destituted. Racism and sexism are two spheres that affect all of us on the planet, actors and institutions that defend the constituted and actors and institutions that are the targets of destitutions. Today the US sanctions in all directions are sanctions projected to the exteriority to secure the constitution of Western civilization. If China, Russia, and Iran were ontically outside Western civilization, sanctions would be a moot point. They are not outside but in exteriority. This is the work of the imperial differential. If Black people and transsexuals were ontically outside, there would be no problem. But people thus labeled are placed in exteriority and subjected to domination. This is the work of the colonial differential. Not only countries and regions (underdeveloped, Third World, emergent) are destituted to the exteriority, but people as well. Racism and sexism are the energies moving the destitutions of people to maintain the privileges of whiteness and heteronormativity. Racism and sexism are problems of whiteness and heteronormativity although they appear to be problems of people of color and transsexuality.[4] However, countries and people destituted to the exteriority of the system never quietly accepted the unilateral decisions of actors and institutions self-endowed with the privileges to destitute. *The Politics of Decolonial Investigations* walks on the paths already opened by the many in the Americas, Africa, Asia, former Eastern Europe, and southern Europe whose thoughts and deeds were propelled by the dignified anger engendered by all levels of destitutions.

III

The original idea for this book came from Francisco Carballo of Goldsmiths, University of London. The story goes like this: Francisco and Luis Alfonso Herrera Robles from the Universidad Autónoma de Ciudad Juárez, Ciencias Sociales, in Mexico, coedited a book (*Habitar la frontera: Sentir y pensar la descolonialidad, Antología: 1999–2014*, 2015) collecting several of my articles in Spanish into a volume published by CIDOB (Barcelona Centre for International Affairs). Shortly after the three of us met in Barcelona for the book's presentation, Francisco suggested a similar volume with articles published in English. We met in Lisbon in April of 2015 and worked on a preliminary list of articles, outlining a rationale. Francisco would write the introduction while I revised the articles, providing short descriptions of when, where, and why the article was published, similar to what we did for the book published by CIDOB. We completed the job and submitted the manuscript to Duke University Press as a proposal to external evaluators. The proposal received positive reviews, but unfortunately Francisco ran into personal problems, preventing him from completing the planned introduction. The Duke University Press editor recommended that I go ahead with the book without the introduction.

When I reread all the articles to outline the rationale for the collection, I came to realize that the articles written between 2000 and 2019 were intermingled with the publication of the following works: *Local Histories/Global Designs: Coloniality, Subaltern Knowledges, and Border Thinking* (2000), reprinted with a new preface in 2012; the afterword written in 2003 for the second edition of *The Darker Side of the Renaissance: Literacy, Territoriality, and Colonization* (1995); the publication of both *The Darker Side of Western Modernity: Global Futures, Decolonial Options* (2011) and *The Idea of Latin America* (2005); and, last but not least, the publication in 2007 of a long essay, "Delinking: The Rhetoric of Modernity, the Logic of Coloniality and the Grammar of De-coloniality," which was rewritten in Spanish and translated into German, Swedish, Rumanian, and French. The fact that it was translated into several languages is due, in my understanding, to the essay's personal summary of the school of thought already recognized by the decolonial compound "modernity/coloniality/decoloniality."[5] These basic assumptions of the decolonial school of thought—that there is no modernity without coloniality and that they both provoked decoloniality—sprang from Aníbal Quijano's seminal article, "Coloniality and Modernity/Rationality."[6]

The title of this book, *The Politics of Decolonial Investigations*, has its reason. I intentionally avoided "research," which in the humanities is a term borrowed from the hard sciences. The *Cambridge Dictionary* offers this general definition: "a detailed *study of a subject, especially in order to discover (new) information or reach a (new) understanding*" (emphasis added). The examples following the definition are extracted from the hard sciences. The humanities have recently also borrowed "lab" from the hard sciences. I surmise that borrowing terms from the hard sciences makes the humanist feel more serious or rigorous, perhaps even scientific (see chapter 14), while at the same time surrendering to the hegemonic coloniality of scientific knowledge. I disagree. By reconstituting "research" into "investigation" (and taking the first step into gnoseological and aesthesic reconstitutions), I am restituting a term in the family of the humanities destituted by the clout of scientific "research." Edmund Husserl titled his work on logic *Logical Investigations* (1900). Ludwig Wittgenstein titled his own *Philosophical Investigations* (1953). If we search for "Sherlock Holmes" on the web, we will find many entries relating Sherlock Holmes to "investigations." Holmes's investigations are neither academic nor scholarly nor scientific. Investigations are needed when a problem has to be solved or a question to be addressed. His strategies have impacted many fields beyond the academy. Here is an example from an organization called the Nonprofit Risk Management Center:

> Recently, many of our clients have focused on increasing their readiness to respond to and manage employee complaints, workplace *investigations*, and employment practices liability (EPL) claims. . . .
>
> While Sherlock Holmes may not be an inspiration for proper workplace etiquette in the 21st Century, his techniques may be useful as you reflect on how your entity manages workplace *investigations*. Keep in mind that conducting effective and ethical *investigations* of workplace issues and employee complaints could reduce your organization's exposure to EPLI claims.[7] (Emphasis added.)

The Politics of Decolonial Investigations takes from Sherlock Holmes his passion to "reveal the mystery" beyond academic strictures. The mystery that decolonial investigations seek to reveal is the foundation, transformation, management, and control of the colonial matrix of power (CMP), from its foundations in the sixteenth century to artificial intelligence in the twenty-first. This matrix has been fueled and run by "coloniality of power," the will to control and dominate, embedded in the politics of Eurocentric knowing. Decolonial investigations are fueled instead by the will to "reveal the mystery of the CMP," disobeying epistemic and aesthetic dictates by taking on gnoseological and aesthetic reconstitutions (see introduction, section III).

In the preface to *The Darker Side of Western Modernity*, I wrote that the book came to be the third volume of a trilogy that was not planned as such. The first part was *The Darker Side of the Renaissance* and the second was *Local Histories/Global Designs*. I realized that the articles that Francisco and I had selected began to look like the fourth volume of a tetralogy as they showed the backstory of the trilogy. I made some adjustments, replacing some of the original articles and adding a few. At the end of the day, the title *Decolonial Investigations* sounded the most appropriate, for literally that is what the articles originally were: decolonial investigations in the framework of modernity/coloniality which at once enacted decolonial thinking in search of decolonial praxes of living.[8]

What all of this means, and what becomes more transparent in chapters 11 to 14 and the epilogue, is that the constitution and hegemony of Western knowledge, along with its regulations of knowing, which together imply the regulation of subjectivity, shall all be questioned for their assumptions (the enunciation) rather than their content. Consequently, to reconstitute knowing and sensing requires starting from non-Western genealogies of thoughts or from Western concepts sidelined by the rhetoric of modernity, like gnosis and aesthesis. To put it more bluntly: reconstitution demands a departure, delinking from Western cosmology, in its theological and secular foundations, in which all knowledges—including scientific ones—are embedded. The shift is accomplished by moving toward non-Western cosmologies, the foundations of their praxes of living and sensing that have been and continue to be destituted by Western cosmology with its epistemic and aesthetic weapons.[9] And by digging into the basement of Western cosmology to recover destituted concepts and histories, as was the case with gnosis and aesthesis (I come back to gnosis in the introduction). In this volume, aesthesis is unpegged from aesthetics in two ways: it refers to (a) the realm of the senses, beliefs, and emotioning, where "art" is one aesthesic sphere, and (b) sensing underlying science, mathematics, philosophy, and theology since the actors are human beings and the rationality of their arguments cannot be detached from the subjectivity that animates what they are doing. However, in these spheres of knowing and understanding, the aesthesic dimension was destituted and silenced by the privilege of the rational and the epistemic.[10] Quijano synthesized this situation in the title of his foundational article, "Coloniality and Modernity/Rationality."

Consequently, the volume that the reader has in her hands is no longer a collection of published articles but a new volume all its own. Every original article has been drastically revised and rewritten while maintaining its original idea and the main thrust of its argument, which required further investigations on the topic of each chapter. *The Politics of Decolonial Investigations* is divided into four parts, including an introduction and an epilogue. And it goes like this: the introduction is the most recently written piece, and it came about after all the previous considerations. In it I revisit basic concepts of the schools of thought identified as modernity/coloniality/decoloniality, and I outline the history, the structure, the levels, and the flows of the CMP. I also revisit my own previously introduced concepts, such as colonial/imperial differences, border thinking, and epistemic/aesthesic reconstitution—all of which provide an overall *analytics* of the CMP's contents (the said, the enunciated) for chapters 1 to 10. Chapters 11 to 14 and the epilogue tackle *terms* (the saying, the enunciation) and work on paths for decolonial reconstitutions.[11]

Part I, "Geopolitics, Social Classification, and Border Thinking," explores diverse ramifications of race/racism, starting from Quijano's distinction between social classification and social class, the making of racism as a foundational concept of modernity/coloniality. Racism is a problem created by the classifier; it is not a problem created by the classified. Hence, race is an epistemological, not an ontic, question. That means there is no "race'" in the world beyond the "concept of race": race is a concept that serves to classify human beings according to preselected features: blood, skin color, religion, nationality, language, primitive/civilized, economic world ranking (developed/underdeveloped), etc. The concept of race is a classification upon which racism was construed. I explore this point in chapter 1. In chapter 2, I turn to how race and racism work in the constitution of the CMP, from the sixteenth century to today. Foregrounding the classifiers that established complicities between Islamophobia and Hispanophobia, I argue that race/racism was a determinant in the constitution of the CMP and its power for destitution. In chapter 3 I look at the economic and political consequences of racism, connecting the African slave trade in the colonial foundation of modernity to the Holocaust in the first half of the twentieth century. I argue that the modern/colonial slave

trade operated by doubly subjective transformations. Slave traders and plantation owners assigned to themselves the privileges of taken human beings as a
commodity (and for that, racism was a useful concept). In turn, the enslaved
persons lost their dignity and self-esteem. Enslaved persons were, for traders
and plantation owners, commodities and, therefore, dispensable or disposable.
Five hundred years later, the Holocaust introduced the political dimension of
disposability: bare lives. Bare lives were not commodities but persons whose
legal rights had been disposed. State politics took the place of slave traders and
plantation owners. At the end of the twentieth century and in the first decades
of the twenty-first, economic and political dispensability of human life worked
together in the bodies and lives of immigrants and refugees in Europe and
the United States. Colonialism ended but coloniality has persisted. The last
chapter of part I tackles the race question in the historical foundation of the
nation-state in nineteenth-century Europe and its impact in the concurrent
foundation of Zionism in the creation of the nation-state of Israel. The common element of all nation-states' form of governance is a care for the nation
more than for human beings. These four chapters are connected through the
geopolitical scope of racial classification, the colonial difference that sustains
racial classification, and border thinking as decolonial perspectives of racism,
geopolitics, and social classification.

Part II, "Cosmopolitanism, Decoloniality, and Rights," is connected with
part I by the following question: who speaks for the human in human rights?
I have explored this question in an article published elsewhere.[12] The basic
presupposition, outlined in part I, is that race and racism are—as I just said—
epistemic, not ontic, matters. Or, if you wish, they are ontological matters that
cannot be dealt with empirically. Which means that race and racism came
about from epistemic classifications of the ontic signs (like blood or skin color).
Consequently, those who control knowledge have the privilege of projecting
an institutional image of the "real" that hides that the real is an epistemic
projection. Chapter 5 explores the difficulties and restrictions that cosmopolitanism has to overcome racial dehumanization and racial discrimination as
well as dehumanization embedded in the concept of human rights, an issue I
explore in more detail in chapter 12. Chapter 6, "Cosmopolitanism and the Decolonial Option," connects with the issue of globalism/globalization explored
in chapter 5 and with the problem of the nation-state explored in chapter 4. In
chapter 6 I investigate the vogue of cosmopolitanism in North Atlantic scholarship that succeeds the decades of the vogue of exploring nationalism in the
1980s. The question raised in chapter 5 is that the cosmopolitan trend in philosophy runs parallel with the trend of globalization in the social sciences. In

chapter 7, I come back and expand on the question of rights explored in chapter 5 and argue that, seen from the experience, history, and perspective of the former Third World, the demands for "living" rights extend beyond "human" ones to the rights of our Earth since life—decolonially speaking—cannot be detached from the limited and restricted sphere of human life.

Part III returns to the geopolitical question focusing on the formation and transformation of the modern/colonial world order from 1500 to 2000, approximately, or for the period of Westernization of the planet. This is the era of the second nomos of the Earth and the epoch of changes when "newness" and "post-" are key markers. In chapter 8, I argue that around 2000 the signs of a shift from the Western to the Eastern Hemisphere were noticeable, and 9/11 was a signpost that legitimized the counterrevolution I call re-Westernization, motivated by the closing of the cycle of Westernization (1500–2000)—initiated with the colonial revolution in the sixteenth century—and the imperative to contain de-Westernization, with China, Russia, and the other BRICS leading the way at the time. However, after the weakening of BRICS following the judicial coup in Brazil and the election of Jair Bolsonaro as president, de-Westernization had three pillars in the CRI (China, Russia, and Iran) and a monumental mover, the BRI (Belt and Road Initiative). I continue this discussion in chapter 9 in a conversation with Christopher Mattison, who at the time of the conversation was assistant director of the Advanced Study Institute of the University of Hong Kong, where I was a research fellow for a semester. I mention these details because the conversation was conducted during the first semester (January–June) of 2012 in the *living* experience and *atmosphere* of East Asia and the spirit of rebalancing the change of hands in Hong Kong in 1997. I traveled to Beijing, Shanghai, and Singapore during the semester, and the sense of de-Westernization became palpable to me (I sensed it; it was something different rather than reaching a rational conclusion over statistics and diagrams). I sensed that the state-led Bandung Conference of 1955 had two outcomes: one toward the South with the creation of the Non-Aligned Movement, and the other to the North, toward Singapore, China, and the Asian Tigers. In chapter 10, I tackle the coming into being of the expression "Global South" as successor of "Third World," after the collapse of the Soviet Union, when the expression "Third World" lost its meaning once the Second World didn't exist anymore. This exploration connects with the issues of classification explored in part I. While in part I classifications refers to bodies, in part III it refers to regions. Race and racism conjoin the classification and ranking of bodies with the geopolitical classifications of the regions the bodies inhabit. Geo- and biopolitical classifications complement each other, for it is assumed that underdeveloped regions of the planet (a geopolitical classification) are inhabited by people of color who speak non-European languages and embrace belief systems other than Christianity; and therefore men, women, and trans/nonbinary people in these regions are ranked below their equivalents in the First World, Global North, and Global West.[13]

Part IV focuses on the geopolitics of gnoseological and aesthesic reconstitutions by exploring in some detail the works and thoughts of José Carlos Mariátegui in the South American Andes and Antonio Gramsci in the South of Europe. The parallel, not the comparison of their lives and thoughts (in the sense that their thinking was entangled with their praxes of living), allows for a better understanding of knowing, thinking, and believing emerging from their geo-body locations, explored in parts I and III, in the colonial matrix of power. Focusing on Sylvia Wynter, chapter 12 examines the meaning of being human: when and for whom. When an Afro-Caribbean woman from the Third Word (or the Global South, if you prefer) asks, "What does it mean to be human," the answers would most likely not be the same as the answer given by a white man from the First World (or the Global North, if you prefer). The answer is no longer a question of an abstract universal definition of "the human," but is affected by the geo-body political location of the answer to an abstract concept created by white males of the North. Hence, gnoseological and aesthesic reconstitutions are of the essence. Wynter's questions and answers allow us to reframe the coexisting perspectives on the posthuman and the inhuman in continental philosophy and North Atlantic cultural studies.[14] Shifting the geography of reasoning toward the gnoseological and the aesthesic relocates the answers to the questions that are taken up from the perspective of the destituted who are supposed to not be properly human.

In chapter 13 I push gnoseological and aesthesic reconstitutions further, exploring the geo-body politics of knowing, sensing, and believing introduced in chapter 11. This time the parallel is between Aníbal Quijano, a thinker from the South American Andes who anchored a particular school of decolonial thought (which has permeated my work since 1995 and the decolonial investigation in this book) and for whom Mariátegui was a political and intellectual ancestor, and Edmund Gustav Albrecht Husserl, a German philosopher who established the school of phenomenology. Gnoseological and aesthesic reconstitutions are here a means to redress the hierarchies by epistemic and aesthetic relevance. The geopolitics of meaning and the geopolitics of money complement each other in the simultaneous movement, the constitution/destitution, of the colonial matrix of power. Those hierarchies worked well in an era of Westernization, the second nomos of the Earth, and the era of changes that come to light in chapter 14. In this chapter I devote my attention to the advent of the third nomos of the Earth, to the politics of decolonial investigations, and to the meaning of gnoseological and aesthesic reconstitutions.

Finally, the epilogue. The epilogue is a continuation of the investigations reported in chapter 14, but in a more personal way. It is a more personal account of why the politics of decolonial investigations is necessary to shake off five centuries of modern/colonial epistemic and aesthetic regulations. It is also a complement to chapter 13 in the intent to redress five hundred years of epistemic and aesthetic regulations and enforced abstract universals. And it is a follow-up to a previous argument on epistemic disobedience, independent thought, and decolonial freedom.

The final steps in the preparation of this manuscript coincided with the beginning of the COVID-19 pandemic. The sense of an ending was for me doubled: the closing of a long and consuming project of writing and editing and the beginning of what revives the sense of an ending. The meaning of "apocalypse," as Moulay Driss El Maarouf, Taieb Belghazi, and Farouk El Maarouf remind us, has been inscribed in different ways (movies, TV series, books) in the popular consciousness by mass media of all kinds, as the final catastrophe (like the one announced in 2012 following the misinterpreted Mayans' prophecy): a catastrophe of such dimensions that it leaves no one to tell the story. However, the authors rescue the Greek meaning of the word *apokalyptein*: "uncovering, disclosure and revelation."[15] In that sense, Francis Fukuyama's infamous sentence could be proven right: we on the planet may be experiencing "the end of history"—the end of a history that fabricated the ontology of the present, the slow disintegration of the CMP; the end of an era, the era of Westernization and of the second nomos of the earth. The advent of the third nomos is not, however, a *transition* as if there were only one line to transit from A to B. That is the logic of the second nomos. The third nomos is not a transition but an *explosion*: the universal does not transit but explodes into the pluriversal; the unipolar doesn't transit but explodes into the multipolar. That is the mark of the change of era and of the advent of the third nomos of the earth. By rescuing the forgotten and destituted meaning of *apokalyptein*, El Maarouf, Belghazi, and El Maarouf have indeed performed a singular work of gnoseological and aesthesic reconstitution.

The politics of decolonial investigations is indivisible from gnoseological and aesthesic reconstitutions. These ideas are, in the last analysis, the main thrust of this book.

Acknowledgments

My first and foremost gratitude and my greatest debt is to Aníbal Quijano (1930–2018). Our interaction and collaboration during the early years of the formation of my thoughts—which unfolded via personal conversations and email exchanges starting in 1996 and in conversation with friends of the collective modernity/coloniality—have radically changed the orientation of my thinking, my sensing and emotioning, my research, and my own praxis of living. Many of those conversations were interspersed with several of the articles that became chapters of this book, which is in constant dialogue with his ideas, proposals, wisdom, intellectual honesty, and political commitment.

Specific thanks to Francisco Carballo, who, as I mentioned in the preface, put this project in motion.

I am indebted to all my coeditors, and to all the publishing houses and scholarly journals where these articles were originally published and where they became preliminary versions of this book's chapters. None of the previously published essays remain in their original form. They were rewritten to fit the main thrust of the book: the politics of decolonial investigations and gnoseological and aesthesic reconstitutions. Most of the original titles were modified. Others remain the same.

Chapter 1, "Racism as We Sense It Today," was originally published in "Comparative Racialization," special issue: *PMLA* 123, no. 5 (October 2008). It was revised in light of a volume on the same topic published the year before: Margaret R. Greer, Walter D. Mignolo, and Maureen Quilligan, eds., *Rereading the Black Legend: The*

Discourses of Religious and Racial Difference in the Renaissance Empires (Chicago: University of Chicago Press, 2007), and rewritten for this volume.

Chapter 2, "Islamophobia/Hispanophobia," and chapter 3, "Dispensable and Bare Lives," were originally published in *Human Architecture: Journal of the Sociology of Self-Knowledge*, the former in vol. 5, no. 1 (2006), and the latter in vol. 7, no. 2 (2009). Mohammad H. Tamdgidi is the journal editor.

Chapter 4, "Decolonizing the Nation-State," was first published in *Deconstructing Zionism: A Critique of Political Metaphysics*, ed. Gianni Vattimo and Michael Marder (London: Bloomsbury Academic, 2013).

Chapter 5, "The Many Faces of Cosmo-polis," was published in *Public Culture* 12, no. 3 (2000). It was rewritten in light of "Cosmopolitan Localism: Overcoming Colonial and Imperial Differences," chapter 7 of *The Darker Side of Western Modernity: Global Futures, Decolonial Options* (Durham, NC: Duke University Press, 2011).

Chapter 6, "Cosmopolitanism and the Decolonial Option," was published in *Studies in Philosophy and Education* 29 (2010). I eliminated the hyphen in "de-colonial" from the original title. It felt necessary back then.

Chapter 7, "From 'Human' to 'Living' Rights," was originally published in *The Meaning of Rights: The Philosophy of Social Theory of Human Rights*, ed. Costas Douzimas and Conor Gearty (Cambridge, UK: Cambridge University Press, 2014). I replaced "Life" with "Living." It is a sequel to "Who Speaks for the 'Human' in Human Rights?," reprinted in Walter D. Mignolo and Madina V. Tlostanova, *Learning to Unlearn: Decolonial Reflections from Eurasia and the Americas* (Columbus: Ohio State University Press, 2012).

Chapter 8, "Decolonial Reflections on Hemispheric Partitions," was published in FIAR: *Forum for Inter-American Research* 7, no. 3 (2014).

Chapter 9, "Delinking, Decoloniality, and De-Westernization," was originally published in HKAICS (Hong Kong Advanced Institute for Cross-Disciplinary Studies) when both Chris Mattison and I were visiting fellows during the first semester of 2012. It was reprinted in *Critical Legal Studies: Law and the Political* (May 2012).

Chapter 10, "The South of the North and the West of the East," was originally published in *Ibraaz: Contemporary Visual Culture in North Africa and the Middle East* (November 2014). I modified the title.

Chapter 11, "Mariátegui and Gramsci in 'Latin' America," was published in *The Postcolonial Gramsci*, ed. Neelam Srivastava and Baidik Bhattacharya (New York: Routledge, 2012). It originally had the subtitle "Between Revolution and Decoloniality."

Chapter 12, "Sylvia Wynter: What Does It Mean to Be Human?," was published in *Sylvia Wynter: On Being Human as a Praxis*, ed. Katherine McKittrick (Durham, NC: Duke University Press, 2015).

Chapter 13, "Decoloniality and Phenomenology: The Geopolitics of Knowing and Epistemic/Ontological Colonial Differences," was published in the *Journal of Speculative Philosophy* 32, no. 3 (2018). The journal editor was Alia Al-Saji.

Chapter 14, "The Rise of the Third Nomos of the Earth," was originally published as the foreword to *The Anomie of the Earth*, ed. Federico Luisetti, John Pickles, and

Wilson Kaiser (Durham, NC: Duke University Press, 2015). The original title was "Anomie, Resurgences and De-Noming." The original argument remains, but it was extended and projected toward the change of era and emergence of the third nomos of the Earth (de-Westernization and decoloniality).

The epilogue, "Yes, We Can: Border Thinking, Pluriversality, and Colonial Differentials," was originally published as a foreword to Hamid Dabashi's book *Can Non-Europeans Think?* (London: Zed Books, 2015).

My gratitude extends not only to friends and colleagues who read and commented on these chapters, or those who have been in the same campus and buildings for many years, or even those with whom I had conversations on the specific topic of this or that chapter. Coloniality is everywhere, and everything connects with everything, such that a conversation on decoloniality and music could illuminate some aspects related to the economy and governance or to knowledge and racism. This is perhaps a significant departure of decolonial investigations from the standardized research mode of the Western Hemisphere and its model of scholarship promoting "expertise" in one area or discipline. Decolonial investigations are tantamount to the politics of decolonial thinking. In every case the conversations and exchanges of ideas enriched my own argumentations and praxis of living. All those unquantifiable experiences that help many of us intellectually, emotionally, and politically cannot be quoted in the footnotes or stored in an archive. Behind and before a book, an artwork (i.e., a skillwork), a public discourse, a TV news program, etc., there lies a world of energy, emotions, interactions, and memories that are irreducible to scientific, technological, and corporate metrics.

Specifically and chronologically, my thanks go to Catherine Walsh, who invited me to join as a faculty member and dissertation advisor in the Program of Latin American Cultural Studies at the Universidad Andina Simón Bolívar in Quito, established at the beginning of the twenty-first century and whose future is uncertain after Catherine's retirement. Over almost twenty years, my collaboration with Cathy has been constant. Its fruit is the coauthored book *On Decoloniality: Concepts, Analytics, Praxis* (2018), and the book series published by Duke University Press. My thanks to Pedro Pablo Gómez Moreno, currently coordinator of the PhD program in Artistic Studies at the Universidad Distrital Francisco José de Caldas, in Bogotá. I have collaborated with Pedro Pablo since 2010 organizing events and publications. In Argentina, thanks go to Zulma Palermo and María Eugenia Borsani, two decolonial thinkers from the South with whom I have been in conversation and collaboration in several activities, though mainly in coworking on the book series *El desprendimiento* ("delinking"), published by Ediciones del Signo in Buenos Aires. Concomitantly

I also benefit by working as director of the book series with Malena Pestellini, director and guiding light of the publishing house, and with Pablo Martillana, Malena's right hand.

In Europe, my thanks go first to Rolando Vázquez, with whom we started the Middelburg Decolonial Summer School in 2010 in the Netherlands, which occasioned yearly summer think tanks. I appreciate the brilliance and generosity of all the teachers involved: María Lugones, Gloria Wekker, Patricia Kaersenhout, Jean Casimir, Jeannette Ehlers, Madina V. Tlostanova, Ovidiu Tichindeleanu, and Rosalba Icaza. In 2012 Alanna Lockward, who unfortunately and unexpectedly passed away in January of 2019, created Be.Bop (Black Europe Body Politics). Being her advisor from 2012 to 2018 put me in yearly contact with curators, artists, activists, and filmmakers who enlarged my relational understanding of what gnoseological and aesthesic reconstitution means for other people (although they are not using those terms to ponder what they are doing). More to the point was the collaboration between Be.Bop and the Middelburg Decolonial Summer School, where in addition to the aforementioned core faculty were periodic collaborators like Quinsy Gario, Manuela Boatcă, and Artwell Cain. All of that was happening during the period (2015–2019) when I worked on rewriting the original articles for this book.

Beyond my appreciation for the communal experiences mentioned above, there were also personal learnings I would like to acknowledge. Leo Ching shared his wisdom on East Asia, mainly China, Japan, and Taiwan. In the fall semester of 2016, we cotaught a graduate seminar at Duke titled, "The Irreversible Shifts of the World Order: The Global South and the Eastern Hemisphere." We repeated the seminar at the undergraduate level in the summer of 2017 at Duke in Kunshan, where we had twenty students from Mainland China, Taiwan, and Hong Kong, and one student from Brazil based in the US. Both seminars were indeed a life laboratory exploring the students' responses to the mutation of the global order. On this matter I benefitted from the opportunity to test ideas and arguments on coloniality, decoloniality, and global order in Taiwan, thanks to a generous invitation by Joyce C. H. Liu to deliver three lectures under the auspices of the Institute of Social Research and Cultural Studies at National Chiao-Tung University and the National Taiwan University.

During the period in which most of the essays collected here were written, I coauthored several articles and a book with Madina V. Tlostanova, who is also a core faculty member of the Middelburg Decolonial Summer School. Since the school's move to the Van Abbemuseum of Contemporary Art, I have benefited from conversations and collaboration with its director, Charles Esche. I was fortunate to be invited to present and test my ideas at CISA (Centre for

Indian Studies in Africa) in July–August of 2014 by director Dilip Menon. The three lectures I delivered there were titled "Decolonial Thoughts" by Dilip himself. Remembering a few years later that CISA's portrait of Mohandas Gandhi hung not too far from the poster announcing my lectures, I realized a fateful proximity to the man whose decolonial thoughts (not exempting criticism of his unfortunate racist underpinnings) centered his very praxis of living. The image of that wall remains vivid in my mind and nourishes my thoughts on Gandhi, some of which I incorporate in the introduction to this book (section III.3). During three six-week periods at STIAS, the Stellenbosch Institute for Advanced Study (2015, 2016, and 2018), while I was writing the second part of *On Decoloniality: Concepts, Analytics, Praxis* (2018), coauthored with Catherine Walsh, I experienced the prelude of Rhodes Must Fall and the intensification of decolonial struggles, decolonizing the university and the curriculum. I learned much in conversation with Nick Shepherd and Siona O'Connell, at the University of Cape Town back then, as well as from Stephanus Muller, creator and director of Africa Open Institute for Music, Research and Innovation. He and Marietjie Pauw taught me to think of music decolonially. And related to them both is the filmmaker, writer, and activist Aryan Kaganof, a STIAS colleague in 2016. He had just finished his film *Decolonising Wits* and was beginning to film *Opening Stellenbosch*, both investigations on decolonizing the university and its curriculum. The documentaries incorporate numerous conversations with faculty and students.

I owe thanks to the graduate students in my seminars on decolonial thinking, and to undergraduate students who understood coloniality and decoloniality without addressing the issues directly, but through the racial, sexual, political, and economic histories of "Latin" America and through the Indigenous thinking of the present grounded in the cosmological ancestrality of the great civilizations of what is today the American continent.

Immense gratitude to Tracy Carhart and Katja Hill. Tracy painstakingly transcribed and adjusted published articles into Word, going two or three times over my editing of each essay, compiling bibliographies, and framing the manuscript under Duke University Press's publication format. When Tracy retired in December of 2019, Katja came to the rescue in the last stage.

Last but by no means least, my gratitude to Reynolds Smith. His savoir faire as former editor of Duke University Press, his familiarity with my work, and our mutual understanding after many years of collaboration on the book series Latin America Otherwise, informed by his understanding of the larger issues addressed in each essay, greatly improved my arguments in detail and clarity.

Introduction

All things organic are dying in the trap of organization. An artificial world is permeating and poisoning the natural. Civilization has itself become a machine that does, or tries to do, everything in mechanical fashion. We think only in horsepower now; we cannot look at a waterfall without mentally turning it into electric power; we cannot survey a countryside full of pasturing cattle without thinking of its exploitation as a source of meat supply; we cannot look at the beautiful old handwork of a lively and primitive people without wishing to replace it by a modern technical process. Whether it has meaning or not, our technical thinking must have its actualization. *The luxury of the Machine is the consequence of a necessity of thought.* In the final analysis, the Machine is a *symbol*—like its secret ideals, perpetual motion—a spiritual and intellectual necessity, but not a vital one.—OSWALD SPENGLER, *Man and Technics: A Contribution to a Philosophy of Life*, 1932, emphasis added

Yet, if we reflect upon our experience as observers, we discover that whatever we do as such happens to us. In other words, we discover that our experience is that we find ourselves observing, talking or acting, and that any explanation or description of what we do is secondary to our experience of finding ourselves in the doing of what we do.—HUMBERTO R. MATURANA, "Reality: The Search for Objectivity or the Quest for a Compelling Argument," 1988

A theory in its most basic form is simply an explanation for why we do the things we do.—LEANNE BETASAMOSAKE SIMPSON, *Dancing on Our Turtle's Back: Stories of Nishnaabeg Re-Creation, Resurgence, and a New Emergence*, 2011

From this brief review, it can be readily seen that Aboriginal traditional knowledge has a very different paradigmatic base from that of Western knowledge. Whereas Western knowledge operates from a linear, singular view, whereas Western knowledge views the world from order beneath chaos, whereas Western languages are very noun oriented, knowledge is about you (first person) in relation to everything else in a relativistic sense. Aboriginal knowledge has a very different "coming to know." It is holistic and cyclical; it views the world from chaos underneath order; its languages are process and action oriented. Knowledge is about participation in and with the natural world. Policy and research implications arising out of Aboriginal paradigms cannot be underestimated. . . . If Aboriginal paradigms are not taken into consideration, policy, research, and the "humanities" will simply miss the mark.—LEROY LITTLE BEAR, "Traditional Knowledge and Humanities: A Perspective by a Blackfoot," 2012

Biskaabiiyang [looking back, returning to ourselves] research *is a process through which Anishinaabe researchers evaluate how they personally have been affected by colonization, rid themselves of the emotional and psychological baggage they carry from this process, and then return to ancestral traditions.* . . . With Biskaabiiyang methodologies, an individual must recognize and deal with this negative kind of thinking before conducting research.—WENDY MAKOONS GENIUSZ, quoted by LEANNE BETASAMOSAKE SIMPSON, *Dancing on Our Turtle's Back*, 2011, emphasis added

Within Nishnaabeg theoretical foundations, Biskaabiiyang does not literally mean returning to the past, but rather re-creating the cultural and political flourishment of the past to support the well-being of our contemporary citizens. *It means reclaiming the fluidity around our traditions, not the rigidity of colonialism.* It means encouraging the self-determination of individuals within our national and community-based contexts; and it means recreating an artistic and intellectual renaissance within a larger political and cultural resurgence. When I asked my Michi Saagiig Nishnaabeg Elder Gidigaa Migizi about Biskaabiiyang, the term immediately resonated with him; when English terms such as "resistance" and "resurgence" did not.—LEANNE BETASAMOSAKE SIMPSON, *Dancing on Our Turtle's Back*, 2011, emphasis added

According to the prevailing traditional European epistemologies, knowledge has mainly been gained through observation and reasoning. However, in traditional Chinese thought, knowledge has been understood in a much broader sense, namely as something which also (or primarily) stems from moral contents and which cannot be separated from (social) practice. The method which determined most of the epistemological teachings found in the Chinese classics was *based on a holistic world view*, and was directed towards a comprehension which could be achieved through education and learning. The basic contents of these teachings were rooted in the premises of pragmatic and utilitarian ethics. *Chinese epistemology was relational . . . meaning that it understood the external world to be ordered structurally, while the human mind was also structured in accordance with its all-embracing but open, organic system (li, 理). The relational correspondence between the cosmic and mental structures thus represents the basic precondition of human perception and comprehension.*—JANA ROŠKER, "Epistemology in Chinese Philosophy," *Stanford Encyclopedia of Philosophy*, emphasis added

I Prolegomenon

The Politics of Decolonial Investigations aims at healing colonial wounds and shrinking the wide spectrum of Western overconfidence to its own size.[1] Colonial wounds are inflicted in all areas of lived experience, human and nonhuman, physical and mental, by the recursive enactment of the "arrogance of power."[2] No living organism at this point in time is immune to coloniality, no less the changing cast of actors running the institutions that maintain coloniality under the rhetoric of modernity celebrating change, development, the cybernetic revolution, AI, and democracy as unquestionable victories. These decolonial investigations shall unveil the underlying logic that has tricked all of us on planet Earth under the mirage of the universality of knowledge and of human destiny, as well as reconsider the cosmogonies and cosmologies that never sought to divide us from the living energy of planet Earth and the cosmos. These investigations shall contribute to rebuilding and reenacting our parameters of knowing and sensing and to the restitution of our love and mutual respect; it aims to restore the *communal*, encompassing the relationality of the human species with/in all the living universe, which has been destituted by the *social*, severing the human species from the cosmic planetary energy and the will to live for far too long.

Most of the newspaper accounts and other mass media discussions I have witnessed in the US since COVID-19 appeared in China have a common concern, a spine that connects their different points of view: when and how the coronavirus will affect the financial markets and the economic prospects for the nation. It reminds me of similar news and the discussions during the 2008 "crisis": their main concern was to save the banks and capitalism. While it was acknowledged that capitalism was not perfect, an understatement under the circumstances, it was concluded that there was not a better alternative.

In both crises, two levels of knowledge have been at work: the *doxa* (common belief, popular opinion) on the one hand, and the *episteme* (knowledge, logical and scientific understanding) on the other. Mainstream political economy and political theory have provided the epistemic foundation transmitted within the public sphere. In this book, I try to show how and why the politics of decolonial inquiry and analysis must be oriented toward changing the assumptions and presuppositions—not just the contents—that currently validate Western political economy, political theory, and the opinions transmitted by the corporate media to the public at large. Following Aníbal Quijano I call this reorientation *epistemic reconstitution*.

In his groundbreaking short essay, published in 1992, Quijano reoriented the task of decolonization vis-à-vis what decolonization meant during the Cold War: to expel the settlers so the natives could govern themselves. The governing institution was the nation-state without questioning the political theory and political economy upon which nation-states came into being. In view of the failure of the nation-state as a means to decolonization, Quijano turned to confront the hegemonic totality of knowledge that constituted the idea of Western modernity and to conceive the task of decolonization as epistemological reconstitution. He wrote:

> The critique of *the European paradigm of rationality/modernity* is indispensable, even more, urgent. But it is doubtful if the criticism consists of a simple negation of all its categories; of the dissolution of reality in discourse; of the pure negation of the idea and the perspective of totality in cognition. It is necessary to extricate oneself from the linkages between rationality/modernity and coloniality, first of all, and definitely from all power which is not constituted by free decisions made by free people. It is the instrumentalization of the reasons for power, of colonial power in the first place, which produced distorted paradigms of knowledge and spoiled the liberating promises of modernity. . . . First of all, epistemological decolonization, as decoloniality, is needed to clear the way for new intercultural communication, for an interchange of experiences and meanings, as the basis of another rationality which may legitimately pretend to some

universality. Nothing is less rational, finally, than the pretension that the specific cosmic vision of a particular ethnie should be taken as universal rationality, even if such an ethnie is called Western Europe because this is actually pretend[ing] to impose a provincialism as universalism. (Emphasis added.)[3]

Although Quijano's expression is "epistemological reconstitution," the overwhelming attention he has paid since then to subjectivity and the control of the senses, rendered by Nelson Maldonado-Torres as "coloniality of being," suggests that the reconstitution shall be both epistemological and ontological, which is a claim in this book.[4] Furthermore, as ontology cannot be reduced to pure materiality, coloniality of being in the world involves and presupposes coloniality of the senses. In the European paradigm of modernity/rationality, the coloniality of the senses has been enacted by modern and Western aesthetics: the entire field of philosophical aesthetics has been, since the late eighteenth century, an effective instrument to colonize aesthesis. Because knowledge (both epistemic and doxastic) controls and manages the subjectivity (aesthesis) of the population affected by it, decolonial reconstitution needs to be both epistemic and doxastic (which carries the weight of sensing and believing).[5] My goal for this book is to help change the terms of the conversations (the presuppositions, assumptions, and enunciations), sustaining the "European paradigm of modernity/rationality" and hiding its darker side, coloniality. I will return to this point in section III.3.

This is a book about "coloniality of power" and its consequences, topics on which I have spent virtually the last twenty-five years of my life, researching, teaching, writing, thinking, and working with other people in the same path. Quijano's concepts of "coloniality" and "coloniality of power" have revealed to us the darker side of modernity. They have uncovered the reality that there cannot be "power" without a modifier. Power without a modifier is a modern concept posited as the universal.[6] It remains caught within the regional limitations and the too often dubious assumptions of Western universality. What options are left for decoloniality as epistemic reconstitution after the closing of the Third World and the demise of the socialist bloc in a world order reshaped by, on the one hand, the projects of de-Westernization and multipolarity and, on the other hand, the efforts to maintain the privileges of five hundred years of Westernization, by engaging in a renewed effort of re-Westernization to maintain the privileges of unipolarity?[7] Yet in the turmoil of everyday life, the attention of millions of people across the planet is sucked into the increasing flow of traffic on the information highway, to the extent that no time or energy is left for thinking beyond the demands of the iPhone to which our eyes are glued like magnets. The magnitude of the geopolitical sphere, including the mass and social media that manipulate sensing and emotioning, is such that no future can be glimpsed beyond the offices of the current managers of global designs. COVID-19 made many aware that technological control of the population could find in the pandemic a reason to be increased. Yes, I would say: management and control of the population has always been inscribed in the colonial matrix of power. This is just the latest turn of the screw.

We only and always live in the constant flux of the present. What is being done in the present will guide the future of the global order and of everyday life—what shall be preserved, what shall be changed, who shall participate in decision making, and who is being made destitute. The COVID-19 pandemic has put a lot of pressure on the present; decisions and options have been made that would orient what is to come. Never in the history of humankind have pandemic and economic turmoil happened at the same time. The darker side of Western modernity has emerged in all its "splendor." Under these conditions and given the present world order, the near future seems to hang on three trajectories. One is offered by re-Westernization—a counterrevolution that many like myself believe is getting out of hand—to retain the privileges of unipolarity. The second is offered by de-Westernization's confrontation of unipolarity, opening up a world order that is multipolar and already here. Both are state-led politics. The third trajectory is decolonization/decoloniality led by the emerging global and diverse political society, taking their/our destinies in their/our own hands.[8]

Decolonial epistemic reconstitutions, and the politics of decolonial investigations, aim to overcome the hegemony of the "European paradigm of modernity/rationality" and take the first two trajectories (de-Westernization and re-Westernization) as a field of investigation. As a matter of fact, setting up the current world order as the conflict between the rise of de-Westernization and the counterrevolution of re-Westernization is a decolonial conceptualization of epistemic reconstitutions to understand the current world order emerging from five hundred years of Westernization. Decolonization as decoloniality, as I present it here, having epistemic and ontological reconstitution as its main goal, offers a conceptual apparatus of knowing and understanding and a visionary *utopia of sustainable economies* (not sustainable development) to live in harmony and plenitude. (See chapter 14.)[9]

In the meantime, the scenario depicted by Oswald Spengler in 1932 in the epigraph to this introduction will continue to deteriorate. The machine alienates the human species from its own kind, distancing the killer from the killed.

Thousands of miles may span between the decider and the target, with the button-presser carrying out orders somewhere in between. Spared any risk of personal accountability, institutions' public call for the care of human beings diverts attention from their profit at the cost of lost lives. The disruption of the planet is justified in the name of "development," destituting the possibilities of sustainable economies to live in harmony. COVID-19 has made this hypocrisy hard to watch: while civil and political society confronting the state and corporations worried about their grandparents, their sick sisters, their friends without face masks, and their jobs, corporations carefully watched the cost.

The arguments that I unfold in this book are the results of two decades of sustained investigation into questions outlined in the previous paragraphs: our global order, daily life, and the intersection between them. All are embedded in the overall frame of modernity/coloniality, and they both encompass the international, the domestic, and the private and public spheres. All the chapters in this book deal with diverse aspects of the historical foundation, transformation, management of, and consequences to the rhetoric of modernity and the logic of coloniality, as well as dissent thereof, and the praxes of reconstitution and restitution, all of which I address in more detail in section III of this introduction. The basic presuppositions guiding these investigations are as follows. By "coloniality of power" I mean the energy driving the beliefs, attitudes, and desires of actors that built an apparatus of management as well as the colonial matrix of power (CMP) sustaining them. Coloniality of power is the *technics* of domination and CMP the instrument. I am building here on Oswald Spengler: "*Technics is the tactics of life. It is the inner form of the process utilized in that struggle which is identical with life itself. . . . Technics is not to be understood in terms of tools. What matters is not how one fashions things, but the process of using them*" (emphasis in the original).[10]

I will use in this book the term "praxis/es of living" instead of "tactics of life." The change of vocabulary is made, simply, to reflect Spengler's life experience and disciplinary training on the one hand and my own grounded praxis of living on the other. At stake here is the geopolitics of knowing, sensing, and believing.[11] Both coloniality of power and CMP are disguised by the rhetoric of modernity: a overwhelming set of discourses, oral and written, write this script. Both fixed and moving images accompanied by soundtrack wind round and round the reel, projecting an image of the world, natural and cultural, upon the mind of the people as if it were the world itself. The rhetoric of modernity settled and maintains the "European paradigm of modernity/rationality," in Quijanos's words. Apart from modernity, which is a concept that emerged in Europe, the rest are decolonial concepts that emerged in and from the South American Andes: Third World concepts in a way. You won't find them either in the social sciences and the humanities or in their North Atlantic hub; neither in western Europe nor in the US. Modernity is a European concept of which the Renaissance and the Enlightenment are two historical pillars. Modernity/coloniality is a decolonial concept, and though some distinguish between modernity and coloniality, I never do because coloniality is constitutive of modernity. This is a basic premise of the collective whole known by the compound modernity/coloniality/decoloniality. Coloniality and modernity/coloniality did not emerge in academe either and are unrelated to any specific discipline. Both concepts became prominent in public sphere debates in the early 1990s as an outcome of previous conversations about economic dependency in South America in which Quijano was heavily involved. Consequently, the sustained decolonial investigations I submit to the reader of this book are grounded in the genealogy of thoughts inherited from the 1960s by debates on economic dependency. At the time, economic and political dependency was the main concern. But Quijano expanded it to all domains of life (culture, subjectivity, everyday life) and explored the historic-structural dependency managed by the European paradigm of modernity/coloniality. In other words, he broadened the scope by the coloniality of power technics and its instrument, the CMP. However, this book intends to continue the energies of dissent that the rhetoric of modernity and the logic of coloniality provoked: decoloniality both in its variegated manifestations in the political society and in the domain of decolonial investigations, epistemological (knowing) and ontological (being, sensing, emotioning—aesthesis) reconstitutions.

Although Quijano was trained in sociology, coloniality—short for the coloniality of power (*colonialidad del poder*)—was not introduced as a sociological concept but as a decolonial one. This means that coloniality of power and decoloniality, in this specific sense, were mutually created. Coloniality was a decolonial concept, and decoloniality, in this local configuration and not as a universal concept, acquired its meaning by bringing coloniality of power to light. There are many other meanings and uses of "decolonization," either in a strong political sense or sometimes as a metaphor, that are based on different presuppositions and do not necessarily take coloniality of power (and CMP) as the basic frame of analysis and as the prison house that decolonial doing and thinking aim to delink. My own work is limited to and grounded on the indissociable foundation of the decolonial analytics of the coloniality of power on the one hand and its political, ethical, and epistemic/philosophical consequences on the other.

The correlations between coloniality of power and decoloniality can be illustrated by analogy to the correlations between the unconscious and psychoanalysis. In Freud's work, the unconscious is a psychoanalytic concept, regardless of whether the word existed before his coinage of it and regardless of the fact that human beings (and animals too) have had dreams since the beginning of time: dreams aren't exclusive to the end of the nineteenth century, nor is their analysis. People have been analyzing their dreams from the moment they began to dream. But thanks to Freud, psychoanalytic analysis is credited to him and catalogued to that time. Freud created an indissociable bond between the analysis of the unconscious and the human mind itself to the extent that psychoanalysis and our unconscious workings became mutually constitutive and remain so to this day. Following this analogy, in the same way that psychoanalysis reveals hidden dimensions of the mind inaccessible to our conscious thought, decolonial thinking and decolonial analytics reveal the work of the colonial matrix of power, the hidden structure of Western civilization. This book is about the coloniality of power and its world-making instrumentalization, the CMP. The colonial matrix of power is—allow me to repeat—the instrumental and conceptual structure (which I will analyze in section III of this introduction) that the coloniality of power creates to enforce its regime of domination, management, and control. Going a step further with my analogy to Freud, I would add that while psychoanalytic investigations foster a therapeutic cure, decolonial investigations invite decolonial healing. Psychoanalysis deals with traumas, decoloniality with colonial wounds. This book is about understanding how the CMP governs us, and, in its boomerang effect, governs the actors implementing control and domination in the name of progress, development, and democracy. Such understanding is of the essence to know when, where, and how to delink and engage in communal praxis of decolonial healing through epistemic (of knowledge and ways of knowing) and aesthesic (being, sensing, and believing) reconstitution, which was the task Quijano assigned to decolonial thinking and doing at the end of the Cold War. This book, thirty years later, offers a decolonial praxis of Quijano's concept for our time.[12]

Colonial wounds are inflicted epistemically (based on knowing, knowledge), although their effects are ontological/aesthesic: they transform a person's sensing, believing, and emotioning. Physical colonial wounds always have a psychological dimension. It's one thing to be physically wounded in an accident, for example, and another to know that the physical wound is related to coloniality of power. Dehumanization is likewise epistemic/aesthesic, justifying violence and physical wounds in turn. If you are labeled a terrorist, an epistemic/aesthesic wound is inflicted on you, opening the gates to all kinds of physical violence by this name. Someone's "knowledge" makes you a terrorist, not what you do, and that affects your sensing and emotioning (aesthesis) for better or worse once you know you have been identified as such. Replace "terrorist" with "Black," "gay," "LGTBQ," "Chinese," "Iranian," etc., and you will understand the vast domain in which imperial and colonial differences operate to inflict colonial wounds (and imperial ones, too, when interstate relations are at work). Knowing and sensing are interrelated and indissociable dimensions of human cognition and of our human praxis (set of practices and routines) of living. You cannot know without sensing and you cannot sense without knowing. Mathematics is *not* an exception, for it is the rhetoric of modernity that separated math and logic from the senses. The body in pain (moral and physical) is altered and diminished in its potentialities for knowing, sensing, and believing. In effect, the body's potential is restricted and/or deformed in its ability to know, to feel, to believe, to emotion. (I am indeed using "emotion" as a verb intentionally.) Beyond physical acts of violence legitimized by coloniality in the name of modernity (e.g., wounded protesters, Blacks harassed as suspected criminals, Indians feared as dangerous, LGTBQ persons shamed as disturbing, etc.), colonial wounds can be inflicted in a wide array of harm beyond the physical and emotional pain of individuals alone.

Indeed, colonial epistemic and aesthetic wounds affect vast sectors of the population of a given country via domestic policies and international relations, such as sanctions and debts on the receiving end. (By "aesthetic," I refer to an effect on the senses, not the perception of beauty.) Two marks of colonial wounds are racism and sexism. Neither racism nor sexism (across the entire spectrum from gendered heteronormativity to LGTBQ and "Two Spirits" people) are based on any ontic "substance" but are the outcomes of social classifications. Furthermore, social classifications are a question of knowledge (epistemic) that encroaches on and modulates sensing and believing (aesthesis). Decolonially speaking, social classifications are *inventions* not *representations*, which means that "race" and "sex" do not carry in themselves the ontic meaning of biological organs and the organism in which they are imbedded; rather, they are the target of meaning projected and world-making by actors, institutions, and languages (see section III of this introduction) that control knowing and knowledge and regard their own sensing as "normal and natural." If, then, classifications are created that inflict colonial wounds as a result, then they are not created ex nihilo. No, they are made by presumptive creators of the world order who intend to imply that their classifications unquestioningly represent the world "as is." Such classifications that *count*, that are accepted as representations of fact, are human, subjective classifications that bring with them a larger, institutional legitimacy that disqualifies and dehumanizes other human beings. "Representation" is a keyword in the rhetoric of modernity. It presupposes that the purpose of existence is to be represented, and by so doing manages and controls its meaning. That is the world of the coloniality of power and the instrumental structure it creates, CMP, and that is the rhetoric of its disguises. As a result, healing colonial wounds becomes an epistemic and systemic issue rather than a personal one. It is not the personal history that provokes the wound, but the systemic history of coloniality of power that inflicts colonial wounds, regardless of your personal experience. Furthermore, healing colonial wounds cannot be achieved without delinking from CMP because individual healing cannot happen in the same epistemic frame of CMP that inflicts colonial wounds. Psychoanalysis operates within the same frame that provokes the trauma in the individual. The ego is confronted by a society that creates desires that not all individuals can fulfill. Decolonial healing requires one to delink from the paradigm of European modernity/rationality that engenders the wound in the same society it creates.

If colonial wounds are consequences of systemic and hierarchical social classifications, and social classifications are hierarchical epistemic inventions disguised as representations, then healing colonial wounds becomes a matter of epistemic and aesthesic reconstitution, as I have explained so far. It is an epistemic matter because social classifications disguised as (scientific) representations must be reconstituted in response to the needs and sensibilities of the people classified and ranked, rather than of those doing the ranking. The aesthesic comes into play as well, because colonial wounds are epistemic modi operandi that affect the sensibility and the emotions of the people classified. Racism and sexism, invoked above, are clear cases in point. Hence, epistemic (of knowledge and knowing) and aesthetic (sensing, believing, being) reconstitution are two aspects of the same phenomenon, and they are of extreme relevance in decolonial arguments. Their conjoining simply reflects the fact that decolonial epistemic and aesthetic reconstitution restores to the sphere of knowing and understanding the fundamental role of the senses, beliefs, and emotions in all ranges of knowledge, knowing, and understanding.

At this point it should be clarified that by "knowledge" I am not referring here only to encyclopedias, libraries, and canonical figures in every discipline, whether theological or secular.[13] I am saying that hegemonic knowledge is stored and canonized, and this storage and its all-too-often later canonization is grounded on the myth of the archive—the notion that our knowledge simply grows, creating a body of truth, rather than a dynamic reality that knowledge changes with knowing over time, much of it being discarded as false in the sphere of science or modified in the knowing of everyday living in communities for whom academic, scholarly, and scientific knowledge is perfectly irrelevant. Other areas in which scientific knowledge could be irrelevant are in state and corporative politics, as we have witnessed with climate change and COVID-19. The threat that this process embodies—from the introduction in the West of the Chinese printing press to the digital archives of today—is that this accumulation and conceptual hegemony becomes legitimized by the materiality of the archive. Grounded in church teachings, the conquistadors' "knowledge" that Indigenous peoples either had no souls or had souls possessed by the devil utterly set aside and vitiated Indigenous world-sensing and ways of knowing, not to mention enabling acts of murder and enslavement. Archival knowledge, such as that based on fifteenth-century interpretations of scripture, justified the devaluation of oral knowledge as well as a great deal of holistic Indigenous world-sensing concerning humans' place in the cosmos that appear increasingly wise and relevant today. But this is another area in which state and corporate politics will discard, ignore, or, if necessary, repress. Behind the state and its corporations, coloniality of power looms large while the CMP provides the tools for disavowals and repression.

In brief, the constitution of Western knowledge ("the European paradigm of modernity/rationality") and its politics of Eurocentric knowing since the European Renaissance (see part IV of this book) were effective hegemonic weapons of Westernization, the five-hundred-years-long foundation of what is today re-Westernization: the neoliberal designs (and desires) to homogenize the planet without sacrificing any of the modernity/rationality (rhetoric of modernity) paradigm. This paradigm was consolidated in and by disciplinary formations regulating and regulated by universities, museums, schools, convents, and monasteries. In the centuries since then it has been exported/imported to Asia and Africa. Nevertheless, local knowledges and ways of knowing have not been erased. Changing the content won't do. Epistemic reconstitutions target the terms (assumptions, beliefs, principles) of the conversations that regulate the content. To do so, decolonial investigations are of paramount importance. They were simply devalued and forsaken (destituted) with all the painful consequences for the people whose languages, knowledge, and praxes of knowing and living were sidelined.

Coloniality of knowledge (one domain of CMP; see section III below) was and still is an instrumental part of the package of political, economic, and military Westernization. But today, coloniality of knowledge is being heavily contested by de-Westernization: China is being accused of "stealing" Western technology—both as *technics* and as instrument—when indeed China is disputing the control and management of the CMP. However, coloniality of knowledge had and has a special Westernizing function: possession and dispossession of lands, for example, were not just acts of grabbing, dispossessing, and keeping silence. Possessions and dispossessions were legitimized through and by knowledge. Provisions of international law were created in the sixteenth century precisely to that end. For this reason, epistemic and aesthesic reconstitution are foundational decolonial tasks. Contesting the coloniality of established knowledge and the coloniality of power behind it requires changing the terms of the conversations in both spheres: the sphere of state-directed de-Westernization and the sphere of the political society's decolonial drive to reconstituting the communal. The politics of decolonial investigations in and beyond the academe is of the essence. Reconstituting the *communal* cannot be pursued, and even less achieved when taking for granted the assumptions and knowledges on which the current *social* has been structured.

At this point the distinction between the *particular meaning* of "decolonization" during the Cold War and of "decoloniality" after the Cold War becomes relevant. I emphasize "particular meaning" because it will be pertinent for the distinctions between decolonialization (i.e., establishing governance by the natives forming their own nation-states) and decoloniality (epistemic reconstitution) that I am about to outline. First, there are many local histories affected by the past five hundred years of Westernization, and therefore there are diverse decolonial responses to it (such as the Zapatistas or Feminismo Comunitario in Bolivia and Guatemala; the Peasant Way, Sovereignty of Food, and Idle No More in Canada; or Black Lives Matter in the US; etc.) as well as responses that do not claim to be decolonial yet direct their efforts toward overcoming coloniality and healing colonial wounds.[14] Second, there are many ways of struggling and confronting the consequences of coloniality without explicitly embracing the presuppositions of the coloniality of power, of CMP, and of the decolonial energies that they provoke in their mutual configuration. To question and struggle against injustice doesn't require decoloniality. It can be pursued in several frames of knowing and being. It is in this respect that I have been arguing that decoloniality is an option; it's neither a mission of conversion nor a field of "disciplinary studies." Delinking from the colonial matrix of power is not a question of content or a question of what we talk about: it is about the presuppositions and assumptions on which we ground our talking and doing; it is *about the terms of the conversations, not just the contents*. But what are the terms of the conversation? Decolonial delinking means delinking from the *enunciation* of the CMP, not just its content. Delinking from the enunciation means to delink from the coloniality of power's regulations of ways of knowing and understanding. Opposing and being "critical" of the content without delinking from the enunciation keeps you trapped in the enunciation of the CMP (see section III below). What I mean is that undertaking decolonial investigations depends on the local histories and the context in which decolonial undertakings materialize. Decoloniality has particular meanings in Africa, among the First Nations of Canada, the Maori of New Zealand, and Indigenous populations in the Andes, among the Afro-Caribbean population in former Eastern Europe, among immigrants, or among LGTBQ populations in Europe, the US, or Indonesia. One global decolonial model cannot serve all local histories. However, what connects the diversity of local histories is the long-lasting and wide-ranging invasion of Westernization and the export/import of the European paradigm of knowledge and knowing. From the decolonial diversity of local histories around the globe, entangled with global designs, no local history can ever be enunciated as global, since every enunciation cannot be but local.[15] The only local history that managed to become the headquarters of global designs was that of Western civilization.

I've already mentioned the distinctive features of decolonization during the Cold War, and decoloniality at the end of it and in the present, but they are important to be considered further. Decolonization during the Cold War was motivated by the need to expel the colonial settler from the colonized territory so that the native or Indigenous population could have its own governance, taking the form of the nation-state. The nation-state was created in Europe by the emerging ethno-class composed of merchant bourgeois and laborers (farmers, artisans, etc.—i.e., the Third Estate that confronted the First and the Second, the clergy and the aristocracy), who led the Glorious Revolution in England (1688) and the French Revolution (1789). This was the first radical transformation of the CMP since its foundation in the sixteenth century with the colonization of the Americas. We could call it the "second modern/colonial revolutions." These revolutions inaugurated the groundwork for the modern nation-state to come into being and, with time, to take over the global order (now in dispute). Imported by liberated colonies, the model of the European nation-state resulted in the formation of modern/colonial nation-states in the former colonies, and in direct interdependency with their former colonists. Power differentials dividing the First, Second, and Third Worlds during the Cold War established exactly that order of priority: the Second and Third Worlds were subordinated to and dependent on the First World. The division was not ontic but epistemological—that is, it was invented in the First World, which posited itself as one component of the classification although it was the locus of enunciation that invented the classification. That is simply the power of coloniality of knowledge and the work of coloniality of power.

The inherited dependency in the formation of modern/colonial nation-states in the former colonies, not surprisingly, touches every area of experience, including and beyond governance, the financial and corporate sectors, and the public sphere. Dependence is political, economic, epistemological, and cultural—it touch the senses and emotions of people at both ends of the spectrum. You feel your dependence and it hurts: that is why you want to be in Paris, London, or New York instead of back home in the Third World or in some other newly emerging economy. And if you are driving the institutions that in those places make decisions for the rest of the world, you sense the superiority of your being; your senses are secured by the institutions that support you. Immersed in feelings of dependence, epistemological dependence manifests as the geopolitical "sense of inferiority" at one end of the spectrum and "sense of superiority" at the other. For officials of the nation-state formed after liberation, it manifested as the desire to become "like" the First World and its people, bypassing the fact that coloniality of power works, in different ways, at both ends of the spectrum: as the locus of exporting global designs and the locus of importing them. Into this sea of feelings, the entertainment industry and television have been powerful tools to project First World images and generate desires for emulation, resulting in the mixed atmosphere of modern/colonial states. The inclination toward decolonial liberation has persisted, while at the same time power differentials and codependent relations have made the horizon of liberation more distant. Not only have Western political theory and political economy remained in place in the newly formed nation-states; Western knowledge and schooling have joined forces with them, overshadowing long histories of local education in the former colonies too. Local knowledges were despised by both the exporter and the importer of the European paradigm of modernity/rationality. The restitution of disavowed local knowledge is an important aspect of decolonial projects of epistemic and ontological reconstitutions. Today, European and US universities have remained world attractions and promote symbols of knowledge as yet another Western commodity exported to the Middle East, Singapore, and China.[16]

However, powerful signs of reversing colonial destitutions were awakened during the Cold War that could not have been incorporated in the emerging modern/colonial states. Here, signs pointed in other directions, along with increasing attention to independent thought rather than to nation-states simply caught in the tentacles of modern thinking. State politics after decolonization truly wanted to modernize. And that was the kiss of death for decolonization and a convenient dependency for the local political, financial, and corporate elites who were able to benefit from the newly created nation-states. There were signs of epistemic disobedience that could not be absorbed by modern/colonial nation-states' falling back into the fold of modernity, and, consequently, maintaining coloniality under the umbrella of decolonization. Epistemic disobedience under these conditions are the seeds of the variegated eruption of political societies. We find such signs in the great thinkers of the time, whether they were directly involved in the struggle to expel the imperial settlers (like Amílcar Cabral, Patrice Lumumba, Kwame Nkrumah), participated as national foreigners in the liberation of another country (like Frantz Fanon in Algeria), fought national settlers (Steve Biko confronting the Afrikaans), or were simply "present" at a metropole (e.g., thinkers in Paris writing for *Présence Africaine*). All these intellectuals engaged in epistemic and aesthesic reconstitution in different ways, yet still confronted the dismissive power of Western epistemology (knowledge) and aesthesis (ways of being, sensing, and systems of belief).

These lines of thought unfolding in Africa were chronologically parallel to the dependency debates in South America, both in their intellectual genealogy that brought about the conceptual "coloniality of power" in the early 1990s and in giving a new meaning to decolonization: decolonization as epistemic reconstitution. For Quijano, from that moment on decolonial horizons were no longer defined by modern/colonial nation-states (see chapter 4). Decolonization required delinking (to extricate oneself) from the colonial matrix of power (the CMP) and engaging in the labor of epistemic and aesthesic reconstitutions. By the end of the Cold War, it was clear to Quijano that decolonization and the nation-state were not compatible—as incompatible indeed as democracy and capitalism. Quijano was not oblivious to the impact of the CMP in the daily lives of the people, in their/our beliefs and sensing emotions. And indeed we cannot detach Quijano's own sensing and emotioning from his powerful conceptual thinking and argument-making. He perceived and noted the equivalences of certain phenomena at the inception of CMP, in the sixteenth century and the last decades of the twentieth century and first decades of the twenty-first, intruding (shaping and forming) in "every aspect of social existence of people." That is, invading our subjectivities, making us subjected to the CMP. He wrote:

> Desde la crisis mundial que comenzó a mediados de los 70s. se ha hecho
> visible un proceso que afecta a todos y a cada uno de los aspectos de la

existencia social de las gentes de todos los países. El mundo que se formó desde hace 500 años está culminando con la formación de una estructura productiva, financiera y comercial que es percibida como más integrada que antes porque su control ha sido reconcentrado bajo pocos y reducidos grupos. . . . Por eso mismo, no es difícil admitir que ha producido una profunda y masiva modificación de la vida de todas las sociedades y de todas las gentes. Se trata de una real mutación, no sólo de cambios dentro de una continuidad.[17]

Since the world crisis that began in the mid-1970s, a process that affects each and every aspect of the social existence of the people of all countries has become visible. The world that was formed five hundred years ago is culminating in the formation of a productive, financial, and commercial structure that is perceived as more integrated than before because its control has been concentrated under a few and small groups. . . . For that very reason, it is not difficult to admit that it has produced a profound and massive modification in the life of all societies and of all peoples. It is a real mutation, not just changes within a continuity.

At the present time equivalent phenomena occur. Following up on Quijano's coloniality of power, which implies coloniality of knowledge and of being in the world, I posit that the basic tasks of decoloniality are to delink from the CMP and to engage in epistemic (knowing) and aesthesic (sensing, being) reconstitutions. Decoloniality of knowing and sensing are two anchors of any project to reexist—to liberate ourselves, our subjectivity from the tentacles of the CMP. The world cannot be changed if the people who inhabit and make it do not change. The goals of decolonial investigations are nothing else than knowing and understanding how the CMP manages all of us without our knowing it to illuminate the paths toward our envisioned self (to borrow Steve Biko's decolonial vision).

To take into account additional factors relevant to the distinction between decolonization and decoloniality in interstate relations, we have to go back to the Cold War. The Bandung Conference (1955) was and still is a marker of decolonization and a point of reference for three ensuing outcomes (chapter 9)—one explicit, the second implicit, and the third indirect. The explicit outcome was the creation of the Non-Aligned Movement (NAM) in 1961, which like Bandung was a state-led project. The leading figures of this organization were Yugoslavia's Marshal Josip Broz Tito (who was not invited to the Bandung Conference), India's Jawaharlal Nehru, Egypt's Gamal Abdel Nasser, Sukarno from Indonesia, and Kwame Nkrumah from Ghana. These were the NAM's five founding fathers. Though the NAM stripped away the decolonial elements of race and religion fundamental at Bandung, it also called neither the nation-state nor capitalist economies into question. The nation-state was assumed to be the "natural" structure of governance and capitalism the "natural" type of economy, as long as both were managed by natives of the land rather than by foreign settlers. The NAM is still operative, but the conditions it addresses have changed radically since the Cold War. The goal was no longer decolonization but socialism, distinguished from Soviet and Chinese communism. The NAM today has been sidelined by the advent of a world order in which capitalism is the common ground and the political conflicts surface when calling the shots is in question. The United Nations Security Council has been in the past decades a thermometer of the dispute for the control and management of the CMP. States that during the Cold War were under the influence of either the Soviet Union or the United States (i.e., either communist or capitalist) are now caught in the conflict between de-Westernization and re-Westernization, both driven by a capitalist-oriented economy.

This outcome grew from the seeds of de-Westernization—and in this regard the Bandung Conference was as much an explicit effort to promote decolonization as it was an implicit state-led attempt at de-Westernization. At that moment both directions were undistinguishable. It was then a different world order dominated by the interstate conflict between liberal capitalism and state communism. What shall be remembered is that Bandung as a state-led—*qua* state—project was not conducive to decolonization. But that became clear later. What do I mean by this? In 1955 no decolonial thinker or state leader foresaw that the prevailing nation-state was incompatible with decolonization. Why? For the simple reason that the nation-state was the modern/colonial institution of governance par excellence, and no decolonial thinker (except Gandhi and Fanon) at that point could foresee that Bandung would, for instance, seed the rising of Singapore in the 1960s and of China in the 1980s. Singapore's Lee Kuan Yew was only five years younger than Nasher, for example, but unlike Nasher, who led the overthrow of Egypt's monarchy in 1952 and was the country's second president in 1954, Yew became the first prime minister of Singapore, its "founding father," in 1959, four years after the conference. Yew, age thirty-two in 1955, was also quite younger than Nehru (born in 1899), who became prime minister of India in 1947. It would have been clear to Yew that the path of liberation from Westernization was through capitalism. That is the spirit of de-Westernization and was also the meaning of Bandung.

Although he was not in a position to be invited, a political figure like young Lee Kuan Yew would have been well acquainted with the Bandung

Conference, which took place just next door in neighboring Indonesia. His political analysis of international relations, his sensibility to manage public relations, and his vision for Singapore are indications of his de-Westernizing political thinking through capitalism, as was his understanding that sovereignty could be attained only by embracing and appropriating a financial capitalism rather than fighting it.[18] The point I am driving at is that de-Westernization uncoupled capitalism from liberalism and neoliberalism and usurped it to advance de-Western liberation. It is well known, and Kuan Yew himself reports, that the conversations he had with Deng Xiaoping after Mao Zedong's death contributed to China's shift from socialism to "market Leninism."[19] Refusing to be "developed" by others following the Western models of modernization and development, Deng Xiaoping delinked (as Kuan Yew had already done) from Western dictates, guidelines, and hope. Deng Xiaoping appropriated the rules of economic accumulation and growth (capitalism) and rejected liberalism instead of confronting it as Mao Zedong had done. The end result was uncoupling capitalism from liberalism (and later on neoliberalism) to manage the economy in China's own way. "Capitalism with Chinese characteristics" was a sarcastic comment in Western media. And indeed it was and it is. And one could ask: what is wrong about that? That is what de-Westernization means in the history of the CMP and it explains a good deal of the conflicts and the hybrid warfare between the US and China, as well as the US's numerous conflicts with Russia and Iran.[20] De-Westernization has contributed to ending the cycle of Westernization and Western hegemony, forcing a reorientation of US foreign policy from Westernization to re-Westernization, initiated first by Barack Obama's globalism and later by Donald Trump's nationalism.

The above are inferences derived from the history of the colonial matrix of power (CMP), not from world history or the history of Western civilization or any other relevant imperial narrative of historical "facts" as they are ordinarily taught in secondary schools and the university. The history of the CMP is the narrative of the creation of a matrix of domination propelled by the coloniality of power, which, as I suggested earlier, in a pedagogical mode, is analogous to the unconscious of psychoanalysis. And it could be seen also as the *technics* of domination, rather than survival, building on Spengler's noninstrumental concept of technics. The coloniality of power—as I've already suggested—is the unconscious of Western civilization and the CMP its instrumentalization. And let's remember that the coloniality of power we are talking about is not a feature of "human nature" but is a reorientation of the *tactics of living for domination* that surfaced in the sixteenth century with the possibilities opened up to European monarchs, clergy, adventurers, and businessmen in the triangulation of the Atlantic: New World lands, African enslaved labor, and European global designs.

What coloniality of power has created, the mechanism of its enforcement (the instrument), is the CMP, and the history of the CMP is the history of an underlying structure of the world order, managed and controlled by North Atlantic imperial states from 1500 to 2000 (Westernization) until its management began to be disputed by the rise of de-Westernization and the making of a multipolar world order. What I am saying is the result of decolonial analytics grounded in the coloniality of power and the history of the CMP. From a decolonial perspective, this history—from the sixteenth century to today—illuminates the mutations arising from seventy years of struggle between two poles of Western civilization, liberalism and socialism/communism. Standing in confrontation with and delinking from this history is the multipolar world order prompted by de-Westernization and the disputes centered on the control and management of the CMP. The three diverse pillars of de-Westernization today are, first, China, Russia, and Iran; second, the ambiguous foreign policies of India and Turkey, which are still playing their game between de- and re-Westernization; and third, the ever-changing heads of state in Latin America. Once Lula da Silva, Hugo Chávez, Néstor Kirchner and Cristina Fernández de Kirchner, Evo Morales, and Rafael Correa were gone, Latin American governance turned from its de-Western orientation to rejoin the path toward re-Westernization. Re-Westernization has resorted to sanctions while supporting "democratic" protests against disobedient states (Hong Kong, Iran, Russia), yet it remains mute when protesters rise against re-Westernizing states such as the massive protests in Chile before COVID-19 and the quiet support of the coup-d'état destituting the democratically elected Evo Morales from the presidency. The point these examples illuminate is the double standards driving, on the one hand, the rhetoric of modernity while, on the other, implementing the logic of coloniality.

An additional outcome to emerge from the Bandung Conference, by indirection, was the mutation of decolonization into decoloniality in the early 1990s, by which I mean that decoloniality after Quijano and seen through his perspective can neither be a state-led project nor be associated with nation-states. The most that a state dissenting from the West can do is to embrace a politics of de-Westernization and join China, Russia, and Iran rather than the US/UK and the European Union. The Bandung Conference was, no doubt, a marker of decolonization, and it remains in the genealogy of decoloniality, as I will describe in more detail later. It belongs there due to two radical elements Sukarno introduced into political theory that deviate or delink from Western political theory as it evolved from Plato and Aristotle to Karl Marx and Carl Schmitt. These two missing elements are race and religion.[21] In his inaugural speech, Sukarno, the first president of Indonesia (and a figure comparable to Amílcar Cabral, Patrice Lumumba, or Kwame Nkrumah) stated forcefully that the conference he convoked was the first intercontinental conference of "colored people." And he followed up by mentioning that the invitees were affiliated with many different religions: Islamism, Shintoism, Hinduism, Buddhism, Taoism. He did not mention Christianity and Judaism. This was the component of Bandung, missing in the NAM, that connects with decolonial thinking during the Cold War, in spite of and parallel to the politics of nation-state formation that I mentioned above.

While decoloniality has common features with de-Westernization, their goals are widely divergent. What decoloniality and de-Westernization share is the need to delink. De-Westernization seeks to delink from the political and economic dictates of Western institutions in order to dispute the control and management by the CMP, while decoloniality aims to delink from the CMP (see section III.3). De-Westernization needs strong states to prevent further disruptions by Western intrusion, while decoloniality turns its back to the state and reorients its task by delinking from the CMP and rebuilding communal relations in spite of social structures. Last but not least, de-Westernization is a concept incorporated into *decolonial analytics* of the world order, while decoloniality names a particular project of *decolonial liberation* by the epistemic and aesthesic reconstitution in which this book is inscribed.

II Signposts in the Formation of the Modern/Colonial World Order

The politics of decolonial investigations I pursue in this volume are framed, first, by the historical formation, transformation, and management of the CMP from 1500 to 2000, the period coinciding with the Westernization of the planet; second, by the dispute over the past two decades for the control and management of the CMP (de-Westernization); and third, by the decolonial political, epistemic, and ethical orientation to delink from both. Re-Westernization is the adjustment made by the North Atlantic states (the US, UK, and EU) to maintain the hegemony and the privileges of a unilateral world order they are in danger of losing and desperately trying to maintain. The coexistence of these three forces explains to a great extent the global disorder that all of us on the planet are experiencing. Pandemics and global warming are of secondary relevance in the dispute to maintain unipolarity, on the one hand, and to uncouple from it and create a multipolar world order on the other. Just as the five hundred years of the formation and transformation of the CMP mark the period of Westernization of the planet, so also are Westernization and Western civilization two facets of the same period, two faces of the same phenomenon: Western civilization came into being in the European Renaissance (1300–1600 are the standard dates), and it was consolidated with the advent of the coloniality of power that propelled European expansion (Westernization) after 1500. The coloniality of power (the technics) and CMP (the instrument), I argue, constitute the underlying structure of Western civilization and Westernization, two different but entangled trajectories. The first concerns the history of Europe (and more recently of the US); the second concerns the rest of the world. The concept of coloniality could have hardly appeared in Europe: Europeans see and sense modernity; the rest of the world senses and sees coloniality.

The so-called discovery and conquest of America was quickly deemed a crucial event in the history of humankind. By 1550 the Spaniard Francisco López de Gómara believed that this was the most momentous event since the creation of the world. By 1776, the Scottish philosopher and moralist Adam Smith had made a similar statement, most likely not knowing de Gómara's dictum. And in the middle of the nineteenth century, Karl Marx—knowing Smith but most likely not de Gómara—also made a similar statement. More specifically, de Gómara wrote the following in the dedication of his book, *Historia General de las Indias* (1553), to Charles I, king of Spain (1500–1558): "The most important event after the creation of the world, with the exception of the reincarnation and death of its Creator, was the discovery of the Indies. God wanted the discovery of the Indies to take place during your time and *for your vassals, so they could be converted to your sacred law.* . . . The conquest of the Indians began just after the expulsion of the Moors, so Spaniards are always at war about the infidels."[22]

Notice the assumptions that the "Indians" were vassals of the king and that they were destined to be converted to "your sacred law," which is the first epistemic destitution in this paragraph. The second one appears right after: the expulsion of the Moors, who are labeled "infidels." Their knowing, knowledge, beliefs, and praxes of living are invalidated and nullified. They, the infidels, are a "problem" that requires war to keep them at bay or to destroy them if they cannot be controlled. The naturalization of this nullification is one of the pillars of Western universalism: the "problem" is displaced onto the other when in fact it is the ostracizing Spanish who have the "problem" with their invented other. Constitution and destitution are two simultaneous epistemic procedures, and it is in this double movement that what I term "colonial" and "imperial" differences are created. The first impacts decoloniality, the second de-Westernization, although there is not a sharp division between them. Racism is an overlapping zone that encroaches on both. We will see the nature and impact of these two types of differences later in this book (chapters 8, 9, 10). For now, it is enough to note that in the period preceding the "discovery" of "the Indies," the Umayyad Caliphate, the Emirate of Córdoba, and the Emirate of Granada were in control of the Iberian Peninsula and had been controlling it for seven centuries (see map in chapter 1). The reconquest of the peninsula by the Spanish coincided with the beginning of Spain's New World conquest. We will see how what I call the "imperial difference" was then projected onto "enemies" who were not or could not be dominated. Once an imperial difference was constituted and projected toward such people, it remained in place from the sixteenth century to today. Eventually, after the expulsion of the Moors from the Iberian Peninsula, the imperial difference was bestowed on the Ottoman sultanate, and has more recently been projected onto Russia, China, and Iran (heir of the Muslim Safavid sultanate).

Significantly, Adam Smith (later recognized as the founder of political economy) issued a statement very similar to de Gómara's: "The discovery of America, and that of a passage to the East Indies by the Cape of Good Hope are the two greatest and most important events recorded in the history of mankind. Their consequences have been very great; but in the short period of between two and three centuries which has elapsed since these discoveries were made, it is impossible that the whole extent of their consequences can have been seen. What benefits, or misfortunes to mankind may hereafter result from those great events, no human wisdom can foresee."[23]

Smith's observations make necessary a few reminders about "discoveries" in view of the argument I make in this book. The Cape of Good Hope was "discovered" by the Portuguese navigator Bartolomeu Dias in 1488. He named it "Cabo das Tormentas" (Cape of Storms) four years before Columbus landed among unknown islands he thought were the Asian Indies, which were later named by Europeans the "Indias Orientales." The word "discover" goes in quotation marks because, of course, the New World and the Cape of Good Hope were known by the people inhabiting the areas. Naming the Cape of Storms, the Cape of Good Hope in Africa, as they have done before by naming the New World, Indias Occidentales, and finally America, a continent that Europeans did not know, accomplished a double destitution of the frameworks of knowledge and spatial reference: one was the erasures of the names that Andean and Mesoamerican civilizations, as well as myriad other existing cultures, gave to their territory and the physical and semantic appropriation of places, locating them in the European consciousness, and the other was the self-affirmation of European legal and economic rights to use and administer them according to their convenience.

This action simultaneously accomplished the invalidation and nullification of the original names and meaning that these places had had for the people who for centuries had inhabited what for Europeans was a New World, and the North Atlantic universals were in the making, in the origins of comparative ethnology, cartography, and international law. Beyond appropriating the planet legally, militarily, and economically, Europeans possessed the world epistemically: *epistemic constitution was simultaneous with epistemic destitutions*, and both provoked the need of *epistemic and aesthesic reconstitutions*, which we will see in more detail in section III, below. In other words, the simultaneous and heterogenous field of forces of modernity/coloniality, that is, constitution/destitution, were here at work. In section III.3 we will see the emergence of *decolonial reconstitutions*. But for the time being I am limiting myself to the work of the coloniality of power and the formation of the CMP. Since modernity/coloniality work through the coloniality of knowing and being, of epistemology and aesthetics (aesthetics is a modern concept, aesthesis a decolonial one), the reconstitution of both calls for the politics of decolonial investigations bringing back gnoseology (the conditions of all knowing, not only disciplinary) to denaturalize epistemology, and aesthesis (sensing, being in the world) to denaturalize aesthetics (the beautiful, sublime, a work of art). Healing colonial wounds and reducing Western modernity to its own size is a foremost political task of decolonial investigations and liberation.[24]

Hence, I propose modernity/coloniality/decoloniality as a complex concept that could be rendered in Aníbal Quijano's vocabulary as heterogeneous historic-structural nodes. This is also a decolonial concept that does away with the unilinear historical time of the North Atlantic universals. Historic-structural heterogeneities are temporal/spatial nodes in motion (e.g., the knotted experience of chronology and geography, of global designs and people's desires and fears, their/our sensing and emotioning, and the constant flows *in* space and time) constituted in the process of the Western epistemic designs and appropriations of planetary histories and locations and the variegated local responses to them. They disturb modes of knowing, being, sensibility (aesthesis), and belief of places and people invaded by imperial settlers, and this disturbance creates colonial wounds that turn into physical and emotional disequilibrium caused by humiliation and dehumanization, which are beyond (although emotionally related to) the aggressions of genocide, rape, and other forms of physical viciousness. For the survivors, healing colonial wounds requires regaining destituted dignity and restoring respect for people's own gnoseological and aesthesic principles of knowing, knowledge, and ways of being. Our decolonial work of reconstituting what has been destituted in the name of modernity, progress, civilization, development, and democracy is an unavoidable "remedy" to heal colonial wounds. And this is a distinctive trajectory of decoloniality today (see chapter 14).[25]

Another point that deserves attention in Smith's statement is that while he recognized the two events mentioned as the most significant in the history of mankind, he did not need the caveat "with the exception of the reincarnation and death of its Creator." Moreover, while noting the indisputable significance of these events, he was cautious about their consequences, "which no human wisdom can foresee." Today, five hundred years after the first statement and three hundred after the second one, we are experiencing their consequences globally. Interpretations vary, but decolonially speaking, the consequences Smith intuited could be seen either to consolidate modernity or to intensify coloniality, though today the issue is no longer either/or but both/and. There are *contributions* that modernity made to the history of the human species that cannot be denied, although the *benefits* of modernity for a quantitative minority of people, the growing inequality, and the increasingly destituted population is the aberration that has to be denied. Both phenomena occur simultaneously and are co-constitutive. Poverty cannot be corrected, let alone erased, as long as the economy of accumulation carries the day. Constitution/destitution, modernity/coloniality are the movers of the coloniality of power and the engine of the CMP.

About a hundred years after Smith, Karl Marx was not indifferent to what in the previous century were labeled the most significant events in the history of mankind. Marx was certainly familiar with Smith, though I doubt (as I already mentioned) he was familiar with de Gómara. In any event, Marx was not impressed by the significance of the "discovery" of America in the history of mankind but in the history of capitalism:

> The discovery of gold and silver in America, the extirpation, enslavement and entombment in mines of the indigenous population of that continent, the beginnings of the conquest and plunder of India, and the conversion of Africa into a preserve for the commercial hunting of *blackskins* are things which characterize the dawn of capitalist production. These idyllic proceedings are the chief moments of primitive accumulation.

The different moments of primitive accumulation can be assigned in particular to Spain, Portugal, Holland, France and England in more or less chronological order. These different moments are systematically combined together at the end of the seventeenth century in England; the combination embraces the colonies, the national debt, the modern tax system, and the system of protecting. These methods depend in part on brute force, for instance the colonial system. But they all employ the power of the state, the concentrated and organized force of society, to hasten as in a hot-house, the process of transformation of the feudal mode of production into capitalist mode, and to shorten the transition.[26]

Marx's narrative is told top-down. He was already witnessing the Industrial Revolution and the role of England in concert with western European imperial states, enumerated at the beginning of the first paragraph. And because he was conceptualizing and analyzing capital through the experience of the Industrial Revolution in England, he conceived the sixteenth-century economy opened up by the commercial circuits of the Atlantic as "primitive," sometimes "original," accumulation. "Primitive" was introduced in the eighteenth century and was a mutation of "barbarian located in space" into "primitives in time," the origin of the human species that "evolved" to civilization.[27] "Original" is a theological concept borrowed from "original sin." In any case, the route from primitive accumulation to the formation of capital reveals a unilineal historical time, and the destitution of geopolitical spaces, in which Marx was conceiving the history of capital(ism). I will come back to this issue shortly, but before I do, I need to consider a second observation of Marx's paragraphs.

England at that time came to be, for Marx, the culmination of the combined colonial impact of all previous European colonialism—"Spain, Portugal, Holland, France and England in more or less chronological order" (see Ottobah Cugoano's perception, below, of the combined forces of European colonialism). Chronology is the narrative logic here: the last in the sequence supersedes all previous contributions of Spain, Portugal, Holland, and France. For Quijano this would be a heterogeneous historic-structural node, a complex of diachronic and synchronic accumulation. Furthermore, the sequence exemplifies a further distinction I explore in part III of this book. Just as it is important to grasp *colonial and imperial* differences, so also should be understood that there are two types of imperial difference. One establishes the distinction within Europe itself: the *intramural imperial difference* from the North to the more inferior "South." The other establishes the distinction between Europe and coexisting strong governance: the *extramural imperial differences* projected onto the Umayyad Caliphate, the Ottoman sultanate before the making of southern Europe, and, more recently onto Russia/Soviet Union/Russian Federation, China, and Iran (heir to the Safavid sultanate).

It should be remembered that race and racism are fundamental factors driving the coloniality of power.[28] However, if we shift the geography of knowing, sensing, and believing and look instead at the Industrial Revolution from the lived experience in and of the Americas since the sixteenth century, we will form a different picture. Marx was looking *backward* from the nineteenth century and from Europe. Quijano was looking *forward* and sideways from the sixteenth century (heterogeneous historic-structural nodes) and from the Americas to the world. Here is what he perceived and described in an article he coauthored with Immanuel Wallerstein: "The modern world-system was born in the long sixteenth century. The Americas as a geosocial construct were born in the long sixteenth century. The creation of this geosocial entity, the Americas, was the *constitutive* act of the modern world-system. The Americas were not incorporated into an already existing capitalist world economy. There could not have been a capitalist world economy without the Americas" (emphasis added).[29]

In the same year as the excerpt above appeared, Quijano published in Peru (and in Spanish) his celebrated "Coloniality and Modernity/Rationality," turning his attention from the economy to knowledge and underscoring the economy as a question of knowledge, or better yet, of knowledge legitimizing the material pursuit of wealth with all its sociological, psychological, and historical consequences. Coloniality of power is the epistemic driver of politics and ethics in all areas of experience (sensing, emotioning, being) through both the economy and knowledge/understanding (i.e., the rhetoric of modernity):

> In the beginning colonialism was a product of a systematic repression, not only of the specific beliefs, ideas, images, symbols or knowledge that were not useful to global colonial domination, while at the same time the colonizers were expropriating from the colonized their knowledge, especially in mining, agriculture, engineering, as well as their products and work. The repression fell, above all, over the modes of knowing, of producing knowledge, of producing perspectives, images and systems of images, symbols, modes of signification, over the resources, patterns, and instruments of formalized and objectivized expression, intellectual or visual. It was followed by the imposition of the use of the rulers' own patterns of expression, and of their beliefs and images with reference to the supernatural. These beliefs and images served not only to impede the cultural production of the dominated, but also as a very efficient means of social

and cultural control, when the immediate repression ceased to be constant and systematic.[30]

Quijano's shift to knowledge as the dominant factor of the colonial matrix of power (CMP) was the preliminary step to shifting the meaning that decolonization had during the Cold War (i.e., the foundations of the native population's own nation-state). In South and Central America, and particularly in Spanish America, the ending of Spanish colonialism began in the first half of the nineteenth century, and in Brazil at the end of the same century. By 1990 it was obvious to Quijano that decolonization could not be achieved, not even advanced, by the modern, secular, and bourgeois nation-state, because the nation-state is fundamentally a tool of the CMP for the control of governance in both domestic national territories and in the interstate global system.[31] The formation of the nation-state in Europe, later exported/imported beyond Europe, was an instrument to lay waste to other forms of governance. Currently, the rhetoric of spreading democracy and human rights through the formation of Western-style nation-states has become an explicit tool—especially of the US—to legitimize interstate humanistic interventions. Hence, Quijano envisioned that an epistemological reconstitution (and the consequent restitution of sensing, being, and emotioning disqualified by the politics of Eurocentric knowing) had to be the fundamental decolonial task since, in his argument (which I incorporate in this book), the control of knowledge and the regulation of ways of knowing and being control the subjectivities of both governing actors (political, economic, epistemic, artistic, religious) and governed actors. White supremacy is nothing but a consequence of the coloniality of power in the sensing and emotioning of actors in ruling positions.

Here is one more vignette to illustrate the formation of the North Atlantic and the impact of the Western totality of knowledge. This time the protagonist is Sigmund Freud, writing about seventy years after Marx. Freud noticed the relevance of the two previously discussed events underscored by de Gómara, Smith, and Marx, but he saw them in relation to the "malaise of civilization." Obviously, he was not talking or thinking about Chinese, Islamic, Incan, or Persian civilizations but of Western civilization: his unconscious assumption of the universal totality of knowledge. Yet by the time Freud was writing his well-known essay *Civilization and Its Discontents* (1930), the "decline of the West" was already an issue debated by European intelligentsia.[32] Taking into account the existing discontent with civilization, he asked himself what "may have happened that so many people have come to take up this strange attitude of hostility to civilization." These reflections evolved around Freud's concern with the conditions of happiness, as they confronted a generalized feeling among the European middle class. Freud observed that what "we call our civilization is largely responsible for our misery, and that we should be happier if we gave it up and returned to the primitive conditions." Asking himself how humans had arrived at this situation, Freud speculates, "I think I know what the last and the last but one of those occasions were. I am not learned enough to trace the chain of them far back in the history of the human species, but a factor of this kind of hostility to civilization must already have been at work in the victory of Christendom over the heathen religions. For it was very closely related to the low estimation put upon earthly life by the Christian doctrine."

After preparing the terrain, Freud makes his point:

> The last but one of these occasions was when the progress of voyages of discovery led to contact with *primitive* peoples and races. In consequence of insufficient observation and a mistaken view of their manners and customs, they appeared to Europeans to be leading a simple, happy life with few wants, a life such as was unattainable by their visitors with their superior civilization. Later experience has corrected some of those judgements. . . . The last occasion is especially familiar to us. It arose when people came to know about the mechanism of neurosis, which threatens to undermine the modicum of happiness enjoyed by civilized men. . . . A person becomes neurotic because he cannot tolerate the amount of frustration which society imposes on him in the service of its cultural ideals. . . . The abolition or reduction of those demands would result in a return to possibilities of happiness. (Emphasis added.)[33]

In his efforts to understand the discontents that civilization has generated, he moves into a consideration of humans' power over nature and technology. Notice that he is writing about a decade before cybernetics would revolutionize technologies by introducing "thinking machines"—the technological automation of the Industrial Revolution that Charles Chaplin has rendered unforgettable in *Modern Times* (1936), made six years after Freud's *Civilization and Its Discontents*. Freud observes that the "newly won power over space and time, this subjugation of the forces of nature, *which is a longing that goes back thousands of years*, has not increased the amount of pleasurable satisfaction which they may expect from life and has not made them happier" (emphasis added).

Freud's concern about the negative effect that civilization has on happiness calls for clarification. The first is to question the assumption that the "pursuit of happiness" (which to this day has increasingly been attached to having more) is a universal, not regional, obsession in a civilization that has made of the individual (individual pleasure and the pursuit of happiness) the fundamental meaning of life. Shall this be the only one for all, or just for Western civilization? (See chapter 14.) Concurrently, the second clarification queries the assumption that for thousands of years mankind was longing to "subjugate the forces of nature." Two counterexamples should suffice to cast some doubt on these assumptions. But notice that both assumptions, the pursuit of happiness and the longing to subjugate the forces of nature, are already constitutive of the *Western civilization*, which Freud renders simply as "civilization" as if it were the only (universal) one or that members of any other civilization would have set for themselves the same principles and goals.

The first counterexample questions Freud's taking for granted that the "pursuit of happiness" is the horizon of all mankind (another assumption of the universal totality of knowledge), and in so doing he preempted asking questions about his assumption, forestalling not only other possibilities but also other circumstances in which different pursuits would have been the main concern of non-Western civilizations. Freud was far removed in space, time, and frame of mind from the world and philosophy of Náhuatl-speaking people in ancient Mexico, also known as the Aztec civilization. Happiness was not the main concern in Náhuatl philosophy, if it was a concern at all. The main concern for them was "rootedness," in which humans valued both "truth" and "good life" (not to be confused with the capitalist "better life"; see chapter 14) in the sense of how life should be lived according to their philosophy. Their image of existence was that we, humans, live on a slippery earth. By this they meant that living well and maintaining one's balance and equilibrium is what should guide people's vision, emotioning, and behavior. Hence, "rootedness" could be translated as "truth" as well as "grounded life," for they are synonymous in Náhuatl philosophy. In that philosophy the horizon of life was not to be happy (whatever happiness may have meant for the Náhuatl); rootedness, balance, and equilibrium were their horizon and praxis of living.

> *Nahua tlamatinime* [man of wisdom] conceived the raison d'être of philosophy in terms of this situation [that we live on a slippery earth], and turned to philosophy for practicable answers to what they regarded as the defining question of human existence: How can humans maintain their balance upon the slippery earth? This situation and question jointly constitute the problematic which functions as the defining framework for Nahua philosophy. Morally, epistemologically, and aesthetically appropriate human activity are defined in terms of the goal of humans main-

taining their balance upon the slippery earth. All human activities are to be directed towards this aim. At bottom, Nahua philosophy is essentially pragmatic.[34]

The "pursuit of happiness" is a Western obsession connected to the Western glorification of the individual (see my previous observations on "trauma") and of material possessions, which also explains the social burdens, demands, and expectations that engender neurosis and create the conditions for its "remedy," in this case the psychoanalytic cure, which brings us to the second observation. Let me add more about Náhuatl philosophy and the meaning of life: the search of rootedness and balance on the slippery Earth:

> The word the Aztecs used is *neltiliztli*. It literally means "rootedness," but also "truth" and "goodness" more broadly. They believed that the true life was the good one, the highest humans could aim for in our deliberate actions. This resonates with the views of their classical "Western" counterparts, but diverges on two other fronts. First, the Aztecs held that this sort of life would not lead to "happiness," except by luck. Second, the rooted life had to be achieved at four separate levels, a more encompassing method than that of the Greeks.[35]

By the time Freud was writing, the *constitution* of Western civilization had *destituted* Aztec civilization four hundred years before. That is how the rhetoric of modernity works (constitution) and how it hides and disqualifies what is on its way forward (destitution).

The second counterexample I offer here calls into question "the mechanism of neurosis," which results from the amount of frustration society imposes on individuals. Needless to say, the individuals in question are most likely middle-class western Europeans. At the time Freud was writing these essays, millions of people around the world had been destabilized by European invasions, projecting racism and inflicting colonial wounds. Psychoanalysis came into being precisely to deal with the destabilized members of the western European middle class, due, as Freud knew well, to the imposition that society enforces "in the service of cultural ideals."

Decolonially speaking, the phenomenon described here is a manifestation of the rhetoric of modernity (cultural ideals and promises of progress, change, and happiness) that are imposed not by force but by creating desires that cannot be satisfied by the majority of the population. Generating desires is what counts, and for that the rhetoric of modernity is an essential tool of the CMP. The rhetoric of modernity goes hand in hand with the logic of coloniality:

happiness (rhetoric of modernity) is the reverse face of frustrations and neuroses (logic of coloniality). Outside Europe, in Asia, Africa, South/Central America, and the Caribbean, colonial wounds were inflicted in the colonized not by unsatisfied desires of the modern middle class but by the relentless work of humiliation and dehumanization (e.g., by racialization and racialized sexualities) of the majority of the non-European population. In psychoanalysis, the analytic cure deals with neurosis. Colonial wounds could hardly be "cured" by psychoanalysis, as Fanon clearly witnessed in Algeria. Colonial wounds had to be *healed* (not cured) by the wounded herself/himself in communal work, not in isolation. And here is where epistemic and aesthesic reconstitutions come to the foreground. These wounds are mended only by decolonial healings, which are communal endeavors initiated and joined by persons affected by colonial wounds. One case in point, among many, is Lorena Cabnal, a communal feminist Maya-Xinca from Guatemala:

> El objetivo político de la Red de Sanadoras es partir de nuestro abordaje ancestral cosmogónico y feminista comunitario territorial para colaborar en la *recuperación emocional, física y espiritual* de las mujeres indígenas defensoras de la vida en las comunidades, quienes actualmente sufren los efectos de múltiples opresiones sobre su cuerpo. (Emphasis added.)[36]

> The political objective of the Network of [female] Healers is to start from our ancestral cosmogony and territorial communitarian feminism, to collaborate in the *emotional, physical and spiritual recovery* of indigenous women defenders of life in the communities, who currently suffer the effects of multiple oppressions on their bodies.

"Emotional, physical and spiritual recovery" requires epistemic and aesthesic reconstitutions, and these goals cannot be achieved within the epistemology and subjectivities of the actors and institutions running the CMP, who operate by means of the double movement of constitution/destitution. Global health is a case in point. Physical and spiritual recovery from the self-constitution of a so-called "global health design" that legitimizes the destitution of ancestral praxes of living and knowing requires healing the colonial wounds that global designs has caused, and this healing can only be achieved by reconstituting acts of knowing and sensing/emotioning, that is, by epistemic/aesthesic reconstitutions. For Indigenous people, the reconstitution of the communal means a constant recalling of ancestral cosmogony and territorial spirituality destituted by Christianity and by dispossession of land and exploitation of Indigenous labor. "Communal" and "communitarian," in Indigenous praxes of living and thinking, mean common union with the living cosmos, not limited to the human community. The *social-human* of Western civilization destituted the *communal-cosmic*. Without epistemic/aesthesic reconstitutions there cannot be restitution in the search for balance and harmony as the horizon of communal life. Put another way, the reconstitution of knowing (gnoseology), sensing, and emotioning (aesthesis) by Indigenous people themselves ("cosmic" in Cabnal's vocabulary) reestablishes the priority of the communal over the glorification of the individual, and the *society of individuals* separated from the living cosmos (nature) and enclosed in their own ego.

Neurosis is not of necessity a problem for Indigenous females, at least as far as taking their destiny into their own hands is concerned. Psychoanalysis and psychoanalysts are not needed. The cosmo-political healing of colonial wounds (as Cabnal articulates it) is not quite the same as dealing with and curing a trauma. When I say—as I often do—that psychoanalysis is irrelevant to healing colonial wounds, I am not making a critique of Freud and psychoanalysis. I am underscoring the consequences of assuming universal totality of knowledge, which is the politics of Eurocentric knowing. I am saying only that in many contexts psychoanalysis is out of place because the "individual" is not the center and the communal is not the Western social. When Fanon perceived the limits of psychoanalysis for the Berber and Arab population (probably not for the *pied noir*), he was well acquainted—as a psychologist—with psychoanalysis, and he embodied the colonial wound of his own Black Caribbean experience in France. Psychoanalysis was born to deal with issues of an increasingly industrial and capitalist Europe at the end of the nineteenth and first decades of the twentieth centuries. When it was reincarnated in the 1960s in Paris, the civilizational discontent that Freud perceived in the 1930s was the same in kind: the frustration that society imposes on individuals. But there was an added element: racism, which could have been in Freud, but he did not thematize it as Fanon did. Even later, following the sophisticated psychoanalytic recasting of Freud by the French psychoanalyst and philosopher Jacques Lacan, the socioeconomic conditions that provoked destabilization and frustration did not change. And if Lacan was aware of racism, it was not a significant element in his psychoanalytic theory. In that regard, there is a function for, indeed a need for, psychoanalysis in the large sector of the world's population trapped in the *interiority* of Western civilization, as Freud perceived early on. And that explains why in Buenos Aires, a society of European immigrants mainly, psychoanalysis found a home. For other sectors of the population, such as Indigenous men and women, *neither neurosis nor other mental trauma* was their problem, though long-lasting colonial wounds, inflicted by racial and sexual dehumanization, pushed the population of European descent in the colonies into the disorders Freud was observing in the European middle class. In many places in South America psychoanalysis is limited to a small portion of the Eurocentered population. Even the middle class at large prefers "*curanderas* and *curanderos*" (healers) who know how to deal with colonial wounds. Trauma names psychological disorders of the European bourgeoisie; colonial wounds name the humiliation and dehumanization of people around the world, of women and men mainly of color but not only.

I close here the four historical sketches that illustrate the constitutive rhetoric of modernity, the underlying assumptions that guide the narratives (celebratory and critical) of Western civilization in its constitution, simultaneous with intended and nonintended consequences: destitutions effected by the logic of coloniality. I move now to the conceptual structure of the CMP. At this point we—you, reader, and myself—are plunged and plunging into the conceptual apparatus of the politics of decolonial investigations.

III The Constitution of the Colonial Matrix of Power: Domains, Levels, and Flows

III.1 Constitution

The time has arrived to take a closer look at the colonial matrix of power (CMP).[37] Coloniality and the coloniality of power can for convenience be thought of as shorthand for a grid of complex and diffuse fields of forces that Quijano described as "patrón colonial de poder" and I translated into English as the "colonial matrix of power."[38] It should be remembered that *since 1500, the singular feature of the coloniality of power is the driving energy in building, maintaining, transforming, and managing the* CMP. The question here is "power." In that regard, Quijano writes:

> Tal como lo conocemos históricamente, *el poder es un espacio y una malla de relaciones sociales* de explotación/dominación/conflicto articuladas, básicamente, en función y en torno de la disputa por el control de los siguientes ámbitos de existencia social: 1) el trabajo y sus productos; 2) en dependencia del anterior, la "naturaleza" y sus recursos de producción; 3) el sexo, sus productos y la reproducción de la especie; 4) la subjetividad y sus productos materiales e intersubjetivos, incluido el conocimiento; 5) la autoridad y sus instrumentos, de coerción en particular, para asegurar la reproducción de ese patrón de relaciones sociales y regular sus cambios. (Emphasis added.)[39]

As we know it historically, *power is a space and a mesh of social relations* of exploitation/domination/conflict articulated, basically, on and around the dispute over the control of the following areas of social existence: (1) work and its products; (2) depending on the foregoing, the products of "natural resources"; (3) sex and its products in the regeneration of the species; (4) subjectivity and its material and intersubjective products, including knowledge; (5) authority and its instruments, in particular of coercion, to ensure the reproduction of this pattern of social relations and regulate its changes.

Through the years, Quijano offered changing modulations of the CMP. However, the core remains in all of them. The CMP cannot be formalized. That is why it shall be conceived as both a structure of management and a frame of mind. The first is a mobile structure, and the second a structured frame of mind that cannot be fixed in mathematical formulae, which would kill the fluidity of the frame of mind/structure of management that the CMP is. Quijano's philosophical argument behind his outline of the CMP as shown in the previous quotation is expressed in this paragraph: "The current model of global power is the first effectively global one in world history in several specific senses. To begin with, it is the first where in each sphere of social existence all historically known forms of control of respective social relations are articulated, configuring in each area only one structure of systematic relations between its components and, by the same means, its whole."[40]

This partial paragraph, although abstract, is crucial to understand the scope of what Quijano was sensing and perceiving: nothing less than the underlying structure of Western civilization. Quijano makes this abstraction more specific in the second part of the paragraph, which I take as a launching pad for the three simultaneous movements described in the following pages. He adds:

> It is [also] the first model in which each structure of each sphere of social existence is under the *hegemony of an institution produced within the process of formation and development of that same model of power*: thus, in the control of labor and its resources and products, it is the capitalist enterprise in the control of sex and its resources and products, the bourgeois family in the control of authority and its resources and products, the nation-state, and in the control of subjectivity, the domain of knowledge/understanding.[41]

He adds that "each one of those institutions exists in a relation of interdependence with each of the other. Therefore, the model of power is configured as a system [a structure of management and frame of mind in my vocabulary]; finally, this model of global power is the first that covers the entire population of the planet."[42]

Over twenty years have elapsed at the time I am writing this introduction since Quijano formulated the concept of "coloniality" in the essay "Coloniality of Power, Eurocentrism and Social Classification," from where I extracted the previous quotations.[43] His insights have not lost the force of their initial formulation.[44] The transformations of the world order since the publication of his essay have enriched the scope of Quijano's vision. Maintaining his basic discernment, in the previous excerpts, I slightly modified his wording and his ordering of the various areas of human existence. I elaborate on these four areas of existence in the double movement of the *constitution of the* CMP's *interiority simultaneous with the* CMP's *destitution of its exteriority*. Exteriority is not an ontic "outside" that exists beyond the CMP; exteriority is the ontological outside created in the process of its epistemic (knowledge and understanding) and subjective (aesthetic) constitution. Both exteriority and interiority parallel the extramural and intramural acting out of the colonial and imperial differences that I mentioned above. Each area of existence is affirmed and established at the expense of those made destitute. Epistemic and aesthesic responses healing colonial wounds emerge in this double movement.

To better understand the responses, let's outline the four basic domains of the CMP, slightly modified:

1 KNOWLEDGE/UNDERSTANDING. From 1500 to 1800, theology was the hegemonic frame for knowing and understanding. From 1800 to today, secular sciences (natural and social sciences and the humanities) displaced theology. Both frames were instrumental in the long processes of Westernization of the planet. Subjectivities (personal sensing, emotioning) and subjective relations are constituted by the overarching frames of knowledge/understanding that the subject is subjected to, even when the subject opposed the subjection.

2 GOVERNANCE/LEGAL AUTHORITY. In the formation and transformation of the CMP, between 1500 and 1800, Western states were theological/monarchic, while bourgeois governance (control of labor and its products) displaced monarchic states and consolidated the nation-state form after the French Revolution. The republics (*res-public*) in South America were the first former colonies that gained independence from peninsular monarchies, formed nations, and transformed monarchic viceroyalties into nation-states. Something similar happened in the second half of the

twentieth century (starting with India in 1947): nations were formed over colonial settlers' governance.

3 ECONOMY. From 1500 to 1750, the type of economy generated in the Atlantic (America, Africa, and Europe) is described in the canonical economic histories as mercantilism; from 1750 to 1945, the Industrial Revolution mutated mercantilism into industrial capitalism; from 1945 on, technology and financialization restructured the sphere of labor and its outcome.

4 HUMAN/HUMANITY. The concept of the human, and its derivation, humanity (i.e., the domain human/humanity), was established after the European Renaissance as the conceptual point of reference and point of arrival of all theologies of human destiny. Knowledge/understanding and governance presupposes human leadership, and therefore the economy, both in its practical regulations and in its political economic conceptualization, was assumed to be the task of the humans. As we will see in chapters 1, 2, 3, and 13 of this book, racism and sexism, civilization and progress, development and modernization are all keywords/concepts in the rhetoric of Western modernity, anchoring a regional image of man/human (see chapter 12) to legitimize domination and exploitation. Human and "culture" were in collusion to expel "nature" out of its realms to the extent that lesser humans were placed near nature. After the Industrial Revolution (in the domain of culture), nature became natural resources. "Standing reserve" was identified more recently by Martin Heidegger. Obviously, such abuses of humanness generate conflicts, and the abuses of "nature" are an overwhelming concern in the twenty-first century. The hierarchies of humanness that human/humanity regulates and justifies have a distorted effect in human relations in all areas of experience—that is to say in the domains and the levels of the CMP, and so in our human relations with the living universe, reduced in the rhetoric of Western modernity to one noun: nature.

These areas of experience or domains of the CMP have not been built by the creator of the universe but by human beings who appointed themselves to be the human model of humanity, concealing the circumstances that the human species and planet Earth were created by the same cosmic energy. The four domains arose at certain points in time and in certain places, and they came into being through a kind of storytelling (theological, literary, philosophical, scientific, artistic) that I call "the rhetoric of (Western) modernity." The rhetoric of modernity created and naturalized areas of experiences that are taken for granted. My analysis of the CMP aims to show that

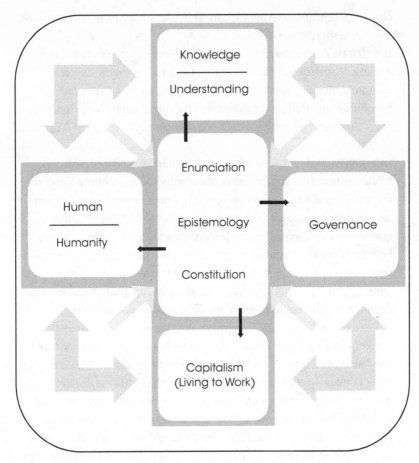

FIGURE I.1 The *constitution* of the colonial matrix of power, the four domains, and the concealed level of the enunciation that governs and interconnects all of them.

it was constituted to have certain purposes and to achieve particular results, as specified in figures I.1 and I.2. The first step in this analysis is to recognize that the domains as described are a decolonial abstraction of what storytelling narratives—their pros and cons that either way legislate Western epistemic and aesthetic management—have built since 1500. The rhetoric of modernity is the visible manifestation of a hidden structure, the logic of coloniality, and both form the colonial matrix of power: the first as the public mask, and the second as the underground logic of domination, exploitation, expropriation, and control. When I write "modernity/coloniality," the CMP described in figure I.1 should be graphically appended to the bottom or the top of "/": the

CMP is both the rhetoric of modernity and the logic of coloniality, while the coloniality of power is the *technics* that calls for instruments of domination, control, and management.

Figure I.1 shows the four domains of the CMP just mentioned: Knowledge/ Understanding, Governance, Economy (in this case, Capitalism), and Human/ Humanity. Each domain has been abstracted from the narratives that in their totality form the rhetoric of modernity. These narratives are based on specific purposes: salvation, progress, development, democracy, happiness. If you pay attention to all the advertising that lands on your computer screen, you will notice that the people in the advertising are either jumping, smiling, running, or doing all these at once. The domains are specific provinces of meaning built as independent units in Western civilization's structure of knowledge. That is, political theory and political economy were built in the sector of knowledge/ explanation (epistemology), while arts and the humanities, cultural anthropology, and history were built in the sector of understanding/interpretation (hermeneutics), ultimately derived from master disciplines such as theology, science, and philosophy (which includes aesthetics). The domain of knowledge/understanding was modeled on the figure and needs of man/whiteness, and therefore patriarchy and masculinity came to be the spirit of the CMP's legitimization of racism and sexism. The autonomy of each domain has been increasingly framed by disciplinary formations to the extent that it has been necessary to invent the role of "the expert" within each domain, ignoring the relationality that makes each domain dependent on the other three, connected by the invisible logic of coloniality. To disclose this hidden logic, the darker side of modernity, is the urgent and constant task of decolonial investigations. Although knowledge-explanation/understanding-interpretation permeates all four domains (and emanates from the level of the enunciation), it also has its specific sphere. (Knowledge/understanding names simultaneously both the process of explanation and meaning and the events, phonemes, and things that are known and understood.)

The other three domains, Governance, Economy, and Humanity, obviously assert and lay claims to knowledge, but it is important to grasp that these domains are distinguished by their specific ways of knowing what is asserted to be known. Think, for example, of how political theory, political economy, science, philosophy, or theology, all of which presuppose human/humanity, are all procedures for *inventing* what they know and understand and do not necessarily *represent* things that exist independently of these domains' particular processes of knowing and understanding. The agencies of knowledges and understanding are granted by the level of enunciation (see below). The domains of the economy and governance, for instance, frame areas of human experiences at the crossroads of knowing/understanding (and they presuppose professional and human ranking of the actors managing each domain). To get a PhD or an MBA you have to conform to disciplinary regulations and social-institutional expectations. Economy frames a domain of experience established by the junction of codified words and deeds—those governing financial exchanges, labor, and so forth—but only those words and deeds that apply to what you do under the presuppositions of what the domain of economy is established to embrace. "Capitalism" in the vocabulary of Western modernity (liberal and Marxist) names the domain of economy in the CMP but sidelines the relevance of the other three domains and the enunciation that regulates and interrelates all four domains. In this regard, political economy is a discourse that clearly reveals the latent presence of discourses in other domains (the rhetoric of modernity) as well the logic of coloniality. Yet often the domain of economy, confused with capitalism, seems to preclude asking questions about the larger issues that are embedded in the functioning of the economic domain: for example, the destitution of economic reciprocity, the administration of scarcity, and the morality of this administration.[45] For that reason, most economic debates today are about "improving" the economy and defending capitalism rather than questioning what role the economy should play if not at the service of accumulation, engendering corruptions, and related crimes. "Improving" in the previous sense points toward changes in the content of what is assumed to be the only alternative—the taking for granted in the CMP that the domain of the economy equals capitalism. The emphasis on "improving" precludes, not by law or public policies, but by the outright rhetoric of no better alternative, that indeed alternatives abound but are not welcome. However, asking questions about the role of the economy should go deeper to address the terms of economic conversations (i.e., the enunciation), namely, the regulations governing the ways of knowing, understanding, and acting on that domain. It implies uncoupling economy from capitalism and reconstituting the etymology of the word *oikonomie* (the regulation, *nomo*, of the household, *oiko*)—that is, the administration of scarcity rather than the administration of wealth. The frame of mind regulating and enacting the CMP's designs has been taken up by the administration of wealth without considering the consequences, which we, on the planet, are experiencing in 2020.

When Karl Marx stated that a society's economic infrastructure determines its superstructure, he articulated a necessary and welcome move to place the economic structure of accumulation (capitalism) in the foreground of our understanding of society. The correlation was critiqued in Europe within

Marxism itself. However, more than 150 years after Marx, and looking at the world order from the South American Andes, the correlation between knowledge/understanding (superstructure) and economy (infrastructure) needs to be significantly reformulated from the perspective of coloniality (that is, from a decolonial perspective), particularly given that in the modern/colonial world order, sensing, knowing, and believing are highly conditioned by the economy, and being aware that the actors who run the economy (the state, the banks, and the corporations, supported by the mass media and the advertising industry) are motivated by their own desires, emotions, perceptions, and beliefs in ways in which their individual interests and the well-being of (a sector of) the nation are difficult to separate. For this reason, the economy (meaning here economic coloniality or capitalism) cannot be changed if the actors running institutions do not change their assumptions, convictions, and beliefs in redirecting their desires toward the well-being of humanity at large and in harmony with living Earth.

To achieve such a difficult task, *decolonial horizons of life placing the economy at the service of life instead of life at the service of the economy are inevitable.* By "decolonial" here I mean horizons celebrating life and harmony instead of competition, exploitation, and war. Put another way, the horse of the economy must again be placed in front of the cart of life rather than having life pushing the cart of the economy, as has been the case especially since the 1950s. If hope is to be preserved, and it should be, that reconstitutions of the destituted be pursued, it will likely not be achieved by diplomatic agencies, by meetings of the UN, the G7, or the G20, for they all operate within the CMP, driven by the rhetoric of modernity and the logic of coloniality. Perhaps the economy needs to be changed by the gargantuan efforts of a political society working beyond or beneath the state and the corporations, the banks, and the mass media to re-create what was devastated by Western modernity and the advent of capitalism. The politics of decolonial investigations shall contribute to and walk into the horizon prompted by the gargantuan work—and the signs of this eruption are already visible—of the *global* political society. Decolonial investigations should assist such a planetary undertaking, an undertaking that is pluriversal—meaning that it will not be a "universal" decolonial design—to reconstitute and restitute what Western modernity and its darker side, coloniality, left destituted. As a result, because decolonial knowledge/understanding permeates all the domains of the CMP, then all efforts of restitution—not returning to the past, but affirming in the present what should be preserved for the future—can only be achieved by a constant task of gnoseological reconstitution of what epistemology destituted and aesthesic reconstitution of what aesthetics destituted. This alone will not complete such a transformation, but without it, the calamities—next to the achievements—brought about by Western civilization cannot be repaired. Albert Einstein's dictum that problems cannot be solved with the same mindset that created them is relevant today and in general, not only to the field of theoretical physics.

Whatever is done by labor—whether it be the production of commodities or of military armaments, whether it be the circulation or distribution of goods, or the administration and organization of a given economic sphere, or the acquisition of products by consumers, or the handling of those products when they are discarded, whether it be the creation of advertisements that harass you to make purchases or banks that offer you low interest on your credit card for three months, or international institutions that offer your government loans to solve the economic problems in your country without disclosing the resulting enslavement of debts—all such activities are interwoven with discourses, narratives, concepts, conversations, and a knowledge and understanding that are shared by those who are part of the game (not merely those who regulate it) and all who give their/our meaning to these activities. The meaning may be controversial. Liberal, neoliberal, and Marxist interpretations of the economy differ, but they all agree on the assumption that economy equals capitalism. Communal economies are destituted, out of the conversation (see chapter 14). The situation is similar with political theory. Political theory is an expression enclosing a vast domain of human experiences and discourses/narratives into regulations that in their unfolding always exceed one set of regulations and the enclosing. However, that frame, the frame of political economy (the domain of the economy), is a frame of Western modernity and nothing else.

If the enclosure of Western political theory, from Plato and Aristotle to Machiavelli and beyond, is now known in Zimbabwe, Bolivia, and China, its span was achieved by the expanding process of Westernization, not because the local histories of these places were the same as the local histories of the West. The epistemic colonial/imperial difference is at work here. No other civilization on the planet conceived the economy (meaning all the activities to produce, store, and exchange what is necessary to live) as an activity of exploiting labor and reinvesting the surplus to produce still more, not to mention dealing with the downstream consequences, seen and unforeseen, of such activities. Reinvesting the surplus to produce more and to satisfy the needs and desires of a global market was a radical shift that the larger, diverse, and planetary sphere of the economy made in the sixteenth century, in the Atlantic, to become the CMP's economic domain. In the making were activities that created a type of subjectivity and of discourses managing desires that affected both the managed and the managers. The concept of *oikonomie*, derived from the Greek *oikos*, meaning "house," and *nomos*, meaning "regulations," was similar to the administration of the *ayllu* in Andean civilizations or the administration of the *calpulli* among the Aztecs. However, the concept of *economy* was not derived from Aymara, Quechua, Quichua, or Náhuatl, but from the Greek language, and the transformation made sense of an activity and a knowledge that mutated the administration of the *oikos* and of scarcity into managing wealth. If you would like to know more about what the *ayllu* and the *calpulli* were, I would say that *oikos* is similar to both, and that we shall see the *oikos* starting from the *ayllu* and the *calpulli* and not the other way round. To do this would be a small step toward delinking from epistemic and aesthetic hegemony and opening them up to gnoseological and aesthesic reconstitutions: the larger frame of knowledge, knowing, sensing, and believing that epistemology and aesthetic enclosed.

I could discuss every domain of the CMP and engage in a lengthier description of each of them, but for the purpose of this introduction it should suffice to say that the domain of government, for example, has a similar configuration to the domain of the economy. It consists of a sphere of doing (governing) and of discourses (storytelling and theories attributing meanings to the doing and world-making and governing). Likewise is the domain of knowledge/ understanding. Knowledge/understanding belongs to the sphere of doing (creating, transforming, and managing knowledge, and regulating knowing and understanding, like governance and economy), and also to the sphere of discourses (storytelling and theories) that attribute meanings and world-making to knowledge and understanding. In this sense, this domain has the privilege above all others of confusing the sphere of doing with the sphere of discourses. Science and philosophy are framed in and by epistemology (explanations of the known); art and aesthetics in and by the frame of hermeneutics (understanding and interpretation of meaning). Actors in the domain of knowledge/ understanding are identified by role names: scientist, theologian, philosopher, scholar, sociologist, artist, curator, journalist, etc. Hegemonic knowledge and knowing have been created, managed, and transmitted by these social roles, the institutions they/we are associated with, and the Western (modern) imperial languages. Overall, epistemology belongs to the family of science and philosophy, and hermeneutics to the realm of the humanities, each of which is an extension, within the domain of knowledge/understanding, of the domain of human/ humanity. Knowledge/understanding do not exist and operate by themselves. They are created, transformed, and administered by human/humanity. What is irrelevant to the constitution of this domain enters the sphere of destituting knowledges and understanding.

Let's explore a little further the domain of human/humanity. Unlike the previous three domains, human/humanity includes neither specific work assignments of its own (no labor of producing, distributing, or consuming commodities; no labor in governing, ruling, establishing social laws; no labor in producing and disseminating knowledge and understanding) nor the products of such labors (knowledge and interpretations; commodities; laws and edicts). Human/humanity seems, indeed, to be itself the "product" of the labor of knowledge/understanding—a product that serves well the surveillance of who fits the requirements of human/humanity and why the living universe, conceptualized as nature, became "natural resources." (See figure I.2.) The discourses bestowing meaning to the domain of human/humanity reside elsewhere in the domain of knowledge/understanding and, as we will see later in this book, at the level of the enunciation: labor in the domain of human/humanity is in the invisible hands of the enunciation. The two words "human" and "humanity" *identify the doers, the actors* of the enunciation as well as *of the other domains*, which are not separated actors but separated functions. The main function of this domain is to maintain its boundaries and to ensure that the other three domains are regulated by actors that belong to the domain of human/humanity and that any lesser humans, or any nonhumans, are kept at bay by the labor of knowledge/understanding.

The interrelations among the four domains are indicated by the double-ended arrows connecting them. Not all participant actors and observers will be aware of how the domains encroach on their lives, and this is precisely the function of the rhetoric of modernity—to hide, to divide, to obscure, to misinform. Knowledge regulates subjectivities, and this is why the decolonial epistemic and aesthesic reconstitution into gnoseology and aesthesis is necessary to disclose the hidden effects of the rhetoric of modernity and its visible and enchanting promises. This awareness comes out in decolonial analysis (hence, the need for decolonial investigations) and self-reflection, making explicit what remains implicit for actors and participants of a given domain. In writing this introduction and this book I become a *participant* in the domains of human/humanity and knowledge/understanding, and at the same time I become an *actor* who is striving to delink from the enchantments of modernity. Engaging in uncovering the logic of coloniality, and engaging in efforts to reconstitute epistemology and aesthetics into gnoseology and aesthesis, I become an actor operating in the *exteriority* of CMP (see figure I.3). Which means that, in Escher's well-known lithograph of two hands, each drawing the other, I am a *participant* in the domains that I describe and an *actor* enacting decolonial gnoseological and aesthesic reconstitution of epistemology and aesthesis.[46]

Let's move finally to the promised enunciation. The four domains configure *the level of the enunciated* (i.e., what is said, the content of the conversations) in which all actors (those running the domains), all participants (those using the domains, e.g., clients using banks or patients using hospitals), and/or all observers (i.e., analysts of a given domain that are not actors or participants in it) engage in or observe conversations—oral, written, and/or communicated through imagery. "Level" here means that the domains (the content of the conversations) are in the open, visible at the surface level, but the enunciation (regulating the terms of the conversation) remains hidden. That is precisely why the politics of Eurocentric knowing was able to make us believe in the universality of the domains (knowledge, what is known as fact and/or sustained by theories) assuming that and acting as if their enunciation were universal: the universal subject of knowing, the totality of knowledge, the politics of Eurocentric research, knowledge, and knowing. "Below" the enunciated (theories circulated in books and specialized magazines, information in the mainstream and social media, in courses and seminars in colleges and universities), the hidden level of the enunciation regulates the effects of the said, implanting the images of the world or reality that appear to us in front of what is being said, managing and framing what is supposed to be there. That is why "representation" is a powerful word in the rhetoric of modernity and one to be avoided at all costs in decolonial thinking.

No domain is a homogeneous or harmonic arena of conversations. Conflict of interpretations in all the four domains and within the CMP are taken for granted. However, what is not often seen is that a conflict of interpretations in a given domain may become muddled in two ways: one is the effect of the totality of knowledge that each domain engenders, and the other is that no domain is independent of the other and of the enunciation. The enunciation connects a given domain with the rest. None of the domains are closed in themselves; they are interlocked with the enunciations and through them to the other domains. The economy is not enclosed in the totality of capitalism. Capitalism is an interpretation of a type of economy interconnected with the other domains and managed by the enunciation. This is the secret force of the imaginary of Western modernity: the constant transference of meaning among the domains through the labor of the enunciation. There are disputes, contentions, arguments, misinformation. All conversations transpire via personal, face-to-face contact or via mediated contacts (TV, internet, newspapers, radio). The conversations and the disputes revolve around the control of a given domain. Quijano outlined the harmony and disharmony in each domain, pointing out that *inherent to the structure and flows of the* CMP *is the coexistence of an underlying threefold energy: domination/exploitation/conflict.* In the domain of human/humanity, the triple energy generates and maintains racism and sexism through diverse strategies of knowledge/understanding that legitimize humiliations and dehumanization. In addition, the commodification of "nature" is the product (as Quijano would say) of an epistemic labor (knowledge/understanding) in collusion with the domains of governance and economy.

In figures I.1, I.2, and I.3, I am attempting to render the triple energy of *domination/exploitation/conflict* (the spirit of coloniality of power) as the triple movement of *constitution/destitution/reconstitution.* The *constitution* of the CMP is achieved by the simultaneous *destitution* of the inconvenient and undesirable. This act of destitution brings into being colonial and imperial differences, and these differences secure the *interiority* of the CMP by inventing its *exteriority,* which generally is the place of danger and the locus of provocations to execute "imminent attacks" against the interiority. That rhetoric was common among Western Christians in the sixteenth century and among Western politicians in the twenty-first. The exteriority, conceptually expelled with all its consequences (imposing sanctions today, for example) from the interiority, now consists of forsaken places and borderlands where gnoseological and aesthesic reconstitution must take place, for once placed in the exteriority, the effects of colonial and imperial difference last a long time. Exteriorities (see figure I.2) are the zones of conflict from where the energies of reconstitution emerge and are nourished (see figure I.3).

Underneath, metaphorically speaking, the level of the domains (what has been said, what is being said, the content of conversations), lies the level of the enunciation (the saying, the terms of the conversations that regulate their content (see the center of figure I.1). In fact, the very *constitution* of the CMP and the *destitution* that creates its exteriority are regulated by enunciated knowledges (establishing the normal and identifying the enemy based on established and canonical knowledge on the side of the accuser). In other words, a leading and determinative function of the enunciation is to orient the subjects through knowledge and understanding which, at the same time, conform to the subjectivities of the manager, asserting itself as the gatekeeper of true knowledge and normal behavior for all. Power differentials between managers and between manager and managed reside at the core of the foundation, operative transformations, and governing and administering the CMP. But what do I mean more specifically by the "level of the enunciation"? Let me begin to explain by listing its three *components*: languages, actors, and institutions.

LANGUAGES The formation of the CMP, during the sixteenth century, was implemented mainly in Latin, Italian, Spanish, and Portuguese, along with the backing provided by translations of Greek texts into Latin. French was very important in Europe, but France did not have a colonial strategic posi tion, in the sixteenth century, to intervene in the making of both the New World and the Atlantic commercial circuit. French commerce and language gained ground in the colonies and in the Atlantic commercial circuits in the seventeenth century, as did English. French and English world dominance was manifested in the eighteenth century (the Enlightenment), simultane ous with the decay of imperial Spain and of the influence of Spanish language vis-à-vis the growing influence of French, English, and German. It was in the languages of the European Renaissance and the Enlightenment that the figure and the image of human/humanity was created by and modeled on the imagi nations of the actors who invented themselves as such and used their own self image of the human as a weapon to disempower "lesser" humans racially and sexually. The decisive factor of vernacular European languages in the forma tion of the CMP was and still is their hegemony over the control and manage ment of knowledge, especially the hegemony enjoyed by six modern European tongues: Italian, Spanish, Portuguese, French, German, and English—in that chronological order since the Renaissance—all of them grounded in Greek and Latin. Further, not only is English the dominant language of international business and diplomacy; its supremacy is complemented by the power of the dollar in international transactions, rendering other languages (Mandarin, Urdu, Hindi, Arabic, Persian, Russian, to name just a few widely spoken ones) to the level of the local and less significant.[47]

ACTORS Each domain has its own primary and secondary institutions, and these are run by actors trained to run them, with specialized training and education required for the management of each domain (human/humanity, economy, governance, and knowledge/understanding). In the founding of the CMP, the original actors were generally European, Christian, and white and also mostly heterosexual, or at least they publicly endorsed heteronormativity. So cial class and educational institutions ranging from private schools to private universities and private teachers constituted a preliminary filter for those who were to become actors guarding the domains, and this guardianship meant that they controlled the level of the enunciation.

INSTITUTIONS In the formation of the CMP, monarchies set up the rules of the state (governance). Next to them were the papacy and the Renaissance university, contributing to statecraft via the domain of knowledge/understanding; banks, mainly in Italy's three financial and commercial city-states—Florence, Genoa, and Venice—were the relevant city-states of the domain of the economy. Eventually, the nation-state was to become the main governing institution; secular science and philosophy established patterns for the control of knowledge/understanding (e.g., Descartes, Newton, Kant); and banks' roles continued and expanded to serve new transatlantic "companies" (e.g., the British and Dutch East India Companies in South Asia [India] and Southeast Asia [Indonesia]) that had been established to control mercantilism. The advent of the Industrial Revolution redefined the overall sphere of the economy, consecrating the values of material conditions of living that naturalized the instrumentalization of exploitation, expropriation, accumulation, and reinvesting surplus income. The pursuit of happiness was pegged to the horizon of life framed by the economy of having more. We could follow the story from the sixteenth century until the creation of the International Monetary Fund, the World Bank, and similar economic institutions. Today the nation-state remains in place in the area of governance, while the Western university, which has gone through significant transformations, remains the main institution for the coloniality of knowledge. Its expansion beyond Europe since the sixteenth century (the creation of, for example, the University of Mexico in 1552 and Harvard in 1636 and the recent opening of Harvard in Singapore, Northwestern in Doha, and Duke in Kunshan) has made it a fundamental institution for the Westernization of knowledge, beyond the collaboration of local elites creating national universities and importing the model of Western universities, with all the attending consequences, in the domains of governance, economy, and humanity/human.[48]

The three components of the enunciation merge human/humanity and knowledge/understanding and both define and regulate (knowledge, knowing, sensing, emotioning—subjectivity) the domains of governance and economy. Although the three also define and regulate the domains of knowledge/understanding and human/humanity, there is a crucial difference between the former and the latter, and it is this: while governance and economy are not integral parts of the act of enunciation (that is, governance and economy are both domains of what is enunciated), human/humanity and knowledge/understanding are both inherent in all enunciations, and both regulate governance and the economy. The difference between governance and economy on the one hand and human/humanity and knowledge/understanding on the other, is that the latter are the heart of the enunciation while the former are the results and consequences. That politics and economy return like a boomerang to actors and institutions regulating them is certainly true. But what is undeniable is that governance and economy are not regulated by themselves, even if it is a machine who does the work. In this case, the machine is not governance and the economy but the program that regulates politics and economy. Human/humanity and knowledge/understanding both have privileged positions in the CMP for being at once the *content* of two domains and the *manifestations of actors and languages, which, through institutions, regulate the four domains*. Epistemology and aesthetics are two key concepts regulating knowledges, knowing, and subjectivities. *Herein lies the urgency to delink from both and take on the decolonial gnoseological and aesthesic reconstitutions of both.* This doesn't mean suppressing them (which cannot be done now), but reducing them to their own deserved local size. In this regard, the *constitution* of the CMP, decolonially construed, echoes the emphasis that liberals and Marxists place on political theory and political economy: governance and economy are epistemic fabrications managed by human elites who saw and still see themselves as human/humanity, believing in the universality of their knowledge/understanding. Liberalism and Marxism are after all two heirs of the Enlightenment. And the Soviet Union was a failed way to deal with the imperial difference, because it was acting on a Western system of ideas which did not correspond with or emerge from Russia local history. What was local were the rage and the anger against the Russian czarate. But the instrument, in this case communism, was borrowed.

The flows between the domains and the two-way exchange between the level of the enunciation and the level of the domains are what secures the logic of coloniality and sustains the rhetoric of modernity. The imaginary constructed by the rhetoric of modernity—progress, development, democracy, growth, happiness, terrorism, national security, all Trojan horses of the rhetoric of modernity—is carried on by the destitution power of the logic of coloniality. It is in these *flows* (indicated by the arrows connecting the domains among themselves and the enunciation with the domains) where one can perceive the interdependence between the content and the terms of the conversations that regulate the saying. The domains jump to your eyes and senses; the enunciation is hidden. That is why, as mentioned before (but it is helpful to repeat it here), the politics of Eurocentric knowing was able to posit its regionality as universal. The enunciation was hidden under the belief that European men, institutions, and languages (grounded in Greek and Latin) were easily transplanted to the rest of the planet and good for all the rest of *men*. Since the enunciation controls the domains enunciated, no single domain can be properly understood without connecting it to the other domains and to the enunciations and attending to the double and simultaneous movement of constitution/destitution. Attaining this understanding is the fundamental task of decolonial analytics. It is the first step in the process of delinking—to know from what one should delink—and then to focus on the work of what needs to be reconstituted. There is no universal model of such needs. They depend on the geopolitics and the body-politics (where and who is responding to destituted humanity-racism and -sexism) of the actors engaging in gnoseological and aesthesic reconstitutions.

Let's now look closer at the *flows*. Economy, for instance, is obviously related to governance, to knowledge/understanding, and to human/humanity, and it cannot be properly understood if it remains within the limits in which the domain has been framed by the discipline of political economy that, as common wisdom goes, began with Adam Smith. However, economic praxis among humans did not begin with Smith! The flows between the domains find their consistency and coherence in the level of the enunciation. It is there that the holistic configuration of CMP can be perceived, hidden under the domains constructed as specific fields of investigations requiring the labor of "experts." The implicit prohibitions—a consequence of managing belief and subjectivities—to investigate the domains beyond disciplinary regulations and actors' expertise within the discipline ensures that questions are not asked about the assumptions sustaining the domains, which are taken for granted by the gatekeepers: the actors, institutions, and languages. The particular language in which something is said carries the connotations of the *levels* of authority, prestige, persuasiveness, and so forth, and all together are essential to the impact of what is said. However, what it is said generally deviates the attention from the saying (the enunciation). Social media has taken advantage of this: what counts in social media is what is said—not who said it, why, when, and with what purpose. In national politics, Republicans and Democrats differ in the content (the enunciated), but their saying partakes of the same locus of enunciation. There is no fundamental disagreement, for example, between Republicans and Democrats when it comes to the very foundations of capitalist economy in its corporate, financial, technological, and military branches, or when it comes to supporting Israel and demonizing Iran. The content and the said place the two parties in opposition and hides that they share the enunciation. Similarly, the divergent schools and tendencies in art and literary histories are all grounded in a Western idea of what art and literature are. Conflicts of interpretation and "new" histories are divergences in the content, but not in maintaining the regulatory power of the enunciation. These types of histories, and the historians securing their continuity and changing the contents but not the terms regulating the practice, do not call into question the entity or phenomena of which they are writing. As long as the discourse remains within the enunciative framework of Western modernity, judgements can be made about the "truth," or the appropriateness, or the justice, or whatever, of a particular enunciation. Stepping outside Western modernity, however, brings other factors into play. Asking when, why, and by whom a certain concept came into being in order to designate and analyze a fluid set of phenomena and experiences is a decolonial concern for the simple reason that epistemic and aesthesic matters cannot be pursued by accepting the meaning, definitions, and conceptualizations provided by the rhetoric of modernity and anchored in the enunciative level of the CMP. Here I close the overall description of the CMP's *constitution*. I move now to the simultaneous movement of destitution. In the pages, one comes after the other. But in *reality* they are simultaneous.

III.2 Destitutions

Figure I.2 maps the general areas of *destitution*, which are simultaneous with the *constitution* of each of the CMP's domains. However, destitutions are regulated by the level of the enunciation where the systemic logic of coloniality is at work in all the domains at once, although the surface effect is that it happens only in the domain in question. Take unemployment, for instance. It appears to be an issue of the economy. But who are the unemployed in the domain of human/humanity? Why does governance allow this to happen? What is the knowledge/understanding that naturalizes unemployment as the consequence of economic and financial "crisis"? Last but not least, the justification and legitimation in each domain are secured by the hub, so to speak: the enunciation regulating each domain and all domains.

Again, figure I.2 maps the general areas of destitution simultaneous with the process of the constitution of the CMP, as well as its subsequent transformations. For example, the destitution of barbarians in space in the sixteenth century became the destitution of primitives in time in the eighteenth century and of terrorists located ideologically rather than spatially or chronologically in the twenty-first century. How does destitution work? Knowledge/understanding and governance, for instance, complement each other to invalidate the communal wisdom in which labor and knowledge are necessary to live, rather than

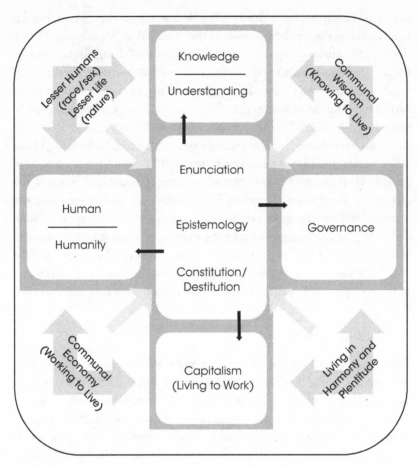

FIGURE I.2 The double and simultaneous movements of *constitution/destitution*. Each domain is built by destitution and is managed by the enunciation, which, like the unconscious, is not visible but working behind the scenes.

the inversion that CMP enacted: one lives in order to work and to know; life at the service of the economy and knowledge instead of economy and knowledge at the service of life. Governance and economy work together to promote competition, success, and innovation, and in so doing divide society and prevent the possibility of living in the harmony and plenitude essential to the philosophy of epistemic and aesthetic reconstitutions promoting harmony with communal wisdom and a communal praxis of living. Remember: the communal implies *vincularidad* (relationality) with all the living that surrounds us and the cosmic life that made that possible. "Nature" is no longer a needed concept for decolonial communal thinking. "Nature" is a concept, not a "reality." Try to live and think while concentrating on the energy of life instead of on an object, nature, and you will most likely live without "nature." When nature is destituted (hidden from view), so are the marvelous and multifarious energies of life that cannot be rendered with one single noun. Instead, coloniality of power works in tandem through economy and human/humanity to demolish communal and sustainable economies in favor of economies of accumulation and growth, in which racial and sexual discrimination manipulated in the domain of human/humanity add their antagonisms to a government and economy that threaten the Earth and the biosphere. These "realities" solidify the arrogance of some to the detriment of colonially wounded others, yet they become the sites where decolonial energies for epistemic and aesthetic reconstitution emerge and work to confront and delink from the component of enunciation which, as I mentioned before, regulates all the domains in the double movement of constitution/destitution (see section III.3). With these general maps in mind, let's look for signposts of reconstitution coexisting with the signposts of constitution/destitution examined in the previous section.

Briefly, the constitution of each domain implies the destitution of the undesirable and the inconvenient. And since the enunciation regulates the constitutions of the domains, de facto coexisting enunciations are suppressed. That is why the idea that non-Europeans cannot think was established and thrived (see the epilogue). However, that is not all; constitution/destitution provokes the drive and will to reconstitute. Here is where decoloniality and de-Westernization, two different responses—one in the sphere of governance and interstate relations and the other in the sphere of knowing, knowledge, understanding, and subjectivity—come to the fore. Constitution/destitution engenders reconstitution, and modernity/coloniality engenders decoloniality and de-Westernization.

III.3 Reconstitutions

III.3.1

At this point I will introduce a conceptual clarification that was left ambiguous, on purpose, up to this point. This is the issue: epistemology and aesthetics, two Western concepts delineating the sphere of knowing and knowledge (the first) and the sphere of sensing and sensed (the second). My claim, after Quijano, that the basic decolonial task consists of "epistemological reconstitution" doesn't mean that what we want is to "fix" epistemology and aesthetics. It means that it is necessary to disengage and delink from them. Quijano said "to divest oneself": "It is not necessary, however, to reject the whole idea of totality [of knowledge] in order to divest oneself of the ideas and images with which it was elaborated within European colonial/modernity. What is to be done is something very different: to liberate the production of knowledge, reflection, and communication from the pitfalls of European rationality/modernity."[49] Now, to divest oneself from the politics of Eurocentric knowing and knowledge, one needs to start from someplace else. Which means that epistemic and aesthetic reconstitution cannot be advanced, providing new interpretations of the already constituted domains and hegemonic vocabulary. A decolonial political theory, for example, cannot be a "new" theory with the CMP regime of constitution/destitution. It has to start from the exteriority of the destituted. There are two ways of doing it. Coloniality, for example, was a concept that emerged in the Third World, not in the North Atlantic, although it is derived from Western vocabulary: "colonial" referred to Roman colonies and Spanish, French, British settler colonialisms. One could argue that instead of striving for democracy and happiness, which are two key concepts in the Western rhetoric of modernity, one should strive for harmony, equilibrium, and plenitude. From this perspective, the philosophies of Ubuntu (a Nguni Bantu term, living for the extended communal) or Sumak Kawsay (a Quichua term, living in harmony and plenitude with the living Earth) would allow us to divest ourselves from *democracy and development*. Or one could appropriate Western concepts that have been destituted from the hegemonic vocabulary constituting the totality (universality) of knowing and knowledge—for example, *gnosis* and *aesthesis*. From this point on I reframe the epistemic and aesthetic into gnoseological and aesthesic reconstitutions. I am not proposing to "replace them." Epistemology and aesthetic will continue to exist; they have been hegemonic options for a long time. What I propose is to bring forward with force the decolonial option by reducing epistemology and aesthetics to its own size and reconstituting gnoseology and aesthesis. This double move sustains the politics of decolonial investigations.

For several reasons, "gnosis" has been sidelined in the Western vocabulary, and "epistemology" took over. The Greek word "gnosis" means "a knowing, knowledge; a judicial inquiry, investigation; a being known." In Christian writings, it means "higher knowledge of spiritual things" (from PIE, *gnō-ti-*, from the root *gno-* or "to know").[50] My use of the term here goes back to my own book *Local Histories/Global Designs*.[51] Back then I followed up on Valentine Y. Mudimbe's recourse to "gnosis" in his classic book *The Invention of Africa: Gnosis, Philosophy, and the Order of Knowledge*.[52] The reason Mudimbe revamped the concept, as he explains it, was that he was asked to write a report on African philosophy. When he began to explore the issue, he realized that African thoughts, in African languages, which verbalize knowing and the known, did not match what Europeans called "philosophy," which is verbalized in vernacular European modern and imperial languages grounded in Greek language. His move revealed to me the colonial epistemic difference, which was the concept around which I built the argument of *Local Histories/Global Designs*. The global scope of "philosophy" beyond its regional sphere was due to both global political and economic expansion and with it the assumed universality of Western knowledges and ways of knowing. Which means that if in Europe, philosophy is a way of thinking, it must be the same all over the planet, and if is not, then there is an epistemic deficiency that has to be remedied. Coloniality was the remedy. The fabrication of the epistemic difference to provide the cure (destitution) presupposes the ontological difference of people who are epistemically deficient.[53] What Mudimbe did was in fact pure and simple gnoseological reconstitution, which is expressed in the book's subtitle: *Gnosis, Philosophy, and the Order of Knowledge*. He did not elaborate on aesthesis but it was implicit: knowledge and knowing control subjectivity—sensing and emotioning. That is, knowledge cannot be standardized and measured according to the politics of European knowing, and especially of philosophy. What Mudimbe referred to as African gnosis (African thinking and wisdom) is not based on ancient Greek philosophers but on the ancestrality and languages of Africa. However, the entanglement with coloniality of knowledge makes the colonial epistemic difference unavoidable and therefore yields the difficult task of epistemic reconstitution.

The second concept, aesthesis, has been colonized by aesthetics—which means it has been destituted in the processes of constituting aesthetic regulations. Looking for the etymology of "aesthetics," I found this: "1798, from German *Ästhetisch* (mid-18c.) or French *esthétique* (which is from German), ultimately from Greek *aisthetikos*, 'of or for perception by the senses, perceptive,' of things, 'perceptible,' from *aisthanesthai*, 'to perceive (by the senses or by the mind), to feel,' from PIE *awis-dh-yo-*, from root *au-* 'to perceive.'"[54] "Perception by the senses" was displaced and replaced by aesthetics: "the sense-perception of the beautiful and the sublime" and, in Hegel, the perception of the beautiful and the sublime in the "fine arts."[55] Aesthetics colonized aesthesis, which means that it destituted the overall meaning of "perception by the senses," reducing it to the regulation of "fine arts." However, a certain sense of aesthetics was established that we see today in the expression "aesthetic surgery" as well as in fashion and design. In so doing, Kant and Hegel standardized "art," and art became, like philosophy, the universal concept to name, describe, refer, and explain what has been done and is being done in non-European culture that can be appropriated or destituted by the concept of "art." To the extent that asking why aesthetics is defined in relation to art and why art provided the ground for aesthetic education was literally out of the question. So I am disobeying, asking the question and delinking from aesthetics to encounter aesthesis. When it comes to coloniality, art and aesthetics were used to talk "about" objects and people's attitudes outside of Europe and to label them art and aesthetics. Such a method serves well to devalue and destitute the meaning that a given object or performance has for the community in which the object has been made and the relations that the community establishes with the object or performance. "Perception by the senses" is beyond "art" and "aesthetics." It is in our daily praxis of living, professional and personal; it invades all we do and shapes our subjectivity. Gnoseological and aesthesic reconstitutions, then, mean to recover and restitute gnosis and aesthesis and to delink from epistemology and aesthetics. In fact, what I am describing here as gnoseological (knowing and knowledge) and aesthesic (being and sensing) reconstitutions are not new phenomena; they don't need to wait for independence or decolonial state formation, as happened during the Cold War. I will identify historical moments of reconstitutions, describing the genealogy of decolonial political theory from Guaman Poma de Ayala, Ottobah Cugoano, Mohandas Gandhi, and Frantz Fanon (see below). Gnosis and aesthesis name the energy of liberation that emerges at the very moment of colonial domination and at any moment in which the simultaneous movement of constitution/destitution is at work.

III.3.2

Let's now consider the work of reconstitution illustrated in figure I.3. In the following pages I trace a genealogy of decolonial thinking: the responses to modernity/coloniality as soon as they emerged in the sixteenth century. In Anahuac (the Aztec territories), the Maya area, and the Tiwanaku and Tawantinsuyu, the areas first invaded after the extermination of Arawak/Taino First Nations in the Caribbean, the population did not receive with joy the Spaniards' invasions. Rejections (what today is called anticolonialism) were the first manifestations. With time, reorganization followed and presupposed reconstitutions based on the knowledge, knowing, sensing, believing of the original population. Of course, reconstitutions of their praxes of living at that time were not framed as decolonial gnoseology and aesthesic. There was no place for second-order self-reflections on what they were doing. But the energy, the will, the indignation, the anger were there and did not go away through the centuries. The seeds for the genealogy of decolonial thought (all action against

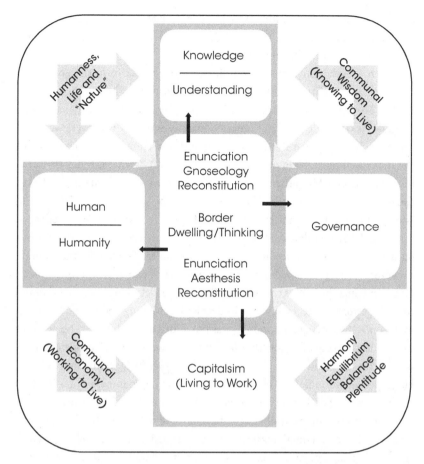

FIGURE I.3 The movements of *gnoseological and aesthesic reconstitutions* indicate the myriad of responses rising from the energy, experiences, and knowledges of the destituted, both in the sphere of de-Westernization and in decoloniality at large.

the Spanish invasions and for their own reconstitutions presupposes reasoning and thinking) were planted. With time, and as European expansion moved from the New World to the Old World, the decolonial rejection and reconstitutions were manifested and continue to be so. In what follows I outline a genealogy of decolonial thoughts without which this book could not have been written. I am not reporting as a detached and scholarly observer based in the social sciences and the humanities. What I am saying and arguing is embedded in the genealogy of decolonial thought, without which the gnoseological and aesthesic reconstitutions that I am proposing could not have been possible. Hence, I am delinking from the genealogies of the social sciences and the humanities to embrace and dwell in the genealogy of decolonial thought that I outline in the following pages.

With these clarifications in mind, I return once again to the end of the sixteenth and beginning of the seventeenth century in the South American Andes. The opening character of this story is Guaman Poma de Ayala, born around 1535 (three years after Francisco Pizarro entered Cuzco). He was born into a noble family that lived at a certain distance from Cuzco (the center of the Inca dwelling and administration, the Incanate) in what is today the province of Ayacucho. His father, based on what we know, was a lord (i.e., leader) of the dynasty, a group conquered by the Incas. In his adult life he worked as an administrator in the Spanish viceroyalty of Peru, an invaluable experience for knowing the Spaniards and sensing the power differential shaping the emotions on both ends of the spectrum. This was a reason for Guaman Poma to build his argument in a sustained double critique, to the Spaniards and to the Incas. Guaman Poma showed us the way (the "method"): delinking from dichotomies (e.g., either/or) is a necessary step in decolonial thinking and living. For Guaman Poma, disobeying dichotomies was not a "discovery" but just the praxis of living and thinking of people that for centuries did not need European (Spanish, in this case) modes of thinking. Furthermore, in Quechua and Aymara languages, dichotomies are always complementary, two moieties of a totality. Each element of dichotomy in a duality is half the story. From the entanglement and power differential of distinct modes of reasoning, border thinking emerged: Guaman Poma's reasoning was grounded in the millenarian memories of his language and praxis of living, but it had to negotiate with the Spaniards, who were in a dominant position, politically and intellectually.

Guaman Poma appropriated the Bible and took it to task, claiming to be Christian and yet rejecting the Castilian missionaries' intentions of converting the people of Tawantinsuyu (the Incas' territory) to Christianity. Claiming to be Christian allowed him to reveal the brutalities and violence of Spanish soldiers and adventurers, legitimized in the name of Christianity. He corrected the stories about his people told by Spanish missionaries, soldiers, and men of letters and anchored his narrative in the collective ancestral memories, praxes of living, and ways of being of Tawantinsuyu. The structure of governance he reconstituted (a truly gnoseological and aesthesic reconstitution) conveyed the force of his sensing, belief, and emotioning. Disregarding Castilian political theories derived from Plato and Aristotle, which he may have learned from his everyday experience rather than by doing careful scholarly work on Western political theories, and attentive to the demographic composition of the

Spanish-named viceroyalty of Peru, he proposed to Philip III, king of Spain, to solve the chaos engendered by the Spanish invasion and Indigenous resistance, to deal with the Tawantinsuyu. To have an idea of what that situation may have been, imagine Iraq after the US invasion in 2003. The analogy is more than pedagogical: it is connected by the persistence of the coloniality of power through the centuries (which I outline in the chapters of this book). By the end of the sixteenth century, the viceroyalty of Peru was built on the destitution of Tawantinsuyu. Its demography had changed significantly. Beyond the inhabitants of Tawantinsuyu, there were Spaniards, Muslims, and Africans (some of them could have been Muslim, too). "Tawantinsuyu" is generally translated as "land of the four regions"; sometimes "bounded together" is added. Indeed, it means "the land of the four (*tawa*) united *suyus*." The four suyus were named Antisuyu, Collasuy, Chinchaysuyu, and Contisuyu. Based on what we know, Guaman Poma was born into a noble family in today's Ayacucho, in the Collasuyu area, south of Cuzco. To better understand Guaman Poma's emotional and rational turmoil, it is important to note that the Inca territory was not an "empire," as it is most often called. Since the ruler was an Inca and not an emperor, the territory was an "Incanate." Without making this distinction, the colonial differential in which Guaman Poma was operating would be misunderstood. Furthermore, this distinction illustrates how coloniality of knowledge works by constituting a universe of meaning and by destituting, in the same move, coexisting knowledges and knowing. Imagine if I referred to the "Roman Incanate" instead of the Roman Empire. Hence, Guaman Poma's proposal was to reorganize not an "empire" according to Roman legacies in Europe, but to reorganize Tawantinsuyu while being attentive to his own language and memories as well as to his own present. Guaman Poma had to deal with the viceroyalty form of governance, the transplantation of the Spanish monarchic state over the ruins of Tawantinsuyu. Now you see how border thinking emerges from dwelling in the border, where entangled praxes of living and thinking are structured by power differentials.

Guaman Poma was confronted with four demographic groups. He proposed that each group have its own suyu. Originally, each suyu, and the relations of each suyu with the other three, embodied a complex communal (economic and cultural) organization based on Andean praxes of living and thinking. Guaman Poma was not proposing to replicate that, but simply to inscribe in the present the governing structure that his people had sustained for thousands of years and that the Spaniards were hard at work to destitute and replace with their own. The Spaniards' past was neither that of Guaman Poma nor that of his people. Why should Spaniards' comfort prevail? The reconstitution of Tawantinsuyu resulted in something different from what it had been; at the same time, the viceroyalty governance was unacceptable and, consequently, Spanish political theory was also unacceptable. The outcome of Guaman Poma's efforts was sustained border thinking to achieve the gnoseological and aesthesic reconstitutions (his knowing and sensing prevailed) of Tawantinsuyu. His monumental *New Chronical and Good Government* (1616), which was the work of several years (presumably starting in the 1580s), is just that: *a monumental effort of gnoseological and aesthesic reconstitution of Western epistemology and aesthetics.* It was composed as a letter of about four hundred folios addressed to His Majesty, King Philip III.

Most likely, Philip III did not pay much attention to the letter and proposal. But he must have saved it, for in the early twentieth century Guaman Poma's letter was "discovered" in the Royal Library of Copenhagen. How it ended up there is for another argument. Relevant to the point of gnoseological and aesthesis reconstitution is the following: the manuscript was lost to sight for three hundred years, and when it reappeared, it was a scholarship gold mine. However, the underground praxes of living and thinking persisted in the body memories of the Quechua- and Aymara-speaking people in the Andes. The spirit of Tawantinsuyu did not go away although the Inca ruling class was dethroned and physically destituted. The recent debates in the rewriting of the Bolivian and Ecuadorian constitutions, in which the first is declared a "plurinational State" and the second "a multicultural secular State," cannot be understood as non-Indigenous initiatives. Looking back to Guaman Poma de Ayala's "good government," it is obvious that he was proposing a multiethnic or plurinational reorganization of Tawantinsuyu. Guaman Poma may have read some of the canonical text of Western civilizations circulated by missionaries and men of letters. He names some authors. I surmise that his reading was to know what needed to be avoided (delinked) rather than looking for models to solve the problem of governance. He had his own tradition, no need to borrow from the Spaniards' traditions. Furthermore, when we look at the Zapatistas' Juntas de Buen Gobierno, a governing organization based on Indigenous knowing, knowledge, sensing, and praxes of living, it is inviting to think that invisible channels of memory run through what Rodolfo Kusch described as "América Profunda" (Deep America). Guaman Poma's sensing and emotioning (and through him the Andean memories) saturate the *New Chronicle*. His work is a paramount decolonial monument of gnoseological and aesthesis reconstitution grounding and nourishing decolonial thinking today. It is not by chance that Aníbal Quijano, in the territories of the Inca civilization, came up, right at the end of the Cold War, with the concept of coloniality of power.

The 1980 publication of Guaman Poma's work, edited by Rolena Adorno and John V. Murra with translations from the Quechua by Jorge Urioste, disseminated the book beyond the somewhat limited circulation it had had to that point.[56] Beyond revamping scholarship on the work and the author, the edition fostered the resurfacing of decolonial conversations in the 1980s. Kenyan writer Ngũgĩ wa Thiong'o published a landmark collection of essays, *Decolonizing the Mind* (1987), revamping the tasks of gnoseological and aesthesic reconstitution that was already at work during the Cold War (Aimé Césaire, Amílcar Cabral, Frantz Fanon, Patrice Lumumba, Steve Biko). "Decolonizing the mind" would have been a project out of place in the middle of revolutionary struggles during the Cold War. However, in the 1980s the struggles for decolonization and nation-state building had run their course. The potent thoughts that paralleled and intermingled with the revolts that expelled the colonial settler for occupied territories did not go away. Today we could say that while the goals of expelling the settler and building nation-states in the colonized territories is no longer a viable project, decolonial thinking and gnoseological and epistemic reconstitutions are beginning to run their course.

III.3.3

A second decolonial political treatise and exemplar of gnoseological and aesthesic reconstitutions was composed in the eighteenth century. The author, a former enslaved African in the Caribbean, was taken to London by his master, where he became politically active to end the slave trade. His name was Quobnah Ottobah Cugoano. Like Guaman Poma, Cugoano appropriated Christianity in his own terms, turning the tables to ask what kind of Christians would engage in the exchange of human beings for guns and alcohol, later selling them to slave owners in the Caribbean. For Cugoano, there was no difference between Portuguese, Spanish, Dutch, French, or British colonists: all of them were part of a large family of lawbreakers and wrongdoers, criminals.

Contrary to Guaman Poma, Ottobah Cugoano did not have his own territory to reconstitute. He was extracted from his African community, transported, and enslaved in Caribbean plantations. His master, Alexander Campbell, took Ottobah Cugoano with him upon his return from the Caribbean to London. Cugoano was in London when he wrote *Thoughts and Sentiments of the Evil and Wicked Traffic of the Slavery: and Commerce of the Human Species, Humbly Submitted to the Inhabitants of Great-Britain* (1787), a powerful analytic narrative and a radical proposal based on his own grounded normativity, chronicling his experience of being captured, transported, and sold like millions of other Africans.[57]

What he proposed was the reconstitution of slavery narratives, to that point dominated by traffickers, plantation owners, and European intellectuals, and of the concept of sovereignty. On the narrative side, Ottobah Cugoano offered a narrative from the perspective and experience of an enslaved person. It was parallel to Guaman Poma's narrative from the perspective of an inhabitant of Tawantinsuyu. Both narratives have one element in common with Bartolomé de Las Casas's *A Short Account of the Destruction of the Indies* (1552): the critique of European brutalities, from the Spaniards to the British. But they have one important difference: de Las Casas was neither an Indigenous inhabitant of Tawantinsuyu nor a Black African enslaved person. The stakes were significantly different—the enunciation makes the difference, while the three of them share the repulsion toward the conqueror's inhumanity in the name of humanity.

Ottobah Cugoano decoupled sovereignty from the state and placed it in the sphere of human relations, claiming that no single human being had the right to appropriate, buy, sell, and enslave other human beings. This fundamental principle of human rights was absent when the French imperial revolutionaries published, adopted (in the National Constituent Assembly), and extolled the *Declaration of the Rights of Man and of the Citizen* (1789). Humans who were not citizens were not considered "Man" and therefore held no rights. Indirectly, Cugoano reversed Adam Smith's *The Theory of Moral Sentiments* (1759) by directing attention in his title to a different kind of "sentiments": those of Black enslaved Africans coexisting in power differentials with the sentiments of white liberal Europeans. Cugoano's *Thoughts and Sentiments* was published in England about a decade after Smith's *The Wealth of Nations* (1776), and one cannot avoid the inclination to read it as an indirect but explicit indictment both of European wealth at the expense of a plundered Africa and of liberal moral sentiments vis-à-vis the sentiments of enslaved human beings generally (see part II for more on the issue of human rights).

The two cases made by Guaman Poma and Cugoano teach us several lessons. The first is that the restitution of people's dignity cannot be achieved within the same epistemology that destituted them and others like them. Gnoseological and aesthesic reconstitutions need to start from someplace other than the epistemology and aesthetics that negated their knowledge and their humanity, and legitimized the negation in the name of humanity and *rationality*. The second lesson is that there cannot be a universal model and even less a method telling you "how to do gnoseological and aesthetic reconstitution." The answer is by doing it, and if you need it your body will tell you how to do it. Think of Guaman Poma and Ottobah Cugoano in these terms. They both appropriated the Bible to throw it in the faces of Christians who claimed to carry its truth. Their thinking and arguing were not learned by digging into theological treatises. It was through their experiences, not experiences in general, but their grounded normativity and experiences of being dispossessed in their own territory and of being extricated from their community, transported, and forced to work for others (living to work), not for themselves (working to live).[58] And the third lesson is that gnoseological and aesthesic reconstitutions bring forward the geo-body politics of knowing, sensing, and believing of the interested actors, the same way that the CMP was constituted to the benefit of interested actors. The global designs imprinted through the CMP touched all local histories and people on the planet. Meaning that while all local histories have their own ancestral grounding, and in that sense are diverse, they all have in common being touched, interfered with, intervened in, and destituted by the CMP. Consequently there cannot be a universal model for gnoseological and aesthesic reconstitutions. Decoloniality is an option, but neither a universal model nor a universal mission. Of necessity it has to be pluriversal. From this pluriversality emerges the third nomos of the Earth (the topic of chapter 14).

III.3.4

A third case in the genealogy of decolonial political reconstitutive thinking and doing is the Haitian Revolution, which in the nineteenth century introduced a distinctive outcome of decoloniality: the foundation of a colonial nation-state governance in the hands of former African enslaved people, alien to the history and memories from where the modern nation-state emerged. The outcome of the Haitian Revolution, seen in the context of decolonial revolution in Africa in the second half of the twentieth century, is parallel and inverse. Parallel because liberation and the foundation of colonial/modern nation-states was the outcome. Inverse because the Haitian Revolution was carried out by people of African descent in the New World, where all the previous struggles for colonial liberation had been achieved by people of European descent. Between 1776 and 1830, numerous "republics" or nation-states were formed in the Americas, by then a universally established name of the continents. The Haitian Revolution was the exception and an anomaly: Black enslaved Africans were not expected to take freedom into their own hands; it was expected that they would wait until the master liberated them.

Today, the meaning of the "Haitian Revolution" is being reconsidered by Haitian intellectuals who see the true decolonial revolution as residing in the organization and survival of the Haitians themselves, in spite of the state, which, as history has shown, has been the pendulum of the local governing elites according to the interests of France and the US. Jean Casimir's detailed decolonial investigation of the history of Haiti breaks away from the modern/ colonial historiography of state formation to focus on the Haitians as social subjects, a situation similar to the Zapatistas in southern Mexico. The people, former captives and the enslaved, took their destiny into their own hands as the Zapatistas did: they created and developed complex forms of organization that enabled them to fight against the plantation system and to reconstitute, in the process, their own praxes of living, thinking, being, and doing. While traditional history has always focused on the state and the heroes of independence, Casimir concentrated on the nation beyond the state and on the people as a whole within their history.[59] The lessons to be learned here are of the parallel and harmonizing streets: Casimir tells the story not as a detached historian observing the history and the present of the people to which he belongs; his work runs parallel to the gnoseological and aesthesis reconstitutions he reports and reflects upon. In this sense he continues the legacies of Ottobah Cugoano that have continued in the Afro-Caribbean intellectual and political histories. Scholarship on the one hand complements the living praxis of the Haitian people while on the other moving toward the decolonization of scholarship by engaging in gnoseological and aesthesic reconstitution (see chapter 12).

Having said this, the historical significance of the Haitian Revolution and the formation of the Haitian state should not be overlooked, though they also should not be considered in isolation. Today, I would say—after Casimir—that the Haitian Revolution might profitably be regarded alongside the Bandung Conference, two nation-state-oriented projects in which race was a paramount topic and mover of decolonization. Of course, de-Westernization was not a possibility at the time of Haiti's revolt; yet in retrospect the Haitian Revolution remains a signpost of decolonization carried on by people of non-European descent; that was the case for decolonization during the Cold War. Whether this overstates its importance today or not, the Haitian Revolution and decolonization during the Cold War are paramount references and points of encounter between African and Caribbean decolonial thinkers in Paris and in *Présence Africaine* of the 1950s: Nkrumah, Lumumba, Cabral, Senghor, Biko on the African side, and Césaire and Fanon from the Caribbean side. The intellectual and political decolonial legacies, the wealth of ideas and proposals emanating from then, cemented the long lasting decolonial trajectories that we have seen arising in the works of Guaman Poma and Ottobah Cugoano. The Americas and the Caribbean were the initial signposts of Westernization, of the implementation of global designs and the foundation of the CMP, which eventually reached Asia and Africa through a long and divergent process beginning in the seventeenth century (the Dutch had been in South Africa since 1652) though flourishing primarily in the nineteenth century: the British settlement in India, the Dutch in Indonesia, the French in North Africa. It is consequential that the decolonial emerged in the Americas, denying the march of Westernization. Briefly restated: decolonial politics of investigation and gnoseological and aesthesic reconstitutions, as Casimir's argument and twenty-five years of the Zapatistas' struggle suggest, cannot be carried on through the Western-style nation-state and within the frame of the politics of Eurocentric knowledge/understanding designed to justify the economy of accumulation and the nation-state as the basic institution of governance.[60]

III.3.5

In this quick outline of the political genealogy of decolonial thinking and of gnoseological and aesthesic reconstitutions, I would like to highlight two more important signposts: Mohandas Gandhi and Frantz Fanon. They are certainly very different from each other (just as Guaman Poma, Ottobah Cugoano, and the Haitian Revolution were distinctive in their formations, claims, and outcome), but at the same time they are extremely relevant to the pluriversal aims of both decolonial thinking and the geopolitics of knowing, sensing, and believing in which all the diversity of gnoseological and aesthesic reconstitutions come into being. Chapter 12 is devoted to the work and thought of Sylvia Wynter, who significantly has been added more recently to the genealogy of decolonial thought. And, of course, Aníbal Quijano, whose work has provided an orientation of mine and that undergirds the entire argument of this book. Regarding placing Fanon and Gandhi alongside each other, I am not concerned here with the debate over nonviolence versus violence (which is a common topic when the two are brought into the conversation)—that is, with what Gandhi meant by nonviolence or what Fanon meant by violence, either domestically or in international contexts. What I am focusing on is their unquestionable contribution to decolonial gnoseology (knowledge, knowing) and aesthesic (sensing, emotion, believing) reconstitution. Their achievements were shaped both through their thinking and through the acts of living their lives—in short, in their praxes of living. These praxes should give us pause in the twenty-first century, sobering any false pride we may take in our decolonial victories, as well as chiding those current critics who claim that decoloniality has become an academic discipline detached from action. Certainly the modern dichotomy of theory versus practice is applicable today, but how many of the critics making these claims are living as Gandhi or Fanon did? Where are the equivalents today of the fights they fought? What would be the corresponding challenges today to the ones confronted by Gandhi and Fanon that ask us to conjoin our thinking with our actions? Shall we be motivated to create modern/colonial nation-states, or to take hold of one like the Cuban and Iranian revolutions did? I do not have an answer for those questions. But I am convinced that the nation-state at this point is no longer a desirable decolonial horizon. Which doesn't mean that certain political gains could be attained by a progressive government. The limits, however, are set today by the dispute for the control of the colonial matrix of power between de-Westernizer and re-Westernizers, between globalists and nationalists. Nevertheless, the radical legacies of all previous decolonial thinkers are the core of the politics of decolonial investigation and reconstitutions, as much as the Greeks, the European Renaissance, and the Enlightenment are the legacies of modern and postmodern thinkers. With these caveats let's elaborate on two of their texts and bring them forward to our praxes of living and thinking today: *Hind Swaraj* (1909) and *The Wretched of the Earth* (1961).

Gandhi's arguments in *Hind Swaraj* are exemplars of what gnoseological and aesthesic reconstitutions mean. The argument is set up as a dialogue between two characters, the Editor and the Reader. To understand the thrust of my argument, it suffices to read the chapters devoted to law, medicine, and railways. One paragraph in particular makes my point clear, taken from chapter 9, on railways. The previous chapter is devoted to the Indian and British suppression of outlaw gangs in Central India (the Thugs and the Pindaris), whose members would make the list of "terrorists" today, according to the hegemonic Western view of terrorism as well as the imperial belief (or make belief) that the control of terrorism in a colonial country is beneficial, in fact liberating, for that country when, indeed, the so-called terrorists may very well be a force of liberation from imperial enforcement in that country. However, things are muddy today when the terrorists are mercenaries employed by and at the service of global designs. In any event, in the *Hind Swaraj* dialogue, the Editor and the Reader both discuss common concerns and share opinions regarding India's liberation from the British. Responding to the Reader's question, the Editor, who carries Gandhi's arguments, confronts Thomas Babington Macaulay, engineer of British education in India. The Editor says, "Macaulay betrayed gross ignorance when he libeled Indians as being cowards. Have you ever visited our fields?" He continues: "I assure you that our agriculturalists sleep fearlessly on their farms even today, and the English, you and I would hesitate to sleep where they sleep.

Strength lies in absence of fear, not in the quantity of flesh and muscle we may have on our bodies."[61]

The conversation carries on into the next chapter. The Reader responds, "I do now, indeed, fear that we are not likely to agree at all. You are attacking the very institutions which we have hitherto considered to be good." Indeed, how could someone—common sense will tell—attack institutions that carry the enunciation of "law" and in this case of the British Empire? (See section III.I.1 in this introduction, on the components of the enunciation.) You can bomb a building, but that will not dismantle the institutions that are founded on rules of knowing, on knowledge, and on the presupposition supporting that knowledge. You dismantle an institution with arguments, and it is here precisely where gnoseological and aesthesis reconstitutions come into play, "attacking" (like a virus) the enunciation that sustains the CMP: the "British version of Western knowledge." Which means that reconstitutions do not call out only the contents of each domain but mainly the assumptions on which the contents are grounded—the enunciation. Reconstitution(s) is (are) not only a question of contesting but of rebuilding what has been destituted and what needs a parallel enunciative apparatus: actors; uses, appropriations, and disobedience to imperial languages (a revamping of destituted languages); and institutions, using existing ones and building decolonial institutions. But it is above all a question of decolonial investigations that mean to call into question the presuppositions, concepts, archives, and built institutional knowledge that manage and control the lives of the people and, by a boomerang effect, the lives of the controllers who want to preserve their privileges.

The argument on the railway may illuminate the point I am making. The Reader asks the Editor to address the introduction of railways in India in the name of progress and civilization (and here you have assumptions, concepts, narratives people live by), which the Editor has metaphorically labeled as a disease (which means disobeying, delinking, and engaging in a counternarrative of reconstitution). In this context, the Editor addresses the railways issue in medical language:

> It must be manifest to you that, but for the railways, the English could not have such a hold on India as they have. The railways, too, have spread the bubonic plague. Without them, masses could not move from place to place. They are the carriers of plague germs. Formerly we had natural segregation. Railways have also increased the frequency of famines, because, owing to facility of means of locomotion, people sell out their grain, and it is sent to the dearest markets. People become careless and so the pressure

of famine increases. They accentuate the evil nature of man. Bad men fulfil their evil designs with greater rapidity. The holy places of India have become unholy. Formerly, people went to these places with very great difficulty. Generally, therefore, only the real devotees visited such places. Nowadays, rogues visit them in order to practice their roguery.

What do we perceive in this paragraph regarding the constitution/destitution/restitution and the parallel formulation of modernity/coloniality/decoloniality? Do you perceive the Editor's response to colonial differences or border dwelling and border thinking? First of all, the Editor, taking advantage of questions and observations from the Reader, confronts assumptions and reasoning that are ingrained in the lives and bodies of the British settlers in India and in their metropolitan counterpart, England: the rulers justifying the invasion and settling of India. The Editor challenges these assumptions, starting from the memories of the history in the bodies and the language of his own people (*Hind Swaraj* was written in Gujarati, which confronted the language of the CMP enunciation), and he does so by *reconstituting* Indian praxes of living that the British had *destituted*. Gandhi's was the perspective of someone speaking while dwelling on the border: he knew well British ways of thinking and reasoning, and he knew well and better his own. That is dwelling on the border, the precondition of border thinking. And that is what the Editor does: look at the British from his Indian body's memories and praxis of living so that border thinking saturates his arguments. Moreover, dwelling on the border in the *exteriority* of the empire (India was exteriority in relation to the British Empire), and manifesting a full awareness of his location, the Editor is in a position to highlight what English officers like Macaulay could not understand and even less sense. The British could not understand the resistances' expressions of emotion, could even less understand that Gandhi (through the dialogue between the Reader and the Editor) was building a comprehensive argument for reexistence: *Hind Swaraj* means "Home Rule." That is, gnoseological and aesthesic reconstitution at work. This is building—not just opposing or resisting—and building requires reconstitution of knowing and of being: knowledge and emotional strength, not muscle or weapons.

Gandhi is known for his "civil disobedience," which he took from Henry David Thoreau, but unlike Thoreau, Gandhi's civil disobedience led him through gnoseological and aesthesic reconstitutions to question the colonial episteme that Indians were cowards and effeminate, a charge that echoed the Spanish rationale to destitute Indigenous humanity. Gandhi broke the convention by asking the questions that the rhetoric of modernity prevents being asked because of the taken-for-granted assumptions of the universality of knowledge grounded in the politics of Eurocentric knowing. In this regard, Gandhi, like Guaman Poma, released the politics of decolonial investigations. The differences between Thoreau and Gandhi come to the fore if we ask when, who, why, and to the benefit of what or whom is the argument for civil disobedience being made? If we remain at the level of the content, we flatten the meaning of "civil disobedience." Addressing the enunciation by asking "w" questions, we bring forward the politics of decolonial investigations as well as the geopolitics of knowing, sensing, and believing. Delinking from and fleeing the controlling paws of the epistemic ("know as I know") and the aesthetic ("be as I am"), and entering the wider realm of disobedient gnoseology and aesthesis, is the first step to entering the politics of decolonial investigations.

Gandhi's gnoseological and aesthesic reconstitutions of Indian communal praxes of living through his creative rendering of "civil disobedience" and the Hindu concept *Satyagraha Ashram* couldn't have been done without engaging the politics of decolonial investigations. Ajay Skaria helps us understand Gandhi's move in this direction when he explains the meaning of "Satyagraha" in this way: "'*Agraha*': seizure of or by, Gandhi's translation of 'resistance.' '*Satya*': not just truth, but being; Gandhi's equivalent initially of 'passive.' Satya is conceived moreover here not as some shared inert substance but as an active force that is everywhere constitutive of being as care and love for all beings: hence the additional translations of *satyagraha* as 'love force' or 'soul force.'"[62]

And what about "Ashram"?[63] Skaria again:

My question here is a simple one: what was the politics of the Gandhian ashram?

Mainstream nationalists such as Nehru, frustrated about the amount of time that the principal leader of the nationalist movement spent on the tiny ashrams, had a simple answer: eccentricity. Gandhi, obviously, did not feel this way. He said of the Satyagraha Ashram that it "set out to eliminate what it thought were defects in our national life."[64]

Skaria saw Gandhi's ashram as a response to Western liberalism, which he, Gandhi, rejected. If Nehru was frustrated, it was because his vision for India was the liberal British political concept of the nation-state: one nation, one state. In places like India, however, this concept fails for at least two reasons: one is that one nation, one state is difficult to achieve in a territory possessing many languages, memories, and belief systems, and the other is that the nation-state form of governance did not unfold in the history of India as it did in the history of western Europe and the Americas, where the nation-state was always ruled by people of European descent (the Haitian Revolution, of course, was an exception). In the former colonies, you can have one state, but hardly one nation. The end result is that only one nation among many nations is identified with the state, and the rest are considered "minorities," which is an important factor in the failures of colonial/modern nation-states built after decolonization. Gandhi's ashram was in line with his gnoseological and aesthesic reconstitutions to restitute Indian governance (like Guaman Poma did in the South American Andes and the Zapatistas have been doing) and praxes of living that were disrupted by British intrusions: first commercial, followed by their settlement. Here is not the place to evaluate whether the ashram was realistic or idealistic, possible or impossible. Rather, I view Gandhi's project for Hindustan as emerging from a grounded normativity that parallels the Zapatistas' *Juntas de Buen Gobierno* (Councils of Good Government, which also arise from an Indigenous normativity), and from the consolidation of the communal sovereignty of the people (the *Lakou*) that Jean Casimir has illuminated for us.[65] Gandhi's *Ashram*, the Zapatistas' *Juntas de Buen Gobierno*, South America Andean's *Sumak Kawsay/Suma Qamaña*,[66] Nishnaabeg *Mino Bimaadiziwin*,[67] Sub-Saharan Africa *Ubuntu*,[68] and Haitian *Lakou*[69]—all of them carry the weight of destituted praxes of living, knowing, sensing, believing to be reconstituted gnoseological and aesthesic, in words and deeds (see chapter 14).

Frantz Fanon is the fourth and last character of my narrative to serve as a signpost in this genealogical outline of decolonial reconstitutions. I have already advanced some of his deep-rooted decolonial contributions in the few comments earlier on Freud and psychoanalysis. Now I want to stress three additional points: (a) his introduction of *sociogenesis*, a fundamental decolonial concept; (b) his analytics of decolonization in Algeria and in the Third World generally (the analytics of the logic of coloniality in my vocabulary), and (c) his uncompromising delinking and invitation—or, better, outcry—for all of us to build what he called "a new man": this was his call for gnoseological and aesthesic reconstitutions, which he had already practiced in *The Wretched of the Earth* as well as in his previous publications. His call at the time was equivalent to today's Indigenous demands for "resurgence," "to live in harmony and plenitude" (*Sumak Kawsay, Mino Bimaadiziwin*), and for "the belief in a universal bond that connects persons among themselves and with life" (*Ubuntu*).

A pause now to briefly comment on three points of sociogenesis's relevance for gnoseologic/aesthesic reconstitutions.[70] Many readers may remember when and why Fanon needed a concept not available in Western vocabulary to account for an experience that shook him up. It was the moment, he tells us, when he encountered a mother walking with her child who said, "Mom, look, a Negro." *Sociogenesis* was the concept he needed to account for this experience, the lived experience of the Negro, as he titled one chapter of *Black Skin, White Masks* (1952). Fanon knew he had black skin but did not know he was a Negro. Being a Negro is not just having black skin; it is being seen and classified by people with white skin. Racism is not biological but sociogenetic. Black skin is an ontic fact of life on planet Earth. Being a Negro is an ethnosocial classification, ontological, not ontic. This means that such classifications were not embedded in certain human beings when this species of living organisms originated on the planet but that they were invented by certain members of the human species who were successful in making many believe that classifications are *representations* of what there is. *Sociogenesis as a classification of what one sees* instead of a *representation of what there is* evinces a decolonial locus of enunciation that is parallel and coexists with the CMP enunciation. It would be like saying, "I am a Negro; yes, so what? That is your problem not mine."[71] Sociogenesis negates the constitution of whiteness by the destitution of Blackness and anchors a decolonial locus of enunciation that makes gnoseological and aesthesic reconstitutions possible. Reconstitutions mean to affirm oneself in the destituted zone of nonbeing, the zone of nonbeing needed for the constitution of human/humanity by actors and institutions who appropriated for themselves the zone of being.[72]

A second point that is relevant to my argument emerges from virtually the entire narrative of Fanon's *The Wretched of the Earth*.[73] Fanon moves from the Algerian struggles for decolonization to the pros and cons of violence, the pitfall of nationalism, national consciousness, and the simultaneous foundation of national culture and decolonial struggle. In the last chapters he gives a detailed analysis of the colonial wounds he singles out in psychological vocabulary as "mental disorders." His narrative, analysis, and arguments could be read and interpreted following two simultaneous paths: one is the immediacy of the situation in Algeria, in the Third World, and in his own praxis of living. The others lead to the larger picture of the CMP, the colonial matrix of power, how it works in all its domains and levels, both the level of the said and its content as well as of the enunciation and its saying. Following these paths allows us to understand the *flows* relating the domains to each other and to each domain anchored in the overarching work of the enunciation that connects the domains without showing the thread of those connections. His argument has two sides: one is the analytics of the CMP, and the other is the affirmation of another enunciation, the decolonial enunciation, that allows him to enter into the mechanisms of the CMP. Here Fanon took a significant step toward decolonial reconstitutions. His arguments are affirmations of disobedient gnoseological and aesthesic reconstitutions. By so doing Fanon negates what the rhetoric of modernity affirms to justify the destitutions enacted by the destructive logic of coloniality and simultaneously announces the paths toward what he called a "new man." I read this statement as a call to delink from the social—built by the "old man" (patriarchy, masculinity, whiteness) and limited to human beings detached from "nature"—and to reconstitute the *communal* where the "new man" is one with Earth and the cosmos. "I am Black; I am in total fusion with the world, in sympathetic affinity with the Earth, losing my id in the heart of the cosmos—and the White man, however intelligent he may be, is incapable of understanding Louis Armstrong or songs from the Congo. I am Black, not because of a curse, but because my skin has been able to capture all the cosmic effluvia. I am truly a drop of sun under the Earth."[74]

My third point: Fanon's conclusion of *The Wretched of the Earth* is the moment of his unapologetic delinking and marching toward reconstitutions of knowing and being (aesthesis). Rereading his argument on decolonization from the perspective of his concluding chapter, one finds it possible to clearly identify the prior signs that have nourished the argument. A few excerpted lines will, I hope, help the reader to understand the point I am making regarding Fanon's place in the genealogy of decolonial thoughts. His is a signal contribution to the ongoing labor of taking the CMP's enunciation by assault, affirming ourselves by negating the double processes of constitution/destitution, undermining the assumptions and the instrument that secured its domination. Here are a few well-known excerpts and the invitation to read them in relation to my argument. In 1961 Europe was still leading the world order. It was in the 1960s that the US displaced Europe in the global imaginary. Although well known, a few of Fanon's words from his concluding notes to *The Wretched of the Earth* could be beneficially reread in the context of this introduction and of this book.

1 Now, comrades, now is the time to decide to change sides. We must shake off the great mantle of night which has enveloped us, and reach for the light. The new day which is dawning must find us determined, enlightened and resolute.

2 Let us leave this Europe which never stops talking of man yet massacres him at every one of its street corners, at every corner of the world.

3 For centuries Europe has brought the progress of other men to a halt and enslaved them for its own purposes and glory; for centuries it has stifled virtually the whole of humanity in the name of so called "spiritual

adventure." Look at it now teetering between atomic destruction and spiritual disintegration.

4 Europe has taken over leadership of the world with fervor, cynicism, and violence. And look how the shadow of its monuments spreads and multiplies. Every movement Europe makes bursts the boundaries of space and thought. Europe has denied itself not only humility and modesty but also solicitude and tenderness.

5 So my brothers, how could we fail to understand that we have better things to do than to follow in that Europe's footsteps. . . . Let's decide not to imitate Europe and let us tense our muscles and our brains in a new direction.

6 Two centuries ago, a former European colony took it into its head to catch up with Europe. It has been so successful that the United States of America has become a monster where the flaws, sickness, and inhumanity of Europe have reached frightening proportions.

7 So comrades, let us not pay tribute to Europe by creating states, institutions, and societies that draw their inspirations from it. Humanity expects other things from us than this grotesque and generally obscene emulation. If we want to transform Africa into a new Europe, America into a new Europe, then let us entrust the destinies of our countries to the Europeans. They will do a better job than the best of us.[75]

Fanon's words from 1961 read as if they were written yesterday, except for the event of Europe falling in desuetude in the global imaginary. They forcefully outline the three movements of the CMP: its constitution, how Europe and then the US built themselves, and the consequences of this self-building—the destitution of the larger part of the human species. Finally comes the delinking and restitution—let's abandon, delink, Fanon says, from what Europe and the US want us to be and to do and create what he called a "new man" for a new humanity. This will require a set of guiding principles on humanness, but today, with the added devastation of planet Earth, these principles will allow us to live in plenitude and harmony, built by the people/us and not by modern philanthropic institutions who will maintain control and management of their vision of man/humanity, telling the people/us what to do according to their ideas of harmony. Restitution will not come by itself. It requires the reconstitution of knowing and knowledge and sensing and believing. This is Fanon's strong summons and the task of decolonial politics today, and what I suggest should be preserved for the future, by us and by upcoming generations.

III.3.6

I close this section on gnoseological and aesthesic reconstitutions with two legacies from Gloria Anzaldúa. While Quijano taught us to look what modernity/rationality hides and, consequently, to look at the history of the colonial matrix of power (CMP) in the formation of the world order since 1500, Anzaldúa taught us that the majority of the planetary population dwells in the borderland and endures colonial wounds. And she taught us that the way to delink from modernity/rationality is by embracing *la facultad*.

On the conjunction of borderland and colonial wounds Anzaldúa has this to say: "The U.S.-Mexican border *es una herida abierta* where the Third World grates against the first and bleeds. And before a scab forms it hemorrhages again, the lifeblood of two worlds merging to form a third country—a border culture. Borders were set up to define the places that are safe and unsafe, to distinguish *us* from *them*."[76] Borderlands are border lines, global linear thinking at work, and the lines divide the ones who traced the line and benefit from it and the ones who have been sent to exteriority, wounded by destitutions. Border lines are both geographic and body-graphic: the subtitle of her book is *The New Mestiza*. "Mestiza" in this case refers to both "impurity of blood," but also to sexuality: the "impurity of gender." Anzaldúa's lesbianism turns the plate around in her gnoseological and aesthesic reconstitution of "heteronormative purity." Here is where *la facultad* comes forward and to the rescue. *La facultad* erupted from the praxis of living of Chicanas (i.e., women of color) and lesbians that without mentioning it invites us to recall a German white male, Immanuel Kant, and his work *The Conflict of the Faculties* (1798). "Faculties" translated into Spanish is *facultades*, which in itself and following dictionary definitions means the "natural" capacity to do something. Kant employs the word to mean the disciplinary organization of the university during his time and the role that corresponds in it to philosopher and philosophy. Kant proposed a reorganization of knowledge and ways of knowing at the university, which was part of the state. That is, he was proposing a reorganization and management of knowledge to educate the citizens of the emerging nation-states—the raising of a secular European bourgeoisie. As Chicana and lesbian, Anzaldúa had little interest in fitting into the university structure of knowledge and regulation of knowing. She was rather interested in liberation of women of color and herself in the communal "we." She highlighted the crucial concept of *la facultad*. What is it?

La facultad, Alzaldúa tells us, "is the capacity to see in surface phenomena the meaning of deeper realities. . . . It is an instant 'sensing,' a quick perception arrived at without conscious reasoning." What, then, is *la facultad* if not the living energy that propels and stores tacit or implicit knowledge? To talk about tacit or implicit knowledge is to talk about something we know. However, *la facultad* is not knowledge but the capacity of knowing in any and all changing situations; it is the living organism's readiness to know, the knowing capacities of living organisms. But she says something more interesting to help us understand the managing and controlling institutional function of philosophy. Anzaldúa adds that "possessing this sensitivity" and being aware of it, releasing it, not suppressing it (philosophy is a mechanism of suppression of sensitivity) make us "excruciatingly alive in the word." And, Anzaldúa adds, those who are in readiness to release the energy of *la facultad* are those who feel the repression of the coloniality of knowing, sensing, and believing, and philosophy is one important component of the coloniality of knowing. By "coloniality of knowing" I mean the taken-for-granted evaluation that reason classifies and ranks what is valid knowledge and what is not, and what is correct knowing and what is not. Anzaldúa thus writes that *la facultad* is always in readiness among "those who are pounced on the most have it the strongest—the females, the homosexuals of all races, the dark-skinned, the outcast, the persecuted, the marginalized, the foreign. *The one possessing this sensitivity is excruciatingly alive in the world*" (emphasis added).[77]

IV Days Ahead

We on the planet today—and COVID-19 has been an eloquent sign—are experiencing a change of epoch, no longer an epoch of changes where the prefix "post-" can be added wherever a "novelty" or a change is sensed or perceived.[78] The prefix "post-" retains the hegemony of the epoch or era framed by the affirmation of Western civilization and the Westernization of the world from 1500 to 2000, where "newness" and "post-" celebrate changes within the same epoch. The change of era we on the planet are experiencing reduces the prefix to its own deserved size, to its regional Western scope, at the same time that it increases the proliferation of planetary temporalities. The two most perceptible manifestations of the change of epoch are the tempos of the *multipolar* interstate world order (which is forcing the US into counterreformation responses, maintaining that it is "the beacon" of the world order, according to Joe Biden's presidential acceptance speech) and trimming down the *unipolarity* that dominated the era of Westernization.[79] On the other hand, the decolonial tempo of *pluriversality* is shrinking the domination (if not the hegemony) of Western *universality*. While multipolarity is an interstate world affair, decolonial pluriversality is a matter of the global political society either ignored or contained by the state and institutional mass media. The global rise (if not insurgencies) of decolonial claims for pluriversal ways of knowing and being in the world, the gnoseological rights to know at every level and areas of experience, the aesthesic rights to sense and taste disregarding and disobeying epistemic and aesthetic restrictions and regulations—these are coming into being at the margins, within and beyond institutional and administrative frames. This book intends to be a contribution to the decolonial tempo of pluriversality.

Critiques to decolonial academicism have proliferated in the past two decades. The decolonial during the Cold War did not originate in the academy, but after the Cold War it made it to the university and museums. While it is an open decision not to be involved in institutional decolonial undertakings, to withdraw the decolonial from research and educational institutions would facilitate the tasks of academics and administrators that are already fighting to prevent and/or expel the decolonial from the academy and contain its spread in the museums.[80] Hence, since universities and museums have been and are two pillars of the coloniality of knowledge (epistemology) and of being (aesthetics), the decolonial options shall not withdraw. Which means that delinking from Western epistemology and aesthetics doesn't equate with delinking from the institutions. The question is what kind of decolonial work could be moved forward at existing institutions that enable the institutions to *be used for* decolonial projects instead of *being used* to preserve modern/colonial regulations of knowledge, knowing (epistemology), and sensing (aesthetics). Introducing gnoseological and aesthesic reconstitutions of the domains, levels, and flows of the CMP at existing institutions must be done carefully to avoid tainting decoloniality with academicism. I do understand that, as is generally the case, decoloniality could be fashionably consumed. But the political tasks of decolonial work shall not be distracted by its fashionable consumption.

This is a book published by a university press. For the reasons given above, I am not apologizing. The options that decoloniality submits were not in place, as conscientious projects, until the second half of the twentieth century. There were, as I stated in section III.3, manifestations, expressions, feelings, and thinking that today could be interpreted as decolonial because the interpreter recognizes in them a pattern that, in the past seventy years, carries the name of decolonization, which I rendered as the decolonial option. Why an option? Because the colonial matrix of power (CMP) was a machine of generating *options* sold as *representations* and gatekeepers of what there is. Here is an outline of what I mean and where we all are today. Starting from the middle of the nineteenth century, three clusters of ideas mapped the modern/colonial frame of Western civilization. The three clusters were secular liberalism, Marxism, and conservatism.[81] Conservatism was the secular version of Christian theology, although toward the end of the nineteenth century there were alliances between liberalism and Protestantism and today between neoliberalism and Pentecostalism. Catholicism remained in general associated with conservatism. Liberalism was the cluster of ideas of the emerging bourgeoisie confronted with the theological aristocracies. Socialism was a newcomer with precedents that socialists themselves (like Saint Simon or Karl Marx) may not have recognized: the sixteenth-century theological/socialist ideas of Spanish Dominican friar Bartolomé de Las Casas. A manifestation of these underground connections is the merging of Marxism and "Lascasism."[82] In its turn, conservatism is a secular mutation of the position advocated by Ginés de Sepúlveda, the conservative contender of Las Casas "socialism," while liberalism was a mutation of the theological legalists like Francisco de Vitoria and Hugo Grotius and John Locke. In sum, the three secular systems of ideas (ideologies), consolidated by the mid-nineteenth century, have their roots in the theological humanism of the sixteenth century, which were the three theological ideologies (the enunciation) securing the foundation of the CMP in all its domains: knowledge, governance, economy, and the imperial idea of the human (the enunciated).

Starting from the middle of the nineteenth century to the end of the twentieth and beginning of the twenty-first centuries, the three clusters mutated and divided. From the liberal cluster emerged neoliberalism, without of course superseding liberalism: liberalism and neoliberalism coexist in tension. Neoliberalism favors a free-market economy while liberalism requires the role of the state to maintain domestic cohesion and interstate coordination. Conservatism, for its part, exploded into radical nationalism in the first half of the twentieth century, in forms known as Nazism and Fascism, and in the second half of the century into Falangism and Franquism. Socialism became Marxism/Leninism. In Russia it generated the Bolshevik Revolution, and in China under Mao Zedong it became Maoism. In the second decade of the twenty-first century, always in the Western sector of the planet, neoliberal globalism (in the US under Barack Obama) engendered its own opposition: fundamental nationalism (in the US under Donald Trump, and in Poland and Hungary, and in the UK as Brexit). This reconfiguration and these internal conflicts are all sidelined with re-Westernization. De-Westernization belongs to a different configuration since China, Russia, and Iran have not been active players in the constitution of the CMP and its preservations through the centuries, but they have been entangled as destituted actors. Which explains why de-Westernization today delinks from the three Western clusters of ideas and their mutations in the twentieth and twenty-first centuries.

This quick outline of clusters of ideas—their formation and mutation from 1500 to 2000—is important to understanding the missing pieces: colonialism and the responses to it. The three major clusters (conservatism, liberalism, and socialism)—their source in the sixteenth century and their mutations since— were all complicit with colonialism; colonialism provided the motivations for the cluster of ideas, but colonial subjects did not participate in their formations and transformations. However, a coexisting cluster of decolonial ideas emerged simultaneously with colonialism. They were destituted and placed in the exteriority of the cluster. But since the second half of the twentieth century they can no longer be contained; decolonial energies have broken the chains that kept the gates locked: the decolonial cluster found its way in the second half of the twentieth century, and the de-Westernizing cluster in the first decade of the twenty-first century. The decolonial and de-Western trajectories did not originate in Europe, obviously. It was the affirmation that non-Europeans can think on their own (see the epilogue). Both types of responses to historical colonialism and to the overall rhetoric of modernity and logic of coloniality come, obviously, from former European colonies and from locales that did not endure the experience of settler colonialisms but that did not escape coloniality: Russia, China, Iran, Turkey. Not surprisingly, these current nation-states (and also India) are mutating into civilizational states. The mutation to civilizational states is a signpost both of de-Westernization and of a change of era.

Concomitantly, the physical struggles of liberation from Western settlers' colonialism in the second half of the twentieth century (the Cold War) were paralleled by a cluster of ideas, analyses, critiques, and visions outlining decolonial horizons. Decolonial energies flourishing during that time were, in retrospect and implicitly, the mutations of precedent struggles and prospective ideas perceived in the work of Guaman Poma, Ottobah Cugoano, the Haitian Revolution, and Mohandas Gandhi. That is, there was a parallel unseen river running under the mirages of the Western clusters sketched above: the decolonial option coexisting with the conservative, liberal, and socialist, their theological historical foundations and their unfolding in the present. This is one simple example of what the politics of decolonial investigations and the gnoseological and aesthesic reconstitutions could do: to understand the change of era and its consequences, and to reorient the praxes of living and knowing toward the reconstitutions of the communal "we" that has been destituted by the Western modern social "I."

When Quijano illuminated coloniality under the guise of Western modernity, at the beginning of the 1990s, he was not yet foreseeing that a change of era would be on the horizon. However, toward 2010 he sensed the eruptions of what he called a "new historical horizon" and forcefully argued that the financial crisis of 2008 was no longer one of the cyclical crises of capitalism; it was something different, a shift in the colonial horizon of modernity.[83] Decoloniality and de-Westernization are the two trajectories, with much in common albeit with irreducible differences, that are bringing about the change of epoch. This argument, however, is a decolonial not a de-Western one. The disputes over the control of the CMP from the side of the US and for the liberation of it from the side of China is not a replica of the dispute between the US and the Soviet Union. There is a significant difference between, on the one hand, the confrontations between liberal/neoliberal capitalism and state communism during the Cold War and, on the other, the confrontations between neoliberal globalism and civilizational resurgences; or, in the expressions I use in this book, between re-Westernization and de-Westernization. What do I mean by "neoliberal globalism" and "civilizational resurgences"?

The Cold War involved the politics of either/or from both sides. Unsurprisingly, both sides acted on Western dichotomies: you are with me or with my enemies. Both actors in the contention operated on the foreign policy of alliances, by diplomacy or by force. With the Soviet Union gone, the foreign policy of alliance has been the weapon of the US. But China did not play that game. It delinked from it. Chinese foreign policy is of *partnership* instead of *alliance*.[84] An alliance means you have two choices, A versus B. That was also how Carl Schmitt conceived domestic policies. He defined the political as confrontations between friends and enemies.[85] We have experienced the consequences of the domestic politics of alliance during the Donald Trump presidency and internationally since George W. Bush and Dick Cheney invented and created the "terrorists." Partnership, instead, means association in business rather than alliances and politics. You are not forced to do business with me, and I will not consider you an enemy if you do not. Responsibility is placed on the ethics of small and medium states: to engage in the politics of alliance or of partnership? That is the de-Western option, its opening to multipolarity and the resulting march of a change of epoch. Multipolarity could only be achieved through a politics of partnership in foreign policies. However, none of the existing nation-states are at this point willing or able to make this move. Decoloniality and the nation-state are strange bedfellows. The politics of partnership promoted by China is a significant factor in the change of epoch in international relations, while the decolonial politics of investigations is a marker of pluriversality in the sphere of knowing, sensing, and being in the world. Both are initiating the advent of the third nomos of the earth (see chapter 14).

At this point, what are the movers of decoloniality at large, by which I mean the global proliferation of deeds and thoughts rejecting the coloniality of power, the explosions of the global politics of gnoseological and aesthesic reconstitutions? They include: the irreversible struggles to break the chains of gender heteronormativity and racial classifications and hierarchies, exposing white innocence and privileges; the growing awareness of the inadequacies of the modern nation-state, both in the place of its foundations and in the colonies where it was transplanted (by force or by a decision of the native population); the myriad publications, workshops, seminars, and blogs embracing decoloniality; the many debates calling into question the coloniality of universities and museums, and of biennial and triennial exhibits within but also beyond university and museum cloisters. All of these and more have the following in common: the *rejection* of established knowledge, of the regulation of knowing and sensing, and of the management of subjectivities to conform people's sensibilities, tastes, and orientations to one dominant, overarching, abstract universal.[86] Decoloniality did not emerge in academic intellectual circles of the North Atlantic but in the struggle for decolonization in the Third World, and entered the academy and North Atlantic intellectual circuits at the end of the twentieth century. Consequently, because the history of decoloniality that I outlined in section III.3, the politics of decolonial investigations is not, cannot, should not be limited to the academy although the academy is an important site to re-direct knowledges and the regulations of knowing (gnoseology) and sensing/believing (aesthesis). After all, universities and museums are factories of knowledge and sensing that regulate epistemology and aesthetics.[87]

While universities and museums are two pillars of the coloniality of knowledge, the control of seeds and the uses of transgenic procedures, the exploitation of natural resources and the commodification of health, are distinct modalities of the colonialization of life, which implies the coloniality of knowledge and sensing. The coloniality of life in these three areas presupposes epistemic regulations that destitute the necessary balance of life without modified food, with access to pure air and clean water, and with healthy bodies in harmony with Earth and with the culture that the human species has created. Gnoseological and aesthesic reconstitutions have gigantic and hopeful tasks ahead to help to restitute communal horizons of living.

Beyond the two signposts of the coloniality of knowing and sensing, universities and museums, there are other areas in which decoloniality at large is making its mark beyond and detached from the nation-state: actors involved in the sovereignty of food, local environmental movements, and local health care have been attentive to what decoloniality has to offer to basic areas of existence that have been transformed into commodities. And decolonial actors have been attentive to the trajectories of the Zapatistas[88] and the Peasant Way,[89] both organizations that are delinked from modern/colonial conventions of knowing and sensing and that have established their own ways (methods) to investigate what they need to know to advance their projects. In between these groups at one extreme and state and private universities at the other, the Global University for Sustainability, spearheaded by professor Lau Kin Chi from Lingnan University in Hong Kong, has conjoined the history of the institution-university with the knowing and sensing generated from praxes of living and doing rather than from disciplinary regulations.[90] What I propose in this book, building on Aníbal Quijano's groundbreaking vision of decoloniality as epistemic reconstitutions (which I render as gnoseological and aesthesic reconstitutions), has indirect relations with the state and faces strong opposition within the academy. Both "deficiencies" are convincing signs that the decolonial option is touching some chords that shall not be overlooked. I mentioned above the French intellectuals' manifesto revealing the increasing discomfort of right-wing academics with decoloniality at large.

All in all, while during the Cold War decolonization was a mixture of decolonial thinking and decolonial state politics, decoloniality after the Cold War has an overarching duty in the wide sphere of knowing, knowledge, sensing, and believing. Decolonial work at this point may not do much to change a world controlled by finances, technology, and interstate capitalism, whether re-Western or de-Western in politics, by an overwhelming presence of mass media, and by sophisticated military power associated with capitals, states, and technology. But decolonial work can and must have an irreplaceable task in shifting the ways that we, members of the human species, are and live in the world. With *The Politics of Decolonial Investigations* I am aiming to add a grain of sand to the change of epoch and to the decolonial earthquake underway.

GEOPOLITICS, SOCIAL CLASSIFICATION, AND BORDER THINKING

1   Racism as We Sense It Today

RACE, A MENTAL CATEGORY OF MODERNITY
The idea of race, in its modern meaning, does not have a known history
before the colonization of America. Perhaps it originated in reference to the
phenotypic differences between conquerors and conquered. However, what
matters is that soon it was constructed to refer to the supposed differential
biological structures between those groups.—ANÍBAL QUIJANO, "Coloniality
of Power, Eurocentrism and Latin America," 2000

I

Race and gender are two concepts of Western modernity that make us believe
they "represent" something that exists. Behind race there is an implied logic
of classification (the logic of coloniality) assuming that people belong to different races and the markers are blood and skin color. Behind gender there is
an implied logic of classification assuming that there are women and men. The
classifications shape and guide our perception of society. However, decolonial
gnoseological assumptions say that names and classifications *do not refer to what
there is* but *frame what we perceive*. Who is behind racial and gender classifications? Both classifications hide the classifiers. The classifiers are actors that
assume the privileges of Christian blood and of whiteness. He who classifies
racially belongs to the same kind of actor that classifies gender and assumes
the natural privilege of patriarchy and masculinity.

The research that I reported in *The Darker Side of the Renaissance: Literacy,
Territoriality, and Colonization* (1995) was driven by my desire and need to

understand the opening up of the Atlantic in the sixteenth century, its historical, theoretical, and political consequences. How was it that coexisting socioeconomic organizations like the Ottoman and Mughal sultanates, as well as the Incanate in the Andes and the Tlatoanate in the Valley of Mexico, were described as inferior by Christian narratives or were almost absent in the global historical picture of the time depicted by Western Christian men of letters?[1] I became aware, for example, that the Spaniards surmised that people in the Valley of Mexico inhabiting the Aztec Tlatoanate were of Jewish descent. Jews were cast out (racialized) in the Iberian Peninsula, and Aztecs, Incas, Mayas, and many other less-well-known communities in the Tawantinsuyu, Anahuac, or Turtle Islands (what Europeans called the "New World") were also ranked as lesser humans. It was even suggested that inhabitants of what for Europeans was a New World descended from the seven tribes of Israel. This association was twofold: on the one hand, "Indians" (that is, the people of the great Aztec civilization) and Jews were dirty and untrustworthy people; on the other hand, the Indians (including the inhabitants of the Maya and Inca civilizations) in the New World may have been part of the Jewish diaspora. So what amounted to a false identification got into trouble, because Indians and Jews may have been the same people.

When the Jesuit priest José de Acosta, in his *Historia natural y moral de las Indias* (1589), asked whether the Indians descended from the Jews, he addressed a question that had been on everybody's mind since the second quarter of the sixteenth century. He dismissed the possibility of a connection because the Jews had had a sophisticated writing system for a long time while the Indians were illiterate (in the Western sense of the word). Jews liked money, Acosta pointed out, while Indians were not even aware of it; and while Jews took circumcision seriously, Indians had no idea of it. Last but not least, if Indians were indeed of Jewish origin, they would not have forgotten the Messiah and their religion.

"Indigenous" was not a word used at the time. The word had not yet been invented in Western vocabulary; it was registered around 1640. However, to name inhabitants of the New World "Indigenous" would have contradicted the argument that they were of Jewish descent. Let's remember the etymology:

INDIGENOUS *(adj.)*
"born or originating in a particular place," 1640s, from Late Latin *indigenus* "born in a country, native," from Latin *indigena* "sprung from the land, native," as a noun, "a native," literally "in-born," or "born in (a place)," from

Old Latin *indu* (prep.) "in, within" + *gignere* (perfective *genui*) "beget," from PIE root *gene- "to produce, give birth, beget" (see genus)[2]

As this etymology suggests, the "Indigenous" of what Europeans also called America are the only Indigenous in the world that are known as Indians, due to the well-known miscalculation and confusion of Christopher Columbus. Furthermore, if Europeans had used the word "Indigenous," at least some of the educated ones should have been aware of its etymology, which tells us that Europeans are the Indigenous people of Europe. If they are not Indigenous, where do they come from? As masters of the narratives, ordering and classifying the world, hiding their own true indigeneity may have allowed them to consider non-European Indigenous people lesser than themselves.

Then came the question of enslaved Africans in the New World. Early in the sixteenth century, Indians were considered vassals of the king and serfs of God. Consequently, they couldn't be enslaved. This prohibition fostered and legitimized the massive enslavement of Africans. Bartolomé de Las Casas, as is well known, first supported the dictum about Indians and Africans, but then he corrected himself and condemned slavery. Indians and Africans were the objects on which the concept of colonial difference was established: they were cast as ontologically inferior and epistemically disabled. Later, in the twentieth century, Jews became targets of colonial difference—manifested internally in host countries, rather than externally in remote colonies—not so much because of their claimed (in Western secular narratives and arguments) ontological or epistemic inferiority as because they endangered the homogeneity of the nation-state. In both cases, however, the state control of knowledge was the basic weapon for racial classification.

Racial classification is tantamount to establishing hierarchies that, in the language of modernity/coloniality, manufacture colonial differences. Colonial differences are not merely and not simply cultural differences. Or, to put it another way, they are cultural differences that are manipulated by power differentials that rank world populations according to a Western category of "the human" (see chapter 13). Colonial differences have been established since the sixteenth century both racially and sexually. Thus, racial and sexual classifications were and still are epistemic. But this epistemology created an ontology that among the persons classified, the classifiers, and the population belonging to the ethnicity of the classifier ends up promoting the idea that some people are ontologically deficient due to "material" (and visual) racial and sexual features. Race, therefore, is always already a racist concept. Moreover, in Europe the difference between man and woman was established among people of the same ethnicity, but in the colonies, it was impossible for the classifiers to see sex as independent of race: colonial females, in the eyes of those who sat in the house of knowledge (who generally were man/human; see chapter 13), were of a different race.[3]

Although Africa and Africans were already classified in Christian cosmology as descendants of Ham, Noah's cursed son, and although Christians and Jews have been in tension since the origin of Christianity, neither difference was understood as colonial. Colonial difference was an invention of Christianity in the sixteenth century, and, perhaps needless to say, its consequences have been enormous. One of the meanings of "Ham" was "black." The conjunction of being cursed and being Black, plus the fact that Ham's descendants expanded throughout Africa and into the current Middle East, brought into the picture the blackamoors (or Moors, as some came to be called). When Elizabeth I of England launched a campaign countering Spaniards' brutal behavior against the Indians (a campaign known today as the "Black Legend"), the Spanish were likened to blackamoors, which underlined the close connections between Spain and Muslims from North Africa.[4] Moors and Blacks were thus conflated as undesirable persons in Christian Europe and were used to establish the internal imperial difference between England (a wannabe empire) and Spain (a leading imperial force).[5] All in all, colonial differences were both intramural (Jews) and extramural (Muslims, Africans, and Indians).

The resulting historical configuration is as messy as it is foundational: racism as we sense it and live it today—its specific historical circumstances, its conceptual and ideological apparatus—has its blueprint in the sixteenth century. It is also a foundational aspect of the rhetoric of modernity (the narratives of the superior race that creates, manages, and controls the "knowledge" that grants the privilege to classify) and the logic of coloniality (the spheres of the classified). It is a messy, heterogeneous, historico-structural undertaking to map the emergence of the racial matrix, the modern/colonial world, and the foundation of the capitalist economy.[6] Differences in previous and coexisting civilizations can be found, certainly. But none of the previous and coexisting civilizations were capitalist in the sense that we understand capitalism today (see the discussion of the colonial matrix of power, or CMP, in the introduction).[7] It was racism that was needed to justify the massive exploitation of labor through slavery and land dispossession leading to the incipient Atlantic commercial circuits displacing the Mediterranean trade and commercial center for southern Europe, North Africa, and West Asia. All of that amounted to an embryonic coming into being of the modern/colonial world system and therefore of the CMP.[8] Economic coloniality (called "capitalism" after Weber and Lenin) was one aspect of an emerging civilizational ideal in tension but not in conflict with Christianity.

This messy historical configuration has therefore an underlying logic that justifies opportunistic and circumstantial structure: Christian theology was confronted with equivalent and competing religious ideas (Jewish and Muslim).[9] It was also confronted with a diversity of people in the New World, all of whom the Christians, applying Occam's razor, called Indians; they were deemed to lack religion and were therefore victims of the mischievous and perverse designs of the devil. And finally there existed a complex population who descended from Ham and constituted a confusing mixture of blackamoors—that is, Moors as Muslims and simultaneously Black, who could have been Muslim or not in Europe and Africa—and African Blacks, who were enslaved and transported to the New World from different African kingdoms, and who were varied in language, religion, and history. The Spanish Inquisition in 1505 established some order within this field; it was a unique and innovative (in the sense that "innovation" is used today to mean an advance in progress and development) modern *state*-political-regulating institution. In retrospect, the racial matrix (and the historical foundation of racism as we know it today) is a combination of two structures, one religious and one secular. Both Christian theology and European egology (in the sense of René Descartes and Immanuel Kant) controlled and managed racial classification.[10] Racial classification is one aspect of staging *colonial* differences (later I will discuss imperial differences) into colonial racial differences.

II

The special issue of the PMLA in which this article was originally published was devoted to "Comparative Racialization." Apropos of this topic, the question asked was the following: Where shall we place comparative endeavors in understanding racism? To that question I added my own: Who is comparing what and when and with what purposes?[11] What are the purposes of comparative work, and what can comparison tell us about how racism is sensed today? A broadly comparative perspective on the question of race may only scratch the surface of the problem, missing the underlying structure (the CMP) according to which, for instance, racial manifestations in sixteenth-century Spain and the New World differed from those in eighteenth-century France or late nineteenth-century Japan after the Meiji Restoration.

All my work on this issue consists of the unfolding of a hypothesis introduced by Aníbal Quijano: racism (more than classism) as we know and sense it today is *constitutive* of the colonial matrix of power put in place in the sixteenth century. Race is already a racist concept. There are no races out there in the world, entities that by themselves are "races." Race is a construct to classify and rank what is in the world; since race is a concept, racism is epistemological: *He* who controls and manages knowledge and the regulation of knowing classifies and places *himself* as the model and reference of the classification and ranking. It is on the basis of racial classification that race provides the epistemological foundation for the colonial and imperial differences and, as such, is the engine of the CMP. Coloniality of power (the will to dominate, the technic, Greek *techné*) and the CMP (technology, the instrument of domination) were cemented by the idea of race. Quijano writes:

> The idea of race, in its modern meaning, does not have a known history before the colonization of America. . . . In America the idea of race was a way of granting legitimacy to the relations of domination imposed by the conquest. After the colonization of America and the expansion of European colonialism to the rest of the world, the subsequent *constitution* [see the introduction to this book for this concept] of Europe as a new id-entity needed the elaboration of *a Eurocentric perspective of knowledge*, a theoretical perspective on the idea of race as a naturalization of colonial relations between Europeans and non-Europeans. . . . So the conquered and dominated people were situated in a natural position of inferiority, and as a result, *their phenotype traits* as well as their *cultural features* were likewise considered inferior. (Emphasis and bracketed phrases added.)[12]

That paragraph exemplifies both Quijano's groundbreaking argument as well as a pillar of my argument on the politics of decolonial investigations. Do not look for race/racism before the sixteenth century either in Europe or in the rest of the world. Once you uncouple "race" from the ontic domain it frames and accept that "race" is an epistemic invention of the ontology of the human species, you can better understand how the idea of race *selected physical features and cultural traits* to create the ontologically inferior and epistemically deficient. The politics of decolonial investigations shall dismantle the racial fictions of modernity that were invented to legitimize the logic of coloniality; this is of the essence to deal with an issue that has become a cultural planetary virus.

Atlantic slavery was one leg of the historical foundation of racism in the sixteenth century. Although slavery was known in Greece and Rome, there is no antecedent of a structure of knowledge and management such as the CMP. This matrix came about from the processes of classifying and diminishing the value of people to justify either their expulsion from "our territory" (Jews and Moors) or their control and exploitation (Indians and enslaved Africans). But racism also had another manifestation, internal to Europe and among empires. The Black Legend initiated *imperial* racial difference, and the Spaniards became seen as blackamoors.[13] The assumed divide, today, between the South and the North of Europe is an outcome and a continuity of the fabrication of the South of Europe in the eighteenth century, demoting the Iberian Peninsula from its imperial role and playing down the Italian Renaissance by highlighting the northern European Enlightenment—a demotion that evinces the imperial intramural racial differences that I mentioned above and that is today alive in the northern imaginary of the "South of Europe." The technologies of racialization have common features within the modern/colonial world order and across time and space: the control of knowledge (i.e., the level of the enunciation) to devalue an imperial adversary (e.g., the term "yellow race" to devalue China and Japan), an enemy that has to be kept at bay or eliminated if necessary (e.g., communists and terrorists), and control of the sector of the population that needs to be dominated.

Figures 1.1 and 1.2 contain two simple illustrations of this underlying process and its geohistorical mutations. Let's think about two triangles: The first triangle has Christians at the top and Muslims (Moors) and Jews at the bottom (see figure 1.1). Moriscos (Muslims who converted to Christianity) and conversos (Jews who converted to Christianity) were the religious mestizos, the result of the mixing of Christian and Moorish "blood" and Christian and Jewish "blood," respectively and figuratively.[14]

The scheme was clear in the Iberian Peninsula, at the heart of the emerging empire. In the colonies, the situation was different. Spaniards considered Indians to be people without religion and thus in the hands of the devil, because for Christians, religion was only what resembled their concept of it. Later Kant would laugh at the so-called religions of India and China. The ancient (and not sacred) meaning of *religare* and *relegere*, "to reunite" (in Lactantius and Cicero), was lost; "religion" meant having one God, even if that God was the wrong one, as with the Jews and Muslims. Being Christian was supplanted by national identification, like being Spanish or Castilian.

At the bottom of the second triangle (figure 1.2) we have Indians and Blacks (Africans). Religious conversion in the Iberian Peninsula engendered the new categories of moriscos and conversos. In the New World, the categories were mestizos/as and mulattos/as. But in this case the categories referred to intermarriage and blood mixtures, whereas in the Iberian Peninsula "moriscos" and "conversos" referred to religious conversion, not to intersexual and

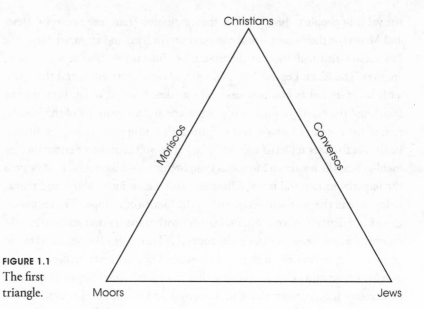

FIGURE 1.1
The first
triangle.

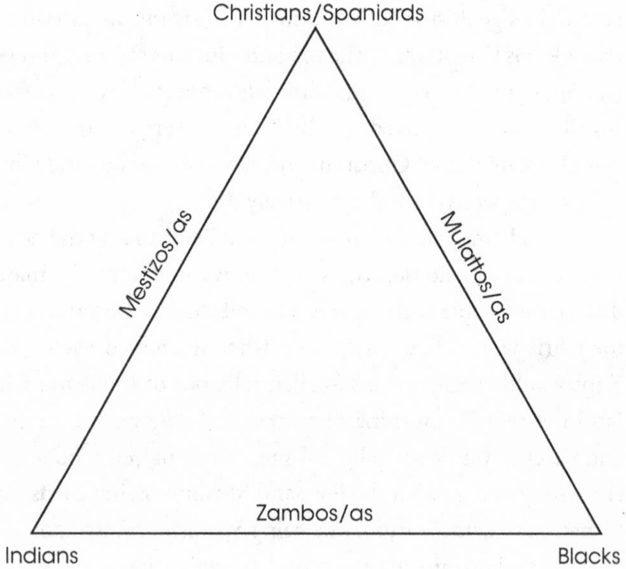

FIGURE 1.2
The second
triangle.

intermarital blood mixtures. But while in the Iberian Peninsula the blood mixture between Moors and Jews was not accounted for (and probably not very common physically), in the New World the mixture of mulattos and mestizas or of mulattas and mestizos engendered a new racial category, *zambos* and *zambas*, *cafuzos* and *cafuzas*. From here on, classifications multiplied, but all of them were displayed under the discourses, narratives, and arguments highlighting the privileges of "purity" of Spanish/Castilian blood or "Cristianos Viejos" (Old Christians). The logic of racial classification was established as a fundamental component of the CMP.

III

Quijano's insight made me understand that logically and historically, race was an epistemic category to legitimize *racism*, and that modern/colonial racism was a Western theological construction at the confluence of the expulsion of Moors and Jews from the Iberian Peninsula and the colonization of the New World, which brought Indians and Black Africans into the picture.[15] The motivations in each case were different, but the rhetoric was similar, justifying expulsions on the one hand and expropriations and destruction on the other: the rhetoric of rightfulness and of salvation. At the same time, I became aware of racial legacies today and their impact on my own subjectivity. The history of European immigrants in South America and the Caribbean (I was not a Creole, of Hispanic descent since colonial times, but part of a European immigration that started toward the end of the nineteenth century) was ingrained in the logic of coloniality as it was and also by my personal migration to France, where I was identified as "Sudaka" (referring to South American migrants to Europe), and then to the United States, where I became a Hispanic/Latino.[16]

In that peregrination, I became aware of actualities. First, given the epistemic and ontological *colonial* differences that structure the imaginary of the modern/colonial world order, I enjoyed, as an Argentine of Italian descent, the (second-class) privileges that immigrants of Italian descent in South America have in the CMP. In that regard, I had an edge on the diversity of Indians and African descendants in South America, while falling short of the privileges of first-class citizens in Argentina (traditional families who settled toward the eighteenth century and are of Spanish descent) and also by virtue of being not European but *of* European descent. Furthermore, racial geopolitical hierarchies were already established in the CMP between the European diaspora in the US and in Canada (mainly from the UK and France) and in South/Central

America and the Caribbean (mainly from southern Europe). The racial geopo-litical divide in Europe, consolidated during the eighteen century, was repli-cated in the Americas (see chapter 8, "Decolonial Reflections on Hemispheric Partitions"). Added to all of this, at the time I was coming of age, I belonged to a Third World country and a Third World subcontinent, which contributed to my understanding of the latitudes, the scales, and the diversity of colonial wounds (see chapter 12 and epilogue).

For all these reasons—and also because of the European and US models of the human and of knowledge—I was deficient: not quite European and not quite white, even if I have white skin. My Spanish accent in France and the US (although I was born and raised among Italo-Argentine families) colored me. The Spanish language (in the mix with German, French, and English) was already carrying the weight of the imperial difference in Europe that trans-lated into colonial difference by my coming to the US from Spanish America, where the Spanish language, and I should add Portuguese, was the official language of the Third World. In the Iberian Peninsula, Spanish and Portu-guese have lost the clout they had as the imperial languages from the six-teenth to the eighteenth centuries, before France, Germany, and Britain took over the leadership of Western epistemology, and before the epistemic hege-mony (secular philosophy and the sciences) became grounded in their national languages. Racism works in all spheres of experience; it conforms people's subjectivity, our sensing and emotioning. Knowledge built and framed in the Spanish language is today, in the European Union, less influential and less en-during than knowledge built in English, French, or German—English above all, because of the global imperial extent to which the UK superseded Spain and then the United States followed in the steps of the UK. Believe me, I am not complaining: I am analyzing geo-body politics decolonially through my own experience, since the politics of decolonial investigations cannot be de-tached from our senses and emotions (which is how coloniality acts on every-one on the planet). I understood that racism expands beyond the metaphor of blood and skin color and is grounded in social classification managed by insti-tutions, languages, and actors who control knowledge. "Sociogenesis" was the term introduced by Frantz Fanon to make visible the routes of racialization. I am noting here the routes of racialization that nourish and are nourished by the CMP.

Thus, I approach racism in the modern/colonial and imperial/colonial world orders as a South American of Italo-European descent (identified as a Hispanic in the United States) and as someone trained in philosophy, liter-ature, and anthropology in Córdoba (Argentina) and in semiotics, discourse analysis, and literary theory in Paris (France).[17] However, to understand the imperial management of human subjectivities through racism, I am not starting from an academic discipline but from the subjective sensing and emotioning of my own history and the history of others who are not immigrants in South America. Rather, these others are dissenting Creoles of Spanish descent or mestizos and mestizas. On the complex issues of mestizos/as, I need only mention here that the majority of mestizos/mestizas may have mixed blood but no Indigenous political spirituality because their/our upbringing and education were derivations of European cosmology, knowledge, and institutional models, which served well to destitute Indigenous and Afro-descendant cosmologies and praxis of knowing.[18]

Once I understood where I fit into the patterns of racial classifications—I leave aside here sexual classifications[19]—sociogenesis, in Frantz Fanon's vocabulary, inspired me to join forces with those who, instead of using their privileges in South America, turned toward the struggle carried on by progressive Indians and progressive Africans and Caribbean Americans. I am not, of course, representing or speaking for Indians and Africans in the Americas, nor for immigrants, for that matter. I *do* speak *as* an immigrant; immigrants have been speaking for themselves/ourselves since we became immigrants, and that happened when the nation-state and the invention of citizenship came into being in the formation of the CMP. My decolonial analysis of racism is driven by semiotics, discourse/visual analysis, and literary theory, but I do not regard the implementation of these tools as separable from my own experience of (sensing) racism. In other words, I make no pretense of complete scientific objectivity, analyzing racism as if I were not trapped in a racial matrix but observing it from a location where I am not racialized and implied in racialization (and no one else is), pretending that my praxis of living and the embodiment of disciplinary training were unaffected by the modern racial matrix or by the epistemic formations embracing it.

In a sense, I have inverted an analytic process, and this inversion is my methodology: there is no way for me to hide—within any discipline—from infection by the racial matrix and pretend that racism, or my existence, or humanness itself, can be described and explained from the uncontaminated nonracial eyes of, say, God (theology) or scientific reason (Man egology; see chapter 12).[20] By inverting the process (and with the aid of Gloria Anzaldúa), I discovered border thinking and became undisciplined. Disciplines in the colonial matrix of power can be like surrogates for religious and ethnic identities. Although disciplinary identities are formed on the principle of objectivity, neutrality, reason without passion, mind without the interference of affects, and so on (formed on the basis of beliefs posited as detached from individual experiences and subjective configurations), they are no less identities than religious or ethnic ones. The modern/colonial, well-hidden paradox is that disciplines are tools to analyze identities but are not identities in themselves. That is how the rhetoric of modernity hides the logic of coloniality.

In sum, from the sixteenth century on, the technology of racism was always enacted and supported by the imperial control of knowledge, and the imperial control of knowledge consists in disciplinary formation, theological and secular: the warrantor of scientific and scholarly objectivity. The success of racism in devaluing (in the name of human/man; see chapter 12) certain human beings who did not conform to the norm and model of humanity—that place at the top of the pyramid—serves as a point of reference to trace the many variations of the chain of being. The consequences have been and continue to be devastating for society at large: the economic and legal-political dispensability of human lives, not to mention life on/of Earth (climate change). In the sphere of the state and the economy today, the technologies of racism may operate somewhat differently from days gone by but the logic is essentially the same. The racialization of China and Russia at the global level is no less "racial" than that of immigrants in Europe and in the United States at the national level. Although China is now a serious competitor in the capitalist economy, the Chinese are still—in the global racial unconscious—yellow.

There is an obvious (for those who want to see it) racist underpinning in Western critiques of the governments of China (the "yellow race" and the "yellow peril") and Russia (Orthodox Christianity, Soviet communism). Not only "the people" are racialized but also the officers of the states and of economics and financial institutions at both ends of the spectrum—he who racializes and he who is racialized. Not to mention Iran, which carries the traces of Islam although they are not Arab but Persian and disobedient to Western global designs. Accusations of violating human rights, lacking democracy, or manipulating media propaganda are on the one hand manifestations of well-known double standards, and on the other the replication of the logic of deficiency and lacking that was the distinctive feature of both racially classified dehumanization and racially classifying humanity: the one who classifies belongs to humanity, the one who is classified is marked by the doubting of his/her humanity. Restoring gnoseology through the politics of decolonial investigations and deserting epistemology that regulates the disciplinary field is like planting a seed that will grow out of the complicities between the ontology of race invented and sustained by epistemology and disciplinarity, trickling down to the mass media and the public sphere.

IV

I have explored here in some detail the logic of racialization that classified as Indians/Indigenous the native inhabitants in the Americas and as Indigenous the native inhabitants in other parts of the world. I have also discussed the racialization of both Africans in Africa and enslaved Africans transported to the New World, who include Afro-Americans in the large sense of the continent "America"—denoting both North and South, that is, the Western Hemisphere—as well as those Africans described as Afro-Caribbean, who are further divided by different imperial classifications: Spanish, English, French, Dutch. And I have described the racial foundation in the Iberian Peninsula since the second half of the fifteenth century and its legalization after Castilians recovered their lands and expelled the last Muslims.

In the following three chapters I will explore the racialization of Jews and Muslims in the formation and transformation of the CMP. My exploration will not be thematic but conceptual, beginning from Aníbal Quijano's insight that one of the pillars of the modern/colonial world system is social classification rather than social class. Social classifications are basically racial and sexual (that is, classifications that are invented and managed by ethnic Christian Europeans and are heteropatriarchal by constitution). Of course, they are also described as "natural" representations of races and genders—bypassing the fact that "nature" is not something existing but is as much a fiction as are racial and sexual classifications (see figures I.1, I.2, and I.3 in the introduction to this volume).

Racial classifications have distributed and ranked ethnicities; sexual classifications have distributed and ranked bodily biological features and ethical and political behaviors; natural classifications (the invention of "nature") have reduced the splendors of life on the planet to one single noun, "nature," to distinguish it from culture, the world of the human. However, culture is where classifications take place and the classifiers and those endorsing their classifications situate themselves. Social classifications are not, then, the "representation" of a given ontological social and "natural" order, or organization, or hierarchy but a creation of them. And these representations/inventions are conceptual, cognitive, and emotional. The classifiers (and whoever accepts their classifications) operate through language, institutions, beliefs, and no doubt primitive feelings toward the classified.

In the four chapters of this section (including this one), I explore the entanglements and consequences of racial classification and concomitant state formation, specifically in chapter 4, where I interconnect epistemic classification of the social with the institutional sphere of the state form of governance. The issues explored in this and the next chapters cut across the entire argument: racial and sexual classifications are the spine of the CMP and traverse all areas of experience, from the domestic issues of the state and daily life (see part II of this book) to interstate relations (see part III); from the geopolitics of knowledge to the geopolitics of knowing (see part IV). Classifications and ranking create colonial and imperial differences and provoke decolonial responses of reconstitutions. Epistemology and aesthetics become an encumbrance, and so reconstitutions resort to gnoseology and aesthesis. Coexisting in disobedient confrontation with epistemology and aesthetics, thinking gnoseologically and aesthesically demands border thinking. At this point we—you, reader, and I—are immersed in the politics of decolonial investigations.

2   Islamophobia/Hispanophobia

I

My argument on the historical foundation and transformations of race/racism as we know it today will require jumps in epochs and continents, between the New and the Old Worlds and between the sixteenth century, the eighteenth century, and the present. To maintain the line of the argument (which defies the linear time that is required by the politics of decolonial investigations), it will be important to bear in mind that the anchor is the historical foundation of the colonial matrix of power (CMP) in the sixteenth century, of which the concept of "race" is a fundamental piece to unlock Western management of knowledge—its ontological assumption as well as the "classification" of mainly non-Western, lesser humans beings. Classification is a modern concept grounded on the presupposition that classifications are representations of what there is. I do not walk the path of current assumptions and debates on the topic. I delink and rebuild, engaging in gnoseological and aesthesic reconstitutions, walking on the politics of decolonial investigations.

The expanding culture of fear that in recent years has identified Islam with the specter of terrorism—mainly in Europe and the US, but also in the Russian Federation—was my motivation for exploring Islamophobia alongside Hispanophobia, two racial specters highlighted by Samuel P. Huntington while he hunted the imaginary of Western foreign and interstate relations (the clash of civilizations) and the domestic ghosts of the increasing Hispanic (his word) population in the US.[1] There is no need here to review the transformation of subjectivities and social consciousness in the West, where Islamophobia resurfaced after 9/11. Islamophobia, under a different name, has a long tradition—although I have not gone into a *historical ethnography* of events since then until today. My focus is on the racial configuration and the *logic of coloniality* in the modern/colonial world order (that I outlined in chapter 1) and its political and emotional underpinnings. Huntington may have perceived that war today has been displaced by interstate conflicts in their impact on civil society: there is an obvious but silenced "supplement" to interstate wars by means of sanctions and trade wars that intrude on the well-being of the population. What interests me in this chapter is the historical period when the Moors were expelled from the Iberian Peninsula and therefore from what was becoming Europe. In fact, this expulsion may have been one of the determinant moments of an emerging European self-consciousness. I will sketch this history in order to explore racism in the forming of the modern/colonial world, or, to put it another way, racism's role in the establishment of a modernity/coloniality of knowing, sensing, and believing.

Literature, as well as the mainstream and independent media, has responded profusely to 9/11, which either confirmed Huntington's thesis or alerted us to an event that he was preannouncing. The Soviet Union being out of the way, the US had a "problem" with national security—there was no powerful enemy to justify national security.[2] In the Russian Federation, which followed the collapse of the Soviet Union, however, this fear was less nourished by the downfall of the twin towers than it was in the US; for the federation, it was the conflict with Chechnya, which, of course, preceded 9/11. Nevertheless, the two events continued the traces of two interrelated and at the same time singular histories—a heterogeneous historic-structural node, if you will. We shall treat them in their singularity rather than try to subsume them within a universal Western linear history. Both histories, however, like the history of Christianity—i.e., Western Christianity (Catholics and Protestants) and Eastern Orthodox Christianity in Russia—have a common origin and moment of divergence. Although I am not familiar with the particularities of Islamophobia in the Russian Federation, I think it is important to keep it in mind to avoid the illusion that what happens in the West (that is, in western Europe and the US) carries the same meaning and significance all over the world.[3] Another approach would have been to take into account Islamophobia in South Asia and in East Asia, where Christianity has made inroads but is not the dominant religion. I will limit my observations, however, to the locales where Christianity became increasingly hostile to Islam, while at the same time improving its complicity with Judaism and above all with Zionism in the state of Israel (see chapter 4).

In the United States, the specter of Islam on a global scale has been accompanied—I have already mentioned—by the rising specter of Hispanophobia.
Interestingly enough, Samuel Huntington has been the ideologue who has
connected both in two influential books. The first (and better-known) one,
The Clash of Civilizations (1996), came out after the collapse of the Soviet Union.
The second, *Who Are We? The Challenges of America's National Identity* (2004),
was published after 9/11, which gave the US legitimacy to intensify its politics of
national security. In March of 2017 we witnessed the trajectory of Huntington's
concerns. A chapter of his second book was prepublished with the title "The
Hispanic Challenge." How are these two historical scenarios and the social
imaginaries they presuppose intermingled in the CMP and in imperial global
designs? In what manner can the politics of decolonial investigations assist in
making sense of the two phobias and their underlying connections? Neither
of them (Islamophobia or Hispanophobia) nor social imaginaries are "natural
happenings" that carry with them their own meaning. On the contrary, the
meanings projected on Muslims and Hispanics build the imaginary of the two
"phobias," which nourish the configuration of the CMP and of global designs.
Hence, the two terms are meaning-making although they are presented as a
mere description of what happened rather than as modeling the events. How
then does the Western imperial imaginary manage to create Islamophobia and
Hispanophobia as challenges or even as threats to the West and to the US
especially? I suggest some answers to these questions in the following pages.

II

A common history connects Western and Eastern Christians. The division between Rome and Constantinople is well known in the history of Western Christians and certainly among Eastern Christians.[4] Eastern Christianity unfolded
collectively in Greece, the Balkans, and Eastern Europe.[5] Western Christians
(or Christendom) were located in the territory that eventually became secular Europe. The differences between both were based on languages, theological
principles, and political projects. Religious divisions and distinctions were
complemented by differing ethnicities. The Slavic peoples are defined by their
use of the Slavic languages. They have inhabited—since the sixth century,
about a century before the emergence of Islam—what is today central Europe,
Eastern Europe, and the Balkans. Meanwhile, the Latin language became the
trademark of Western Christianity and so part of the ethnicity of the inhabitants to the west of Jerusalem and to the north of the Mediterranean Sea.
Anglo-Saxons occupied the territories to the west of the Slavic populations. For

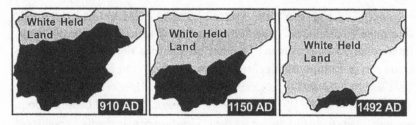

FIGURE 2.1 The long process of the expulsion of Muslims from Western Christian territories: from today's southern France through the Iberian Peninsula. *Source:* Arthur Kemp, *March of the Titans: The Complete History of the White Race* (Burlington: Ostara Publications, 2011), 171.

the people inhabiting the territory northeast of the Mediterranean Sea (from Greece to Spain), there is not a single name but several: Hispania, Gaul, Italia (originally Vitalia). Thus, Western and Eastern Christians, in spite of their diverse ethnicities and languages, confronted Judaism and Islam. However, the Judeo-Christian tradition, especially after 1948, has remapped the relationship between religion and the state in both the US and the Russian Federation, although Islam has remained a rival.[6]

Wide ranges of both Islamic and Christian traditions defined a variety of interrelationships, conflicts, and instances of cooperation in the long stretch from India to Central Asia, the Caucasus, and eastern and western Europe, where people of Islamic or Christian beliefs, persuasions, and institutions interacted. All that began to change, radically, toward the end of the fifteenth and beginning of the sixteenth centuries. The change was initiated by Western Christians' expulsion of the Muslims from the lands of Christendom in Garnhata (Granada) in 1492. It is true, of course, that this singular event did not immediately affect the wide range of relations between Christian and Muslims from Spain to Central Asia and India. There was no CNN at the time to provide simultaneous coverage of the immediate consequences of these events and to nourish hatred, as there was no photographer in Granada at the moment the Christians raised their flag over the Alhambra.

The map in figure 2.1 comes from a publishing house, founded in 1999, devoted to rewriting Eurocentered histories to claim the right of European people to exist. Which of course is right. My claim in this book is not to deny the achievements of Western civilization and the contributions made under the banner of "modernity." What I denounce are the aberrations. The map is described as follows: "The invasion of Western Europe by a non-White Muslim army after 711 A.D. very nearly extinguished modern White Europe—certainly the threat was no less serious than the Hunnish invasion which had earlier created so much chaos. While the Huns were Asiatic, the Moors were a mixed-race invasion—part Arabic, part Black and part mixed race, always easily distinguishable from the Visigoth Whites of Spain."[7]

The lack of a CNN notwithstanding, the conflict between Christianity and Islam was to become more focused in the Iberian Peninsula, and it ushered in the rapid rise of Castile from a kingdom to a capitalist world empire, a circumstance that remapped the long history of conflicts between Muslims and Christians. It is to this radical qualitative transformation that we must turn our attention.

III

Tariq Ali's opening for his novel *Shadows of the Pomegranate Tree* (1992) describes a week in early December of 1499 when Cardinal Francisco Jiménez de Cisneros, associated with the Spanish Inquisition, gathered in his house in Toledo a group of selected knights. A few days after the meeting, the knights, along with a few dozen soldiers, begin the ride to Garnhata. When the knights and soldiers arrive, they enter the houses of the Muslim elites and confiscate their libraries. They make a pile of books in the central plaza, except, as Cardinal Cisneros ordered, they hold back a few books on medicine, astrology, and architecture. At the end of the day, when all the books are piled up, one of the soldiers ignites the fire. A beggar jumps into the pile and immolates himself. His last words are "What is life without knowledge?" Ali's opening chapter closes with Cardinal Cisneros, a few days later, walking around the ashes and celebrating this "final victory." Not quite.

The novel tells the story of the persecution of Muslim families in the following two decades. An additional aspect of this narrative relevant to my argument occurs in one of the final chapters when a new character is introduced. This unnamed, red-headed, young, and merciless *capitan*, described as a ruthless soldier in the service of Cardinal Cisneros, leads one of the most violent scenes near the end of the novel, when the last Moors are expelled. The novel's closing chapter, which takes place several years later and in a different geography, parallels the opening, with both printed in italic typography. At this point, the *capitan* is no longer in Garnhata. He walks through hills until the view of a valley opens to his astonished view. He is not walking alone. A local guide accompanies him. They stop at the top of a hill, looking down in admiration on the spectacle of an urban center, a majestic city built over and surrounded by water. "Do you know the name of this fabulous place?" the *capitan* asks his companion. "The city is named Tenochtitlan and its King is Moctezuma. . . . It is a very rich nation, Capitan Cortés," the guide says.[8] Tariq Ali underlines, at the beginning and end of the novel, a structural and heterogeneous moment of history setting the stage for the foundation of the modern/colonial racial matrix. Islamophobia today, I contend, has resulted from the accumulation of meaning in building the rhetoric of modernity, from the expulsion of the Moors to the war in Iraq and the conflict with Iran.

Hispanophobia has its seeds in the so-called Mexican-American War of 1846–1848, which ended with the US possessing a vast expanse of territories that had belonged first to the Spanish Empire and, after independence, to the republic of Mexico; and also in the so-called Spanish-American War of 1898, when Spain lost its last colonies in the Caribbean (Dominican, Puerto Rico, and Cuba) and the doors were opened to US interventions. Aren't these claims too big to sustain and be supported in a single chapter, you may wonder? However, and paradoxically, the end of the novel preannounces what could not be predicted at that point in history: the emergence of Hispanophobia four hundred years later. Huntington's framing of both "phobias" in the US takes us back to the Christian expulsion of the Moors from the Iberian Peninsula around 1500, to the conquest of the New World, to the present in-migrations from the former Spanish territories that were conquered and repossessed by the US through the Guadalupe-Hidalgo Treaty (1848), and to the economic, political, and military interventions in Central America and the Spanish Caribbean in the second half of the twentieth century. These complex historical configurations— properly, heterogenous historic-structural nodes that defy linear historical chronologies—become more evident when the events and processes are looked at as surface signs of the logic of coloniality and the transformation of the CMP. We are getting deeper into the politics of decolonial investigations.

IV

In the sixteenth century, Christian theology offered a frame and a conception of the *human* (see chapter 12) that took a particular turn in relation to coexisting civilizations (generally called empires), like the Mughal and the Ottoman sultanates, the Russian tzarate, and the Incanate in the New World. Christian theological classification overruled, with time, all the others and served as the basic structure for the secular classification of races in the late eighteenth and nineteenth centuries. In 1526, shortly after Charles I of Castile and Charles V of the Holy Roman Empire came to power, Babar (one of the descendants of Genghis Khan) was on his way to founding the so-called Mughal sultanate. His son Akbar was the sultan (not the emperor) of the Mughals from 1556 to 1605, during almost the same years that Elizabeth I ruled England and Philip II, son of Charles V, reigned in Spain (1556–1598). Sultan Suleiman the Magnificent's period of dominance and the preeminence in the Ottoman sultanate (1520–1566) coexisted with the reign of Emperor Charles V of the Holy Roman Empire of the German Nation (1519–1558) and the king of Spain (1516–1556). While the Mughal and Ottoman sultanates coexisted during the sixteenth century with the emerging Spanish Empire, in the so-called New World the Incanate (the territories ruled by the Inca) in Tawantinsuyu (which became the viceroyalty of Peru under Spanish rules) and the Tlatoanate (the territories ruled by the Tlatoani) in Anahuac (which became the viceroyalty of New Spain under Spanish rules) were destroyed—the former around 1548, sixteen years after Francisco Pizarro set foot in the lands of Tawantinsuyu, and the latter in 1520, a few years after Hernán Cortés, the merciless red-headed *capitan*, moved from the coast of Veracruz to Tlaxcala and finally to Mexico-Tenochtitlan. At this time the Russian tzarate was engaged in its increasing expansion, after Moscow was declared the Third Rome around 1520 and Muscovite Russia ended its tributary domination by the Golden Horde.

Thus, the point of my argument is over current debates about whether "race" is an eighteenth- and nineteenth-century discourse, or whether in the sixteenth century "caste" was the proper system of classification. In both debates it is assumed that the classifications concocted by Renaissance men of letters or Enlightenment "philosophes" were universal, and that "race" had an ontological existence before the Renaissance. It is the same logic that leads Western scholars and intellectuals to label as "empire" every territorial organization that is not a nation-state. The systems of classification and hierarchies formed during the Renaissance or during the Enlightenment were local in this precise sense: people in India, China, Ottoman, Tawantinsuyu, Anahuac, etc., certainly became part of this system of classification, but none of them, except Christian theologians, had any say in the classification. The only possibility open to those who did not participate in this imperial organization of planetary knowledge was either to accept how they were classified or to reclassify themselves for their own pride but with little effect on the larger and increasing organization of knowledge, economy, politics, and culture that impinged on, classified, and destituted their knowledges and praxes of living. Coloniality of power was at work and being established, and the conditions for differential consciousness and border thinking were following close behind.[9] What I just described was not to inform you about "facts" but to expose and invite you (reader) to think about the implicit hierarchies that have been built, epistemically, from Christian theology and secular philosophy and social sciences. Let me elaborate with the following premise in mind.

Discourses of racial and religious differences in the European Renaissance went hand in hand with discourses of fear.[10] There is plenty of evidence regarding Christians in Spain but also Christians from England outside their homeland. British travelers to the Hapsburg or Austro-Hungarian empires expressed their feelings of strangeness and their discomfort vis-à-vis the Turks. The European Renaissance can be taken as a reference period in which several "empires" coexisted ("empire" became a general name extended after the title of the Roman Emperor in preference to, for example, "sultanate" or "tzarate"); it was during the European Renaissance that the discourses of Christianity and later of political theory and political economy emerged as the dominant discourses of the Western empires that ran economies of accumulation, exploitation of labor, and reinvestment of the surplus. Racism, I am suggesting, went hand in hand with the historical foundation of economic coloniality (capitalism) as we know it today.

The Black Legend, commonly understood as a sixteenth-century discourse demonizing Spanish people and culture, is in fact also a good and early example of the propagation of the Muslim "menace" from the Iberian Peninsula to the Atlantic countries north of the Pyrenees. The Black Legend is, first and foremost, an internal conflict in Europe and for that reason I will describe it as a manifestation of imperial internal difference.[11] The Black Legend, propelled by Elizabeth I of England, shared the same Christian cosmology with the Spaniards (it was a family feud) by which Spaniards were distinguished from the Muslims, the Turks, and from Eastern Christians, the Russian Orthodox Church. That is, the Black Legend contributed to the reinforcement of an imperial intramural divide (the imperial difference between the North and the South of Europe) that had been inaugurated by the Spanish kingdom of Charles I and the Spanish Empire under Philip II.

We all know the story I told above: in 1492, the Moors and the Jews were prosecuted in the Iberian Peninsula, "Indians" were "discovered" in the New World, and massive contingents of captives and enslaved Africans were transported across the Atlantic. Narratives, maps, and drawings built the image of triumph and salvation (the rhetoric of modernity) over pagans and barbarians (the hidden logic of coloniality at work). The "discovery" of the New World posed a different problem for Western Christians dealing with Muslims, Jews, and Turks: if Jews and Moors were classified according to their belief in the wrong God, Indians (and later Black Africans) had to be classified assuming that they had no religions. Christianity had already foreclosed spirituality so as not to recognize it among Africans and Indians. If Christians did perhaps recognize it, they attributed it to the devil. Thus, the question of "purity of blood" acquired in the New World a meaning totally different from the one it had on the Iberian Peninsula. Following the double expulsion of Moors and Jews from the Iberian Peninsula, the New World brought a different dimension to the classificatory and hierarchical system. In Spain, Jews and Muslims were racialized by their religious assumptions, even though, basically, Jews, Christians, and Muslim worship the "same" God.[12] However, in the New World Indians were racialized because they had no God and were subjected to the will of the devil. These distinctions last until today, with some transformations that occurred in the eighteenth century: racial classifications operate at the level of religion (Moors, Jews) and the level of ethnicity (Blacks, Indians). Today, Islamophobia is projected on multiple spheres: ethnic (Arabs), national (Iranians), and religious (Muslims). Interestingly enough, in these cases "blood" is the common thread. The expression "purity of blood," employed by Western Christians in the Iberian Peninsula to justify their distance from and control of Jews and Muslims, was also the distinctive feature to distinguish in the Americas the Spaniards from Indians and Blacks, and to invent the category of mestizo/a (blood mixture of Spanish and Indians) and mulatto/a (blood mixture of Spanish and Black).[13] In other words, whatever the system of classification in the Iberian Peninsula and in the New World, it was controlled by Christian theology as the overarching and hegemonic frame of knowledge. Neither the "Turks," nor the Mughals, nor the Christian Orthodoxy in Russia had any say in it—even less, of course, Indians and Blacks. After the eighteenth century the system of classification was taken up by secular science and philosophy. However, the foundation was already established in and by Western Christian theologians. Racism, in other words and again, is not ontological but it is rooted in the Western structure of knowledge and the principles of sensing and knowing: Christian theology and secular science and philosophy.

V

Let's take a closer look at this first outline of the sixteenth-century scenario in the Mediterranean and in the Atlantic. Three foundational commentaries on the logic of the articulation of "race" into "racism" at the end of the fifteenth century and during the sixteenth century are: Aníbal Quijano's seminal paper introducing the concept of coloniality, mentioned in chapter 1 (1990/2007); Sylvia Wynter's article (1992); and the article coauthored by Aníbal Quijano and Immanuel Wallerstein (1992), also mentioned in chapter 1.[14] These three articles have radically shifted the perspective and conceptualization of race/racism from the internal history of European modernity (Foucault) to the entangled histories of modernity/coloniality. They began to change the terms of the conversation. Which means that in all three arguments the common grounds are: (a) the reconfiguration of previous mutual conceptualizations among Christians, Moors, and Jews; (b) the new configuration among Christians, Indians, and Blacks in the New World; (c) the interrelations between (a) and (b); and (d) the translation of race into racism that took place in the late fifteenth and sixteenth centuries and that was (and still is) strictly related to the consolidation and expansion of Western Christianity and the historical foundation of capitalism. The complicity between capital accumulation and the devaluation of human and animal life, and later on of life in general with the invention of the concept of "natural resources," was absent in the coexisting sixteenth-century sultanates like the Mughal, the Ottoman, the Aztec Tlatoanate, and the Incanate in the Andes, as well as in the Chinese dynasties and the emerging Russian tzarate. The dispensability of human lives emerged in and with the Indigenous genocide and the slave trade. I am talking here about interstate perceptions of Western Christian monarchies and theological knowledge. Obviously, in each of the civilizational formations I mentioned—for example, the Incanate and the Russian tzarate, to name just two cases—domestic distinctions were made with respect to servants and peasants. Inequalities existed, but local organizations and hierarchies were not grounded in the global system of classification being advanced by Western Christians. The complicity between political economy and political theory in the West, based on the racialization of human beings, languages, places, cultures, memories, knowledge, etc., is what distinguishes the CMP from coexisting civilizational organizations, and what constitutes the grounds of Western civilization and of Eurocentrism.

This was the "novelty" of the sixteenth century that is still at work today. The actors and institutions have been changing, as has the rhetoric of modernity (from conversion to Christianity, to progress and civilization, to development and modernization, to market democracy, and to re-Westernization), but the logic of coloniality preserves the same movement of constitution/destitution. The most drastic changes in the twenty-first century are that the West (the EU, the US, NATO, and the International Monetary Fund) cannot unilaterally manage and control the CMP as it did for five hundred years. De-Westernization is disputing its control and management. As a result, racism is alive and well and nourishes the current scenario of the imperial difference

(United States-European Union on the one hand, Russia, China, Iran on the other). I am talking about interstate formation or civilization and not referring here to the local and domestic hierarchies in the civilizations disputing the management and control of the CMP. The Black Legend should be understood in this scenario as the historical foundation of an intramural form of racism among European Christians and across the North-South divide in Europe itself: the imperial intramural difference. Orientalism, understood in these terms, was a manifestation of extramural colonial difference and became the seed of extramural imperial difference today—once the "Orientals" asserted themselves as de-Westernizing forces confronting Westernization (1500–2000) and forced re-Westernizing counterreformation, evident since the presidency of Barack Obama.

Let's first pause to explain the merging of race into racism, which became one of the historical foundations of modernity/coloniality. Racial classification overdetermined "social class." *Enslaved* exploitation of labor created the conditions for the later *waged* exploitation of labor and the classification of social class instead of human race. Enslaved exploitation of labor in the sixteenth century, next to massive appropriation of land and production of commodities (gold, silver, coffee, cotton, sugar, tobacco) for a global market, could only have been conceived as "primitive accumulation" for a nineteenth-century local European gaze that only perceived capitalism in the Industrial Revolution of the late eighteenth century and not in the colonial revolution of the early sixteenth century. "Race" was, in sixteenth-century Spain, a concept that referred to a lineage, particularly applied to horses. Horses had, in Arabic history, a distinction they did not have among Christians.[15] In Spanish dictionaries, horses became the primary example of lineage—and still are today. "Blood purity," an expression applied to distinctive horses, invaded the vocabulary of the English and Spanish languages; *pureza de sangre inglesa* or *pura sangre española* is said of a person as well as of an animal of pure breed. This is telling in that animals were classified by "race" and people by "ethnicity" (Greek *nous*, Latin *natio*). "Ethnicity" refers to a lineage of people for whom blood is not the only factor (and I wonder when blood became a crucial factor to redefining ethnicity), but one among others such as memories and common histories, languages, rituals, everyday practices, food, songs, and other music—all are elements connecting a community of people through history. How "pure blood" was displaced toward the end of the eighteenth and into the nineteenth century by "skin color" is a part of the history of the transformation of the rhetoric of modernity and the people targeted by the new racial rhetoric.[16]

However, in the Renaissance, when Spanish Christians defined "race" after the example of horses then added the slippage toward the human, as happened in the classic Covarrubias's dictionary that I refer to above, they planted the seed for the merging and the historical foundation of race into racism as we sense it today. Hence, following this line of decolonial reasoning and the politics of decolonial investigations, it may be understood why I have been stating that racism is not a question of blood or skin color but of the logic of discursive classifications entrenched in the foundation of the CMP. The task of the politics of decolonial investigations is not to retell the story of racism by changing its content, or to keep repeating how bad it is and how it should be erased. Rather, the task is to change the terms of the conversation, to unmask the enunciation that created and maintains the logic of coloniality, regulating debates, thoughts, and sentiments without addressing the state of mind that the historical foundation of racism in the modern/colonial world system created (see chapter 1). This is a telling illustration of how the control of knowledge makes it possible to manage subjectivities. The result of this unmasking would require reorienting education, which will require institutional and media support. Taking such a step would foster serious opposition, for unmasking the invention of racism and working toward erasing epistemic and aesthesic (sensing) grounding would go against the exploitation of labor and the domestic control of the population necessary to advance Western domestic and global designs. In a multipolar world order, racism would be diminished, but while capitalism/economic coloniality guides the global economy, multipolarity would weaken but not erase racism (I will come back to this issue addressing "de-Westernization").

The entangled histories of the West (the EU and the US) with Russia, China, and Iran are not homogeneous. However, the assumption that the West is entitled to dictate, manage, and lead the world order is ingrained in the mentalities of Republican and Democrat alike and lies at the core of the EU. The assumptions legitimizing the entitlement are manifest in the modern/colonial interstate system, since their purposes are to maintain the extramural imperial differences disguised in terms of violations of international law and subjected to *political and economic sanction*. The actors ruling the countries (the state, corporations, religious institutions, and the media) are not exempt from "sensing" that in the modern/colonial order they are not neutral or outside the racial system. Diplomacy bypasses racism when convenient politico/economic agreements are beneficial for both parties in spite of colonial or imperial differences. When politico/economic interests are in conflict, politico/economic disputes are no doubt undergirded by racial differentials that no one can escape.

This double bind comes to the foreground in the embassies' control and management of granting visas to personnel who are highly ranked in the political and economic sphere.

"Race," in the famous Spanish dictionary by Sebastian de Covarrubias, is synonymous with "blood," and by implication (c.f., the common knowledge of "purity of blood") with "religion"—meaning the wrong religion (Jews and Muslims).[17] In the New World, the situation was different. There were no native people of the book. Indeed, Christopher Columbus surmised that the people he met in the Caribbean had no religion. Later, Spanish missionaries in the powerful Inca and Aztec "empires" had difficulties figuring out what kind of "religions" were these that were so different from the three religions of the book they were used to. They decided that people in the Tawantinsuyu and Anahuac lived in spiritual idolatry and under the guidance of the devil. Spanish missionaries assigned themselves the task of extirpating idolatries. Indians, therefore, were cast aside and placed in a different category from Jews and Moors. Thus, while in the Iberian Peninsula the terms "conversos" and "moriscos" designated ex-Jews and ex-Moors who had converted to Christianity, in the New World the term "mestizo" was coined to identify an emerging population of mixed blood, Spanish (and Portuguese), and Indian. Blacks mixed with Spanish were mulattos and Blacks mixed with Indians zambos. In the process, Blacks in the New World lost their European identification and relationship with the Moors.

In fact, "Moor" was the identification given to Indigenous nomadic Berber people in North Africa who were converted to Islam around the seventh century. "Moor" then came to mean Muslim people of Berber and Arab descent. The name itself, as is well known, comes from the kingdom of Mauri (Mauritania), a province in the Roman Empire located in what is today North Africa and more specifically Morocco. Since the Mauri were dark-skinned people from Africa, the description "Moor" was extended to African populations beyond the North of Africa. As Fuchs points out, in the growing vocabulary of the Black Legend, Spaniards were sometimes pejoratively referred to (by Britons), as Moors and as Blacks. Shakespeare's "Moor of Venice" is indeed a Black person, a "blackamoor."[18] Blackamoors were not just Spaniards but, from the perspective of those who lived in the North, like Shakespeare, they were in the South of Europe. Detached from European imaginary of the blackamoors, for European Christians (Spaniards to British), Blacks in the New World were just ontologically slaves. From Europe it must have been difficult not to see Africans and born slaves so that their memories, ways of livings, desires, and spiritual belongings were not taken into account. In the New World, Blacks were not Moors but Ethiopians.[19] In the Spanish and Portuguese colonies a new word was coined—"mulatto/a"—to designate people of a new breed, a mixture of Spanish and Black. The seeds of Islamophobia in the twentieth century were planted several centuries before, when the Moors were finally expelled from the Iberian Peninsula. The Black Legend established an idea and feelings that are still alive today: the inferiority of southern Catholic Europeans who were to transplant themselves to the South of the New World (as the British and French transplanted themselves to the North). Hence, the divide in Europe between the intramural north and south was transplanted to the New World. And so did the Christian animosity towards Islam.

VI

Now we have the basic elements to locate racism in the colonial matrix of power. Christians placed themselves at the center, enjoying the epistemic privileges of theology and benefiting from the theopolitics of knowledge,[20] as members of the right religion, as members of the hegemonic theological discourse, and as white Spaniards and Portuguese. Racism, in other words, was at the heart of the coloniality of knowledge. On the one hand, we have Christians and, confronting them, Moors and Jews. On the other, we have Spaniards and Portuguese and, confronting them, Indians and Blacks. Between the first triad, we have conversos/as and moriscos/as. Between the second triad, we have mestizos/as and mulattos/as. The first triad is based on religious differentials. In the second triad, religion is not the basis for classifications so national entities take the place of religion (see the figures in chapter 1). Spaniards and Portuguese in the New World become the substitute for Christians in the Iberian Peninsula. When, in the late eighteenth and early nineteenth centuries, the concept of "race" was reconfigured, it was reconfigured in a secular frame— translating religious belief into ethnicity and blood into skin color. In the eighteenth century, Moors became Arabs and Jews became ethnic Jews (I pursue the consequences of this transformation in chapters 3 and 4). Consequently, skin color and ethnicity (for the secular *nation*-state mentality) began to replace blood and religion as racial markers. As a further consequence, the peninsular triad (Christians, Jews, and Muslims) fell into oblivion when secular thinking sidelined religious and—in the Western mind—Jews became ethnic people (see chapter 4) and Muslims became Arabs. The second triad (Spanish, Indians, and Blacks) fell into oblivion because of what happened in the colonies. Hence, secular philosophy and science took charge of racial classification from the end of the century on. Immanuel Kant significantly contributed to the oblivion and to the secular pattern of racial classification.[21] This was one aspect of the reconfiguration of the CMP in the eighteenth century.

Today, scholars revisiting the concept of race—most of them in England, the US, Germany, and France—start in the mid-eighteenth century. H. F. Augstein's edited volume *Race: The Origins of an Idea, 1760-1850* (1996) evidently was not aware of what happened before 1760, as if racism emerged in the heart of Europe (England, France, and Germany) without any relation to the Iberian Peninsula and its colonies in the New World. Michel Foucault also dated the question of race to the same period and to the heart of Europe. More to the point, and surprisingly humorously, the first chapter of *Histoire naturelle* (thirty-six volumes published 1749-1788)—by Georges-Louis Leclerc (aka Comte de Buffon), French naturalist, mathematician, cosmologist, and encyclopedist—is on what? On the *natural history of the horse*! There is no indication that the origin of the modern/colonial idea of race emerged when the practice of improving the bloodlines of horses became the explanatory model for Christians to discriminate between so-called desirable and undesirable human beings, here Moors and Jews. This double-blindness among intellectuals and scholars from and in the heart of Europe is the (unintended) consequence of the Black Legend. At this point we are making new inroads into the politics of decolonial investigations since established Eurocentric knowledge and Eurocentric critiques of that knowledge are necessary but hardly sufficient. Why?

What I have said up to this point (and I remind you of the first paragraph of this chapter) has been a sketchy summary of the idea of race/racism as it emerged in the sixteenth century. Theology was the master epistemic frame and offered the tools to describe and classify people with the wrong religion and people without religion. Christianity was only one among the world's religions, but its practitioners found themselves in the privileged situation to classify and to occupy two positions in the CMP: it was, on the one hand, part of the classification (the content), but was the only enunciation controlling and managing the classification (the enunciation) (see introduction, figure I.1) How was that decided? Christians made the classification on the basis of a theology that saw Christianity as the supreme Archimedean point ("universe," "universal," and "university" come from Latin words in a theological hegemonic frame of mind) from which the entire world was properly observed and classified. Christians, who were also Castilians and Portuguese in the New World, found themselves among Indians and Blacks, who were regarded as inferior for having no religion. Thus, theology allowed for a conceptualization of humanity for which Castilians and Portuguese, and their Greek and Roman ancestors, were taken as the exemplar. Those assumptions justified and still justify evaluating everyone on the planet according to the theological model of humanity.

Elizabeth I put in motion a discourse of race in England that was mainly directed toward the Spaniards, and by so doing she inaugurated the emerging intramural imperial difference, and the conflict is between Christians: Protestants in the North, Catholic in the South. Bartolomé de Las Casas's *Brevísima relación de la destrucción de las Indias* (A short account of the destruction of the Indies) was published in Spanish in 1552 and translated into English in 1583.[22] Elizabeth I's intervention was one in which the dice were already cast: the logic of coloniality, which includes racial classification, was already drawn. What Elizabeth I did was to introduce the intramural imperial difference that lasts until today in the North-South, Protestant-Catholic divisions of the European Union. Supporting de Las Casas's descriptions of Spanish brutalities allowed her to hide the pivotal role England was playing in trading enslaved African human beings. Yesterday, as well as today, interstate denunciations hid the misgiving of the accuser. Already in the making here was the intramural imperial difference between the Protestant North and the Catholic South.

British men of letters and officers of the state did not look at the Ottoman sultanate with friendly eyes. But that was another story—the story of the extramural imperial difference that has mutated today toward China, Russia, Iran and made even more virulent the previous racial differences within the Muslim population. The tribulations of Roger Ascham at the frontiers of Western Christianity with the Ottoman sultanate (*Report and Discourse of the Affairs and State of Germany*, 1550), where he felt the disturbing presence of the Turks, are a telling sign of the fundamental and self-inflicted fear of difference. With respect to the New World, England was more interested in following the Castilian example of empire building and benefiting from a plantation economy than in debating whether Indians and Blacks were human beings. Thus, the discourse of race in England during the European Renaissance did not contradict the Spaniards' classification; on the contrary, the British made the Spaniards the racial target, since Spaniards were, for Britons, what the Moors, Jews, Indians, and Blacks were for Spaniards. Here we see the colonial and imperial racial differences at work—a heterogeneous historic-structural node irreducible to a linear timeline. In the Black Legend, we see a racial intramural to Europe: the racialization of the Latin and Catholic South in the mouth and pen of the Anglo and Protestant North.

The logic underlying the discourses on race during the European Renaissance went hand in hand with the historical foundation of economic coloniality and the imperial conflict to rip economic benefits from the New World. Bartolomé de Las Casas offered a blueprint of the logic of both colonial and imperial racial differences in his well-known classification of five types of "barbarians."[23] Let's follow the path in the making of the extramural imperial difference. Long after the end of the Crusades, Christian Europe continued to be under pressure from the expanding Ottoman Sultanate. The Ottomans had impressive victories, including the capture of Constantinople, last outpost of the Roman Empire and spiritual center of Orthodox Christianity. Eventually Western Christians would mount effective counterattacks and keep Ottoman forces out of central Europe, but for a long time the "Turkish Menace" would haunt European dreams. The Turks and the Moors were not, of course, the same in any Christian mind. However, Christians knew that the Moors had a royal Islamic past and the Turks an imposing and bright present. Thus, calling the Turk and the Moors barbarians was a way to construct the *extramural imperial difference*. By extramural I mean that the difference was with non-Western non-Christians and therefore non-Europeans. And it was imperial because neither the Moors nor the Turks were colonized in the way Indians were colonized and Africans enslaved. The Jews were expelled, but most of them remained in Europe and were subjected to the *intramural colonial difference*—that is, they were the subjects as much as Indians and Blacks were subjected to the extramural colonial difference. Aimé Césaire pointed out in his *Discourse on Colonialism* that regarding the German Holocaust, what western Europeans cannot forgive Hitler for are *not the crimes against man*—not *the humiliation of man as such*—but the crimes against the white man, the humiliation of the white man, and the fact that Hitler made use of European colonialist procedures which until then had been reserved exclusively for the Arabs of Algeria, the "coolies" of India and China, and the "niggers" of Africa.[24]

What was the weight of the Black Legend in the logic of racialization I am uncovering? And what is its relevance to actual Hispanophobia? Philip II became king of Spain in 1556, and he would transform the kingdom he inherited from his father, Charles I of Spain (and Charles V of the Holy Roman Empire of the German Nation), into the glorious moment of the Spanish Empire. Philip II was also a German archduke in the House of Hapsburg. The Austro-Hungarian Empire came after the demise of the House, and the Habsburgs became one of the dual monarchy of the new imperial formation. All in all it was itself in a long process of transformation extending from the second half of the sixteenth century to its downfall during WWI. The Austro-Hungarian Empire became a buffer zone between the Ottoman sultanate and western Europe, and it turned out to be a marginal region of Western Christendom when the center of the world economy moved to the Atlantic, from Spain and Portugal to Holland and England. Vienna and Munich still today conserve the garb and the magnificence of imperial cities (while Moscow and Istanbul entered a process of visible decay). It was in that scenario that Richard Eden traveled from England to the limits of the lands of "the Turk" toward the middle of the sixteenth century and wrote a report that could be considered a blueprint of the aforementioned Black Legend.

The promoters of the Black Legend took advantage of the logic already in place to describe and classify people in relation to a model or standard of humanity. By so doing, they contravened Spanish Christians' will at the height of the crisis of the church in the middle of the nineteenth Council of Trent.[25] By accusing Spaniards of being barbarians (for the atrocities they committed in the New World), and naming them Moors, Blacks, and Saracens, the British disqualified Spaniards from the sphere of humanity with which the British themselves self-identified and that they defended. It was a strategy consisting in recasting the logic of racial colonial difference to enact the imperial intramural difference. The clash between Protestants and Catholics was at stake. No Englishman or Englishwomen of the time would fail to make the distinction between a Christian, Catholic or Protestant, and a Jew. While the previous racial classifications were maintained, what was added was the intramural imperial difference: the invention of the South of Europe, which would soon be complemented by the mutation of the extramural colonial difference, previously bestowed on Indians and Blacks, to propel the invention of Orientalism.

What the Black Legend hides is that the British were as brutal and greedy as the Spaniards. In fact, the Black Legend was part of a constellation of imperial behaviors, as well as a discourse, that we have seen at work since then in England and the present-day United States. Ottobah Cugoano's descriptions of Western empires make the point. As an African living in London after having been enslaved in the plantations of the New World, Cugoano saw no difference among western European slave traders, whether they were Spaniards, Portuguese, Dutch, French, or English.[26] And all of that was happening at the historical foundation of Western civilization and of the CMP.

The Black Legend is a piece of a larger puzzle that transcends the particular moment of its origin and connects Islamophobia with Hispanophobia. Similar ideas filtered into the US in the nineteenth century and informed widely read narratives like William Prescott's *History of the Conquest of Peru* (1847) and

History of the Conquest of Mexico (1843). Needless to say, Islamophobia was res-
urrected in the US after 9/11 and joined the already existing Hispanophobia.
President Donald Trump has been rehearsing both since his candidacy for
president of the US and during his mandate (2016–2020).

Prescott's book on the history of Mexico was published a few years before the signing of the Treaty of Guadalupe-Hidalgo (1848), which gave the US
possession of a vast territory previously belonging to Mexico.[27] The book was
published at a moment in history when history was repeating itself (as a farce,
as Marx would say) and the US of the nineteenth century, like England of the
mid-sixteenth century, was affirming its imperial ambitions. Imperial ambitions that had already been mapped by the discourse of race/racism during the
European Renaissance had given imperial authority to regenerate themselves
and their sense of superiority as agents in a position of epistemic legitimacy
to classify the world. A few decades before Prescott, Hegel in Europe had collected the legacies of the Black Legend and asserted the superiority of the
heart of Europe (England, Germany, and France)—that is, the three countries
that in the nineteenth century consolidated and expanded Western capitalism
and imperialism. With this consolidation, the CMP was launched on another
trajectory of transformation, followed by the advances made by the US that
would place it as the world leader after WWII.[28] Hegel clearly captured the unfolding of this story when he wrote, at the end of his introduction to *Lectures
on the Philosophy of History*, "The three sections of Europe require therefore a
different basis of classification." He went on to offer the following geopolitical
map (in my paraphrasing):

1 The first region is southern Europe, looking toward the Mediterranean.
   North of the Pyrenees, mountain chains run through France, connecting
   with the Alps, which separate and cut off Italy from France and
   Germany. Greece also belongs to this part of Europe.
2 The second region is the heart of Europe, in which France, Germany, and
   England are the principal countries.
3 The third consists of the northeastern states of Europe—Poland, Russia,
   and the Slavonic Kingdoms. They came late into the series of historical
   states, to form and perpetuate Europe's connection with Asia. In contrast
   with the physical singularities of the earlier division, these are already
   noticed, not present in a remarkable degree, but counterbalance each
   other.[29]

Hegel wrote about states but neglected to mention that the states of the
heart of Europe constituted the new imperial states. He claimed that these

states were pure and clean, had no connection with Africa, as in the case of Spain and Portugal (which is why it was important for him to highlight Italy and Greece), and no connections with Asia, like the northeastern states. Then in 1853 (a few years after Prescott's *History of the Conquest of Peru*), Joseph Arthur, Comte de Gobineau, published a new configuration of the discourse on race/racism, a discourse that would serve the purpose of the emerging empires in the heart of Europe. The title was *Essai sur l'inégalité des races humaines* (Essays on the inequalities of human races).

The rhetoric of intramural imperial difference that the Black Legend put in place became more restrained once Europe—meaning England, Germany, and France—attained their goals to become the strong players of the European Union. The Latin and Catholic south next to Orthodox Greece carry memories of being the South of Europe and the present neoliberal label of PIGS countries. England and the US joined forces, in spite of their differences, after Ronald Reagan and Margaret Thatcher opened the way to the fatal alliance of Tony Blair and George W. Bush. Five hundred years after the expulsion of the Moors from the Iberian Peninsula and five hundred years after the invasion and invention of America, Samuel Huntington identified the Moors as enemies of Western civilization and Hispanics (that is Latinos and Latinas) as a challenge to Anglo identity in the US. Racism dies hard and the specter of the Black Legend is still alive and well, helping to diminish Spaniards in Europe and criminalize Latinos and Latinas in the US. If Indians were the victims of Spaniards that the Black Legend denounced, enslaved Africans were the victims of England that the Black Legend helped to hide under Spanish barbarism.

However, none of the discourses on race/racism went uncontested. In the first era of modernity (i.e., the Renaissance), racist discourse was challenged by Guaman Poma de Ayala in colonial Peru, and in England in the eighteenth century the former Caribbean slave Ottobah Cugoano contested it. Before Gobineau and before Prescott, Frederick Douglass in the nineteenth century published (in the US) *Narrative of the Life of Frederick Douglass, an American Slave, Written by Himself* (1845). In France, the Haitian Anténor Firmin published a well-documented study against Gobineau, titled *De l'égalité des races humaines* (1885). W. E. B. Du Bois and Frantz Fanon followed suit in the Americas, and in more recent times Gloria Anzaldúa stood up, as a Latina, to claim, "Por la mujer de mi raza hablará el espíritu" (For women of my race the spirit shall speak).[30] These voices of dissent contest not only the Black Legend but all imperial discourses on race and racism (including those against Spaniards, which are markers of the imperial difference; see the introduction to this book), of which the Black Legend is one piece.

The borderlands and borderlines traced by the colonial matrix of power have never been uncontested. Decolonial energies were released at the very founding of the CMP. Contestations to the politics of modernity/coloniality bring about decolonial politics, not just in the sphere of government but also in the larger sphere of being in the world. The double meaning that was explicit in Mahatma Gandhi's title, *Hind Swaraj* (Home Rule), stands for both sovereignty of the person (which was Ottobah Cugoano's strong argument) and sovereignty of the nation (see the introduction to this book). Delinking prompts reexistence, and reexistence brings about the experience of dwelling in the borderland and, consequently, motivates border thinking and border doing. The politics of decolonial investigations requires decolonial subjectivities and decolonial subjects healing their/our colonial wounds to be no longer subjected to the coloniality of power and captives and captivated by the promises of modernity.

VII

Time to return to the "white lands" I invoked at the beginning of this chapter. There was a parallel between the appropriation of land and racism in the Iberian Peninsula (in the process of expelling the Moors), and the appropriation of land and racism in the New World. Complementary to the possession of land in the New World was massive slavery, exploitation of labor, and racism. In that configuration, racism was the frame of mind that allowed actors who were involved in these processes and were in control of knowing and knowledge to justify their inhumane behavior to themselves and to protect it in the name of God and in the name of the law.

As is well known, the process of expelling the Moors from Western Christians' lands (referred to by the author of the book *March of the Titans*—a vade mecum of white supremacy—as "white-held lands"; see figure 2.1) was supported by papal bulls authorizing the dispossession of pagans' lands and legitimizing their Christian appropriation (see, for example, the edict of Pope Nicholas V, January 8, 1455).[31] Thus, when Western Christians arrived at Indias Occidentales on Columbus's map, they already had the experience of dispossessing people from their land and legitimizing Christian appropriation. The (in)famous Spanish *Requerimiento*, granting the right to take possession of the lands of the New World and to subjugate its inhabitants, remains the signpost of a long, brutal process of victimizing the Indigenous population. The enormously diverse populations of Tawantinsuyu and Anahuac (as well as the land in between, named Abya-Yala) and of the islands renamed the "Caribbean" collectively became known, in spite of themselves, as Indians. And all of them were constructed as people without religion and therefore victims of the devil. Accordingly, there was an empty space in their souls that the devil took advantage of, as there were empty lands the Christian monarchs and adventurers began to take advantage of. Theology and law came together in the school of Salamanca and in the pioneering work of Francisco de Vitoria, *Relectio de Indis* (1539), the justification of Christian land appropriation with the "recognition" that Indians had to keep possessions of their "parcels." In this regard, Francisco de Vitoria is the direct antecedent of John Locke's legitimation of land dispossession in the British colonies.

The difference between them is that de Vitoria not only was concerned with the relationships among theology, law, and land possession; he also charted the principles of international law that, from then on, would go hand in hand with Western imperial expansion. In that regard, de Vitoria is also the forerunner of Hugo Grotius's (1583–1645) international law and Immanuel Kant's cosmopolitanism. While de Vitoria devised a system of international law to legitimize land (dis)possession, Grotius extended it (during the first half of the seventeenth century) to the opening of the sea. In *Mare Liberum* (Free Seas) he formulated the new principle that the sea was international territory and all nations were free to use it for seafaring trade. Global designs changed hands but never faded from the imaginary of North Atlantic empires. They are evident still today in the efforts to re-Westernize the world order. One notorious episode is the *mare nostrum* conflict in the South China Sea. Grotius, by claiming "free seas," provided suitable ideological justification for the Dutch's breaking up of various trade monopolies with their formidable naval power (and then establishing their own monopoly).

The *Requerimiento* was a double-edged sword.[32] On the one hand, it responded to the complaints of many theologians who protested the Spaniards' treatment of the Indians and the way they took possession (dispossession) of their land. On the other hand, it served as a legal-theological document justifying (dis)possession of Indian land whenever the Indians (i.e., the rulers of the great existing civilizations at the time of the Spanish and British invasions: the exterminated Tainos and Arawaks, the Mapuches, Incas, Aztecs, and Iroquois) did not comply with regulations imposed by the king and the church. You see here how racism worked backstage, as the driving force was presumed to be not racism but the rule of law. And we know how easy it is to fabricate violations of the rule and to criminalize the people that the dominant system needs to marginalize or dominate. The *Requerimiento*, read in Spanish and sometimes in Latin to the Indians, "offered" them the opportunity to surrender and obey or to be captive and dispossessed. At this initial moment of the consolidation of Western empires, of the colonial matrix of power, and of economic coloniality, in the emergence of the Atlantic economy, land possession went together with its theological and legal (racial) justifications. The sixteenth century was the turning point in what Carl Schmitt in 1950 described as the "nomos of the Earth" (we could invent the expression "land-nomia" in parallel to "astro-nomia," the law of the stars): the appropriation of land (together with the exploitation of labor) to produce commodities for the global market.[33] The African political theorist Siba N'Zatioula Grovogui, writing in 1995 from the silenced half in Schmitt's narrative, describes it as the complicity between racism, international law, and justifications for the appropriation of land and exploitation of labor.[34] The turning point here was the economic transformation and the emergence of economic coloniality that Quijano describes as the transformation of capital into capitalism before the Industrial Revolution and what he saw as the role the invention of modern racism played in that transformation. A similar turning point reoccurred more radically during the seventeenth century, when the Dutch, the French, and the British intensified the slave trade and established their profitable Caribbean plantations.

While Spaniards and Portuguese concentrated on the extraction of gold and silver (from Zacatecas in New Spain to Potosi in Bolivia to Ouro Preto in Brazil), the northern Atlantic economy (England, France) was based mainly on sugar, tobacco, coffee, and cotton.[35] The economic variances and approaches also reveal the national interests that propelled the emergence of the Black Legend. However, what is important for my purposes here is that in both economic configurations (extraction of gold and silver, and cultivation of sugar, coffee, cotton, and tobacco), capitalism emerged—as Anibal Quijano has explained—as the happy complicity between several forms of labor (serfdom, slavery, handicraft, small-commodity production, and reciprocity) and capital (economic control by the use of currency and other means).[36] This conjunction in the New World of the massive appropriation of land and the massive exploitation of labor (mainly by enslaved Africans) prompted the emerging global capitalism market. And this market was created from the *Requerimiento* in the early sixteenth century, from the intensification of labor through slavery and its massive production of "natural" commodities (e.g., sugar) from the nomos of the Earth that justified the confiscation and exploitation of the land, all deriving from the racialization of the New World population (Indians and Blacks).[37]

VIII

And what happened to the Moors in the meantime? Let me jump three centuries ahead and focus on the end of the nineteenth century and the beginning
of the twentieth. Alfred Thayer Mahan (*The Influence of Sea Power upon History,
1660–1783*, published toward the end of the nineteenth century) is credited
with the invention of the geopolitical region today known as the Middle East.
There was no Middle East before the name was invented and got us used to
"seeing" that a region existed that was not invented. Mahan was tremendously
helped in his task by the officers of the British Empire. Roger Anderson described the already constituted region in his book *London and the Invention of the
Middle East: Money, Power, and War, 1902–1922* (1995). At the time of the collapse
of the Ottoman Sultanate (1922), the Moors of the early Christian imaginary
had been converted to Arabs in the secular European Enlightenment imaginary. The Arabs were located in the "Orient," as Moroccan philosopher Ab-
delkebir Khatibi taught us in the early 1970s and Edward Said popularized in
the late 1970s. Orientalism was an invention of the second modernity dominated by England, France, and Germany in the economic, political, and epistemic domains. Orientals—in the great collective mind of the new imperial
powers and their intellectuals—took the place of Occidentals for the Spanish
and Portuguese, a reminder that America was named Indias Occidentales in
all Spanish and Portuguese documents. Indias Occidentales was the land of
the Indians and enslaved Africans. Racism that was articulated geopolitically
in the sixteenth century (by virtue of the terms "Indias Occidentales" and
"Indias Orientales") was mutated under the secular transformation of hemispheric partitions (see chapter 9). Henceforward the Orient became the land
of Arabs, Indians, Chinese, Japanese, and, of course, Muslims. But at the time
of secular nation-states (in which Immanuel Kant and George W. Friedrich
Hegel imagined a cosmopolitan world and a world history), ethnicity (e.g.,
Arab) took precedence over religion (e.g., Islam).

Another transformation relevant to my argument was the Industrial Revolution, which required "natural resources." Capitalism at that point was adding to the production of "natural products" (everything related to agriculture
for human consumption) and exploiting natural resources (everything related
to machines' consumption). The invention of the Middle East marked a territory within the larger region of the Orientals, one rich in natural resources,
particularly oil. The history, from the discovery of oil and the invention of the
Middle East to the Gulf War and the invasion of Iraq, has been told many times
and is well known in a general sense. Of interest for my argument here is the

transformation—in the imaginary created and propagated by Western capitalist empires—and the continuation by Christian theologians dating from the sixteenth and seventeenth centuries of the racializing discourses directed first at ancient Moors and later at modern Arab nations that control vast amounts of natural resources. Also of interest here is that after WWII it was no longer only London but mainly Washington that took the lead in directing the public relations and the wars with the Middle East. This situation was further complicated by the existence of the Soviet Union.

Once again, during the Cold War, we witnessed the transformation—within the colonial matrix of power—of the role of the Russian (Orthodox) Empire (an empire after Peter and Catherine the Great; before then it had been a tzarate) in the sixteenth century. The Eisenhower Doctrine, enunciated in a "Special Message to the Congress on the Situation in the Middle East" (January 5, 1957), set the stage for a triangulation between the US, the Soviet Union, and the Middle East. Then the Soviet Union collapsed, after which Condoleezza Rice expressed her concerns about lacking a reason for maintaining a strong national security profile.[38] Shortly thereafter, the events of 9/11 marked, by themselves as well as by the political consequences fostered by the reactions of the Western media, a turning point in the connection between economy, racism, and national interests/security. Metaphorically, the collapse of the twin towers of the World Trade Center, as a symbol of a capitalist society, could be seen as closing a cycle that started in Granada in 1499 with Cardinal Cisneros's burning of the books, symbols of Islamic society (while appropriating some texts that contained relevant Muslim knowledge, particularly in medicine).[39] Islamophobia today, it seems to me, is a fear that cannot be dissociated from the need of the natural resources "provided" by the Middle East to the former industrial and developed First World (today the Global North/West), the consequent instability of the regions, and the in-migration of Arabs and Muslims to the former First World. As the dictum goes, "We are here because you are there."

IX

Let me close this chapter with two stories that, I hope, will bring together all of what I've said up to this point. The setting of the first story is the US, where neither Arabs nor Muslims were visible in what David Hollinger described as Nixon's ethno-racial pentagon: that is, whites, Hispanics, Asian Americans, African Americans, and Native Americans.[40] In the ethno-racial pentagon, the grouping of people by religions (common in the sixteenth century Christian classification) was erased. The ethno-racial pentagon is the rearticulation of the secular imaginary of the late eighteenth and nineteenth centuries, when racial classifications became "scientific" instead of "religious" and purity of blood was replaced by skin color. Thus, declaring whether you were Christian, Islamic, Buddhist, or Hindu was not a requirement on official state census forms used to keep track of ethno-nationals without a hyphen (i.e., "American") as well as ethno-nationals with a hyphen (e.g., Native-American, Afro-American, or Asian-American). As far as I know, the Nixon ethno-racial pentagon has not been changed on official forms. But we all know that Arabs, Middle Easterners, and Muslims are no longer invisible. Not only that, the racialization of the Middle East created an imagined entity that is both visible and feared—as were communists during the Cold War. For Condoleezza Rice, the events of 9/11 presented the opportunity to justify and intensify national interests related to security, a topic she was promoting before the election of George W. Bush.[41] For contractors and the oil industry, 9/11 offered an excuse to intensify and justify the control of the economy (e.g., what happened to Saddam Hussein) and the efforts of the US to demonize Mahmoud Ahmadinejad in Iran.[42]

Thus, I am making here a general distinction between interacting spheres and flows of levels and domains in the CMP: the control of the economy, the control of authority, the extraction and management of "natural" resources, and the management and manipulation of the civil society through schooling and mass media. We can understand how Western imperial configurations (e.g., political and economic complicities between the US, France, and England, mainly) administer fear through the mass media. Thus, domestic designs to control the civil society, and international designs (foreign policy) to rule and manage the global order, are both different and complementary levels in modulating people's sensing and emotioning, that is, subjectivity. Domestic and global designs are geared toward actively reinscribing the racial dimension of the colonial matrix of power, which since the sixteenth century has been the consistent imperial instrument—exerting control of authority, control of the economy, control of labor and natural resources, and control of knowledge and subjectivity (i.e., control of the population)—by all those who have been integrated into the Christian civilizing missions of the market economy at the expense of those who cannot be integrated and who may rebel.

The political society (often identified as "social movements") has always existed in all regions of the planet wherever Western modernity/coloniality extended its tentacles (sometimes through anti-imperial reactions, other times through clear decolonial projects). Today, multiple and diverse configurations of political society are coming together to pursue a common yet diverse (pluriversal, not universal) agenda, delinking from the magic bubble of universal totalitarianism to engage in relentless decolonial processes—decolonizing authority, decolonizing the economy, decolonizing knowledge and being. Islamophobia is nothing more than a reinscription of racial fears toward a sector of the population (the civil society) the hatred of which the empire needs as a buffer zone.

The setting of the second story takes us back, full circle, to the sixteenth century: to the common ground of Islamophobia and Hispanophobia. Samuel Huntington provided a new map of the two phobias, as indicated at the beginning of the chapter. Imperial and colonial phobias, however, will not make invisible the emergence of decolonial forces. Without these decolonial energies consolidated through the second half of the sixteenth century and reappearing here and there ever since (e.g., at the Bandung Conference of 1955 and the ensuing initiatives by the Non-Aligned Movement, and in the numerous sagas of liberation in Asia and Africa and South America and the island nations of the tropics), I would not be making the argument I am making and searching to articulate the meanings of decolonial politics.

There are enormous historical and social differences in the imperial creation of Islamophobia—the fear and the hatred of a powerful and widespread religion—and the making of Hispanophobia. To appreciate these differences it is imperative to understand, on the one hand, how the imperial imaginary constructs phobias in the minds of *civil society* although hardly in the minds of the *political society*, which is always alert and suspicious toward the state and mainstream media. On the other hand, one must remain aware that on the opposite side of the imperial/colonial phobias, potent decolonial forces are at work, among Muslims, among Hispanics in the US, among Indigenous scholars and activists throughout the Americas, among Africans in South America, and among others. There are significant differences between them: between what each wants to preserve and what mode of reexistence they are striving for. They have in common the awareness that modernity/coloniality demands decolonial responses and that decolonial responses start by emancipating ourselves from mental slavery, by overcoming the belief in abstract universalism and in the dream that the proletariat or the multitude will provide one all-encompassing solution for the wretched of the Earth. It so happens that the wretched of the Earth know that if they are proletarians or part of the multitude, they are also the imperial/colonial wretched—that is, racialized beings marked by the colonial wound and existing at the lowest rank on the human scale of being that, built by Christian theology during the Renaissance, has been reactivated and maintained by secular philosophy ever since the Enlightenment.

Islamophobia and Hispanophobia are entrenched in the colonial landscape of modernity, and even as decolonial projects move forward these phobias remain deep-seated in the minds of Muslims and Hispanic/Latinx people.[43] Unveiling and uncovering the imperial foundations and reproductions of phobias (Islamic or Hispanic) are necessary tasks toward decolonizing (and denaturalizing) the ideas and images of "reality" that imperial rationality constructed and maintain. Thus, understanding imperial designs and how the CMP works are the necessary first steps to engage in epistemic/gnoseological reconstitutions.

Tariq Ali's novel *Shadows of the Pomegranate Tree* is indeed prophetic (published in 1992, before Samuel Huntington's alarming article). It reveals the underground of Huntington's fears. And it shows that the politics of decolonial investigations shall not and cannot be restricted to academic disciplines. It could and should be done in all areas of experience where it is felt and needed. By associating, at the beginning and at the end of the novel, Cardinal Cisneros's hateful campaign to expel the Moors from the Iberian Peninsula with the conquest of Mexico and the appropriation of the Aztecs' land, Ali connected two radical heterogeneous historico-structural moments that are the consequences of the racial matrix holding together the modern/colonial world. The colonial matrix of power is continuously unfolding and updated in what we witness today as Islamophobia and Hispanophobia. I will continue these explorations in the next chapter, which focuses on two major consequences of racism: the economic (disposability of human life) and the political (bare life). Overcoming racism cannot be achieved by public policy. It requires a massive labor of historical and conceptual gnoseological/aesthesic reconstitutions, to which this book attempts to be a small contribution. Epistemic decolonial *reconstitutions* cannot be pursued without the analysis of the epistemic modern/colonial *constitution* (the constitution of the CMP) and the simultaneous *destitutions* (denials, disavowals, erasures of coexisting nonmodern epistemologies) that its constitution implied. Racism (i.e., the destitution of the humanity of human beings who are unwelcome to the CMP's builders and gatekeepers) was and is a consequence of the simultaneous work in the constitution and conservation of the CMP that still exists today, transformed on the surface but sustained in its logic. Racism is systemic, not conjunctural.

3   Dispensable and Bare Lives

I

In this chapter I pursue further the historical narrative of the previous one and expand on the epistemic foundation of racism and its ethical and political consequences on international law and human rights. I examine some key moments in the history of the colonial matrix of power (CMP): the "naturalization" of disposable and bare lives that traps the mindset of the racialized as well as that of the racializers in a game of power differential, of suspicion, fear, and hate and the aftereffects that involve the entire population, disregarding the degree to which each of us is implicated, accused, involved, or fingered. Racism touches all of us, racializers and racialized, one way or another and in different scales so that none of us can say that race and racism are "realities" out there that can be studied scientifically and objectively by detached observers; or say that we are not racist or involved in racism. The double task of the politics of decolonial investigations (and of decolonial politics in general) concerning racism—as I conceive it in this book—consists in, first, disclosing the hidden connections beyond the surface markers of racism (blood, skin color, religion, nationalities, linguistic accents), and showing how these signs reveal the underlying structure that gives them the meaning society at large attributes to and projects toward people, nations, and regions of the planet (e.g., the Third World).[1]

And, second, delinking from the accepted belief in the biological and ontological racial ranking of people, regions, languages, and religions in order to relink with communal forms of being that were and continue to be destituted in the name of modernity, progress, democracy, peace, development, growth, and civilization. To do so requires a global engagement in epistemic/gnoseo-logical and aesthetic/aesthesic reconstitutions grounded in the experiences of local histories and memories entangled with coloniality through the promises of modernity. Both tasks—the analytic disclosure of the CMP and the praxical engagement in the reconstitutions of knowing, knowledge, and sensing—begin with each of us. Whatever is "out there" is nothing without us, the perceivers (in the vocabulary of Blackfoot thinker Leroy Little Bear) or the observers (in the vocabulary of Chilean neurobiologist Humberto Maturana) who are mak-ing sense of the "out there."[2]

II

I have already described, in chapter 1, the comparison Christians made be-tween Jews and so-called Indians. But then there was also the question of en-slaved Africans.[3] Where did they fit into the Christian scheme of things? Be-fore the Atlantic slave trade began in earnest, Africa and Africans were already classified, in the Christian's cosmological frame of mind, as descendants of Ham, Noah's cursed son. Africans were portrayed in the Bible as people to be expelled from religion. The seed of the colonial difference that framed the role of enslaved Africans in the sixteenth century was already planted in Christian narratives. The conjunction of "cursed" and "black," plus the fact that Ham's descendants—in the Biblical narrative—spread through Africa to the current Middle East, prompted the scenario in which the British described Spaniards as blackamoors.[4] When Elizabeth I of England launched the campaign against the brutality exacted by the Spaniards on the Indians (known today as the Black Legend), thus disguising her own violence, the Spanish were likened to blackamoors, underlining the close connections between Spaniards and Mus-lims from North Africa.[5] "Moors" and "Blacks" were thus conflated and desig-nated as undesirable in Christian Europe, a classification used to establish the *intramural imperial difference* between England (a wannabe empire at the time) and Spain (a leading imperial force).[6]

Now, what you have here is a messy historical configuration, the emer-gence of the racial matrix of the modern/colonial world, that is, of Western imperial global designs. Racial classifications (which mean racism in disguise) were worked out according to the epistemic supremacy of Christian theology first; later on, the epistemic supremacy of secular philosophy and science were added as the ultimate proof of the empirical existence of "races." The classifica-tions both dividing and ranking were and still are an epistemic praxis authorizing an ontological invention. Moreover, this configuration's underlying "logical" and "historical" structure has additional proportions: Christian theology was confronted with equivalent and competing religions of the book (those espoused by Jews and Moors); with people like Indians, who lacked, in Christians' epistemic theological eyes, religion (according to Spanish missionaries, who had already lost track of what spirituality means), and were victims of the mischievous and perverse designs of the devil; with a complex population who had descended from Ham and become a confusing mixture of blackamoors; and with Jews, with whom Christians had much in common but who also problematically denied that Jesus of Nazareth was the Messiah, and who were consequently found undesirable in the Spanish kingdom of Castile. Linking Jews with Indians was therefore a judgement that worked in two ways: to discredit Indians and to discredit Jews.

When I convinced myself that logically and historically "race" was an epistemic category regarded as having an ontic status, I realized this was due to the confusion in Western epistemology between what one sees and what there is. While definitions tell you that "epistemology" means discourses and experiences related to knowledge ("episteme-"), and "ontology" means discourses and experiences related to entities ("onto-"), they are both "-logies," that is, they are discourses or logos *about* entities. But no entity has its own logos. Entities do not have meanings; meanings are creations of human enunciations by humans who enunciate (see introduction, figures I.1, I.2, and I.3). Thus, Western categories of thought hide the enunciation (the saying and doing) and highlight the enunciated (the said and done).[7] And that is what confuses you. Your attention is driven toward the content (knowledge, ontic) so that the terms of the conversation (-logy) are made transparent and hence invisible. All good reasons to recognize the limited scope in which epistemology operates and—on the other hand—simultaneously to depart from it (delink), restoring gnoseology and wisdom over epistemology and knowledge. The coexistence of epistemology in the vocabulary of Western modernity and gnoseology in the vocabulary of decoloniality becomes the anchor of border thinking and of the politics of decolonial investigations, which I am talking about and enacting in this book.

When "race" is seen as having material existence (ontic) rather than being merely a discursive (logos) topic, the transparency of the discourse (logos) is accepted as merely a "representation" of what is there. What I am decolonially arguing is that "race" is an epistemic category; it is not a representation of what there is but a modulation of what is "seen" and projected into what is "there." In other words, there is not a "reality" to be "represented" but the modulation of what is taken for granted as there. As Humberto Maturana would say, we do not see what there is; we see what we see.[8] I decolonially argue, furthermore, that "race" is an epistemic invention embedded in the CMP and, as such, is a noun that legitimizes and disguises an action, racism.[9]

I did not reach this conclusion by reading philosophical treatises and essays but through my own experience—which I've mentioned in previous chapters—of migration to the US after being a migrant in France and growing up in a family of migrants in Argentina. When I arrived in the US, I was classified as Hispanic/Latino.[10] I realized that:

a   Given the epistemic and ontological colonial differences that structure the imaginary of the modern/colonial world, I enjoyed a privilege of which I had not been previously aware: that an Argentine of European descent (even if from a family economically and professionally nonprivileged) has privileges over all Indians and people of African descent;

b   Nevertheless, in relation to the European and US model of man and of knowledge, I felt epistemically and ontologically deficient: not quite European (only of European descent) and indeed in the US not really white. My accent revealed my color. The Spanish accent tainted me. The Spanish language has been demoted from modernity three times: first, in the eighteenth century, when Spain became the South of Europe (an intramural imperial difference; see chapter 1); second, during the Cold War, when Spanish was the language of a huge portion of the Third World; and third, in the US, where Spanish is the language of Latinos/as (immigrants).

Thus, it is both as a South American of European descent cum a Hispanic/Latino in the US (an ethnic identification), and as someone trained in semiotic analysis and literary theory, that I approach "racism" in the modern/colonial world order.[11] This context is relevant, since to understand the Western management of human subjectivities (through racism), I am not starting from a purely disciplinary standpoint, but, on the contrary, from my subjective feelings, sensing, and emotionally experiencing the different shades, intensities, and scales of racism. I am using the rationality of disciplinary training to make sense of my experience and explain to the reader how this emotion guides, and disciplinary reasoning explains, what emotions dictate. I am evincing here my understanding while performing the politics of decolonial investigations.

I am thus inverting the processes of knowing and understanding in an effort to change the terms of epistemological and ontological conversations—hence, to advance gnoseological reconstitutions—and this inversion is indeed my methodology: the problems at hand (whichever ones we select), racism in this case, are always already infected by the colonial/imperial differences inscribed in the modulations of the CMP. Once one enacts this inversion, s/he realizes that there is no way to hide from this infection in any of the existing disciplines (semiotics, sociology, political science, biology, biotechnology, computer science, nanotechnology, what have you), and thus no way to pretend that "racism" and "human being" or "humanity" have *objective* ontic existences that can be described and explained from the perspective of the uncontaminated eyes of God (theology) or of reason (egology).[12] (I return to this topic in chapter 12 and the epilogue.) Furthermore, secular disciplinary formations (that is, since the eighteenth century) are a surrogate for religious and ethnic identities. Disciplinary identities (semiotician, sociologist, computer scientist, lawyer, and even those in the humanities) are formed under the principles of objectivity, neutrality, reason without passion, minds without interference of affects, etc.

III

With this premise in mind I argue that from the sixteenth century on, the imaginary construction of racism was projected onto the construction of sexism in the colonies on the principle of humans lacking something (knowledge of God or possession of rational acumen that allows Christians to see promiscuity in men and women) or of humans being otherwise intrinsically deficient (e.g., incapable of human spirituality as theologically conceived). This European projection of racism onto sexism (colonial difference) in the colonies had two major devastating consequences: the *economic disposability* of human life that materialized for the first time in the Western-led Atlantic slave trade, and the *legally/politically bare life* whose paradigmatic manifestation occurred during the Nazi genocide. Both events are the most visible tragedies of Western civilization, and both are consequences of the constitution of the idea of the self-assumed privileges of Man/Human (see chapter 12) in the CMP over the rest of humanness. Both continue today, and we see them at work in the crises of immigrants (in the EU and US) and refugees (now mainly in Europe). Immigration at the inception of economic coloniality demonstrated how reducing costs and increasing profits were more important than human well-being; refugees at the other end of the coloniality timeline exemplified how the secular, bourgeois nation-state placed nationals over all other human beings. Dispensable lives are necessary to secure economic gains; bare lives are necessary to secure the well-being of the nationals over the well-being of the human species.

Slavery was sustained under a basic premise: some human lives are dispensable or disposable, like any other commodity. Disposable life is an economic category. The Holocaust was sustained under the principle of bare life, which is a political category. In both cases human lives are considered dispensable, one for economic reasons, the other for national-political reasons, and the state is the main agent; both scenarios were stamped into the formation and transformation of the CMP's global racial designs.

My understanding of anti-Semitism and of the Nazi genocide is in accord with my continuing explorations of the colonial matrix of power, how it works in specific domains, how it mutates, how it is connected with other domains. I am not "applying" the colonial matrix to the Nazi genocide. On the contrary, I examine the Nazi genocide to understand the mutations and manifestations of the underlying structure and flows that mobilize the rhetoric of modernity and the logic of coloniality, that is, the CMP.[13] The Nazi genocide, in which sixteen million people were believed to have been exterminated, six million of whom—according to statistics—were Jews, is a crucial chapter in the story of racism perpetrated in the name of the purity and homogeneity of the nation by a structure of government that was conceived as a one-to-one correspondence between the nation and the state. The principle was defended in late 2016 by Israel's prime minister, Benjamin Netanyahu. The former US secretary of state, John Kerry, summarized the contradiction in Israel's state formation by saying that Israel can be a Jewish or a democratic state, but it cannot be both.[14] A democratic state is supposed to be a plurinational state. But this is another matter.

Deeming some lives as dispensable is a practice that did not exist before the sixteenth century for the simple reason that the racism that motivated human dispensability did not exist. Dispensability was directed toward the enslaved African population—and after the Industrial Revolution until today toward every manifestation of life that has to be sacrificed to maintain capitalism (in spite of, e.g., climate change, the responsibility of a certain kind of anthropos in the Anthropocene era). Dispensable life is an economic category, though political economy was not yet an established subject in the sixteenth century. Only recently did it become an imperative concept for the politics of decolonial investigations and of the gnoseological reconstitutions of knowing, sensing, and understanding that what racism does is to legitimize the dispensability of certain lives and to inflict dehumanizing colonial wounds. Yesterday was the slave trade, more recently the Armenian and European Holocausts, currently the lives deemed unnecessary by neoliberalism. "Dispensable lives" has two complementary meanings: labor and commodity. The life of an enslaved person is dispensable because once an enslaved body is no longer labor efficient, it can be replaced by another. The person vanishes; only the body counts. Behind this naturalization of economic dispensability were European imperial/colonial merchants and the monarchic states to which they belonged (Portugal, Spain, France, England, and Holland), all preaching the marvels of discovery, conquest, and colonization of the New World. Ottobah Cugoano's *Thoughts and Sentiments on the Evil of Slavery* (1787; see chapters 1 and 2) makes many observations directly relevant to the economic aspect of dispensable lives, for example:

> The vast carnage and murders committed by the British instigators of slavery, is attended with a very shocking, peculiar, and almost unheard of conception, according to the notion of the perpetrators of it: they either consider them as their own property that they may do with as they please, in life or death; or that the taking away the life of a black man is of no more account than taking away the life of a beast. A very tragic instance of this happened around the year 1780 as recorded in the courts of law: the master of a vessel bound for the Western Colonies, selected 132 of *the most sickly of the black slaves, and ordered them to be thrown overboard into the sea, in order to recover their value from the insurers, as he had perceived that he was too late to get a good market for them in the West Indies.*[15] (Emphasis added.)

Cugoano's observation was echoed, some 160 years later, by Eric Williams, a Trinidadian scholar and politician. Williams recast the making of enslaved Africans' dispensable lives and reframed the legacy of the racial/colonial wound in a context that was not visible at the time of Cugoano. For Cugoano, Christian ethics was the weapon available, and he used it to build two complementary arguments, one about the barbarian attitudes he found in colonizers from Spain and Portugal to Holland, France, and Britain; the other about the Christian struggle against the expansion of economic horizons that transformed humans into predators who will go to any length to obtain economic benefits. Williams, on the other hand, had the Marxist analysis of capitalism to replace the ethical dimension Christianity offered to Cugoano. Yet both Cugoano and Williams introduced a dimension that was alien to both Christianity and Marxism: the radical critique of racism, which meant the radical critique of the imperial/colonial foundation of economic coloniality (viz., capitalism). Both made singular contributions to gnoseological and aesthesic reconstitutions in the genealogy of the politics of decolonial investigations.

The second meaning of dispensability renders human beings into commodities. Both meanings highlight coloniality in the economic sphere. A telling passage by Eric Williams (in *Capitalism and Slavery*, 1944) underscores the bottom line of racism in the CMP and in the management of the modern/colonial world order.[16] It reads: "One of the most important consequences of the Glorious Revolution of 1688 and the expulsion of the Stuarts was the impetus it gave to the principle of free trade. In 1698 the Royal African Company lost its monopoly and the rights of a free trade in slaves was recognized as a fundamental and natural right of Englishmen. In the same year the Merchant Adventurers of London were deprived of their monopoly of the export trade in cloth, and yet later the monopoly of the Muscovy Company was abrogated and the trade to Russia made free. Only in one particular did the freedom accorded in the slave trade differ from the freedom accorded in other trades—the commodity involved was man."[17] That Atlantic slavery, as a particular form of the exploitation of labor, was consubstantial with capitalism was Williams's fundamental insight based on the British colonial management of Caribbean plantations. His insight helps us also to understand the same connection that Aníbal Quijano made forty-five years after Williams, based on the Spanish colonial invasion of the Andean region. While slavery in the form it acquired in the sixteenth-century Atlantic economy officially came to an end during the first half of the nineteenth century, in reality it never ended. Coloniality operates beyond particular colonial histories: it is the underlying logic that sustained colonialism and the constitution of the idea and ideals of modernity. Not only did people of African descent continue to be enslaved, even when they were not they were racialized and marginalized in society. Furthermore, slavery and the dispensability of human lives continue to affect a wide sector of the population, and new technologies and rhetoric are used to justify or silence it. New forms of slavery have continued to develop into the present; what has never ended is the commerce in human bodies and, now, also the commerce in human organs.[18]

It so happened that the human agents who controlled meaning (knowledge) and money (institutions and actors serving the institutions) and who claimed and claim the authority to classify and manage sectors of the human population, their self-fashioned privileges imprinted on their bodies and minds, have been and are shaped by racism as much as the humanness of planetary regions that they racialize (see part III of this book). Otherwise, how would you explain the minds and sensibilities of officers of the state, of the IMF, of the World Bank, of bankers overlooking a large world population during the 2008 bailout? Their sensibility persists today. The invisible structure—behind the market's invisible hand—and the flows that shape subjectivities and belief, which ultimately provide institutions with a structure of knowledge that justifies legal crimes, is the colonial matrix of power in its synchronic as well as diachronic dimensions. Sigmund Freud unmasked the work of the unconscious in individual human beings. Similarly, decoloniality, after the work of Aníbal Quijano, allows us to expose the invisible and intangible sets of beliefs that drive certain people to derive their well-being from sacrificing other human beings.

Manifesting good intentions to end poverty is misleading in the sense that the very concept of poverty was invented and introduced into the rhetoric of modernity to hide the fact that the "poor" (who are in the majority racialized) live lives that are dispensable and so can be either discarded or when necessary made indispensable as a labor force or as consumers.[19] Indeed, it is not surprising that at the end of the twentieth century it was necessary to insist that one "remains convinced that poverty and wealth-creation are but two sides of the same historical process."[20] This entanglement of wealth creation and poverty was extensively and convincingly argued by Henry George in 1879.[21] But the coloniality of knowledge disguised his influence beyond the rhetoric of modernity: progress was related not to poverty but to civilization.

Another example, among many, of how modernity/coloniality works in the simultaneous processes of constitution/destitution outlined in the introduction to this book is health care centers in the US. The *New York Times* reported the story of Habana Health Care in Tampa, Florida; in 2002 it was purchased by a private investment firm, which bought, around the same period, another forty-eight clinics in the country.[22] "Efficiency" and "management" were put to work. There was an immediate personnel reduction; costs for providing patients' daily needs were also reduced. But the prices charged to the patient were maintained. Consequently, patients received less and less attention, and several died as a result, while the private investors increased their economic returns. President George W. Bush was reported as defending private health care: "Democratic leaders want to put more power in the hands of government by expanding federal healthcare programs. It's so incremental a step towards government-run healthcare for every American." He added that federal programs would lead to "European style government-run health care."[23] If we put together the US government-run invasion of Iraq and the government's abdication of health care, we have two outstanding examples of the dispensability of human lives for the benefit of the corporate-run economy and the politics supporting it. The brutal transformation of slavery in the sixteenth century and the Nazi genocide in the twentieth century were two cases of the "naturalization" of dispensable—the first—and bare lives—the second. In our present era, as the example of health care shows, the governing philosophy may be different (economic in the case of slavery, political in the Nazi case), but in all these cases lives are made dispensable to protect the economic well-being of communities from the menace the lives pose to economic security, to the security of the nation-state, and, though rarely spoken of in official circles, to the homogeneity of the nation.

IV

As I have tried to suggest, behind the economic reasons for the African slave trade in the Atlantic, and behind the political reasons for the Nazi genocide, as well as its consequences beyond state politics, common threads link them in the colonial matrix of power. Slavery practiced on African bodies was the tip of an enormous iceberg that encased a fundamental perversity: human beings turning human lives into commodities and making them dispensable for profit. Five centuries later, Norbert Wiener saw related dangers in the domain of technology when he adverted to "the human use of human beings."[24] He was writing in the wake of the Holocaust. While Africans were the victims of a multinational economic manifestation of imperial subjectivity, the victims of the Holocaust were the consequences of the modern nation-state: purity of (religious) blood in the sixteenth century became purity of (national) blood in the twentieth. Human lives became disposable in the domain of the economy and bare lives in the domain of state politics. That is, as technologies to manage both the economy and authority—two domains of the colonial matrix of power—they had a double function: to secure growth and order and at the same time to dispense with whatever was an economic or political hindrance. The sophisticated technology of the Industrial Revolution was implemented in the Nazi genocide—modern rationality working efficiently to eliminate human beings, as Zygmunt Bauman brilliantly argued.[25] And Wiener sensed the danger of technology at the inception of the technological revolution that he was unintentionally initiating.

Hannah Arendt provided a detailed analysis of the political dimension of bare lives that is at once historical and conceptual. Historically, it traces the trajectories of the Jews in Europe after they were expelled from Spain at the end of the fifteenth century. Although I'm not claiming that all Jews in Germany and Poland who were victims of the Holocaust were descendants of those expelled from Spain, I do claim a direct link between the Spanish Inquisition, the expulsion of the Jews, and the Holocaust. However, the Holocaust affected a larger population than Arendt accounts for. She connects transatlantic slavery (dispensable lives in my vocabulary) with "naked lives" in political (not economic) terms in her pursuit of an explanation of the decay of the nation-state form of governance and its failure to keep up with the legacy of the *Declaration of the Rights of Man and of the Citizen*. Arendt writes:

> Slavery's crime against humanity did not begin when one people defeated and enslaved the enemies (though of course this was bad enough), but when slavery became an institution in which some men were "born" free and others slave, when it was forgotten that it was man depriving his fellow men of freedom. . . . Yet in the light of recent events [the Holocaust], it is possible to say than even slaves still belonged to some sort of human community; their labor was needed, used, and exploited, and this kept them within the pale of humanity.[26]

And she adds, "Only the loss of a polity itself expels [a person] from humanity." Arendt's perception of slavery differs from that of Williams. Williams embodies the cultural memories and colonial wounds of the Atlantic trades and the Middle Passage in the Caribbean. Arendt embodies the cultural memories of Jewishness in Europe. For his part, Williams did not make reference to the Holocaust. However, a few years later, Aimé Césaire connected the Holocaust with Atlantic slavery (see below). Still, decolonially, the conversion of human beings into dispensable lives, making them belong to a community of enslaved people (as Arendt points out), is of little comfort knowing that their lives are dispensable when they no longer are necessary for labor. And being forever a commodity is also of little comfort: the feeling of being a member of a community of commodities cannot be a desirable and comfortable feeling. Because of that, the enslaved ran away and built the communal *palenques* and *quilombos*. What interests me here, however, is the distinction between dispensable lives (as an economic category) and naked lives (as a political/legal category). Following up on her statement that only the loss of a polity expels a person from his or her humanity, Arendt writes, "The calamity of the rightless is not that they are deprived of life, liberty, and the pursuit of happiness [see the introduction to this volume on this concept], or of equality before the law and freedom of opinion . . . but that they no longer belong to any community whatsoever."[27]

Now it should be understood why dispensable lives are an economic category and naked lives a legal/political one. But today, dispensable and bare lives coalesce in the experiences of immigrants and refugees from the former "Third World" to Western industrialized countries. They are the current targets of both the economic and legal/political destitutions in the intensifying superfluity of life under the exuberant pursuit of happiness under capitalism.

The connector for both is the reiteration of intramural colonial differences directed at European Jews and making them subject to internal colonialism. Once we understand the underground work of the colonial matrix of power, we begin to make sense of the slave trade in the Atlantic, slavery today, the expulsion of the Jews from Spain, and the Holocaust—all of which were consequences of economic coloniality perpetrated by the modern, secular nation-state, which displaced the church and the monarchic state, and which was in turn a consequence of the economic coloniality of the sixteenth century.

Yet the Holocaust and the world's reaction to it cannot be explained only by reference to the history of Europe—a fact clearly understood by the Martinican poet, essayist, and activist Aimé Césaire. Césaire observes that what the very humanistic bourgeois of the twentieth century "cannot forgive Hitler [for] is not *the crime* in itself, the *crime against man*; *it is not the humiliation of man as such*; it is the crime against the white man, the humiliation of the white man, and the fact that he [Hitler] applied Europe colonialist procedures which until then had been reserved to the Arabs of Algeria, the 'coolies' of India, and the 'niggers' of Africa."[28] Césaire's insight reveals the links between two interrelated manifestations of racism: one at the inception of the CMP, in the sixteenth century, and the other four and a half centuries later, in the first half of the twentieth century. The first was enacted on Africans by Europeans in the triangular Atlantic trade; the second by white Europeans on other white Europeans in Europe. Furthermore, Césaire noted the parallel between the Germans' genocide of the Herero in Namibia and the Holocaust—the first in the colonies, the second in the national territory.[29] The scenario had changed but the logic remained: Christians acted on religious belief, the German state on secular national beliefs. The radical shift in the configuration of the CMP occurred in the eighteenth century with the advent of secularism and the Jews being seen on the basis of their ethnicity rather than their religiosity.

An added consequence of this shift was the rise of Zionism and the foundation of the nation-state of Israel (1948), guided by the Western model of governance privileging nationals over human beings (see chapter 4). The Nazi genocide cannot be explained within merely the internal history of Europe; on the contrary, the Holocaust "reflects" back to Europe itself what European merchants, monarchs, philosophers, and officers of the state did in the colonies. It is a heterogeneous historic-structural node, neither a linear history nor two separate events (Atlantic slavery and the Holocaust) that can be compared. Their interconnectedness brings to light the hidden logic of coloniality and racism, the two main forces legitimizing exploitation and extermination, to create institutions and actors/subjectivities willing to make fellow humans dispensable and bare, stripped from the benefits that the state is supposed to bring to the nation. Hannah Arendt also perceived the connections between the Holocaust and European colonization of South Africa, but her view was still "centrifugal" (looking from Europe outward), while Césaire shifted the geography of understanding by making his observation "centripetal" (looking from outside Europe toward Europe). He thus provided a decolonial understanding that is fundamental to any aspect of the politics of decolonial investigations.

Césaire (like Cugoano and Williams) investigates and narrates, analyzes, and conceptualizes coloniality at the intersection of the historical legacies of African slavery and Western categories of thought, while Arendt proceeds in a similar manner but at the intersection of the historical legacies of Jewish people and Western categories of thought. However, Jews and Africans are differently located in the CMP; that is why I distinguish between the economic underpinning of dispensable life and the political underpinning of bare life. Jews are entangled in the long-lasting conflict between the so-called religions of the book, but have been updated in Christian theological narratives since 1492. Africans, in contrast, were cast at the margins of theology (as the descendants of Ham) and of universal history (Hegel). In both cases, nevertheless, the theological and secular (egological) narratives are embedded in the memories of communities degraded, suspected, or expelled from the official rhetoric and sensibility controlling the colonial matrix of power but also, above all, from the sphere of knowledge that made possible the management of subjectivities. This is what Césaire outlined, having been in France after WWII and close to the impact of the Holocaust.

Césaire's intuition was confirmed—indirectly—by Claudia Koonz's magisterial investigation, *The Nazi Conscience* (2003). Koonz observes, "What surprised Jewish Germans during this period was not the cruelty of kleptocrats, fanatics, and malcontents, but the behavior of friends, neighbors, and colleagues who were not gripped by devotion to Nazism. . . . Germans who, in 1933, were ordinary Western Europeans had become in 1939, anything but."[30] The telling lesson of Césaire's investigated suspicion and Koonz's scholarly conclusion is how subjectivities are formed under the naturalization of dispensable and bare human lives. Beyond these events, what I am pursuing is an understanding of the double work of the colonial matrix of power: how it is managed by actors and institutions at the same time that actors and institutions are managed by it to the degree that they justify and naturalize the horrors of Western civilization in the name of modernity, that is, in the name of the benefits of capitalism and the protective and just function of the nation-state.

During the period of heavy slave trade, the process of making lives dispensable for economic reasons implied that the people involved, who benefited either directly or indirectly from it, did not subjectively care about the crimes they were committing or supporting. And if they did not care, it was because they had accepted that Africans either were not quite human or were dispensable, even though they might be necessary as workers, be they enslaved, servants, or employed at minimum wage and without health insurance. Progress and poverty are two sides of the same coin: progress expresses the rhetoric of modernity; poverty evinces the logic of coloniality. The task of decolonial politics of investigations starts from showing that these are not isolated events but that there is something major behind them that still manages us today.

In the Nazi genocide, the main victims were Jews, although other "irregular" people and citizens were also considered dispensable ("gypsies" as well as "Aryan citizens" who were alleged to have damaged genes or homosexual inclinations, despite sharing a heritage, language, and culture with their tormentors). Jews were, in the discourse of the state, a "problem" to be solved.[31] To solve the problem, it was necessary to invent strategies ("technologies" we say today) to eradicate them from the community, to make them noncitizens, to deprive them of all citizenship rights, and, once they were converted to "things" (but not into "commodities"), to exterminate them.

Hannah Arendt offered the first conceptualization, to my knowledge, of bare life (*nuda vita*). Like Césaire, who saw the problems in Europe from his experience of colonial histories, Arendt saw the problems in Africa and Asia from her experience as a Jew in Germany. That is why, as noted earlier, Arendt's view is centrifugal while Césaire's is centripetal: a geopolitics of knowledge is necessary to delink (or to decouple) from the imperial assumption that categories of knowledge are one and universal, and that knowledge is and should be centrifugal, flowing out from a center. Centrifugal epistemic assumptions sustain Eurocentrism, which in this case is a descriptive, not an evaluative, category. There is nothing wrong with Eurocentric epistemology as long as there is an awareness of its locality and its status as neither global nor universal.

V

We have seen up to this point the matching relations, rather than isolated instances, of coloniality and racism (disposable/bare lives). We turn now to the conformity between coloniality, racism, and human rights (a topic to which I devote chapter 7). Pursuing further the geopolitics of knowledge in our understanding of dispensable and bare lives, Arendt elaborates on the philosophical implications and shortcomings of the concept of the rights of man. She was writing near the moment of the *Universal Declaration of Human Rights* (*The Origins of Totalitarianism* was published in 1951), though she reflected instead on the very foundations of the question of rights: the circumstances of the French *Declaration of the Rights of Man and of the Citizen*, simultaneous with the advent of the European ethno-bourgeoisie and the secular nation-state (see chapter 4). She perceived insightfully that "man, and the people" have been taken out of God's tutelage and placed under the frame of man: "The people's sovereignty (different from that of the prince)—was not proclaimed by the grace of God but in the name of Man, so that it seemed only natural that the 'inalienable' rights of man would find their guarantee and become an inalienable part of the rights of the people to sovereign self-government."[32] Arendt underscored, on the one hand, the links between the rights of man and the emergence of nation-states in Europe after the French Revolution, and, on the other, the *Universal Declaration of Human Rights* (1948). What are the connections? She writes:

> The full implication of this identification of the rights of man with the rights of peoples in the European nation-state system, came to light only when a growing number of people and peoples suddenly appeared whose elementary rights were as little safeguarded by the ordinary functioning of nation-states in the middle of Europe as they would have been in the heart of Africa. The Rights of Man, after all, had been defined as "inalienable" because they were supposed to be independent of all government; but it happened that the moment human beings lacked their own government and had to fall back upon their minimum rights, no authority was left to protect them and no institution was willing to guarantee them.[33]

And so, the "Rights of Man" and the rights of citizenship came together. One of the dramatic consequences (particularly today for immigrants in Europe and the US) is that lack of citizenship implies lack of protection. There are no instances in the *Universal Declaration* to protect people who are not citizens or who have been deprived of their citizenship. Thus, bare lives become disposable today for either economic reasons (different technologies of enslavement) or state reasons (different technologies of depriving human beings—immigrants, refugees—of legal rights). The extension and transformation of these two basic technologies of death can be traced geopolitically to European interventions in Africa, Asia, and South America, and, lately, to the US outside its borders: in Guantánamo and Abu Ghraib.[34] The logic of coloniality did not end with the end of settler colonialism. Colonialism mutated into coloniality without colonies, preserving the subject formation at both ends of the spectrum, the emotional and subjective naturalization of disposable and bare lives, and securing the conviction that economic growth and social order have priorities over any other possible consideration. "Financial fascism" is an expression that appeared in the *Washington Post* about a decade ago.[35]

At the time she was writing, Arendt still believed that "never before had the Rights of Man, solemnly proclaimed by the French and the American revolutions as the new fundament for civilized societies, been a practical political issue."[36] The problem with this observation is a generalized one that mainly afflicts scholars and intellectuals whose sensibilities and subjectivities have been shaped by their dwelling in countries and regions (the North Atlantic) where the Glorious Revolution, the American Revolution, or the French Revolution took place. Notice Arendt's unconscious move: she mentions first the French and then the American revolutions, altering the chronology by privileging geography. Why has she reversed their chronological order? Is it because this order has been displaced by the unconscious hierarchical structure of the coloniality of knowledge and of being in the world, wherein the imperial internal differences of France (and Germany and England) come first and the US second? Racism is pervasive; it operates at all levels. Arendt overlooks that the rights of the people (*ius gentium*) became a practical political issue in the sixteenth century with the European discovery/invention/invasion of "Indians" in the New World. Here is a blindness, or silence, revealing the hidden work of the coloniality (destitution) of knowledge and manifested in the intramural epistemic racialization of regions and people through knowledge-making, to which, by the way, Immanuel Kant significantly contributed: Spain, for Kant, as later for Hegel, belonged to Europe's South, mixed with the Moors.[37]

The history of "rights" (of people, of man, and of citizen—human rights) is consubstantial with and constitutive of the CMP. (I will come back to these issues in chapters 5, 6, and 7.) Human rights violations can be invoked in defense of human rights, as has been evident in the past three decades.[38] Arendt has a point when asserting that the rights of man and of citizens, in the history of Europe since the Glorious Revolution (for her, the American and the French revolutions), is part and parcel of nation-state building. What is missing in this picture is that the British, American, and French versions of nation-state building were pioneered by the undertaking (which became the foundational modern/colonial project of the West), initiated by Spanish and Portuguese monarchies in the sixteenth century. The colonial project installed monarchic management in the New World, displacing and marginalizing the existing structure of governances and of economies among Maya, Inca, and

Aztec while disrupting the existing order in Africa by extricating human beings from their communities. Arendt perceived, however, that from the rights of man to "the recent attempts to frame a new bill of human rights" (she refers to the *Universal Declaration of Human Rights* being drafted while she was finishing her manuscript), there was something slippery and hazardous.

She writes, "No one seems able to define with any assurance what these general human rights, as distinguished from the rights of citizens, really are. Although everyone seems to agree that the plight of these people consists precisely in their loss of the Rights of Man, no one seems to know which rights they lost when they lost these human rights." For Arendt, the historical situation she witnessed in Europe between 1930 and late 1940 was unprecedented—not in the fact that many people lost their homes, "but [in] the impossibility of [their] finding a new one."[39] This presented a historical situation that prompted her to recall slavery, as noted previously, that "to be a slave was after all to have a distinctive character, a place in society—*more than the abstract nakedness of being human and nothing but human*"[40] (emphasis added). "Nakedness of being" (also "bare life," another expression used by Arendt and picked up by the Italian philosopher Giorgio Agamben), then, is not just the condition of losing specific rights, "but the loss of a community willing and able to guarantee any rights whatsoever . . . the calamity which has befallen ever-increasing numbers of people." Arendt concludes, "Man, it turns out, can lose all so-called Rights of Man without losing his essential quality as man, his human dignity. *Only the loss of polity itself expels him from humanity*" (emphasis added).[41]

We arrive here at the crux of the matter, announced by Césaire: the equivalences of two institutions in constructing and transforming dispensable lives and bare lives, one at the heart of the economy of accumulation (capitalism) in the Atlantic triangle, the other at the core of the nation-state in Europe. Bare lives are the consequences of racism manifested in the legal-political language of Western modernity at work in and for the control of authority. The symbolic figure of that authority is Man/Human theorized by Sylvia Wynter (see chapter 12). Thus, the concept of citizenship fulfilled the role attributed to certain human beings that at the same time insured the authority of the state (the giver of rights) to keep people in and out legally. Citizenship is a legal/administrative and abstract entity that is generally confused with the nationality of a person identified by a document. It is this confusion that encourages another, major one: the idea that one state (constituted by the legal apparatus of citizenship) corresponds to one nation (constituted by the ethnicity of a group of people). Under such assumptions and structures of authority in the colonial matrix of power, undesirable nationals (in Arendt's case, German Jews), could be legally deprived of their citizenship because of their nationality; being Jewish was not simply or even necessarily to belong to a given religion but to a given ethnicity. Those who were born free but had the bad luck of being born to languages, religions, histories, memories, and styles of life that were not the norm of a given nation-state (say, Spain, France, or Germany) could run into trouble. The Holocaust was an extreme and dramatic exercise of the state controlling the nation(s). Today that problem continues, as manifested by the immigration of refugees to the EU and the US. But not only here. A boomerang effect is felt strongly in all the nation-states that build and reproduce the rhetoric of modernity and implement and enforce the logic of coloniality.

Dispensable lives are not adequately explained today by "the loss of polity itself," as Arendt would have it, but arise as consequences of the racist foundation of economic capitalist practices. Cost reductions, financial gains, accumulation to reinvest for further accumulation—these are the economic goals that make human lives dispensable (financial and economic fascism; see note 35). Race is a necessary keyword in the rhetoric to legitimize and devalue—to justify devaluing—dispensable and bare lives. Racism is the outcome of the colonial difference—the technology to inflict colonial wounds. The bottom line of racism is dehumanization and not the color of one's skin. Skin color is merely an excuse for dehumanization, and dehumanization turns human lives into *commodities*. That slavery achieves this transformation means that human beings did not just lose their rights but lost their humanity. *It is not only "the loss of polity itself that expels him [Man] from humanity"* (emphasis added); enslaved Africans were not *expelled* but were *pulled out* from their community. It was perhaps short-sighted and self-serving for Arendt to claim that "in the light of recent events it is possible to say that even slaves still belonged to some sort of human community," and to place bare lives and the Holocaust somehow above dispensable lives.[42]

Both crimes against humanity—dispensable lives and bare lives—are ingrained in the very logic of coloniality and are always disguised by the rhetoric of modernity. Certain lives become dispensable in racist rhetoric to justify economic control, chiefly the exploitation of labor and the appropriation of natural resources. Lives are dispensable when *expelled from humanity, not because of the loss of polity* but because they are pulled out of their community (enslaved Africans yesterday, young women and children today). Lives become bare in the racist rhetoric that justifies national prosperity for a homogenous population of "ideal" citizens, a rhetoric that President Donald Trump consistently invoked to justify the "need" for a wall between the US and Mexico.[43] In the first case, *consumerism* is preferable to humanity (human beings are not physically enslaved but are converted into consumers); in the second, *citizenship* is preferable to humanity (the law is the tool to convert human beings into illegal aliens or second-class citizens). Thus, we have knowledge working in tandem with racialization in the service of managing both economy and authority— two pillars of the modern/colonial world, that is, of Western civilization. Aimé Césaire's view of the Holocaust comes again to mind at this point. What counted for Césaire was the application of "colonialist procedures" to the "white man." "Colonialist procedures" had been invented by imperial actors and institutions to be implemented on people classified as inferior or outcast, closer to animals than to man: unbelievers, pagans, those derailed by the devil. Five centuries after the origination of the colonial matrix of power and its implementation on non-Europeans, it returned to Europe to resurrect its past, disrupting the dreams Europeans wanted to preserve.

Let's return to some of Arendt's helpful observations for understanding the invisible work of coloniality. For Arendt, slavery constituted a crime against humanity when it became "an institution in which some men were 'born' free and others born a slave, when it was forgotten that it was man who had deprived his fellow-men of freedom, and when the sanction of the crime was attributed to nature."[44] The ethical and political principles of freedom and sovereignty, *from the perspective of an enslaved person, mean "no right" of any human being to enslave or deprive any other human being of their rights.* This was one of the crucial arguments of Ottobah Cugoano, in his *Thoughts and Sentiments on the Evil of Slavery*. However, Cugoano's argument didn't come from the framework of European political philosophy, the genealogy of thought in which Arendt was dwelling. Cugoano articulated a decolonial political philosophy, but as a Black African ex-enslaved man, he did not have the ontological and epistemic privileges that would have allowed his cause to be heard. Consequently, he resorted to the gnoseology and aesthesis of his own lived experiences of being captive and coexisting with his master. Added to these obstacles are also the difficulties in verbalizing the suffering, which is implied in Arendt's argument. What connects the very act of verbalizing the suffering with the experience of the suffering that is verbalized?

Both Cugoano and Arendt were expressing injustices and abuses committed by human beings against human beings, which Norbert Wiener has perceived in the darker side of cybernetic technology (although industrial technology had already introduced it at a lower scale). Human beings inflicting physical and psychological wounds and suffering on people enslaved and exterminated, and by extension on the ethnic descendants of the people enslaved and exterminated, *have been trapped and dehumanized themselves* by the very mentality and sensibility that created the CMP to prioritize economic prosperity and development at the expense of racialized human beings. And above all, at the expense of the self-dehumanization of the enslaver/master and all those who racialize, whether or not they/we are aware of it. However, the scale to which "crimes against humanity" cause lasting wounds varies according to the proximity in time or space each human being has with those who are or were victims of injustices. Consequently, the connections between the act of verbalizing the suffering (enunciation) and the suffering that is verbalized (enunciated) depend on the degree to which the one that is suffering impinges on the body/subject that is verbalizing the suffering. Cugoano's experience of slavery and Arendt's experience of genocide are dissimilar, not only because Cugoano endured capture, the Middle Passage, and enslaved labor while Arendt was able to flee the genocide. Both were arguing from their sensing, knowing, and believing, in languages that were not native to Cugoano, but on the basis of assumptions that in Cugoano's time were theological and in Arendt's were secular. Both sets of assumptions were not personal or contextual; they were collective assumptions shaped by the rhetoric of modernity and by the logic of coloniality.

Let's move on to further explore how disposable lives and the coloniality of the economic domain (capitalism in liberal and Marxist vocabulary) join bare lives in the coloniality of the political domain of governance (the nation-state).

VI

In the previous section I elaborated on the coalescence of coloniality, racism, and rights. In this section I bring international law and land into collusion with coloniality and racism. International law is intrinsically embedded in the CMP. Or better yet, it is an outcome of the colonial frame of mind and the coloniality of power provoked and demanded by Spaniards first and by the competing European would-be imperial states (the Netherlands, France, UK), as well as the US by the end of the nineteenth century. Carl Schmitt traced the trajectory of international law and its basic technology: global linear thinking, a topic I have explored before and to which I will return in chapter 14.[45] Therefore, if international law in the sense of linear global thinking, hemispheric partition, and nation-state territoriality is intrinsically embedded in the CMP, it has been and still is a contributing, if not a determining, factor to racism and consequently to the maintenance of the logic of disposable and bare lives.

Césaire's perception, quoted above, of the Nazi genocide from the experiential memories of the African slave trade in the Atlantic provided the connection between the economic order (human commodities, dispensable lives) and the political order (the nation-state, bare lives). In the economic sphere of Atlantic slavery, human beings were *extracted* from their communities and transported elsewhere, like any other *merchandise*. In the political order, human beings are *expelled* from their community and left *bare*: abandoned to their own destiny (e.g., refugees) or eliminated (e.g., Jews, Roma). Césaire observed that the white man's burden, in the Nazi genocide, was to endure the crime against white people without necessarily noticing that Hitler was applying in Europe the same principles that Europe originally applied to their colonies. Césaire connected the two events. Colonialism, in his words, was the overall frame for both of them. Today we would say coloniality and the colonial matrix of power, the underlying logic and structure of Western colonialism. In short, Césaire offered a decolonial narrative, political and historical in substance, and invisible from the perspective of the political narratives of modernity.

We can advance along Césaire's line of inquiry and make his perception more explicit. International law is the legal mechanism interconnecting both events. International law was a sixteenth-century invention to cope with the realities of an unexpected enlargement of the world and the sudden European encounter with massive amounts of land and unknown people. While records exist of the Europeans' bewilderment and their efforts to accommodate into Christian cosmology people and lands not accounted for in the Bible, records of the Incas' and Aztecs' equal bewilderment at the unknown people arriving and settling in their land do not abound. Nevertheless, in spite of the unbalanced archival material reporting the European side of the encounter, we can expect—on the basis of common human behavior—that both sides tried to understand and accommodate each other into their own cosmology. But Europeans' will prevailed over the Incanate and the Tlatoanate. And knowledge of the European encounters with the Indigenous people of the New World began to proliferate in European languages (based on Greek and Latin), and this knowledge prevailed over narratives in Indigenous languages (Aymara, Quechua, Aztec, Tojolabal, Maya-Quiché, etc.) of Anahuac and Tawantinsuyu. The proliferation of these European narratives expanded the conversations of the European Renaissance, and they changed the subjectivity of those who had access to the novelties the narratives recounted, perhaps especially those who ventured to live in the New World for expanded periods of their life or who otherwise became part of the Atlantic commercial circuits.

Modern/colonial (i.e., from the Renaissance to WWII) international law was first formulated by Francisco de Vitoria, who initiated the so-called School of Salamanca. De Vitoria introduced *ius gentium* (the rights of the people, the rights of nations) into the debate, provoked by the Spaniards' "discovery" of people whose existence they were unaware of and who were not accounted for in Biblical narratives.[46] All of this happened at a time when the distinction between *ius naturalis* (natural rights) and *ius divinus* (divine rights) was being theologically debated. *Ius gentium*, in Francisco de Vitoria, contested theological authority to regulate human affairs. De Vitoria called into question the emperor's and the pope's authority as "rulers of the globe" (*orbis*). In this regard, de Vitoria was joining the arguments of other Renaissance humanists who were increasingly self-liberating from the dictates of the church. He is also recognized for admitting that the "Indians" were endowed with *ius gentium*, as much as the Spaniards. However, de Vitoria couldn't avoid falling into the Western Christian's overconfidence in his supposed privileged superiority. De Vitoria considered "Indians" like women and children: they could not govern themselves and needed the guide of Christian European males.[47]

In 1529 Juan Ginés de Sepúlveda published his *Exortación al Emperador Carlos V para que, hecha la paz, con los príncipes cristianos, haga la Guerra contra los turcos*. One of the central issues in this text was about just and unjust wars, and the target was the Ottoman Turks, who were a menace for the kingdom of Castile.[48] Two decades later (in the 1550s, during the debate of Valladolid) Sepúlveda extended his exhortation about the humanity of the Indians. The declaration of war against Indians was justified *not* because Indians were "menacing" Western Christians and invading Spanish territories, but because Indians presented an obstacle to the expansion of Christianity. Not invited to this debate were sub-Saharan Africans, no matter that the Portuguese had been invading their territory and *pulling out* and enslaving a significant part of the population. Modern/colonial international law came into the spotlight in Christianity's double bind: to defend itself in western Europe from the "pagan menace," mainly the Muslims from the South and the Ottoman Turks, and to justify the conquest of the New World (as de Vitoria needed to do). De Vitoria was aware that the land could not be taken on the grounds that the land did not "belong to" Indians. However, he found a way to legitimize possession and dispossession of the land on the grounds that—as mentioned above—the Indians were like children and unable to govern themselves. This is plainly a racial justification of the law that was based on neither religion or skin color but on a notion of lesser humanity.

Francisco de Vitoria's sustained reflections on *ius naturalis* and *ius gentium* and his concern with order as a way to achieve justice were followed (without direct reference) by Immanuel Kant, in the eighteenth century, in his reflections on perpetual peace and cosmopolitanism. "Without direct reference" is not meant to imply that Kant was a dishonest scholar who plagiarized de Vitoria. I am saying something else: de Vitoria and Kant were of the same frame of mind and activated the same logic and subjectivity of modernity/coloniality. This is why Kant was concerned about similar issues two centuries after de Vitoria, and also why his perceptions were closer to de Vitoria's than to Sepúlveda or Las Casas. Instead, Marx (also indirectly), arguing from the Kantian-Hegelian philosophical paths but focusing on the economy and industrial waged labor that displaced the less economically efficient enslaved exploitation of labor, changed the contents of the argument and turned the proletarians into the industrial equivalent to the colonial Indians. Marx arrived at a position similar to the one adopted earlier by Las Casas confronting Sepúlveda. Contemporary to Marx was Juan Donoso Cortés—a Spanish, Catholic, conservative political theorist and diplomat—who followed the legacies of Ginés de Sepúlveda and placed himself vis-à-vis the legacies of both de Vitoria/Kant/Hegel and Las Casas/Marx.[49] De Vitoria's theological legacy became liberalism under secularization; Las Casas's theological defense of the Indians became the secular Marxist defense of the proletarian; Donoso Cortés's Catholic conservatism updated the humanistic legacies of Sepúlveda. Liberalism, Marxism, and conservatism were the three secular systems of ideas that emerged from the mutation of the CMP from the theological/humanist Renaissance legacies into the secular Enlightenment frame of mind. What all of this means is that the CMP, by the mid-nineteenth century, was configured by three rival ideologies, all assuming the universality of Western regionalism and therefore oblivious to coexisting languages, memories, and praxes of thinking and living. That obliviousness cannot be disconnected from the mindset taking for granted that certain humans are disposable and lack the rights that other humans have, be they enslaved Africans, Indigenous people dispossessed of their lands, people under the rule of apartheid in South Africa, or Arab/Palestinian citizens of Israel.

International law was a primary component of the historical foundation of the coloniality of power (the CMP) and of the Westernization of the planet: it legalized the rhetoric of modernity while simultaneously enforcing the logic of coloniality. It was prompted by the "discovery" of unknown lands and unknown people, and by the trafficking of enslaved Africans to the New World. The foundation of international law to defend European interests destituted and prevented the possibilities of dissent by the people who were subjected to it. But in the second half of the twentieth century, processes of epistemic/gnoseological reconstitutions began. Reconstitutions are not welcome by the defenders and gatekeepers of the constituted, while the politics of decolonial investigations cannot avoid dealing with gatekeepers. In 1979, Oji Umozurike from the University of Nigeria published a report titled *International Law and Colonialism in Africa*. However, given the nature of the intellectual book market and the publisher's (Nwamife's) lack of international celebrity status, the book did not get much attention beyond the few who had a professional interest in the topic. The other reason for the lack of interest is that it was a book written by a Nigerian scholar and published in Nigeria, which at the time was located in the Third World. This is one example of the difficulties that the reconstitution of knowing and knowledge confronts: the impact and visibility of de Vitoria's work when it was reprinted and published by the Consejo de Investigaciones Científicas y Técnicas in Madrid, or the impact of, say, a study of international law published by Oxford University Press cannot be matched by a book by a Nigerian author published in Nigeria. It is a case in point of the indirect consequences of the racialization of people, countries, and continents: ontological and epistemic "deficiencies" have been naturalized, and the division of intellectual and scientific labor is inscribed in the racial distribution of hemispheric partitions.[50] Hemispheric partitions since the sixteenth century have been legitimized by international law, which was not developed by Africans but by Europeans to benefit the interest of Europeans.

In the 1990s, Siba N'Zatioula Grovogui, another African political theorist, but based at Johns Hopkins University, followed up on Umozurike's legacy and wrote about international law from its receiving end. Aware of the fact that racism is ingrained in the distribution and hierarchy of intellectual labor, and that he was being published by an American university press, he reviewed international law in the modern/colonial era and its impact in the partition and apportionment of Africa, by 1900, between all western European countries. The experience upon which Grovogui based his arguments was the colonial history of Africa instead of the imperiled history and experience of Europe. Here is a paragraph that will help us to unveil the interconnections between international law and dispensable and bare lives:

> As a constituent element of Western culture, the law of nations has been integral to a discourse of inclusion and exclusion. In this regard, international law has formed its subject and objects through an arbitrary system of signs. As rhetoric of identity, it has depended upon metaphysical associa-

tions grounded on religious, cultural, or racial similarities and differences. The legal subject, for the most part, has been composed of a Christian/European self. In contrast, the European founders of the law of nations created an opposite image of the self (the other) as a legal object. They materialized this legal objectification of non-Europeans through a process of alterity. The other has comprised, at once, non-European communities that Europe has accepted as its mirror image and those it has considered to be either languishing in a developmental stage long since surpassed by Europe or moving in historical progression toward the model provided by the European self.[51]

The history of the epistemic processes of inclusion/exclusion cannot be separated from the consequences of racial classification of people and continents. Led first by Christian theology, later on by philosophy and science, and lately by political economy supported by political theory, international law was and continues to be a decisive factor in the imperial/colonial transformation of the modern/colonial world order, which, let me say again, operates on the assumptions of racial classification of people, nation-states, and continents (see part III of this book). Consequently, international law was instrumental in the making of extramural colonial and imperial differences. An implicit instrument of classification, international law built Europe's exteriority as "legal objects," their language, religions, families, communities, sensibilities, memories destituted. In sum, legal objects became, for European international law, not only bare but above all dispensable lives. If Western people were and are targets of the objectivation and commodification of life (human and nonhuman natural resources impacting human lives), they are also targeted to be outlawed. As legal objects, subjects beyond the global lines had no say in international law, unless they agreed to the terms stipulated by European lawmakers.

Let's return now to Aimé Césaire's assertion that Hitler had applied to the white man what Europeans had previously created to deal with non-Europeans. Césaire made this statement in 1955, and it, along with his discourse on colonialism, clearly shifted the geography of reason: now international law was seen from the perspective of those most wounded by the consequences of its implementation. Five years earlier Carl Schmitt had published *The Nomos of the Earth* (1950), in which he also clearly noted the Eurocentric nature of international law. Both statements were to assume distinctive positions in the geopolitics of knowledge. Schmitt had not been concerned about the colonies and the colonial world struggling for liberation but about the crisis in Europe, particularly in Germany. Yet now Schmitt had to take European colonies into account. Césaire had not been concerned with Europe and Germany, but with the colonized world and the people converted into legal objects. And now he had to take Europe and Germany into account. Decoloniality of knowledge and of being begins with the shift illustrated in Césaire's statement and secondarily recognizes the contribution, though partial, that Schmitt made from the perspective of Europe in critiquing the Eurocentrism of international law.

VII

Christianity and international law were two racial pillars in the historical formation of the modern/colonial world order concurrent with the emergence of the Atlantic economy—an economy of investment and accumulation of wealth (the wealth of nations for Adam Smith) that we call "capitalism" (after Karl Marx, who did not talk about "capitalism" but about "capital").[52] The salient aspects of these concurrent moments could be summarized as follows:

a   Christianity detached God's heaven from people's Earth, a detachment unfamiliar to coexisting cosmogonies such as those of the Aztecs and Incas in the New World, to those of the populations of the African continent, certainly to those of Buddhists and Hindus in Asia, and even to those of ancient Greece. Secularization sidelined God and detached Man from Nature. In Frances Bacon's *Novum Organum* (1620), Nature became the sphere of living organisms to be conquered and vanquished by Man.

b   As Christian theology became the privileged, imperial locus of enunciation, it prepared the terrain for two compound articulations of racism illustrated in the two triangles found in chapter 1. One was built on the Christian theological epistemic privilege over the two major competing religions (Judaism and Islam). The other articulation of racism was built on the secularization of the already existing theological detachment: God was separated from Earth, and Man was separated from Nature.

c   Secularization in eighteenth-century Europe sidelined religion and underscored ethnicity, and ethnicity became the foundation of the nation in the secular state. Consequently, Muslims and Jews were considered to be ethnic communities of birth rather than religious communities of believers. Not all Jews, however, saw themselves as ethnic Jews, but some did, and this transformation prompted the emergence of Zionism (see chapter 4). The same logic applied to the emergence of ethnic Arabs, which displaced the religious concept of Muslims. Certainly, not every Muslim abandoned their religious identification, but some endorsed secularism. By the same logic, secularism sidelined Christianity within Europe itself although it was necessary as a Western buffer zone to keep out other religions.[53]

In the next chapter I explore the consequences of the secularization of Judaism, while in the previous chapter my explorations of Islamophobia presupposed the secularization of Islam as translated into Arabness. Human rights and international law come onto the scene in the foundation of the state of Israel, which was achieved in 1948 with the support of the United Kingdom. Nationalism was not a Jewish tradition but a secular concept, as is the concept of the nation-state. Three years after the foundation of the state of Israel, in 1951, the American Israel Public Affairs Committee (AIPAC) was created in the US; it remains a visible and influential institution. AIPAC's mission is straightforwardly expressed on their web page: "The mission of AIPAC . . . is to strengthen and expand the U.S.-Israel relationship in ways that enhance the security of the United States and Israel."[54] Racial assumptions about dispensable and bare lives are implicit in the resolve of human rights, the foundation of international law supporting the politics of national security, and the building and transformations of the CMP.

4   Decolonizing the Nation-State

|

The original version of this chapter was written for the book *Deconstructing Zionism*.[1] My goal then, and which I intend to push further now, was not to address the Zionist state per se but to reflect on the nation-state form of governance by exploring Zionism. Hence, the target is the invisible threads that connect the nation-state with the colonial matrix of power (CMP), and the goal is to advance the politics of decolonial investigations. I do not start from Western political theories but from an already constituted state to understand its place in the CMP.[2] President Trump's words, in this and many other cases, brought into the open what was there before but disguised: that the rhetoric of modernity (which was tantamount to the goals of Westernization and now with re-Westernization) is an empty rhetoric to disguise and deviate attention from the unavoidable and necessary logic of coloniality. There is no modernity without coloniality, so that the rhetoric of re-Westernization goes hand in hand with the logic of coloniality (see chapter 9).

Three serious issues loomed over the nation-state form of governance that emerged after the Peace of Westphalia, which attempted to overcome the limits of monarchical states and the church. Nation-states were built in Europe by an emerging ethno-class called the bourgeoisie, and these bourgeois European states conceived of themselves as national communities having a specific type of governance, one which assured that nationals (citizens) had privilege over human beings who were not nationals. The nation-state form of governance undertook to marginalize, expel, and eliminate when necessary spurious nonnational human beings destituted to bare life. Such governance, of course, was also intended either to invite a needed population or to prevent inflows of immigrants and refugees. This is the first challenging issue. The second issue is that the same principle that allowed states to invite, limit, or repel immigrants and refugees also legitimized states' efforts to defend themselves in the name of "national security" and, hence, to destroy whatever could not be controlled. Consequently, and not surprisingly, the European modern/national state form has been—since the nineteenth century—a strong weapon of Western expansion. The third issue is that in the interstate system in place since the nineteenth century, a world order is structured on power differentials and on the dependencies between strong and medium and small states that are formalized in alliances and treatises. Which leads us, in the twenty-first century and after the closing of the Third World, to the confrontation between de-Westernization and re-Westernization.[3]

I return, in this chapter, to some of the issues addressed in chapter 3. Any conversation on Zionism generally leads to a polarization of positions, for Zionism and Judaism are often conceived of as interchangeable: to be critical of Zionism is frequently interpreted as being anti-Judaism. I am following here Marc Ellis's formula: "Judaism does not equal Israel."[4] I myself am not Jewish. As I mentioned in the previous chapter, I am a son of Italian immigrants to Argentina, and I was educated as a Catholic. What has endured throughout my life is my awareness of the immigrant condition and my immigrant consciousness, which were activated when I went to France to study and to the US to work, and which made me conscious of the fact that secularism and modernity were only half the story of Western civilization.[5] The other half, coloniality, was hidden. I began to sense the question of the state and the nation first in Argentina and then abroad. But it was through my investigations of the conquest and colonization of the Americas and of the struggle for decolonization in Africa and Asia that I learned to perceive the emergence of the nation-state in nineteenth-century Europe as a benefit for some (the national bourgeoisie) and a problem for others (the nonnationals). The form and the ideology of the nation-state established a clear-cut divide between national citizens and nonnationals (as well as noncitizens). However, the consequences were more drastic in the colonies. There, the formation of nation-states after independence was taken for granted, as it was in locales invaded by coloniality though not actually colonized, such as China, Japan, Russia, Turkey, Persia/ Iran, and Israel.

The argument in this chapter, consequently, is that while the State of Israel offered a solution for the stateless Jewish people, it became a problem for the Palestinians. Modernity/coloniality are two sides of the same coin; the Zionist project was simultaneously a liberation on the model of the modern European nation-state as well as a rehearsal of the long-lasting program of Western colonialism. The model of the Zionist state was and is already entrenched in European state-forms projected around the world. As a result, resolving the conflict between Palestine and Israel requires more than peace agreements—it requires decolonizing governance as it was established by the modern European nation-state. One of the last remarks of the former US secretary of state John Kerry—mentioned previously—was that Israel could be a Jewish or a democratic state, but not both. Why the statement was made at the time and not earlier I leave out of my argument, as pursuing it requires a discussion of US domestic rather than international politics.

Since its coming into being and its consolidation after the Glorious Revolution of 1688 in England, the American Revolution of 1776, and the French Revolution of 1789, the nation-state form has been a political solution benefiting the emerging European bourgeoisie, which desired to establish its independence from the church and the monarchical state. In the US, the revolution of 1776 provided a political solution for Anglo-Creoles (born in the British New World colonies) by delinking them from the British monarchy. But the revolution was no solution for Indigenous people of the New World and enslaved Africans. The processes that changed the world order over the century from 1688 to 1789 were, clearly, good solutions for some (modernity) and humiliations for others (coloniality). Modernity/coloniality are not two chronologically distinct events; they are not contradictory nor binary opposites of each other. They are two in one: a single concept with two faces. They are always the same event, but only half of their story surfaces in state discourse, the story of modernity, for the simple reason that the tellers of the story believe in modernity and take it for the totality. Beyond modernity, the rest is disposable and dispensable.

The Glorious Revolution and the French Revolution consolidated political control by the emerging bourgeois ethno-class, while the American Revolution consolidated political and economic control by a newly emerging class, namely the New World–born elite. This elite asserted itself in the name of freedom, while at the same time depriving of freedom and dispossessing millions of Native Americans. In short, the secular nation-state in the former US colonies reproduced coloniality in the name of liberty, equality, and fraternity.

In Europe, the story was different. There was not a lower social stratum of a different "race" to dispossess. I do not mean that there was not racism.

I mean that for the homogenous ethnic *majority* racism was not an issue. In the colonies, though, it was unavoidable, for the colonies had been founded on racism. There the racial dispossessions took place within the colonies. In fact, from the sixteenth century onward, Europe had grown stronger based on the economic benefits derived from the racial exploitation of the colonies. Modernity and progress in Europe meant stagnation and misery (coloniality) in much of the rest of the world. Modernity and progress constituted the two key concepts in the rhetoric of salvation. Stagnation and misery were and still are phenomena about which the rhetoric of salvation is silent, hiding the logic of coloniality behind the rhetoric of the redemptive power of modernity. Revolutions became signs of progressive changes. Their darker side, coloniality, was sacrificed for the benefit of the brighter side, modernity.[6]

The State of Israel itself is not, of course, an imperial state similar to England, France, or the US. It has some similarities to the nation-states that emerged in the former colonies of the Americas, Asia, and Africa after decolonization, and it was created during the same period of decolonization. It has also some similarities in that people previously without a state managed to create one, either by expelling imperial settlers (not true of Israel) or (specifically in Israel's case) working with the imperial forces of the time to forge one. Coloniality in both cases did not end with decolonization; it mutated. Internal colonialism is the form the modern European state took in its colonies after independence. Revolution and independence were keywords in the discourse of modernity that reproduced coloniality in these colonies. However, the discourses legitimizing the foundation of modern/colonial states were also made possible by the dispossession of land, and they replicated previous imperial discourses that invoked the Bible. Irish theologian Michael Prior has argued convincingly that similar biblical arguments, based on the chosen people and their rights, were appealed to in the Spanish conquest of America, in the foundation of the US nation-state, in the European colonization of South Africa, and in the foundation of the State of Israel.[7] It is worth noting that at the time of Israel's founding, other nation-states were also being founded: India (1947), Egypt (1953), and Algeria (1962). The last three came into being against the will of England and France, while Israel was founded with the support of both, as well as of the US. In any case, the circumstances in which the State of Israel came about, the underlying links with the expulsion of the Jews from Christian Spain at the end of the fifteenth century, and the temporality of its foundation parallel to the national-states emerging from processes of decolonization in Africa and Asia combine to highlight how nation-state formation illustrates the mutation of the CMP after WWII.

Let us start with anti-Zionist arguments. One of the most radical voices here is the Jewish US citizen Marc Ellis. A Jew who takes sides with the Palestinians may sound to some like an anti-Semite.[8] The accusation is common and logical within the form of the nation-state. During the Bush-Cheney era, every critique of the American state was chastised as a critique of the nation—not, of course, as anti-Zionist, but as antipatriotic. The content is different, but the logic is the same. Insofar as the idea of "patria" is identified with the modern nation-state—that is, where one state corresponds to one nation—a citizen who is critical of his or her own state is accused of being antinationalist.[9] Such a citizen is assumed to go against his or her nation (antipatriotic), by which is meant the homogeneous community in the process of creating its own state identity; and such state critique may have indeed been un-American by the standards of many in the Bush-Cheney administration, but only for them. For the un-Americanness in the rhetoric of Bush-Cheney indeed ran against the basic principles of the US as the leading democratic state in the world. The rhetoric of modernity got twisted in such a way to defend undemocratic objectives in the name of democracy. In this complex scenario, Ellis is a citizen of the US. However, he assumes his Jewish identity, both ethnic and religious. His critique of Zionism addresses Jews both in Israel and in the diaspora, but it also addresses the role of US foreign policy as it pertains to Israel.

The anchoring point of Ellis's argument is encapsulated in the title of his 2009 book: "Judaism does not equal Israel."[10] The first paragraph of Ellis's preface to the book lays out the argument's framework with unmistakable transparency: "The prophetic is the wild card of Jewish life and its primordial marker. Jewish life cannot be described without the prophetic, which always pushes Judaism to another dimension. In these pages, I hold the prophetic marker of Judaism against its corrupting—and potentially fatal—identification with modern Israel. I also offer a prophetic, life giving way forward for Jewish life in the world."[11]

Although the expression "modern Israel" is not flagged in the paragraph, it is useful to flag it, because the creation of the State of Israel in 1948 was—as I mentioned—contemporaneous with the struggle for decolonization in Asia and Africa. This means that, while in Africa and Asia the struggle for decolonization was at its inception, the State of Israel emerged not as a decolonial state (like India or Algeria) but as a modern one. The problems of the nation-state form are generic and therefore common to both insofar as the founding of Israel and of the other nation-states were the outcome of decolonizing struggles, in spite of the fact that the results and the consequences are quite different.

Ellis's book has a short foreword by Bishop Desmond Tutu that begins with these words: "I thank God for my Hebrew antecedents and their Bible." He continues: "Jews are indispensable for a just and caring world. We need Jews faithful to their scriptures and to their prophetic vocation; these have meant so much for the world's morality—for our sense of what sets oppressed people free and of what is just."

Bishop Tutu acknowledges the relevance of Judaism and the contribution it makes to our current efforts (meaning the efforts of "all of us" who are concerned with injustices, dispossession, exploitation, and humiliation of human beings by other human beings) toward a polyreligious and polyethnic world harmony. Tutu then turns from his experience to the central thesis advanced by Ellis: "Equating the State of Israel with Judaism threatens with irrelevance the prophetic power and truth of the scriptures that have, for millennia, inspired and grounded Jews in their witness to God. Israel's treatment of the Palestinian people reminds me of Cape Town under apartheid: colored thrown out of their homes and relocated in distant ghetto townships, illegal walls encroaching on people's ancient lands, separated families, divided properties and the nightmare of running military checkpoint gauntlets."[12]

Beyond this foreword, Bishop Tutu's efforts to dispute support for the State of Israel are very well known. A few years ago, he urged the US pension fund of the Teachers Insurance and Annuity Association to cut their partnership with Israeli companies. He has campaigned to extend an arms embargo to Israel. In Cape Town, he started periodic meetings of the "anti-Israeli Russell Tribunal," an international organization that had previously met in Barcelona and London. He has also contributed to stopping the cooperation of the University of Johannesburg in South Africa with Ben-Gurion University in Israel.[13] For all of that, Bishop Tutu has been strongly attacked as an anti-Semite.[14] Indeed, he is manifestly and openly anti-Zionist. But from this, it does not follow that he is an anti-Semite. In these debates, it seems impossible to escape from the "you are with us or against us" accusations, implying that if you are anti-Zionist you are an anti-Semite. Overcoming the prison house of religion, nation, and state is one of the most basic conditions for resolving the Palestine/Israel conflict. Another is to understand the State of Israel in the global frame of modernity/coloniality. This is one of the tasks of the decolonial politics of investigations. The difficulties of escaping this prison house should not prevent us from conceptually disentangling the State of Israel from Judaism.

The entanglement and the troubles it creates come from the fact that religious Jews, who had criticized Zionism before the foundation of the State of Israel, have now lent it their clear and strong support, particularly after the Six-Day War in 1967.[15] It should be noted also that in 1948 the State of Israel came into being thanks to the support of Western imperial states, while the victories of the Six-Day War gave Israel the necessary confidence to consolidate and expand its territorial and national project. From the point of view of the Palestinians, both moments were detrimental: 1948, because the creation of the state forced Palestinian displacements; 1967, because the State of Israel implemented the very colonial strategies that had been previously employed by Western imperial powers. Although at this point in time Israel is not an obvious analog of imperial legacies, it does not dispute the management of the CMP (like, for instance, China, Russia, or Iran). On the contrary, it contributes to maintaining, expanding, and benefiting from it, from Westernization, and, more recently, from the US and EU to re-Westernize the world order (see chapter 9).

III

In this section, I look at the State of Israel within the colonial horizon of modernity and, consequently, I focus on the prospect of decolonizing the *idea of* the nation-state form to which Zionism is indebted. Decolonizing the nation-state form of government (previously called "republic"—*res publica*) means first and foremost not taking it for granted, and exploring the reasons, motivations, and needs that brought it into being. It means unveiling the logic of coloniality implicit in it, along with its rhetoric of salvation through national security and democracy. Decolonizing the idea of the nation-state is, to be sure, a conceptual and philosophical issue. It doesn't mean assembling massively in the streets, taking over the current government, and building a new form of government. At this point we may not even know what a new form would be. Such a system may not be accepted by the current population of the nation-state in question, and it would not survive under the an interstate world order where finances, production, military forces, and mass media are interwoven. The modern nation-state is supported by three centuries of Western political theory and political economy, and by deep-seated institutions. As a consequence, decolonizing the state requires—first—understanding and calling into question the conceptual logic of much of Western political theory and its implicit complicity with the coloniality of power.[16]

The State of Israel was established at a historical crossroads of race, religion, nationalism, secularism, and a long history of Western global designs.

Creating it required some mutation of the CMP. The modern and secular European nation-state displaced the theologically grounded national communities of faith (Christians and Jews regulated by the church and the monarchy) and replaced them with communities of birth (*natio*), regulated by the secular state.[17] "Secular Jews" who championed the Zionist project emerged roughly at this juncture in central Europe, since Theodor Herzl, founder of Zionism, was an Austro-Hungarian citizen. Although Vienna was a predominantly racist society, it may have prompted responses from the Jewish community, like Herzl's Zionism and Freud's psychoanalysis. It is difficult to imagine that the political and now predominant branch of Zionism in Israel could have emerged in Australia, Argentina, South Africa, or even the US, where many Jews settled.[18] The geopolitics of knowledge is a fundamental concept of decolonial thinking. It takes us away from the myth of linear universal history and the belief that the West is the universal present and the rest is the past—a powerful fiction in the rhetoric of Western modernity. The splendor of the nation-state in Europe allowed an emerging bourgeois ethno-class to displace the joint alliance of the monarchy and the church that pegged one Christian nation to one monarchical state.

In Europe it was possible to attach one nation to one state, due mainly to the relative homogeneity of the white, European, and Christian populations—Jews and Roma being invisibles. The problems emerged later on, in Europe and in its colonies, since there aren't many places in the world outside Europe where the state could be made to easily correspond to one nation. Of course, today in Europe this correspondence is no longer so apparent. Immigration is causing western Europe and the US to move toward becoming future plurinational states—or some other form of governance we cannot yet imagine. Plurinational states should not be confused with mono-national states that promote multiculturalism. A plurinational state is one managed by various nations within the state's territory. Whatever the future brings, the model of one state/one nation is already untenable and cannot improve. From the beginning, the State of Israel has confronted the unsolvable problem of every modern nation-state: to look after the well-being of its citizens, and to deem everyone else suspicious or lesser humans and so dispensable in relation to a given nation-state. It is imperative to overcome this legalized violence in the nation-state form in every state in the world.

In Europe, an exacerbation of the ideology built on the equivalence of one nation to one state exploded under Nazism (explored in chapter 3). The Nazi state and the bombing of Hiroshima and Nagasaki that ended WWII created the conditions for *The Universal Declaration of Human Rights*: the security of the nation ran parallel to the security of Western civilization. But the discourse of human rights soon became a double-edged sword—used on the one hand to enforce the respect and protection of persons who uphold certain values, but violated others when "necessary" to defend those same values.[19]

Thus, while Nazi-engineered genocide was a consequence of the ideology that pegged one nation to one state, Hiroshima and Nagasaki could be said to be consequences of this same ideology brought to bear in the context of global war on people said to be representatives of the "yellow peril."[20] The model of one nation/one state became a political pillar of Western civilization. The defeat of Hitler by the Allies and the defeat of Japan's supreme ruler, Hirohito, made evident the potential of the modern European nation-state, if only as a justification and legitimation of mass murder in the name of that political form.

However, while the nation-state form of governance came into existence "naturally" in the history of Europe, it was forced by colonial imposition or positively endorsed by local elites in most non-European histories, memories, sensibilities, modes of existence, and communal organizations. In the Americas (North and South), nation-state formation was contemporary with that in Europe. However, in Europe it was an outcome of its own history, while in the Americas the colonial history managed by elites of European descent (England, France, Portugal, and Spain) overruled the First Nations forms of governance— overruled but did not vanquish. Today, First Nations' reclamation of their right to the land is parallel to the Palestinians' struggles in Israel.[21] In Asia and Africa, the importation of the nation-state form came later. With the exception of China's Xinhai Revolution in 1911 and the Russian Revolution in 1917, nation-state formation occurred after WWII and as a consequence of decolonization: the State of Israel was founded one year after the independence of India (1947). The historical trajectories, however, were inverted: Britain gave up on India at the same time that it supported the creation of the State of Israel.

Why was the State of Israel successful while nation-states in Africa and Asia have gone through all kinds of difficulties? We have been witnessing their denouements in the uprisings taking place in North Africa and the Middle East, in Syria, in Iran, and in the nation-states that emerged after the disintegration of the Soviet Union (Ukraine, Belarus, Hungary). Even countries in "Latin" America—the republics formed in the first half of the nineteenth century—are still struggling with the nation-state form of governance. One answer advanced by dependency theorists in "Latin" America, and embraced in Africa and Asia as well, was the political and economic dependency of newly emerged states. Although their argument centered on the economic dependency of these states, implicitly it referred to the reality of their overall dependency. Refounding the state or decolonizing the state form are two distinct options in the questions at the core of current debates. Decolonially speaking, the state can neither be refounded and democratized nor be decolonized—in the sense of having a decolonial government ruling the state. Bolivia under Evo Morales (2006–2019) intended a decolonial form of governance. It turned instead—inevitably, I would argue—to de-Westernization. And even de-Westernization was too much for the conservative elites who supported the re-Westernization that accomplished the coup that destituted him from the government. The nation-state form of governance is essentially embedded in the CMP, such that either option, refounding or decolonizing—is out of the question. And de-Westernization in Latin America runs into all kinds of difficulties, as the experience of Brazil under Lula da Silva and Dilma Rousseff has shown.

The decolonial option argues for delinking, engaging in decolonizing *the idea* of the nation-state by decolonizing Western political theory and envisioning a structure of governance beyond the nation-state.[22] The Zapatistas have a long way to go, but they are showing that it is possible, even if the nation-state is still dominant (but not longer hegemonic). And the current experience in Rojava shows that governance cannot be equated with the nation-state. However, the idea that a state could be plurinational and not necessarily mononational is an important step toward delinking from the modern nation-state formation. The demand for constitutional explicitness of plurinational states in Bolivia and Ecuador was the outcome of Indigenous political demands and arguments, which shows the strength of the politics of knowledge.[23] Be that as it may, the State of Israel did not emerge from a struggle for independence involving the overthrow of imperial administrations. The dates are relevant to understanding the turmoil in the world order after WWII, the colonies lost by Britain, France, and the Netherlands, while the US moved to interstate leadership: India obtained political independence in 1947 and Palestinians lost theirs in 1948.

Although the founding of the State of Israel was dissimilar to that of the states that emerged from decolonization efforts during the Cold War, its territorial occupations were similar to those prevalent in sixteenth-century Castile, or to Holland's occupations in Indonesia, Britain's in India, France's in Algeria, and the US's interventions in the Philippines and elsewhere. Today the US does not attempt to justify the occupation of territory through settlements but instead through its efforts to manage the world order by diplomacy, finance, interventions in foreign states, campaigns conducted by mainstream media, and military deterrence.[24] The contrasts are revealing. Dispossessions in the New World and in South Africa were argued for and enacted by Western imperial states (Spain, England, Holland). In the case of Zionism, dispossession was argued for and enacted by people without a state (e.g., those coming from a diaspora). And yet, the very founding of the State of Israel and its continuity are due in large part to the support of Western imperial states—England at the beginning of the process and the US especially since 1967.

It is a telling paradox that the states which emerged from processes of decolonization either failed (Egypt, Tunisia, Libya, Yemen, Syria), had great difficulties finding their way (Nigeria, India), or had to go through a long fight (South Africa, from Biko to Mandela), while the State of Israel was established and consolidated in a relatively short time. In the process, Palestinians became colonized people like Indigenous people who lived in the "New World" before European settlements and dispossessions. We can perceive here the continuity and mutation of CMP, the rhetoric of modernity, and the logic of coloniality. To the earliest form of colonial dispossession the State of Israel has added a second form.

IV

In this section I explore the relations between secularism and Zionism in nineteenth-century Europe. Whatever the relations between Jews, Christians, and Muslims were before the end of the fifteenth century, those relationships were turned around toward the end of the fifteenth and during the sixteenth centuries. It is from this mutation, which I will argue was first and foremost semantic, that Zionism emerged four centuries later. Why?

The expulsion of the Jews from the Iberian Peninsula, a fundamental chapter in the constitution of the CMP that was taken to an extreme—to say the least—by Nazi Germany, is analogous but also dissimilar to the exodus of the Jews from Egypt.[25] Whether the Jews were released from bondage in Egypt and allowed to leave voluntarily, or whether they were freed and then expelled, or whether they were simply expelled for other reasons (e.g., causing plagues, having a monotheistic faith in a pantheistic Egypt), there are important differences from the Iberian case. But there is one overriding similarity: Jews had come to be considered, both by those they left behind and by those who expelled them, undesirable. When the Jews are said to have left Egypt, Christianity and Islam were still far from being born. On the other hand, when they were expelled from the Iberian Peninsula (1492), Jewish *people* were interacting with Muslims and Christians, but Christians at that point had the *institutional* upper hand and were able to expel both Jews and Muslims from Christian territories. Modern Western Christianity, during the European Renaissance, thus created the blueprint and the spirit of the nation-state: "purity of blood" became an accepted Christian principle upon which homogeneous religious communities could be built. Later, in eighteenth-century Europe, secularization adopted and adapted the notion of purity of blood as that which defined the spirit of the nation (and the nationals). Communities of faith were translated into communities of birth, and purity of blood into skin color. The justification of racism was no longer theology but science—or rather a primitive imposter of science.

The year 1492 witnessed, as we know, a series of decisive events, the expulsions of Moors and Jews from the Iberian Peninsula among them, which I've accounted for in previous chapters of this book. The Moors went to the South, the Jews to the North, and Columbus, sailing to the West, landed on a territory unknown to Europeans and which he named "Indias." (Only fourteen years later it was named "America" by a European cartographer to honor Amerigo Vespucci.) Soon after, the forced migration of enslaved Africans contributed to shaping the demography of the New World/America and created the preconditions for the modern/colonial racial pattern that I explored in chapter 1. Jews became part of a larger picture created by Christians, who were in a position to classify and make their classifications valid for centuries to come: Jews, Muslims, "Indians," and "Blacks" formed the initial racial tetragon that has survived, with mutation and additions, to the present day.[26]

Muslims were expelled from Western Christendom, but at that point Muslims had behind them eight centuries of history, from the Islamic caliphate controlling the Iberian Peninsula and what is today the South of France to the powerful Ottoman sultanate. Some Muslim forms of governance mutated into nation-states (Turkey, Iran), and others remained as monarchies (Saudi Arabia, United Arab Emirates, Qatar, Morocco). By contrast, Aztec, Maya, and Inca civilizations were dismantled and their populations degraded as "Indians." Enslaved Africans were detached from the kingdoms of Africa, transported to America, and identified as "Blacks." Consequently, while Muslims became *extramural imperial enemies* (by virtue of the constant presence of the Ottomans in the North of Africa and the Southeast of Europe), First Nations "Indians" and enslaved Blacks became *extramural colonial subjects*. In Europe, Jews who remained in the lands of Western Christians (soon to become Europe) became *intramural colonial subjects*. What you see in this distribution are colonial and imperial differences at work, their layers and gradations in managing and classifying the population. As for the Jews, the reinscription of Zion within nineteenth-century Europe was a consequence of their saga as a people without a state and as internal colonial subjects during the dissolution of European monarchies, the marginalization of the Christian church, and the formation of the European nation-state.

V

We are now in a position to map the state of Israel in the colonial horizon of Western modernity. Its foundation, supported by a western European coalition, invites the question about the historical nature of the modern nation-state form of governance in the transformation of the global order since the eighteenth century. Two issues are relevant for my argument:

1 The larger picture of interstate relations under the hegemony of the nation-state form of government in the US, England, France, and Germany
2 The *idea* of the "nation" upon which the modern European state apparatus was established

To elaborate on these issues, we need to revisit some events of the sixteenth century and their mutation in the nineteenth century. The thread connecting these events will give us an understanding of the underlying colonial matrix of power (the CMP) and its transformation, which occurred at the same time as its rationale was solidified. Concomitantly, of course, the rhetoric of modernity has also changed. As is well known, before the sixteenth century Muslims were not only residing in Spain and North Africa. They also resided in the territories of the Islamic caliphate—which united the communities of believers (*ummah*) ruled by a single caliph—that extended from Spain to the southeast through the North of Africa, across the Persian shahanate, all the way to today's South Asia and Southeast Asia.[27] The largest colony of the British Empire was in South Asia. The British invasion of India started by the dismantling of the Mughal sultanate, based in Delhi and extending from Kabul in the North to Calcutta in the East and Madras in the South—almost the totality of India and Afghanistan today. By chance or design, the first large colony of the British Empire was in a sultanate. In the Palestinian region, the historical trajectory of interest for this discussion goes from 1517, when the armies of the Turkish sultan Selim I conquered the Levant; to the period 1538-1555, when Suleiman the Magnificent, a contemporary of Charles V (emperor of the Holy Roman Empire of the German Nation, 1519-1556), restored the Jerusalem city walls; to 1916, when Britain and France, anticipating the demise of the Ottoman sultanate, signed the Sykes-Picot Agreement defining their respective areas of influence in the control of Western Asia—a specific chapter of global linear thinking, hemispheric partition, international law, racial configuration, and imperial management of the CMP.[28]

Certainly, the first incursions by the British were commercial, through the East India Company, but the political control of Bharat (India) in 1858 was set in place by overruling the sultanate and implanting modern/colonial institutions. A second wave by the British entered the Persian/Iranian sultanate after oil was discovered in the region. Britain and the Soviet Union invaded Iran after WWII. Reza Shah was forced to abdicate and was replaced by his son, the pro-British Mohammad Reza Shah Pahlavi, who lasted until 1979, the year of the Iranian Revolution. Following a third incursion, the Ottoman sultanate fell under British rule in 1922. From the debris of the Ottoman sultanate emerged the republic (nation-state) led by Mustafa Kemal Atatürk (Turkey), and another new state was formed in the territories occupied by the Ottomans: Iraq. Again, oil had been discovered in this area at the beginning of the twentieth century.

In 1917 the British entered and took possession of Jerusalem, until then under Ottoman rule. The city was in turmoil, with constant confrontations between Muslims, Jews, and British. In 1947 the United Nations approved the partition of Palestine into two territories, one Arab and one Jewish—Israel and Jordan. With the fall of the Ottoman sultanate and the removal of Reza Shah in 1941, Britain managed to control a vast area from the Mughal sultanate territories, contiguous with the Persian and the Ottoman sultanates. The founding of the State of Israel occurred not only with the Jews' return to their Promised Land, but also with the securing of a key territory: the eastern buffer zone of Europe. President Barack Obama's early declaration of the "unbreakable alliance with Israel" (which turned sour at the end of his mandate, but was strengthened during the Donald Trump presidency, perhaps on the advice of his son-in-law) means much more than maintaining the ties between the two countries with the largest Jewish populations and whose affinities are bolstered by a common Judeo-Christian tradition. It also means geopolitical alliances with important economic and military implications: Iran and Syria on the other side of the border, Russia in the north, and China in the east.

The spread of the nation-state carried with it the implicit idea of one nation/one state. This idea and its implementation, or the implementation of a form of governance that became named and described as the nation-state form of governance, did not emerge in the early nineteenth century in China, India, southern Africa, West Asia, or Central Asia. And it was not born in South America either, although in South America and in Haiti the adoption of the nation-state was coeval with European and United States governance. In all these locales, it was a form of governance that *destituted* in the same movement that was *constituting* Europe and the North Atlantic; today, NATO is defending a world order that is no longer viable.

The fall of the Ottoman sultanate brought about the modern/colonial republic (nation-state) of Turkey, ruled by Atatürk, and one of the shameful episodes in this transformation involved the genocide of Armenians in the name of national defense and unity. Although the genocide occurred during the era of the Ottoman sultanate, the nation-state model was already in place and most likely convinced the Turks there was no room for "nonnationals" like Armenians, an attitude that is not registered in the history of Muslim caliphates and sultanates before the nineteenth century. In fact, the idea of the nation infiltrated Armenian communities, which were between Ottoman control and the Russian czarate's advance toward the Caucasus. Armenians saw the possibility of liberating from the Ottoman and forming their own state with Russian assistance:

> The Turkish "provocation thesis" blames the Armenian victims for the genocide, asserting that Armenian peasants living in the eastern vilayets (provinces of the empire) had nationalist aspirations and were thus prepared to join the Russian invaders at the beginning of World War I. Further, these Armenians aspired to carve out an independent Armenia in eastern Anatolia, and this, according to the thesis, would spell the demise of Turkey. Armenians therefore had to be eliminated in order that Turkey might survive. What Turkish deniers leave out is any discussion of independent Turkish nationalist motivations or of policies that included the destruction of Christian minorities in the empire.[29]

As a matter of fact, Suleiman the Magnificent has been recognized by historians for his domestic policies accommodating non-Muslims until the advent of the idea of the nation and the nation-state took on a life of its own. The concept spread rapidly and widely. The independence and partition of India and Pakistan derived as a consequence of this idea, mounted on the already existing perspective offered by global linear thinking and the constitution of the second nomos of the earth (see chapter 14), the consolidation of modernity, and the instrumentalization of coloniality. The control of the Mughal sultanate made it possible for the British to promote the cultivation of opium in India, leading eventually to the Opium Wars with China that contributed to weakening and eventually ending the Qin's Dynasty. After the revolution (1911–1912), China entered a period of political reorganization in which the

Western model of the nation-state served as a starting point in the search for a form of governance that would balance what China had with what the West was compelling them to have.[30] Similarly, the concept of the nation-state prompted the mandates that created Iraq out of the ruins of the Ottoman sultanate. Once Iraq became a nation-state, it subjugated the Kurds and invaded Iran in 1980 to prevent potential uprisings of suppressed minorities.[31] Hence the nation-state form not only *governs and divides the nation (the people) but is governed by* the underlying logic of coloniality. One nation/one state translated democracy into one person/one vote. All of this—genocides and wars—was done in the name of unity of the *nation and the nationals.* In short, it is abundantly clear that the nation-state form has been, since the nineteenth century, the power instrument of the CMP for managing and defending authority, chaining both those who govern and the governed.

I turn now to how the idea of one nation/one state nourished the Zionist project in the nineteenth century.

VI

That political Zionism originated in Europe during the nineteenth century is not a random event of universal history. It is a logical consequence of the modern/colonial world (i.e., Western civilization) and its underlying structure—the colonial matrix of power. The unfolding of European history, self-fashioned as "modernity," needed and invented the nation-state that Zionists began to claim in the nineteenth century. At this junction, Jews were perceived in secular Europe, and many perceived themselves also, as ethnic Jews. I mentioned above that in like fashion, Muslims became Arabs.

Statistically, today's worldwide Jewish population is estimated at between 14 and 15 million. Of that total, 5.7 million live in Israel and 5.2 million in the US. Close to a million live in Europe (France, Belgium, the Netherlands, Britain, Germany, and Hungary), and about 300,000 in South America. South Africa, Australia, Ukraine, and Russia account for, approximately, an additional half million. Even considering the geopolitical scope of the Jewish diaspora, it was a politician, intellectual, and activist in the Austro-Hungarian Empire, Theodor Herzl (1860–1904), who during his short life accomplished so much to establish the basic foundation of the Zionist state. The quest for the State of Israel that Herzl pursued with determination was doubly marginal—both in its Jewishness and in Herzl's origins in the decaying Austro-Hungarian Empire as it confronted the forces of western European and imperial nation-states. (As mentioned, at about the same time, Sigmund Freud, 1856–1939, was in Vienna, a city that did not welcome Jews.) Herzl was not the first to come up with the idea of Zionism, but he was its engine and engineer, and he was no doubt helped by living in Europe at a time when the nation-state was being consolidated in the core western European countries. The nation-state was a secular institution. And so was Herzl's Zionism.

A sign of modernity and progress, the European secular form of governance was an institution modeled for and by the emerging ethno-class, the bourgeoisie, whose legacies were the Glorious Revolution and the Industrial Revolution in England, and the French Revolution in continental Europe. The nation-state was the major consequence of the Westphalia treaty that ended the deadly Thirty Years' War (1618–1648). Herzl's Zionism was no doubt motivated by the examples of western Europe and the US. Both continents provided a model for a possible Zionist state to which he gave birth. However, in the Americas, the nation-states did not emerge from religious wars among Christians, but from the expulsion of the colonists and the subjugation of First Nations people and people from the African diaspora. The logic of coloniality not only regulated relations between states but also engendered desires and shaped subjectivities. In this mutual complicity, the legal dimension of the state entangles the subjectivity of those who govern and those who are governed. The state cares for national interests and creates legislation that, while necessary to maintain the coherence of daily life, legalizes national interests and legislates from top to bottom, overdetermined by the colonial difference. The colonial difference, by the way, is the foundational difference in the domestic issues of any state. The imperial difference regulates interstate relations, generally named international relations (see chapter 3).

The nation nourishes and is nourished by national sentiments; the state is driven by legal rationality. However, the officers of the state (e.g., the government) are also driven by sentiments and emotions that stain both the written legislation and its interpretation. Racism is unavoidable and is muddled in the triangulation between the laws of the state, the subjectivities of its officers, and the sentiments of the people (e.g., the nation). Herzl lived in a place and time when the world order was being remade, in Europe and its former colonies, over the crumbling monarchies and the diminishing role of the church and, in the Americas, over the first wave of decolonization (called "revolution" in the US and Haiti, and "independence" in South America). This remaking was a consequence of the decay of the European monarchies that had led the colonial enterprise from 1500 to 1800.

Secularism in Europe established the separation of the state from the church and put an end to the monarchic-state form. However, neither the church nor the monarchies vanished from sight. They kept their domains of influence behind the scenes, as we know by looking at the so-called developed and industrialized countries in Europe. Still, nation-states, as the compound name indicates, were conceived as legal, administrative, and economic organizations based on communities of birth (nation) and not on hereditary family lineage or undemocratic elections in the Roman papacy. National subjects were also united by the national language, national literature, and national culture (the concept of "culture" had acquired a different meaning from the one it had in Latin-derived languages during the Middle Ages). National subjects were protected by the law and shared the same national "culture." They became "citizens" in the modern sense of the word, profiled in the *Declaration of the Rights of Man and of the Citizen.*[32]

In contrast to Europe after 1500, where classification and hierarchy were based on the racialization of religion (Christianity, Judaism, and Islam), which triggered conflict among class/church/state, in the Americas (both North and South) conflicts were grounded from the beginning on classification and hierarchy established in the racialization of ethnicities: Spaniards, Indians, Blacks. Americans ("Pueblos Originarios" in the South, First Nations in Canada) and enslaved Africans, transported to the New World, were the equivalents of the Moors and the Jews in sixteenth- and seventeenth-century Spain (when Europe was still known as Western Christendom). In the US, "Manifest Destiny" was the explicit justification for the appropriation of Native American lands. In Canada, state politics followed the same logic of coloniality. The parallels, then, between the formation of the United States and its politics of Manifest Destiny, whose religious origins are well known, had repercussion in the politics of the State of Israel. Conrad Cherry has outlined those repercussions, and Michael Prior has followed the path of the Bible and colonialism from the Americas to apartheid South Africa to Israel.[33] We should remember the message of Desmond Tutu, after the end of apartheid, to the people of Israel: liberate yourself by liberating Palestine. Tutu was addressing an issue much larger than the relations between South Africa and Israel: underneath the seemingly unrelated local histories lay the belief and the assumptions that maintain and sustain the colonial matrix of power. Tutu's indictment was an act of decolonial politics not only for what he said but by the act of his saying it.[34]

Zionism in the vision and action of Theodor Herzl was basically a secular project driven by the nation-state model. Secularization—as I've already mentioned—changed the European Enlightenment perception of Jews as an ethnic more than a religious group. After WWII, there was a second mutation in the Western perception of the Jews and in the Jewish community in the US: Jews began to be perceived as white.[35] None of this, of course, erased the foundational religious origins of Judaism. But it alerts us to the mutations of the rhetoric of modernity (i.e., the imaginary component of the CMP) with significant consequences in the mutations of the logic of coloniality: hence the alliance between the US and Israel after 1948. This also means that the Zionist vision of the state assumed that Jews were ethnic-nationals rather than (or instead of/also) religious-nationals. Who is who and what they believe would be a matter of ethnographic investigation. My intention here is to outline how the rhetoric of modernity and the logic of coloniality work in the infrastructural network of the global order. One task of the politics of decolonial investigations is understanding precisely how the CMP works beneath the surface of everyday news. Once Jews saw themselves as ethnic and became ethnic in the eyes of non-Jews, the secular Zionist project had to confront the leaders of the Jewish religious communities who opposed it. Michael Brenner in 2003 described the position as a "paradoxical international nationalism."[36] It is paradoxical if your argument is grounded in the presupposition of modern social sciences. In fact, it is not a paradox but rather the interpretation of the visible surface hiding the underground mutations of the logic of coloniality. In Brenner's line of reasoning, another paradox could be that a political movement that at its inception was secular, and therefore emphasized ethno-Jewish nationality rather than theological Judaism, was very much criticized by religious Jews who considered Zionism an affront to Judaism. But it is not a paradox if our attention is on the mutation of the CMP rather than on what happens on the surface.

VII

Legalizing dispossession has been a foundational strategy of the rhetoric of modernity (constitution) and the logic of coloniality (destitution) since the (in)famous *Requerimiento* at the beginning of the sixteenth century.[37] Following the reasoning I have been pursuing to this point, the Palestine/Israel question is far more than a local issue. Understanding it within the colonial horizon of modernity illuminates how the CMP works and the fundamental role that the nation-state played in its formation and its transformations. The Palestine/Israel question is entrenched in the global order whose historical foundations are to be unearthed in late fifteenth-century Europe and the "discovery" of America.

The global order I am talking about is the one that Carl Schmitt described as the "second *nomos* of the earth," regulated by global linear thinking (which I introduced in chapter 3 and will return to in chapter 14). The "second nomos" is the European vision of the world order to be achieved, it is a vision of global designs, and it is one half of the story. The other half, the vision from the receiving end of global linear thinking—the colonized end, so to speak—is the founding moment of the CMP and of Western civilization.[38] International law (explored in chapter 3) regulating the "second nomos" is one aspect of the CMP. Both narratives (that of the second nomos and that of the CMP) have dispossession at their core. In Schmitt's argument, global linear thinking is tantamount to international law. Remapping the globe brought the second nomos into existence, and international law legalized dispossession from its inception.[39] The foundation of the State of Israel benefited from one of the strategies of imperial expansion. In the vocabulary of the CMP, international law legalized the control and management of authority. Legal dispossession, regulated by international law, was an affair of the state, both monarchical and secular. And this is the constellation in which the State of Israel was founded: the return to the Promised Land was supported by a long-lasting trajectory of legalizing dispossession in the name of progress and civilization.

In principle, dispossession has serious implications beyond the law and couldn't be justified in the name of sacred texts: dispossession is both illegal and unsacred and in both cases immoral. However, an argument could be made, and has been made, that the Bible has been interpreted to legitimize dispossession, and that such interpretations have become legal principles of international law.[40] It may be said also that here we confront another paradox. But decolonially speaking there is neither paradox nor contradiction. It is another case in which the rhetoric of modernity shows its face and hides the logic of coloniality. Paradoxes and contradictions belong to modern epistemic frames of mind; they dissolve when they are seen decolonially: modernity/coloniality is the overarching frame of all supposed paradoxes and contradictions. But if you start from a frame that separates modernity from coloniality, you only see paradoxes and contradictions. There seems to be no law or sacred truth that can justify a human being's right to dispossess other human beings of what they have. The continuity and complementarity in Western civilization—since its colonial foundation at the end of the fifteenth century (i.e., with the expulsion of Moors and Jews, and the "discovery of America")—between the law of the state and the truth of the sacred text have contributed to the ranking and racialization of regions, territories, and human beings.

Dispossession is, first and above all, dehumanizing and psychologically degrading. People disposed are both physically and psychologically wounded. The colonial wound is more than physical, or it is both physical and psychological. Healing colonial wounds therefore requires not only legal justice but the self-gnoseological and aesthesic reconstitution of the wounded people. Colonial healing cannot be enacted by the state. But the officers of the state should be aware that in their unilateral decisions in the name of the well-being of the nation, the beneficiaries of the imagined nations are not necessarily all the people inhabiting a given state. However, dehumanization is not a concern that is prioritized in modern/colonial relations, both domestic and international. The main concerns and goals are to control, to manage, and to possess. When it comes to nations, the primary goals are articulated in the name of the state. Second in importance are the benefits to the citizens of the state who enact the dispossession, and third are the interests of the nonnationals being dispossessed. The underlying logic of dehumanization is propelled by racism. Here we touch again on one of the major drawbacks of the modern nation-state: *nationals have priorities over nonnationals*, which means that *the nation-state privileges nationals over other human beings*. Second, nationals ethnically identified with the state have priorities over nationals (that is, legal citizens) who do not belong to the monoethnic nationality identified with the state. That is why the idea of plurinational states (such as Bolivia and Ecuador) is important, if for no other reason than to reveal the fiction sustaining the idea that to one state shall correspond one and only one nation. One of the tasks of decolonial politics is to show how the nation-state has become a dead end of governance and how it must open its horizons of authority in ways that also constrain its rulers, as the Zapatistas have been telling us (see chapter 13). This dead end is the open violence the state can no longer hide. The Nazi genocide was one such instance, "justified" by the assumed priority of ethnic Germans over German Jews, who supposedly endangered the nation-state's homogeneity. Today, Palestinians are at once foreigners in the State of Israel, and even those who live there, though they be considered citizens, do not belong to the ethnicity with which the State of Israel identifies.

VIII

The point of this section is to sort out the politics of anti-Zionism from the politics of calling into question the nation-state. I have been arguing that it is necessary not only to uncouple Judaism from the State of Israel but also to uncouple Zionism from Judaism. If Judaism does not equal the State of Israel, then it is also important to uncouple Zionism (not limited to Jews, as Joe Biden pointed out and as I mentioned above) from the Hebrew faith of Judaism. The problem the international community has with Zionism is indeed a problem with the modern form of the nation-state and not with Judaism. There cannot be solutions to the Palestine/Israel conflict, neither within the nation-state form of governance, nor in the network of international conflicts and struggles for natural resources and territorial control—not so long as solutions are sought within the canonical concept of the nation-state. Let's recall Einstein once again: no solutions can be found by the same mindset that created the problem.

When Jewish Zionism came into being in the nineteenth century, it was the necessary response to, on the one hand, the long history of the Jewish diaspora and, on the other hand, the isolation and persecution the Jews had endured historically. Religious Jews were included in the formation of national communities, but the European Enlightenment and secularization prompted the emergence of secular Jews (*hiloni*, nonreligious Jews). Therefore, if Zionism is a Jewish national movement claiming the right of Jews to return to their historical birthplace (Zion, the land of Israel and Jerusalem), then it is consistent with the desire and the right of any community that has been dispossessed. In this regard, the formation of the Zionist project in nineteenth-century Europe responded to a predicament similar to that of all the Indigenous people of the planet who have been consistently dispossessed of their land since 1500: in the sixteenth century in America, in the nineteenth in New Zealand, Australia, and South Africa, and, following the Berlin Conference in 1884, the entire African population dispossessed by the European imperial states.

It is at this crossroads that Herzl's project played two cards: one, the liberation of the Jewish people, and two, the appropriation of discourses of dispossession. Regarding where the State of Israel might be created, Herzl considered obtaining land in Argentina, as described in chapter 3 (titled "Purchasing of Land") of his pamphlet *The Jewish State*: "Argentina is one of the most fertile countries in the world, extends over a vast area, has a sparse population and a mild climate. The Argentine Republic would derive considerable profit from the cession of a portion of its territory to us. The present infiltration of Jews has certainly produced some discontent, and it would be necessary to enlighten the Republic on the intrinsic difference of our new movement."[41]

However, Argentina was not so desirable as Palestine. Herzl's implication, discussed in chapter 5 of his pamphlet, is occupation (and dispossession) of the land from the people who were already living in Palestine: "Palestine is our ever-memorable historic home. The very name of Palestine would attract our people with a force of marvelous potency. If His Majesty the Sultan were to give us Palestine, we could in return undertake to regulate the whole finances of Turkey. We should there form a portion of a rampart of Europe against Asia, an outpost of civilization as opposed to barbarism. We should as a neutral State remain in contact with all Europe, which would have to guarantee our existence."[42] Argentina could not offer what Palestine could, and not only because the latter alone was the "ever-memorable historic home." Imagining that the Ottoman sultan would give Palestine to the Jews, Herzl declared that the State of Israel would form "a rampart of Europe against Asia, an outpost of civilization against barbarism." The two cards he played further imply that the Jews themselves would no longer be seen as "barbarians" but would be integrated into Western civilization in its struggle against barbarism.[43]

While the modern European nation-state provided a solution for nationals over foreigners and for ethnic-nationals identified with the state over nationals of other ethnicities not so identified, in the US this issue was sidestepped by the notion of "multiculturalism." Many "cultures" were acknowledged, particularly those that had not been assimilated in the "melting pot." Cultures became "minority" nationals identified with a hyphen (e.g., Asian-American, Native-American, Afro-American). National "Americans" do not require a hyphen because they are the citizens with whom the state is identified. Creation of the idea and the image of communities of birth (nationalism) also created their opposites, whose members would become targets of xenophobia. In the process, the larger picture of "humanity" was, and continues to be, lost. The consequences have been disastrous. I have already mentioned the Armenian genocide (1915), triggered when the idea of "national" was incorporated into the official discourse of the Ottoman sultanate, which contrasted with the conviviality the sultanate had been known for during the sixteenth and the seventeenth centuries.[44]

Other violent episodes of nationalism include the massive slaughter in Rwanda after the Belgians left the country, both at the time they left and again later, when the strong remaining nationalist sentiments produced the murderous clashes between Tutsis and Hutus. Beyond genocide, nationalism armed with the power of the state has, around the globe, created a sickening catalog of further dispossessions, wars, and violence. Not surprisingly, the State of Israel, once established, has not escaped the logic of coloniality embedded in the form of the nation-state. Before the creation of Israel, Jewish Zionism was a movement of liberation by and for the Jewish people, be they religious or secular. To what extent Zionist Jews had a clear geopolitical vision of what it would mean to create a Zionist state in the Middle East, and to what extent that was also an ambition of the western European imperial states supporting the Zionist project, are matters that deserve special attention. Here I am concerned only that Zionism was a project of liberation that sought support from the western European imperial states (mainly England), and that, most important, once Israel was created, Zionism became a state ideology with a legal and military apparatus to defend the interests of Israeli national citizens. The recognition of the humanity of nonnationals was lost.

This is one of the points Marc Ellis has made: that in coming into being Israel has become not only un-Jewish but also, and because of that, unhuman. Significantly, this is not an ad hominem charge against the State of Israel. It is a charge leveled against the modern European, imperial nation-state form of governance, of which Israel is one specific manifestation.[45] The creation of the State of Israel was not only due to the actions of secular Jews who, in Europe, worked hard to advocate for the right of the Jewish people to return to their native Promised Land. That idea could not even have emerged in the seventeenth century, when the concept of the nation-state was not in place; nor in nineteenth-century Australia, Argentina, or South Africa, all places with significant numbers of Jews, but where the nation-state was either unknown or known merely as a distant species of government. Furthermore, as I have argued, the State of Israel came into being due to the work of Western imperial interests playing a double card: "solving" a problem that a European state had created (the Jewish genocide under Hitler) while keeping an eye on the checkerboard of international politics to find a solution to the mess the British created in the Middle East. From the viewpoint of Jews themselves, at some point in the process they had two different ways to regard their future: *having* their own land (a secular solution) and *returning to* their own land (a religious solution). In the first case, the main issue was that the creation of a state could have been established in other places; Argentina was one such place. In the second case, a *return* meant the creation of a state in Zion. All this was due also to the particular circumstances in which England found itself after defeating the Ottoman sultanate and taking control of Jerusalem from 1922 until 1948.

IX

In closing, the nation-state form of governance has two faces: one domestic, the other interstate (equivocally named "international"). Because of the systemic articulation of the nation-state in the colonial matrix of power, the prospect of solving the Palestine/Israel conflict does not look hopeful in the short term. Given this situation, it may be helpful to reflect, briefly and separately, first, on a moment occurring in the territory shared by Israelis and Palestinians,

President Barack Obama's visit to Israel in 2013; and second, on the international problems posed by Iran and Syria. However, the view of these events is affected by President Donald Trump's recognition in 2018 of Jerusalem as the capital city of the State of Israel, and by the more recent signed agreement between the US, Israel, and the Arab Emirates.[46]

Obama's 2013 visit to Israel had several overlapping agendas and a clear message, which was to continue the talks toward a peaceful resolution of the conflict and to reiterate that "a two-state solution is possible," a formula for delaying the solution that did not fool the Palestinians.[47] Second, Syria and Iran, two nations that in the Arab world were once roughly comparable in terms of the way they were governed and the relative level of development they had achieved, are territories that in Western perspectives seem to be viewed as economically and geopolitically very constrained by much greater powers outside their borders. They might be said to stand for two opposite arguments on a continuum that includes present-day Iraq between them, at least in Western eyes. The "unknowns" in their future are Russia to their north and China to their east. The State of Israel may very well be situated at the crossroads of global forces and conflicts, beyond the local tension with Palestine. From 2013 to 2017 the state of affairs did not improve, and it may yet not improve, for the Palestine/Israel conflict is related not only to the reconfiguration of the field of forces in the Middle East, whose center of focus in 2017 was Syria, but also to the increasingly evident fact that the Middle East is also West Asia.[48] The bottom line at this point is that the US and the European Union, and in a more ambiguous way the state of Israel, are confronted by three Asiatic powerhouses: Russia, China, and increasingly Iran.[49]

It is worth repeating, as the outcome of my argument, that being anti-Zionist is not being anti-Jewish (a confusion that is still prevalent among many people); rather, it is being anti-nation-state, or, better yet, calling into question the idea and the assumption that the nation-state is and should be a global/universal form of governance for all time. What are the options? No government? Of any kind? I see three possible directions. I have no blueprint, but trajectories are being worked out toward possible futures and unknown outcomes, and in all of them I see the nation-state nearing exhaustion. Whether it will remain the model for governance and the broker of interstate relations is difficult to say. The bottom line is that, while the State of Israel presupposed the secular European and modern nation-state form, a solution to the Palestine/Israel conflict will hardly be found within the same framework that created the conflict. Meanwhile, the planet is experiencing the politicization of civil society (growing constituencies demanding dignity) as well as the emergence of a political society that is global. The solution to the Palestine/Israel conflict must be thought out in forms of governance that offer alternatives to the nation-state, which created the conditions by which Zionism could emerge in the modern/colonial world order.

It should be remembered that Jews were perceived by Western Christians with suspicion when Western Christians' territories became European territories, before Western civilization was conceived. There were good reasons then for Christians to expel Jews and Muslims from the Iberian Peninsula. The Western imaginary changed after the creation of the State of Israel. On this topic, see Reyes Mate, *Memory of the West*, and Santiago Slabodsky, *Decolonial Judaism*. Last but not least, it should be remembered that by "decolonizing the state" I mean first and foremost decolonizing the Western political theory that made sense and supported the state. Not much can be done by changing administrations and legislating public policies that change the content but leave the logic and the frame of mind (terms of the conversations) of such form of governance intact. Second, decolonizing the state means also working toward communal forms of governance that integrate the social with Earth and the cosmos and are predicated on the principles of harmony rather than competition, love instead of hate, reciprocity instead of consumerism, care for life and creativity rather than justifying death and destruction.

Related to these issues, in part II of the book I explore aspects of cosmopolitanism, human rights, and life rights. The first two issues have served well in the rhetoric of modernity to justify the implementation of the logic of coloniality. The third is an issue addressed by many today on the planet in projects that allow people to live in harmony in spite of the fact that the nation-state (bourgeois or monarchic) discourages and prevents them/us from living in plenitude.

COSMOPOLITANISM, DECOLONIALITY, AND **RIGHTS**

PART II

5   The Many Faces of Cosmo-polis

I   The Scenario

In this and the following two chapters, I explore the invisible collusion between cosmopolitanism, human rights, and life rights—life rights for humans on the planet and for the planet itself. My argument in these chapters—as it was throughout part I—is that the rhetoric of modernity regarding salvation, peace, progress, democracy, human rights, development, rough and dangerous states, etc., hides or diverts attention from global designs advanced by the logic of coloniality. The actors (Man/Human; see chapter 12) who created the problems of coloniality are trapped in the rhetoric to justify coloniality. Maintaining and intensifying the rhetoric of Westernization has driven re-Westernization under former presidents Obama and Trump, in spite of their differing rhetoric, to an anxious defense of Western modernity. Re-Westernization has become the global counterrevolutionary politics. However, Western global designs, in the past and in the present, did not go without contests, dissents, and responses. One type of response concerns me here: the advent of border thinking and the emergence of decoloniality (without this name) in the sixteenth century, a development that runs its course, increasing in visibility and influence, into the twenty-first century (see the introduction to this volume, specifically section III). I begin with cosmopolitanism.

II   Cosmopolitanism, Globalization, or Globalism?

How shall cosmopolitanism be conceived in relation to globalism, globalization, capitalism, and modernity? Globalism drives our attention to global designs, which presuppose actors and institutions. Designs do not make themselves, and they have been made neither by God nor by such an abstract actor as "history." Designs are necessarily made by human agencies, supposedly before something happens. But they can be made to give sense and orientation to what is happening and that did not have yet a design. Coloniality of power is such a case: the will to power that presented itself with the unexpected "discovery" of America had to be reoriented, and that reorientation resulted in the making of an instrument: the colonial matrix of power (CMP). In this sense, designing an instrument to reorient the will to power resulted in "the coloniality of power." We could call this breakthrough the "colonial revolution"—the revolution that established the foundations of the European idea of modernity. The "discovery of America" was such a black swan. Global designs emerged at this point. Global linear thinking appeared after this "discovery," not before. Globalism is the projected design (or set of designs) that began to emerge in this moment, while "globalization" is the recent term in the rhetoric of modernity to make believe that history just happens without human designs. Although there is truth in that statement, the rhetoric of modernity provides the designs that highlight and interpret historical events while covering with smoke the unaccountable.

Although in some contexts I use "globalism/globalization" to invoke the full spectrum of responses these terms give rise to, "globalization," as distinct from "globalism," hides the moment of creation in which the global designs of globalism emerge and instead directs our attention to the outcome of these designs, as if this outcome were a "natural" consequence of universal history.[1] The geopolitical imaginary nourished by the term and the processes of globalization at the end of the twentieth century lay claim to the homogeneity of the planet from a perspective high above it—economically, politically, and culturally. Behind this homogenizing scenario were neoliberalism and the continuation of a long-lasting tradition of global designs. I use the term "cosmopolitanism" as a counter to "globalization," although not necessarily in the sense of globalization from below, not from a grassroots level, so to speak. Interestingly, no one talks about "cosmopolitanization" being parallel to globalization as "cosmopolitanism" is parallel to globalism. Cosmopolitanism is accepted as a project, while globalization suggests that it is history itself, independent of the *anthropos*/humans doing the work. My take on it is summed up in the term "cosmopolitan localism." If there is room for cosmopolitanism today it cannot be top-down, as per the Kantian legacy. Cosmopolitanism cannot be a single and global design. It should come from the diversity of planetary *locals* that are embarking in common, horizontal, and plural global designs. Cosmopolitan localism is tantamount to pluriversality. Modern and postmodern cosmopolitanism are tantamount to universality.

How shall we understand cosmopolitanism in relation to these two sides of it and in relation to globalization/globalism? Notice first of all that two decades into the twenty-first century the meaning of globalization/globalism is changing, for today there is no longer only the West projecting global designs, *but so far only the West conflates globalism with universalism.* China's "new Silk Road"—its commitment of billions of dollars to new infrastructure financing and development aid throughout Asia, the Middle East, Africa, and Europe—is countering the unipolarity of globalism, and China, together with Russia, is disrupting Western neoliberal designs to homogenize the world. China and Russia are capitalist but are not neoliberal.[2] Disrupting the last global design (neoliberalism) means disputing the controlling management of the CMP.

Let's assume, then, that globalization covers up (via the rhetoric of modernity) the outcome of a set of designs to manage the world (globalism), while top-down cosmopolitanism is a set of projects directed toward planetary conviviality according to a single cosmo-experience and cosmo-vision based on monocivilizational experiences. Coexisting with both *decolonial* cosmopolitan, localism would be *one set of* many other designs toward harmony and conviviality. *Cosmopolitan localism is horizontal, not vertical—neither top-down or bottom-up.* And it is not, of course, a global blueprint. If the goal to achieve is cosmopolitan localism, there cannot be a universal model of how to achieve it. For if decolonial cosmopolitan localism were the only one, it would be a universal cosmopolitanism, à la Kant, under the mask of Kant's projected cosmopolitan designs from above. Decolonial cosmopolitan localism, being horizontal, is from the South, the North, the East, and the West (see chapters 8, 9, and 10). One suspects that globalism and cosmopolitanism may then be two synchronized projects mutually supporting each other. However, they are far apart from cosmopolitan localism. The first seeks profits through competition and conviviality under capitalism; the second seeks harmony and conviviality in spite of capitalism and globalism.

The first global design for the modern world was Christianity, a cause (Western Christianity's need to expand after its defeat in the Crusades) and a consequence of the incorporation of the Americas into the global vision of an Orbis Christianus.[3] The unexpected "discovery" of the Americas, a land ready to be absorbed into the Orbis Christianus, was exactly what sixteenth-century

Christianity needed. It preceded the British and French secular civilizing mission: their intention to civilize the world under the model of the modern European nation-states. Christianity's global designs (e.g., globalism) were one sphere of the European Renaissance and were constitutive of modernity, while seen from its darker side, coloniality, the rhetoric of salvation meant submission, facilitating the merchants' and the adventurers' search for wealth through dispossession of land, exploitation of labor, the slave trade, etc. All aspects of life in Europe and their colonies in the New World (their only colonies at that point) began to change. At the moment that the secular cosmopolitan project (cosmopolitanism) arose, the centrality of the Christian project was displaced. Conversion was displaced by civilization achieved in the name of secular progress: this was Kant's cosmopolitanism.

Both cosmopolitanisms, in spite of their significant differences, have been at work in their respective historical periods of the modern/colonial world order. During the Renaissance, the expression was the Latin *orbis* and *universum*; during the Enlightenment, "cosmopolitanism" was derived from the Greek *kosmos*, not from its Latin translations. "Orbis Christianus" named a religious project; "cosmopolitanism" a secular one. Both, however, were ingrained with coloniality and with the modern/colonial world order. The colonization of the Americas in the sixteenth and seventeenth centuries, and of Africa and Asia in the nineteenth and early twentieth centuries, consolidated a particular idea of the West, a geopolitical image that reflected a chronological movement toward global ordering. Three overlapping macro narratives contributed to building and maintaining this image. In the first narrative, the West originates temporally and geographically in Greece and moves northwest of the Mediterranean to the North Atlantic. The point of origination is Greece, even though the narrative itself was created during the European Renaissance.

The second narrative is an outgrowth of the first. In it the West is self-conceived, by actors controlling narratives and institutions, as *"les modernes"* (the moderns) distinct from *"les anciens"* (the old). This binary chronological idea and image was devised during the Renaissance and with the expansion of capitalism through the Atlantic commercial circuits. In the third narrative, Western modernity is located in northern Europe, where it bears the distinctive trademark of the Enlightenment and the French Revolution. While the first narrative emphasizes the geographical marker "West" as the keyword of its ideological formation as Western civilization, the second and third narratives correlated the West more strongly with modernity. Since the three narratives are not generally distinguished, their cumulative effect has been instrumental in establishing the idea of Western universality relevant for all rather than just for Westerners. The confusion of the said (universal) with the saying (western Europeans), the confusion of the enunciated with the enunciation was a successful confusion to secure Eurocentrism. Eurocentrism is not a geographic but an epistemic concept. In the process, coloniality was enacted but hidden. Coloniality, as the constitutive side of modernity, emerged from the latter two narratives and their corresponding global designs, which, as a consequence, bound cosmopolitanism intrinsically to coloniality. We could add that the fourth and fifth narratives were eventually set in place, these being development and modernization after WWII, and globalization since the late 1970s and 1980s, when the word "globalization" masked neoliberal globalism.

I am not implying that it is improper to conceive and analyze cosmopolitan projects beyond these parameters.[4] I am simply stating that I look at cosmopolitan projects within the scope and the frame of modernity/coloniality (i.e., the CMP)—that is, located chronologically in the 1500s and spatially in the northwestern Mediterranean and the North Atlantic. While it is possible to imagine a history that, à la Hegel, would begin with the origin of humanity (instead of beginning in ancient China), it is also possible to tell stories with different beginnings, which are no less arbitrary than to proclaim the beginning with the origin of organic life on earth, or of Western civilization, or more recently of the era of the anthropos (the Anthropocene). The crucial point is not when and where the beginning is located, but where and why, what for, and by whom. The enunciation (the act of enunciating, which presupposes actors, languages, and institutions; see introduction, section III) takes precedence over the enunciated, although the perceiver perceives the enunciated first (be it oral, written, visual, or aural). That is: what are the geohistorical and ideological motivations that shaped the frame of such macro narratives grounded on the common presupposition of Western universality? Narratives with a cosmopolitan orientation could be at the same time managerial and emancipatory. For example, expelling the Muslims from the Iberian Peninsula was a liberation for Christians, while at the same time, Christians' occupation of First Nations territories in the Americas was the seed of their imperial consolidation and subsequent expansion. Kant encouraged people to emancipate from our nonage at the same time that the emancipation founded his managerial cosmopolitan project: "Enlightenment is man's emergence from his self-imposed nonage. Nonage is the inability to use one's own understanding without another's guidance. This nonage is self-imposed if its cause lies not in lack of understanding but in indecision and lack of courage to use one's own mind without another's guidance. *Dare to know*! (*Sapere aude*.) 'Have the courage to use your own understanding,' is therefore the motto of the enlightenment."[5] Marx proposed emancipation from liberalism and capitalism, simultaneous with the managerial project of a proletarian dictatorship. The need for decolonial cosmopolitan localism arises from the shortcomings of the three previous projects. The specific cosmopolitanism I am arguing for here is decolonial in that it consists of delinking from the universal aims of previous ones. It promotes a pluriversality grounded in dwelling on the borders between universal cosmopolitanisms and the local histories that the three (as well as the fourth and fifth) versions of Western cosmopolitanism attempted to erase. Conviviality cannot be attained by the imposition of the "right and true" cosmopolitan project. Conviviality is only possible if each locale recognizes the limits of its own understanding of cosmopolitan conviviality and accepts that there is no one single design to be imposed over all others. Cultural relativism? No. Pluriversality as a universal project instead. Once universal global designs are no longer in place and the aim is to live together convivially instead of competitively, the will to cooperate displaces the will to dominate.

III Modern/Critical Cosmopolitanism and Decolonial Cosmopolitan Localism

Decolonial cosmopolitan localism is in itself critical and doesn't need the modifier, but modern and postmodern cosmopolitanisms, to be distinguished from Kantian (modern critical cosmopolitanism) legacies, need the modifier. My story begins, then, with the emergence of a rhetoric of salvation in Renaissance modernity and a logic of coloniality that arose and was implemented in the emerging colonies of the Atlantic world with the slave trade. Cosmopolitan narratives as well as narratives of global designs shaped the imaginary of modernity. Coloniality, the darker side of modernity, remains elusive due to the fact that most stories of modernity have been told from the perspective of modernity itself, including, of course, those told by its internal critics, like Las Casas and Marx, Nietzsche and Freud. There is a need to reconceive cosmopolitanism from the perspective of the consequences of coloniality—which I conceive as (decolonial) cosmopolitan localism. Decolonial cosmopolitanism has to be conceived historically, from the sixteenth century until today, and geographically, from the interplay between a growing capitalism in the Mediterranean and the (North) Atlantic, as well as from an expanding colonialism in other areas of the planet: South and East but also North and West. Thus, to the geohistory of modernity/coloniality correspond the geohistorical decolonial responses worldwide (from *kosmos* to *orbis* to *world*). The two types of variegated responses are de-Westernization (state-led projects) and decoloniality (people-led projects).

In this conception, I need to uncouple, on the one hand, cosmopolitanism from global designs and, on the other, cosmopolitan projects from decolonial cosmopolitan localism. While global designs are driven by the will to control and homogenize—either from the right or from the left, as in the Christian (theological) and the civilizing (secular) missions, or in the planetary revolution of the proletariat—cosmopolitan projects can be complementary or antagonistic with regard to global designs. Cosmopolitanism from above (modern and postmodern) complements globalism; local cosmopolitanisms (decolonial or not) are dissenting and delinking from both globalism and cosmopolitanism from above. This is the tension we find in de Vitoria, Kant, and Marx, for example. In the sixteenth century, after emancipating from Islam, the Christian mission embraced both global designs of conversion and the justification of war, on the one hand. On the other, dissenting positions emerged, denouncing the double standard of Christian salvation: Bartolomé de Las Casas preached salvation from the devil by converting to Christianity the people inhabiting the land at the same time that their codices were burned, their civilizations destroyed, and their land expropriated. De Las Casas's rhetoric of salvation by conversion set up the foundation of the rhetoric of modernity for centuries to come: salvation by civilization and progress, by development and modernization, by market democracy. In the same movement of constitution, the rhetoric of modernity legitimizes destitutions: book burning, expropriation of land, exploitation of labor, manipulation of debt, etc.

A similar argument could be made with respect to global designs articulated by the British and French colonial projects of civilizing missions as well as the declaration, in France, of the "rights of man and of the citizen" as an emancipating project (see the next two chapters). Such arguments open up an internal critical perspective on theological Christian global designs at the same time that the civilizing mission was a secular continuation of the Christian conversion: the rights of man and of the citizen left out women, racialized people in Europe, and non-Europeans. The first enacted the intramural colonial difference, the second the extramural, which impinged on the making of imperial differences: civilizations that did not endure settler colonialism but did not escape coloniality. Hence, the imperial difference undergirds imperial discourses of Westernization and re-Westernization (e.g., today's Western demonization of Russia and China). One could say that colonial and imperial differences are the inherent contradictions of modernity. Decolonially speaking, however, they are not contradictions as explained above; they compound the double standards of the salvationist and the civilizing rhetoric of modernity hiding the logic of coloniality. In the first case, secularization (a civilizing mission) of the theological mission (salvation by conversion) was a Western intramural change of hands managing the coloniality of power narrated as progress; in the second case, global designs hid the assumptions that the designation of Man/Human was not to be projected to all human beings who were considered—by the cast of actors and institutions projecting the racial colonial difference—to be not properly Human (see the introduction, section III.2, and chapter 12).

The Haitian Revolution was one of the visible signs of the compound rhetoric of modernity and logic of coloniality: revolutionaries appropriated both the meaning of revolution and the rights of men taking freedom in their own hands when imperial global design, epistemic and political, did not grant them the knowledge and the savoir faire reserved to Man/Human (see chapter 12). The splendors and miseries of the Haitian Revolution are the same ones that have plagued all decolonial revolutions during the Cold War. Global designs *appear contradictory* because they are narrated in the name of goodness for all (e.g., modernity), especially for those whom the narratives claim to save (by conversion, civilization, development, globalism) and because, according to this one-sided narrative, "they need to be saved." There is no contradiction if you read the narratives and the events decolonially: the rhetoric of modernity carries with it the logic of coloniality. Any project to "do good for others," without allowing the others to do what they need to do, is a modern/colonial one. It is how modernity/coloniality works: there is no modernity without coloniality—no contradiction here, but a compound of global designs—a thesis that is central to decolonial thinking after Aníbal Quijano. "Capitalism's contradictions" is an expression of high currency. You could see contradiction in capitalism if you expected capitalism to be democratic and to care for equality, but that requirement is not imbedded in capitalist projects. So, no contradiction here either: progress and poverty are two sides of the same coin. Contradictions are perceived from the perspective of Western modernity built on the binary opposition either/or.

Salvation by conversion and civilizing by progress are two chapters of Western globalist and cosmopolitan designs. The Christian (theological, Renaissance) and civilizing (secular, Enlightenment) missions shared the will to dominate as their final goal, while cosmopolitan projects such as de Vitoria's and Kant's were attentive to the dangers and the excesses of global designs. Being attentive, however, did not prevent them from falling into the trap. Since 1959, modernization and development have been the keywords of a renovated mission and, therefore, of a renovation of the colonial matrix of power that displaced the Christian (Spanish) and civilizing (English, French) missions at once after WWII. Development and modernization became the new rhetoric displacing progress and civilization. The road was paved for the revival of cosmopolitanism in the 1990s, parallel to neoliberal globalism (market democracy), which follows the historical pattern. De Vitoria's *ius gentium* runs parallel to the first wave of Western expansion, Kant's cosmopolitanism with the second wave, and today's cosmopolitanism follows with a third wave: neoliberal globalism. None of these cosmopolitan projects fomented globalism from below. They offered, nonetheless, a counterposition to state (theological-monarchic or secular nation-state) imperial global designs, although within the same cosmology (Western civilization) in which global designs were thought out, transformed, and implemented.

The cosmopolitan projects I have identified arose from and constituted the narratives of modernity after the Renaissance. For that reason, they could not escape coloniality because coloniality is constitutive of modernity. Thus, their critical dimensions remain modern and must be distinguished from what I am describing here as (decolonial) cosmopolitan localism, which I conceive as the necessary project of an increasingly transnational (and nonnational) world order, at once both multipolar and pluriversal, confronting Western efforts to maintain leadership in a unipolar world order supported by the universality of knowledge. And I place "decolonial" in parentheses to highlight that by using the modifier "decolonial" I understand and construct cosmopolitan localism as pluriversal localism rather than as a "new" universal design. Decolonial cosmopolitan localism emerged and prospers from the energy of exteriority: the destituted of coloniality justified by the rhetoric of modernity (see introduction, section III.2 and III.3). By "exteriority" I do not mean something lying untouched beyond and outside the CMP and untouched by narratives promoting modernity. On the contrary, without modernity/coloniality there is no exteriority (i.e., the idea of the outside that legitimizes the idea of the inside), and without exteriority there would be no need for decoloniality. Exteriority therefore is the outside *made, invented* by the inside in the process of constituting itself as inside: exteriority is the ontological consequence of epistemic colonial and imperial differences whose enactment impinges on people's subjectivity (aesthesis) and on interstate world order. Traditions, barbarians, primitives, communists, terrorists: all are labels fabricating and portraying exteriorities. They are the effects of knowledge, not representations of realities. None of these concepts name a reality that preexists modernity; they are epistemic concepts intended to pass for ontological ones.

Exteriority is the mark, the line, of the borderlands. The line that indicates who is in and who is out, people and regions, knowledges and beliefs, languages and ethnicities, gender and sexualities. If you happen to feel and/or to know that you inhabit the exteriority, that you are seen as such, and you sense/know it because of dominant narratives in which you do not fit racially, sexually, nationally, religiously, epistemically, etc.—then you inhabit exteriority. You inhabit the borderlands and "see and sense" the borderlines. Then whatever you sense, think, and do will be border sensing, border thinking, border doing. And if you engage in cosmopolitanism then you will want to engage in decolonial cosmopolitan localism with people who in diverse regions, histories, and languages sense that they have been placed in exteriority. Cosmopolitan localism becomes the path and design of world making that creates global communal sites where the praxis of living, sensing, and doing does not fit in modern global designs or modern global cosmopolitanism. If CMP is held together by the energies of domination/exploitation and oppression/conflict, decolonial cosmopolitan localism is the energy of gnoseological and aesthesic reconstitutions.

Decolonial cosmopolitan localism, in the last analysis, intends to put on the table other options beyond both benevolent recognition and humanitarian pleas for inclusion.[6] The problem with recognition and inclusion is that benevolence and humanitarianism serve as masks to protect the privileges of those who recognize and include. It so happens that many of, if not all, the people to which recognition and inclusion are extended do not want to be recognized or included.[7] Although not speaking the language of "cosmopolitanism," First Nations scholars, intellectuals, artists, and activists in Canada are already well advanced in the arguments rejecting the discourse of recognition and inclusion. Their languages are anchored in both the resurgence of indigeneity and in a decolonial delinking from settlers' regulations.[8]

The difference, the enormous and irreducible difference, between modern (critical) cosmopolitanism on the one hand and decolonial cosmopolitan localism on the other is that the former operates within the *interiority* that invents the outside, that builds *exteriority* to maintain cosmopolitanism within and to eject to exteriority the undesired; while the latter builds and operates in the *exteriority* (e.g., the invented "other" confronting the inventing "same").[9] *Decolonial cosmopolitan localism, operating in exteriority, puts in motion gnoseological and aesthesic reconstitutions* (see introduction, section III.3). Today, modern (critical) cosmopolitanism uncoupled from the nation-state cannot absorb immigrants and refugees. Decolonial cosmopolitan localism is limited at this point to influencing public policy as long as the policy remains in the frame of mind of modern states and modern nations, but it is contributing to creating another frame of mind showing the injustice of globalism and the shortcomings of modern and postmodern cosmopolitanism. However, and in spite of its current limitations in this respect, decolonial cosmopolitan localism is instrumental in changing the terms of the conversation by changing the questions asked and reorienting the public opinion that could make powerful appeals to state institutions. These are the junctions where decolonial and cosmopolitan (convivial) modes of reexistence could be and are being built.

IV Cosmopolitanism and Quijano's Heterogeneous Historic-Structural Nodes

Grasping the distinctions I have drawn between global designs, modern (and critical) cosmopolitanism, and decolonial cosmopolitan localism (a concept I explore in *The Darker Side of Western Modernity*) presupposes that they have in common the complex geopolitical scenario that I explore in this chapter.[10]

I will examine here three historical and mutually complementing manifestations, and will sketch a fourth, all of which help us to understand the overall operation of the CMP (which cosmopolitan localism confronts) and the two faces of modernity/coloniality from the sixteenth century until the end of the twentieth century. It is a premise of my argument that I am not constructing a historiographical narrative but *a conceptual understanding of the CMP's history*. The four manifestations should be conceived not within a single linear narrative of succession but rather in terms of their multiple diachronic coexistences in the global times of their geohistorical locations. Rather than imagining events in a linear succession, the narratives that follow tell the story of events occurring at heterogeneous historical-structural nodes, coexistences, and multiple temporalities: one set of events took place from the sixteenth to the eighteenth century, the second from the eighteenth century to WWII, the third from WWII to the end of the twentieth century, and the fourth after the end of the Cold War and into the twenty-first century. However, because of the epistemic hegemony of the Western concept of time, the structural nodes cannot be perceived outside of it but shall not be absorbed into and limited by it: linear is the modern way of understanding complex heterogenous historic-structural nodes. The concept of historical-structural nodes allows us to examine coexisting ontic temporalities that have been relegated to the past by the rhetoric of modernity: what Johannes Fabian described as a "denial of coevalness."[11] Western epistemic appropriation of the concept of time is constitutive of the rhetoric of modernity in its devaluing and destitution of coexisting temporalities (e.g., civilization and progress/barbarism and tradition; development/

underdevelopment; globalization/localism). Western universal linear time locates the narrated events into one single and homogenous space in which all localities lose their singularity, absorbed into the unlocated universal.

Historical-structural nodes entangle the unilinear temporality of the CMP with the multiple temporalities of global exteriorities (from the parallel times of Abya-Yala and Latin America, to the times of Asia and of the African continent). Hence, while each node is determined by the unilinear temporality of the CMP, each node actualizes at the same time the multiple temporalities that it entangles. For instance, the temporality of Western civilization, narrated from its local time, is not the same temporality of the history of First Nations in the Americas (before and after 1452), China (before and after the Opium Wars), or Africa (before and after the Dutch invasion, 1652). Western history maintained its own local temporality that was rendered as universal time. All coexisting temporalities had to either bend and accept it, or engage in gnoseological and aesthesic reconstitutions to regain and affirm what had been destituted and disavowed.

Historically, the ideological configuration of one moment or node (let's say one year in the global—not universal—calendar) does not vanish when the second moment arrives, but it is reconfigured. None of the local histories in every continent stopped when the Europeans arrived. They were entangled and absorbed into the single time frame of Western narratives *about* the entire planet. People began to live in two temporalities, in a time borderline in all dimensions of their lives: coexisting in the local time of the invaded settlers and their own local Indigenous temporality. On the other hand, in the linear time of Western historical narratives, the Renaissance did not disappear with the Enlightenment. Neither did liberalism vanish with the emergence of Marxism, nor Christianity after its displacement by liberal and Marxist projects. However, the temporality of Islam is not the same, and it did not stop when Christianity, liberalism, and Marxism became dominant narratives. It has coexisted and coexists in conflict until now. Confucius may have been sidelined in Chinese memory and history with the invasion of Western concepts, but he never went away, and today he is returning, adumbrating the cultural heterogeneous historic-structural node that is also manifested in the trade war between the US and China. All these are coexisting temporalities of Western and non-Western civilizations, are the consequences of the simultaneous movement constitution/destitution of the CMP. It is from the destituted exteriority that the decolonial option emerges as processes of reconstitution of the destituted.

The fourth manifestation I promised to sketch above is chronologically located after the end of the Cold War and could be characterized as a new chapter of the modern/colonial world order. De-Westernization is halting the unilinear march of global designs by disputing the management and control of the CMP (see chapters 8, 9, and 10 of this book). The current heterogeneous historic-structural node—in which political confrontations between re- and de-Westernization dispute control of the CMP, while a wide range of people's uprisings defy both—is the sign of a change of epoch, not merely an epoch of change. The epoch in which changes, revolutions, and various "post-" phenomena were the engine of the CMP within Western and re-Westernizing global designs (from Christian theology to secular neoliberalism and the efforts to reconfigure Marxism) is closing. The change of epoch is marked by the dispute over control of the CMP and by the global awakening of people's understanding that neither re-Westernization nor de-Westernization—neither the state nor the banks and the corporations—will care for them or have much to offer. I call decoloniality at large an orientation toward the awareness and the will to delink from re- and de-Westernization, and a call for the politics of decolonial investigations to assist in gnoseological and aesthesic reconstitutions to break the chains of all either/or prison houses of the imagination.

The first of the four heterogenous historic-structural nodes brought about the foundation of the CMP and was led by Spanish and Portuguese settlers and commercial colonialism in America and Asia (Philippines, Macao, Formosa, now Taiwan), which ran parallel to the Christian mission. Stated more simply: the political and economic spheres ran parallel to the cultural sphere that was dominated by Christian theology and humanistic education (e.g., the university transplanted to the Americas). Western temporalities interfered with local temporalities of the Americas and Asia. Africa was different. It had two types of disruption: the long-lasting slave trade, and the settlements beginning in 1652 led by the Dutch and British East Indian Companies.

The second node occurred in the eighteenth and nineteenth centuries when French and English colonialism took the lead in global design, secularizing the Christian mission of conversion and mutating it into the civilizing mission of the Enlightenment. The nation-state form of governance displaced the monarchy after the Peace of Westphalia (May–October 1648), the Glorious Revolution (1688), the American Revolution (1776), and the French Revolution (1789). China and India were disrupted in their temporality by the mid-nineteenth century in the concurrent events of the British settling in India, disrupting the Mughal sultanate, and managing the opium trade and the Opium Wars. The third node arose in the second half of the twentieth century—after WWII—when the US took over the leadership of the CMP.

Coloniality without settler colonialism, the fourth node, has run from the end of the Cold War to the present. It is centered in market democracy of neoliberal design, finances, and military bases that replaced colonial settlers. But this fourth stage also runs into the emergence of de-Westernization. It shows that the five hundred years of Westernization, consolidation, and expansion generated their own capitalist dissidence and reorientation. De-Westernization is nothing less than the resurgence of temporalities derided by the triumphal march of Western global designs and the colonial matrix of power. De-Westernization is not challenging the CMP; it is disputing who manages and controls it. Cosmopolitanism has many faces. Western modern cosmopolitanism (Kantian) aimed to homogenize the planet concurrent with the civilizing mission. It was refurbished by neoliberalism's attempts to homogenize the planet under market democracy. Modern (critical) cosmopolitanism looks like refurbishing liberalism to confront neoliberal designs. However, de-Westernization put a halt to all cosmopolitan projects that maintain Western global designs, even if critical.

De-Westernization may not have cosmopolitan programmatic ambitions and therefore a cosmopolitan theory. As for decolonial cosmopolitan localism, it promotes the resurgence of exteriorities that modernity disavowed (see chapter 13). Now, as we enter the third decade of the twenty-first century, we all are in the fourth node. We are witnessing, within the sphere of interstate relations, the flourishing conversations conducted in the de-Western vocabulary of multipolarity and the decolonial vocabulary of pluriversality.[12] These are conversations that involve all people who find themselves dwelling on both actual and figurative borders, be they the borders of de-Westernization or of decoloniality. The borders of de-Westernization are manifested in the sphere of interstate relations. De-Western border politics has to confront what Westernization wanted and wants them to do: by "them" I mean China, Russia, Iran, and to a certain extent Turkey. The US and the core of the EU do not enact border politics but rather territorial politics: the persistent aim to contain de-Westernization. Decoloniality, however, doesn't operate in the sphere of interstate politics but in the sphere of the political society, delinking from rather than disputing the management and control of the colonial matrix of power. Hence, "multipolarity" and "pluriversality" are two key terms that distinguish de-Westernization from decoloniality. All four historical nodes are characterized by conflicts between globalism and nationalism (the EU nightmare), and by an acceleration of multipolarity in interstate relations, and all this appeared in stark clarity with the campaign and election of Donald Trump and his rhetoric for re-Westernization ("Make America Great Again").[13] In contrast Xi Jinping has his "Vision of a Community with a Shared Future for Humankind." He has also been explicit that this is a vision that China proposes for a community of shared future, not a universal model but a Chinese model to share with other models for shared futures, not of competition but of cooperation. In his address to the Davos World Economic Forum of 2017, he said:

> China stands on its own conditions and experience. We inherit wisdom from the Chinese civilization, learning widely from the strengths of both east and west. We defend our way but are not rigid. We learn but do not copy from others. We formulate our own development path through continuous experimentations. . . . No country should put its own way on the pedestal as the only way.[14]

The point here is the following: from Kantian cosmopolitanism on, modern and postmodern have been formulated in the frame of Westernization from the perspective of Western civilization, and of *unipolarity in international relations*. De-Westernization, instead, introduced another vision: "a shared future for humankind." The proposal is formulated with full awareness of *multipolarity in international relations*. Multipolarity, by definition, prevents the possibility of a unipolar model for a multipolar shared future! But I suspect that this would be a Western interpretation based on unipolarity in international relations and universalism in epistemology and aesthetics.

Laying aside the sphere of interstate (or international) relations where neither modern (critical) nor decolonial cosmopolitan localism has much to say but little possibility of being heard, let us focus on the politics of decolonial investigations to advance cosmopolitan localisms in education at large (in and beyond institutional education) and in the public sphere. In this context, the question of "rights" is of particular import in cosmopolitan conversations, albeit with low hopes that intellectual and scholarly decolonial conversations in the public sphere will reach the United Nations Human Rights Office of the High Commissioner. The question of "rights," however, is crucial for cosmopolitan considerations within the frame of Western civilization as well as in de-Western and decolonial politics. We on the planet have arrived at the point where no one has the final word regarding who is violating "rights." Consequently, Western declarations of rights can no longer be legislated by Western actors, institutions, and laws. The Vision of a Community with a Shared Future for Humankind offers another platform to legislate questions of rights, domestically and internationally. Decolonial principles such as Sumak Kawsay (to live in harmony and plenitude among all the living on Earth, including the human species) offer still another platform, which I explore in chapter 7.

In this chapter, however, the question of rights is connected to cosmopolitan projects. Let's thus begin at the beginning.

In the sixteenth and the seventeenth centuries, "rights" were conceived as the rights of the "people" or the "nation" (territorially and ethnically conceived before the nation-state was constituted; see chapter 4) and were called *ius gentium*. From the eighteenth century onward, "rights" were discussed in terms of "man" and national citizenship (see chapter 12). After World War II, "rights" have been discussed in terms of "humanity" (as in, e.g., crimes against humanity). In light of these various conceptions, the continuity of global designs appears unimpeded and without mask for the simple reason that the rhetoric of defending human rights has been a justification to violate human rights. Human rights and democracy are, as Gandhi said about civilization, good ideas. Human rights therefore throw down the gauntlet to both (critical) modern and decolonial cosmopolitan localism: what do "human rights" and "global citizenship" accomplish when defending the nationals is more relevant than caring for human beings? Decolonially speaking, both have to be framed in relation to and across colonial differences. Immigrants and refugees have asked: Do human rights and global citizenship have meaning? Do they have status? Critical cosmopolitanism, modern and postmodern and cosmopolitan localism, must negotiate human rights and global citizenship without losing the historical dimensions in which each has been reconceived, today, within the colonial horizon of modernity. How they are negotiated will depend on where we begin the story. Do we begin with the history of Europe and the legislation of *ius gentium*, or do we begin from the European violations of *ius gentium* in the New World and from the principles of good government as stipulated by Guaman Poma de Ayala (see introduction, section III.3)? Or do we begin with similar cases, the specific times and local histories of the peoples whose "rights" were violated by European invasions through the centuries? The first beginning maintains the march of constitutions/destitutions, while the second beginning starts from the reconstitution of the destituted. Critical cosmopolitanism (modern and postmodern) operates within this frame. Cosmopolitan localism operates from the second. And here is where the politics of decolonial investigations is of the essence for gnoseological and aesthesic reconstitutions of the principles and assumptions on which the question of rights was established in the simultaneous movement of constitution/destitution. What cosmopolitanism can be will depend on the assumptions upon which cosmopolitan claims are made. Cosmopolitan claims that do not question the rhetoric of modernity remain within the movement of constitution/destitution in which the CMP operates. Decolonial cosmopolitan localism starts, instead, from the destituted and calls for gnoseological and aesthesic re-constitution, activating border thinking and advancing the politics of decolonial investigations. To which shall be added the de-Western approach in search of "a community with a shared future for humankind," in which the Western question of rights is approached from a Confucian (rather than a Christian theological and secular liberal) perspective.[15] Both cases, decolonial cosmo-politan localism and the de-Western vision of a shared future for humankind, argue from someplace else—from destituted locations. For that reason, border thinking is unavoidable since the question of rights has already been estab-lished. Hence, it cannot be ignored at the same time that it shall not be obeyed based on the terms and principles in which rights have been constituted in order to destitute.

Let us explore in more detail the coexistence (by which I mean not linear succession but rather several coexisting temporal lines entangled in historic-structural temporal nodes) of the four heterogenous historic-structural nodes, mentioned above, from the perspectives of religion, nation, and ideology in order to better understand the history of the CMP and the present scenario in which critical (modern and postmodern) cosmopolitanism became thinkable. Analysis of the CMP to which modern and postmodern critical cosmopolitan-ism respond is a necessary step toward understanding when and why cosmo-politan localism—as well as de-Westernizing rhetoric of a community with a shared future for humankind that demands Confucian (not liberal) human rights arguments—became thinkable.

V   From Orbis Universalis and Occidentalism
to Cosmo-polis and Eurocentrism

The sixteenth century was the first time in the history of humankind that a world map was drawn on which the continents of Africa, Asia, America, and Europe could be seen at once and connected on the basis of empirical information. The diversity of local cosmographies in complex civilizations (of China, India, Islam, Europe, Tawantinsuyu, Anahuac) were unified and subsumed by a world map drawn by cartographers of Christian Europe. The map, rather than the internet, was the first step toward the imaginary of the modern/colonial world order built in and by European visual images. "Orbis," not "cosmos" (as in the eighteenth century), was the preferred figure of speech, and it was a vital rhetorical figure in the Christian imaginary. The emergence of this imaginary happened in tandem with the growth of the Atlantic commercial circuits at the historical foundation of capitalism/colonialism that was also the initial configuration of modernity/

coloniality and of the CMP. I even suggest, following Quijano's pioneering work, that it was with the emergence of these Atlantic commercial circuits that the CMP arose and continued to expand, managed and controlled by Western Atlantic empires until the fall of the Soviet Union and the end of the twentieth century. This is the epoch of Westernization that is now closing.

Simultaneous with the mapping (constitution) of the planet and the suppression of local territorialities (destitutions), a turbulent intramural European situation unfolded that arose with Martin Luther's *Ninety-Five Theses* (1517) and continued throughout the century leading to the religious Thirty Years' War, which concluded with the Peace of Westphalia (1648). Parallel to these Christian conflicts, the search was underway for laws of the natural order that challenged, if did not completely dispense with, the need for an intervening God. Isaac Newton provided the "map" of nature (Earth and the universe) that was quickly taken as a model for the organization of society; Kant projected his own cosmopolitan vision following Newton's steps. Since the laws of nature applied to the universe (or at least to the solar system), the regulation of society by their principles could be conceived as universal, or at least as planetary. Finally, the path toward a universal secularism (or a secular universalism) was laid open by competing interpretations of Christian doctrine and continuing conflict between the three religions of the book: Christianity, Judaism, and Islam—all of which worked to render dubious the universality of the Christian God and the Christian's singular vision of the Orbis Christianus. One of the outcomes of this turbulence was the surfacing of cosmopolitan vision and ambition. The laws of nature could now be declared universal, precisely when a Christian God no longer could, and the law of nature (the cosmos) provided the basis for an idea of cosmopolitanism: the law of the *cosmos* discovered by Man displaced the law of the *orbis* regulated by God.

Within this local history, I am interested in a particular aspect of the idea of the cosmo-polis existing parallel to, and simultaneous with, the concept of the nation-state (see chapter 4). Once God became questionable, the pope and the emperor became questionable as well, and Orbis Christianus lost its power to unify communities. As the church came under scrutiny by an increasingly secular European world, the secular (modern and European) nation-state became sovereign. Those who were labeled infidels (gentiles, Jews, pagans) and were expelled from the Orbis, to its exteriority, mutated into the category of the foreigner of the state.[16] If Christians were those who inhabited the interiority of a transnational Orbis Christianus, citizens were then also inhabitants of the new, emergent space of the nation-state. In due course, the Renaissance idea of Man (for "human beings"; see chapter 12) was also reconfigured in the

Enlightenment and given center stage, thus eventually transcending the division between citizen and foreigner.[17] Philosophers who during the Enlightenment proposed the "rights of man and of the citizen" had difficulty understanding (or accepting) that Black "men" were taking their "rights" into their own hands. Michel-Rolph Trouillot has recently underlined this point in an argument that explains the silence surrounding the Haitian Revolution.[18] Silencing the past, as Trouillot words it, is precisely how the denial of coevalness works as the Haitian temporality and the dense history of the slave trade and of plantations that enriched Europe are absorbed and silenced. Philosophers who during the Renaissance asked themselves, "What is Man?" could not escape the fact that colonization was going on as they spoke. Man (European) was conquering, killing, dominating, and enslaving other beings thought to be equally human, if only by some. The European version of cosmo-polis shows its limits when the coeval colonial question is considered.

The logic of coloniality at work (destitution) was set in place in the sixteenth century during the well-known debates of Valladolid, between Juan Ginés de Sepúlveda and Bartolomé de Las Casas, concerning the degree of humanity of the "Indians."[19] By the eighteenth century the religion based on the rights of the people (ius gentium) was supplanted by the secular nation-state concomitant with the rights of man and of the citizen. This was the process of mutation between Man1 (the Renaissance) and Man2 (the Enlightenment; see chapter 12 of this book).

The debates removed the assumptions of Western Christianity about humanity and planted a doubt that would encumber future cosmopolitan ideals. Philosopher-theologians in Salamanca examined the ethical and legal circumstances of Spaniards in the Indias Occidentales, or the New World. The "Indian doubt," a doubt about their humanness, was defined around two issues: the right of Amerindians to the possession of their land, and the right of Spaniards to declare war against Indians. These inquiries circulated in Europe, first in manuscript form and later as the book entitled *Relectio de Indis*.[20] In published form, the inquiries were organized into three major issues:

1 Whether the original inhabitants of (for Spanish) the New World of Indias Occidentales were true "owners" of their lands and other properties and in control of their own social organization

2 Whether, instead, the emperor and the pope were "owners" and had the right to control both Amerindians and other non-Christian people (infidels), and

3 What the "legal entitlements" were that justified (from a Spanish point of view) Spanish domination of Amerindians

In today's terminology, de Vitoria's inquiry was principally concerned with the idea of "the inclusion of the other," which carries implications for both cosmopolitanism and human rights. Because he was concerned with legal justification for the crown's appropriation and (when necessary) dispossession of land, the political aspects of society and its international relations were examined with the assumption that every human and rational being (under Greek/Christian parameters) has a "natural right."[21] De Vitoria extended this principle to mean the "rights of the people" to adjudicate new questions of international relations raised by developments in the New World. Theology in de Vitoria (divergent from secular philosophy in Kant) was the ultimate ground on which to examine all kinds of human relations among individuals and among nations (pueblos, peoples). But his inquiries included also a profound ethical concern: to be a Christian meant to be self-conscious and to act consciously on behalf of the common good. Certainly, Christian ethical concerns were to de Vitoria no less honest or earnest than philosophical concerns were to philosophers of the Enlightenment, and the laws of nature were, of course, no better foundation on which to build arguments on behalf of the common good than were natural rights. De Vitoria did not have a fully developed notion of the nation-state (he was living under a monarchy and had Plato and Aristotle in his training), as there would be after the eighteenth century (viz., the bourgeois secular nation-state), but neither was one necessary given the historical conditions under which he was operating. While de Vitoria's horizon was the planetary realm opened to sixteenth-century Renaissance intellectuals and the encounter with people they did not know existed, the Enlightenment operated according to a different set of parameters—namely, European peace and the construction of the secular Europe of nations.

However, the seed of the future secular state did begin to emerge in de Vitoria, although it remained coupled with the church. An ethno-class that would take over the monarchy and the church would have been unimaginable to him. He removed the emperor and pope as "owners" of the world and of all imaginable communities, and he conceived a Christian theocratic state as the civil and spiritual center of society. The cosmopolitan ideology of possession enjoyed by the pope and emperor was replaced by de Vitoria's proposal in favor of international relations based on *derecho de gentes*, or the "right of the people" (community, nation). *Derecho de gentes*, which required the discussion and regulation of theology and jurisprudence, was then assigned to the monarchic-religion-state, instead of to the pope and emperor.

In the third part of *Relectio de Indis*, de Vitoria examined the "legal entitlements" that justified war against the Indians and enunciated a series of "fundamental rights" for people—meaning nations of human communities—the violation of which was justification of war. De Vitoria had a vision of a "natural society" grounded in communication, conviviality, and international collaboration. The word "cosmo-polis" was not used, but the concerns were there. De Vitoria's utopia was an Orbis Christianus: a planetary society or a world community of monarchic-religion-states founded on the principle of natural rights (instead of on the laws of nature) and subject to regulation by the religion-state. The "Indian doubt" was prompted at the same time as the emergence of the Atlantic commercial circuit—a crucial step in the formation of capitalism after Christianity's victory over the Moors and the Jews. Consequently, the question of "humanity" emerged in complicity with the question of "rights," both questions setting up the foundations of the CMP at the confluence of the law and the question of who has the right to legislate over whom. The management and control of authority encroaches on the management and control of the idea of the Human who legislates (see introduction, section III).

I have the impression that if one stripped de Vitoria of his religious principles, replaced theology with philosophy, and replaced his concern to deal with differences in humanity with a straightforward classification of people by nations, color, and continents, what one would obtain, indeed, would be Kant, or at least the Kant who was preoccupied with these specific issues. Is that much of a difference? In my view, it is not. De Vitoria and Kant are two different faces of the same imaginary—the imaginary of the modern/colonial world order as an interstate system regulated by the CMP in the first case under the frame of Christian theology and in the second under the frame of secular philosophy. The reason why the "Indian doubt," the "rights of the people," and the Christian idea of orbis were erased in the eighteenth century cosmopolitan debates is another matter, and one of the issues with which I deal in section VI of this chapter.

Relevant to my argument is a change that de Vitoria introduced into the principle established by Gaius, the Roman jurist who related *ius naturalis* (natural law) to *homines* (human beings). De Vitoria replaced *homines* with *gentes* (people)—perhaps an almost imperceptible change, but one of enormous significance. De Vitoria was facing a situation in which the *gentes* in question had been previously unknown to Christianity and, obviously, were not clearly *homines* (see chapter 12 for a full exploration of this issue). Certainly, there was a difference between the inhabitants of Indias Occidentales on the one hand and the Moors, Jews, or Chinese on the other. But this was precisely the difference that would become the historical foundation of colonial and imperial differences. Thus, it was no longer the question of thinking of men or human beings (*homines*), but of thinking of different people and relating to them through a new structure of power and rights: the right to possess, the right to dispossess, the right to govern those outside the Christian realm, the right to dictate, the right to declare war. De Vitoria began to rethink the international order (i.e., the cosmo-polis) from the perspective of New World events and from the need to accommodate, in that international order, what he called the "barbarians," that is, the "Indians" of the New World.

De Vitoria's rethinking required him to accommodate two levels in the world order. On one level, de Vitoria had Orbis Christianus as the ultimate cultural space in which he would justify the rights of barbarians and pagans; on the other, he had a spectrum of Christian-European (monarchic) "nations" already established in the sixteenth-century imaginary (Castile, France, Italy). How these two levels interact was never made explicit by him; he treated them as equals in his thinking on international rights and international communication, although it was obvious at the time that barbarians or pagans were considered unequal to the French or Italians. He was more explicit, however, in considering the rights of Indigenous nations against the need to legitimate the rights of Castilians to preach and convert Indigenous nations and their rights of commerce and settlement. The second ended up overruling the first. This was the domain in which the monarchic-religion-state became instrumental as a replacement for the emperor and the pope in international relations, and in which Christian cosmopolitanism (without using this term) was advanced as a correction of the Castilian crown's imperial global designs.

VI Cosmo-polis, Eurocentrism, and the Rights of Man and of the Citizen

I rolled over my discussion from the sixteenth to the end of the eighteenth century because this period is often forgotten in North Atlantic scholarship (Carl Schmitt's *The Nomos of the Earth* is one exception). Debating cosmopolitanism and human rights without paying due attention to the historical foundation of the colonial matrix of power and the role in its founding played by cosmopolitanism, international law, and the ideas of man/human and rights, is like beginning to read a novel in the second chapter.[22] In the sixteenth century, "the rights of the people" had been formulated within a planetary consciousness—the planetary consciousness of the Orbis Christianus. In the eighteenth century, the "rights of man and of the citizen" were formulated, instead, within the planetary consciousness of a cosmo-polis more dominated by the secular thinking of the Enlightenment and the laws of nature, with (western) Europe—the Europe of nations, specifically—as the frame of reference. It was a significant change within the system, or, better yet, within the Eurocentered imagination of the modern/colonial world order.

For cosmopolitanism, what is still missing is the link with the sixteenth century. In saying this, I am not making merely a historiographical claim, but a substantive one, political and epistemic, with significance for the present.

What nowadays we call multiculturalism has its roots in the sixteenth century, in the inception of the modern/colonial world, in the struggles of jurists/theologians like de Vitoria or missionaries like Las Casas, struggles that were at the time similar to the struggles of liberal thinkers such as Jürgen Habermas and Will Kymlicka.[23] If Kant needs today to be amended to include multiculturalism in his cosmopolitan view, as Thomas McCarthy suggests, then we must return to the roots of the concept of cosmopolitanism—that is, to the sixteenth century, when racial classification, as a labor of knowledge creation, established the rules governing "who shall be out" and the conditions required to be "in."[24] The logic of constitution/destitution is something that critical (modern and postmodern) cosmopolitanism has to deal with. Instead, decolonial cosmopolitan localism and the platform of a shared future for humankind (based on Confucian principles) begins from the destituted. Hence, from the borders, from dwelling in the borderlands between destituted histories and memories and the presence of the constituted (e.g., human rights, the concept of the human, of human rights, of cosmopolitanism), none of which existed in destituted memories and languages. For that reason, destituted people in the Americas (and also in Asia and Africa) are today rebuilding their memories destituted from the moment European invaders disrupted their mode of existence; they are engaged in gnoseological and aesthesic reconstitutions.

To understand cosmopolitan thinking since the eighteenth century, as well as the oblivion of sixteenth-century legacies, I offer here two historical instances and two structural issues that I would like to elaborate on from the previous section. The two historical instances are the Thirty Years' War that concluded with the Peace of Westphalia in 1648 and the French Revolution of the eighteenth century. The structural issues are the connections made by eighteenth-century intellectuals between the law of nature (*cosmos*) and the ideal society (*polis*). One of the consequences of the structural aspect was to derive *ius cosmopoliticum* (cosmopolitan law/rights) from the law of nature to model social organization. For eighteenth-century intellectuals in France, England, and Germany, their own existence and praxes of living were the beginning.[25] And such a beginning was oblivious to the historical conditions that made the Enlightenment possible: the Spanish and Portuguese proving the historical foundation for what the Enlightenment came to be. That oblivion has important repercussions. It was one aspect of making the intramural imperial difference: the fabrication of the South of Europe. The philosophical invention of the South of Europe (Kant, Hegel) was contemporary to the work of philologists inventing the Orient, which, at that point in time, was the fabrication of extramural imperial differences.

China in its long dynastic history, the Mughal sultanate, the Ottoman sultanate, the Russian czarate—none of them endured the experience of settler colonialism, and none of them escaped the logic of coloniality. All of them were and are *destituted*, legislating the extramural imperial difference in the processes of *constituting* Western modernity. The current confrontations of re- and de-Westernization have their ground in the history of the CMP. One of the tasks of the politics of decolonial investigations is precisely to bring to light what remains buried in the logic of either/or.[26] By the same token, the extramural colonial differences were rearticulated when French and German philosophy recast the Americas (its nature and its people) in light of the "new" ideas of the Enlightenment, rather than the "old" ideas of the Renaissance.[27] That beginning is reproduced today, in so far as the eighteenth century is accepted as the "origin" of modernity. From this perspective, the emergence of the Atlantic commercial circuits, which created the conditions for capitalist expansion and the French Revolution, remains relegated to a premodern world. "Premodern" is indeed a Eurocentered expression to hide the fact that the nonmodern coexists with the European modern. The expression "premodern" presupposes a teleological unfolding of history, which is necessary to enrich the fiction of modernity.

The structural issues I mentioned next to historical instances are the historical events that reveal decolonial analytics in intramural and extramural colonial and imperial differences drawn in the eighteenth century at the same time that Orientalism and Kantian cosmopolitanism were being thought out. The inception of secular cosmopolitanism was simultaneous with (and part of the same move as) the updating of the extramural colonial difference involving the New World (the Occident) and the emergence of Orientalism (the Orient) that located and ranked Asia and Africa in the imaginary of the modern/colonial world order. Eighteenth-century Orientalism was in fact a reorienting of the extramural colonial difference engendered in the sixteenth century, a mutating continuity between the European Renaissance and the European Enlightenment.

All of the above counts when the narrative is grounded in European formation (constitution) and expansion (destitution). The "other" beginnings—the narratives grounded in the exteriority of the modern/colonial world or set up by the constitutive/destitutive movements of the CMP—are more complex, spatial, and planetary than the punctual space/time of eighteenth-century Europe that is assumed to be the narrative center. The "other" beginnings connect the commercial circuits before European hegemony with the emergent Mediterranean capitalism of the period and with the displacement of capitalist expansion from the Mediterranean to the Atlantic.[28] Interestingly enough, the extramural colonial differences were relevant in devaluing the people and nature of the New World.[29] All of this coincided with the mutation of the extramural colonial difference in the making of Orientalism and has been sidelined in cosmopolitan debates. Not, of course, because of national pride opposing cosmopolitanism or for historical accuracy, but because of the impediment imposed by the linear macro narrative that constructed modernity (from Ancient Greece to western Europe) and obstructed what is today evident: that these macro narratives were told from the perspective of modernity hiding coloniality while, in that hiding, mutating the intramural and extramural colonial and imperial differences.

Bearing in mind the conceptual and historical frame of mind of the modern/colonial world order in the European imagination, there are at least two ways to enter critically into the modern European conception of cosmopolitanism and, simultaneously, into its racial underpinning and Eurocentric bias. Since Kant was the artifice of Enlightenment cosmopolitanism, let's focus on Kant. I see two promising paths to pursue my argument. One would be to start with an analysis of his writings on history from a cosmopolitan point of view and on his writings regarding perpetual peace.[30] The other would be to start from his lectures on anthropology, which he began in 1772 and published in 1797.[31] In these lectures, Kant's Eurocentrism clearly enters into conflict with his cosmopolitan ideals.[32] The first way of reading Kant will take us to Habermas and Taylor. The second way will carry us back to the inception of coloniality under the salvationist rhetoric of conversion, to Las Casas and de Vitoria and the first chapter of European entanglement with Africa and Asia narrated by European actors. Kant built his cosmopolitan ideals on the basis of these one-sided stories. It will also take us to his racial classification of the planet by skin color and continental divisions. In short, it takes us to the disobeying of epistemology and aesthetics—to the gnoseological and aesthesic reconstitutions of the destituted.

I would like to explore these ideas further by bringing into the picture the associations of cosmopolitanism with Eurocentrism. Argentine philosopher Enrique Dussel coupled modernity and Eurocentrism (i.e., modernity is a narrative, not an ontological unfolding of universal history), and he proposed the notion of "transmodernity" as a way out of the impasses of postmodern critiques of modernity. Dussel argues that if emancipatory reason is one of the features of modernity, genocidal reason is its hidden marker: a singular case in which the rhetoric of modernity (emancipation) works in tandem with and disguises the logic of coloniality (genocide). Here you have in a nutshell what modernity/coloniality means. In this specific historical node, it means emancipatory reason/genocidal reason. It also illuminates why gnoseological and aesthesic reconstitutions are the vehicles to implement the politics of decolonial investigations. Decolonial investigations cannot be limited to epistemology and aesthetics, two of Kant's weapons that are still with us.

While "postmodernists criticize modern reason as a reason of terror," Dussel writes, "we criticize modern reason because of the irrational myth that it conceals."[33] The pronoun "we" situates the enunciation in the extramural colonial difference, in this case no longer projected on Indigenous and African people but on people of European descent in the Third World. And it situates modernity in the sphere of "them." In other works, Dussel has highlighted the irreducible difference, the exteriority (with all its various local histories, racializations, and sexualizations) that indeed structures the imaginary of the modern/colonial world and the experiential locations of decolonial (the people) and de-Western (the state) thinking.[34] Much like the awareness of the person enslaved—who understands the logic of the master *and* of the slave, while the master only understands the master's logic—Dussel's argument reveals that the narratives of modernity, and their postmodern versions, are half the story that consistently conceals coloniality. Decolonial investigations and narratives, instead, bring about the other half of the story: coloniality. Thus, there is a need for Dussel (as there is also for African philosophers) to read Kant decolonially (that is, from the different levels of extramural colonial differences).[35] Dussel observes:

> Kant's answer to the question posed by the title of his essay "What Is Enlightenment?" is now more than two centuries old. "Enlightenment is the exodus of humanity by its own effort from the state of guilty immaturity," he wrote. "Laziness and cowardice are the reasons why the greater part of humanity remains pleasurably in this state of immaturity."
>
> For Kant, immaturity, or adolescence, is a culpable state, laziness and cowardice is existential ethos: the *unmündig*. Today, we would ask him: an African in Africa, or a slave in the United States in the 18th century; an Indian in Mexico, or a Latin American mestizo: should all of these subjects be considered to reside in a state of guilty immaturity?[36]

In fact, Kant's judgement regarding the Indigenous population in the Americas was bound together with his view of Africans and Hindus; for him they all shared an incapacity for moral maturity, owing to what he perceived as their common ineptitude and proximity to nature. And you can see what "nature" means in the European imagination. African philosopher Emmanuel Chukwudi Eze provides several examples in which Kant states that the race of the American Indians cannot be educated since they lack any motivating impulse, they are devoid of affect and passion, and they hardly speak and do not caress each other.[37] Kant introduces then the race of the Negroes, who are the opposite—in his view—of the First Nations in the American continent: the Negroes are full of affection and passion, very lively, but vain; as such, they can be educated, but only as servants or slaves. Kant continues, in tune with the naturalist and philosophic discourses of his time, by noting that inhabitants of the hottest zones are, in general, idle and lazy—qualities that are only correctable by government and force.[38]

In part II of *Anthropology from a Pragmatic Point of View*, devoted to "Classification," Kant's argument comes into full force. It begins with a consideration of the character of the person, moves next to the character of the sexes and then to the character of nations, and concludes with speculation on the characters of races and species.[39] The fact that the "person" is Kant's beginning and recurring reference point is already indicative of the presuppositions implied in his idea of the universal neutrality of the imaginary that for him constitutes the "person." The survivors of the dismantled civilizations (Maya, Incas, Aztec, and the millenarian memories of their ancestors) in the New World were not paradigmatic examples of Kant's notion of "persons" and "nations." Neither were Africans and Asians in all their diversity.

Here you see extramural colonial differences at work. "Person" was for Kant the sign naming an entity according to the European sense of humanity. "Person" seems to be at first glance a noun around which all ontological differences might be accommodated and classified, generously. But it turned out that "person" (according to European standards) was also the entity upon which the classifications of races and sexes and the conceptualization of nations were and are still built.[40] And the classifications were made by "persons"! If the idea of "person" was projected toward non-European people, it did not mean that there were ontological "persons" dictated by Kant. It was merely Kant naming an entity according to his own German language, thoughts, and vocabulary, disregarding how "persons" (or those who may have been "persons") in Africa, Asia, and the Americas identified themselves and what words they had for the European "invading persons."

But let us pause for a while over Kant's discourse on the character of nations, since it more strictly relates to cosmopolitanism. "Cosmo-polis" implies the possibilities and the capabilities of people (*populus*) to live together when they are organized around the concept of nation. It was too early for Kant to see the nation together with the state. The modern secular bourgeois state was not yet in place at the time of these reflections, two decades after the US Revolution and shortly after the French Revolution. A nation, for Kant, was not (like the ground on which it is located) a possession, a patrimonium (*patri-*, meaning "father"; *-monium*, meaning "state, condition"). It was a society of "men" (my quotation marks) whom no one other than the nation itself can command or dispose of. Since, like a tree, each nation has its own roots, to incorporate it into another nation as a graft denies its existence as a society of moral persons, turns it into a thing, and thus contradicts the concept of the original contract, without which a people (*Volk*) have no right.[41]

As time passes and the nation-state form comes into being, it happens that the nation has roots, the state has laws, and the people have rights. But, of course, the character of each nation varies, and a successful cosmopolitanism and a perpetual peace would very much depend on the character of (the peoples in) nations and on the state they constitute together. However, the state is not the people. It is not clear then to what extent modern cosmopolitanism means nation-cosmo-polis or state-cosmo-polis. Thus, England and France (and Germany, by implication of the enunciating agency) are "the two most civilized nations on earth."[42] Kant clearly forgot China, the spread of the Islamic caliphate, and the Mughal sultanate (present-day India). Perhaps he should have said "most civilized in Europe" rather than on Earth.

The fact that France and England constantly feud because of their different national characters does not, for Kant, diminish their standing as paragons of civilization. One could say—to justify Kant—that he was entitled to his own opinion. The French and the English are the first national characters he describes in the section titled "The Characters of the Nations," and significantly it was only in Europe that the concept of "nation" made sense. Perhaps Kant thought that in every other civilization, thinkers thought in terms of "nation," but they did not. Ibn Khaldun was not common reading for European philosophers of the Enlightenment. If Kant had read him, he would have found out that "nation" was not a concern for Khaldun, who was more concerned with the state. "State" here doesn't mean a European monarchic or bourgeois state, but a legal-administrative organization of sedentary people. Nomads do not require a state. The term often used by Ibn Khaldun was *asabiyyah*. Syed Farid Alatas suggests, correctly in my view, that the term used for translation is less important than understanding what the concept *asabiyyah* means: "By *asabiyyah* Ibn Khaldun meant a sense of common cause and destiny, and the binding ties of loyalty that are founded to a great extent but not exclusively on blood ties. . . . There are three types of relationship that make *asabiyyah*. These are blood ties (*silat al-rahim*), clientship (*walá*) and alliance (*hilf*). . . . The most powerful type is the *asabiyyah*."[43]

When Ibn Khaldun thought about the state (the legal and administrative organization of sedentary people), he was not thinking about the European nation-state that would emerge in the late eighteenth century. Nor was he thinking "nation" in terms of national character. There is no straight line going from Ibn Khaldun to Kant as there is from de Vitoria to Kant. Extramural colonial difference separated the latter while intramural difference (e.g., distinguishing the South of Europe from the heart of Europe) separated the former. It is noteworthy that Kant made this latter distinction—he was proud of Western civilization—and his opinion that France, Germany, and England were the three countries most civilized on earth was indeed his own opinion, not, of course, a matter of fact.

For Kant, the third national character is the Spanish. Here you see intramural imperial difference at work. It's almost a preview of the Third World in the second half of the twentieth century, except that in this case it was the colonial extramural difference, but the logic is the same. Only the content changed in the rhetoric of modernity. Kant's ranked order of countries is not alphabetical, but imperial: Spain, the empire in decay, is followed by England and France, the new and emerging imperial nations. Significantly, the first feature that Kant observes in the Spaniards is that they "evolved from the mixture of European blood with Arabian (Moorish) blood." Here you have intramural imperial difference mounted on extramural colonial difference. Perhaps because of this the Spaniard "displays in his public and private behavior a certain solemnity; even the peasant expresses a consciousness of his own dignity toward his master, to whom he is lawfully obedient." Kant adds, "The Spaniard's bad side is that he does not learn from foreigners; that he does not travel in order to get acquainted with other nations; that he is centuries behind in the sciences. He resists any reform; he is proud of not having to work; he is of a romantic quality of spirit, as the bullfight shows; he is cruel, as the former auto-da-fé shows; and he displays in his taste an origin that is partly non-European."[44] All the philosophical debates of the sixteenth century, the contributions of Las Casas and de Vitoria, are here abandoned in favor of negative features of national characters. The mixture of Spaniard with Moorish blood sets the character of the nation in racial terms, this time not in relation to Africa, Asia, or the Americas, but to Europe itself—the South of Europe. In this regard, Kant's contribution to drawing the intramural imperial difference between the modern/North (England, France, Germany) and the traditional/South (Spain, Portugal, Italy) should not be overlooked. Russians, Turks, Greeks, and Armenians belong to yet another division of national character. The first two are dispatched by their extramural imperial difference from northern Europe. Russia was a czarate and the Turks were a sultanate. Greece instead has descended from its classical pedestal to now reflect an intramural colonial difference—that is, perhaps, until today, when it belongs to the European Union. The underlying forces of the CMP, the flows between its levels and domains, arise out of an invisible structure that forms subjects who are accustomed to accepting human history as virtually a "natural order."

Kant paved the way for Hegel's tripartite division of Europe: the core (England, France, and Germany), the South, and the Northeast.[45] Thus, according to Kant's geopolitical distribution of national characters, which anticipates Hegel's geopolitical distribution of Europe, a modern cosmopolitanism presupposes that it can only be thought out from one particular geopolitical location—the heart of Europe, where reside the most civilized nations. Kant's cosmopolitanism turns out to be a global imperial design.

Indeed, as much as we owe to Kant's cosmopolitanism today, we must not forget that it plagued the inception of national ideology with racial hierarchical classification. It is indeed Kant's imperial cosmopolitanism (modern/colonial) that requires us to confront it with decolonial cosmopolitan localism. It is not difficult to agree with both de Vitoria and Kant on their ideas of justice, equality, rights, and planetary peace. But it remains difficult to carry these ideas further without clearing up the Renaissance and Enlightenment prejudices that surrounded their concepts of race and manhood. One of the tasks of decolonial (critical) cosmopolitanism is precisely to clear up the encumbrances of the past. The other is to speak the present toward nonexisting possible futures. For instance, when Kant thinks in terms of "all nations of the earth," he assumes that the entire planet eventually will be organized according to the terms he has envisioned for western Europe and will be modeled by his description of national characters.[46] Today this dream remains alive, although it is diminishing, especially in the Western expectation that such a world order in perpetual peace will follow the Western example of democracy, now in desuetude in both the European Union and the US and in perpetual war.

VII Cosmopolitanism and Human Rights: The Changing
Faces of the Modern/Colonial Imaginary

De Vitoria and Kant founded cosmopolitan projects and conceptualizations of rights that responded to specific needs. For de Vitoria, it was the inclusion of the "Indians" as Spaniards, including millenarian civilizations like Mayas, Tihuanacotas, and Incas. For Kant, it was the redefinition of "person" and "citizen" in the Europe of nations, and the advent of new forms of colonialism. Similarly, the United Nations' *Universal Declaration of Human Rights* that followed World War II also responded to the changing faces of the coloniality of power in the modern/colonial world order.[47] Soon after the declaration, the classification and ranking was rewritten into developed and underdeveloped nations. Top-down cosmopolitanism kept running into a wall. During the Cold War, human rights were legitimized in defense of Western values and against the danger of communism, as if communism were not a derivation of Western enlightenment values. Led by the US, the *Universal Declaration of Human Rights* was established a few years after two nuclear bombs were dropped on Nagasaki and Hiroshima. Later, at the conclusion of the Cold War, human rights became associated with world trade and with the diversity of capitalism.[48] Neither de Vitoria nor Kant had to deal with a world in which consolidated modern, secular, and bourgeois nation-states had to assume a leading role in conflicted discussions over human rights.[49] (See chapter 7, on "human" and "living" rights.)

The conclusion of World War II reconfigured a narrative in which the first chapter was in effect written in Salamanca and the second by Kant's conception of a universal history from a cosmopolitan point of view—a history of perpetual peace and cosmopolitan rights. This chapter of Western history could be read today as a prolegomenon to the model for planetary (cosmopolitan) liberal democracy, but that reading has indeed become an impossibility because of the persistence of extramural colonial and imperial differences. Rather, this second chapter ended with WWII and the realization after the war that such dreams were no longer viable. The conditions were ripe for the advent of the neoliberal and the seeming end of history fifty years later, following the collapse of the Soviet Union.[50] The Cold War was not convivial. And the struggles for decolonization in Africa and Asia brought to the foreground an experience that Kant could not have foreseen in a time when British and French colonization were not yet fully in place. Globalism and cosmopolitanism where two bad bedfellows within the CMP, as much as capitalism and democracy.

Kant's horizons were very limited in retrospect, but were very wide compared with de Vitoria's. De Vitoria was in the thick of an emerging world order in which he could not have known what was to come. Kant, on the other hand, was not paying attention to the three centuries of Iberian colonization in the New World and in Asia. Curiously, the scenario that presented itself after World War II brought us back to de Vitoria and the school of Salamanca. Not curiously, though, the Cold War and the intensification of conflicts between the two previous phases of the modern/colonial world order (the Renaissance and the Enlightenment) left the exteriority of the system in shadows as an expectant Third World contemplated the struggle between the First and the Second while advancing decolonial liberation. Coloniality remained hidden behind the smoke to advance the ideal of modernity and to implement it as modernization. The horrors of National Socialism that contributed to the transformation of the "rights of man and of the citizen" into "human rights" were horrors whose traces stretched back to the sixteenth century (the expulsion of Jews from Spain) and to the eighteenth-century imaginary of "national characters." The sentiment, in Europe, of the decay of the West and the discontent of civilizations had its reasons. During the Cold War, human rights appeared to be a strategy for controlling communism rather than a gesture toward cosmopolitanism. It was similar to the control of pagans, infidels, and barbarians by the model of international relations devised by the school of Salamanca, or of foreigners, in Kantian cosmopolitanism. Thus, while for de Vitoria and his followers the master discourse was theology, and for Kant and the Enlightenment it was philosophy, after World War II the master discourse was political science and political economy unfolding on two fronts: specialized studies in the social sciences to deal with the Third World; and neoliberalism and Pentagonism to set up the domestic politics in the US and to regulate US expansionism.[51]

The Universal Declaration of Human Rights followed by a few years the constitution of the United Nations, which had to be named "Nations" because the title "United States" was already taken, and it would have been either confusing or, worse, explicitly hegemonic to give the conglomerate of planetary states the same name as one powerful member that had the idea for the new institution. The document announced, paradoxically, the closing of the international order and of international laws as conceived since Kant. A couple of decades later, dependency theory in Latin America voiced concerns that interstate relations were indeed relations of dependency and the promised development just a myth.[52] But ideologues who supported transnational (or trans-state) corporations did not agree with that view. In one stroke, they put a closure to Kant's trust in the nation and transformed dependency into interdependency (that is, with the 1973 Trilateral Commission between the

United States, Europe, and Japan).[53] They ended the sovereignty of the nation-state and revamped the language of developing and underdeveloped nations as an alternative to communism. Thus, as communists (no longer pagans, infidels, or foreigners) represented the danger to the system, parallel to the decolonization occurring in Asia and Africa, dictatorial regimes were on the rise in Latin America (Brazil, Uruguay, Chile, and Argentina). Human rights commissions, no doubt, played a fundamental role in abating the atrocities of some dictatorial regimes, at the same time that the encouragement of human rights served as an instrument to promote the rhetoric of liberal democracy over communism to legitimize humanitarian interventions (settler colonialism being no longer acceptable). Planetary conviviality and perpetual peace could no longer sustain the cosmopolitan ideal within the CMP. Here again are the double standards or apparent contradictions we saw at the historical foundations of modernity/coloniality that Dussel highlighted in the Enlightenment: the coexistence of emancipatory and genocidal reasons, modernization, and democracy on the one hand, and dependency, control, and exploitation of labor and natural resources on the other. From de Vitoria to Kant to *The Universal Declaration of Human Rights*, the three acolytes of modernity/coloniality form a continuity linking heterogeneous historic-structural nodes that correspond to the changing hands of Western leadership in the world order and in the management of the CMP.

Extramural imperial and colonial differences were updated during the Cold War under the epistemic and intellectual leadership of the US. When the planet was divided into three geopolitical areas (First, Second, and Third Worlds), human rights were caught in the middle of the transformation of liberal into neoliberal democratic projects. In this battle within the new imperial borders of the modern world, the problem was no longer the racialized South, as in Kant's time, but the communist East, which included Mao Zedong's China. Decolonized countries were striving to become nation-states at the same time that ideologues of the new world order no longer believed in them. Zbigniew Brzezinski, in 1970, was promoting interdependence—apparently a good ground for cosmopolitanism—while despising the nation-state. He believed, or at least said he believed, that in the formal sphere global politics operated much as nation-states had in the past, but the inner reality of that process was increasingly shaped by forces whose influence or scope transcended national lines.[54]

Still, in the increasing enthusiasm for globalization, which was the goal of neoliberal globalism, many political leaders were and are not aware of the memories of extramural imperial and colonial differences. And they could not be aware, for it is in thinking decolonially that these differences become visible in two ways: through de-Westernization (and the rise of the influence of Russia, China, and especially the BRI, Belt and Road Initiative), and through the emergence of the decolonial option, which this book is about. Extramural imperial differences would erupt in the twenty-first century with Russia and China growing both economically and in confidence as world actors, and in the eruption of thousands of political organizations emerging from civil society, struggling to recover the dignity that modernity had erased (via racism, sexism, the commodification of "nature," linguistic and epistemic hierarchies, artistic and aesthetic Eurocentrism, etc.), and fighting for their rights. Decolonial cosmopolitan localism could be conceived at this moment as the decolonial imaginary proposing an active cosmopolitan localism—the global network of political societies taking their destinies into their own hands, de-linking from hegemonic global designs.

In the sphere of interstate dependence, the lines of extramural imperial differences were redrawn between the First World (the West), which controls the classification of the "Three World" division, and the Second World (the Soviet Union). The First World, consequently, remapped the transfigurations of previous extramural imperial differences ("Orientalism") and invented the Third World, to which China and India were demoted. What we see in this untold story, from de Vitoria to Brzezinski through Kant, is the modern/colonial imaginary continuously growing and transforming itself while simultaneously maintaining the colonial space as derivative, rather than as constitutive, of modernity. Modern and postmodern (critical) cosmopolitanism continued to be discussed without any attention to the persistence of coloniality, the hidden half of the story.

The difficulties for the modern and postmodern versions of cosmopolitanism that I am trying to convey here have been cast in different words by Abdullahi Ahmed An-Na'im, a lawyer and Muslim advocate for human rights. He points out that the universality of human rights is undermined by both Western and non-Western cultural relativism. Similar to the claims of some elites in non-Western societies that their own cultural norms should prevail over international human rights standards, Western elites are claiming exclusive rights to prescribe the essential concepts and normative content of human rights for all societies to implement.[55] Both types of relativism not only take a variety of conceptual and practical forms, but also play an insidious role in inhibiting even the possibilities of imagining supplementary or alternative conceptions and implementation strategies.[56] This dilemma calls for a radical reconceptualization of the human rights paradigm as the next step toward establishing cosmopolitan values (ethics) and regulations (politics). This is the topic of the next section, and of the entire chapter 7.

VIII Border Thinking: A Step toward Pluriversality and Decolonial Cosmopolitan Localism

I have drawn three stages of cosmopolitan projects of the modern/colonial imaginary. In the first stage, cosmopolitanism faced the difficulties of dealing with pagans, infidels, and barbarians. This stage was characterized by a predominantly religious and racial "perception" of society—a "perception" that constituted the modern/colonial imaginary. In the second stage, cosmopolitanism faced the difficulties posed by the existence of communities without states and the dangers of foreigners who, at that point in time, constituted those populations residing at the edge of the Europe of nations. In the third stage, communists replaced pagans and infidels, barbarians and foreigners, as the difficulties of cosmopolitan society were reassessed. Throughout these three stages we see the visible faces of modernity and the hidden faces of coloniality that decolonial analytics are undraping to reveal the modern (critical) cosmopolitan visions and ambitions trapped in that imaginary. My argument is that the intention to be decolonial requires the perspective of distance, only achieved by detaching and delinking from modern (critical) cosmopolitanism. At the time when the first version of this argument was published (2000), it was necessary to add a fourth stage to the scenario that Kant observed, which had changed again with the "dangers" presented by recent African and Middle Eastern immigration to Europe and Latin American immigration to the United States. Now, at the end of the second decade of the twenty-first century, Western modern (critical) versions of cosmopolitanism are exhausted. Immigration continues to disturb the "Europe of nations" (now the EU), refugees have increased, state-supported "terrorists" are growing in numbers, and, last but not least, drug cartels (also supported by states, banks, and corporations) are growing.

I believe it is now possible to talk more specifically about a fourth stage. Global coloniality, hidden under the promises of globalism, is drawing a new scenario. Economic coloniality is no longer concentrated in the Atlantic (as in de Vitoria's time), or in the Europe of nations and the North Atlantic (as in Kant's time), when liberalism joined forces with Christian Protestantism and skin color began to replace blood and religion in the reconfiguration of the colonial difference. At that time, capital, labor control, and whiteness created a new paradigm under which intra- and extramural colonial differences were redefined. In the second half of the twentieth century, and especially after the end of the Cold War, economic coloniality (i.e., capitalism) transformed the former colonial difference with the Orient (Orientalism) and re-created it as an imperial difference with China—thereby entering territories in which Christianity, liberalism, and whiteness are alien categories. Perhaps Samuel Huntington had a similar scenario in mind when he proposed that in the future, wars would be motivated by a clash of civilizations, rather than by the pursuit of economic advantages.[57] Which means that when capitalism crosses the border of imperial differences, it brings civilizations into conflicts of a different order (e.g., current conflicts between the US, supported by the EU, with Russia and China). But now, imperial differences are being contested, and this contestation brings about de-Westernization: the appropriation and management of economic coloniality (capitalism, if you wish) to delink from Western political and economic domination. In any event, relevant to my argument is the fact that while capitalism expands, and the rage for accumulation steadily grows out of control (as for instance, through the weakening of nation-states, or the irrational exuberance of the market), racial or religious or political-ideological conflicts emerge as new impediments to cosmopolitan societies.

The new situation we are facing in the fourth stage is that cosmopolitanism and democracy can no longer be articulated—if they ever truly could—from some foundational point of enunciation that maps what is good for the rest of the world. The rest of the world always knew what was good for it but needed a while for the energies of discontent to take the stage and say, "Basta!," using the famous Zapatista finger pointing. Cosmopolitanism, human rights, democracy cannot be achieved by unipolar orders and decisions. De Vitoria, Kant, the ideologues of interdependence, the champions of development, the neoliberal managers of globalism, the technocrats who believe in the wonders of technology to promote peace and conviviality—all of them leave little room for those on the other side of the intramural and extramural colonial and imperial divide. All of those/us who have been mapped began to remap themselves/ourselves and to map those who mapped them/us. This moment, which has many geographical and historical anchors, is the moment of the emergence and the emergency of border thinking and doing. These are the moments in which decolonial energies and visions erupt. But they are also the moments in which de-Westernization (by way of state projects now supported by the states' own growing economies) erupts. The recent Chinese replies to Secretary of State Rex Tillerson's statements about what China was doing in the South China Sea were immediately and forcefully answered by direct confrontation. China has endured a long list of humiliations from the West since WWII, and now it is in a position to refuse to take any more.

Obviously, managed cosmopolitanism could (and most likely will) remain as a benevolent form of control. In the New World order, how can modern (critical) and dialogic cosmopolitanism be thought out without falling into the traps of cultural relativism (and the reproduction of colonial difference), as pointed out by An-Na'im? I have been suggesting, and now will move to justify, that cultural relativism should be dissolved to concentrate on colonial and imperial differences—both intramural (domestic) and extramural (interstate) differences—and that those differences should be identified as the locations of the politics of decolonial investigations and of cosmopolitan localism. Instead of cosmopolitanism managed from above (that is, via global designs), I am proposing decolonial and pluriversal local cosmopolitanisms, emerging from the various destituted spatial and historical locations of colonial differences.[58] In this vein, I interpret the claim made by An-Na'im. Defenders of modern (critical) cosmopolitanism would have its place and its right to participate. But the aberration of there being one definitive cosmopolitanism proposed and managed from the West is unsustainable. Decolonial cosmopolitan localism is not a blueprint of what to do; it is only the call for nonimperial cosmopolitanisms (in plural), which are tantamount to cosmopolitan localisms. Border thinking has to be the guiding light for all local cosmopolitanisms emerging from the past of local colonial histories. Imperial locals will have to confront their own past, both the virtues and the crimes that have been committed in the name of justice and peace.

Replacing "cultural differences" with "colonial and imperial differences" helps change the terms, and not just the content, of the conversation. The first term, "cultural differences," hides power differentials, that is, hides coloniality. The second, "colonial and imperial differences," exposes it. "Culture" is the term that in the eighteenth century and in the Western secular world replaced "religion" in a new discourse of colonial expansion.[59] The notion of cultural relativism transformed the coloniality of power into a semantic problem. If we accept that actions, objects, beliefs, and so on are merely culturally relative, we hide the coloniality of power from which different cultures came into being in the first place. The problem, then, is not to accommodate cosmopolitanism to cultural relativism, but to dissolve cultural relativism and to focus on the coloniality of power and the colonial difference produced, reproduced, and maintained by global designs.

Critical postmodern cosmopolitanism and new democratic projects imply negotiating the coloniality of power and colonial differences in a world dominated by global capitalism and the sacred belief in growth and development. In a pluriversal world the rights of man, or human rights, would, of course, have to be negotiated across gender and sexual lines.[60] Human rights cannot any longer be accepted as limited to what de Vitoria, Kant, and the United Nations invented and established. The problem is not the inventing, but the arrogance of the establishing. Such expressions, as well as democracy and cosmopolitanism themselves, must be opened up to others beyond their inventors and establishers, not simply by listening to these others but by opening up the mechanisms of decision-making to the victims of Western human rights and imperial/colonial violations, freeing the victims from the racial and sexual humiliations experienced over five hundred years of Western expansion, hegemony, and domination. "Cosmopolitanism," "democracy," "the human race" will then become connectors rather than merely enunciated content with exclusively political and dubiously universal intentions. These terms will then not merely be preserved as the property of the European Enlightenment. Rather they will promote the benevolent inclusion of the other and make room for the multicultural—which in the last analysis is a modern and critical cosmopolitanism to deal with colonial differences while maintaining a region's own idea of cosmopolitanism.

Take for instance the Zapatistas. They have used the word "democracy" while giving it a meaning that deviates from its use by the Mexican government. This obviously is not a question of semantics but of decolonial politics. "Democracy," in Zapatista usage, is not conceptualized adopting European political philosophy but following current Mayan conceptions and enactments. Reciprocity is stressed instead of individual rational interests; communal values are preferred over individual values; wisdom of life is valued over an epistemology of science and philosophy; complementarity of the opposite is prized in all orders of existence, both of the human species and that of the cosmos. From this scenario, a different concept of "cosmopolitanism" could be derived, because it still needs to be maintained as a useful idea. Indigenous cosmopolitan localisms include the river and the mountain, the sun and the moon, the wind and the rain, the dog and the horse, and so forth. The Mexican government's understanding of democracy is that of a modern/colonial state: government of the whole population by elected representatives. There is no need to elaborate on the masquerading function of governmental uses of Western democratic ideals whose deterioration is obvious (by the second decade of the twenty-first century) in the EU and the US, the promoters and guardians of the word. The difference is not an ethical matter of right and wrong, for right and wrong are not detached universals but are based on premises argued by actors grounded in institutions. The point I am making is different.

The point is that the Zapatistas have no choice but to use the word "democracy" to bring Indigenous cosmology forcefully into the conversation, and in so doing to expose the fiction of governmental cover stories. "Democracy" is a word entrenched in the rhetoric of modernity. It serves to hide coloniality. Decolonial politics would consist then in (1) exposing this fiction and (2) underscoring that what matters for human civilization is to be in harmony and plenitude with the living energy of the planet (which in Western vocabulary turns to be an object: nature). Two more points are crucial here: to embrace decolonial politics it is not necessary to rely on Western legacies and even less on the word "democracy." Democracy may or may not be a useful concept if the goals are to overcome its short history of Western modernity. Democracy calls for certain forms of living together in *societies* among humans separated from "nature." The *communal* instead implies living together with all organisms in the constant relational flow of life on Earth and in the cosmos. In this context, "democracy" is out of place rather than a hopeful ideal. It was through the confluence—in the mutations of the CMP that have obtained since the eighteenth century—of the nation-state and the Industrial Revolution that we have arrived where we are: the human species appropriating life on Earth as natural resources; democracy becoming a fight between contending economic and financial interests; and nation-states becoming a place to encircle the nationals and expel nonnational human beings from the territory.

Democracy can be one among many concepts, useful in certain regions of the planet and for certain organizations, but it cannot be universal. It should be open to transmutating the social (only for certain human beings) to the communal (for all life on Earth), to ending the exploitation of "nature," and to respecting living rights (see chapter 7). The pretense or claim to universalize democracy is a recipe for disaster, as has become evident in US foreign policy since the 1950s.[61] Once democracy is separated from its deformation by the state, the word becomes a connector through which liberal concepts of democracy and Indigenous concepts of reciprocity along with communal social organization for the common good all must come to terms with each other. This is not only a question of Indigenous philosophy confronting liberal political philosophy. The same issue is being debated in Chinese political philosophy's revamping of Confucianism. It is being debated in Islamic political philosophy, Muslim thinkers evaluating what they want to preserve beyond and above Western liberal and economic neoliberal expectations.[62]

The word "democracy" is not universal, although it is assumed to be so in Western political philosophy. Nevertheless, "democracy" has been used globally since the eighteenth-century European philosophers built their legacy on Greece, which espoused the legacies they wanted to preserve. Being conservative in this sense, they fashioned themselves as progressive. For all other civilizations, the question became: either accept and try to apply democratic bureaucracy to your memories and modes of existence (millenarian in many cases) that did not fit democracy, or contest the injunction to be democratic.[63] Since democracy came out of Western conceptual histories and subjectivities but did not come from the conceptual histories of non-Western civilizations, it ended up being imposed or imported by local Western agencies. The results are superficial and the consequences far from Western expectations.[64] The first case leads to failure, and to advance the second it is necessary to change the terms of epistemic and philosophical conversations. Democracy cannot be contested within the same cosmology from which it emerged. Any contestation within the same cosmology would remain, important no doubt, but limited to one single story or half the story. Contesting democracy from another cosmology requires border thinking. Why? Because you cannot avoid the word "democracy" or any other keyword of the rhetoric of modernity (e.g., "religion," "capitalism," "state," "gender," "race," etc.). And you cannot remove the colonial weight from any vocabulary you invent within the same cosmology from which the word "democracy" emerged (e.g., "biopolitics," "hegemony," "capitalism," "city," "human," etc.). You need recourse to vocabularies from non-Western cosmologies.[65]

Border thinking is what I am naming the political and ethical move from the Zapatistas' perspective to rework the concept of democracy. Border thinking is not a possibility, at this point, from the perspective of the Mexican government, although it is necessary for those in subaltern positions. In this line of argument, a new Western abstract universal (such as de Vitoria's, or Kant's, which replaced de Vitoria's, or the ideologies of transnationalism, which replaced Kant's abstract universal) is no longer possible either, or desirable.

Abstract universals are what hegemonic perspectives provide, be they neoliberal or neo-Marxist. The perspective from the exteriority of modernity— be it the imperial difference (de-Westernization) or the colonial difference (decoloniality), illustrated in the dilemma formulated by An-Na'im and further developed with the example of the Zapatistas (i.e., the nonhegemonic perspective)—opens the possibility of imagining border thinking as the necessary condition for a future decolonial and dialogic cosmopolitanism. Such a decolonial and dialogic cosmopolitanism would lead to pluriversality instead of toward a new universality based (again) "on the potential of democratic politicization, as the true European legacy from ancient Greece onward."[66] A new universalism recasting the democratic potential of the European legacy is not necessarily a solution to the vicious circle between (neo)liberal globalization and "regressive forms of fundamentalist hatred."[67] It is hard to imagine that the entire planet would endorse the democratic potential of the "European legacy from ancient Greece onward." The entire planet could, in fact, endorse a democratic, just, and cosmopolitan project as long as democracy and justice were detached from their "fundamental" European heritage, and as long as it was accepted that a Western vocabulary would here function as connectors around which a decolonial cosmopolitanism (cosmopolitan localism) could be articulated.

Border thinking and decolonial cosmopolitan localism lead us to epistemic and, therefore, political, economic, ethic, and religious pluriversality. In other words, pluriversality becomes the horizon of any decolonial work: decoloniality fosters pluriversality, and pluriversality means to live in communal harmony and balance with all humans and other life forms. In this regard, pluriversality aims to be a universal project irreducible to one global design: a universal project with many designers. It is a horizon rather than a design. Which means that the only accepted universal would be pluriversality: conflicted and/or pacific coexistences in which no one would have the last word on how pluriversality should be attained. For that reason, pluriversality cannot be designed. Cultural relativism? I do not think so, for cultural relativism is a concept that retains the legacies of thinking from a universal frame of mind. Cultural relativism changes the content, not the terms, of the conversation. Pluriversality instead requires changing the terms of the conversation, to imagine and act toward abandoning (delinking from) the concept of "culture" to focus on decolonial "projects" that no given "culture" could contain. What I do know is that the processes leading toward pluriversality will have to overcome colonial and imperial differences held together by the coloniality of power. The idea of "cultural relativism" is blind to colonial and imperial differences and the power entanglements implied in them. It questions, once again, the content of the conversations, not the terms (assumptions, principles).

Decolonial cosmopolitan localism should be based on regulative principles that demand yielding generously ("convivially," said de Vitoria; "friendly," said Kant) toward pluriversality, toward universal and cosmopolitan projects without the directives of a commander in chief, projects in which everyone would participate instead of "being participated." A regulative principle like pluriversality would replace and displace the abstract, universal, cosmopolitan ideals (Christian, liberal, socialist, neoliberal) that helped (and continue to help) hold together the modern/colonial world system and preserve the managerial role of the nations that have dominated the North Atlantic region.

Here is where local histories and global designs come into the picture. Cosmopolitanism was thought out and projected from particular local histories that became the local history of the modern world system: any history that pretends to be global cannot be enunciated from the global. Every enunciation is local, including that of Western modernity that tells stories (enunciated, counted) about the global and globalization. For this reason, cosmopolitanism, if it is to be at all viable, cannot remain within the territorial, imperial, and top-down Kantian legacy. To be viable, cosmopolitanism has to become border thinking, decolonial and dialogic, from the perspective of those local histories that had to deal all along with global designs. Cosmopolitan localism is unavoidable. But decolonial cosmopolitan localism is an option. It must involve the relentless practice of decolonial and dialogical reconstitutions of the destituted praxes of living of any top-down and unilateral pretense to offering a blueprint for a future and ideal society projected from a single point of view that would take us back (again!) to the Greek paradigm and to European legacies.

Obviously, I am not proposing my own unilateral decolonial perspective. What I am proposing is that the cycle of pretended universalism and unipolarity is closing. That is why I have been arguing that the decolonial is an option and not a mission. And if the decolonial is to be an imperative, it would be for all who embrace it, without pretending that it has to be an imperative for everyone. A possible critique—one that imagines that pluriversality would degenerate into a patchwork of local practices in which each locality is ruled by a warlord and for the primary benefit of the warlord—would be a critique made from a modern (or postmodern) frame of mind. If pluriversality degenerates to that extent, it would not be pluriversality anymore and no longer a decolonial project. What would prevent this? Placing democracy at the service of life, to name one example, and not life at the service of democracy; working for living rather than living to work would be another; living in harmony with planet Earth rather than exploiting nature would be a third. When the logic of coloniality that regulates destitution is overcome; when the top-down pyramidal control and management of authority, economy, and knowledge is overcome; when the disastrous modern/colonial hegemonic horizon of life that brought the planet into an unprecedented compound of health and economy is overcome; when vertical domination and exploitation turns into horizontal care and respect for life—then cosmopolitan localism in its pluriversal configuration will have a place in the shared communal future of humankind. Pluriversality demands an economy at the service of the communal ("society" in Western terminology) rather than the communal at the service of the economy (capitalism, economic coloniality).

All of this cannot be expected at this point from state politics. Hence, decolonial politics cannot be state politics, and the politics of decolonial investigations shall be oriented toward gnoseological and aesthesic reconstitutions, delinking from the restricted territoriality of Kantian and Hegelian legacies. The politics of decolonial investigations shall work toward restituting and preserving dignified modes of existence (reexistence) that have been shattered by the ideological juggernaut of salvation, progress, civilization, development, modernization, and universal democracy.

IX Concluding Remarks

At the beginning of this chapter, I suggested that cosmopolitanism, in any of its conceptualizations and enactments, cannot be today a state-led project. There is a state rhetoric of peace, but it is just that, rhetoric. Cosmopolitanism, if it is still relevant, has to be a project of political society, a society that turns its back to the state and builds communal ways of living and being in the world. Hence, it is imperative to distinguish between my decolonial analysis of cosmopolitan localism and my decolonial proposal for cosmopolitan localism. If this distinction is not made, then the reader will remain trapped in the confusion of modern epistemology: identifying the description with what is described, and confusing the politics of decolonial investigations with the proposals of the decolonial option. The politics of decolonial investigations is no doubt one horizon of the decolonial option, and the decolonial option, in this case, is one option in the planetary scenario of cosmopolitan localisms.

I have outlined a framework in which three modern and Western cosmopolitan designs (*ius gentium* in the sixteenth century, the "rights of man and of citizens" in the eighteenth century, and *The Universal Declaration of Human Rights* in the first half of the twentieth century) run parallel to the three different stages of the modern/colonial world order: the Spanish Empire and Portuguese colonialism (de Vitoria), the British Empire and French and German colonialism (Kant), and US imperialism (human rights). All three cosmopolitan designs should be seen not only in chronological order, but in their synchronic coexistence with an enduring concern articulated, first, through the Orbis Christianus, second, through the nation-state and democracy, and, third, through the policies of development and modernization activated by neoliberal globalism. I concluded by arguing that pluriversality should be a universal project and that border thinking is the necessary way (i.e., method) to engage and enact pluriversality.

Isn't this a new form of cultural relativism? No, it is not. Cultural relativism and pluriversality belong to distinct loci of enunciation: cultural relativism belongs to the epistemic frame of Westernization, *constitution/destitution*;

pluriversality belongs to the gnoseological and aesthesic frame of *reconstitutions* (see introduction, section III for more on this concept). Cultural relativism is a compound of a philosophical concept (relativism) and an anthropological one (culture). Philosophically, relativism is defined by the *Stanford Encyclopedia of Philosophy* as follows: "Relativism, roughly put, is the view that truth and falsity, right and wrong, standards of reasoning, and procedures of justification are products of differing conventions and frameworks of assessment and that their authority is confined to the context giving rise to them. . . . Relativists characteristically insist, furthermore, that if something is only *relatively* so, then there can be no framework-independent vantage point from which the matter of whether the thing in question is so can be established."[68] Cultural relativism means then that variations between cultures (where cultures are supposed to be identifiable, peoples sharing language, memories, praxes of living, and the like) cannot be considered better or worse than others, and right and wrong are questions to be decided within cultures and not between them. Cultural relativism defies hierarchies while at the same time projecting the feeling of chaos, a world in which everything goes. What cultural relativism misses, decolonially speaking, are the power differentials (colonial and imperial differences) that coloniality has established between Western descriptions and constitutions of cultures and civilizations (although the talk of "civilizational relativism" is not in circulation). Pluriversality confronts the imaginary of a universally imagined world order structured by power differentials, so that even if the concept of "culture" is maintained (which is not necessary in decolonial pursuits), power differentials are incongruent with philosophical relativism and anthropological cultural relativism. The first presupposes autonomous abstract philosophical frames, and the latter the coexistence of autonomous entities (e.g., cultures). Decolonial aims toward and claims to local cosmopolitanism and pluriversality cannot be equated with the imaginary of cultural relativism for the simple reason that in the modern/colonial world order there is no autonomous culture. All cultures, and all civilizations, have been interfered with by the expansive designs of Western civilization since 1500.

Let me put it this way. I—we, for the sake of argument—say that modern cosmopolitanism and modern (critical) cosmopolitanism aim at a cosmopolitanism without parentheses, while decolonial cosmopolitan localism aims at a universalism in parentheses (meaning that each cosmopolitan proposal is sustained by its own truth in the awareness that one truth cannot be *the* truth).[69] Cultural relativism is a concept within Western hegemonic frames of knowing and knowledge (constitution/destitution). Decolonial cosmopolitan localism, instead, confronts but doesn't replace modern and modern critical cosmopolitanism. They coexist in conflict. Hence, pluriversality reduces Western universalism to its own size: it has the right to exist, but the aberration of being valid for all has to be shattered. And that is one of the tasks of the politics of decolonial investigations. They are already coexisting. The coexistence of both is what "pluriversality" and "universality in parentheses" mean. Furthermore, at this point, power differentials and entanglements cannot be ignored, and what is already in place cannot be eliminated next week. It is not a question of Houdini's magic trick. It is not as though by saying "Pluriversality will be generated and universality will vanish," the one will appear, the other disappear, and the "new" will be celebrated, maintaining the linear chronology of when one arrives the other goes away. That is the mindset of Western modernity. Pluriversality doesn't belong to it; it is already delinking from the existing (set of) Western universalities (theology, liberalism, neoliberalism, Marxism). It can be argued the Confucianism and Islamism also aim toward universality. It could be. But today, the power differential (in this case imperial differentials) between Western theological-secular universalism still rules over other coexisting claims. Pluriversality shall obtains in the sphere not only of the colonial but also of the imperial differences. This last one is precisely what characterizes de-Westernization.

What all of this means is that each pluriversal project aims at a totality that cannot be totalitarian if it claims the pluriversal. Totalitarian totality is a claim grounded in universal fundamentalisms. Fundamentalisms, and modern and modern (critical) cosmopolitanism, belong, decolonially speaking, to one sphere of the pluriverse; once they are divested of their assumed universality and therefore become an option among many, rather than the only option, only then can they be confronted with "alternatives." Modern and modern critical cosmopolitanism have the right to exist, but they do not have the right to assume that what is desirable for some will be desirable for all. Modern and critical modern cosmopolitanisms are inclusive—they aim to include—but generous inclusions prevent *recognizing* that there are millions of people who do not want or desire to be included or recognized (see chapter 14). Pluriversality is not an "alternative" to the universalism without parentheses. It is an option that reduces universals without parentheses to just another option.

Modern and critical modern cosmopolitanism, divested of their pretense, sometimes arrogance, become, then, a sphere of the pluriverse, coexisting with decolonial cosmopolitan localism. That is, decolonial cosmopolitan localism reduces modern and modern critical cosmopolitanism to its locality. It would be too modern and postmodern to think that decolonial cosmopolitan localism is a "new" universal that overcomes and leaves behind the "previous one." No, it is not that. The power of decolonial cosmopolitan localism doesn't come from universality without parentheses but from the claim that universality in parentheses changes the terms (not the content) of the conversation. Pluriversality as a universal decolonial project is universal not for everyone but only for those who embrace it, in the same way that Western universals are—from a decolonial perspective—*universals only for those who believe in them, be they theologians, Marxists, or neoliberals.* Decolonially speaking, Western or North Atlantic universal fictions are just options that have been successful in making many believe (including the promotors) in their universality (on this, see chapter 7).[70] Universality is not ontological; it is epistemological and aesthetic: there is nothing ontologically universal beyond the statements that are enounced and the people who believe in the ontic universality of what the statements propose. Pluriversality is gnoseological and aesthesic. There is nothing behind the claim to universality other than the apparatus of enunciation that claims it (see introduction, section III.3). For that reason, decolonial universality is universality in parentheses and in full awareness of its local enunciative and praxical claim.

In chapter 6 I further explore cosmopolitanism and the decolonial option. In chapter 7 I return to the question of human rights, and I expand on it to examine the rights of all life, leaving behind the coloniality and anthropocentrism of the notions of the rights of man and citizens, and of the universal declaration of human rights.

6   Cosmopolitanism and the Decolonial Option

I   The Scenario

A dear friend and colleague of mine who is sympathetic to decoloniality was not convinced about it being an option. In our conversation, he brought up counterarguments, one of which was that if we follow the logic of the argument for decoloniality, the white supremacists and Tea Party are also options. And I responded yes, of course. For him that was a problem while for me it was precisely what I mean. I realized that my friend was expecting "option" to be something singular to decoloniality, where only the decolonial is an option. His comments were very helpful, for they made me realize that I need to underscore that the decolonial is on the one hand an option, but in the very act of presenting it as an option, decoloniality makes everything else an option too. We all live among options. That is "reality." It is a reality made of options (e.g., in words, concepts, sentences, narratives, theories oral and/or written). It doesn't matter where we live or who we are, we all live among options; thus, ethics emerges at the moment that, willingly or not, we endorse and engage with a given option. Ethics is the responsibility we assume when engaging and endorsing whatever option we select, whether we live in the city or in the country, in the former Third, Second, or First World. My argument is not so much that the decolonial (in the sense I am conceiving it—as a response to coloniality, or better yet to modernity/coloniality) is an option, but that decolonial thinking and doing, our cultural praxes of living, unfold from birth to death between and among options. Our praxis of living is not what we do when we engage with one or two options; it is in the act of engaging, moment to moment, in the options that guide our living. A second counterargument from my friend was that decoloniality should be conceived as an imperative, not as an option. The question is that options are always imperative for those who engage and endorse a given option: for Republicans, their party is an imperative; for Marxists, Marxism is an imperative; for Muslims and Christians, theological beliefs are imperative. In academia, we live among disciplinary options, and the discipline is imperative for its practitioners. But from a decolonial perspective, they are all options that are imperative for the believers (secular or theological) but not for the nonbelievers. And that is the way it is.

The article from which this chapter evolved was published a decade after the one that was the basis for the previous chapter. In retrospect, it is evident that "globalization" was a term introduced into the vocabulary of political theory and political economy when markets were deregulated and profit was equated (for all practical purposes) with growth. "Globalization" (a term that indeed disguised neoliberalism's projected "globalism") became in the 1980s the replacement for "development," which invaded the field of political theory and political economies from approximately 1950 to 1975. In the 1990s, "globalization" joined forces with postmodern thinking in celebrating a world order without borders. The debates on nation and nationalism that were at center stage in the 1980s moved to second place when globalization, in the 1990s, announced a future with markets increasing to infinity and neoliberal globalism achieving what Christianity couldn't achieve: the neoliberalization of the world.

The theories of Milton Friedman began to take hold in the late 1970s and were institutionalized by Ronald Reagan and Margaret Thatcher in the following decade; "globalization" (the mask for neoliberal globalism) was the rhetorical term to describe imperial designs for remaking global coloniality. Global coloniality, the darker side of postmodern globalization/globalism, explains the frequent concern with the fact that during the past quarter century, globalization meant also a rising poverty line and the growing divide between the haves and have-nots. "Cosmopolitanism" instead was a term reinvigorated by progressive humanists of liberal, postmodern, and Marxist bent. Furthermore, cosmopolitanism was a concern of mainly Western scholars and intellectuals. I did not encounter any interest in cosmopolitanism in Bolivia and Ecuador, South Africa or Indonesia, China or Iran, to name just a few places. I wonder what cosmopolitanism may mean in the Middle East or in Central Asia. Cosmopolitanism, like globalism, was (and may continue to be) unidirectional and housed in the North Atlantic.

Thus, in the article on which the previous chapter was based, I was asking myself what is the place of "cosmopolitanism" in the dreary scenario at the end of the twentieth century? My response at the time started from Im-manuel Kant's cosmopolitan ideals (and by extension from Enlightenment ideals, which clearly reflected his cosmopolitan ambitions), which coexisted with, indeed rested upon, his noted racism. So, the question was, how could cosmopolitanism be possible when the designer of the project had a hierar-chical view of humanity around the planet? It became clear to me then that "cosmopolitanism" was willingly or not a project of Western expansion whose implementation was accomplished through the "civilizing mission" that today is named globalization (disguising that it was a globalist neoliberal design now escaping neoliberal management), and it is implemented by a free market in the economy and by democracy in politics. It became clear to me also how the colonial matrix of power (CMP) works both in the continuity and in the complementarity between different domains and flows to connect domains and levels. The enunciation of "cosmopolitanism" was no longer voiced from liberal frames of mind operating behind progress and the civilizing mission, but by neoliberal principles operating behind development and market de-mocracy. In any event, cosmopolitanism could run and indeed was running parallel to political and economic Westernization. Cosmopolitanism in the twenty-first century could either dissent from re-Westernization or play into its hands. My question then was what would decolonial cosmopolitanism look like, and what decolonial arguments could be advanced to confront the his-tory of Western universal cosmopolitan since the sixteenth century?

Once I reached this conclusion, I set myself to explore the issue in two directions: one historical and the other coeval with the particular "faces" of cosmopolitan projects. Historically, I realized that Kant's cosmopolitanism was coeval with the *Declaration of the Rights of Man and of the Citizen*. While cos-mopolitanism was a world (or global) project, the *Declaration* was concerned with what would be the modern (and European) nation-states. It didn't take too much effort to conclude that the *Declaration* in France, and by extension in England and Germany, by appearing alongside the formation of the modern nation-state, would become—directly or indirectly—associated with cosmo-politan projects. Why? First, because of the complicity between the rights of man, the nation-state form of governance (secular bourgeoisie), and universal cosmopolitanism. Second, if the *Declaration* in Europe were to warranty the civil security of man (let's say of human beings), and if the civil security of man (a singular set of human beings; see chapter 12) were tied to citizenship, then *Declaration of the Rights* worked in two complementary directions. One was chronological, as the *Declaration of the Rights* secured these rights for the life-time of citizens under the secular rule of government within the span of the history of Europe itself. The other was geographical, as the *Declaration* was to become the measuring stick with which to judge social behavior that, according to Western standards, was uncivilized and, therefore, violated the rights of man, a measurement that would eventually be applied outside Europe. The silent assumption was to assume no violation of the rights of citizens, because there was no such social function (citizenship was a European invention for Europeans only) operating outside Europe. Thus, the civilizing mission and cosmopolitanism appeared ultimately to be the underlying project of secular Western expansion (Westernization of the planet).[1]

September 11, 2001, whatever the reasons and motivations behind it, was a wake-up call with many possible outcomes, and not only with respect to globalization/globalism but for cosmopolitanism as well. It was perhaps the first global event that called a halt to the dreams of Kantian cosmopolitanism and neoliberal globalism, and it also revealed the imperial underpinning of the Kantian vision and legacy. If cosmopolitanism were to return to the realm of possibilities after the fall of the Soviet Union and 9/11, it could not have been neoliberal because humanists that promoted cosmopolitanism before had taken a decisive critical stance against globalism. Hence, within the bubble of Western civilization (in the sense that, as I said, cosmopolitanism was not a concern outside the North Atlantic), it had to be either liberal or Marxist. Cosmopolitanism was not debated at this time, as far as I know, among Western Christians. They had other more pressing concerns. In the North Atlantic, the old dream of an Orbis Christianus had been taken over by secular forces. For that reason, any renewed impetus for cosmopolitanism remained within the cosmological orbit of secular Western civilization and thus contributed to maintaining the CMP. In light of these events, then, we return to the question of what the decolonial cosmopolitanism option (decolonial cosmopolitan localism, argued in the previous chapter) would look like. In the following pages, I explore some answers.

II   The Cosmopolitan Call at the Close of the Twentieth Century

Needless to say, what follows is an exercise in decolonial analysis of Western cosmopolitanism. It constitutes a search for decolonial cosmopolitan localism, one option emerging from the experiences and memories of dwelling, thinking, and doing in the borderlands and on the borderlines. Let's begin. "Cosmopolitanism" was a buzzword in the late 1990s and continued to attract interest in the first decade of the twenty-first century, when I published the article on which this chapter is based. Why the widespread interest in cosmopolitanism in the 1990s? I see four main motivations.

One was the previous concern (i.e., in the 1980s) with the limits of national thinking. Nationalism was what cosmopolitanism was trying to overcome. Cross-cultural and planetary dialogues were advanced as roads toward the future, much preferred over leaping to defend and enclose the borders of the nations. Immigration contributed to the surge of cosmopolitanism. Nationalists saw immigration as a problem, cosmopolitans as an opening toward global futures. I explored the complicities between cosmopolitanism and globalism in the previous chapter and the double standards of the nation-state in chapter 4.

The second motivation was the need to build arguments that, moving away from nationalism, did not fall into the hands of the proponents of neoliberal and economic globalization/globalism. Neoliberal ambitions to erase borders to increase economic gains did not coincide with the aims of humanist cosmopolitans to erase borders as a means to end territorial control by nation-states. Thus, one of the strands of cosmopolitan thinking, confronting globalization/ globalism, was caught between honest liberals opposed to neoliberal globalization/ globalism and a renovated Marxism that saw new global players invited to conceive of cosmopolitanism beyond the international proletarian revolution.

A third motivation, related to the first two, was to move away from closed and monocultural conceptions of identity in order to support state designs to control populations by celebrating multiculturalism. At this level, cosmopolitanism focused on the individual: the person was invited to see herself as an open citizen of the world, embodying several "identities." In a word, this was a liberal conception of cosmopolitanism born out of dissent and was simultaneous with the formation in Europe of modern nation-states, which at the end of the twentieth century needed to update their masked imperial vocabulary (the rhetoric of modernity), always hiding but nevertheless enacting the logic of coloniality. Multiculturalism served to prevent the recognition that in reality it was a plurinationality that was at stake. The mononational (one state for one nation) legacy of the eighteenth century was now translated into an ideal of flexible and open cultural citizenship occurring in tandem with the process of neoliberal globalization/globalism.

The fourth motivation, compatible with but also distinct from the second, was the legal proposal to put on the agenda "cosmopolitanism from below," which was eventually connected with the agenda of the World Social Forum.[2] Cosmopolitanism from below should not be confused with decolonial cosmopolitanism. Decolonial cosmopolitanism is neither from above nor from below, neither from the right nor from the left. It is cosmopolitanism created from "the border," the global border mapped by modernity/coloniality—the "/" being the mark that unites and divides modernity from coloniality and signifies the simultaneous unity and division between colonial and imperial differences.

III To Uncouple the Racial Compound of One Nation
to One State

Let's come back to Kant. In his lectures published as *Anthropology from a Pragmatic Point of View*, published toward the end of his life, Kant brought cosmopolitanism into the section he devoted to the "characters of the species." With regard to his cosmopolitan ideas and ideals, the "characters of the species" must be understood in relation to two preceding sections in *Anthropology*: "the character of the nations" and the "character of races." The scope of the character of the nations is limited to six European nations: France, England, and Germany in the first round; Italy, Spain, and Portugal in the second. Racism is manifested in its tracing of intramural imperial difference—within the South of Europe (Italy, Spain, and Portugal) and the northeast heart of Europe (Germany, France, and England)—and its tracing of extramural differences as well (Russia). This last brings it to the very frontier of "nations" and circumscribes the section by stressing its limits: "Since *Russia* has not yet developed definite characteristics from its natural potential; since *Poland* has no longer any characteristics; and since the nationals of European Turkey never have had a character, nor will ever attain what is necessary for a definite national character, the description of these nations' characters may properly be passed over here."[3] If you wonder about the paranoia of the liberal media in the US confronting Donald Trump and accusing Russia of conduct unbecoming a civilized nation, here you find a historical thread: the extramural imperial difference traced to the eighteenth century.

Kant then moves to the "character of races," which is a short section in which "nature" takes the place of "nations" in the previous section. Kant brackets the question of race by focusing instead on the "character of species." And in this section the character of the species "human" (of the race "animals") deserves close scrutiny. Cosmopolitanism comes into the picture in the section "Basic Features Concerning the Description of the Human Species' Characters." Here is how Kant envisioned cosmopolitanism, quoted at length:

> The human race taken collectively (as the entire human species) is a great number of people living successively and simultaneously. *They* cannot be

without peaceful co-existence, and yet they cannot avoid continuous dis-agreement with one another. Consequently, *they* feel destined by nature to develop, through mutual compulsion and laws written by *them*, into *a cosmopolitan society* (*cosmopolitismus*) which is constantly threatened by dissension but generally progressing toward a coalition.

The cosmopolitan society is in itself an unreachable idea, but it is not a constitutive principle (which is expectant of peace amidst the most vigor-ous actions and reactions of men). It is only a *regulative principle* demanding that *we yield generously* to the *cosmopolitan society as the destiny of the human race*; and this not without reasonable ground for supposition that there is a natural inclination in this direction.[4] (Emphasis added.)

In the previous chapter I made reference to Xi Jinping's global "commu-nity of shared destiny."[5] The community of shared destiny for humankind is a diplomatic policy for domestic and foreign affairs. It is not a statement of manifest destiny to rule the world according to China's will, but it is a call that a community of shared destiny should be built by all states involved. *It is a proposal of what should be done, not a blueprint of how to do it.* "Socialism with Chi-nese characteristics" is China's contribution to building the global community of shared destiny.[6] In this sense, there is a significant difference between the universalism of modern Western/Soviet communism and Chinese socialism. Both are proposals that reject globalism as the only game in town. Globalism is the Western neoliberal project; the community of shared destiny is the project of socialism with Chinese characteristics. *Now, it is not an "alternative" to global-ism but a coexisting path to globalization.* China is proposing its own view: a multi-polar state-led cosmopolitanism coexisting with Western scholarly cosmopoli-tanism and state-led unipolar globalism. The closing of Western unipolarity, in knowledge and state politics, should be added to Pope Francis's encyclical *Fratelli Tutti*. It is no doubt a cosmopolitan call that is neither state-led nor a scholarly/political proposal. Referring to "Dark Clouds over a Closed World," Pope Francis stated:

> "Opening up to the world" is an expression that has been co-opted by the economic and financial sector and is now used exclusively [to mean] open-ness to foreign interests or to the freedom of economic powers to invest without obstacles or complications in all countries. Local conflicts and disregard for the common good are exploited by the global economy in order to impose a single cultural model. This culture unifies the world, but divides persons and nations, for "as society becomes ever more globalized, it makes us neighbors, but does not make us brothers."

Reflecting on the consequences of co-opting the expression by economic and financial sectors, he added:

> These are the new forms of cultural colonization. Let us not forget that "peoples that abandon their tradition and, either from a craze to mimic others or to foment violence, or from unpardonable negligence or apathy, allow others to rob their very soul, end up losing not only their spiritual identity but also their moral consistency and, in the end, their intellectual, economic and political independence." One effective way to weaken historical consciousness, critical thinking, the struggle for justice and the processes of integration is to empty great words of their meaning or to manipulate them. Nowadays, what do certain words like democracy, freedom, justice or unity really mean? They have been bent and shaped to serve as tools for domination, as meaningless tags that can be used to justify any action.[7]

One of the most interesting responses to the encyclical was from the World Economic Forum (WEF). Having launched the platform for "The Great Reset," celebrating the opportunities that COVID-19 had opened, the WEF posted the encyclical on its web page with the following comment: "In a striking, 43,000-word-long encyclical published last Sunday, the pope put his stamp on efforts to shape what's been termed a Great Reset of the global economy in response to the devastation of COVID-19."[8] The WEF jumped on the bandwagon, distancing itself from neoliberalism and implementing the "Great Reset" (the topic of their meeting scheduled for January 2021), pushing the re-Westernizing counterreformation facing China's "community of a shared future" that is being advanced through the "Belt and Road Initiative."[9] I am bringing current events into the picture of cosmopolitanism and the decolonial option to underscore, once again, that the cycle of Westernization (1500–2000)—in the middle of which Kant launched his cosmopolitan vision for "perpetual peace"—is closing. We all on the planet are experiencing a change of epoch and no longer an epoch of change. The most visible and palpable sign, as I argue in this book, is that the closing of Westernization (an epoch of changes, newness, novelty, linear time progress, unipolarity) is over. This doesn't mean that it is the end of the West but of Westernization. The West will remain one regional civilization among others. This is perhaps the main reason why China, Russia, and Turkey are looking into a reconfiguration of their territories as *civilizational-states* rather than *nation-states*.[10]

Decoloniality (the people's project of delinking and reexisting) and deWesternization (a state-led project of delinking from Westernization and reconstitution of the destituted) have provoked the counterreformation I describe as re-Westernization. Furthermore, the forceful intervention of the papacy with the encyclical *Fratelli Tutti* introduces a new dimension in which cosmopolitan localism opens up pluriversality in the sphere of knowing and sensing as well as in interstate multipolarity and the papacy's interreligious coexistence. Cosmopolitan localism shall be a multilocal and multilayered co-existence of concurrent projects for living in harmony and plenitude.

IV Revisiting Kant's Cosmopolitanism

The time has arrived, with awareness of the current scenario, to take a closer look at Kant's cosmopolitan proposal and his legacies. The idea and the horizon of a cosmopolitan society is predicated, by Kant, on the bases of a previous consideration he has established between freedom and law, the two pivots or pillars of any civil legislation: "If authority is combined with freedom and law, the principles of freedom and law are ensured with success." He considers four conceivable combinations of authority with freedom and law:

1　Law and freedom without authority (anarchy);
2　Law and authority without freedom (despotism);
3　Authority without freedom and law (barbarism);
4　Authority, with freedom and law (republic).[11]

Needless to say, Kant privileges the last one. And, therefore, cosmopolitan ideals presuppose the republican organization of society in which authority goes hand in hand with freedom and law. As Kant himself recognized, cosmopolitanism is an idea that may become despotic and anarchic if authority with freedom and law in Nation A is considered the ideal of social organization for Nations B, C, D, E, F, G, and the failure of Nations B, C, D . . . G to attain this organization then becomes a reason for Nation A to intervene in their affairs and attempt to remake them. This was precisely the presupposition underlying Kant's vision of a global order he conceived as cosmopolitan. Since the entire planet beyond France, England, and Germany (the core of Europe) was deficient in one way or another, the conclusion was obvious: cosmopolitanism would become the tool of the civilizing mission.

There is another aspect of a cosmopolitan social order that we must bring to the foreground because it raises important implications that were already recognized in the eighteenth century. In his landmark book *Cosmopolis: The Hidden Agenda of Modernity* (1990), Stephen Toulmin cast the idea of a cosmopolis in a new light: cosmopolis was a significant aspect of the hidden agenda of modernity. Why the hidden agenda? Because what motivated Toulmin to write this book was the moment in which he recognized that the images of *modernity* he had absorbed in England in the decades of the 1930s and 1940s were faulty, partial, and overtly celebratory. Toulmin uncovered two dimensions of the idealistic and triumphal image of modernity ingrained mainly in Protestant Europe. One was that the seventeenth century, far from being a golden age of Europe that prompted the advent of science and philosophy, was a moment of economic crisis marked by the decay of the Spanish Empire and the not-yet flourishing of a new imperial era. Holland was enjoying a moment of commercial glory provided by the Dutch East Indies Company, but Western Christians were killing each other in the Thirty Years' War, a religious conflict with economic and political underpinnings.[12]

The second factor prompting Toulmin's thesis was the humanistic tradition he discovered in his early reading of Michel de Montaigne's *Essais*. This humanistic tradition ran parallel to the advent of modern science and secular philosophy; it was the humanistic tradition, initiated during the European Renaissance, that broke away from the theological and epistemological control of the church and the papacy. That, in a nutshell, was for Toulmin the hidden agenda of modernity: the inauguration of cosmopolis, which, in his argument, arises out of this humanistic vein, although of course mixed with the emerging Western scientific models of the universe. For him the idea of the cosmopolis (the intersection of the cosmos and the city) was not so much a translation of the Greek word as it was the model of the cosmos that physics and astronomy were making available at the time (from Galileo to Newton). However, at that time the cosmos was already separated from the city (and the social), which was not the case in ancient Greek cosmology.

Toulmin adumbrates the issue in the following manner: "We are here concerned, not with 'science' as the modern positivists understand it, but with a *cosmopolis* that gives a comprehensive account of the world, so as to bind things together in politico-theological as much as in scientific or explanatory, terms."[13] He explains that the cosmopolitical reconstruction of European society after the Thirty Years' War was based on two pillars or principles: *stability* and *hierarchy*. *Stability* applied to interrelations among sovereign nations. "Sovereign nation" (in reality, the sovereign state) was a conception in the mind of European thinkers (like Kant, for example), and it applied to the very society in which they were dwelling and thinking, based on the legacy they wanted to preserve in order to exist in the manner they desired—the outcome of which was basically the six modern and imperial European nations (Germany, England, France, Spain, Italy, and Portugal, with Holland interregnum). The imperial question was not part of the picture of stable relations among sovereign nations in the process of becoming states.[14] *Hierarchy* applied to the domestic organization of society and to the internal organization of each individual state. The presupposed *totality* was that of the six Western countries: three of them the core of Europe, two of them the South of Europe, and one, Holland, neither in the core nor in the South of Europe but an imperial commercial force in the Caribbean and in Southeast Asia (see the previous chapter on the making of the South of Europe).

Toulmin further explains—and reminds us—that by 1700 social relations (*hierarchy*) within nation-states were defined *horizontally* based on superordination and subordination of class relations: "Social stability depended on all the parties in society 'knowing their place' relative to the others, and knowing what reciprocal modes of behavior were appropriate and rational."[15] The planetary model of society was based on the *hierarchical* domestic relations in each nation-state. And the model was, Toulmin observes, "explicitly *cosmo-political.*" How come?

Toulmin observes that without a justification, the imposition of hierarchy on "the lower orders" by "the better sort" of people would be arbitrary and self-serving. *To the extent that this hierarchy mirrored the structure of nature*, its *authority* was self-explanatory, self-justifying, and seemingly rational.[16] The cosmopolis is the organization of society mirroring the structure of the cosmos (nature). *Indeed, it was mirroring the scientific (ontological) image of the cosmos, not the ontic structure of the cosmos itself*, for the cosmos could be conceived as a structure governed by law or as constant movements and flows that cannot be fixed in mathematical formulas. Leaving aside the synonymy of *cosmos* and *nature* (to which I will return in chapter 14), here we encounter *authority* and *law* (posited by Kant) to manage hierarchies, but not yet *freedom*. So, let's take it one step further and see how the *polis* could be organized following the model of the *cosmos* so as to find the place of *freedom* in Toulmin's understanding of cosmopolitics. In this effort we understand the following as the undisclosed assumptions:

a   The *hierarchical organization* of each nation-state (*polis*) should follow the model provided by the law of the *cosmos*.
b   The *stable relations* among nation-states should also be modeled on the law of nature (*cosmos*) that serves as the model for the organization of each state within itself (*polis*).

Toulmin puts it this way: "The philosophical belief that nature obeys mathematical 'laws' which will ensure its stability for so long as it pleases God to maintain it, was a socially revolutionary idea: both *cosmos* and *polis* (it appeared) were self-contained, and their joint 'rationality' guaranteed their stability. As recently as 1650, people worried that the World was grinding to its End: by 1720, their grandchildren were confident that a rational and omniscient Creator had made a world that ran perfectly."[17] By 1776 this idea had been applied to the economy, and the belief took hold that economic transactions were guided by an "invisible hand," which, like God or nature, regulated and balanced the field of economic forces. This idea lasted until the autumn of 2008, when Wall Street exploded, blowing off the fingers of the invisible hand and depriving it from playing the strings and guiding the marionettes.

V   Kant's Traces and the Traces That Kant Erased

If *cosmopolitan* ideals are maintained *in* and *for* the twenty-first century, *cosmopolitanism* should be accountable for its crimes: the very foundation of *cosmopolitanism* as envisioned by Kant and explained by Toulmin was in complicity with the formation of European imperial powers and with the European expansion into America, Africa, and Asia, as well as with the continuation of Europe in the United States, as Hegel was anticipating.[18] To maintain *cosmopolitan ideals* we (all those who engage in this conversation) need to decolonize cosmopolitanism (which I have been trying to do in this chapter and the previous one), and this task requires us to communally seek paths of reexistence that are no longer modeled on the law of nature and are not state regulated, but are modeled on a praxis of living in harmony and joy, recovering to reexist in the biology of love (see preface). The horizon of decolonial cosmopolitan localism must be pluriversal and horizontal rather than universal and vertical. The politics of decolonial investigations shall assist us in unlearning the modeling of society cut off from the *cosmos* by the *human invention* of *its law*, to relearn modeling the communal immersed in the constant flow and movement of the *life of the cosmos* (see chapters 7 and 14).

In what follows I will argue this idea, but I will take a step forward from the seventeenth century, where Toulmin learned that the idea of "modernity" found its energies in the Renaissance, and especially from humanists, where he discovered modernity's hidden agenda, beyond the celebration of science and secular philosophy. This step forward will take us to the formation of the United States and the early twentieth century's transformation of European cosmopolitan ideals. Here massive immigration from Europe agitated the quiet waters of two centuries of Pilgrims' procreation, Native American repression, and enslaved African exploitation.

About 130 years before Immanuel Kant gave his pragmatically oriented lectures on anthropology (1772–1773), the need for international law emerged in the consciousness of Western Christians. In Europe the Council of Trent was setting the stage for a bloody scenario that would consume Western Christian Europe until the Peace of Westphalia (1648), ending both the Thirty Years' War and the eighty-year war riding on the conflicts between Spain and the Netherlands. We encounter here again the legal theologians of Salamanca, who were starting their long journey in quest of a solution to two interrelated problems: to what extent Indians in the New World were human, and to what extent, as a consequence, they had property rights. Far from the minds of Castilians was simply to think for a minute that property rights were not universal, and that in the Inca, Maya, and Aztec civilizations, as well as in other communities in the Caribbean, land as property was unthinkable, and when these communities were informed about private property, it was nonsense to them. "Land" was not divided into distinct marketable parcels in the minds of wiser men from Pachamama in the Andes and Tonantzin in the Valley of Mexico. Since such a way of thinking was not understood by Spaniards, they attributed it either to the ignorance of the "Indians" or to the work of the devil upon them. By Kant's time, the memories of Andean and Mesoamerican civilizations had been twice forgotten. Spaniards had already disqualified and destituted, by the middle of the eighteenth century, what the "Indians" thought. Simultaneously, Kant marginalized the Spaniards. In the first case, the extramural colonial difference continued its work of destitution; in the second, the intramural imperial difference initiated the destitution of the South of Europe. But Kant, who was already into the same logic of destitution (coloniality) that the Spanish Christians applied to Incas and Aztecs, projected it toward Asian and African civilizations. Except that Kant did not attribute to the work of the devil what he did not understand. For him, it was just the reality of barbarism confronted by civilization.

What Kant couldn't know (nor de Vitoria before him) was that the Greek cosmopolis had more in common with the Quechua-Aymara Tawantinsuyu (the world, cosmos, and city, organized into four suyus or sections connecting heaven with earth and with the underground) than with Kant's cosmopolis. Indeed, one could surmise that Tawantinsuyu could have served equally well as the model image for the human species. But the mathematic and geometric projection, in Europe, to understand the cosmos separated the human from its living energy, which is the living energy that engendered the human species. As a matter of fact, Guaman Poma de Ayala did exactly that 250 years before Kant when he laid out his *Nueva corónica y buen gobierno* and proposed to Philip III a conceptual model of a vast communal space in constant flow (*pacha*)—"The Indies of the New World," as Guaman Poma de Ayala referred to the mixed coexistence of Incan and Spanish rule in the viceroyalty of Peru and the Inca Tawantinsuyu (see preface).[19] And Tawantinsuyu was a complex communal organization modeled on the Southern Cross.[20] I am not emphasizing Guaman Poma because his decolonial politics were based on *pacha* instead of cosmos at a time "before" Kant. I am saying that Kant's cosmopolis was a regional and imperial conception of social organization, just as Guaman Poma's was. Why should Indigenous people in the Andes (or for that matter Latin Americans of European descent) have to rely on Aristotle and the European Enlightenment, rather than beginning from Guaman Poma de Ayala? His conceptual model of the first imperial/colonial society since the sixteenth century was meant to solve a cosmopolitical problem of a particular kind: the formation of a modern/colonial domestic society and its intertwined forms of governance (Tawantinsuyu in the Andes and monarchy in Spain).

And here is precisely the catch. Why should we in the New World be limited to cosmo-politics and not also to *pacha*-politics, given that *pacha* philosophy was already an expression in circulation here?[21] There is no reason other than the coloniality of knowledge to think of "cosmopolitanism" universally instead of pluriversally. Instead of planning such social organizations on the basis of a colonially determined hierarchy and intergovernance (enforced stability), Guaman Poma, in accordance with everything else we know of the history of civilizations and *pacha*-sophy in the Andes, thought first about *relations and balance/equilibrium*.[22] That is, he considered the relationality (in Spanish the word is *vincularidad*) existing among all the manifestations of the lifeworld: lightning, thunder, water, darkness, plants, mountains, animals, rivers, plants, *runa* (the human species *in* the cosmos, which cannot be translated as "human" because human is *separated from* the cosmos), etc. For that reason the social is not equivalent to the communal. The former is a Western concept that separates society from the cosmos. The latter is a concept from the First Nations—the communal includes *runa* in the cosmos. Relationality makes the concept of "nature" both unnecessary and aberrant; and "balance/equilibrium" refers to those conditions among the forms life on the planet. In the Western vocabulary "relationality" is equivalent to "animism."

Guaman Poma's decolonial political treatise remains exemplary. The concept of "good governance" recently entered the vocabulary of international relations and international law.[23] The meaning of this term as used by the United Nations belongs to the rhetoric of modernity. In contrast, its meaning for Guaman Poma de Ayala (*buen gobierno*) and its meaning in the twentieth-century Zapatista expression (*juntas de buen gobierno*) are decolonial concepts that delink it from what the United Nations calls "good governance." Similarly, radical Indigenous thinkers and activists in Canada who reject "recognition" build decolonial arguments in the sense that their actions are responses to both the rhetoric of modernity and the logic of coloniality, while the United Nations' use of the term continues modernity/coloniality's legacies inscribed in the colonial tradition.[24] My use of the expression "good government" here and in all my work follows the genealogy of decolonial thinking from Guaman Poma to the Zapatistas to the Indigenous thinkers in Canada. The meaning of the term as used by the United Nations, however, belongs to a different genealogy of political thought.

VI The Atlantic Detour

Let's get back to the "Atlantic detour" before Kant advanced his ideas on cosmopolitanism. For Kant, a thread of cosmopolitan thinking led directly from ancient Greece to eighteenth-century Germany. But eighteenth-century Germany could not have been what it was without three centuries of European economic, political, and epistemic consolidation benefiting from the Atlantic economy in the double movement of constitution/destitution. Let's review how *ius gentium* and Orbis Christianus mutated into the *rights of man and of the citizen* and ultimately into cosmopolitanism. Antony Anghie has made two decisive points about de Vitoria and the historical origins of international law: "My argument, then, is that de Vitoria is concerned, not so much with the *problem of order among sovereign states but the problem of order among societies belonging to two different cultural systems.* De Vitoria resolves this problem by focusing on the cultural practices of each society and assessing them in terms of the universal law of *jus gentium. Once this framework is established,* he demonstrates that the Indians e.g., barbarians in Vitoria's vocabulary are in violation of universal natural law. Indians are included within a system only to be disciplined"[25] (emphasis added).

To be included only to be disciplined is a modern Western political belief and strategy that continues until today. That is why there is not ontic outside the CMP but *exteriority* created in the double processes of constitution/destitution (see introduction, section III). That is also why the decolonial politics of Indigenous people in Canada reject recognition: they know that to be recognized is to be submitted to settler-state discipline. And that belongs to a different sensibility, knowledge, belief, and conviction from what they themselves hold. Therefore, thinking decolonially and doing decolonial politics, we find three parameters affecting cosmopolitan ideals (from Orbis Christianus to globalism) that deserve attention. The first is that the distinction between the two cultural systems underscored by Anghie has not been proposed by "Indians" (or barbarians), but by de Vitoria unilaterally. Unilateral decision-making has been a prerogative of the manager of the colonial matrix of power from the imposition of Spanish government in the sixteenth century to the foreign interventions of the US in the twenty-first. Unilateralism in this case means that the *colonial difference* was inscribed in the apparent equality between people belonging (thinking, doing, sensing, being) to two different cultures or nations both endowed by natural law with *ius gentium*. The colonial difference was foremost *epistemological*, not ontological. It was *made up*, not a description of what there is. That is, by recognizing equality by birth and by natural law, Spaniards and barbarians were said to be ontologically equals. However, epistemically barbarians were not yet ready to govern themselves according to the standards established by *human law*. And here is where de Vitoria's distinction between divine, natural, and human law pays its dividends.

The second parameter affecting his cosmopolitanism is that the legal framework existed to regulate its violation. And when a violation occurred, then the creator and enforcers of the framework had a justification to invade and use force to punish and expropriate the violator, a system still at work today. John Locke wonderfully rehearsed this logic in his *Second Treatise on Government* (1689). One can say that "coloniality" in de Vitoria set the stage not only for international law but also for modern and European conceptions of governmentality. It seems obvious that Locke did not get as much from Machiavelli as from the emergence of international law in the sixteenth century, and in the way that de Vitoria and his followers in Spain and Portugal discussed both the question of "property" and "governance" in the interaction between Christians and barbarians. Machiavelli was thinking politically in the context of a conflicted Italy of the first half of the sixteenth century. His concern was to advise the Prince about how to obtain or maintain power and how to regulate conflict in Italy, not between Spaniards and barbarians. So, for Machiavelli there was no "thief," as in Locke, and no violators of natural law, as in de Vitoria. What happened in the Atlantic was not of Machiavelli's concern, but it was of the essence for Locke and de Vitoria.

The third parameter is that the "legal framework" is not established by divine or natural law but by human interests, and in this case, the interests of Christian Castilian males. Thus, the "framework" presupposes a very well pinpointed, singular locus of enunciation that, guarded by divine and natural law, is presumed to be universal. And fourth, the universal and unilateral frame "includes" the barbarians and/or Indians (invoking a principle that is valid for all politics of inclusion we hear today) in their difference and so justifying any action Christians might take to tame them. Thus, the making, transforming, and maintaining of the *epistemic colonial difference* goes hand in hand with the establishment of *exteriority*: the invented places outside the frame (barbarians, primitives, communists, terrorists) that are created by the frame so the frame (Western civilization) can be controlled and legislated. A jump to the present shows that since the collapse of the Soviet Union, the rhetoric of modernity used to control and legislate has been "national security."[26] A concern with national security is common to both neoliberal globalism and the extreme forms of nationalism that contest globalism and are on the rise in the West (in the UK, Hungary, Poland, the US). National interests and national security obstruct cosmopolitanism as well as globalism. At this point, however, they are responses to neoliberal globalism in both the European Union and the US, where neoliberalism originated. If *exteriority*, in other words, is the outside invented in the process of building the inside, the rise of nationalism is a response from intramural colonial differences in the cases of Poland and Hungary, from intramural imperial difference in the UK (Brexit), and from *intramural conflicts* (there is no exteriority in this case) between globalists and nationalists in the US.

Anghie made a second observation that coincides with one of the basic principles upon which modernity/coloniality has been built: "Clearly, then, de Vitoria's work suggests that the conventional view that sovereignty doctrine was developed in the West and then transferred to the non-European world is, in important respects, misleading. *Sovereignty doctrine acquired its character through the colonial encounter*. This is the darker history of sovereignty, which cannot be understood by any account of the doctrine that assumes the existence of sovereign states"[27] (emphasis added). De Vitoria developed without planning to the initial narrative of international law that built the idea and the goals of Western civilization by employing its basic tools: the rhetoric of modernity to promote salvation while hiding the logic of coloniality to advance dispossessions. Here Anghie helps us read de Vitoria decolonially by highlighting the initial moments in the gestation of the CMP and the complicities of modernity/coloniality in discourses, conversations, arguments, and procedures. So, then, if the imperial praxis was and is supported by narratives, arguments, conversations, and discourses, and this praxis built the edifice of Western civilization—coloniality and the idea of modernity—the structure of the edifice was hidden in the basement while the rhetoric of modernity promoted the edifice, promising an open front door. At this juncture, decolonial praxes find in the politics of decolonial investigations two fundamental tasks: on the one hand, the analytic of the strategies to promote modernity and hide coloniality, of constituting and building over the ruins of the destituted; and, on the other, to build decolonial ways of knowing and knowledge leading to the healing of colonial wounds and the building of communal paths of reexistence. Here is where border thinking (because of the variety of local histories entangled with Western civilization) enters the picture of decolonial praxis and the politics of decolonial investigations.

Anghie points us toward the radical epistemic shift necessary to decolonize our inherited view of Eurocentered modernity: after the Peace of Westphalia, international (more properly, interstate) relations based on the concept of sovereignty emerged in Europe to regulate the embryonic interstate system where, within Europe, states were considered sovereign. This is the local as well as the regional situation in which Kant was thinking about cosmopolitanism. But beyond the heart of the Europe of his time (England, France, and Germany), when Kant faced Russia, Turkey, and Poland, what he faced was indeed a constellation of *colonial and imperial differences*. And these *differences*, in Kant's era, were being refashioned in two directions that matched each other:

1 COLONIAL DIFFERENCE (EXTRAMURAL). Orientalism, as analyzed by Edward Said, was nothing other than an updating of the colonial difference that de Vitoria had already established between Christian Europe and the barbarians, now applied to secular Europe's difference from the Orient. With regard to Poland, the colonial difference was intramural.

2 IMPERIAL DIFFERENCE (INTRAMURAL). The invention of the South of Europe (apparent in Kant and Hegel) recast colonial difference into *internal imperial difference*; the emerging imperial countries (England, Germany, France, now leading the European Union) separated themselves from Christian and southern countries (Greece, Italy, Spain, and Portugal), with France occupying an intermediary position. Being a Latin country, it was neither Catholic nor Orthodox and shared with England and Germany the making of the South of Europe. The traces of this mutation of the CMP are still felt in the organization and hierarchies of the European Union. With regard to Russia and Turkey (really the Ottoman sultanate), the extramural imperial difference was enacted. Notice also that at the time of conceiving the nation-state, what was then the Ottoman sultanate became Turkey the nation-state.

Kant's cosmopolitanism was fashioned by the implicit assumption that beyond the heart of Europe was the land of those who had yet to be brought into civilization. His cosmopolitanism was a companion of the civilizing mission. To a significant degree, the South of Europe was rather too close to the Moors and showed evidence of mixed blood, so that a touch of civilization was desirable to "bring" them into civilized northern Europe. Kant's cosmopolitanism looks today like the runner-up in a contest to identify the most strident rhetoric of national interests and national security.

VII Looking Forward from Kant to the Present: *Homo Economicus* and *Homo Technologicus*

If we jump from the era of European "cosmopolitan" modernity and its civilizing mission (with England and France leading the way) to the post-Soviet world order guided by globalism, we have a time-lapse image of the continuities and diachronic accumulations of the rhetoric of modernity (salvation, conviviality, prosperity, and freedom) as well as its darker side, the logic of coloniality (discrimination, racism, domination, unilateralism, and exploitation). Manfred Steger's distinction between globalization and globalism was not misled by all the noise about "globalization." He saw the trick, that revamping the logic of coloniality (not his words) required a new rhetoric and vocabulary, one that would hide in plain sight that what was concealed under globalization (the march of history) was globalism (neoliberal global designs). For Steger, globalism is "an Anglo-American market ideology that reached its zenith in the 1990s," and was inextricably linked to the rising fortunes of neoliberal political forces in the world's sole remaining superpower.[28] Globalism in the last analysis was a neoliberal cosmopolitan state project, similar to Kant's cosmopolitanism in philosophy. Anchored in ideas launched and unfolded after World War II by Friedrich Hayek and Milton Friedman—in radical confrontation with the state-regulated economy of the Soviet Union—neoliberal ideas were implemented by Ronald Reagan and Margaret Thatcher in ways that contributed to the spectacular collapse not only of the Soviet Union but also to the Wall Street stock market in September-October 2008. The compelling interest of globalism—in relation to previous periods of (1) theological international law and (2) secular state and interstate regulations after Westphalia (Locke, Kant)—is that while the first (Orbis Christianus) employed Christian theology (divine, natural, and human law) as its overarching frame, and the second (secular cosmopolitanism) endorsed secular philosophy and science (the physical law of the cosmos formulated from Copernicus to Galileo to Newton) to regulate society and imagine a cosmopolitan world, the third (globalism) had the "invisible hand" of the market guiding the economy and reigning supreme over much other state regulation. What is less noted about the "invisible hand," introduced by Adam Smith, is that Smith conceived it during the same years Kant was imagining cosmopolitanism and conviviality. Both Smith and Kant were searching for underlying determinants of worldly phenomena at a time when the natural sciences were translating natural laws into mathematical formulas, almost as if they shared a hidden and unconscious complicity with de Vitoria and (Christian) divine and natural laws.

As we move forward to neoliberal globalism from "good governance" in the sense de Vitoria and Locke imagined (the first through international law, the second through regulation by the nation-state), we put *Homo economicus* in the driver's seat (instead of a Christian and civilized confrontation with the barbarians), and as a consequence it might be said to have contributed to civilizing ourselves in one dimension and to barbarizing and uncivilizing ourselves in another. At this point "barbarians" of all kinds lose their fascination and their power to affect us. Globalism is not so much concerned with taming barbarians or the legality of international relations as it is with reducing costs and increasing gains. Barbarians have been replaced by primitives, then by communists, and now by terrorists in the sense that any dissenting voice is a "terrorist," that is, a threat to the system. But now what globalism has to defend are not civilizations, nor Christianity, but *Homo economicus*. *Homo economicus* and concurrent neoliberal globalism have given the final coup to democracy.

Democracy and capitalism have become an oxymoron; cosmopolitanism and capitalism are another oxymoron. Thus, the turmoil in which the EU finds itself after Brexit and the election of Donald Trump is the historical consequence of five hundred years of an effective rhetoric of modernity hiding the logic of coloniality, made possible by the control of knowledge (linguistically, institutionally, through trained actors, and via the concentration of wealth in the West, etc.). Decolonial investigations are bringing to light that the Western idea of "good government" is not only different from the decolonial politics of Guaman de Poma and the Zapatistas, but also from de-Westernization (see chapter 8).[29] Shall we still rely on Plato, Aristotle, Locke, etc., to maintain unipolar global governance? Or it is time to bring back reconstituted Confucian principles of harmony under heaven and the shared destiny of humankind, as well as First Nations principles of good governance, elaborating on the experiences and narratives of Guaman Poma de Ayala and the Zapatistas?

When *Homo economicus* took the field, questions related to the nature of humanity, of who is human or less human, lost their relevance for the state and for banks, corporations, and other interstate economic institutions (e.g., the International Monetary Fund, the World Bank). *Homo economicus* came with a powerful companion to support his/her ideals: the so-called Number 2, the cybernetic machine that talks to us on the telephone and tells us what is the best route from point A to point B.[30] While Newton mutated theological natural law dictated by God into mathematical natural law dictated by humans, Kant's cosmopolitanism was modeled on Newton's scientific law of the cosmos rather than on theological narratives about the creation and the ordering of the cosmos. About two hundred years after Kant (following WWII), cybernetics came into being simultaneously with the US taking over as world leader, displacing Germany, France, and England, which had regulated the world order during Kant's time. These changes were coupled with the mathematization of the economy (*Homo economicus*), to provide the foundations and celebration of a technological revolution that made it possible to liberate the economy from state regulation. Cosmopolitanism at this point may have become an unwilling companion of both *Homo economicus* and Number 2 (see the four reasons for the advent of cosmopolitanism at the beginning of this chapter). Citizens mutated into consumers. Hence, cosmopolitan consumerism is not a project but a de facto consequence of market regulations.

Modern and postmodern cosmopolitanism today confront *Homo economicus* and *Homo technologicus* (Number 2—which corresponds to Man/Human3 in Sylvia Wynter's narrative; see chapter 12). Life, human and otherwise, receded to second place and was subjected to both. What counts now are people who can work and consume regardless of their religious belief, their skin color, or their sexuality. "Globalism" is the global neoliberal design of a particular type of economy coupled with the civilizing mission of a homogenous government and culture under neoliberal dictates. Cosmopolitanism is a liberal rather than a neoliberal design. Globalism and cosmopolitanism are, then, different versions of an underlying expression of power in the long history of Western imperial expansion. Both would like to have a planetary order to conform to the West. On the one hand the ruling neoliberal economic and political elites, and on the other the ruling liberal intelligentsia that is critical (and this is the "critical" in "critical cosmopolitanism") of globalism. I arrived at an answer to my initial questions in the first paragraph of this chapter: what are the correlations between cosmopolitanism and globalism? Today neoliberal globalism may have loosened the grip it once had on the CMP. Globalism has been stopped and defied by de-Westernization (see chapters 8 and 14). De-Westernization has been possible because of the consolidation of economies that delinked from Western political theories (neoliberal democracy) and Western political economy (liberal and neoliberal ideologies tied to the economy). So today, modern and postmodern cosmopolitanism (confronting neoliberal globalism) also have to confront the conflict between re-Westernization (former president Barack Obama's foreign policy) and de-Westernization (the failure of neoliberalism). Decolonial cosmopolitanism, too, must confront both trends. My argument is one beginning of this confrontation: a decolonial analytics of the confrontation between re-Westernization and de-Westernization and the decolonial project of gnoseological and aesthesic reconstitutions for reexisting.

VIII Decolonial Cosmopolitan Localism

I have been engaged in a decolonial analytic of Western cosmopolitanism from the perspective of decolonial cosmopolitan localism. It is time now to switch gears and move from the analytic to the perspective and to concentrate, decolonially, on cosmopolitan localism to propose a double departure aimed at a radical shift in the geopolitics of knowing, sensing, believing, and being (*estar*).[31] The scenarios in which decolonial cosmopolitan localism could be thought out (conceptual praxis) and enacted (education and communal and institutional building) are the following:

1 The mutations from universal and monocentric to pluriversal and polycentric thinking, sensing, and doing. What you sense and do depends on what you think, and vice versa, for the simple reason that living is doing and doing is living. From 1500 to 2000, the world order became increasingly unipolar in interstate relations and universal in the sphere of knowledge and understanding. Since 2000, the world order has mutated to a multipolar order in interstate relations and pluriversality in the domain of knowing and sensing (very evident in 2017 when I first wrote this chapter and more evident in the fall of 2020 when I am editing it). Where decoloniality is more evident now is in the growing decolonial responses—all over, and not just in the US or the European Union—confronting racism, sexism, religious fundamentalism, disciplinary control, and regulation (by, e.g., universities, museums, elementary schools, communal organizations); fighting extractivism; protesting the state's regulated abuses; protesting climate change and the robotic replacement of labor; etc. All of this coexists with re-Westernization (unipolar and universal), de-Westernization (multipolar in political theory), and the changing intensity of Vatican politics in global affairs. The decolonial option, an affair of the political society in the public sphere, coexists today with de-Westernization and re-Westernization in interstate regulations and with religious, disciplinary, ideological, and artistic options in the public sphere at large (i.e., everyday praxes of living).

2 An economic and political polycentric and multipolar world order is not, of course, a decolonial world order because the colonial matrix of power

is still at work. Pluriversality is an option coexisting with the current conflict between unipolarity and multipolarity. Multipolarity means, in the current world order, that the control of the colonial matrix of power is being disputed, no longer solely controlled by the West—led by the US—in spite of its effort to maintain domination once hegemony has been lost. The decolonial option calls into question the CMP and therefore detaches and delinks from both. As an option in the public sphere and in education, it simply means that it has existed as an option, in variegated forms, since the Bandung Conference of 1955 provided a signpost and a point of reference. In tandem, decolonial cosmopolitan localism is not (yet) thought out and activated in the sphere of the state, due to the fact that the state form of governance (the monarchic or secular nation-state) is a crucial institution for maintaining the CMP, although today there is dispute over its management. The decolonial is an option that falls in the domain of what Partha Chatterjee describes as "political society."[32] That is, the sphere of "civil society" described by Hegel in the framework of liberal cosmopolitanism and the secular order of society has been expanded, mainly in the twentieth century, by the irruption and disruption of the "political society," a part of which includes "social movements," the variegated feminist and LGTBQ organizations, scholarships, blogs, reconstituting gnoseological and aesthesically what has been destituted, while simultaneously affirming and restituting praxes of living that no one and no institutions have the right to prevent if such praxes don't intrude on coexisting praxes of living. Pluriversality means just that.

The decolonial option, then, becomes the connector, the spine of decolonial cosmopolitan localism, the link that connects colonial experiences and colonial wounds in planetary decolonial processes of healings that, at this point, are not coordinated but are prompted by the global awareness of coloniality; while coloniality is the thread connecting a variety of colonial wounds with uncommon local histories but a common sensing of colonial wounds and similar decolonial responses. Therefore, decolonial cosmopolitan localism cannot be a project managed by a mastermind, institution, or computer program; it is a name to identify the nexuses among the revivals and rebirths rejecting the CMP's regulations in their re-Western and de-Western manifestations. In sum, decolonial cosmopolitan localism accounts for and is part of people's manifestations (in deeds and thoughts, arguments and visual and aural signs) enacting the decolonial option; cuts across identities *in* ordinary life and *in* politics.[33] The decolonial option materializes along multiple trajectories where identities *in* politics emerge, reflecting the reality that decolonial politics is about life under regulation by the CMP, and about the kind of governance needed to delink from the state that is the regulator. Decolonial politics confronts the state's controls over life—over politics from the Renaissance to the Enlightenment; over biopolitics from the Enlightenment to WWII; and over technopolitics (Number 2) from WWII on.[34] Beyond individual identities, the commonalties that label peoples and communities as being "not quite human" as well as "not quite X" run like a thread connecting many groups and projects in global processes of decolonial cosmopolitanism localism and aiming toward the horizon of pluriversality as a universal project.

IX Closing Remarks

Frantz Fanon wrote the following paragraph in the middle of Algerian and Third World struggles for decolonization:

> I am ready to concede that on the plane of factual being the past existence of an Aztec civilization does not change anything very much in the diet of the Mexican peasant of today. . . . But it has been remarked several times that this passionate search for a national culture which existed before the colonial era finds its legitimate reason in the anxiety shared by native intellectuals to shrink away from that Western culture in which they all risk being swamped. Because they realize they are in danger of losing their lives and thus becoming lost to their people, these men, hotheaded and with anger in their hearts, relentlessly determine to renew contact once more with the oldest and most pre-colonial springs of life of their people.[35]

Today we might like to replace "men" with "human beings," which is what I think Fanon meant, although at the time the unconscious use of "men" for "human beings" was widespread and ingrained in everybody's mind. How is this paragraph related to the decolonial options and to decolonial cosmopolitan localism?

Let's translate "nativism" in Fanon's vocabulary into "localism" and be clear that local histories have been conformed by the colonial matrix of power projecting its global designs over the planet. "Localism" then emerges, helped by the advent of a powerful Third World intellectual at a time of decolonization during the Cold War. "Localism" now exists, created out of existing local histories before the invasion of Europe's own local history, which then devises and implements its imperial designs (with the US taking over the management of these designs after WWII). After the invasion, each local history mutated into borderland/borderline local histories. At this point, the search for "national culture," in Fanon's words—which is the search for the need to reemerge out of the ruins (physical and psychological) left by European invasions (physical and psychological)—becomes an existential need not to succumb to these global designs. The *forced* mode of existences in the borderland created by the invasion of the idea of modernity *provokes* decolonial responses to the colonial wounds caused by coerced modes of existence. These responses are driven by decolonial healing through the search for modes of *reexistence*. This is the moment in which the past, in whatever form of expression it takes, becomes essential to decolonial healing and decolonial cosmopolitanism. Decolonial cosmopolitanism then becomes the connector among people and projects around the world. At this level, decolonial politics is not about the state; it is about modes of reexistence and forms of governance needed in each local history.

I close by adding to Fanon's quotation a parallel one from Taiaiake Alfred, from the Kahnawake Nation in Canada. Arguing for the need to reemerge and reexist in preference to being recognized by the state, Alfred says, "The principles underlying European-style representative government through coercive force stand in fundamental opposition to the values from which Indigenous leadership and power derive. In Indigenous cultures, the core values of equality and respect are reflected in the practices of consensus decision-making and dispute resolution through balanced consideration of all interests and views. In Indigenous societies, governance results from the interactions of leadership and autonomous power of the individuals who make up the society. *Governance in an Indigenist sense can be practiced only in a decentralized, small-scale environment among people who share a culture*"[36] (emphasis added).

Decolonial cosmopolitan localism contributes to highlighting the commonality between very diverse projects of reexistence arising from heterogeneous modes of existence that have been demonized (primitive, barbarian, gay, lesbian, LGTBQ, Indian, Black, Muslim, those of underdeveloped countries and emerging countries, etc.) but cannot be reduced and managed—once again—by a mastermind, institution, or computer program. Or if they are, they no longer advance decoloniality but have been incarcerated by coloniality.

7   From "Human" to "Living" Rights

I   The Limits of the *Declaration of Rights of Man and of the Citizen* and *The Universal Declaration of Human Rights*

This chapter explores the limits of rights when restricted to *human social rights* and argues instead for *communal living rights*, which encompass all life on the planet, including life that has evolved in recent history (i.e., "recent" in terms of planetary chronology). The politics of decolonial investigations will assist us in this endeavor at the same time that walking in this endeavor will show the potential of decolonial investigations.

The historical trajectories of "rights" encompasses both modernity and coloniality. What this means is that the question of "rights" and the question of "the human" have followed close and often interconnected trajectories since the European Renaissance, jointly undergoing important transformations by the invention of America, the founding of modern/colonial racism, and the subsequent expansion of Western civilization (Westernization).[1] It may sound strange to hear that "rights" have something to do with coloniality, for the very rhetoric of "rights" suggests that "rights" are necessary precisely to avoid and correct their violation. The problem is that this formulation prevents calling into question the source and scope of the formulation. That is how modernity and coloniality work in tandem. The formulation doesn't prohibit this questioning explicitly. Rather, it obstructs it by assuming that whoever proposes, defends, or stands for human rights would not violate the rights that the formulation says should be defended. This logic is known but often forgotten: the best way to hide your guilt—when in a position of power to make decisions—is to accuse someone else of the misdeed you yourself have committed and wish to conceal. Project that tendency onto the level of interstate relations and you will understand the imperial rhetoric of modernity. This is one of the notorious but seldom noticed blind spots in the discourse on human rights.[2] Another is that the history of rights (from *ius gentium* in the sixteenth century to *The Universal Declaration of Human Rights* in the first half of the twentieth century) is also a chapter in the history of modernity, which means that the discourse on rights is only half the story; the other half, the darker one, is coloniality. Growing awareness of this situation prompted the discussion of human rights from a Third World perspective.[3] A Third World perspective means that the need and formulation of human rights emerged in the North Atlantic (western Europe—now the headquarters of the European Union—and the mainstream US), where it was half of the history based on the needs and experiences of modernity while Third World responses were prompted by the experience of coloniality. The Third World also sensed the violation of "nature" rights to the benefit of corporations from the First Word. Beyond the North Atlantic, which ended WWII with two atomic bombs dropped on Japan before the existence of *The Universal Declaration of Human Rights*, only modernity was sensed. For this reason, decolonialization in all its distinct local histories and configurations emerged from the Third World, and after the formation of the European Union, Western coloniality, supplanting Soviet coloniality, came to the fore in Eastern Europe.[4]

Although it seems incongruous to think that "rights" could be used to enforce coloniality rather than to prevent or correct it, this feeling of incongruity parallels the incongruities between "progress" and "poverty" and between "democracy" and "capitalism." Human rights were declared to advance modernity, not to prevent coloniality, which is embedded in modernity. They work in tandem, the first masking the second: democracy becomes authoritarian when the capitalist economy is in turmoil. We are taught to believe that progress should prevent and correct poverty, while upon closer inspection it is progress that engenders poverty.[5] Poverty cannot be corrected when progress (and now development) remains the overriding goal, just as violations of human rights cannot be prevented or corrected if human rights had not been recognized merely to be violated by the actors and institutions who instituted them. We are made to believe that democracy will correct the imbalances of a capitalist economy. My take is that it is necessary to accept that progress engenders poverty and democracy protects capitalism. Therefore, poverty cannot be erased and economic equality cannot be superseded under these two regimes of words and deeds. The basic assumption of decolonial thinking is that modernity engendered coloniality, and coloniality cannot be ended without ending the principles and values that created and sustain modernity. That is how the colonial matrix of power (CMP) works; thus, the task of decolonial investigations is to understand how it works in all areas of experience, and to delink from it.

A Third World perspective on human rights begs the question of the "human" before the question of "rights" throughout the entire history of "rights" since the sixteenth century (see chapter 12).[6] Narratives (including arguments and explanations) are created and told to make sense of human doing, and they also orient and reorient this doing. Three major narratives have recently surfaced that call into question not only who has the right to have rights but who, when, and why human rights came into being. The fact that human rights are a good thing should not prevent us from asking why we have them. One of the narratives, already mentioned, is that of human rights from the Third World perspective (Barreto); the second is that of the posthuman, which begs the question of what "posthuman rights" would be; and the third is that of the Anthropocene era, which prompts the question whether the entire population of human beings is responsible for the excesses and violations committed during this era. In this chapter, I will unfold the first. I will address the second in chapter 12 and the third in chapter 14, and I will suspend the third. The emergence of these three narratives doesn't supersede or nullify the existing narratives, particularly in their last version: *The Universal Declaration of Human Rights*, written in 1948.

The strong thesis of this chapter is that *The Universal Declaration of Human Rights* was not only a Euro-American and North Atlantic invention; it was an invention to correct the errors and mistakes made by a handful of western European states and the US (fascism, Nazism, Francoism, Stalinism, the bombing of Nagasaki and Hiroshima, 450 years of colonialism). The document was prompted by the crimes committed by actors supported by institutions of the First and Second World; both were off-springs of the Enlightenment. The Third World had nothing to do with these crimes, but soon it became the principal place where violations of human rights were perpetrated. In that manner, the Third World was subjected and brought into the regulatory regime of human rights violations by actors and institutions violating the rights that they proposed to regulate. Let's call this the inaugural moment of the declaration. Violations of human rights in the Third World favored advancing global designs for economic development and dissemination of democracy. If violations of human rights occurred in the process, it was for the good of the rights of the people being violated. Very similar to the logic of *ius gentium*.

Former First Lady of the US and delegate to the United Nations Eleanor Roosevelt delivered a speech titled "The Struggle for Human Rights." The date was September 28, 1948. Hitler had been defeated, and Hirohito had surrendered after the US dropped two atomic bombs, one on Hiroshima and the other on Nagasaki.[7] Her speech was delivered at the Sorbonne University in Paris, to an audience of thousands of French citizens and delegates of the United Nations. "The Struggle for Human Rights" was addressed not so much to her audience as it was to the "rogue" states. What were those states in 1948? The communist one, certainly—the USSR—and the states under its influence such as Yugoslavia, Belarus, Albania, Bulgaria, and Korea, which had refused to accept the unilateral declaration of human rights and freedoms. The liberal and democratic fight to defeat communism justified all potential violations of human rights to benefit the people under authoritarian states—this is similar to today's situations in Iraq, Syria, Ukraine, Byelorussia. One can surmise that the "rogue" states of the Second World that refused to join the UN were states that felt their own human rights had been violated and wanted to maintain their freedom. The strategy was to delink from the UN and from the global designs of the US. The apparent paradox—although in reality only the two sides of modernity/coloniality—was that most of the Third World became the target of human rights violations perpetrated by the First World: coloniality was the hidden name that identified these violations. For this reason, the Third World is reclaiming its own perspective on human rights.[8]

II   The Four Spheres of Human Rights

The two previous chapters (5 and 6) laid out the hidden tensions between cosmopolitanism and human rights. In this chapter, I would like to explore four spheres in which questions of "human rights" occur daily and become a hindrance to the conciliation of human rights and cosmopolitanism. One is the sphere of migration, mainly migration to the core countries of the European Union and to the US. These migrants come mainly from Asia (more recently from West Asia) and Africa to western Europe, and from Latin America and the Caribbean to the US. The second sphere is that of "humanitarian intervention" invoked by major Western states (I have not yet seen these arguments advanced by Russia or China) to prevent authoritarian rulers from abusing their power against the populations of their own countries, even when their rulers were democratically elected, according to the rules of democracy established by Western political modernity. You could maintain that Russia and China cannot make this argument because they do not qualify for humanitarian interventions (although during the pandemic Russia and China assisted without fanfare even some of the countries of the European Union). Or you could say that the US is the only state that is qualified to make humanitarian interventions. Then the question of why would arise. But let's leave it at that. The third sphere is the violation of life rights by the mining industry, particularly open-pit mining or mining in any form that as a result of competition in the extraction of "natural resources" leads to war and genocide (as in the crisis in the Congo and the invasion of Latin America by mining companies from the North and the Australian South). The fourth is the commodification of food that leads not only to market speculation and food shortages, but also to the uses of chemical poisoning to accelerate and increase the production of food as a commodity, not as a need for recycling and regeneration of life.[9] These are obvious violations of the "rights to life" that escape the classical paradigm of rights, from the rights of the people (*ius gentium* in the sixteenth century), the rights of man and of the citizen in the eighteenth century, and human rights in the twentieth century. Obvious violations that are attributable to the interests of corporations are not regarded as violations, but as corporations' "right" to increase productivity and supply the demands of technological innovation, for example.

The first two spheres of violation fall squarely within the traditional paradigm of "human rights." The third and fourth spheres demand urgent reconceptualization to bring to public attention the limits of the traditional paradigm illustrated by the first two spheres.[10] The emphasis on the legality of rights has, on the one hand, placed the "expert" above the ordinary "human," and on the other hand has obscured the fact that the "expert" is as human as the rest of us—that is, subjected to emotions, political and economic interests, and ideological preferences. However, the "expert" is endowed with the objective authority conferred by a naturalizing and legitimizing racism. The expert is supposed to be untouched by racism. Although *The Universal Declaration of Human Rights* states that we are all born equal, it doesn't mention the fact that we stop being equal shortly after we are born and that one of the reasons for losing our equality in the modern/colonial world is racism.[11] Racism is not a matter of skin color, but of the social place assigned to people being classified according to a ranking of "humanity."[12] Colonial and imperial differences, as seen in the previous chapters, touch every one: those who devise and implement them, and those who are affected by their implementation. As a matter of fact, colonial and imperial differences are built at the same time that social classification maps human beings into racial hierarchies. If people are classified, it is because there are people with the privilege to classify. In short, whoever is ranked in first place controls the knowledge system that ranks and classifies people in second or third place; classification is not ingrained in "nature" but is a cultural, human-made phenomenon.

The pragmatic model of "human rights" has three agencies: a perpetrator, a victim, and a savior, so that the question of "rights" for humans is always related to what kind of "humans" are the perpetrator and the victim. In the sixteenth century, the perpetrator was the devil, at the end of the seventeenth century it was the Oriental despot (John Locke dixit), in the late eighteenth and the nineteenth centuries it was the monarchy, in the twentieth century it was communism, and in the twenty-first century the perpetrators are non-compliant dictators and terrorists. The savior is s/he who formulates the question of "right" and, of course, puts him-/herself in a safe spot, lest one think the savior is the perpetrator—a trick much exploited in mystery narratives. The saviors and defenders of human rights would apply Occam's razor and accuse of violating human rights all those who do not follow the script written according to the criteria of the regulator. In that way, the doors are locked to any intent and attempt to liberate oneself from the totalitarianism of human rights: the logic of coloniality consists in violating human rights justified by the rhetoric of defending human rights, as Franz Hinkelammert brilliantly argued.[13]

By "pragmatic model" I mean that human rights are not just a set of principles established in and by *The Universal Declaration*; they materialize when a violation of them occurs. The violation of human rights is already something that has been codified in the declaration. It is in the declaration that we find out what is considered a violation of human rights. Actors and institutions who detect human rights violations and work to eliminate them are the "saviors" that act in favor of the "victim" to punish the "perpetrator." As a result, the declaration of and action on behalf of human rights do not prevent violations from happening again; rather they guarantee that the perpetrators are punished and that the savior maintains his judging and policing privileges. Violations are not acts that in themselves carry a tag saying, "Be aware, this is a violation of human rights." What constitutes a violation of human rights is an interpretation based on a code, explicit or implicit, clear or ambiguous. This is Hinkelammert's argument uncovering Locke's inversion of human rights as endowing the savior to violate human rights in the name of defending human rights. Hinkelammert made his argument by analyzing the US's humanitarian intervention in Kosovo. But we can just as easily extend it to all the interventions in West Asia (the Middle East in the Western vocabulary), from Iraq to Syria. The paradox here is that the "despotic" perpetrator is at the same time the victim of the imperial saviors (US and allies). That situation could now, in the twenty-first century, provoke the emergence of another savior: a non-compliant state (Russia) to rescue the perpetrator as victim (al-Assad). Since a code is needed in order to interpret a given act as a "violation of human rights," the perpetrator and the victim can then be recognized as such depending on their location in an overarching power structure and on the controllers of knowledge who legitimize interpretations. The role of savior would depend on who the victim and the perpetrator are. In general terms, it is assumed that the perpetrator and the victim suffer the consequences of the delinquent act and the savior is the person or institution that keeps things in a just order. The question, as we will see, is that the rules of human rights and life rights could legally be violated by the savior because it is the savior who writes and interprets the rules. Therefore, explicitly or implicitly, the savior prevents the asking of any questions about his own violation of the rules he established.

In the standard model, the victim is generally a person (journalist, academic, activist, dissenter, or defender of democratic values, for example) who becomes a victim of the state of which she or he is a citizen. The victim could also be an ethnic community or an ideological community. The perpetrator could be a noncompliant state (like North Korea). Compliant states have more latitude; human rights could perhaps be violated by such states insofar as a compliant state aligns itself with a state that manages human rights and has the approval of that managing state. Consequently, individual victims would be judged according to the status of the state of which they are victims: a compliant state criticized by outsiders might have the support of the savior with which the perpetrating state is aligned, thus placing the victim in a precarious position. Saudi Arabia, suspected of ordering the killing of Jamal Khashoggi in Turkey, was able to get off the hook with the support of the US government and mainstream media. On the other hand, if the state is not compliant with the managers of human rights, individual or collective victims would likely be supported and helped as refugees. But there could be limits to such support, as was the case in the European Union's having to confront massive numbers of refugees from Syria in the summer of 2016. Violations of human rights in Syria by all parties involved helped to create the refugees, which in turn prompted violations of human rights in the savior states that accepted refugees.

Human rights violators have targeted various types of victims. When the violators are state officers of noncompliant countries—for example, Hitler (before *The Universal Declaration*) and Milosevic (after)—their victims have been ethnic communities. In Chile under Augusto Pinochet and in Argentina under Jorge Rafael Videla, the victims were ideological communities. In Syria, the victims of the state have in large part been Syrian citizens, while the "opposition" to the Syrian state (the saviors), who represent no single ethnicity, ideology, or religion, are the "moderate terrorists."[14] That was the expression used by the media to profile terrorists supported by the Western alliance that violates human rights in defense of human rights and that justifies such violations as punishment for the declared perpetrator, the Syrian government. The Islamic State (ISIS) established another layer of human rights violations: it was not judged for human rights violations because it was supported by states managing human rights violations and was at their service.[15] These are just a few examples to stress that human rights are a good idea, as Mahatma Gandhi said about Western civilization, but they can also be used to defend the advancement of Western global designs. This is precisely how the rhetoric of modernity and the logic of coloniality work in tandem.[16]

Saviors can also be NGOs with the support of democratic (compliant) states. In international conflicts, saviors are often major states working with the UN. In some cases, a state can be the perpetrator and the savior at the same time. For instance, the government of Israel has violated the human rights of Palestinians, but has joined the international coalition to stop violations of human rights in Syria. The US has condemned the violence and the human rights violations in Syria while at the same time remaining silent regarding Israeli violations of the human rights of Palestinians. The US government has accepted or excused, typically after paying some form of compensation to the victims, the violation of human rights by killing civilians in Iraq, ostensibly in a war to defend human rights. China stands accused of violations of human rights by the US, while the Chinese have well-documented incidents of the US as violator of human rights. Although in what follows I will keep in mind the four spheres, I will concentrate on open-pit mining and other massive-scale extraction industries as cases of the legal violation of rights (nature + human, i.e., life rights) that demand substantial revision of the classical concept of "human rights." He—whether an officer of the state, a corporation, a financial institution, the police, an army—who speaks for the human in "human rights" must be open to questions about his own violation of human and life rights.

III   Living Life Rights: "Nature" Rights *Are* Human Rights

We humans are nature, not separated from it. Without the water and air and sunlight and food that come from the Earth we are nothing; poisoned air and poisoned food kill us in the long run. "Human" and "nature" are two universal North Atlantic nouns that make sense to people in that particular culture.

The words do not name what there is, but what the name *tells* you there is. This is a question of the enunciation and of meaning-making (epistemology), not the "representation" of what there is (ontology; see chapter 14). Living organisms or the human species are what they are because of the capacity for languaging and conversations, enabling them to coordinate their deeds. Humans do not come to the world with a self-identifying tag saying, "I belong to the human species." "Human" is a noun created in the process of building the images of Western civilization based on a series of distinctions between humans and lesser humans and between humans and nonhuman entities (e.g., rocks, plants, animals, air, water, etc.—that is, what we call "nature"). Racism and sexism were built on the first distinction; naturism (if I can create a parallel neologism) was built on the second distinction. Actors that built and maintained all the civilizations on the planet created their own vocabulary to conceive of themselves and their relation to the cosmos. *Runa* in Quechua cannot be translated as "human" because human is separated from nature while *runa* is interrelated with the living Earth and the cosmos (Pachamama). Similarly, in Mandarin, *rén* (人) is generally mistranslated as "human," but *rén* is a person in relation to other persons (similar to *ubuntu* in Bantu cosmology) within *all under heaven* (*tianxia*). A human, in Western civilization, is an individual unit in a society composed of similar units, all preserving their individual freedoms and separated from nature and the cosmos.[17]

Human rights are caught in the web of these fictions. Consequently, my argument in this section and the next operates at two levels: at the level of the *constituted* (modernity; i.e., *The Universal Declaration of Human Rights* and its pros and cons within the rhetoric of modernity and the logic of coloniality), and at the level of the *destituted* (coloniality). My own argument builds on the gnoseological and aesthesic reconstitution of the destituted (see introduction, section III.3). The politics of decolonial investigations calls into question the very presuppositions and privileges of the actors and institutions managing the discourses of human rights, preventing (not by explicit prohibition but by control and management of knowledge) any probing of the assumptions supporting their claims.

The question to be asked is not "What is human?," a question that has infinite answers (in fact, there is a history from Aristotle to today), but "Who has the privilege and control of the knowledge, institutions, and discourses to decide what is human?" The first question addresses the content, the second the enunciation (actors, institutions, languages) controlling the content (see introduction, section III). In this respect, *The Universal Declaration of Human Rights* has to be repositioned from law to ethics. Ethics brings to the foreground racism and sexism as well as the commodification of life under the heading of "natural resources" and the exploitation of labor (as well as its companion, unemployment), all in the name of "human resources." Finally, racism resides in the subjectivity of individuals (the racist and the racialized), but it is a category inscribed in individuals. Individuals are the carriers of the cosmology of Western civilizations: they/we are formed by the CMP. Racism and sexism are not universal; they are global and exported in the process of Westernization. If there were classifications in civilizations and cultures before Western incursion and expansion, those classifications could not have been based on the same assumptions as they were not capitalist civilizations, and therefore the perceived differences were not colonial and imperial in the sense that racism and sexism acquire in Western cosmology (see chapter 1).

Adopting the standard model of human rights described above, and observing the global scenario, it is obvious that what are being violated are not only "human rights" but the "rights to life," which are threatened by climate change and the alteration of the environments (e.g., via forest fires engineered to promote agribusiness and building construction) of communities living in and from the land, the ocean, and the rivers. At this juncture, immigration, humanitarian interventions, the exploitation of "natural resources" (including the commodification of life on the planet), and the commodification of food and water are consequences of the logic of capital accumulation and the dispensability of life.[18] All of these combine to impact living species at large, including those who describe themselves as part of the human species. The "human rights" paradigm focuses on "bare lives" (chapter 3): persons who in one way or another are stripped of their citizen's rights, human beings who become legally naked and can be persecuted and/or killed (or if not killed, humiliated as persons, as human beings). Dispensable life rights are the blind spot of human rights, perhaps because they are the excesses of capitalism; to query dispensable life rights implies querying the spirit of capitalism.

Colonial wounds are another blind spot of human rights. Since the human rights paradigm was framed in the sphere of political theory and the philosophy of law, ethics (concern for the colonially wounded) were peripheral. Therefore, the answer to the question of "who speaks for the 'human'?" is the self-appointed humans who are oblivious or blind to colonial wounds. Decolonial healing would be difficult to integrate into human rights because it would be necessary to support the "victim's" own healing rather than being cured based on the criteria of the "savior." Decolonial healing is the task of the wounded. And decolonial investigations are part of the healing: understanding the modern/colonial system that engenders and perpetuates colonial wounds, as well as the subjectivities of the actors ruling and maintaining it, is the necessary diagnosis for a proper prognosis.

The human rights paradigm is limited by a Eurocentered vision of both "human" and "rights," and it should be extended to give equal weight to ethics, to coexisting civilizational gnoseology and aesthesics, and to life rights. It is not right to have a universal, enunciated declaration of human rights when all of us on the planet are already exiting universalism and entering pluriversalism (Western universalism being one of the pluri-gnoseologies), and exiting unipolarity and entering multipolarity (unipolarity being one of the multipoles of interstate relations). That is, we are not "transitioning" to anything, for Western universalism and unipolarity have the right to exist within Western civilization without pretense and expectation to global status. Extending human living rights on Earth (the rights of nature/Pachamama/Gaia) would mean changing the terms of the conversation and reducing the foundation of Western civilization to its own size. When "nature" (the abusive noun that reifies the splendors of the living and the energies of life) is included in the paradigm of ethics and rights violations, the racialization of regions of the planet becomes apparent: why is it the Third World that provides "natural resources" to the First, and what are the implications for planetary conviviality? Coincidentally, many regions rich in "natural resources" are also regions with a poor population that tends to migrate to wealthy countries that have fewer natural resources but are enriched by an industrial economy, technological innovation, and market concentration, and that violate the right of "nature" in the former Third World.[19] Coincidentally also, the management of knowledge that justifies exploitation of natural resources to secure "development" destitutes local knowledges that for millennia were built and transmitted to perceive, sense, and exist in harmony with all living organisms and energies that are not "natural resources." These are two paradigms with a variety of manifestations: all existing cosmogonies before the institutionalization of the Christian cosmogony and the so-called religions of the book built narratives of coexistence and *vincularidad* (relationality) with living organisms on Earth and with cosmic energies. The constitution of the CMP since 1500 implied the destitution of all coexisting cosmologies that in the twenty-first century are reconstituting their own long-lasting gnoseology and being in the planet (aesthesis).

For these reasons, in the last two decades a radical shift in the geopolitics of human rights has been announced. Calling for living rights (the rights of nature/Pachamama/Gaia) brings a different philosophy that unfolds mainly in the sphere of the economy and exposes the reality that the ethics of corporations violate rights to life in the name of development.[20] "Development" in the domain of economic coloniality, rather than democracy and justice in the domain of governmental authority, legitimates violations and legalizes the illegal. Neoliberalism has exacerbated the priority of the economy over state legislation, growth over life on the planet, including humans (and including the very actors promoting and driving neoliberal ideals and ethics). The victims are not only reduced to bare or naked life, as in the case of refugees or victims of state genocide; their lives are made disposable as well. *The victims are not only stripped of their rights but are mainly deprived of their lives*, in both the short and long run.

Dispensable or disposable lives manifest themselves in two complementary ways (see chapter 3 and above). Persons becoming commodities, as in the Atlantic slave trade, have been at the root of Western civilization since the sixteenth century.[21] The phenomenon continues today in the trafficking of women and children, as well as in the organ transplant trade. All these abuses are possible and are encouraged in a society whose horizon of life is dominated by the preoccupation with increasing wealth and possessions. Life becomes a commodity, and wealth is accrued, violating the law and suppressing communal ethics. But these actions are compounded via straightforwardly legal means through financial markets and corporate maneuverings to exploit natural resources and labor. A consequence is that society today is embedded in the economy rather than the economy being embedded in society. To the degree that economic gains and increasing wealth have become the priorities of life on the planet and of the lives of all humans, who are also nature, the race to misery and death will continue.

There is an urgent need to shift the basis of such reasoning to put the economy and the law at the service of life. To do this, changing the law and public policy is not enough. The terms of the conversation must change, and doing so requires sustained processes of delinking from current cultural horizons, assumptions of knowing, and constituted knowledges and subjectivities. It will involve the long process of shifting the existing modern/colonial subjectivities in the reconstitution of epistemology into gnoseology, and aesthetics into aesthesis: *restituting, in other words, the communal subject over the social individual*. Shifting the geography of reasoning and sensing requires a robust ethical movement in which "dignity" prevails over "rights." And when dignity of life defines our horizon, *individual experts* move backstage and acquire a secondary role: there is no single person but all of us together who can reorient the horizon of life so that it embraces dignity, the communal over individual success, working to live in plenitude over living to work to consume.

Exploitation of natural resources to fulfill the needs created by the industrial and the technological revolutions leads to poisoning the environment and to the deterioration of the life of all living organisms, including organisms that in the vocabulary of the state and transnational corporations are "human."[22] Migrants are organisms changing territory, and in so doing they disrupt the territories of the other organisms (the nationals) who have previously settled in that territory and hence are protected by a nation-state that cares for nationals but not for human foreigners. Human rights without life rights remain regional and Eurocentric, both in Europe and in locales outside of Europe where they are uncritically adopted. This is an illness that the politics of decolonial investigations shall contribute to curing. The directionality of these displacements and the power differential existing between state-nationals and stateless foreigners is a consequence of established modern/colonial belief systems and the theories and knowledge-building that sustain those beliefs and ground that knowledge. People dwelling in the locales where corporations migrate in search of cheap labor or natural resources can benefit from migrant corporations (the local elites) or be reduced to situations similar to those migrants in foreign lands: the land doesn't belong anymore to the people but to the state in collaboration with the corporations.

The exploitation of labor and the exploitation of "nature" (that is, of living processes) are two strategies of modernity/coloniality and its economy. Recognizing these strategies today, the sixteenth century appears in a new light. What appeared then to be legal justice was in fact a violation of rights, taking place just as the "rights of nations" (*ius gentium*) were being discussed in Salamanca and other legal-theological schools in Europe. At that time, of course, "rights to life" were not an issue, because the industrial and technological revolutions were not yet in place to demand the use of natural resources and to replace human beings with machines; and to conceive bodies and machines. Nevertheless, since individuals and institutions debating *ius gentium* were Spaniards and not Africans, Incas, or Aztecs, they determined the definition of "rights." Spaniards had no problem with violations of life rights, since they were the ones violating them in the name of salvation. Meanwhile, they legalized the rights of nations to control dissenting and noncompliant attitudes that challenged and disrupted the legality of these rights.

You can begin to see, I hope, how the question of "rights" became embedded in the CMP then and persisted through the chronology of modernity/coloniality. Spaniards (and the Portuguese, and later the British, French, and Dutch) were interested in the legality of their invasion. Africans, Aztecs, and

Incas—the populations under their governance—were concerned about their lives and the dismantling of their social order. But Africans and those who were becoming Americans in the European consciousness (i.e., from southern Chile to Alaska, not to be confused with the US) had no way to establish their claims or even to make themselves heard and their dissent understood. Consequently, the violation of life rights (that is, the right to live) was founded on the legalization of the violation of the rights of certain people and under certain circumstances. Modernity established the rules to justify coloniality and to make it invisible within the legal system.

At the beginning of the twenty-first century, life rights are being addressed not only by state institutions and marginally by NGOs (not managed by the state) that have joined the leadership of political society, but also by many organizations disturbed by the deterioration of their niches in the planetary ecosystem and the deterioration of living conditions. Crucial for embracing life rights is breaking up with the Western distinction and separation of the "natural order" from the "human order." There is a space of entanglement—as in Venn diagrams, embedding living organisms with Earth and cosmic energies—where all share this same entangled space and participate in the regeneration of life: violation of nature rights implies the violation of human rights and therefore of life rights (the right to live). If the fundamental question "Who speaks for the 'human' in human rights?" is not asked—thereby maintaining the distinction between nature and human—then the traditional paradigm of human rights would still be of some use but would remain extremely limited in facing the complexity of ethics, economy, and the law in the twenty-first century.

IV Juicio Ético Popular a las Transnacionales (JEPT) on the Violation of "Life Rights"

On October 28, 2011, the Juicio Ético Popular a las Transnacionales (JEPT; the Ethical-Popular Judgement to Transnational Corporations) was initiated at the Faculty of Social Sciences, National University of Buenos Aires. The initiative was promoted by the Center for Research and Training of the Latin American Social Movements and the Popular Education Team Pañuelos en Rebeldía, plus a large number of social and collective organizations of Argentina and Latin America. Participants in the act of inauguration were Adolfo Pérez Esquivel, Nobel Peace Prize winner; Mirta Baravalle, from Mothers of the Plaza de Mayo; Berta Cáceres, coordinator of the COPINH (Civic

Council of Popular and Indigenous Organizations of Honduras); Bernardino Camilo Da Silva, of the Movement Sin Tierra of Brazil; Cristina Castro, of Red Hermandad, Colombia; Tomás Palau, of BASE-IS Paraguay; and Alcira Daroqui, director of the Sociology Department, University of Buenos Aires. The event was the synthesis of a series of previous similar events in which the following transnational corporations were judged for the violations of life rights: Barrick Gold, Minera La Alumbrera, Agua Rica, Ledesma, REPSOL, Pan American Energy, Monsanto, Proyecto Navidad (Pan American Silver), Proyecto Potasio Rio Colorado, Río Tinto, Vales, Cargill, Alto Paraná, Microsoft, Telefónica, Google.[23]

The public pronouncement of the Tribunal Ético Popular (TEP) responsible for the Juicio Ético Popular (JEP) was read out loud in a public act under the rubric of Lectura de la Sentencia (reading of the sentence). It begins as follows:

> After more than 500 years of colonization and re-colonization of the subcontinent, this Tribunal affirms the difference between "living out of nature" and "living with and in nature." The Ethical Judgment against transnational and national corporations in trial, all of them involved in mega-extractivism had—for this Tribunal—a precise and profoundly human meaning: the protection of life and its reproduction, today and in the future and in all its dimensions and implications. The criteria for discerning an ethical scale from the most to the least ethical, has no other reference than life itself: anti-ethical is everything that kills life or that can, in the short and long run, kill life.[24] "Ethical" is every attitude that acts in favor of life, for the integrity of life and on behalf of life. The goal of this Ethical Judgment is to demand that the juridical order be subsumed under the Ethical so that every level of political responsibility and/or other responsibility—public or private that impinges on the communal—act in accordance with a foundation in ethics.[25]

The reading of the sentence was not, of course, attended by representatives of the corporations being judged or by representatives of nation-states that support the corporations (in the name of development, the rhetoric of modernity) rather than supporting the nationals who are paying the consequences. On the contrary, people that raise their voices in protests and in defense of their own lives are criminalized by the state and the media at the service of the state, in defense of progress and development: that is, deploying powerful mediatic versions of the rhetoric of modernity to hide and defend the logic of coloniality.

The respect for, defense of, and acting for the preservation of life rather than for growth and development will not be effective as long as the imaginary horizon in which we live is determined by the belief that development is necessary and good for all, individual economic wealth is the overriding goal of our lives, and billionaires are celebrated as heroes and examples of success. Nor will it be effective as long as artificial intelligence and design are treated as though they will solve the unfortunate misgiving of innovation that takes the human species away from itself, that is, away from the short passage each organism has on the planet while living energy and intelligence continue after each of us have vanished. Cyber dreams would continue to be indulged by dreamers who believe that *artificial* intelligence could tame the *natural* intelligence of the universe which generated the dreamers and which inhabits them (modern Western vocabulary calls it "soul," "mind," and sometimes "spirit"). You have to succeed, to be innovative, to be number one, to grow, to believe bigger is better, to control and defeat whatever interferes with your dreams. Not succeeding (according, of course, to certain regional concepts of success in which the word is understood and makes sense) makes you a loser, and being a loser puts you at a disadvantage around all those who want to succeed. These beliefs cannot be changed by public policy. They are sustained and maintained by a system of knowledge (coloniality of knowledge) and regulations of knowing (coloniality of knowing) that molds subjectivity and behavior. This injunction defines the horizon and the imaginary in which development, designs, and artificial intelligence make you believe that accumulation is necessary for well-being and happiness.

Turning that around and valuing the slow plenitude of living, delinking from the trap of winner-loser, of being faster and first, of growth, of more is better, of individual success—taking these steps causes one to realize finally that what counts is not development, design, or artificial intelligence but the simple marvel of living. Negating all of these will not be sufficient. Decolonial regulations of knowing and building decolonial knowledges are necessary— and are the tasks to which the politics of decolonial investigations shall be oriented. I can imagine someone thinking, yes, of course, but the invention of electrical power, the advances in medicine, the impressive pharmaceutical industries, all have been achieved thanks to the competitive drive for individual success, innovation, and capital supporting research. All that is right, but it is only half of the story. The other is the consequences, what is left behind, who is being sacrificed, why inequality increases, and why health care is under duress at the same time that pharmaceutical companies increase the prices of their products, which are supposed to cure rather than to increase profit. All these issues have been addressed and others are implied in the Juicio Ético to Transnational Corporations.[26] Last but not least, we are learning to unlearn and relearn. In the Americas people are learning to unlearn the legacies of European concepts in order to relearn Andean and Mesoamerican philosophies derived from ancient civilizations, which are the philosophies endorsed by the actors carrying on the investigation and judgement formulated in the final *sentencia* to the transnational corporations. In Asia people are restituting the legacies of Confucius and Mencius, as well as Taoism and Buddhism. In Africa people are reembracing the force of Ubuntu philosophy to restitute the harmonious communal life that has been destituted by competitive Western societal life. And in South America people are relearning *Sumak Kawsay/Suma Qamaña*.[27]

Human rights maintain the idea of the human-social (only for human beings) while silencing the life-communal (the coexistences of the living). Climate change and environmental issues are not only unresolvable within the frame of development goals and policies and the economy of accumulation. They are unresolvable within the limited horizon of human rights. The Western liberal decision to correct Japan's wrongdoing by dropping two atomic bombs—although just before adoption of *The Universal Declaration of Human Rights*—on Nagasaki and Hiroshima (poisoning life in the region, including human life), with the acquiescence of Russian communism, operated on the naturalization of inverted logic. I am not saying that Japan was right in its ambitions. I am underscoring how the violation of human rights to defend human rights operates. It is an interesting ruse that prevents understanding that the inventors and defenders of rights could also be violators. It prevents questions about the legitimacy of authority. The inversion of human rights, as Hinkelammert convincingly argues, is a legal excuse for imperial violence. Whether or not the pretense to universalization will continue to prevail, it is up to "them" to decide. In the meantime, the rest of the world has much to do to move toward non-Western-imperial futures in which life and human rights are intertwined.

If this argument can be sustained, what is the next step? In the next section I will explore the need to think differently and what changing the terms of the conversation may mean for debating human rights and decolonial cosmopolitan localism. I will argue that thinking differently and changing paradigms is a process that has been at work for the past fifty years, but has not been recognized. Today I call the process simply "thinking otherwise," and I believe it is necessary to envision the horizons of living now blocked by the current hegemony of knowing, sensing, and believing.

V Changing the Terms of the Conversation: Toward Decolonial Horizons of Living and Thinking

At the beginning of the twenty-first century, Hans-Peter Dürr, winner of the so-called Alternative Nobel Prize, was requested to write an update of the "Russell-Einstein Manifesto." He and two coauthors, J. Daniel Dahm and Rudolf Prinz zur Lippe, drafted a substantial piece titled "Beyond the Einstein-Russell [sic] Manifesto of 1955: The Potsdam Denkschrift" (a condensed version of which is known as the "Potsdam Manifesto 2005").[28] One hundred thirty-one scientists from around the world agreed with the need to "think differently." In their piece, Dürr and his coauthors recall that the original manifesto was signed ten years after two atomic bombs destroyed Nagasaki and Hiroshima. The atomic bombs, along with Hitler's and Stalin's genocides (two outcomes of the European Enlightenment), were three disastrous consequences of Western modernity that prompted *The Universal Declaration of Human Rights*, which attempted to solve the problems created by the very same agencies that had originated them.[29]

The "Russell-Einstein Manifesto" came seven years after *The Universal Declaration* and points to one of the three major violations of human rights at the time by Hitler, Stalin, and Hirohito. The three human disasters prompting the manifesto were of constant concern because honesty and goodwill in the service of humanity has not been of overriding concern to the ruling political, economic, and military elites. Their concerns have focused more on the legitimation of their values. It is difficult to understand how individuals could be so programmed by the CMP that little to nothing beyond their interests and benefits matter. The planetary population trapped in the CMP's spider web has seen this type of subjectivity hardening over the past three and a half decades of US/UK governmental politics—from Reagan and Thatcher to the first George Bush, to Clinton, to the second George Bush, to Obama, to Trump—with the cooperation of the EU. It has been a consistent line with only superficial differences beyond a common imperial subjectivity that characterizes these entities' thinking and doing. The concern for leadership and success has taken priority over any interest in well-being and global harmony. A dominating focus on the nation-state's *enemies* has constantly been deployed to maintain unipolarity and leadership of the world order.[30] Long before this present moment (2017–2020), Dürr and his coauthors wrote:

> Justifiably worried that Hitler's Germany could get the upper hand in building an atomic bomb, the convinced pacifist Einstein wrote a letter to

President Roosevelt shortly before the beginning of World War II, adding his voice to what led the President to initiate America's Manhattan Project. The resulting fission bombs were used sixty years ago in 1945, soon after Germany's capitulation, against Japan. In great consternation, Einstein called for a fundamental political re-orientation to make wars impossible in the future. But without visible success. The development of fission bombs (hydrogen bombs) increased the deadly potential of nuclear weapons of mass destruction to almost unlimited dimensions and, in the escalating confrontation between East and West, became a mortal danger for all of humanity.[31]

It is now widely accepted that an economy of accumulation and concentration of wealth managed by the corporations, the states, and the army of Western imperial countries from 1500 to today requires war, not peace. Peace is the excuse to justify wars. This may not have been the first, and will certainly not be the last, situation in which double standards rule over honest attempts to solve serious world problems. The international situation has reached (in 2020) a point of no return. For that reason, the "rights of life" (threatened by, e.g., political persecution and open-pit mining and potential nuclear conflicts) are bound either to be ignored (when the situation is not convenient for the ruling states and corporations, like the crisis in the Congo a few years ago) or to be turned into an everlasting conflict like the one in Palestine-Israel (and currently between the US and Iran, with all its consequences for the Middle East and the global order).[32] Or they fall victim to the repressive responses of state politics when people react in their own defense to confront the legalized abuses of the state and the corporations. Only when the situation is favorable to the interests of the rulers, not of the ones being ruled, will humanitarian interventions be invoked to save lives.

There is a memorable, and much quoted, sentence in the "Russell-Einstein Manifesto": "We have to learn to think in a new way. We have to learn to ask ourselves, not what steps can be taken to give military victory to whatever group we prefer, for there no longer are such steps; the question we have to ask ourselves is: what steps can be taken to prevent a military contest of which the issue must be disastrous to all parties?"[33] Let's not forget that these were questions asked by Europeans addressing the mess that Europe and the US had made. These recommendations were not made for the 80 percent of the world that was neither responsible for the crimes committed by European countries and the US nor seriously considered significant voices in the philosophy of human rights. But with time, that 80 percent was to become victim, though they may not have figured in the minds of the framers of the statement, for Russell and Einstein's recommendations were made from within the core of Western civilization and were addressed to the people of Western civilization in order to prevent further catastrophes provoked by that civilization.

The remaining regions of the planet were not asked "to think in a different way." It was not expected that the people being saved by *The Universal Declaration of Human Rights* and the equally important "Russell-Einstein Manifesto" would assume any responsibility. They had to be saved and had to be told what needed to be done. European religious war in the seventeenth century was duplicated by European politico-economic (and secular) war in the twentieth century. I, and many others, was not requested to "think differently," simply because many of us (the 80 percent) belong to the Third World not the First, even if we live in it. There is always the sensation, in different scales and intensities, of being perceived (because of skin color, sexual preferences, religious beliefs, idiomatic accents, nationalities) in the class of the *anthropos* and not the class of *man*. If I felt that I belonged to the people being asked to think differently, I would not be writing this chapter from the perspective of thinking differently—not from within the CMP but from its exteriority. Thinking differently decolonially is not the same as thinking differently modernly. Nevertheless, although I feel that I do not belong to the class of *man* (and this is not a complaint but a matter of fact) writing the manifestos, I strongly support Russell and Einstein's as well as Dürr's plea. Moreover, I hope the plea carries on and is not forgotten and buried in the past, for it was a necessary act of conscience for Western citizens. Which doesn't prevent me from seeing and highlighting its underpinnings. The "we" (Westerners) that the "Russell-Einstein Manifesto" and Dürr's efforts go beyond, all centered in the North Atlantic, is not my "we." That is why I am pushing for the politics of decolonial investigations.

It is imperative at this point that we anthropos (lesser humans), especially scholars and intellectual workers, contribute to unveiling the double standards in the discourse of human rights as well as in all discourses of modernity regarding peace, development, democracy, and the like pronounced by nonstate and noncorporate and nonmilitary agencies, but by the emerging global political society embedded in differing local histories: a few embedded in imperial legacies, many embedded in colonial legacies. Human rights are embedded in the rhetoric of modernity. The rhetoric of modernity is predicated on progress, freedom, and salvation when addressing political actors whom it frames as dictatorial or authoritarian regimes exploiting their nations. Hence, to promote life rights would call into question the salvations promoted by the ideas of progress and development. Today, however, it is obvious that no nation-state on the planet can claim innocence from human rights violations or lay claim to the right to judge without being judged. If the self-proclaimed right to judge that is one of the foundations of Eurocentrism has been disguised since the sixteenth-century goal of saving the "Indians" from the devil, never was this proclamation so obvious and explicit as it has been during Donald Trump's presidency. Perhaps he will be remembered as the president that took off the mask of democracy and human rights.

Let's recall the three major events that prompted the drafting of *The Universal Declaration of Human Rights*: the Hitler genocide and mass murder (about ten million non-Jews were killed), Stalin's genocide or mass murder, and the atomic bombs dropped on Hiroshima and Nagasaki. All these events are grounded in the same logic. Genocide, mass murder, and bombing with nuclear weapons were all justified by the rhetoric of modernity: nationalism, communism, and Western values. But it so happened that "nationalism" and "communism" were Western values that went totalitarian. And bombing Hiroshima and Nagasaki was justified in the name of Western values or of human lives, and the environmental consequences were justified in the name of saving those values: hence, the good and the bad of Western values. I am not defending Hitler, Stalin, or Hirohito. I am just pointing out that Western civilization has promoted, I believe unwittingly, undesirable outcomes that had to be eliminated by the same civilization that prompted them. You may say that indeed there are violations of human rights beyond those of the Western North Atlantic, and indeed there are. But the point is to be aware of power differentials in the uses and abuses of human rights, the silence about living/life rights, and whether nature is invoked in questions of morality.

The logic behind the rhetoric of "rights" is the logic of coloniality: control of authority by means of the state and control of authority by asserting global leadership by means of the atomic bomb. Let's quote again the theologian of liberation Franz J. Hinkelammert, who wrote about the humanitarian intervention in Kosovo:

> The war in Kosovo made us aware of the ambivalence of human rights. An entire country was destroyed in the name of assuring the force of these rights. The war destroyed not only Kosovo, but also all of Serbia. It was a war without combatants of any kind; yet, it annihilated Kosovo and Serbia. The North Atlantic Treaty Organization (NATO) put in motion a great machine of death that brought about an action of annihilation. There were no possible defenses and NATO suffered no deaths; all of

the casualties were Kosovars and Serbs, and the majority of them were civilians. The pilots acted as executioners that killed the guilty, who had no defenses.

When they flew, they said they had done a "good job." It was the good job of the executioner. NATO boasted of having minimal deaths. What was destroyed was the real base of life of the population. The economic infrastructure was destroyed, with all of its important factories, significant telecommunications, potable water and electricity infra-structure, schools and hospitals, and many houses. All of those are civilian targets that involve only collateral damage to military power. The attack was not directed so much against human lives as against the means of living of the entire country. This is precisely what Shakespeare meant when he said: "You take my life when you do take the means whereby I live."[34]

Shakespeare's quotation offers a useful shift from human rights to life rights and from thinking differently (changing the content of the conversation) to thinking otherwise (changing the terms of the conversation). This is crucial now, when the extinction of animal species is alarming, the contamination of the water and the land is without precedent, the poisoning of the air is as never seen before. *The Universal Declaration* and the manifestos remain a necessary and limited chapter of the twentieth century. Also necessary is a double departure: decolonial and demodern, no longer postmodern. It is not a question of "moving forward" on autopilot but of "undoing" the machine of modernity within the machine itself.[35] Decolonial political claims for living/life rights came initially from Indigenous people and peasants who saw their lives, their community, and their descendants in danger from the deterioration of the "environment." Their thinking and doing were not motivated by the desire to *improve* their life with salary increases, but by the need to *save* their lives from destruction by the degradation of their sources of life (land, air, water). Saving their lives was not only a physical necessity; it was a question of human dignity and the ownership of their destiny. Most interesting to me is that this disruption has come not from scientists, Western or non-Western, who were following some Western "scientific" paradigm.[36] The idea of thinking decolonially otherwise (hence the politics of decolonial investigations) has for decades been incorporated into academic reasoning. Its point of origination has not been either academic or grounded in the genealogy of European thinking. It comes from ancestral Indigenous knowledge, peasants knowing through experience (empiricism), not from ritualized or bureaucratized European practices or from the pathological culture fostered by profit-seeking transnational corporations. Thinking decolonially otherwise had to depart from the modern imperial trajectory—from *ius gentium*, to the *Declaration of the Rights of Man and of the Citizen*, to *The Universal Declaration of Human Rights*, and to help in building the planetary consciousness of life rights. Hence, again, we encounter the politics of decolonial investigations and the arguments this book intends to make.

Thinking otherwise and changing the terms (assumptions, principles) locates the thinker within a decolonial paradigm that coexists with Russell and Einstein's and Dürr's efforts to go beyond and to call people to think differently. Scientists' disciplinary knowledge doesn't endow scientists with ethical, political, and philosophical authority. I am not denying the relevance of scientific research. I am sounding an alert to the opposite threat (which we have heard during the COVID-19 pandemic): the sacralization of science to the extreme totalitarianism of knowledge. Ethics and politics are different dimensions that touch all disciplinary and nondisciplinary knowledge. Certainly, scientific disciplinary knowledge has, until the twentieth century, largely been limited to persons whose life experiences for the most part lie at the opposite end of the academic spectrum from the lived experiences of the Aymaras, Quechuas, and Quichuas. Nevertheless, the Indigenous people have won the debate to include the "rights of nature/Pachamama" (right to life) in the Constitution of Ecuador. The formulation of "The Law of Mother Earth" was taken by Bolivian president Evo Morales to the United Nations, its existence as law demonstrating the potent agency of people who are thinking otherwise to effect change on their own behalf.[37]

Let's now come back to Dürr and his coauthors, who took seriously the Russell-Einstein challenge: "Taking this challenge seriously actually means setting off on a path of learning. The essential orientations are obvious: negative, calling for a turn back, and positive, encouraging different alignments. But thinking in a new way also means becoming familiar with other forms of thought than those of the problematical, still prevailing conventions; and even our use of language requires further development and supplementation."[38]

But there is more to consider. A later paragraph of Dürr et al.'s indictment reads:

The modesty demanded by the new insights teaches us that, in a certain sense, the new natural scientific knowledge and its consequences can hardly be called "revolutionary," as it might appear to many modern people whose patterns of thought are oriented toward important partial aspects of the Enlightenment and the reductionist science based on it. We find this "new knowledge" confirmed in one way or another in the broad spectrum of cultural knowledge, in the diversity and forms of expression of human life in history, and in the broad variance of living and cultural realms. We can thus regard the "new" knowledge presented here as an additional scientific confirmation of the diverse ethical and moral value systems (if we, like many today, have thus far assumed an eternal validity of epistemic science). The necessary immaterial opening of the Wirklichkeit [reality] can be caught in a "mental" form that, in this description, however, goes beyond the human to include all life.[39]

There are two interrelated points in this paragraph that I would like to underline and briefly comment on. One concerns the technicalities of scientific knowledge, which requires specific training and learning in the genealogy of those technicalities. The other is that in addition to scientific knowledge (epistemology), there is knowledge in general (gnoseology)—that is, living knowledge interwoven with living labor. Since all human beings (anthropos), beyond and including the elite Humans, basically have to work to live (before capitalism forced them/us to live to work), theoretically living labor and living knowledge cannot be supplanted, even less guided exclusively by scientific knowledge. On the contrary, scientific and technical knowledge, which today guides the scandalous extractive industries and the questionable celebratory propaganda of artificial intelligence, cannot replace (although it is displacing) the living knowledge of the people who for centuries have made their territory the sources of life and communal conviviality.

The moment has come, however, when expert knowledge threatens to completely supplant living knowledge: the "expert" is the authoritative figure whose limited knowledge of one specific domain can make him or her ignorant of the role of that domain in the totality of knowledge. Detached from living knowledge, the expert loses or downplays the guidance of the senses (aesthesis). That is why gnoseological and aesthesic reconstitutions are paramount for the politics of decolonial investigations. The declaration of the rights of nature (rights of living life) in the Constitution of Ecuador is an important call to return to grounded sensing in living labor (whatever labor we do to live) and living knowledge: expert knowledge should be guided and led by living labor and living knowledge, rather than the other way around. Because their relationship has been inverted (following Locke's logic inversion), it is necessary to expand human rights to life rights and to insist that there is no solution to climate change and environmental degradation without a shift in consciousness that places life above economic growth (a dilemma clearly visible during the COVID-19 pandemic), the communal (humans and nonhumans) over the social (only humans), and living to work over working to live.

The "Ethical Judgment" of the corporations mentioned above introduced a significant variant—a shift in the geography of sensing (aesthesis) and reasoning (gnoseology)—vis-à-vis the "Russell-Einstein Manifesto" and Dürr's claim to go beyond it. Contrary to Dürr and his coauthors, the decolonial perspective doesn't aim to go "beyond the beyond" but "to decolonially think otherwise," that is, to delink from the supposedly single genealogy by which "thinking in a different way" has advanced. Decolonial thinking otherwise calls attention to the reality that there is more than one genealogy of "thinking in a different way," and that as important as scientists and experts are to the persistence of civilization, the roads to the future must also be paved by the call for life rights, which can neither be defined nor regulated exclusively by legal experts. To think decolonially otherwise is necessary to both support and delink from Einstein and Russell's and Dürr's assumptions embedded in the belief system of Western civilization.

By agreeing with the "Potsdam Manifesto 2005," we support an honest liberal manifesto. By delinking from it, we cross the road of the colonial difference and join the Ethical Judgment, bringing forward life rights including human rights.[40] It is not just we humans, considered as a single agency, who are destroying the planet, but specific types of humans—self-endowed individuals—operating within transnational corporations that daily perpetrate ethical crimes that make human life dispensable in exchange for the metal they extract from the mountains. Consequently, it is not just the planet, Mother Earth, Pachamama, who is being mutilated, but the humanness of her assailants—the individual actors and larger institutions that have been blinded by the magnitude of potential profits to the destructiveness of their own actions. Racial and sexual dehumanization enacted in defense of whiteness and heteronormativity has returned like a boomerang to dehumanize the dehumanizer. The saviors have become the victims of their own perpetration.

When we shift from human rights to the ethics of life rights, we acknowledge, for example, that "water" is poisoned when it is combined with mercury and cyanide to wash rocks in which metals are embedded and thereafter is no longer a life-sustaining resource, no longer available to some other corporation to own and sell for drinking. It becomes an environmental hazard from which we must be protected. Such violations of life rights are unacceptable for the concerned population, and yet often they are legalized in the name of economic growth and development. We have seen former presidents taken before the Hague Tribunal. We have seen CEOs prosecuted for financial corruption, but we have not yet seen corporations taken to court for their violation of life rights or of the ethics of communal well-being. It has been visible in the increased production of cell phones, which requires the extraction of coltan, a price paid by the Congo between 1960 and 1966 and after, and in the increase in the stock prices of the technological sector.[41] But the expense of such "progress" remains hidden by the mainstream media. The rhetoric of modernity disguises, always, the logic of coloniality. The classical human rights paradigm is not only a set of principles. It is a set of principles that require actions and judgements. The principles materialize and require action when a violation is identified. The government of Israel violates the human rights of the Palestinians but challenges violations of human rights in Syria.[42] The US condemns the violence and human rights violations in Syria but has kept silent regarding Israeli violations of the human rights of Palestinians.[43] Such selective blindness or double standards were also the logic of NATO's "humanitarian intervention" in Kosovo.

When it comes to violations of rights to life—that is, when the violation of Pachamama's (or Gaia's, for that matter) rights affects the quality of life of an entire population and its descendants—it is no longer solely a legal issue: it is an ethical one. Its damage is not to property but to living organisms—to bodies handicapped by reckless profit-seeking and made unable to live fully as "humans" because of birth defects and fatal diseases, and whose destiny is to die early along with other members of the community. The "Base of the Pyramid" theory—which suggests business opportunities by providing credit to people affected by these practices—won't do. Other factors are more relevant for their situation than having money to become better consumers; one powerful factor is dignity. Though "dignity" is an ambiguous and overused word, I use it now to indicate the way out of humiliation and dehumanization. Restoring dignity means healing the colonial wounds that have afflicted—and still afflict—the majority of the global population. Human rights may be of little assistance to that endeavor. Life rights if properly regulated may be empowering for populations destituted of their basic needs: water, food, clean air, and hygienic conditions. Once all of these are secured, the communities themselves will take care of the education of their children and of future generations. The human species has done that for millennia. Universities are recent institutions that don't account for the totality of knowledge in many respects. The ethical judgement to the transnational corporations is about life and dignity: dignity first and rights second. It was not an academically crafted argument or the result of granted research.

At this moment, the standard model of the "human rights watch" runs into argumentative difficulties. The perpetrators are not totalitarian states but "democratic" ones that tolerate the degradation of rights to life by supporting predatory transnational corporations in the name of development and economic growth. Their victims are victims simply by living in regions where natural resources abound, be it the Amazon, the Andes, North Dakota, the Congo, or the Middle East.[44] One day the victims' lives begin to be in danger, not because someone directly attacks their person, but because someone has polluted their rivers and their soils and created the conditions for leukemia and others cancers in their bodies. When these victims take salvation into their own hands, they transform the model for redressing violations and may be accused of terrorism. Now the victims are also their own saviors, and the saviors in the name of progress are the perpetrators. Gnoseological and aesthesic reconstitution is not a platform for protest, but for investigations driven by the need to change the terms of the conversations. Thinking otherwise is not a question of modifying the content (the domains, what is said) but of starting from principles and assumptions derived from experiencing the exteriority of the destituted, dwelling in the borderlands of living experience and Western knowledge.

I end this section by requoting part of a paragraph from the Juicio Ético that brings the memory of coloniality together with the present of global coloniality. "After 500 years of colonization and recolonization of the continent, this Tribunal [of Juicio Ético a las Transnacionales] asserts that it is not the same to 'live out of nature' as to 'live with and in Nature.' However, in defense of the insatiable assignments of the transnational corporations and the deepening of the capitalist logic and the widening of the frontiers for exploitation, the environment is destroyed and with it goes the extermination of entire towns of Indigenous and peasant populations that today are considered 'the rest' of society."[45] Just as the Tribunal of the Juicio Ético identified the "rest of society," the Zapatistas in their struggle underlined the "the rest of neoliberalism." The parallel is not trivial, for both cases are manifestations of decolonial thinking otherwise facing the limitations of modern thinking otherwise. Modern (and postmodern) thinking otherwise are caught in their own web. Decolonial thinking otherwise starts and departs from the awareness that the mindset that created the problems cannot be activated to solve those problems.

VI Concluding Remarks

In closing this chapter I bring back the call to expand the classical paradigm of human rights made in the *Lectura de la Sentencia del Juicio Ético* (LSJE). This call, I insist, comes from thinking otherwise, that is, from taking seriously Indigenous philosophy. A "new way of thinking," called for in the "Russell-Einstein Manifesto" as extended by Dürr and his coauthors, is an important complement to decolonial thinking.

To think otherwise decolonially you have to delink from the same call made by the very respectable "Russell-Einstein Manifesto" and Dürr's statement. They should be supported at the same time that they are reduced to their own North Atlantic size. Delinking from *modern* (and postmodern for that matter) presuppositions and frames of thinking otherwise draws inspiration from the paradigm opened up by the Bandung Conference in both the trajectories it launched. Granted, thinking otherwise in a de-Western mode is not the same as thinking decolonially. However, to think in a de-Western mode cannot draw inspiration from Saint Paul or Spinoza. De-Westernization means finding one's own source of inspiration, praxis of living, and thinking to reconstituted. Most of the countries whose representatives were at the Bandung Conference counted for roughly half the people on the planet. That is why the seeds of both decolonization and de-Westernization were planted there in a still nebulous distinction but with a clear horizon of going "de-" not "post-" (see chapter 9). Further, the countries represented were connected by their non-Christian religious beliefs and by their experience of being racialized.[46] This connectedness within their diversity requires us to reflect on a crowning achievement of the Western civilization constructed by capitalism and communism: the advances in science and technology and their military consequences. Science and technology are not exclusively universal but also historical and local. Better yet, "science" and "technology" (like "human" and "rights") are Western words to name a regional and particular kind of human knowing called "science," and a particular instrumentalization of the extension of the hands called "technology." Human knowing and instrumentalization by the extension of the hands are not privileges of Western civilization but of the commonality of the human species qua species. Coloniality made possible the universalization of the particular and the long-lasting (and in many senses irrelevant) philosophical distinction between the universal and the particular. The praxis named "science" and the praxis named "technology" have reached spectacular heights in Western civilization, and their achievements have come with both splendors and miseries. The misery of science is what the "new ways of thinking" (as identified by the "Russell-Einstein Manifesto") demand be ended, and the splendors cannot be sustained by the same system in which both splendors and miseries were brought forth, that system being most fully built and activated by the visibility of modernity and the invisibility of coloniality.[47] For science and technology as such, development is not a problem. Rather, it is one outcome that the "dumb" (in the sense of being grounded in materialism) tools of science and technology can advance, if employed to do so.

Instead, for the Tribunal Ético Popular, science and technology brought forward the idea that civilization presupposes progress and development, and the expansion of technological and scientific investigations are generously financed to secure the advancement of technology (one of the key sectors in the hybrid war between the US and China, with Russia having a solid background in both). Life has to be sacrificed to secure progress and development: "The Tribunal is convinced that it is not possible to judge transnational corporations without condemning at the same time the so called 'development model' and the capitalist system, which is patriarchal and racist, that generated such a model, maintains and extends it. The core subjects of the system are the values of the white male, bourgeois, owner, heterosexual, Westerner and Christian."[48]

Such a shift in the geography of reasoning takes place when the victim not only becomes the savior but in the process also delinks from the categories of knowledge that generated the history of "rights"—from *ius gentium*, to the rights of man, to the rights of the citizen, ultimately to the declared universality of human rights. This history is the genealogy of Western thought and rights, which proceeded in three stages that were invented to solve problems that emerged in the process of building Western civilization itself. Life rights, on the contrary, come forward precisely in places and from people suffering the consequences of the miseries and splendors of Western modern science and technology (of which Martin Heidegger was well aware) and, therefore, materialized in a state of mind engendered by Western coloniality: the consequences of racism, sexism, exploitation, domination (of which Heidegger was not well aware).[49]

We are ready to move to part III, where I will shift the argument to a terrain that may seem, at first, to be outside the question of racism, human rights, and cosmopolitanism—the main concerns of parts I and II. It may seem so, but the hemispheric partition and racialization of regions and continents are the outcomes of the same logic (coloniality) of racial and sexual classifications and of the modern dreams of homogeneity (globalism). Continents and regions do not carry with them their own ontology: regions and continents are epistemically constructed, their ontology an invention of epistemology. People's sensing and emotions are tied to their regions, country, county, or town, which are hierarchically arranged in the world order, some over others, some below. Classification and ranking are creations of specific actors who speak and write in certain languages, manage map-making, and operate within certain institutions. Hemispheric partitions are essential to the formation (i.e., the invention) of America and the transformation of the CMP. The politics of decolonial investigations, which I pursue in part II, needs to resort to gnoseology and aesthesis to avoid the CMP's regulations of knowing, taste, and sensing.

Hemispheric partitions are also relevant for the division of labor and the appropriation of "natural resources." One could not but be surprised by the fact that most of the "grossest" (in the sense of affecting great masses of people at once) violations of human rights are located in non-Western areas of the world. The global exploitations of natural resources and labor (e.g., outsourcing) also have been located mainly beyond the North Atlantic until the protests in North Dakota brought the issue home. Today, however, the perpetrators of violations of life rights, as well as the saviors of their victims, are all actors and institutions in developed countries. Their victims are elsewhere, mostly in the nondeveloped regions of the planet. This is an important reason why violations of life rights are not condemned. The politics of hemispheric partition has much to do with this (chapters 8 and 10) and with the current political emergence of de-Westernization. The state politics of de-Westernization is also one of the consequences of the Bandung Conference (chapter 9).

PART III

THE GEOPOLITICS OF THE MODERN/ COLONIAL WORLD ORDER

8   Decolonial Reflections on Hemispheric Partitions

About twenty years ago I explored the meaning of the "Western Hemisphere" within the colonial horizon of modernity.[1] Now roughly twenty years into the twenty-first century, the economic and political fields of power that existed at that time are rapidly being reoriented. This reorientation is more than metaphorical. On the one hand, "Orientalism" is being superseded, not reversed: superseded because the "Orient" (from East Asia to South Asia and to Southeast Asia) is no longer a voiceless place and people subjected to Western Orientalism.[2] Now a series of possibilities emerges from a thoroughgoing disavowal of Western Orientalism. I underscore "Western" Orientalism because Orientalism did not emerge from "Oriental" ontology. In other words: the Orient is not Oriental; it has been made Oriental by an observer who locates himself (and him it was) in the West. People inhabiting the Orient did not know they were doing so until they learned from Westerners that they were "Orientals." If you place yourself in China or Japan, for instance, you would realize that the Orient (where the sun rises and thus where you are "oriented" before the magnetic compass established north as the standard point of "orientation") is the American continent, from Alaska to southern Chile.

Today there exists the possibility of an Orientalism in reverse. If Orientalism in reverse takes place, it will be because Western Orientalism provoked it. Further, the possibility of border epistemic and emotional responses to this reversal is now open. These responses consist in reaffirming what the West disavowed: that it invented Orientalism and that this invention acquired an ontological status. Put another way, Hegel's narrative on the philosophy of history has taken a very paradoxical turn. Spirit, in Hegel's narrative, arrived in Europe after a long journey and realized that it was the center of the world; it also realized that it was in Germany, the center of Europe. It was programmed to continue its journey through the Atlantic to the US, as indeed it did. But then the unthinkable happened: Spirit escaped Hegel's cage and took its destiny into its own hands and returned to the East.[3]

This narrative (epistemology) produces an ontological effect: that of the trajectory of the Spirit since its origination, when indeed it was a fiction created by Hegel himself. This ontological effect made us believe that Germany was the end of Spirit's journey when, indeed, it was the beginning—the beginning of a narrative (the enunciation) that created the Spirit's journey (the enunciated). What this means is that the true beginning is the *idea* of Spirit arriving in Germany and not the beginning of a journey that actually happened in ancient China beyond Hegel's imagination. The Chinese did not know that they were at the beginning of a Western narrative of universal history. To justify the itinerary and to create the illusion of "history," Hegel needed the beginning of the journey to be elsewhere. The Chinese people did not have that need. In other words, it was the presence and the present of Hegel's enunciation that generated the effect of the presence of the enunciated in the past: the past of Spirit's journey. That fiction worked well because when Spirit arrived in Germany, it looked like it had made a "natural" journey. It did not appear, as was in fact the case, that it was a narrative *started in Germany* to tell a story that supposedly *started in China*. What mattered was the act of enunciation rather than any "journey" of Spirit. Making the enunciation the focal point is a must of the politics of decolonial investigations. Granted, to arrive at the enunciation one has to go through the smoke, the fog, and the noise of the enunciated. To delink from the enunciated, pushing it aside to look at the enunciation is not something you can achieve through empirical research and a microscope. It requires a different pair of glasses.

Hegel surmised that the route of Spirit would continue, cross the Atlantic, and dwell in the US. And he was right. But, he added, that is the future and his narrative was about the past. South America he dismissed as a place of "caudillos" and civil wars. Africa was out of history. One day, in fact, Spirit was deceived by European history, crossed the Atlantic, and indeed dwelled in the US for a while. But deceived again, it decided to continue its route to the West and return to its place of origination. It was Columbus's dream: to reach the Orient, from Europe, navigating toward the West. The return of Spirit to the East makes us realize that indeed the East is the West seen not from the location of

Europe but from the location of people in the Western Hemisphere, the Americas hemisphere. Again, if you place yourself in China or Japan, the Americas are the Eastern Hemisphere (see chapter 10).[4]

Departing from my essay of nearly twenty years ago, I now introduce two variations in the conversation about hemispheric studies of the Americas. In these variations, I want to twist my original argument toward the hemispheric partition occurring in the formation and transformation of the colonial matrix of power (CMP). The first variation is to ask whether it is "hemispheric studies" we should theorize or the "invention of America(s) and the idea of the (Western) Hemisphere." In asking this, I am calling into question the very invention of the hemisphere proposed for study. I ask, why is there a growing interest in the Western Hemisphere today and why in hemispheric studies? I ask also what it is we would like to know *about* the Western Hemisphere now, at a moment when so many on the planet are witnessing what seems to be an unmistakable shift of attention to the "Eastern Hemisphere"?[5] Or a third question: is there anything specific we would like to know or understand by pursuing hemispheric studies, or are we open to whatever we can "find"? I am interested in understanding the CMP *through* the ontology (the semiotic creation) of hemispheric partitions. I will go through the smoke, the fog, and the noise to uncover the enunciation of hemispheric partitions. That is, I will walk the paths of the politics of decolonial investigations.

I   The Invention of America and
    of the Western Hemisphere

    I.1

In order to theorize hemispheric partitions in search of the enunciation, it makes sense to first ask a historical question since the planet was not created with hemispheric partitions that had any particular significance other than being land masses separated by water masses or vice versa. Hemispheric partitions are a recent phenomenon in view of the age of the planet. The question is, therefore, when did the idea of the Western and Eastern Hemispheres emerge and why? Who was in a position to sanction it, and who benefited from the sanction? Before the invention of America, the possibility of dividing the planet into two hemispheres was unthinkable. But when the CMP began to be formed, international law emerged and with it linear global thinking; ranking regions was part of the racial classification scheme prompted by the desire for domination, and dividing the planet into hemispheres supported this scheme.

The *ecumene* (to use a consecrated Greek word), the known world, was once a continuity from what today is Europe, Asia, and Africa across the Mediterranean Sea. But that was for the Greeks, not for everyone else. It was the "discovery" of the Americas and the navigation through two oceans, Atlantic and Pacific, that generated the idea of dividing the planet into two, Western and Eastern, geographic hemispheres that soon took on epistemic and political significance. Notice that "Western Hemisphere" doesn't equal "the West." Notice also that at that point in time, the division between the Northern and Southern Hemispheres (today the Global North and the Global South) was not a question and it was not *in* question. Why? It was not necessary. The European encounter with a land mass they did not know—although there were managed knowledges to describe and map this land mass—brought about the "hemispheric" conceit, for the West was already a concept in use: Western Christians were Christians who resided west of Jerusalem.

So, both "America" and "Western Hemisphere" are not entities in themselves (i.e., they do not have ontologies independent of the discourse that invented and described them), but are geopolitical ideas to organize the planet. And that has been done in the processes of building the CMP. Further, the discourse of Western and Eastern Hemispheres was not proposed by actors inhabiting institutions created in the Eastern Hemisphere, but by actors that located themselves in the Western Hemisphere. They activated the imperial/colonial differences by inventing its counterpart, the Eastern Hemisphere. And underneath the partition, the CMP was being established. Philological Orientalism followed the cartographic partitions. These ideas did not come about by any universal governing consensus of all existing civilizations either. There was no dialogue of civilizations, but monologues of one civilization. The partition was a product of Western Christians who already conceived the world as divided into three continents: Asia, Europe, and Africa. All was the outcome of the global linear thinking and international law that I explored in chapter 6. Furthermore, the idea that the planet was divided into three continents only made sense for Western Christians, not for Chinese, Mayas, Persians, the kingdom of Benin, etc. But that is not all: the idea of East and West, the Eastern and Western Hemisphere, first needed the idea of the Americas christened—by the same people—"New World." That meant "new" to them, not to the millions of people inhabiting the continent.

To be fair, people inhabiting Anahuac, Tawantinsuyu, Abya-Yala, and the hundreds of other territories on the continent did not know about the Old World (Asia, Africa, and Europe) either. The distinction between Old and New World is tantamount to the distinction between Indias Occidentales and

Indias Orientales for Spaniards, and America for people north of the Pyrenees. In this distinction, the seed of the Western and Eastern Hemispheres was planted: for Western Christians, the lands to the west of Europe were labeled (due to Columbus's confusion) Indias Occidentales, and the lands to the east of Europe Indias Orientales. When Spanish institutions and actors lost control of the knowledge that was taken up by northern Europeans and Dutch mapmakers, Indias Occidentales and Indias Orientales mutated into the Western and Eastern Hemispheres.[6]

Castilian conquerors (Hernán Cortés), Italian explorers (Columbus, Vespucci), and men of letters in Castile (d'Anghiera) were the first, in Europe and in the world, to write about and map the continent that not too many people knew about. Mayan, Aztec, and Incan civilizations dwelling in the continent when Spaniards arrived had a totally different conception of where they dwelled. Written and printed information and conceptualization about land and people unknown to the actors who were writing and mapping had a tremendous effect: they transformed ignorance into ontology and fiction into truth. This is the context in which I propose to investigate hemispheric partitions, looking through to the enunciation and management of the CMP.

1.2

Originally, this argument was presented orally in a lecture at the University of Bielefeld, Germany. I opened my lecture with a two-minute statement by Native American theologian Richard Twiss, from his video "A Theology of Manifest Destiny."[7] If you watch and listen to his statement on YouTube, you will soon see the reasons why I started with it. Twiss talks about the coming to America of the Europeans—for example, William Penn, fleeing persecution, coming to found a community built on biblical ideas, and arriving with a sense of this endeavor as a mission ordained by God. As a consequence, the Indigenous people already here were seen as Canaanites, either as subjects for religious conversion or as obstacles to be overcome.

Twiss's statement underscores a commonality among theologians and secular Native American thinkers, First Nations people in Canada, and Pueblos Originarios in South and Central America. He sketches the first two historical events that I would like to focus on here. The first of these is the invasion by European colonizers starting in the late fifteenth century and going through the sixteenth century. From the perspective of the people being invaded, there was little difference among the invaders. Be they Spaniards, Portuguese, Dutch, English, or French, their different imperial languages, rooted in Greek and Latin, primarily gave voice to the same inhumanity, even among those who defended the "Indians" but considered them somewhat defective in relation to a self-fashioned concept of the "human" (see chapters 7 and 12).

This circumstance also reflects a commonality with thinkers of Afro-Caribbean and African descent in continental South and Central America as well as some US African Americans (e.g., Cornel West), for whom 1492 is the point of reference for the life and death of the continent. Although the slave trade started in earnest during the sixteenth century, 1492 is the date of reference that created the conditions for the transportation of enslaved Africans to America. It is also the date referenced by thinkers of European descent in South America and the Caribbean, of either theological or secular persuasion. In Anglo-America the initial moment is marked by the arrival of Pilgrims to the northeast area of the continent. A considerable difference distinguishes, therefore, the group of European descendants in the Americas and the Caribbean from the knowing and sensing of Indigenous and Africans in the Caribbean and continental America (including the US). People of European descent in the Western Hemisphere are divided between those who considered the invasion beneficial for Indians and the slave trade necessary for economic reasons, and those who considered both conquest and slavery genocidal interventions. We do not encounter that division, at least with such clear outlines, among Indians and Blacks. The majority in both these demographic groups agree that the invasion was genocidal, as was the subsequent organization of the Atlantic slave trade. And, also, there is a noticeable distinction in memories, sensing, and knowing between Anglo- and Ibero-Americans (Spanish and Portuguese).

The bottom line is that all the disputes about the New World were disputes between Europeans in Europe and others of European descent in the New World and between Creoles (people of European descent born in the Americas) themselves and between themselves and their Europeans ancestors. "Indians" (Indigenous) and Blacks had their own opinions and expressed them constantly in different ways but were not allowed to enter into the broader public conversation, even less in institutional education. Their views were not a factor in decisions to appropriate and expropriate lands, which were divided among Europeans and their descendants and named by those Europeans according to their own cultural memories.

The second historical event concerned the later role of the US in this "New World." By the end of the seventeenth century, European cartographers had divided the planet into two hemispheres, the Western and the Eastern.[8] However, in the nineteenth century, the US appropriated the idea of "Western Hemisphere" by claiming US sovereignty throughout the continent and thus challenging European expansionism. This was a crucial move for international politics in the sense that, up to that point, the idea of the "Western Hemisphere" referred to European colonies in the New World/America. Thereafter, the "Western Hemisphere" named and defined "America" from a US perspective and subject to US management: the US became equivalent to America.[9] Theodore Roosevelt made this clear in 1904-1905 by amending the Monroe Doctrine a century after its proclamation to declare that Europe must stay off "American" soils, thereby making the US guardian and putative manager of all countries in the Western Hemisphere and the chief preventer of European colonialism in this realm.[10]

Now (in 2020), the US threatens to do the same in the South China Sea. Here we see US exceptionalism working in two ways: first, asserting the right to reject intervention on its own soil, and second, affirming the right to intervene whenever and wherever it pleases. Since the Monroe Doctrine, the rhetoric of US foreign policy has promoted the US as the primary agent of world order and world freedom. This was an interesting move indeed—to first become the imperial guardian of the Western Hemisphere, and then, increasingly (neoliberalism was the last phase), the manager of the planetary world order. The rhetoric of salvation has changed narratives but maintained its aim. Europe was confronted, in the nineteenth century, by the US and was accused for its imperial ambitions and designs. In the process, the US affirmed its own state autonomy simultaneously with its vision of Manifest Destiny and its own imperial designs molded in the name of liberty.[11] What is unique in this appropriation of the idea of the Western Hemisphere is the complementarity between the US's ideology of liberty, upon which its Founding Fathers established the nation, and, simultaneously, the justification of US imperial expansion as a struggle in the name of liberty and democracy. "Hemispheric America" became first the US's self-hemispheric identification and later that of the entire continent. Here again we could revisit Richard Twiss.

II   The Irreversible Shift to the Eastern Hemisphere

Although the division between East and West, as I described above, was originally based on how Christians imagined and visualized the planet—with Jerusalem first and later Rome as the center (and still later with London and the Greenwich Meridian as the center)—the fiction of East and West eventually acquired ontological status with global partitions and the moveable center taken for granted. At present the rhetoric of the global order is still predicated on the presumed "existence" of two entities, the East and the West. More recently the Global South complicated the picture. "Global South" was a notion that had some currency in the 1970s, when it was taken up by the Third World and the nonaligned states. With the end of the Cold War the division between three worlds lost currency, and the Global South gained ascendency in spite of the fact that South Asia and Southeast Asia are, as the name attributed to them testifies, in the East. Epistemology trumps ontology.

I am bringing this scenario of "hemispheric America" and Western/Eastern Hemispheres into consideration because it is intersected in two ways by the Global South: On the one hand, there are South and Central America, and also North America. In the middle lies the Caribbean, which is also counted as Global South. On the other hand, there is also the South of the North (i.e., the South of the US; see chapter 10). The superposition of the Global South over hemispheric America flags the power differentials within the very same hemisphere—power differentials that can be accounted for by the history of coloniality from 1500 to the present.

Today the expression "Global South" (see chapter 10) is confronted by the rising visibility and the economic and political force of the Eastern Hemisphere (as described by the aforementioned seventeenth-century European cartographers, and, later on, by the US politics of Manifest Destiny). This shift means that for the first time in five hundred years (since Pope Alexander VI divided the planet between Indias Occidentales and Indias Orientales), the Eastern Hemisphere is no longer a complement to the Western Hemisphere but is becoming a counterbalancing force. This new reality erodes the coloniality of cartographic knowledge that divided the hemispheres with an implied (yet subtly visible on the maps) power differential—a differential that became invisible once the cartouches of seventeenth-century cartography no longer appeared on the maps. In these Old World maps, Europe appeared on the top left corner, personified by an elegant lady seated in a *locus amoenus*. In the upper right corner, an elegant lady personified Asia, but she was seated on an elephant. An alphabetic writing civilization, like the Western one, that has privileged the Latin alphabet marks the primacy of the upper left corner over the upper right corner, and, of course, over the bottom corners. In seventeenth-century cartography those corners were attributed to America and Africa.[12]

The rise and resurgence of China since the end of the twentieth century reveals more than the nation's economic growth. It exposes a widespread affirmation and strengthening of China's political decisions in the interstate arena; it exhibits also the dispute for the control and management of the CMP and the shift of global attention to the Eastern Hemisphere. Furthermore, it means that for Western coloniality or power by the end of the eighteenth century (viz., the hidden logic of the imperial discourse of civilization, progress, and development), the monarchic state was out of joint and the idea of the modern nation-state came into the picture concurrently with liberalism and industrial capitalism. That mutation of the CMP would be bad news for China. The Opium Wars mark one telling moment in China's decline and the dismembering of the long-lasting trajectory of the Chinese dynasties. China, which endured 150 years of disarray after the Opium Wars, is now recovering, returning and leading a global shift of focus to the Eastern Hemisphere. By redressing the balance of global forces, it is changing the configuration and profile of the Western Hemisphere. It is provoking the US to struggle to regain the leadership it acquired in the second half of the twentieth century.[13] De-Westernization, which came to the surface by the beginning of the twenty-first century, was destined to happen after the Opium Wars. South and Central America as well as the Caribbean now have open options. Depending on the government of the moment, a given state may realign its political and economic policies and create an alliance with the Eastern Hemisphere or remain tacked to the North of the Western Hemisphere. What this means is that the planetary earthquake in the second decade of the twentieth century is a sign of the CMP's radical mutation: the rise of multipolarity on the one hand and the counterrevolution to maintain unipolarity on the other. In other words, de-Westernization and re-Westernization disputing the control and management of the CMP.

The implications of China's new ascendancy are enormous. But before going further: multipolarity doesn't mean that China pretends to be or could be the new "hegemonic unipolar power." It is only within the frame of mind of Western modernity that this scenario is feared. One of the most overreaching is the dismantling of the basic partition of the world since Alexander VI: now the East is both in the West and in the South. And the South is both in the East and the North (see chapter 10). A multipolar ordering of the world is erasing the modern/colonial partitions of hemispheres and continents. That is to say, economic and political forces establish new transhemispheric and transdirectional alliances. Take the case of the BRICS states (Brazil, Russia, India, China, and South Africa), now in desuetude after the legal coup d'état in Brazil. Certainly, China is in the Eastern Hemisphere, according to the modern/colonial imaginary, and Brazil is in the Western Hemisphere but also in the Global South. South Africa is certainly in the Global South but between Western and Eastern Hemispheres: the Atlantic and the Indian Ocean kiss each other south of Cape Town.

We saw in the recent past many South and Central American countries, for example, following the leadership of Brazil under Ignacio Lula da Silva and

Dilma Rousseff, joining the shift toward the East away from US control of the hemisphere. But that was precisely one of the main reasons for the coup d'état. De-Westernizing geopolitics has been complicated after the judicial and financial coup in Brazil that dislocated the country's membership in BRICS. But the BRICS benefited after Donald Trump was elected president and dissolved the Trans-Pacific Partnership (TPP). The right-wing Brazilian government became an outlier in the BRICS geopolitics promoted by Lula and Rousseff. Brazil, like Argentina under Mauricio Macri, began to court the Alianza del Pacífico and the TPP (if the TPP survives Donald Trump's administration), two sides of the same imperial coin. The formation of the Grupo de Lima (which includes Brazil), and its support of Juan Guaidó as acting president, is another sign that the "turn to the left" from 2006 has been turned around to a "turn to the right."[14] Donald Trump's scrapping of the TPP, which was created by former president Barack Obama and was a globalist project to "contain" China (e.g., to contain de-Westernization) and to re-Westernize the world order, meant ending globalism in favor of Americanism ("America First"). Trump's rejection of neoliberal globalism in favor of his Americanism has left plenty of room for China to take the lead in globalization—that is, to take over what globalism initiated but can no longer control. This is a crucial moment in the dispute for the control and management of the CMP.[15] In short, here is a clear-cut case in which de-Westernization is disputing the control and management of the colonial matrix of power.

The political shift across hemispheres, then, has a name: "de-Westernization," a turning away from five hundred years of Westernization (see chapters 9 and 10), which forced the counterrevolution I describe as re-Westernization. De-Westernization means to dispute the overarching control of global affairs by four states in the Western Hemisphere: Germany, England, France, and the US (GEFU). GEFU is in the Northern and Western Hemispheres, the equivalent to the PIGS countries (Portugal, Italy, Greece, and Spain), that is, the South of Europe, to which Ireland was added to form the PIIGS. Do they belong to the Global South or to western Europe, when "history" unfolded between the Western and Eastern Hemispheres but not between the Global South and the Global North (which literally would include Russia)?[16] Ancient Greece lay just west of Asia, but it was "moved" to the West and has become a pillar of Western civilization since the narratives of the European Renaissance. Then it was relegated to the Global South following the narratives of the European enlightenment, when the North of Europe was fabricated to relegate the South to the exteriority of Europe, which is today the underlying map of the European Union. I'm trying to illustrate, with these few references, the formation and transformation of the CMP—how the content of the conversation changes but the terms created from Western global designs and the accompanying logic of coloniality remain in place. Beyond the moving hemispheric plateau, the CMP regulates the moves. Who are the actors pulling the strings of the CMP? That is a different and far more complicated question. The logic of global linear thinking and the actors and institutions managing it not only remain but maneuver the semantic and epistemic distinctions appearing in the news and in scholarly books, grounded in political and economic fields of force. At this point, de-Westernization disputes the content, not the terms, of the conversation. The logic of coloniality remains (e.g., development and globalization are goals that China has endorsed and appropriated), but the global imaginary is recognizing the irreversible shift to the Eastern Hemisphere (see chapter 9).

To the extent that hemispheric America was predominantly profiled in the regions along one of its coastlines, the Atlantic, the distinction between the Western Hemisphere and the West was blurred or intensified: the Western Hemisphere was US-America, and the West was western Europe. western Europe, and today the European Union, minus Britain, are no doubt in the West (that is, they lie west of Jerusalem, which was where Christians located themselves and for that reason they attributed Europe to Noah's son Japheth), but obviously it was not in the Western Hemisphere. Here it is useful to note the distinction between the "Occident" and the "West." The Occident has its center in the Mediterranean region to the west of Jerusalem, which it shares with Maghreb, also to the west of Mecca and Medina. "The West" has its center in the Atlantic and emerged in the sixteenth century when the Atlantic displaced the Mediterranean.[17] Up to that point, the West in the European imagination was the territory inhabited by Western Christians. In the twenty-first century the Western Hemisphere is, paradoxically, turning to a new "West," that is, to the Pacific. China, after all, is to the east of Europe but to the west of the Western Hemisphere. Recently, the US has started an international project to secure the presence of the West in the East and the South. The project was the Pacific Alliance, announced by Hillary Clinton in her speech in Honolulu in November of 2011, although President Barack Obama's lobbying preceded this speech.[18]

Shortly after Clinton's Honolulu talk, four states in the Global South of hemispheric America (not just the US) initiated their own Pacific Ocean project. It was, apparently, an initiative of mostly South American states in the Western Hemisphere (Chile, Peru, and Colombia, as well as Mexico), that is, the most conservative and neoliberal-prone states—not surprisingly, the ones embracing the project of re-Westernization.[19] Consistent with the turn of foreign policy toward the Pacific, Barack Obama maintained a close connection with Latin American countries, enthusiastically praising the political and economic model.[20] Obama's statements were not difficult to understand since the four countries were joining his own design to re-Westernize the world. Re-Westernization was Obama's response to de-Westernization and to the return of China as a major international political and economic player—as well as to the rise of the BRICS "alliance" during his presidency (and before the judicial coup in Brazil that ousted Rousseff and Lula). The Alliance of the Pacific existed in confrontation with the Latin American efforts at interregional integration represented by Mercosur and CELAC (Comunidad de Estados Latino-Americanos y Caribeños). However, with the turn to the right during 2017–2018, the Alliance of the Pacific and the Grupo de Lima sidelined all previous efforts to form an autonomous block of Latin American countries.

Clearly, then, the Western Hemisphere (as hemispheric America, including the US) is being partitioned between de-Westernization and re-Westernization efforts; the first was led on the South American continent, by Brazil, and the second in the North by the US. In this historic seismic shift, the unity of hemispheric America, or the Western Hemisphere as the US once conceived it, is exploding into pieces, and the pieces are being redistributed in a process of remaking the global order. What is different in this remaking is that western Europe and the US are no longer leading according to their will. Economic growth (meaning here growth not led by the IMF and the World Bank) is becoming a chapter of the past. This tendency will accelerate; there will not be a return to the global hemispheric order that originated in the Renaissance and persisted for five hundred years. But NATO became the Western Hemisphere.

III A Short Interregnum

The buzz on all of this has been, "Oh, things are not that simple. They are more complex." One wonders, then, what do we make of the complexity and the denial of simplicity? This is a question that does not so much affect a theoretical understanding of global shifts as it impinges on how disciplinary territories are mapped and defended. The problem is the epistemic and political lag between the reforming of disciplines and the act of understanding sociohistorical processes in order to orient our actions within them. Disciplinary regulations block creative imagination. The essay is a literary genre that was destituted in the constitution of the social sciences. In the humanities, it also occurred. Peer reviews, disciplinary rigor, and the tyranny of grammatical rules has also contributed to cutting the wings of inventiveness. I do not want to deny complexity, peer reviews, or grammatical restrictions: the colonial matrix of power with its domains, levels, and flows, its history and mutation, and its management of disputes is quite complex indeed (see introduction). Peer reviews provide a fresh reading, and grammatical tyranny helps to ensure that the text is readable. All of that doesn't prevent the need for simplification (not necessarily simplicity) when things are a little messy (not necessarily complex). I am here more interested in shifting the geography of reasoning, uncovering the enunciation under the messiness of the enunciated, and delinking from the obstruction of what—not always, but often—engulfs us into disciplinary decadence.[21]

Decolonial thinking (since I am claiming that these are decolonial reflections on hemispheric partitions) and decolonial doing in all domains, levels, and flows of the colonial matrix of power, with their double movement of constitution/destitution, demand that the politics of decolonial investigations contribute to gnoseological and aesthesic reconstitutions. Decolonial thinking and the politics of decolonial investigations are irreducible to a master plan, a political party, a charismatic leader, or a disciplinary structure. Both claim their existence in the dispersed and pluriversal doing in all walks of life and all regions of the planet—regions with different local histories, languages, memories, beliefs, praxes of living, yet still entangled with the modernity/coloniality that disrupted those local histories. To think, be, and do decolonially in today's world order, when questions are asked about hemispheric partitions, means to think through of the rhetoric of modernity and its successful mapping of the world to understand how the logic of coloniality (the persistent making and remaking of global power relations behind the promise of the rhetoric of modernity) is being remapped in the complex fields of forces in which de-Westernization and re-Westernization are entangled and in conflict, but are still forcing the closing of the unipolar world order by a multipolar one. What, then, should be the politics of decolonial scholarship in the multipolar world order in which all actors and institutions are immersed, willingly or not?

IV The Politics of Scholarship: Critical Theory, Decolonial
    Thinking, and the Underlying Fields of Forces Remapping
    the Eastern and Western Hemispheres

The keynote lecture that was a first draft of this chapter delivered at FIAR (Forum for Inter-American Research) also addressed—at the request of the organizers—the politics of scholarship. While the forum's overall subject was the Inter-American research promoted by FIAR, the themes of their research were addressed by disciplinary approaches from the social sciences and the humanities. Mine was a decolonial approach. The letter of invitation underscored the need to "theorize hemispheric studies of the Americas." My response to the invitation was framed as "decolonial reflections on hemispheric partitions," in which I attempted to underline (and I am pursuing it here) the correlation between the content or the enunciated ("hemispheric partitions") and the enunciation of that saying ("who, when, and why make hemispheric partitions"). Which means that my pursuit is to understand not what the hemispheric partitions *are*, but *how they became what they are*, and what are the political consequences of the content (being what they came to be) and the instances of making that content (the enunciation holding together—in this case—the colonial matrix of power through hemispheric partitions). Hence, decolonial reflection means, on the one hand, to establish a locus of enunciation that delinks from the enunciation controlling the CMP and, on the other, to understand the enunciation managing the CMP and the hemispheric partitions from which decolonial thinking and reflections attempt to delink. Which also means that I am not disputing the content of the hemispheric partition and am not looking for a "better one," but rather am revealing the epistemology of its making and the political and economic consequences. This is for me the most urgent task of the politics of decolonial scholarship—hence investigations.

Given that my own research since the late 1980s has focused on the historical foundation of Western colonialism inaugurated with the invention of America, and has since mutated into an effort to understand Western coloniality generally, I could satisfy the goals of the organizers by exploring—as I mentioned at the beginning of this chapter—the role of the Western Hemisphere in the formation and transformation of the CMP. I looked for a way to address hemispheric and inter-American research as a whole based on what my research was indicating to me, namely, that the invention of America was the constitutive event of modernity/coloniality, an issue that has been forcefully argued by Aníbal Quijano and Immanuel Wallerstein in their classic article on Americanity.[22]

The initial questions I asked were two:

1 The first related to the domains of investigation: hemispheric and inter-American research and study in one case and the analysis of the colonial matrix of power in the other. Of course, research on coloniality, while of great interest to me, is not necessarily the goal of hemispheric and inter-American studies, which can have many other goals than mine,

though admittedly this is not for me to say because I am not an "expert" in hemispheric or inter-American scholarship. Which means that I am not an expert in the content, in the enunciated, and if I am an expert in something, it would be in decolonial thinking, the analytic of the CMP to disengage from the field of forces that established the existing hemispheric partition and its political and ethical consequences. And this leads me to the second question.

2 The second question addresses the principles, assumptions, concepts, and drives that motivate scholarship in one or the other of the two domains mentioned in the preceding paragraph and that were at stake at the conference. In other words, the first question addresses the enunciated: the words naming the field to be investigated or studied. The second addresses the enunciation: the disciplinary formations that create and shape (theorize) the domain of investigation. Exploring both questions establishes a third level, that of my own enunciation, in between the rules of scholarship and the freedom of analytic imagination. Hence, thinking in the borderland, scholarly and existential; evading the prison house of disciplinary restrictions and disciplinary decadence to build places of joy and of the pleasure of thinking.

Having said that, I accept that hemispheric and inter-American research is an interdisciplinary undertaking convoking not only the social sciences and the humanities but the natural sciences as well. There are issues needing urgent attention, like "extractivism," which involves the site of exploitation and the capital needed for the exploitation. The sites are in the South, the capital in the North—not only in the American North but in the Global North (and indeed also in the Global South—Australian mining companies, for example). Hemispheric partitions are the work of imperial states legitimized by international law, which Carl Schmitt outlined, historically and theoretically, by tracing the emergence and the history of the *second nomos of the earth* and of global linear thinking.[23]

At this point, we enter the terrain in which hemispheric and inter-American scholarly investigations require interdisciplinary research, while the politics of decolonial investigations and the analysis of the colonial matrix of power require a praxis of decolonial thinking. What are the differences? Quickly stated: while disciplinary and interdisciplinary research and inter-American scholarship are one domain of disciplinary formation *within* (*interiority*) the colonial matrix of power (see the introduction), and therefore of the domain of the coloniality of knowledge and of being, decolonial thinking and doing come into being from the destituted, the *borders* (*exteriority*) of the CMP: accepting, on the one hand, the scholarly name of the game while, on the other, disobeying scholarly regulations, promoting independent thoughts and decolonial freedom.[24]

Delinking from disciplinary regulations anchored at the university as a fundamental institution of the coloniality of knowledge doesn't mean that you should resign your position at the university because your politics of decolonial investigations doesn't fit in any discipline in particular and, therefore, cannot be neither disciplinary nor transdisciplinary, because to do one or the other presupposes obeying the regulations of the disciplines involved in interor transdisciplinarity. Still, if you do that, there is a price to pay, as always, but there are also gains to harvest: you may not be approved for a research grant, for example, but you gain the freedom of thinking, doing, teaching, and writing. There is always a balancing act that border thinking implies. Thus, while interdisciplinary research has been transformed—as have many academic fields of investigation that have erupted since the Civil Rights movement, and just as transformations have occurred within various social science, humanities, and natural science departments—it nevertheless introduces *changes in disciplinary content*. However, the various departments and programs that have arisen from these transformations (e.g., Women's Studies, Latinx Studies, LGTBQ studies) questioned the terms of disciplinary conversations. For that reason, all these programs had and still have difficulties with canonical disciplinary formations—whether they are in the *-logy* paradigm (e.g., sociology), in the *-ic* paradigm (botanic), or in the *-y* paradigm (geography). All these disciplines have one thing in common: the clear-cut relationship between knowing and the known. All programs emerging from the Civil Rights movement have one thing in common: they all erase the distinction between knowing and the known. Hence, they changed the terms of the conversation. The aim of the politics of decolonial investigations is also *to change the terms of the conversation*, while interdisciplinary hemispheric and inter-American research aims, in my understanding, to change the *content* of the conversation. Which doesn't mean that one is bad and the other good. That is not the point. The point is to be clear about who is doing what and why. Hence, the claim of the politics of decolonial investigations.

Therefore, to conduct hemispheric and inter-American investigations means in decolonial analytics to first have an understanding of when, why, who, and what for the planet's hemispheric partitions came about; how, why, and by whom they are maintained and restructured; and to the benefit of whom. When you look at the BRICS countries, the presuppositions, the logic of hemispheric partitions, and the common sense they created fall apart. Russia is in the Global North, China in the Global East, India in the South of Asia, South Africa in the South of Africa (repetition necessary to distinguish a region from a country), and Brazil in the Global South of the Western Hemisphere! I also mean that hemispheric and inter-American research should be understood and oriented in relation to the oceans and not only to the land for the simple reason that the Eastern and Western Hemispheres are surrounded and interconnected by oceans that have become crucial in political-commercial relations. On the one hand, the TPP and NATO (North Atlantic Treaty Organization) aimed to control the Pacific and the Atlantic. On the other hand, the current tension in the South China Sea due to the US's attempt to contain China and to assert the role of the US as global arbiter is an obvious sign of a larger dispute: the dispute for control of the colonial matrix of power. That is, the dispute between re- and de-Westernization.[25]

Concurrently, the return to international prominence of India and China has prompted the return to importance of the Indian Ocean, a power center of commerce and civilizational exchanges before the Mediterranean displaced its relevance. All of these can be understood as changing manifestations of the colonial matrix of power: its formations and transformations managed by Western states and now disputed by de-Westernization.

Thinking decolonially means focusing on the CMP and not being distracted by the surface of the events, political discourses by state officers, or information from the mainstream mass media. Consequently, one decolonial question for hemispheric and inter-American research should be this: why hemispheric studies of the Americas now? Certainly, the answers to this question are numerous, but the underlying issue may be obscured. The issue is this: why do we need hemispheric and inter-American research now, and why do we need to theorize them? Any theoretical investigation starts with a question—if there is no question, there is no need to investigate or theorize further because there is no problem to address or question to answer. My answer to these questions does not come from within the project of hemispheric and inter-American scholarship, but from thinking decolonially about the making of both topics. By so doing, I am building an argument that delinks from the enunciation that created the ideas of hemispheres and inter-America, which then became topics for scholarly research. The difference is this: the topic of inter-American relations (the enunciated) is regulated by interdisciplinary formations (the enunciation), while for decolonial thinking the topics are both the enunciated and the enunciation embedded in CMP.

In his classic article "Traditional and Critical Theory," Max Horkheimer addressed a similar issue by distinguishing one from the other.[26] Although his important insights remained in the sphere of the CMP, his arguments are very helpful to introduce the further distinction between "critical theory" and "decolonial thinking." One key point of Horkheimer's argument is to blur the distinction between knowing subject and knowing object that is fundamental in traditional theory. Critical theory, on the contrary, starts from the assumption that the known object is a creation of the knowing subject. Or in simpler terms: what common sense refers to as "reality" (which empirical theory takes for granted) is not the known object of critical theory; the known object is the theoretical "cut" or the "frame" that the knowing subject formulates to understand a sector of the constant flux of social life. In that sense, the object is a creation of the subject. Nevertheless, the knowing subject in Horkheimer's argument is still a "modern and Western subject." The decolonial politics of investigations, fostered by decolonial thinking, presupposes instead a decolonial knowing subject, which means two things: (a) that the decolonial knowing subjects dwell in the borders of both Western and non-Western legacies, which are specific to local memories and histories that have been interfered with by Western subjects at different times since 1500, and (b) that the decolonial knowing subjects are border dwellers that become political border thinkers when the border consciousness activates and mobilizes her/his will to delink from the condition of colonial subject in order to retrieve her/his personhood. Knowing, knowledge, and decolonial healing partake of the labor of gnoseological and aesthesic reconstitutions. Further, this personhood can be enriched by the appropriation of whatever is put at the service of her/his benefit to advance reconstitutions of the destituted. In so doing, and at this point, delinking and epistemic disobedience mean that the decolonial person, healed from her or his colonial wounds, is no longer a colonial subject but a human being liberated from the inhumanity of the modern/colonial imaginary of Man/Human (see figures I.1, I.2, and I.3 in the introduction to this book).

Yet, there is still another layer exposed by empirical and critical theory relevant to the enterprise of decolonial thinking. This layer brings the decolonial view of the world into the full picture. The decolonial view exists at the moment that the analysis of the colonial matrix of power is posited as a topic of investigation. At this moment, the questions asked are neither empirical nor critical, in the senses meant by Horkheimer, but decolonial. And this brings geopolitics and the body politics of knowledge forward. Although Max Horkheimer and Carl Schmitt were looking at the philosophy of knowledge

(Horkheimer) and global linear thinking in international law (Schmitt), decolonial thinking surfaces at the moment in which the geopolitical and the body-political encounter each other in the borderlands where modernity/coloniality are united and divided by the slash "/." The consciousness of a body that is crossed by religious, racial, and sexual classifications is also the consciousness of being ranked in reference to a norm that is fictional but is accepted as real. Both, classification and ranking, are two basic operations in the double movement of constitution/destitution (see the introduction), which are direct consequences of (global) linear thinking. The same logic that operates on the bodies (racializing and sexualizing them, and identifying them by religion, nationality, and native spoken language) is projected onto the classifications of regions and countries. Bodies and regions are seen, from Western eyes, as complementing each other: underdeveloped regions of the planet, invented as such by the hegemonic imaginary of developed countries, presuppose underdeveloped bodies also. Which explains why Westerners in general believed that non-Europeans cannot think (see the epilogue). Hence, the sensing and emotioning of bodies growing aware of their/our downgrading become the fire fueling a desubjecting energy of thinking and doing while retrieving their/our decolonial personhood liberated from the prison of their/our colonial subjecthood. The decolonial personhood of knowing and understanding is no longer comparable to Horkheimer's knowing subject: what the decolonial gnoseological and political personhood wants is the knowledge that secures the liberation of all former colonial subjects of scholarship trapped in the demands of modern/colonial scholarship. The concern of decolonial thinking, coexisting with critical theory, is not the philosophical problem of object/subject relation but the epistemic, political, and ethical problem of the coloniality of knowledge hidden under the mirror effect of Western universal categories. My argument here is not intended to devalue Horkheimer's argument or the contribution of the politics of scholarship respecting the modern canon, but to clarify and consolidate the irreversible instance of decolonial thinking and the decolonial option for the politics of decolonial investigations.

If the world is named, described, and conceived in as many languages as exist on the planet, and if the speakers of each language have their own way of understanding and using the language they speak, then the crux of the matter is that Western modern/imperial languages (Italian, Spanish, Portuguese, French, German, and English, which are rooted in Greek and Latin) dominate the sphere of higher learning and knowledge to the point that knowledge in other languages (say Mandarin, Persian, Arabic, or Russian) remains restricted to the speakers of that language, unless they express themselves in a modern/imperial language, like contemporary English. The reverse doesn't pertain: no speaker, scholar, intellectual, or journalist speaking any of the three major modern/colonial Western languages (English, French, or German) has to translate his or her concepts into Arabic, Chinese, or Russian, because none of those three languages (as well as many others) are epistemically global. Having recognized the problem, our first philological task is to address, to undermine, and to uproot concepts sacralized in Western epistemology.

Decolonial questions are addressed not only to entities, phenomena, or relations among entities, but mainly to the vocabulary in which entities, phenomena, or their relations are cast or framed. One can't help but be aware that the disciplines across the entire spectrum of higher education and its continuity in everyday life, as well as in publicly and privately funded research, are conceived, defined, and managed in the vocabulary of modern western European languages derived from Greek and Latin, and are glued in the double movement of the constitution/destitution of knowing and knowledge, of epistemology and aesthetics. The politics of decolonial investigations begins from the awareness that the totality of knowledge encircled in the Western disciplinary spectrum, which trickles down to the larger public and private sphere, is a constituted mirage that legitimizes the destitution of knowledges, ways of knowing, and knowing subjects beyond the circle of the constituted idea of Western modernity. Three departures are basic to the politics of decolonial investigations: (a) delinking and epistemic disobedience; (b) doing so not to redefine the already constituted categories, but to investigate how they came to be what they are and for the benefit of whom; and (c) starting from other places, not by asking what X means in non-European ways of knowing and living, but by asking what is *relevant* in non-European languages, what ways of knowing and living are lacking in European ways of living.[27] These three departures are the foundations of this book: in doing what I am doing and saying what I am saying, I assume to be acting on the politics of decolonial investigations. I am not attempting to tell you *what it is* but *inviting you to decide what it is by understanding what I am doing.* That is, I am inviting you to pierce through what I say and to look at my saying. And my saying is endeavoring to pierce through the said in the rhetoric of modernity by *representing what it is* to understand the saying *governing* the logic of coloniality.

Thus, decolonial ways of knowing are at work in my analysis of the Western Hemisphere's idea, not by interpreting what it is or correcting or providing a better definition, but by looking into the enunciation, that is, of the coming into being of the idea of the Western Hemisphere. Nouns and compound nouns such as "America," "hemisphere," and "inter-American relations" in this case are modern/colonial configurations, keywords of the rhetoric of modernity. Consequently, the politics of decolonial investigations requires, in this case, a philological analysis: interrogating the words and expressions that in the process of naming and describing built and created the illusion of what exists. Certainly, there is something round and tall in front of my front door, and if I do not pay attention, I can break my nose walking into it. But the moment I say that the round and tall thing *is* "a tree trunk," I have confused the level at which the entity exists in the world with my description of that entity—my naming is not the entity I name. That is why the enunciation is so crucial in the decolonial analytics of the CMP as well as the decolonial politics of gnoseological and aesthesic reconstitutions. The narrated events, for example, that illustrate the law of physics that explains the event is not, and can never be, the event itself. The ontic doesn't equal the ontological, which is created by narrative or explanatory procedures. I am not talking either about conflict of interpretations. Sure, there are several physical theories since Aristotle and Galileo, but all of them are within Western cosmology. While they differ in the content they partake of the enunciations. If instead I account for cosmic flows and energies starting from the constant movement of yin and yang, there is not a conflict of interpretation but an activation of the enunciation based on traditional Chinese knowledge, not on traditional Greek knowledge and its update during the European Renaissance. Decolonial investigations and thinking have to confront the belief that one way or another modern epistemology holds the privileges of "truth" that have been granted by five hundred years of Westernization of knowledge. For that reason, the domain of knowledge is a fundamental concern for the politics of gnoseological and aesthesic reconstitutions.

Let's take one more step and focus on the noun "hemisphere" to elucidate the decolonial investigations that can, and have to, be done. Starting from (not negating) the accepted meaning of the word and the belief that *there are hemispheres*, the next move is to depart from it and look toward the underlying conditions that propelled the creation and the conservation of the word in Western scholarship and in the public sphere. (Of "America" as an invention I have already said something; indeed, I have devoted a book to it.)[28]

HEMISPHERE *(n.)*
late 14c., hemysperie, in reference to the celestial sphere, from Latin hemisphaerium, from Greek hemisphairion, from hemi- "half" (see hemi-) + sphaira "sphere"[29]

Now, if one hemisphere is half the planet along the east/west or south/ north axis, then the other half is the second hemisphere—clear and simple enough. The hemispheres have been "cut" above and below the equator and to where the sun rises and sets in reference to Rome first and later to the Greenwich Meridian (when the UK took over the leadership of the West). Both Rome and the Greenwich Meridian are in the West. That's obvious, but it needs to be said. In this division the American continent is only one sector of the Western Hemisphere, the other being Europe. But it happens that Europe lies to the east of the Greenwich Meridian. As for the North/South equation, Russia is clearly in the North but not in the West. It is the "poor North."[30] The Southern Hemisphere more or less coincides nowadays with the Global South. But not quite: half of Africa and a significant portion of South America would be in the North. This may sound strange, but the bottom-line questions are: If both divisions of the semi-spheres—south/north and east/west—are possible and legitimate, why did the second prevail from the late sixteenth century to WWII and then become displaced by the tripartite First, Second, and Third Worlds? And why was the Third World replaced by the Global South and the First by the Global North, leaving Russia in the poor North?[31] And finally, why is the Global East (which gets entangled with the Global South in the maps of *Southeast* Asia, where Singapore, Hong Kong, and Indonesia are the "rich South," playing with Tlostanova's metaphor of Russia as the "poor North") sidelined by the metaphor of the Global South?

Here we go again to the realization that hemispheric partitions do not have much to do with the ontology of the planet but with the epistemology of cartographic partitions in the double movement of the constitution/destitution of the CMP; with who controls and manages knowledge and regulates ways of knowing. Disciplines in the natural and social sciences have confused the unframed flow of Earthly and cosmic life with disciplinary frames of knowledge and the regulations of knowing that create the frames. This is another case of the confusion of the explanation with the explained, and of the coloniality of knowledge. The politics of decolonial investigations digs into the enunciation in the CMP's configuration where the confusion of the ontic with the epistemic is regulated. In the process of constituting the natural sciences, practitioners of the disciplines confused the explanation with the explained, and so the concept of representation became a crucial concept in the rhetoric of modernity: scientific knowledge "represents" what is there. Even in the humanities, countless theses have been written on "the representation of X in Z," where Z is a sign (a narrative, painting, film, etc.) in which something that is not the narrative is represented in the narrative. In other words, the ontic is always mapped and fixed as ontological, creating the illusion that epistemic descriptions and explanations of the ontic are rendered in words or visual signs; the unformed entity (*onto-*) is captured (as in a snapshot) by the formed sign (*-logos*). European Christians who were in control of knowledge and institutions decided on the east/west hemispheric partition, and they had the ability to depict (map) the planet according to their views and needs. What were their views and needs? Let's first attend to their views.

If we look at the famous T and O map (*orbis terrarium*; see figure 10.5), we can see that there is no clear east/west division. There are indeed "three hemispheres" (Asia, Europe, and Africa), which is nonsense if we take seriously the etymology of "hemisphere" (half a sphere). The planet was not divided into hemispheres but into three continental landmasses separated by water. The "three" was not serendipitous and did not depend on the location of landmasses but on the meaning of the number three in Christian cosmology. Each part of the planet "belonged" to one of Noah's sons. We do not see hemispheres but hierarchies: Asia corresponds to Shem, Africa to Ham, and Europe to Japheth. A basic knowledge of biblical narrative is sufficient to understand the implicit hierarchy: Christians did not inhabit the land of Shem or Ham but the land of Japheth. At that point, before the Crusades, the center was Jerusalem.

But Jerusalem was not the center of the world for all. It was the center only for Christians. The Bünting Clover Leaf map is univocal.[32] It was drawn in 1581. For Jews, Jerusalem is the heart of Judaism, dating back to around 1700 B.C. But it was not necessarily the center of the world, as it was mapped in the Christian T and O map around the sixth century A.C. For Christians, Jerusalem is the city of the ministry of Jesus Christ, which is dated between 27 and 36 A.C. For Jews, Jerusalem is the Ancient Testament. Christian Jerusalem is the New Testament. In the Bünting Clover Leaf map, what predominates is Christian Jerusalem, for Western Christians were then in command, the Jews having been expelled from the Iberian Peninsula by Western Christians at the end of the fifteenth century. Donald Trump's support for making Jerusalem the capital of Israel, taking it away from Palestinians, has not only drastic current political implications but also a deep and dense memory (see chapter 6).

In chapter 5 of my book *The Darker Side of the Renaissance*, titled "Geometric and Ethnic Centers," I argue that until the creation of the Renaissance-era world maps (Gerardus Mercator, *Orbis Terrae Compendiosa Descriptio*, 1569; Abraham Ortelius, *Typus Orbis Terrarum*, 1570), each civilization on the planet had its own ethnic center, including of course, Jerusalem as the ethnic center of Jewish and Christian cosmologies.[33] What Mercator's and Ortelius's maps did was to project the ethnic center into a geometric one.[34] The move had tremendous consequences—uplifting for those belonging to the civilization in which the world map was made, and devastating for all the other ethnic centers that did not have the opportunity, ability, or need to project their own ethnic center onto a geographic one. At this point Rome changed status: from being the Christian ethnic center, to being the center of the world. This was precisely the moment at which Pope Alexander VI divided the planet between Indias Orientales and Indias Occidentales, the forerunner of the Eastern/ Western Hemispheres. Here we encounter the advent of the second nomos of the earth, stamped by Western cartography as if the planet were, again, partitioned as such by God.

Rome became the center of the world and, in consequence, the center of enunciation, supported by the Latin language. It managed to impose over other civilizations its own conception of the planet and be recognized as the geographical location of universal knowledge—theological knowledge in this case. The Atlantic Ocean became the *center of trade and commerce* and, for that reason, the *expanded center of the world*, understood to be ancient Rome and the already consolidated Mediterranean.[35] The Atlantic Ocean encompassed the eastern coasts of the New World and the western coasts of Africa and Europe. The "triangular trade" (commodities from the New World to Europe, guns and manufactures from Europe to Africa, enslaved human beings from Africa to the New World) commenced. This reality and no other should be the foundation of any "hemispheric studies of the Americas." The triangular trade meant also the dismantling of coexisting civilizations of the New World, mainly those of the Andes (Tawantinsuyu) and Mesoamerica (Anahuac). Hemispheric studies (not to be confused with decolonial investigations) of the Americas that do not start at the moment of their continental constitution by the destitution of existing cultures and civilizations would be like any study of Europe that ignored that its very constitution has much to do with what it has destituted all over the planet, beginning at the end of the fifteenth century.

V   Five Hundred Years Later: From the Atlantic to the Pacific
    and the Indian Ocean

I have taken you through a detour that started the moment I began to uproot the word "hemisphere" from its reference (the epistemic/ontological partition of the planet) and to expose the ontic ungrounding of epistemic hemispheric partition. It was a decolonial detour, and an exercise in decolonial investigations, starting with the invention of the Americas and the follow-up, the Western/ Eastern hemispheric partition, preceded by the Indias Occidentales and Indias

Orientales divide. To continue our decolonial detour we must acknowledge that the Western Hemisphere or hemispheric America is not essentially a lump of land surrounded by water. It is and always has been, since the name "America" was bestowed on the landmasses that became it, a field of forces in the modern/colonial and European self-consolidation and imperial expansion. If we start from this premise, then, our concern will not be to "study" or "research" hemispheric and inter-American relations, but to ponder what questions should be asked about the inventions of America and the Western Hemisphere, and why we are interested in answering these questions.

A field of global forces, the Western Hemisphere and America were constituted from the perspective of the emerging Atlantic commercial circuit, which by 2009 (during the first period of Barack Obama's presidency) began to turn toward the Pacific: China leading de-Westernization forced re-Westernization. The contest for control of the colonial matrix of power erupted and is escalating today (in the summer of 2020). The turn to the Pacific was a major move and political declaration by Barack Obama's administration, occurring well before Hillary Clinton's own declaration of it in November 2011 in Honolulu (when she was responding to various challenges from China). Obama announced it in Japan in 2009, and coincidentally, at that time, Chile, Peru, Colombia, and Mexico formed Alianza del Pacífico (as I've already mentioned in a different context).[36] Soon after, Obama was invited to serve as a host of honor at a meeting of the Alianza held in Colombia. Interestingly enough, soon after that, Benjamin Netanyahu was invited as an honorary member.[37]

The field of forces and alliances was becoming clear. On the Atlantic side, Brazil was at that time a powerhouse of BRICS, next to Russia, China, and India. The judicial coup and the election of Jair Bolsonaro changed the role of Brazil in the BRICS. Other neoliberal-oriented countries in South America (Colombia, Argentina, Chile, Peru, Ecuador after Rafael Correa, Paraguay) allied with the US, ending the turn to the left during the first decade of the twenty-first century. At the same time, the Atlantic Mercosur (the Mercado Comun del Sur, or Southern Common Market) has been working toward delinking from control and management by the US, but by 2019 the project was undermined by the Alianza del Pacífico. It remains to be seen what foreign policy after Donald Trump will be for Latin America, China, and Russia since the Israel connection was clearly based on family relations. The Alianza del Pacífico is obviously a move to contain China and to assert the US presence in the South China Sea conflicts. At stake is the irreversible shift of power to the Eastern Hemisphere.

The events in Venezuela that started in January of 2019 are a telling sign of the reordering of US foreign policy to maintain global leadership in the continuation of the re-Westernizing policies initiated by Barack Obama.[38] However, de-Westernization (see chapter 9) is growing and forcing the US to increase its politics of domination after losing the privileges of its hegemony. The focus is on oil resources (in Venezuela and Iran), on containing China through a trade war, and, indirectly, on slowing down the Belt and Road Initiative. However, Italy's decision to join the initiative, with other European countries most likely following suit (Hungary), continues to tilt the balance toward the Eastern Hemisphere. The destiny of South America and the Caribbean in the next decades will very much depend on the leftward or rightward orientation of elected governments. The political turn to the right may stay in place for a while, given the lack of visionary orientations from the left and, for the time being, a lack of popular movements and popular leaders to reorient Southern Hemispheric foreign policy toward de-Westernization. By will or default, South America and the Caribbean remain mostly attached to the project of re-Westernization (see chapter 9).

VI Closing Remarks

The cycle that started with the invention of America and gave rise later to the Western Hemisphere is closing. We on the planet are living during a change of era, no longer an era of changes.[39] Hemispheric partitions are pervasive and they naturalize themselves. Events related to them may appear unrelated to global linear thinking and international law, yet nevertheless be closely related. The creation of the State of Israel is one among many cases that are logical consequences of the unfolding of global linear thinking and international law (see chapter 4).

There are many directions that a decolonial inquiry into hemispheric partition could take. What does it mean, in the past and today, when we say "the Americas" or "the Western Hemisphere"? Where are those expressions coming from, who invented them, why, and to the benefit of whom? We see in this question the reappearance of the notions of "Occident" and "Western." Since western Europe has been detached from the US's concept of the Western Hemisphere, tensions have surfaced between the US and the EU under the Donald Trump administration. What do these shallow denominations and partitions tell us about the CMP? These questions cannot be answered from any existing discipline or even from interdisciplinary research, for they are decolonial questions that must be decolonially addressed. I have suggested that hemispheric partitions engendered geopolitical borderlines and borderlands. Dwelling places and dwelling on the borders open up the possibility of thinking and doing in the border in which one dwells. Which brings us back to the politics of decolonial investigations located in the borderland of disciplinary formations (epistemology and aesthetics) and the unavoidable will to know and understand inbuilt in the daily praxis of living (gnoseology and aesthesis) in a world order that has been partitioned, ranked, and managed by actors and institutions. These are the same actors and institutions that made and transformed the CMP that is now, on the one hand, under interstate dispute (de-Westernization, re-Westernization) and, on the other, being refused by the rising global political society, the decolonial option among it.

The tasks of the politics of decolonial investigations and the decolonial option are to understand the changing fields of forces and flows of the CMP we are all immersed in, both in our disciplinary training and in our daily praxes of living. Understanding the constant flow of the CMP could be observed and understood from a distant and place not contaminated by the CMP. We on the planet have all been and are located in the hemispheric partition. The ways in which the living organisms we are sense the Earthly and cosmic energies that maintain it and sense the coexistence with organisms of the same species (human) cannot be detached from the disciplinary schooling that provides us with tools to make sense of our senses (pleonasm intended), at the same time that we are limited to the hemispheric partition in which our organism came into the planet. The politics of decolonial investigations, more than a disciplinary endeavor, breaks open the prison houses of epistemology and aesthetics and opens the windows to the fresh air of gnoseology and aesthesis.

In the next chapter I go into more detail to isolate and detoxify the ontology of continental and hemispheric partitions.

9   Delinking, Decoloniality, and De-Westernization

I   Chapel Hill-Durham, June 2019:
Preface to the Conversation

This conversation was conducted by Christopher Mattison at the former Advanced Center for Cross-Cultural Studies of the City University of Hong Kong. It is actually the outcome of several conversations created in email and combined with personal conversations over coffee or lunches. Although at the time we were at the same institute (two offices apart), where I was a visiting scholar from January to June of 2012, email exchanges mixed with personal conversations in between one question and the next proved to be consistent with the politics of decolonial investigations by not being limited to the library, the lab, and the office. Our chats about issues of everyday life in Hong Kong, the politics of Southeast Asia, and the long-lasting relations with the mainland were as illuminating as consulting documents in the library. And, of course, between one question and its answer, life in East and Southeast Asia was unfolding. I was sensing the shift toward and absorbing the experience of the Eastern Hemisphere I explored in the previous chapter. In the now of those conversations was not just the history of the colonial matrix of power (CMP) and of hemispheric partitions, but the experience of daily living, in its minute details—the smells, the sunlight, the noises, the crowd, the sound of a language one does not understand.

Beyond the attractions of everyday life, I had a particular concern that guided my investigations, always thinking decolonially, and travels during those six months. Convinced as I had been for a long time that Western storytelling about the world order and about the role of Europe (also the EU) and the US as leaders and modelers of the destiny of humanity was only half the story, I wondered when and what arguments would emerge from the other side of the story and the other side of the planet. It was around 2009, three years before my time in Hong Kong, that I read Mahbubani's *The New Asian Hemisphere: The Irresistible Shift of Global Power to the East*.[1] Mahbubani was a former ambassador from Singapore to the United Nations and then director of the Lew Kuan Yew School of Public Policy at the National University of Singapore. I read his book in tandem with the works of prominent public figures in the West like Henry Kissinger, Zbigniew Brzezinski, and Samuel Huntington. I found in Mahbubani's book the view from the East, so to speak, which is not Orientalism in reverse in any imaginable sense of the expression. Several of his arguments reveal the double standards of Western media, public policy, and the imperial will to Westernize the planet that show the missing chapters in the works of the Kissingers, the Brzezinskis, and the Huntingtons.

One chapter in Mahbubani summarized for me the thrust of his argument: "De-Westernization: The Return of History" (117–74). Understanding de-Westernization presupposes first understanding Westernization and also that Westernization would depend on where the narrator or the historian locates its narrative. Narrators that have been experiencing the second wave of Westernization (led by England and France) would locate the origination toward 1650.[2] For those of us who experienced the first wave of Westernization during the Renaissance, we would locate its point of origination in 1500, with the invasion and invention of America, as I did in all my writings. Colonization and Westernization are two different ways of referring to European expansion since 1500: the first refers to control and management, the second to schooling. Colonization carries the image of violence and force; the second suggests the double project of disseminating Western values and their acceptance by governments and people beyond the West in their effort to emulate or at least to follow the leads of Western dictates. That image was alive in Frances Fukuyama's belief, expounded in *The End of History*, which celebrated the collapse of the Soviet Union and hoped, if not assumed, that Western modernity would from then on penetrate all the way down: control, management, and schooling, everyone free under Western regulation. All of this is what the Soviet Union failed to do. Now Western neoliberalism would accomplish the task, fulfilling its manifest destiny. However, de-Westernization has disappointed the overconfident expectations in Western hegemony; what emerged after the end of the Cold War was instead the increased confidence in the appropriation of capitalism in China, the recomposition of the Russian Federation to Russian government, and the affirmation of Iran in its own sovereignty. The end of Western *hegemony* mutated into Western *domination*, which has been explicit since Donald Trump took office in January of 2017.[3]

More recently, Mahbubani has recast his argument in a short and provocative book that did not hide its intention: *Has the West Lost It? A Provocation*.[4] The thrust of his previous argument (2008) lay in his distinction between modernization and Westernization. For him modernization consists of the appropriation of the seven pillars of Western wisdom: free market, science and technology, meritocracy, pragmatism, culture of peace, rule of law, education. The appropriation of these seven pillars led Eastern countries to modernization—not, however, by cloning the West but by appropriating the seven pillars to their own benefit, rebuilding what the West had destituted. De-Westernization presupposes border thinking as state politics: absorbing the seven pillars into the much larger and more powerful memories, knowledges, and praxes of living, and revamping praxes of living transmitted through generations long before Western modernity was constituted. If de-Westernization means cloning and following Western dictates, it would be difficult to understand the increasing tension (in 2020) of the US and the EU's passive followers confronting China, Russia, and Iran.

It was during the semester in Hong Kong that I began to reflect on the legacies of the Bandung Conference and its impact on both decolonization and de-Westernization. At the time, it was not a common topic among humanists and social scientists but a conversation on revisiting the 1955 conference after the celebration of the sixtieth anniversary and the role of China in that celebration. Having read Mahbubani and having paid attention to Chinese conversations about the conference, both personal and in the media, and, perhaps most important, having obtained my information from Asian media without paying much attention to Western media, I began to sense otherwise. I began to sense, more than rational understanding, the feelings among the Asians with whom I was conversing, and in the media I was reading and listening to, the Chinese perspective on Bandung. China, in contrast to India and Indonesia, was never colonized. But it did not escape the tentacles of coloniality. The Opium Wars disrupted the millenarian trajectory of Chinese history. De-Westernization was, by 2012, an issue I had paid attention to before, and it is one of the five trajectories I summarized in the first chapter of *The Darker Side of Western Modernity*, published in 2011. What I began to understand in the first semester of 2012 was that the Bandung Conference of 1955 was a signpost for both decolonization and de-Westernization. A weeklong visit to Singapore, being there and chatting with colleagues and graduate students, confirmed my intuitions. Every nation-state has two faces, domestic and international. Each of them has a distinctive configuration. My colleagues and students were not shy in exposing the domestic shortcomings. I was and still am looking into interstate configurations. Hence, Xi Jinping's protagonism during the sixty-year celebration was not an appropriation of decolonial legacies (for China was not on the same path as India and Indonesia), but one more sign of de-Westernization. In 1955, Zhou Enlai attended, representing communist China, but the Soviet Union was not invited: twenty-nine representatives of Asian and African colonies and former colonies were the attendees. Singapore was not yet an independent nation-state, but I could have imagined, reading Lee Kuan Yew's memories, that he was not disinterested in the Bandung Conference, as I cannot understand the Singapore he built without reference to the philosophy of the conference: Lee Kuan Yew planted the seeds of de-Westernization.

In the process of thinking about and looking into the issues with the eyes of the politics of decolonial investigations, I began to understand the role that Lee Kuan Yew may have played in planting the seeds of de-Westernization. Beyond his writing and public addresses found on the web, reading the discourses of the first foreign minister of Singapore, S. Rajaratnam, once again confirmed my intuitions.[5] In 1955, Lee Kuan Yew was in no position to have been invited to Bandung. Singapore became an independent republic in 1965, and Lee Kuan Yew was its first prime minister. In 1967, he was interviewed about the Vietnam War on the program *Meet the Press*, in New York City. The interview is revealing about the interviewers' disjointed ways of thinking and Lee Kuan Yew's answers. The seeds of de-Westernization and border thinking are there: Yew senses and knows the Asian history and circumstances, and he knows Western ways of thinking. The interviewers only know their own assumptions and the logic of Western territorial thinking that have been presumed to be universal. The journalists show their arrogance and their blindness. Lee Kuan Yew shows that he knows what they do not know while at the same time knowing what they know. Border thinking in action. The interviewers had difficulties, if they didn't find it outright impossible, understanding the power of border thinking. Lee Kuan Yew knows that they do not know. His smile during the interview, and preceding his replies, preannounces the self-control and self-assertion of someone who knows what the interlocutor doesn't know. De-Westernization is not a question of high international politics without self-assertion, sensing, and reasoning by the person who leads the project. When I learned that Deng Xiaoping took China's leadership after the death of Mao Zedong and went to consult with Lee Kuan Yew, I began to better sense the meaning of de-Westernization. It became crystal clear that one of the unintended trajectories of Bandung went through Singapore to the reorientation of Chinese domestic and international politics: de-Westernization and border thinking by absorption of the seven pillars of Western wisdom without relinquishing what they had accomplished through twenty-five hundred years of their own civilization, and during the two hundred years after Western modernity had invaded and disrupted the flow of their history.[6] It was a fact of history, so to speak, destining the course of events leading to de-Westernization and re-Westernization.

My Western friends (because Westerners abound in Hong Kong) smiled at me when I said I read *People's Daily* and *Global Times* and watched the daily CCTV news. They smiled because all these sources of information are biased, a fact they underscored, just in case I was not paying attention to it. I responded that in the US I check the *New York Times*, the *Washington Post*, Fox News, and CNN, which are equally biased, I pointed out. My interest in checking these sources is not to find out the truth, but to know what the government and the media convey in the US, the European Union, China, Russia, or Iran. Remember, my decolonial attention pierces through what it is said to understand the saying, to find the enunciation behind the enunciated. It was through reading, listening to news, and having conversations that I began to see de-Westernization as a distinctive orientation of state politics that was not cloning the West, but taking whatever was useful and running with it. The confidence in their thinking was far from being the submissive attitude of someone who doesn't know what to do and kneels before his or her master, expecting a benediction and instructions to behave properly. My friends smiled at me also because they thought I was celebrating de-Westernization when I was simply acknowledging that something distinctive was happening. The signs of a change of eras were showing but were interpreted as an epoch of changes, which some of them expressed by using the prefix "post-" whenever convenient. De-Westernization involves state-led politics (as Lee Kuan Yew, Deng Xiaoping, Xi Jinping, and Vladimir Putin did it), and as all state-led politics (whether of nation-states or monarchic states) are today (as in the US and the EU), they are tied to the capitalist economy. But there is a difference, the imperial difference: Western states built capitalism; non-Western and de-Westernizing forms of governance were disrupted and had no choice but to learn something that was not built in to their own history (as capitalism was in the history of Western civilization), but had to be appropriated, twisted, and used for their own benefit. Imperial differences were cast, by Western knowledge, on regions that were not colonized but were disrupted, their modus vivendi destituted. Now it is the time to reconstitute what the Opium Wars disrupted. Activating what they have is of paramount relevance: activating their own patterns of thinking activates gnoseology; revaluing their praxis of living activates aesthesis. The imperial differences created border dwelling sites, and border thinking emerged with force among people not ready to submit to Western "truth." However, Wang Hui has made a convincing case for border thinking (without using this expression). The Western dichotomy of "empire vs. nation-state" doesn't work to account for China's past and present. To recover ancient Chinese concepts doesn't work either because they have already been tainted by the intrusion of Western epistemology. However, sensing the presence of ancestral thoughts cannot be avoided. Hence, border thinking calls for gnoseological and aesthesic reconstitution that neither bends to Western thought without Western senses, nor submits to Chinese fundamentalism.[7] I am touching here on one aspect of de-Westernization that I have to leave out: the intellectual and scholarly sphere that plays into the de-Western politics of investigations parallel to the decolonial to which I briefly return in the paragraphs below.

If Bandung in 1955 planted the seeds of decoloniality and de-Westernization, it became clear to me during that period that the third legacy of the conference is neither decolonial nor de-Western. The third legacy is the Non-Aligned Movement (initiated in Belgrade 1961) and the Tricontinental Conference organized by Fidel Castro (1966). However, this continuity sidelined one of the key dimensions of Bandung: race/racism and decolonization, as Sukarno clearly stated in his inaugural speech. Bandung was for him the first international conference of "colored people."[8] Nationalism was instead the solo driver of both the Non-Aligned Movement and the Tricontinental Conference. Decolonization vanished from the vocabulary, and it was maintained mainly by African leaders and thinkers—Patrice Lumumba, Amílcar Cabral, Steve Biko—and in the major decolonial theoretical formulation of Frantz Fanon.

The struggles for decolonization were struggles for national sovereignty by means of the foundation of nation-states. Consequently, the Bandung Conference was organized by the independent state of Indonesia with the presence of governing officers of twenty-nine African and Asian countries, some of them ruled by dynastic governance.[9] I emphasize that it was an event organized *not by "the people"* but by the state. It was concurrent with the struggle for decolonization during the Cold War, and its aim was to get imperial actors out of countries so states could be ruled by their Indigenous or native populations.

It was clear by the end of the century that decolonization during the Cold War was constituted by victories and failures, both for numerous reasons. Two of the major ones in my understanding are that native and Indigenous elites (as Fanon was already guessing in 1961) took control of the state and continued the politics of the imperialists in the name of nationality. The second is that the imperial foundations of political theory and political economy were left intact. Decolonization ended up being a change of hands from foreign to native management, but with the foreign management ever present in interstate relations between emerging modern/colonial states (after decolonization) and the consolidation of the US as leader of the world order after World War II.

All of this is well known. Less known were Bandung legacies for what became the multilayered trajectories of de-Westernization: politico-economic de-Westernization led by the state in Singapore and China as well as—as I mentioned above—de-Western scholarly and intellectual works parallel to decolonial ones. For instance, religious de-Westernization debated principally by Islam; artistic/aesthetic de-Westernization initiated by the Japanese curator Yuko Hasegawa in two of her events, *Sharjah Biennial 11* and the more recent *The New Sensorium: Exiting from the Failures of Modernization*; and the works of the prolific Chinese scholar and intellectual Wang Hui.[10] If "decolonization" was a keyword during the Bandung Conference, the word "de-Westernization" seldom appears. But it must surely have been in the air. Most likely because in the context of the conference the distinction between the decolonial and the de-Western was not necessary. The concept of de-Westernization appeared two decades after the Bandung Conference in Malaysia, in the religious sphere. The controversial book by Syed Muhammad Naquib Al-Attas, *Islam and Secularism* (1978), includes a chapter titled "De-Westernization of Knowledge."[11] Interestingly enough, that chapter, written from a Muslim perspective, connects with one of the chapters in Mahbubani's book *The New Asian Hemisphere*, written in a secular mode, titled "De-Westernization: The Return of History."[12] The need to de-Westernize knowledge in the sphere of religions is more an intellectual and scholarly orientation than a state project. In the case of art/aesthetics, de-Westernization has been advanced in institutions directly state related, like *Sharjah Biennal*, as well as in cultural institutions indirectly related to the state but supported by corporate funding. As for decolonization, the turning point was the collapse of the Soviet Union and the radical mutations of interstate global order. Decolonization became decoloniality, in the sense that decoloniality as conceived by Quijano and those of us who follow his lead was no longer constituted by projects geared toward founding or taking hold of state governance. Decoloniality was reoriented toward "epistemic reconstitution" (which is the main thrust of this book), motivated by the failure of decolonization to question political economy, political theory, and the cultural sphere of religion, art, and aesthetics. Stated more generally:

the failure to question the coloniality of knowledge and understanding, and the failure to distinguish coloniality from colonization.

In sum, the Bandung Conference of 1955 remains the signpost of irreversible shifts in the geo- and biographies of sensing, believing, thinking, and reasoning. It was the first time the West was looked at explicitly from its *exteriority* instead of the West looking at the rest of the world. Critiques of Western civilization within itself have been noticed since the end of WWI. But Bandung was without a doubt an unmistakable signpost and symptom of the disintegration of Western epistemic and aesthetic hegemony and the rise of decolonization and de-Westernization. A mere decade later, a signpost exploded in the West itself: the ascendancy in the US of the civil rights movement (1960–1965) had enormous significance in the academy and in the intellectual arena and in feeding dissenting energies of everyday life—as was manifested after the killing of George Floyd on May 25, 2020, and the responses of the political society, of all ages, sexualities, and skin colors.

The following conversation was my first effort to make sense of de-Westernization and decoloniality after the end of the Cold War. It is a follow-up on the topic in chapter 1 of *The Darker Side of Western Modernity: Global Futures, Decolonial Options* (2011) and in an essay, "The Role of BRICS Countries in the Becoming World Order," that I delivered orally at Tsinghua University, Beijing, in May of 2012.[13] Today, we are neither in a new Cold War nor in a post–Cold War era. De-Westernization and decoloniality opened up the presence of spaces (regions and continents) that were discounted in the linear time of modernity and postmodernity. De-Westernization and decoloniality, in spite of their different locations in the colonial matrix of power (i.e., de-Westernization disputes those who manage and control it; decoloniality aims at delinking from it), have these features in common: the urgent need to reemerge from the ruins of what has been destituted, to work toward epistemic and aesthetic reconstitution, to open up the doors of the prison house into the landscapes of gnoseology and aesthesis as agents of their/our own destinies. Witnessing and experiencing today the conflicts between re-Westernization and state-led de-Westernization, we see that the politics of decolonial investigations is unavoidable for both decolonial and intellectual and scholarly de-Westernization. What I have said so far and in the following dialogue constitutes a decolonial analysis of the transformation of it. State-led de-Westernization disputes who controls and manages it, while scholarly and intellectual de-Westernization (including in the spheres of art, aesthetics, and religion) aims at delinking from the coloniality of knowing and of being the world.

With this context in mind, the Hong Kong conversation that follows and the next chapter explore some of these issues. This conversation has been edited and updated. You will see my parenthetical comments mentioning later dates, but the arguments remain.

II Hong Kong, January–June 2012: The Conversation

CM (CHRISTOPHER MATTISON) To continue our earlier discussion about Bolivia in relation to "refunding" or "decolonizing"—you've stated on a number of occasions that capitalism or socialism, as they are currently constituted, are not the answers. One of the alternatives that you offer to this choice is "delinking." Could you expand on what you mean by delinking in this particular instance and how it integrates into modes of de-Westernization and the various layers of decolonization?

WM (WALTER MIGNOLO) Let me first restate that the world dis/order is currently moving toward both re-Westernization and de-Westernization. Which means a conflict between the Western will to maintain unipolarity, while China and Iran push toward multipolarity. The political ambition of the US (announced by Hillary Clinton in Honolulu and followed up by President Obama) was to integrate the Pacific into the American century. It was in line with President Obama's politics of regaining world leadership for the US, which was severely shaken by the presidency of George W. Bush and Dick Cheney. Obama's famous speech in Cairo, in June 2009, proposing "a new beginning between the United States and Muslims around the world," was one of the first moves in this direction. The turn to the Pacific was the second. However, this second move came too late because of the growing confidence of the rest of the world, most specifically the states of the Pacific.

The unavoidable next step would be the conflictive coexistence of re-Westernization with de-Westernization, which we are witnessing. De-Westernization is not a geographic but a political concept and refers to all states which are consolidating their economies without following the dictates of the US, the EU, the IMF (International Monetary Fund), or the World Bank. De-Westernization presupposes both political and subjective delinking. That is, delinking from Western political theory and from Western manipulation of citizens and consumer subjectivity. Yes, China's middle class is consumerist, but consumerism doesn't presuppose a Western individualistic type of ego manifested in different ways in the population (the nation) and the state leadership that many years ago senator William Fulbright adequately profiled in the sentence (later the title of his book, a collection of his speeches): the arrogance of power.[14] Delinking here does not mean delinking from "a type of economy" (China's economy is as capitalist as Germany's or the US's) but from the instructions of the White House, the World Bank, the IMF, and related institutions. And the recovery of the Confucius and Mencius legacies is telling us that the subjectivities (sensing, feelings) are not being shaped by the same energies, desires, memories, and education as the Western modern subjects. This delinking occurs in the sphere of state politics and policies, as well as in the emotions—those of many people who may be consumerist but do not necessarily want to become "Western subjects and subjectivities." Iran is capitalist, but there is no sign that the country would aspire to be an emulator of France or Germany, although, as always, there would be a sector of the population that would like to do so. That is the sector of the population that is targeted by the politics of re-Westernization.

President Harry Truman introduced the word "underdevelopment": the US foresaw that the waves of decolonization in Indonesia in 1945—followed by India in 1947—were not going to stop there. In 1949, Truman understood that Asia, Africa, and South America were, in his perspective, underdeveloped countries. Thus, the politics of development and modernization became vital in recasting the preexisting idea of progress, which was a cornerstone of the British Empire's hegemony. The US appointed itself to lead the world toward development and modernization. Its first formal step was taken in 1945 with the creation of the Bretton Woods agreement, which was signed by delegates of forty-four nation-states (at the time). Bretton Woods was established to regulate the international monetary system. From this agreement emerged the IMF and the IBRD (International Bank for Reconstruction and Development), which mutated into today's World Bank. Other regional banks were created later, such as the IDB (Inter-American Development Bank). The United States' ascending control of finances, the strength of the US economy, particularly in relation to the enormous wartime devastation in Europe and its creation of European markets as a result of the Marshall Plan, its dominance of international politics from the end of WWII furthered by fears of communism raised by the Greek Civil War, and the blockade of Berlin by the Soviets in 1948, among other things, all gave the US enormous leverage in structuring the global economy. The Bretton Woods agreement had initially pegged the dollar to gold valued at thirty-five dollars an ounce, but in

August 1971, with the French government annoyed that the United States had now become a trade-deficit nation rather than a surplus-producing one and frustrated that the US seemed free to print dollars without apparently any international constraints (oil exports were denominated in dollars), French president George Pompidou ordered that a destroyer be sent to New Jersey with the mission to redeem US dollars in gold. US president Nixon was incensed and four days later announced the end of Bretton Woods and the end of the dollar convertibility to gold. Thus, the dollar, without any backing in gold, was left as the default currency for all international transactions.[15]

De-Westernization is now in the continuing process of ending international dependency on the legacies of Bretton Woods, as well as ending the reign of the dollar. This is one sphere of the dispute for the management of the CMP. Another involves the tensions between the US and China, which we would not likely decrease. All signs point to the US, and the so-called West, losing hegemony and turning to domination. Hegemony is lost because the control and management of the CMP are under dispute, and the dispute means disobedience in place of what once was obedience to hegemony. De-Westernization is, at a basic level, a political delinking from economic decisions that are not beneficial for the states disputing hegemony. The fourth meeting of the BRICS in New Delhi in 2012 was a signpost of political delinking with economic implications and therefore the sign of ending Western hegemony, but not the ending of capitalism. Two outcomes from this meeting are important for this conversation: BRICS countries have, as critics have noted repeatedly, very different local and geopolitical histories. What they do not mention is what BRICS countries have in common: a long history of overcoming Western interventions. Brazil (let's remember that Brazil's membership in BRICS changed after the judicial coup, the destitution of Dilma Rousseff, and the media and legal campaigns against Ignacio Lula da Silva) was colonized by the Portuguese, South Africa and India by the British. China and Russia were never formally colonized, but they were unable to avoid Western intervention—China's Opium Wars and Russia's self-inflicted Westernization by Peter and Catherine the Great, and the subsequent mutation of the Russian tzarate into the Soviet Union. A second point of interest concerns the confrontation with the IMF. A proposal that counterbalances the historical unilateralism of the IMF, contained in point 13 of their resolution, reads as follows: "We have considered the possibility of setting up a new Development Bank for mobilizing resources for infrastructure and sustainable development projects in BRICS and other emerging economies and developing countries, to supplement the existing efforts of multilateral and regional financial institutions for global growth and development. We direct our Finance Ministers to examine the feasibility and viability of such an initiative, set up a joint working group for further study, and report back to us by the next Summit."[16]

Here we have a clear case of de-Westernization as delinking by disputing the management of the CMP. There are two spheres in which de-Westernization is disputing the management of the CMP. One is the politico-economic-military sphere, in which the main actors are state officers. In the other sphere, the cultural, the main actors are located in cultural institutions (e.g., museums in the case of Hasegawa, religion in the case of Naquib Al-Attas; see section I of this chapter, and see the introduction, section III).[17] De-Westernization doesn't mean delinking from a capitalist type of economy, or better yet from economic coloniality using a decolonial vocabulary (Japan and Malaysia are capitalist). Politico-economic delinking and cultural delinking mean delinking from the general spirit of the CMP. Furthermore, religious delinking and de-Westernization scholarly and intellectual delinking (disciplinary, religious, curatorial) need to be broken down in extramural and intramural delinking. For Naquib Al-Attas, de-Westernization operates in the extramural sphere: "Many challenges have arisen in the midst of man's confusion through the ages, but none perhaps more destructive to man than today's challenge posed by Western civilization."[18] Naquib Al-Attas's argument is controversial among Muslims themselves. The controversy in my understanding is not over the need to de-Westernize knowledge (to change the terms of the conversation) but over Naquib Al-Attas's argument (the content of the conversation), which is seen as promoting fundamentalism. The intramural delinking has already been put on the table. Christianity was since 1492 the first mover to Westernize the world; it provided the first global designs. The awareness of the complicity of religion and empire (which goes back to Constantine, three centuries B.C.) reached Christians themselves who aimed to delink from Christianity's imperial legacies, whether Catholic or Protestant.[19] (Eastern Christianity is part of a different story: the story of extramural delinking from Western Christianity.) For Western Christians to delink from the imperial/colonial traps would involve joint processes of de-Western and decolonial strategies.[20] De-Westernizing Christianity—intramural—would be a more complex phenomenon than Islamic de-Westernization (extramural).

Regarding politico-economic de-Westernization, it should be taken into account that de-Westernization (and re-Westernization for that matter) operate in interstate (not domestic) relations. Therefore, criticism of domestic politics in China or Russia, for example, is often fused with interstate politics: if China is domestically authoritarian, the implication is that it is also authoritarian in interstate relations. However, the politics of the two spheres are quite different when the players in question are still dependent on sanctions imposed to advance re-Westernization. Similarly, re-Westernization operates in international relations, not in the domestic affairs of the US and EU. Criticism of their domestic policies should be distinguished from their interstate will to maintain privileges. The dispute for the control and management of the CMP is an interstate dispute. At stake is *who* is making the decisions regarding the global order. The latest divided votes in the Security Council have been three to two. The first (France, UK, and the US) are pushing re-Westernization, and the latter (China, Russia) are determined to advance de-Westernization and multipolarity. More recently, President Trump's threat to dissolve the Security Council is a unipolar move to maintain global unipolarity.

Two distinctions are necessary here in order to understand the different layers and levels of delinking, some being regarded as de-Westernization and others as decoloniality. The first distinction to be made is between civil and political society. I should add that the politicization of civil society is still encroaching on the state and the market, which leads to people questioning unilateral decisions in politics, the economy, and everyday life (when it comes to the basics—health, food, and education). On the other hand, the "global political society" is more radical in its demands: in general it questions the foundations and the beliefs sustaining "economic coloniality," which is an economy based on growth and development that has created and continues to increase poverty; it questions the legitimacy of a state at the service of banks, corporations, and armed forces, and consequently its irrelevance for the nation; it aims at delinking in search of decolonial horizons of reexistence. Two examples of global political society are La Via Campesina (The Peasant's Way), an international organization that works for the sovereignty of food, and the Zapatistas.

But, you can ask, who is actually conceptualizing such activities in terms of de-Westernization and who in terms of decoloniality? Neither de-Westernization nor decoloniality originated in Europe or the US, but in the "Third World." "Decolonization" was the word used at the Bandung Conference. Decoloniality is a more recent term, beginning in the early 1990s. But, in general, the vocabulary of decolonization/decoloniality came out of the Bandung Conference and has had a significant effect in Africa, South and Southeast Asia, South America (among thinkers of European, Indigenous, and African descent), the Caribbean, Native American and Latino/a societies in the US, New Zealand, and Australia. In short, in geohistorical locations with enduring histories of colonization.

"De-Westernization," on the other hand, is more common within the local histories of societies that were not directly colonized but did not escape the logic of coloniality: for example, East Asia and Russia, as well as the Islamic corridor from West Asia (or the Middle East for Westerners) to Malaysia and Indonesia. However, in Malaysia and Indonesia it is common to find use of both terms in Islamic thinkers and philosophers, as well as among social scientists who reflect on the coloniality of knowledge through the social sciences and the need to decolonize them, or, in another expression they commonly use, "the Islamization of knowledge." Interestingly enough, the project that operates under the Islamization of knowledge runs parallel to "indigenizing the academy," which among Native Americans is synonymous with the "decolonization of knowledge." A similar project, under Indigenous leadership, emerged in Ecuador, with the creation of Amawtay Wasi (House of Wisdom), translated in official documents as the Universidad Intercultural de los Pueblos y Naciones Indigenas de Ecuador (Intercultural University of People and Indigenous Nations of Ecuador).

CM And this polycentric discussion relates to your call for the communal, "to start thinking from our bodies, their geopolitical position?"

WM I made a distinction between polycentric, which was the world order before 1500, and a multipolar world order, which is the one emerging, motivated by the rise of de-Westernization. On the other hand, a distinction must be made between multipolarity and pluriversality. Both are outcomes of the disintegration of the unipolar world order and the universal conception of knowledge: de-Westernization is an interstate and economic project leading to multipolarity; decoloniality is a project of the political society, not a state-led project, leading to rebuilding a communal praxis of living and pluriversal ways of thinking.

I have been arguing in different places, but chiefly in my latest book (*The Darker Side of Western Modernity: Global Futures, Decolonial Options*), that the present and the future are being defined by the confrontations and coparticipation of various options. To think in terms of options helps us to understand that "modernity" (i.e., Western civilization, capitalism, and development) is only one option, and that this option was defined by those who lead and benefit from it, which is in part how it became hegemonic. Economic, political, epistemic, and institutional benefits coalesced to suggest that there is only one option and that the best we can do is to improve on this single option. One of the common expressions in the rhetoric of modernity is: "Capitalism is not perfect, but there is no other alternative." To think in terms of "alternative" keeps us hostage to the vocabulary of modernity. For that reason, "option" is a concept that invites starting points from the exteriority of modernity. When I refer to re-Westernization, I am speaking about recent efforts to maintain this option and to argue that there is no better choice; that capitalism and Western modernity are the best options for a majority of the people. This option is founded on what I and my colleagues define, describe, and explain as the CMP. Delinking implies there are other options looming large on the horizon that dispute the monopoly of the CMP, which has been controlled for five hundred years by western Europe and the US. Two trajectories of delinking, as explained previously, are de-Westernization and decoloniality. What does this mean? It means, as I have said before, that de-Westernization is a necessary and welcome trajectory for the future, but, as far as coloniality is disputed but still maintained, the legacy of coloniality prevents the construction of an economically just world, of equitable and ethical future social organizations. De-Westernization is important for political decisions on economic matters, and for ethical decisions on scientific research, but it still remains within the fantasy of development and growth at the expense of life.

Now, the concept of the communal, like many other concepts, needs to be clearly defined so that it is not confused and assimilated into what are known as Western ideas of the "common good" (domestic political horizon) or the "commonwealth" (interstate political horizon, naming the fifty-three territories under the British Empire) or the "commons." The first two are liberal, the third Marxist. Before the eighteenth-century secularization of Western history, the *ekklesia* (*iglesia* in Spanish, "church" in English) referred to the community of Christian believers worldwide. The communal is neither liberal nor Marxist, but decolonial. The communal is a way to advance on one of the legacies of the Bandung Conference: neither capitalism nor communism, but decoloniality. The common good and the commonwealth are political images consistent with republicanism and liberalism; they are consistent with Marxism. The *ekklesia* is consistent with the goal and vision of Christianity: virtue, human good, and the kingdom of God. Beyond these three overarching political frames (con) forming the colonial matrix of power, there are other images orienting the administration of governance and the organization of people living together. The communal is one of them with a long history, as long as that of Christianity and much longer than that of republicanism/liberalism and Marxism. However, because of the coloniality of knowledge and the still-hegemonic idea of the secular and bourgeois nation-state, the rhetoric of modernity is constantly enacted to demonize any other form of governance, be it de-Westernizing states or the communal organizations of the emerging political society. The communal shall not be seen as an "alternative" to the state but as a weapon of the people organizing themselves and disobeying the state.[21] Why should Western ideologies on governance be adopted, endorsed, and implemented by the 190 or so states? I am not saying, either, that the communal shall be imposed as a form of governance and as the people's organization. I am saying that the communal shall be taken seriously in pluriversal ways of thinking and living.

It is in this sense that the communal is consistent with decoloniality. Decoloniality works toward delinking from economic coloniality (i.e., a capitalist economy within which there can be no peace, equality, or democracy). So how do you delink in a decolonial way? First, you need to build knowledge and arguments that supersede the current hegemony of Western knowledge. It is the hegemony of Western knowledge that justifies the hegemony of capitalism and the state, for example, and that also establishes development as a condition of freedom. "Development" is not its own justification! This is why the struggle for the control of knowledge is crucial: it is necessary to build convincing arguments for people to realize that development is an option, justified by actors, categories of thought, institutions, the media, etc. It is one option and not the only option, which carries with it its own splendors, together with certain miseries (e.g., the rhetoric of modernity and the logic of coloniality). This is the struggle for the control of knowledge. Otherwise, hegemonic knowledge has the power to convince people who are dying of cancer because the water and lands around them are being polluted with cyanide, who are rising up to defend their very lives, that they are "delinquents" because they dare to confront modernity and development. This current world dis/order has been challenged by the energies of de-Westernization and decoloniality, by dissenting, disobeying, and delinking—in different ways and with different purposes, to be sure—from Western global designs. At the same time, these actions require other ways of conceptualizing beyond the narrow Western right/left dichotomy, or the republican/liberal common good versus the Marxist commons.

The "communal" means, then, the present-day reinscription of noncapitalist economic organizations and nonmodern knowledges that have coexisted with capitalism but that have been marginalized (e.g., as "informal" economies) or incorporated into a capitalist mentality (e.g., the so-called BoP, bottom of the pyramid, or the Grameen Bank, a microfinance organization founded by Muhammad Yunus). The global political society has organized itself in myriad ways because neither the state nor the market has taken care of everyone. The recasting of spirituality plays an important role here. We know that religion has many faces, and I will not discuss these differences now, but will simply mention that significant sectors of religion, different religions in different parts of the world, are joining the political society without abandoning their religious foundations. One of the tasks is to decolonize religion so as to liberate spirituality.

Returning to your question, the communal in the history of Andean Aymaras and Quechuas was a socioeconomic organization dismantled by the Spaniards. The communal has, however, survived until now alongside the colonial and current ruling government. Now it is being reinscribed, but the reinscription is grounded in the revamping and expansion of Aymara and Quechua categories of thought, which must pass through the Western categories that denied them epistemic legitimacy. Thus, the communal goes hand in hand with border thinking or border gnoseology: thinking from non-Western categories of thought through Western categories of thought. The first step of decolonial delinking is to reinscribe, in contemporary debates and toward the future, social organizations and economic conceptions that were banned and silenced by the progressive discourse of modernity, both in its liberal-capitalist and socialist-communist vein. There is no master model of the communal; the communal is inscribed in all nonmodern memories that, since 1500, have been pushed aside and placed in the past in relation to Western ideas of modernity.

CM Before moving too far into the communal, could we linger for a moment on the role of the church, with a specific focus on the Spanish jurist Juan López de Palacios Rubios's *Requerimiento*—where the "invitation to conversion" takes on more of a fist. In one of your recent lectures at City U, you mentioned Christianity's move to create a measure of "purity of blood" as a way of giving credence to conversion and the subjugation of layers of race. Insidious for sure, but I think that the *Requerimiento* was potentially far more destructive, as it was the basis for the moral justification of colonization and massacres around the globe, and required the collusion of the church hierarchy, economic forces, and the judicial structure. This seems to have been an ultimate moment of enunciation.

WM I am glad that you are bringing the *Requerimiento* into the conversation, for this is certainly a fundamental work that allows us to understand the denial of the communal and to understand what was at stake in the sixteenth century, and why the sixteenth century is undeniably the colonial foundation of the modern world. There are a few things I would like to stress about the *Requerimiento*, in full agreement with the framing that you provided. First of all, the *Requerimiento* was issued after the papal bull *Inter Caetera*, issued on May 4, 1493, by Pope Alexander the VI, granting full possession of "Indias Occidentales" to the Spaniards. (The idea of "America" was introduced in 1505 by a group of scholars in the gymnasium of Saint-Dié-des-Vosges, where Martin Waldseemüller came up with the name "America" to honor Amerigo Vespucci, who realized, contrary to Columbus, that he was not in Asia but in a "Mondo Nuovo.") One year later, with the Treaty of Tordesillas, Alexander VI recognized a portion of Indias Occidentales and donated it to the crown of Portugal. The *Requerimiento* is the second aberration (the first was Pope Alexander VI appropriating and donating Indias Occidentales to the Spaniards and Portuguese), an aberration that became a pillar of modernity, capitalism, and Western civilization.

The second point that deserves attention is that the self-entitlement of Western Christians, in this case Spaniards (for Western Christians were not only Spaniards), was manifested in the *Requerimiento*. Read in Spanish (some say in 1513, some in 1514) by Spanish jurist Martin de Enciso to a group of natives who did not understand Spanish, it stated that the Spanish monarch was entitled to "this land" (they say "this" not "your" land) by God, and that if the natives wanted to remain on the land they needed to pay a gold tribute to the monarch.[22] This move was vehemently criticized by some Spanish missionaries, chief among them Dominican friar Bartolomé de Las Casas. However, what we ultimately take away from this foundational move is that arrogance and racism were the basis for the document. It is arrogance to believe that one's state and beliefs carry a global truth for the rest of humanity. And it is racism based on viewing another human being as inferior (this is what racism is, rather than an issue of skin color), thereby justifying the appropriation of land and the means of production (labor), slavery, and deprivation.

Finally, I will say that if by "ultimate moment of enunciation" you mean a "historical, foundational moment of enunciation"—then I would say yes. It was a historically foundational moment because of the control of knowledge that established Latin and Spanish as the languages of knowledge, and Christian theological categories of thought as the basis for politics and ethics. After dispossessing the natives of their land, the church next began a campaign of dispossessing them of their souls, of attempting to convert them to Christianity. The first assault was successful and the second failed radically, which is what germinated in the decolonial option and the current reinscription of the communal, because Christianization and Westernization (which at that moment was the mission of Western Christians) utterly failed. As you point out, it was a foundational moment of the locus of enunciation upon which Western civilization was built. The British and French, three centuries later, benefited from what the *Requerimiento* achieved and proceeded in their own way. Weren't the Opium Wars another legacy of the *Requerimiento*? Didn't the British feel entitled to intervene and force the Chinese rulers to open up their ports to trade? Weren't the British acting as the bearers of historical destiny (secular at the time), viewing themselves as white and Christian, who were, within their construct, above the "yellow" Confucians and Buddhists?[23]

Before returning to the communal, let me first add something about delinking and border gnoseology, which I introduced in the previous answer. Border gnoseology goes hand in hand with decoloniality. Why? Because decoloniality focuses on changing the terms of the conversation and not just its content. How does border gnoseology work? And once you delink, where do you go? You have to go back to the reservoir of the modes of thought that were destituted by Christian theology during the Renaissance and that continued to expand during the Enlightenment through secular philosophy and the sciences. You cannot find your way out of the reservoir of modernity (Greece, Rome, the Renaissance, the Enlightenment). If you go there, you remain chained to the illusion that there is no other way of thinking, doing, and living. Modern/colonial racism (the logic of racialization that emerged in the sixteenth century) has two dimensions (ontological and epistemic) and one single purpose: to rank as inferior all languages beyond the Greek and Latin and the six modern European languages from the domain of sustainable knowledge and to maintain the privileges of enunciation held by Renaissance and Enlightenment European institutions—men and categories of thought. Languages that were considered ill "suited" for rational thinking (either theological or secular)—Indians have no word for God, Christians say; and Africans are utterly deficient in matters of intelligence, Kant thought—were considered to be languages that revealed the inferiority of the human beings speaking them. What could a person do who was not born speaking one of these privileged languages, and who was not educated in a privileged institution? Either accept his or her inferiority or make an effort to demonstrate that he or she was a human being equal to those who had placed him or her into a second-class category. That is, two of the choices are either to accept the humiliation of being inferior to those who have decided that you are inferior, or to assimilate. And to assimilate means that you accept your inferiority and resign yourself to playing the game that is not yours but that has been imposed upon you. And then there is the third option: border thinking/border gnoseology and decolonial action.

CM We've witnessed the "domain of sustainable knowledge" rear its head at any number of conferences and workshops here in Hong Kong over the past year. Panelists and discussants consistently rely almost entirely on Western theory in English translation—Foucault, Habermas, Hegel, Arendt, Bourdieu—in discussing (post)coloniality as it relates to the Hong Kong/East Asian experience. I realize that this is not exactly what you are referring to as the communal, but it is an aspect, and there does need to be more of a balance between the established canon and "local" thinkers in creating a common philosophical language of dissent—so that the local has equal footing in the discussion about the present and future. One also must remain aware of subjectivity so as not to recolonize through the appropriation of those "established" voices from the West.

WM This is a huge issue for both de-Western and decolonial thinking. You are right, what is most common is the re-Westernizing discussions of sustainable knowledge. And the agents of re-Westernization are not only "local" Western actors (in England or the US) but also "local" actors in non-Western locales—Hong Kong or Argentina, Tunisia or the Republic of South Africa. It is good that those who are still attached to Western categories of thought realize that development, as it currently stands, is unsustainable precisely because the knowledge that supports the arguments in favor of development are no longer sustainable. Certainly, those who rely on the limited scope of Western conceptualization are, like Las Casas or Marx, confronting their own genealogy of thought and the subjectivity of their own local histories. For de-Westernizers and decolonials, that is "their game," and of course we cannot stop them from playing it, but as we have seen, decoloniality moves toward delinking from every domain (economy, authority, gender and sexual heteronormativity, and racism), while de-Westernization moves to delink from every domain except one, the economy of growth and development—in other words, from economic coloniality. When Indigenous people and peasants, as well as mestizos and people of European descent, join forces to stop and denounce the devastating consequences of open-pit mining, they know that the struggle is not only to stop the digging, but rather, and primarily, to halt the knowledge that legitimizes digging and criminalizes the protesters. To disavow knowledge here doesn't mean to stop the technical knowledge that allows extraction, but the "knowledge" that justifies (for the corporation and the state) a type of activity that "sustains development" for the corporations and the state and "destroys life" for those who can no longer drink their water, use their land, or have the resources to deal with illnesses and birth defects that are the consequences of unsustainable development. Now, for sustainable knowledge in South America and in Africa, you do not need Habermas, Bourdieu, Arendt, or Foucault. They know a lot about their own experiences and European history, but are of little use in South America and Africa. And if you rely on them to address problems specific to Hong Kong, Argentina, Zimbabwe, or Tunisia, and not to Paris, Tubingen, or Berlin, then you are demonstrating either that you are afraid to think on your own, or else that you believe you are superior to your local peers because you "know" European thinkers. In this way, you fall, willingly or not, into the hands of re-Westernization (see the epilogue).

For these reasons, I would say that if Foucault, Habermas, and others are invoked at conferences in Hong Kong, it is similar to what happens in other parts of the world. Many non-Western scholars, intellectuals, scientists, and artists still believe in the superiority of the West. They have been self-colonized and are afraid to think for themselves, as if serious thought and innovation require a Western security blanket. Another point is that the discussion of sustainable knowledge in locales such as Hong Kong allows the local community to display its "modernity," and allows the foreign Euro-Americans to maintain the belief that they are "educating the Easterners." This kind of politics is being enacted by scholars and also promoted by foundations such as the Fulbright, Rockefeller, MacArthur, and numerous others. The same thing happens in Africa, South America, and the Caribbean. It is the modern, secular, and capitalist version of Christian missionaries in the sixteenth century; they are secular missionaries and agents of Westernization and re-Westernization.

In the time that I have been in Hong Kong, I have noticed that one of the recurring threads throughout my reading and research has been "coloniality" and not "colonialism." A recurrent observation that comes up in conversation on this topic is that Hong Kong was not colonized like the islands of Cuba, Puerto Rico, and Jamaica, and, as many have pointed out, Hong Kong was not decolonized like India or Algeria. The end of British colonial rule has meant a state agreement and the return of Hong Kong to mainland China. Whether this return is seen as a liberation or a change of colonial rulers is a deep-seated debate in Hong Kong and provides Hong Kong with its singular profile. As you know better than I, Hong Kong was, from the beginning, a city founded by the British, who appropriated the land through a treaty with the Chinese authorities, rather than through presenting a legal writ to fishermen and villagers. It later unfolded into what Professor Law Wing Sang has described as "collaborative colonialism"—that is, a collaboration not with the villagers, but with migrants from mainland China to Hong Kong.[24] Coloniality here runs in two streams. On the one hand, Western coloniality runs through the economy, political authority, knowledge, morality, etc. On the other hand, there is the concern that, after the handover, what transpired was merely a shift of imperial/colonial rulers. This last may very well be the case, but from a decolonial standpoint—which may not necessarily be shared or supported by Hong Kong scholars focused on coloniality—what deserves our attention is that British and Chinese coloniality are similar but different. Interpreting Chinese history and politics in Western terms of either/or, in terms of friends/foes, leads to serious misunderstandings as is obvious in the demonization of China. The Chinese government does not necessarily think in terms of either/or, or of friends/foes. If, then, you do not understand the logic of other thinking, you get trapped in the blind paranoia of your own limited thinking, still assuming that it is universal, truthful, and objective. Win-win is not the same as either/or.

What I describe as coloniality or the CMP was set up, maintained, transformed, and controlled by the Western imperial states—first by theological and monarchic states, and then secular—from Spain and Portugal to the US, through Holland, France, and England. But also by Germany, Italy, and Belgium, who had their own small colonies. China (as well as Japan and Russia) became imperial by following the rules of the game set up by the Western states. These states, as Madina V. Tlostanova argues, were Janus-faced—one eye toward their Western imperial masters and the other toward their own colonies. This created a complex situation from which de-Westernization offers a way out: if Russia, Japan, and China at one time did dutifully follow the teachings of the "master," they have since learned and grown to respect this master, but also to act on their own. From the point of view of Hong Kong, this situation concerns the crossroads between the history of British colonialism and the present-day confrontation between China and US interests in the Pacific. At these crossroads, Hong Kong endures the legacies of Westernization and the temptations that re-Westernization (the US belief that the twenty-first century is the Asia-Pacific-American century) offer. At the same time, however, Hong Kong is well established in a region of de-Westernization (China, Singapore, Japan, Korea, and Taiwan), which doesn't mean that all Chinese, Hongkongers, and Singaporeans are pro-de-Westernization. Some certainly support re-Westernization. What remains an undeniable fact is that Hong Kong is part of the "return" of Asia and the dawn of the "Asian century."

Finally, I would like to remark that I have heard quite a bit about colonization and coloniality in Hong Kong, but not much about decoloniality. The discourse of decoloniality is more common in Taiwan (through outlets such as the journal *Inter-Asia Cultural Studies*) and a result of Malaysia's plantation economy (common to this region and the Caribbean since the seventeenth century, because of the Dutch and British). I mean this not as a critique, but simply to affirm that in Hong Kong—for the moment—the stakes are higher at the crossroads of de-Westernization and re-Westernization than is accounted for by the extent of Hong Kong's discourse on decoloniality.

Coming back to one of your points concerning the question of "sustainable knowledge," I would like to note that the relationship of sustainable knowledge to the communal can't be resolved within the same genealogy of thought that created the problem. This is what I was saying a few paragraphs above by referring to Western limitations in understanding Chinese politics. That is, "sustainable development" (an outcome of sustainable knowledge) cannot be achieved within the structure and archives of knowledge that created "unsustainable development." This debate occurs in the Andean region of South America over *sumak kawsay* (a Quichua word—and I mean Quichua, not Quechua), the concept of living in plenitude and harmony that confronts the myth of sustainable development. Both concepts and projects coexist: one is driven by the UN in the interstate system. The second is a project of the political society. Those who control the knowledge (the UN, mass media, university departments, think tanks) that justifies development argue that *sumak kawsay* is unsustainable because it opposes development, modernization, and progress. And this takes us to the second point of your question about the urgent need to think from the problems and the history of the problems rather than thinking from theories that have been put forward to solve other problems. The example that should be followed is what Habermas, Foucault, Bourdieu *did* and not *what* they said. What they did was to think on and about their own local histories, situations, languages, and subjectivities.

So, the communal, as you mention at the end of your question, is a case in point for people in the Andes, and not for people in the South of France or Germany. European thinkers don't have much to say about the Andean concept of the communal, unless they take it as an object of study and not as a living and lived experience, which is the case for Indigenous people. When the communal was revamped into the debates about a new constitution for Bolivia, the European tradition of political theory (and there goes Habermas and Bourdieu) was displaced: the communal demanded we think in terms of a future plurinational state, while European states have been, since their inception, mononational. Europeans may, however, need to consider plurinational states to solve their immigration problems. In this case, they will have much to learn from Aymara and Quechua thinkers in Bolivia and Peru and Quichua thinkers in Ecuador. There is no tradition in the history of Western thought that matches up with the legacies of Tihuanaco (with the center of what is today Bolivia) and Tawantinsuyu (with the center of what is today Peru).

The idea of plurinational states introducing the communal into the debate is a fascinating case that makes the traditional/modern notions of democracy and socialism obsolete, based on their pretense of universality. The communal option reduces democracy and socialism to merely other options and disposes of their pretense to the universal (or at least the global) truth. Therefore, the open-ended question is: why would democracy and socialism be the only, and universal, visions for a just and equitable society? Certainly, the communal has its problems, and we should not romanticize it. But we also should not romanticize democracy and socialism because, as we know, both *had* and *have* serious shortcomings. Decolonizing democracy and socialism means reducing them down to size, recognizing their contributions but breaking away from their arrogance and their dreams of universal "solutions" for all, and in their place building knowledge that allows for the legitimization and enactment of the communal option.

Last but not least, the communal is not an Indigenous proposal solely for Indians, as democracy and socialism were not a European proposal only for Europeans. And it is not a proposal to be "universalized." (See chapter 13.) The communal is—in different forms and rationales—what we encounter when we look into the history of different societies and civilizations pre-1500. These nonmodern formations and communal organizations— "nonmodern," not "premodern," because they did not vanish with the advent of the European idea of modernity; it is only the narrative of modernity by modern thinkers that made them premodern—are thriving, although constantly being eroded by the expansion of development and by one of its consequences: the concentration of megacities as rural life vanishes, absorbed by developers' thirst for land. The communal as a lifestyle is already a global concern, expressed in different vocabularies. Once we recognize the communal as a legitimate vision for the present and the future, we should expect that parallel contributions will come from other local histories that have been suppressed by imperial global designs. The future is open and lies beyond democracy and socialism, a pluriversal world where democracy and socialism will have their place, but where universal claims are already unsustainable.

It is obvious that a similar potential is being found within Chinese and Asian-Indian histories. Now the problem we (those engaged in these debates) are confronting is—as it has been pointed out in a number of venues—that China, India, and Singapore are "using" a particular interpretation of the past to justify state authority. This is not surprising. The same thing is happening in the US, France, and Bolivia. The vice president of Bolivia, at least on the public stage, talks constantly about decolonization, about Indigenous ways of thinking and government (a clear "use" of a history that belongs to the Aymaras and Quechuas, Chiquitanos, and other Indian nations) to justify the authority of the state. What this all amounts to is the use of Indigenous memories and social organizations to advance a corporate state with a leftist persuasion. Indigenous organizations such as CONAMAQ (Consejo Nacional de Ayllus y Markas del Qullasuyu; National Council of Ayllus and Markas of Qullasuyu) do not for a minute believe the discourse of decolonization, as several of the recent decisions made by the government of Evo Morales have betrayed Indigenous interests and have been made in direct opposition to many of the vice president's statements.[25] What is crucial here is that new elements have entered the economic, political, philosophical, and ethical debates: you cannot give up difference because the state is appropriating it. The struggle between de-Westernization and decoloniality lies precisely here. The "communal" is precisely what CONAMAQ is arguing for and promoting.[26] The vice president is arguing for "the commons" to begin using the language of decolonization within a Marxist frame.

CM Let's return to some of the issues touched upon before, returning to the realm of economics—in terms of polycentric capitalism—and de-Westernization. You have cited Kishore Mahbubani, from Singapore, as a thinker of note in terms of his call to de-Westernize—the rest overtaking the West. You further note that Mahbubani's economic form of hyper-modernization is not an appropriate direction for decolonial thinking but that you admire his resistance to the West. Mahbubani remains a problematical person for me—someone who reads as a natural progression of an authoritarian regime rather than as a nuanced thinker.

WM Not so much a "resistance to the West" as an opening up of a different direction: de-Westernization as an option. Without that option, the only other one will be re-Westernization, which is the neoliberal agenda, which has been the last chapter of the global design for Westernizing the planet since the sixteenth century. What I take more seriously are the arguments he has been making over the years in books, video interviews, printed interviews, and op-eds. Mahbubani is no doubt a controversial figure, as de-Westernization is also problematic. What is important in his arguments is to unveil the double standards of the Western rhetoric of modernity. What I take seriously about him is that now not only do we have the argument of Milton Friedman and the defenders of neoliberalism, and Amartya Sen, the honest (and blind) defender of development, but we have from Mahbubani the counterargument that does not resist, but rather formulates another form of existence, a reexistence. I agree with you: Mahbubani and de-Westernization are as problematic as re-Westernization and the arguments in defense of it—as seen lately via Barack Obama's eight years of American leadership in the world.[27] Twenty or so years ago, statements like those that Mahbubani makes would have been unthinkable. Here's just one example:

The West has been dominant for 200 years in world history, which is a historical aberration. In the 19th century, Europe dominated the world, in the 20th century, the US dominated the world. Many in the

US and Europe assume that this is the natural state of affairs and want their dominance to continue into the 21st century. However, I refer to Western dominance as a major historical aberration, because from year 1 to 1820, the two largest economies of the world were China and India. The US and Europe only took off in the last 200 years. . . . All aberrations come to a natural end.[28]

You are right; in Mahbubani we can see the problem of de-Westernization at the same time as he casts the problem of re-Westernization in a new light. We are not only in a polycentric politico-economic world; we are entering into a polycentric epistemic world. Especially because re-Westernization and de-Westernization are problematic we cannot ignore them. We need to utilize decoloniality. I do not mean to glorify Mahbubani, but I do think that some of his arguments should be considered, for they reveal what I see as an unfolding of global history—the present directed toward the future. In relation to my previous questions, my reading and hearing of Mahbubani arise from the experience of a son of South American immigrants and someone considered Latino in the US. Your experience of living in Hong Kong and at the same time of being educated and trained in the US prepares you to see issues in Mahbubani that I am unable to see or feel.

Now, back to your question and caution about Mahbubani's narrative "as the natural progression of an authoritarian regime rather than as a nuanced thinker." We should keep in mind that he is basically a diplomat and a public thinker in the domain of public policy. He is not a sociologist who attempts to analyze situations in order to correct previous interpretations within the discipline. He is a public intellectual. The question of "authoritarian regime" in Singapore is undeniable in terms of the standards of "democratic governments." But upon closer inspection, the comparison with authoritarianism doesn't hold.

CM Setting aside Mahbubani's disdain for certain liberties, in his various interviews and essays I find little redeeming in his policies—both in his outward disdain for the concept of a free press and his fixation on economic progress as the response to all concerns about Singapore's future. The latter of these two points is perhaps the most problematical in relation to your call for stepping away from economic progress as the ultimate goal, and you do mention here and in other settings that thinkers such as Mahbubani are operating under the false claim that "economic growth will bring peace and happiness on earth."

WM Let's parse some of his statement and take a few examples of his views to better focus our conversation. There are two aspects of Mahbubani's intervention I think important to understand the de-Westernizing option (which is not, as you know, the one I endorse). The first is that his is a powerful intervention that makes the de-Westernization option an option one can no longer ignore. The second is that once the option is in place, the debates about it can take several different routes. On one route, we can concentrate on *what he says*. And of course, I would agree with you that "economic growth and development will bring peace and happiness on earth" is today hardly convincing; doesn't matter if it is President Barack Obama, Dean Mahbubani, Professor Amartya Sen, or the World Bank who is stating it. By supporting development, he is supporting both the current and potential imperial politics—both regionally and globally. This is why if you want to meet Mahbubani you do not look for him at the World Social Forum (where you certainly will meet Walden Bello) but at the World Economic Forum in Davos.

Another route, which is the one I am interested in, is *why is he saying what he is saying, and how is he able to say it?* And what are the consequences? As decolonial thinkers, we are always focusing on the enunciation rather than the enunciated. That is, the enunciated makes sense to us in relation to the enunciation, but the enunciation comes first. Basically, it is in the "why" that the de-Westernizing option is anchored. Why is he advancing the position he is advancing? Because he, like many others, has reached the point of no return with respect to Westernization and re-Westernization. I would say that in different languages the arguments advanced by Mahbubani are the arguments being put forward by the BRICS countries. None of them denies or questions development; all of them question the imperial history of Western civilization and are no longer ready to put up with re-Westernization and to follow its instructions.

CM So then are you suggesting that we should utilize those aspects of Mahbubani that are most useful for reinterpreting the CMP while avoiding engagement with the more problematical aspects of his developmentalism? Perhaps my concern is that it doesn't ultimately matter if Mahbubani's goal is "to awaken the world to the completely different historical era," if development and progress are the same two carrots awaiting us in his new era.

WM I realize now that there is something that I have not yet made explicit, and this question gives me the opportunity to see if I can clarify my argument. The keywords in your question are "utilize those aspects of

Mahbubani that are most useful for reinterpreting the CMP while avoiding engagement with the more problematical aspect of developmentalism." This is really a key epistemic and political aspect that I will now try the best I can to clarify.

First of all, it is not a question of "utilizing" Mahbubani or some aspects of his thesis. I am not doing that, and I am not interested in doing it. The question is to understand how he "utilizes" his own argument. I am not interpreting the CMP through Mahbubani, but, quite the contrary, interpreting Mahbubani from the analytic of the CMP. In other words, since the colonial matrix is a decolonial conceptual framework, what I am seeing is that: (a) the CMP was put in place in the process of Westernizing the world (1500–2000); (b) it was put in place and controlled by Western Euro-American countries (Spain, Portugal, Holland, France, England, Germany, and the US); (c) by 2000 the control of the CMP was being disputed by emerging, non-Western countries who maintained the economy of growth and development but who wanted to have their destiny in their own hands and not in the hands of the former imperial countries; (d) as a consequence of this, we have President Obama's politics of re-Westernization; and (e) all of the above are a decolonial analysis and that decolonial analysis gives ground to formulate and work on the decolonial option. If, within the Western legacies, the decolonial option after Bandung (coexisting with the de-Westernizing options and the neoliberal re-Westernizing options, as well as with the reconfiguration of the left after the fall of the Soviet Union) affirms neither capitalism nor communism but decolonization, today we add neither re-Westernization nor de-Westernization but decoloniality. However, what is important is that de-Westernization (of which, again, beyond Mahbubani we have the BRICS countries) has stopped the neoliberal project of homogenizing the world and continues to eliminate differences and create the conditions for a pluricentered and noncapitalist world. For five hundred years the world was becoming increasingly monocentered and capitalist (that is, ruled by economic coloniality). In the twenty-first century it is becoming polycentered and capitalist. The decolonial road to the future is toward a polycentered and noncapitalist world—that is, an economy that administers scarcity rather than an economy that promotes the rhetoric of growth and development, of invention and creativity, and continues to march toward increasing the death toll of human beings and seriously damaging planet Earth, on which those who promote growth and development are also living with their families and friends.

In more general terms, my observations are focused primarily on Mahbubani's concept of de-Westernization. De-Westernization, as it is clearly explained in his book *The New Asian Hemisphere: The Irresistible Shift of Global Power to the* East, is useful as an explanatory as well as a programmatic exposition of de-Westernization. Programmatically, it lays out the attitudes and the discourses unfolding in the elite classes toward the relation of East Asian countries to the West—and here the West comprises the US, the EU, the United Nations, and the IMF.[29] What I see as relevant for the future is that for the first time in the past five hundred years, the CMP is no longer controlled by Western countries, meaning the countries where Western civilization and Western imperialism emerged and flourished. Of course, you can ask what is good about this. Because, you may argue, if de-Westernization does not *call into question* the CMP but *only disputes its management*, what is the difference from re-Westernization? The difference is that, on the one hand, neoliberalism, as the last chapter of Westernization, and re-Westernization would succeed in the homogenization of the planet under Western unipolar global designs while, on the other hand, de-Westernization halts the prospect of homogenization and unipolarity, opening up multipolarity and all the political and epistemic consequences derived from it.

The importance of the BRICS countries' politics, and of Mahbubani's argument, is that it terminates the illusion of a "global empire" controlled not only by one type of economy but by one set of values (epistemic, political, aesthetical, ethical) and by one superior "race." If the world order is, by 2019, facing the possibility of a global financial collapse and the possibility of a devastating war, it is because we are all experiencing the closing of unipolarity and the opening of multipolarity. Which is "best," I do not know. What I know is that it is what it is. For, in the last analysis, what by 2012 is behind BRICS and what by 2019 is behind the BRI (Belt and Road Initiative) are challenges to "the racial distribution of capital." None of the BRICS countries were Western, and the BRI is not an industrial and financial Western project. For that reason, both BRICS and BRI are racialized in Western media and, therefore, downgraded in the perspectives of Western "knowledge" and considered a threat to unipolarity. From a non-Western perspective, they are not a threat but are projects responding to the need to affirm sovereignty and creativity instead of being servants of Western global designs. One early book by Mahbubani confronted this issue head on: *Can Asians Think?* (1998). Now, in this vein, de-Westernization and decoloniality have something in common. And at the end of the day, the distinction between "left and right" becomes obsolete once options of de-Westernization and decoloniality are on the table.

CM So, there's a certain blurring between the established Cold War discourse and de-Westernization?

WM Hmm, this is a very interesting question. (See the introduction to this volume for more on the question of de-Westernization after the Cold War.) It gives another spin to the right/left distinction. As is well known, the distinction between left and right was one of the consequences of the French Revolution. The assembly in charge of writing the constitution was composed of a number of deputies with different opinions. One of the groups, the Gironde (a group of twelve moderate republicans), sat to the right of the assembly president. The other group, the Montagnards (the radical republicans in power during the Reign of Terror), sat to the left of the president. At the center, facing the president, was seated a mixed and undifferentiated group of people. At one point, before Bonaparte, the idea of socialism (Saint-Simon) was not known, and the idea of socialism-communism (Marx) was not introduced until 1848. So the right/Gironde were the secular conservatives on good relations with the church, and the left/Montagnards, who later joined the Jacobins, were indeed the seed of liberalism. The radicalism of the Jacobins, who were not "socialist," ended up, after Marx, defining communism as the left. The legacy of the Jacobins gave rise to liberalism and the liberal right, while the legacies of Christianity and the monarchy give rise to the conservative, secular right. These legacies framed international politics during the Cold War: the Soviets were the communist left, and the West was the liberal and conservative right (in the US, the Republican and Democratic parties fit to perfection that tradition). The Cold War was still a war of ideology whose historical foundations are in Europe and in the Enlightenment. De-Westernization is breaking up that tradition. It comes from totally different legacies, non-European legacies. The point of origination and enactment of de-Westernization is the non-European world, while the left/right distinction is a regional European issue that went beyond Europe because of Europe's imperial expansion.

The Cold War ended, and it looked for a while as if conservatives (that is, the neoliberals and neocons of the Reagan 1980s) and liberals (the Democrats of the Clinton 1990s) were rightly on top of the world, because the end of history, as Fukuyama's (in)famous dictum had announced, had perhaps actually come to pass. Well, the illusion lasted ten years. Then de-Westernization emerged on the horizon, and decolonial forces reactivated themselves as epistemic and political forces—not in arms but with the pen, as the Zapatistas popularized it.

What we have now is capitalism, but it is no longer Western liberalism and neoliberalism controlling the colonial matrix and ruling the game. If India is investing in Africa, it is not just to compete with China; it is also to compete with Western investment in Africa. A few years ago, I wrote an op-ed, "Bono Contra China," which is the basic point I am making here.[30] Briefly, capitalism is no longer solely neoliberal. Although neoliberal capitalism is the continuing project of Westernization throughout the world, capitalism has escaped the hands of liberalism and neoliberalism, entering a new stage of struggle for management: re-Westernization and de-Westernization are two different political projects within the same capitalist economic frame. I am not endorsing de-Westernization; I am recognizing that it is here to stay and that it opens up fractures within the capitalist order. One of these fractures is the colonial wound that racism has imposed on people around the world and that Mahbubani addresses.

When the idea of de-Westernization and the actions that accompany it emerged into the public sphere—both before and after the articulation of de-Westernization as an idea—it was common to hear people say that with China we are in a new Cold War. That was another narrow, Western-centered, quick, and absurd interpretation. The Cold War was between the international right and left—that is, between the defenders of free-trade capitalism and the defenders of the state-regulated socialist economy. De-Westernization, as we have already talked about, is based on state-regulated capitalism. So what we have is the promoter of free-trade capitalism and the invisible hand of the markets versus the promoter and defender of state capitalism and economic regulations. This is a totally different ball game that not only makes obsolete the division between left and right, but also puts limits on the regional interests of Western political theory and political economy. China and Singapore, for example, are really weird and difficult cases to encapsulate in the principles, values, and beliefs of Western knowledge. Hence, we hear such aberrations as saying that we are in a new Cold War, or that China is neoliberalism in the Asian way. De-Westernization is contributing on the one hand to making that way of thinking obsolete and to forging knowledges and arguments that help to delink economies from what for a long time appeared to be the only game in town.

CM "Contested modernities," then, operate at the local level in response to the previous allocation of authorities by different local histories?

WM I read that expression, "contested modernities," in Jacques Martin's book *When China Rules the World* (2011). It got my attention because, although Martin doesn't refer to de-Westernization, his analysis captures the ideas and debates being advanced in this domain. Now, what does it mean to see the current global order as "contested modernities" and not as "peripheral," "alternative," or "subaltern" modernities, which was the common language used at the end of the 1980s and throughout the 1990s? Peripheral, alternative, or subaltern modernities imply that there is one modernity without qualifiers, the true, original, or authentic one (the headquarters), and then you have its derivatives like peripheral or alternative modernities (the branches). There is indeed a huge problem with this view. Basically it accepts flatly the European version of modernity, which is, as expressed in Hegel's lesson on the philosophy of history, the point of arrival of the Spirit and the leadership of Western civilization. In the long history of the species, this is situated at the center of space and the present of time: that is, modernity is the "natural" unfolding of universal history. Whereas from a decolonial perspective, modernity is nothing more than the self-fashioned narrative of Western civilization.

The success of the fictional narrative of modernity consisted in making many people believe, first, that modernity is a historical period that corresponds to the hegemony of Western civilization (instead of it being the case that Europe is the self-inventor of modernity), and, second, that modernity "elected" Europe as its incarnation. The terms "history" and "hegemony" are inverted: the consequence became the cause. And, further, many people believe that Europe and the US (the leading states of Western civilization) are the incarnation of modernity, which is also the natural unfolding of history, and they are therefore the guardians and the missionaries for spreading modernity (progress, democracy, development) around the world. When this belief was accepted, then the resulting tendency was to want to "become modern." It is telling that when Harry Truman introduced the concept of underdeveloped countries, his analysis justified the plan of development and modernization, that is, a project for countries to "catch up." What happened in reality was that countries wanting to modernize ended up with a huge debt—exactly what is happening in the European Union at the beginning of the twenty-first century. Now Greece, Spain, Portugal, and Italy are in the same condition that many

Third World countries were in during the second half of the twentieth century: indebted and poor.

To make a long story short (that is, a story of the last one hundred years and not five hundred), by the end of the nineteenth century most of the existing countries wanted to "become Western" and join Western civilization. There were others, like India, which began to confront their colonizers in an effort to delink from Western civilization. There is that famous dictum of Mahatma Gandhi, who was asked his thoughts about Western civilization. His ironic response was that it is a "good idea." At that point, and through all the process of decolonization in Asia and Africa that lasted until the 1970s, the tendency of non-Western countries (state and people) was either to Westernize (that is, follow the West's example, its lead, and its instructions) or to decolonize (Gandhi, Bandung, Fanon, Amílcar Cabral, Lumumba, etc.). In the second half of the twentieth century, a third trajectory was to join by will or force the Soviet Union, which was a Western model projected onto a non-Western history. Russia/Soviet Union has a Cyrillic alphabet, its connection with Greece is through the Orthodox church, and its population is mainly slaves. The Soviet Union was indeed a clear case of Westernization through state politics. Now Russia, particularly under Vladimir Putin, has changed strategies and joined other countries (chiefly the BRICS) in the process of de-Westernization. And it is de-Westernization precisely that brings the question of "contested modernity" to the fore. If modernity is a period in the unfolding of universal history, then it belongs to all of us and not just to Europe, and to "be modern" doesn't mean to follow certain predetermined paths or rules. Indian political theorist Partha Chatterjee has put it forcefully in a classical article he titled "Modernity in Two Languages": "It is our modernity."[31]

Now, if "contested modernities" is thinkable, it is because of de-Westernization. And de-Westernization is a process happening not only in the sphere of states and economies—about which we have talked—but in all the domains of the colonial matrix: in the domain of gender and sexuality, in the sphere of racism (e.g., *Can Asians Think?*), in the domain of art and museums (e.g., the Museum of Islamic Civilization in Doha, or the *Sharjah Biennial*), in religious debates (chiefly in confrontation with Western Christianity), in the spheres of knowledge and education. Briefly, in disputing the control of the colonial matrix at every level.

Thus, de-Westernization and decoloniality run along parallel paths, but they march in different directions. De-Westernizers, as I've mentioned in several places, believe in development and growth, and that belief runs through all the other domains of the matrix. It is the same with decoloniality. The radical difference is that decoloniality works toward the displacement of economic coloniality and toward an economy that administers scarcity, a society where rewards are not in money, and where success means to be recognized for working toward communal well-being and not for celebrated individual achievement, where art is produced not for the market but for the exploration and release of human creativity, where the goal of invention is not primarily to succeed in the market, and where innovation is not needed because the race to supersede the former and be the first is no longer a concern of a communal praxis of living.

Chapter 10 closes this section. In it I explore the cartographic and political history of hemispheric partition examined in chapter 8 and query current conceptions of planetary partitions of West/East and North/South.

10   The South of the North and the West of the East

The East was named from the West, never having enjoyed the advantage of a name that sprang from the region itself.—G. ETZEL PEARCY, geographer, US State Department, 1959

I   On the Third World, the Global South, and the Eastern Hemisphere

"Global South" is not an expression or a concept I use very often for two reasons. I am not sure if the South of Europe and the South of the US count as the Global South, and if they do what does it mean? On the other hand, and insofar as the South (global or not) presupposes the North, the East, and the West, I understand that South and Southeast Asia count as the Global South and Global East, but then we are overlooking Central Asia and West Asia, known as the Middle East. I address these issues here. Earth itself is not ontically divided as such. The partitions are ontological, that is, classifications and ranking. Epistemology creates ontologies. Those who control knowledge have the privilege of creating the illusion that the planet is so divided. Those who control money control meaning. Certainly, "Global South" has become a site of contestation. I take a step farther in the politics of decolonial investigations and look into the historical advent of hemispheric partitions.

Though the expression "Global South" dates back to the 1960s it wasn't as trenchant as the expression "Third World," which caught the imagination of politicians and scholars as well as of the economic and financial literature of the times.[1] However, the struggles for decolonization during the Cold War appropriated the expression, which acquired two different sets of meanings. From First World perspectives and sensibilities, the Third World was the variegated underdeveloped region of the planet. For people inhabiting the so-called Third World, it became a site of pride and struggle for liberation. It was not a place, as Vijay Prashad argued, but the "project" that counts. Or better yet it was a "place" (the place of economic underdeveloped nation-states and of lesser people, generally seen as "colored people") in the canonical First World perspective. The expression "Third World" has fallen into desuetude somehow, displaced and replaced by the more "modern" or perhaps "postmodern" (in the sense of newness, the new expression that advanced and supersedes the first) expression "Global South," but the spirit is still there in journals like *Third World Quarterly*.

However, the expression "Global South" incorporates a dimension absent in the expression "Third World": the South of Europe and the South of the US, not just as geography or places but as projects. The South of Europe (from Greece to Portugal, going through Italy and Spain) has become both an epistemic location of the Global North and Global West and a part of appropriating the Global South. Distinctive voices in reclaiming the Global South from the perspective of the Global North and Global West are the Italian scholar and thinker Franco Cassano and the Portuguese scholar and activist Boaventura de Sousa Santos. In the younger generation, the position advanced by Roberto Dainotto has fruitfully activated the encounter of Antonio Gramsci's "Southern Question" with Franco Cassano's "Pensiero Meridiano."[2] When it comes to Africa, South Asia, and South America, we are into a different Global South. The first, the European south, is a consequence of the intramural imperial difference. Beyond that, all the souths are the consequences of the extramural imperial difference. The South of Europe cannot be taken as the guiding light of the global Global South, to be redundant, nor vice versa.

The concepts of "South" and "Global South" have also been very important for thinkers and scholars either based or born and educated in those regions and who therefore carry a vital experience of the South. In the first case, Australian sociologist Raewyn Connell has raised a voice to denounce the blindness of Northern/Western sociologists and to acknowledge that being a sociologist in Australia is not the same as being a sociologist in Germany or the US. The latter have Max Weber and Talcott Parsons behind them; the former have both Weber and Parsons plus the history of British colonization and the presence of the Australian Aboriginal population. Similarly, if you are an anthropologist or sociologist from South Africa or South America and a scholar in the US, you carry with you not only the learning from the anthropological canon and the official history of South Africa and South America you learned in high school but also, above all, the praxis of living that shaped your organism in a particular geo-bio-culture in a particular region of the planet. Beyond disciplinary formation, there is the imprint in your organism of a non-Western praxis of living, as has been the case in Australia and South Africa, modified by British intervention and the formation of the British Commonwealth.[3]

But that is not all. There are two more trajectories I would like to recall. The collapse of the Soviet Union left the expression "Second World" without a referent and a reference. When the notion of the Global South appeared, it so happened that the Russian Federation was counted neither in the Global North nor the Global East and even less (judging by the increasing Russiaphobia in the US and the EU) as a First World member. So what do we do with the reconfiguration of the global order once the Second World vanished from sight if we circumscribe ourselves to the epistemic ontology of the Global South? Instead, I subscribe to border thinking, rather than to southern epistemology. Border thinking (which in this book I am expanding into gnoseological and aesthesic reconstitutions; see the introduction) emerges from all the places (South and North, East and West) undergoing Western interventions. Madina V. Tlostanova has been exploring and charting the territory of the fallen Second World and the emerging border thinking from the North. Russia became the poor Global North (US and the EU) and the Northwest of the East. Russia is between Europe and Asia, that is, Eurasia.[4]

In the US, "Global South" has been a distinctive expression for casting Latinx epistemic and political projects. Although Latinxs live all over the US, the fact that the US expropriated (by the Guadalupe Hidalgo Treatise, 1848) northern Mexican territories that became southern US territories and that Latinx migrations come from the hemispheric south (Mexico, the Caribbean, and Central America, mainly), the appropriation of the concept of the Global South provides to the Latinx political and epistemic project a distinctive profile within the political and epistemic projects of the Global North.[5]

The concept of the Global South changed the pattern. "Third World" presupposed the First and the Second, while Global South invokes the Global North and silences Global East and Global West. When you look at them together, then you see that Global North and Global West are both implicated in "the West" and in NATO (*North* Atlantic Treaty Organization). It was more difficult to think of the South of Europe and the South of the US as "Third World," although the South of Europe underscores disparities within the First World, disparities made up by the intramural imperial difference. Nevertheless, the expression also has weaknesses for self-identified political and epistemic projects in Asia. Activists, scholars, artists, etc., in India could perhaps see themselves as part of Global South projects. But that idea would be more difficult for East Asians and perhaps ambiguous for *Southeast* Asians. Both East and Southeast Asians tend to see themselves aligned or in confrontation with the West rather than with the North. A single case in point is Kuan-Hsing Chen's *Asia as Method: Toward Deimperialization.*[6] His argument goes to the very roots (archeology digging in the foundations of Western civilizations) and the hidden assumptions behind all surface expressions such as First/Second/Third Worlds, Global North/West and Global South/East, an issue that was also intuited in the classical, and often forgotten, article by US political theorist Carl Pletsch, "The Three Worlds, or the Division of Social Scientific Labor, circa 1950–1975."[7] Kuan-Hsing Chen's argument reverts to the epistemic ontologization of Asia: when the discipline of Area Studies was created in the US during the Cold War, Asia (and by extension, the Second and the Third Worlds) became an "object" to be studied by First World social scientists and humanists (see, e.g., Third World literature). The subject located itself in the First World and in the process created two objects, the Second and the Third World. Kuan-Hsing Chen changes the term of the conversation: Asia became a method to understand Asia on its own trajectory before being mapped by the West, at the same time that it became a method to understand the West; the West (or the First World) became an object of investigation in its history of invasion and disruption of Asian history.

Why is it not just a simple inversion? Because Asia as a method has to unfold as border thinking; that is, the memories, manners, customs, rituals, knowledge, and sensibilities that have been preserved generation after generation, in their languages and praxes of living, cannot be recovered in the way they were before Western invasion. At the same time, Western institutions and concepts, including Western imperial languages as instrumental languages, cannot be avoided, but Western praxes of living remain and will remain (perhaps forever) alien to Asia (East, South, and Southeast). Border thinking emerges from the deep praxes of living, the local histories, and the experiences of being disrupted by alien local histories and praxes of living: the West is not a place, but a set of political and epistemic projects of invasion and intrusion throughout the planet since the sixteenth century.[8] Border dwelling is an unavoidable condition of the logic of coloniality projected by the salvationist, and by the progressive and developmental rhetoric of modernity. Once you dwell in the border you have three options: you surrender and want to become a Westerner; you reject and opt for an "anti" politics, which means that you do not call into question Western intrusion but you oppose and resist it; or you become a border dweller and border thinker, a border gnoseological warrior, an identity in which you ground your border praxis of living, doing, and thinking. The appropriation of the expressions "Third World" and "Global South" by people who identified themselves in the sphere that those expressions invoke are of necessity border dwellers and thinkers. But more forceful is actively working on the gnoseological reconstitution by taking Asia as *method*, removing the continent from its role of *object*, changing the focus from Orientalism to area studies.[9]

My approach detaches from the epistemology of the South for three reasons, all of them crossed by diverse manifestations of colonial and imperial differences: (1) the variegated local histories of the "South" in their colonial trajectories (from Australia to South Africa to South America) and their imperial ones (the South of Europe, the South of the US) are blurred in the ontology of a region; (2) the South is as much a place of struggle for liberation as it is of dependency and collaboration with capitals of the Global North (i.e., internal colonialisms); (3) most important, Western global design has created a world imaginary of territories mapped by borderlines and borderlands, by colonial and imperial differences—that is, imperial differences between the North and the South of Europe, between the North and the South of the Americas. But also between the West and the East. Borderlines and borderlands that created colonial and imperial differences between North/South and West/East generated the two overarching political and epistemic trajectories of our time and certainly for the twenty-first century: decolonization/decoloniality and de-Westernization. Border thinking and border epistemologies cannot be anchored in one single geography, as metaphorical as it could be.[10]

This chapter—indeed, the entire book—is an exercise of border thinking, dwelling in the border, to delink from Western/Northern epistemology/ontology and to excavate its foundations (the colonial matrix of power, or CMP) and history. My thesis is that the expressions such as those introduced in the previous paragraphs are surface manifestations of the making and remaking of the colonial and the imperial differences (epistemically ontological, meaning the ontologies created by Western epistemic and political projects), which were the "natural" consequences of global linear thinking. Border dwelling is unavoidable for many people. Border thinking can be activated or shattered. Disciplinary "rigor" is one of the manifestations to shatter border thinking and subjecting it to Western epistemic territoriality; that is, the cultural/territorial praxis of living built in Western epistemology and political theory protect and justify Western interferences in non-Western territorialities and praxis of living. Think, for example, of today's (May 2020) US foreign politics toward China, Russia, and Iran. All of this is not new; it is grounded in global linear thinking that regulates hemispheric partitions, the logic of coloniality hidden by the rhetoric of modernity (justifications to intervene) that have been operating since the sixteenth century.

II Global Linear Thinking: Disturbing and Interfering with Non-Western Praxes of Living

In the introduction to this volume, I described my understanding of "praxis of living" as the basic practice of survival within the organic and cultural compounds of the human species. Contrary to the ants or bees, which for millions of years have been building anthills and beehives without architects, urban planners, and cultural designers, the advent of the species called human materializes in the double movement of the organic (bio-life) and the cultural (bio-semiotic). While the organic has been determined to come to life, follow the bio-cycle and die, it is the cultural that creates narratives of and for living and dying in certain ways. The cultural sphere materializes due to the human's capacity for languaging to coordinate activities and to plan endeavors, and for using the hands to procure nourishment, build shelter, and create instruments. The hands enhance human interactions in languaging (e.g., the creation of aural and visual signs to coordinate their/our doing, their/our praxis of living) and what the hands can build. Furthermore, languaging and hands work together in the expressions of love and care: the loving tonalities of a voice together with caresses bring comfort and the sensations of well-being.[11] And they also work together to write books! They elaborate (reflect) on our doing and coordinate our doing, that is, by creating "theories" or second-order languaging reflecting the first-order languaging to coordinate their/our consents or dissents.

Coloniality seized the logic that made it possible for an elite group of human beings within the divergent and multiple histories of the species to start processes of invasion and interference that became global after 1500. Impinging on and destroying other civilizations is not a singular feature of Western civilizations. The Mongols invaded China, and the Germanic tribes invaded Rome, to name just two examples. Such deeds have been registered many times since at least the Axial Age (starting about 7000 B.C.), but none of the previous invading civilizations attained the global reach that Western civilization did. In consequence, what became a praxis of living in the cultural dimension of Western civilization, and therefore of thinking and knowing, interfered with and disrupted all existing civilizations on the planet while attempting to implant by diplomacy or by military might Western praxes of living and modes of thinking. That is, the double movements of constitution/ destitution, of modernity/coloniality that provoke the responses of reconstitution today in the form of de-Westernization and decoloniality result in the coming into being of a multipolar world order and pluriversal modes of thinking. The gnoseological and aesthesic arguments I am advancing are one manifestation of the rise of the third nomos of the earth (see chapter 14).

In the previous chapter I suggested that the "Global South" has become an expression of high currency after the end of the Cold War; and in previous publications I mapped the Global South in the world (dis)order.[12] The concept replaced—as I outlined above—one of the three worlds in the once tripartite division, shifting to a two-part division (South/North) and thereby obscuring the previously dominant poles of East/West. However, the growing presence of China globally and the efforts by the US to maintain global dominance and leadership bring East/West back, rearranging the field of forces. The China/ Russia alliance and the fact that Russia is in the Global North make the kaleidoscope change colors as we speak. Not to forget that the South of Europe is the South, but it is not the same South as the South of America, the South of Africa, and the South (or Southeast) of Asia and Australasia. If the Global South is a metaphor for "resistance" and "opposition," then the Global South is neither a homogenous block in each location at the same time nor a conglomerate of geopolitical and economic local histories that nourish the kinds of oppositions and resurgences that are at stake. Some regions of the Global South endure colonial legacies (Africa, America), and others endure imperial legacies (Europe).

Dwelling, wherever you dwell, implies a praxis of living. You dwell where you live, and you live where you dwell. And the praxis of living is at once biological (the body needs food and water) and cultural (the body dwells in a cultural imaginary in its various and changing forms through distinct, diverse, variegated, nonlinear, multiple local histories, languages, cosmographies, and cosmologies that have existed since, say, the Axial Age). Whatever the variations in local histories, the organic (i.e., not made by humans) praxis of living, of staying alive (eating, obtaining water, air, sunlight, etc.), is the same all over the planet. You can say that the organic is global or universal, whatever you like. We are organically born equal; culturally we are not. And this is not a binary opposition, as modern and postmodern minds may suppose. They are one in two; the one does not exist without the other. The variations occur in the cultural (human-made) praxes of living. The organic and cultural praxes of living are interrelated, obviously, but they are not opposed as they are in the Western-conceived distinction between nature and culture. Certain organisms (humans) prioritize languaging, which allows them to use the hands, extended through instruments (technology), and to define themselves in different manners in different cultures. "Man," "human," "anthropos," "human being" are nouns of one of the planet's many civilizations and linguistic families, one that is self-constructed as Western civilization. Why did I go into this terrain when talking about hemispheric partitions? Because global and hemispheric partitions, fabricated regionally (i.e., in the enunciations of Western civilization), impinge on the living organism, both in its animal existence (its need for air, water, light, food) and in its cultural niche (language, memories, religions, histories, etc.). And fabrications are constituted and constitutive of the enunciation. The fabricated is its result. Humans' animal needs were not related to hemispheric partition until the sixteenth-century cartographical appropriation of the planet, and until international law legalized the appropriation. For their part, nonhuman animals, be they aquatic or terrestrial, do not need regional, global, or hemispheric partitions; they do not make maps or invent international law.

Cartography and international law were (and still are) two powerful tools through which Western civilization built its own image by creating, transforming, and managing the image of the world. The German legal philosopher Carl Schmitt perceived the complicity between cartography and law starting in 1500. He labelled this complicity "linear global thinking."[13] Linear global thinking is the story of how Europe mapped the world for its own benefit and left behind a fiction that became an ontology: a partition of the world into "East"/"West," "South"/"North," or "First," "Second," and "Third." Cartography carries in it the memories, world-sense, and worldview of the cartographers, political actors, and governmental, cultural, and intellectual institutions. It carries with it the power differentials that naturalize the imposition of map-making and the concept of "cartography" in the single movement of naming what is being done and silencing what was there before the doing: the "modernization" of people living in the error and ignorance of territorial organizations grounded in non-Western concepts and the drawing of maps. Cartography, since the sixteenth century, does not represent the world; it creates an image of the world that became hegemonic. Furthermore, cartography, ostensibly devoted to locating things, is based on assumptions regarding latitude and longitude that allow the cartographer to convince us (based on those assumptions) to believe that things are geographically located where cartography tells us they are. Since Western cartographers assumed that their own mapping of the planet was the real one, reality became the justification of their conviction. Thus, colonial and imperial differences were created by locating places and people in a hierarchical order. Cartography, as a methodology as well as an art, has been a tool in the racialization of space and the racialization of people spatially located.[14]

The overall assumption of my meditation here is the following: the "East"/"West" partition was an invention of Western Christianity in the late fifteenth and early sixteenth centuries between Indias Occidentales (America) and Indias Orientales (Asia)—an invention whose consequences last until today. The seed of this invention was planted in the Christian T and O (orbis terrarum) map that I briefly described in chapter 8: Jerusalem was the center, and in relation to it was conceived the side of the Earth where the sun rises (East) and where the sun sets (West). In the sixteenth century, after Spanish and Portuguese navigators circumnavigated the planet, the partition was used to legitimize the centrality of Europe (no longer Jerusalem but Rome) and its civilizing mission. From the end of World War II onward, there was a shift to a "North"/"South" partition, but this time the partition was needed to legitimize a mission of development and modernization. The first part of this history was led by Europe, the second by the United States. Now, at the beginning of the twenty-first century, the so-called rise—and return—of the "East" is drastically altering five hundred years of global partitions created in and by Western interests (as Schmitt recognized) to advance its imperial designs. The requisite for understanding, and the want to decolonize knowledge, arose from this long-lasting Western hegemony: the coloniality of knowledge that extends from scholarly work to the mainstream media, from science to art and aesthetics, from technology to the market. It all begins with naming, mapping, and international law.

"Knowledge" is a fundamental component of the CMP. By "knowledge" I mean all that is claimed to be known in the oral memories of the human species at some point, complemented with visual signs of all known writing systems, including all the epistemological principles that contribute to Western civilization.[15] These principles include Christian theology, which is of course a system of beliefs rather than knowledge, indeed beliefs that have changed through time and yet for centuries have served as a basis for action in ways identical to what today we refer to as "knowledge." They also include secular philosophies and the natural and social sciences, including practical disciplines like engineering, law, medicine, and of course cartography. It is apparent, as Frantz Fanon clearly saw in 1961, that historical colonialism and the logic of coloniality that undergird all the different incidents of Western colonialism are not limited to political, economic, and military domination. They are fundamentally epistemic, by which I mean that for many political actors, entrepreneurs, and leaders of various sorts, the driving force of the CMP rests on the epistemology that may lack any real, philosophically persuasive authority—indeed may amount simply to beliefs—but nevertheless rationalizes forms of colonialism existing today. For that reason, delinking from epistemology and restituting gnoseology is the basic step of gnoseological reconstitution; gnoseology absorbs and swallows up epistemology, reduced to its own regional sphere: scientific and institutional knowledges. The wisdom of the human species is much larger than the knowledge that is regulated, controlled, and guarded by epistemology.

Epistemic coloniality refers, then, to the double function of Western knowledge (institutions, actors, disciplines, languages). On the one hand, it is the soul of Western civilization, which is building and conceiving itself as such by creating its own history (archives, libraries registering information) and the history of its regulation (written manuals registering rules and procedures). And, of course, there is nothing wrong with that, at least in some respects. The problem appears in its second function: namely to devalue, diminish, undermine, and demonize non-Western forms of knowledge and ways of living. The first function is constitutive, the second destitutive. The first is achieved by the rhetoric of modernity, the second by the logic of coloniality. The demonic function of Western epistemology is the domain of the coloniality of knowledge. Decolonization of knowledge and ways of knowing is achieved by means of gnoseological reconstitutions, and gnoseological reconstitutions demand the restitution of gnoseology. Which I claim I am doing in this chapter and in the book. This is the task that leads to and supports the diversity of decolonial reexistences.

Let's then explore the coloniality of knowledge manifesting itself in Western cartography. I assume that unmasking the cartographic pretense providing an accurate representation of the planet—its bodies of water, landmasses, and hemispheres—is a task of the politics of decolonial investigations. This book is an academic work, to be sure, published by Duke University Press. However, it is also a matter of opening up investigation into the public sphere and making it work in education in and beyond schools and universities. Decolonial pedagogy goes hand in hand with the decolonial politics of investigations. And decolonial pedagogy consists of learning to unlearn the truth of institutional coloniality of knowledge and ways of knowing.

Geopolitical naming and mapping are fictions insofar as they suggest that this naming and marking of territories and boundaries is unproblematic and uncontested. To be clear: the decolonial option (as much as the scientific and the historical options) is constituted also by fictions, fictions built on the assumptions of a pattern of management and control construed as the CMP as much as quantum theory (quantum physics and quantum mechanics) is put together on the assumptions that the behavior of matter and energy can be explained at the atomic and subatomic levels.

Any rational theory, whether we go with Nelson Goodman (ways of worldmaking) or Humberto Maturana (everything said is said by an observer) or Max Planck (quantum mechanics), is founded and sustained on nonrational assumptions, on intuitions and emotional beliefs. Disciplinary theories, in sciences and the humanities as well in our daily expressions or defenses of our ideas, even if our arguments are strongly rational, are based on our nonrational beliefs. No one is convinced by arguments if the arguments do not touch the emotional chords of the person being persuaded. This also means that the human species has built (and continues to build) cosmologies based on assumptions that do not correspond with anything "real"; on the contrary, whatever may be considered real is an imaginary entity built on the basis of nonrational assumptions. But once "real" and "objective" became keywords sustaining the coloniality of knowledge, they shored up the arguments to convince and became synonymous with "true" and with "history." Once those beliefs are brought to light, it becomes evident that we humans live among "options," among narratives (including theological and scientific narratives), which, when seen from the assumptions of someone (be they an actor or an institution) claiming to be objectively real, are fictions. Therefore, the perspective of the decolonial option argues that any claims of reality, objectivity, truth, or history are as much options as the decolonial option, in the sense that they are narratives, storytelling framing and arguing a given option (e.g., science, religion, literature, philosophy, art, etc.), each option claiming *its own* truth. Decolonially speaking, none have the right to claim *the* Truth. Or, to put it other way, each option can claim its own truth, but the pretense of being *the* Truth is by now totally out of place. The decolonial is as much an option as quantum theory and the Bible. The particular power of the decolonial option is that by claiming to be an option it makes of everything else an option. These are all frameworks that sustain our faith in the accuracy of what we see and believe. These frameworks are what I am calling "options." Decoloniality is an option among other options. The domain of knowing and knowledge holds the CMP together through its avatars, transformations, and disputes.

Maps are signs, and signs have creators. Signs are never isolated; they belong to a frame, a grammar, a context, or a set of beliefs that make their meaning understandable. Names are signs. Take the regional name "North Africa," which is more widely used than "Maghreb." If you look for the "meaning" of Maghreb on the web in a standard search, you will find the "reference"—that is, the names of the countries that make up the Maghreb. If you persist in searching, you will find the etymology of the phrase "the place of the setting sun."[16] The source will also tell you, so you do not get lost, that the sun sets in the west. But there is no necessary relation between the rotation of the Earth where you see, wherever you are, the sunset and the word "west." The first is how the planetary system has been made by the intelligence of the cosmos. The second is how certain human beings named the place where the sun sets. In the case of Western civilization and Maghreb, you may wonder, to the west of what? It may take a while to realize that the Maghreb, for people inhabiting the South of the Mediterranean, is located on the side where the sun sets in relation to Mecca and Medina. For people located in the North of the Mediterranean, "west" (i.e., the "west" of "Western civilization") means to the west of Jerusalem.

The act of naming and mapping is always an act of identification, and identification at this level requires someone who is in a position to name and map. Furthermore, effective naming and mapping can only be done from a position of power that overrules local senses of territoriality, overrules different ways of knowing, of world-making, and of creating knowledge. Take Alfred Thayer Mahan, who in 1902 renamed a region that was identified in Orientalist discourse as the "Near East" with the label "Middle East."[17] Thayer Mahan was not interested in people but in natural resources and strategic geopolitical mapping, and a great deal of India's territory became part of his newly identified Middle East. But not everyone in the region was happy with such an identification and proceeded to disidentify from it, making it clear that in this case, naming cartographic regions carried the weight of imperial identification: there is never a direct relation between the name and the map on the one hand and the people and the region on the other.[18]

Here, the consolidation and expansion contained in the act of naming and mapping are not only economic and political, but also—and above all—epistemic. They are signs of authority managing knowledge and identifications. Geopolitical naming and mapping are arbitrary signs in relation to what the signs refer to and name. The acts of naming and mapping are possible only through the assumed authority to control and manage knowledge, and it requires rhetorical persuasion (the rhetoric of modernity) to make naming and mapping believable and acceptable. The fact that naming and mapping territories and peoples create fictional cartographies does not mean that what is mapped and named already had an ontological existence beyond the act of mapping and naming. On the contrary, these actions are grounded in the interests of people, institutions, and languages (modern European vernacular languages grounded in Greek and Latin) that have the privilege of naming and mapping.

IV Reasoning from Western Cartography

So how does all of what I said in section III relate to the terms "Global South" and "Global North" and to the hemispheric partitions? Let us consider how these "regions" are popularly perceived today on the web: "The *North-South divide* is broadly considered a socio-economic and political divide. Generally, definitions of the *Global North* include the United States, Canada, developed parts of Europe, and East Asia. The *Global South* is made up of Africa, Latin America, and developing Asia including the Middle East. *The North is home to four of the five permanent members of the United Nations Security Council*"[19] (emphasis added).

Here you have the answer to the general question suggested by the title of this chapter; North Africa is indeed located in the Global South. The above definition also notes that the Global South includes "developing Asia and the Middle East." I now set about debriefing these mappings by recalling the distribution of the planet's inhabitants as depicted in many European maps of the seventeenth century. I've taken one at random. Figure 10.1 depicts Visscher's world map from 1652.

What do you see in this map? What there is?[20] Or what you see? And how do you see what you see? You have been educated in the coloniality of knowing and knowledge. So you see many things, of course, but for the argument at hand let's concentrate on the four corner cartouches. Europe is a woman in the upper left corner, elegantly dressed and seated in a *locus amoenus*. In the upper right corner, the viewer encounters Asia, also an elegantly dressed lady, this time seated on a camel (though often in such maps the animal is an elephant). Now let's look at the bottom left corner. It is Africa: seminaked and seated on an unidentifiable animal, a sort of four-legged crocodile. Finally, in the bottom right corner is America, also seminaked and seated on an armadillo. Here, visual classification follows the visual logic of alphabetic writing: in Western

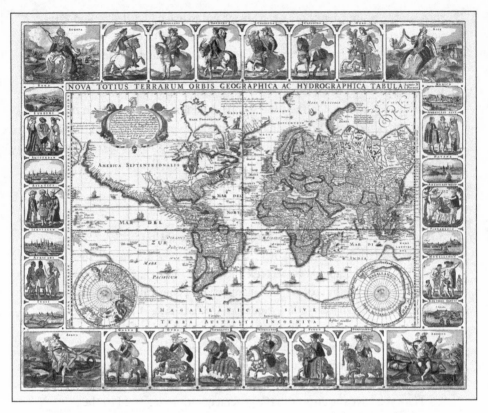

FIGURE 10.1 Claes Janszoon Visscher, *Nova Totius Terrarum Orbis Geographica ac Hydrographica Tabula*, Amsterdam, 1652.

alphabetic writing, words move from left to right and from top to bottom. In this map, the most important native, the one given the primacy of place, is in the upper left corner, where the most important news items in newspapers and on web pages are still located today. In the upper right corner is the second in relevance. Then, at the bottom, Africa and America (exchangeable in other maps) in their seminaked state signal a lack of civilization and a closer relation to the animal kingdom.

In the map depicted in figure 10.1, and thus at that time in history, the North/South divide was already implied, for the magnetic compass (and no longer the rising and setting of the sun) was in use to determine the four cardinal points of the globe. That is why we still use the term "orientation." We say it even if we are "orienting" ourselves with the "North" as a point of reference.

Here, let us consider Russia (the former Second World) for a moment, which was left out of the North/South partition. As Madina V. Tlostanova has argued, the Caucasus is the South of the poor North, an argument that is crucial to understanding how North/South divides operate:

> The erasing of the Second World has resulted in the increased binary organization of world order and the changing of its axis to the North-South divide. Similarly, the West-East partition tends to homogenize various local histories into imagined essential sets of characteristics. Drifting of bits and pieces of the Second World in the direction of either the North or the South has become unavoidable for all its former subjects, yet leaves them with an uncertain, almost negative subjectivity. This article problematizes the role and function of the ex-Socialist world and its colonial others within the global North-South divide through the concepts of colonial and imperial differences. It considers Caucasus as the utmost case of the South of the poor North, and analyses secondary "Australism"—a syndrome that is devastating for the subjectivity of its people. Finally, it dwells on the possible ways of decolonizing being, sensing and thinking in the non-European Russian/Soviet ex-colonies.[21]

Tlostanova's argument and the introduction of the word "Australism" have particular resonance here. It makes us aware that the North/South divide is the displacement and replacement of Orientalism. In this, "Australism" is the appropriate term to understand the invention of the South as much as Orientalism was, in its time, a way to understand the invention of the Orient. Both the East/West and the North/South divides are not ontological but fictional, and also political, since they tell us more about the interests of the enunciators (institutions, people, organizations) than about what is named, classified, and mapped.

These semiotic alignments are not just games. They have real effects.

V Racial Assumptions and Geographic Partitions

When it comes to hemispheric and continental partitions, racism should be seriously taken into account, though it should not be conceived as a biological issue as much as an epistemic one (see chapter 1). Racism is a classification of differences (colonial and imperial) and an organization of these differences into hierarchies that operate not only in the everyday life of nations but also at an interstate level, reflecting the fact that racism is precisely the driving mechanism for how these North/South, East/West, and Third World/Second World/First World divides have operated. In other words, racism is always already implied in linear global thinking and has been since the sixteenth

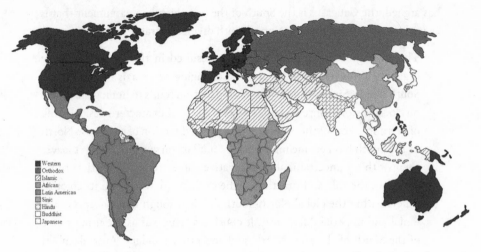

FIGURE 10.2 Samuel P. Huntington, Map of Nine Civilizations, *The Clash of Civilizations and the Remaking of the World Order*, 1996.

century. Racism moves beyond the classification of people by their biological features and overdetermines the entire spectrum of Western global designs. We can see Samuel Huntington's logic of planetary classification as depicted in the legend from the map in figure 10.2, showing the hierarchies evident in this classification.

The "West"—North America, Canada, Europe, and Australia—is positioned at the top of the list and is the civilization that classifies the remaining eight according to the following categories: "Orthodox" (meaning Eastern Christianity), "Islamic," "African," "Latin American," "Sinic," "Hindu," "Buddhist," and "Japanese." Now consider here the mapping of Islam—the civilization that serves as the main reason Huntington wrote *The Clash of Civilizations*—and Africa. As a trick in the mind set up by the rhetoric of modernity, the map pretends to "represent" the world. If you are attentive to the logic of coloniality you realize that the map is not representing the world but, literally, "mapping" the world according to the necessity of remaking it: a new enemy was needed after the collapse of the Soviet Union. In this very step of the rhetoric of modernity (constitution) there is its darker side, the logic of coloniality: destitution. The politics of decolonial investigations aims at gnoseological and aesthesic reconstitutions, which is what this chapter attempts to pull off. The map in figure 10.2 makes clear that it is in North Africa and not sub-Saharan Africa where the majority is Muslim, thus severing Black Africa and Muslim Africa from each other. Indeed, what the BRICS countries

(Brazil, Russia, India, China, and South Africa) have in common—along with the rest of the world order after decolonization during the Cold War—is that all of them have been racialized (ranked below the West, the First World, or the North).

To better understand my claim, let's take a historical detour. Since decolonial geopolitical thinking (distinct, say, from geopolitical thinking in the social sciences and the humanities) is anchored to historical consciousness and the subjective transformation engendered by the invention of America and the circumnavigation of the planet, persons became colonial subjects as a consequence of global linear thinking and the making of colonial and imperial differences. The imperial self was simultaneously built with the colonial other, both entangled by the colonial (e.g., Africans and Indigenous Americans) and imperial (e.g., Ottoman sultanate, Russian czarate) differences. From the sixteenth century, "Being" was no longer the universality of the trajectory from Greece to Germany (e.g., Heidegger) but the entanglement of the imperial subject construing colonial and imperial differences. Eurocentrism was the outcome of these processes, building the territoriality of the self (interiority) by building the exteriority of the other: colonial and imperial differences at work and the work of global linear thinking. To expand on these thoughts, I will draw a picture of the historical geopolitical formation and transformation of the modern/colonial world order, the global cartographic imaging of which we owe to Pope Alexander VI. In fact, soon after Christopher Columbus landed on shores he thought were Indian, Pope Alexander VI partitioned the land and sea as they had been known until that year and donated them to the Castilian and Portuguese crowns. The new land partition was named "Indias Occidentales," and the donation was stamped in a treaty called the Treaty of Tordesillas (1494). Thus, the Atlantic was born as a zone of commerce between the Iberian Peninsula, Indias Occidentales, and Africa (see figure 10.3).[22]

About thirty-five years after the Treaty of Tordesillas, the monarchs of Spain and Portugal reached another agreement, formalized in another treaty, the Treaty of Zaragoza, and signed in 1529. In this treaty, the two monarchs agreed to divide between them the eastern part of the known landmass named "Indias Orientales."[23] (Mind you, people who had lived for centuries in Indias Occidentales, as it was thought of in the European imagination, had no idea that they were living in the European imagination, for both the name and the mapping were fictions of popes and monarchs of Western Christendom and mapmakers in the Netherlands.) It was then that the West/East partition of the planet as we know it today was established. It was a Western Christian invention, pure and simple, which presupposed a center between two poles:

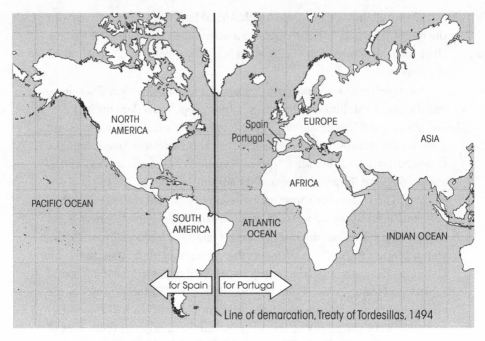

NORTH
AMERICA

Spain
Portugal

EUROPE

ASIA

AFRICA

PACIFIC OCEAN

SOUTH
AMERICA

ATLANTIC
OCEAN

INDIAN OCEAN

for Spain | for Portugal

Line of demarcation, Treaty of Tordesillas, 1494

FIGURE 10.3 Tratado de Tordesillas. The Treaty of Tordesillas, signed on June 7, 1494, was an agreement between the representatives of Isabel and Fernando, queen and king of Castile and Aragon, and those of King Juan II of Portugal, by virtue of which they established a distribution of the areas of navigation and conquest of the Atlantic Ocean and the New World.

Rome (the papacy), and the two monarchs advancing the papacy's project to Christianize the world (see figure 10.4).

About three and a half centuries later, Britain took over the leadership of Western imperial expansion, removed the theological connotation of Rome as the center of the world, and replaced it with the secular Greenwich Meridian. Nevertheless, by the time the Greenwich Meridian displaced Rome, the border establishing the West/East partition was mapped. However, though Rome was simultaneously located in the West and at the center of the world, between Indias Occidentales and Indias Orientales, London—after appropriating the position geographically located to the east of the Greenwich Meridian—was cosmologically self-located in the "West" and therefore at the world's center.

But it should be said that until the first decades of the sixteenth century there *was no single world map*, that is, no map providing a complete view of the land and water masses that we know today. Each existing civilization (Chinese,

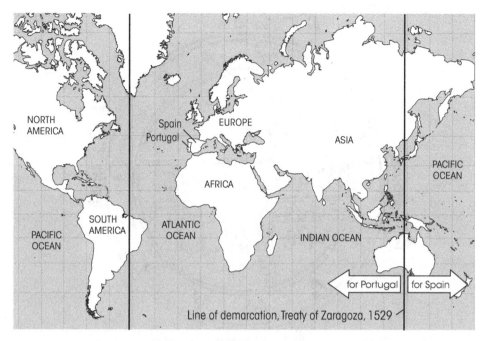

Line of demarcation, Treaty of Zaragoza, 1529

FIGURE 10.4 Treaty of Zaragoza. On April 22, 1529, Carlos I of Spain and Juan III of Portugal signed the Treaty of Zaragoza. The arrival of Columbus to the so-called West Indies raised the need to reach an agreement on the rights of overseas navigation for Castilians and Portuguese.

Indian, Persian, African kingdoms, Mayas, Aztecs, Incas, and so on) had its own spatial configuration of sky, Earth, sea, and Earth's underground. When the first global maps were devised, the previous local territorialities were subsumed and colonized by the *local world map that served as the foundation of Western civilization*. When Pope Alexander VI drew the line of the Tordesillas Treaty, he had an already existing map of the world in his mind: the Christian T and O map, to which I am returning. It was a visual drawing (not, of course, universal) in the imagination of a singular, local cosmology: Western Christianity (see figure 10.5).

By the mid-sixteenth century, Gerardus Mercator and later Abraham Ortelius (*Typus Orbis Terrarum*) drew the world map that is familiar to all of us today. But though we may tend to believe that this is what the planet looks like, it doesn't. Take Asia, Africa, and Europe: at the time, these three "continents" existed as such only in the minds of Christians, who in their minds were inhabiting Europe. Asians did not know that they lived in "Asia" until

FIGURE 10.5 The Western Christian T and O map, from the Middle Ages. It divided the world into three schematic parts: Asia, Europe, and Africa, corresponding to Noah's three sons: Shem (Asia), Ham (Africa), and Japheth (Europe). Before development of the magnetic compass, the top indicated where the sun rises. The center is Jerusalem. Hence, "East" and "West" were directions from Jerusalem, where the enunciation was located, as the point of reference.

approximately 1582, when Jesuit missionaries visited China and told them that according to the Christian concept of the Earth, they lived in Asia![24] For that reason, embedded in the Ortelius map *is* the T and O map, and the drastic consequences of sixteenth-century mapping were the disavowal and devaluation of non-Western cosmologies and territorial imaginaries. The first nomos of the Earth, to use Schmitt's terminology, was *superseded* (Schmitt's own linear thinking) by the second nomos, which homogenized and universalized the belief that the planet really looked the way Christian European mapmakers of the sixteenth century believed it to look.[25] Western cartography shuttered out everyone else and made us see the planet according to the eyes of Western cartographers (see figure 10.6).

Thus, the world map, *though global*, could (and can) *not be but local*, since the "West" is not only an enunciated location *in* the map, but is—above all—

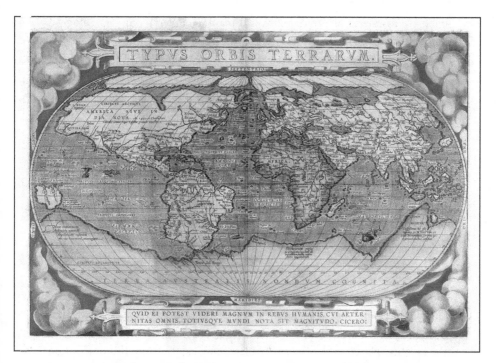

FIGURE 10.6 Abraham Ortelius's classic *Typus Orbis Terrarum* (1570). For the first time, an image of the planet's land/water distributions was available. The Atlantic occupies the center of the map, displacing the centrality of the Mediterranean (*Medi-Terra*) in the T and O map. Both maps enacted the displacement of the previous relevance of the Indian Ocean for trade and commerce between Asia and Africa.

the locus of enunciation *of* the map. It is the locus that has the legitimacy (language, institutions, and social actors) of world-making. But today, there is a shift. Peoples who were once mapped are remapping themselves. The multipolar world order arising as a result of de-Westernization is parallel to the pluriversal gnoseology and aesthesis that is coming into being decolonially. There is no longer a zero point of observation: the Global North/Global West. There is no reason to look at the world from the perspective of Rome first and the Greenwich Meridian second. Now we are seeing the reemergence of pluriversality: the planet as it was before 1500. Decolonial world-making surfaces from gnoseological and aesthesic reconstitutions. Consequently, decolonial enunciation works at the borderlands of the CMP and destituted knowledges, modes of knowing, languages, and praxes of living. Consequently, I am not *talking about* and telling you *how to do it*. I assume that this chapter and this book are instances of decolonial world-making carrying out gnoseological and aesthesic reconstitutions and moving forward the politics of decolonial investigations. I have been excavating, so far, the CMP's enunciation of modern/colonial mapmaking. My excavation delinks from it and, in the process, it cements the terrain of decolonial enunciations and decolonial world-making.

VI The Colonial Matrix of Power: Cartography and Global Linear Thinking

Notice that I am not elaborating a history of cartography, of which there are many good ones. I am tracing a history of cartographic expression of the colonial matrix of power, which is something different. Consequently, my subject matter is not cartography but the CMP through cartography.[26]

Having reminded you of my argument, let me return to the previous definition of the Global North and the Global South as cited from the web. The Global North includes the United States, Canada, and developed parts of Europe and East Asia. Furthermore, Japan and China have been removed from the East and placed in the North. The lesson we can get from this description is the following: until 1945 the world was divided between the Western and Eastern Hemispheres based on civilizational criteria (Orientalism and civilizing missions propelled by British and French imperialism). Then, from 1945 onward, the world was divided between the Northern and Southern Hemispheres, and between three Worlds. The South and the East (China and India) were components of the Third World. The mapping was based on economic criteria (development and modernization led by the US).

What this tells us is that the "North" is defined by economic and not cultural criteria, and it is done by people and institutions in the North: he who controls money also controls meaning. (Otherwise, it would be absurd to count East Asia as part of the Global North.) And from the economic perspective of the North, the Global South refers to regions that are "underdeveloped" and "emerging." Curiously enough, from a political and decolonial perspective, the Global North includes places where forces of liberation from the South have been at work.

After all, to be classed as a "Third World" person places you in an inferior position—third, not first. But this could also be taken as a sign of pride, as a way to denunciate such a hierarchical, derogatory naming and turn it into a space of struggle and reidentification. When this happens, gnoseological and aesthesic reconstitution is at work. "Third World" is the enunciated of two different enunciations. It is not a conflict of interpretations within the same enunciation, but a conflict of enunciations: the terms of the conversation are changing; decoloniality at large (reconstitution) is at work.

In this changing panorama of naming and renaming, the configuration of the BRICS states is of great relevance here because, among other things, it dismantles East/West and South/North divides. It would be limiting to say that this is a "post" world order, for it maintains the logic upon which spatial partitions were drawn within the linear time that the North and West were the partitioners. Rather than a post-world order, it is "de-," in this case a de-Westernized order, because it is not a change happening in a linear concept of time, but a rebuilding, resurgence, and reemergence of ways of living, thinking, and doing that were disavowed by both Western modernity and postmodernity.

The BRICS states are located—within the current divide between North/South and West/East—both in the North and the South, and in the East and the West (see figure 10.7). Yet to modern/colonial ways of thinking, it would be impossible for the BRICS countries to form a viable union of any sort because they do not have common languages or common religions, they are not in contiguous territories, they do not have a common memory, and their people look and act and experience the world differently. None of them drank from ancient Greek and Roman fountains. Modern/colonial common sense assumes that people who do not have a common language or memory or who do not live in contiguous regions—and thus are only bound together for and by economic interests—cannot remain together for long. However, the five countries have a profound and unforgettable common memory: coloniality. That memory has been erased and destituted by modern/colonial narratives.

The BRICS countries were approached with the promises of modernity—progress, civilization, development, modernity—and the weapons of coloniality. From a decolonial perspective, attentive to coloniality and always piercing through Western triumphalism, the commonalities are obvious. Three current states (India, Brazil, and South Africa) have formed over the ruins of previous Western imperial colonies (of variously British, Portuguese, and Dutch settlers). The Dutch had been settled in South Africa since 1652, but the full colonization of Africa (including, of course, northern Africa) started around 1870 and was completed by and after the Berlin Conference of 1884.[27] China and Russia were not affected by settler colonialism, as the other three countries were, yet they did not escape coloniality. The nineteenth-century Opium Wars were the strategy used by Britain, with the support of France and the US, to undermine the Chinese government and population. As for Russia, there is its

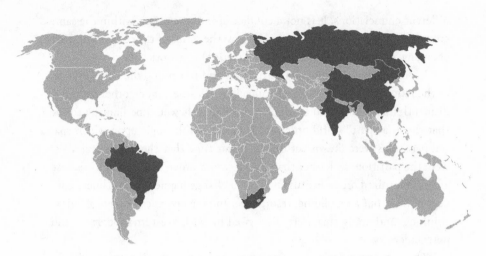

FIGURE 10.7 The BRICS (Brazil, Russia, India, China, and South Africa) countries. A common question at the time the association was formed was whether a state organization spanning different continents would work out. I dealt with this issue in an essay explaining that their common interests were grounded in their respective locations within the colonial matrix of power (CMP). See Walter D. Mignolo, "The Role of the BRICS Countries in the Becoming World Order," 2012.

long history of being viewed from the West, and sensed by Russians themselves, as a "second-class" empire, parallel to but less significant than the rising Western civilization and imperialism.[28]

The fact that Brazil, unlike India and South Africa after Nelson Mandela, is ruled by people of European descent rather than by natives (as India and South Africa are) evinces a difference of scale rather than of nature. It is a long story to repeat here, but the fact that Samuel Huntington, political scientist and author of *The Clash of Civilizations*, placed Latin America (which of course includes Brazil) in the Third World and also located Australia and New Zealand (Aotearoa, for the Maori people) within Western civilization, is not something that has been passed over. Australia and New Zealand were already placed in the First World. Have they been "demoted" to the Global South, or are Australians and New Zealanders/Aotearoa claiming their "belonging" to it? The classification and ranking reveal how the people of British and Portuguese descent are seen from the perspective of the First World in the Global North, which turned their imagining into "civilization": the people of British descent in Australia and New Zealand are located in the First World, while the people of Portuguese descent in Brazil are located in the Third World. What you see here is a replica of the European intramural imperial differences, turned into extramural colonial differences. The logic is the same; only the membership has been moved around. Without Mandela and the end of apartheid, China may not have invited South Africa to join BRICS.[29]

Thus, what these five BRICS states have in common is the infliction of modern/colonial disdain, destitution, and humiliation according to Western perceptions of interstate relations. Geopolitical wounds, either colonial (India, South Africa, Brazil) or imperial (Russia, China), are the threads that connect the BRICS countries. By colonial wounds, as I've mentioned in previous chapters, I mean the racialization and dehumanization of colonized and enslaved human beings (Aztecs and Mayas, Africans in the sixteenth century, and Indians in the nineteenth century). Imperial wounds are a derivation of colonial wounds projected onto people and countries that were not subjected to settler colonialism. Colonial and imperial wounds have one feature in common: racial assumptions and classifications. Imperial differences, and therefore imperial wounds, are as humiliating as colonial wounds, and the responses to one or the other (de-Westernization or decoloniality) differ in their respective configurations and aims. China, Russia, and Iran have been distressed by imperial differences, and their de-Western responses correspond to the level of interstate relations. On the other hand, and in spite of the Gulf states' compliance with re-Westernization, cultural institutions like the *Sharjah Biennial* can take a de-Western attitude. It happened with the organization of *Sharjah Biennial II*, which was an open and clear call for de-Westernization in the cultural sphere. More telling was that the Japanese curator, Yuko Hasegawa, took an openly de-Western stance (which is also a trend of her work), even though the Japanese state is openly pro re-Westernization.[30]

VII The Political Meaning of "North Africa" and the "Middle East"

In this light, I ask the question, where are "North Africa" and the "Middle East"? (See figure 10.8.) I write these names in quotation marks to remind you that they are signs, not entities. "Near East," for example, was a translation of the French expression "Proche-Orient" and referred roughly to the regions under the control of the Ottoman sultanate at the beginning of the twentieth century. But by 1922, the sultanate had collapsed under global designs led, at the time, by England and France. This collapse brought about the Republic of Turkey, which is now counted in the so-called broader MENA (Middle East and North Africa), though technically it is located in western Asia. Imperial and

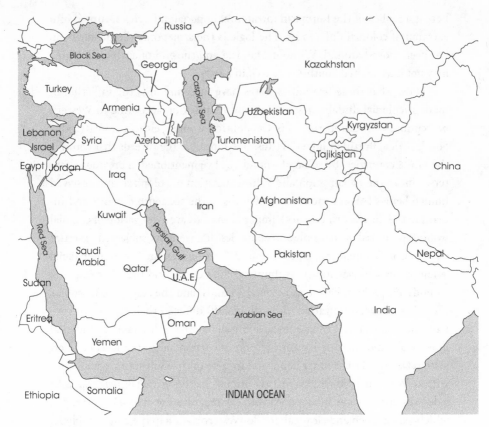

FIGURE 10.8 The invention of the Middle East. Alfred Thayer Mahan, the US mastermind of sea power, in 1901 invented the region that came to be known as the "Middle East." The Sykes-Picot Agreement of 1916 was a series of lines drawn to establish British and French "areas of influence," and the expression was popularized that year by Sir Mark Sykes, a British member of Parliament. The invention was established. In 1916 the Ottoman sultanate was still standing. The mapping of the Middle East began the destitution of the sultanate's territories.

colonial differences were remapped on the surface, but the logic of coloniality remained guided by global linear thinking and international law.

Iran has a different history: the history of the mutations of the Persian shahanate (misleadingly called an "empire," for the shah was not an emperor in the same way that an emperor was not a shah—this observation is a small example of delinking from the CMP's enunciation, disobeying and bringing forward epistemic and aesthesic reconstitutions). Modern Iran traces the beginning of its history to the end of the Safavid shahanate (1502–1736), based in Baku in present-day Azerbaijan. An Islamic state, Iranian dynasties existed from 1736 to 1979, when the Iranian Revolution ended the system of dynastic government. But in looking at Iran, which will most likely continue its alliances with Russia in the North and with Indonesia and Malaysia in *Southeast* Asia (emphasis mine), as well as with Turkey, we see that a state which emerged from the ruins of the Ottoman sultanate and to which present-day Iraq also once belonged is located in a region conceived as West Asia.

Clearly, in the first quarter of the twenty-first century, the world order is being remapped in a way that cuts across the North/South and West/East divides. Pulling away from Western dominance, the politics of BRICS states and other emerging economies of the Middle East (e.g., Turkey) and Southeast Asia (Indonesia) have foregrounded the rising trajectory of de-Westernization. Economic growth has brought new self-esteem and confidence in the political arena to "former Third World territories" and "people of color," and provided them with the energy and creativity to overcome racial hierarchies (of both regions and people) that were invented and implemented during five hundred years of Westernization. But of course, actors and institutions in the Western world do not want to lose the privileges they gained over the centuries. Thus, the politics of Westernization have increased in the Middle East since 9/11. One of the distinctive features of modern/colonial designs is the logic of cause-effect promoted by the rhetoric of modernity while the events themselves suggest that the effect is the cause: the intensification of US politics in the Middle East was not caused by 9/11, but 9/11 happened to legitimize the politics of Westernization after the fall of the Soviet Union.[31] Re-Westernization (the expansion of the Global West/North) is what the world is witnessing in Ukraine and in the Middle East. De-Westernization is also visible in Ukraine by its stopping the march of the West toward Central Asia.

I would mention, however, an important movable variable: while re-Westernization is diminishing middle class consumer privileges, de-Westernization is creating an enormous middle class with consumer privileges. In both cases, the gap between the concentration of wealth and the expansion of poverty is disproportionate. On the other hand, Middle East Arab–dominated countries, while in between re- and de-Westernization, have created a wealthy middle class supported by migrant labor. Cultural de-Westernization takes place in this mixed context of political and economic forces. The Sharjah Foundation enjoys a healthy budget to program biennials and purchase expensive art works. Similarly, so does the Museum of Art in Doha. Compare the annual budgets of the Museum of Modern Art in New York ($32 million) and the Metropolitan Museum in New York ($30 million) with the annual budget of the Islamic Museum of Art in Doha ($1 billion). That fancy amount allowed

Sheikha Al-Mayassa bint Hamad bin Khalifa Al-Thani to spend, in 2012, $250 million for Cezanne's *Card Players* (1890–1895), about four times the budget of the two New York museums combined.[32] The point is not the pride of having an expensive Western art work but, on the contrary, to make a statement of de-Westernization: if a Western museum exhibits non-Western art, why shouldn't non-Western museums exhibit Western art? Sheikha Al-Mayassa asserted this goal in a well-drafted TED Talk.[33]

What I have written here about cultural de-Westernization is a decolonial analysis of gnoseological and aesthesic reconstitutions that have been made possible by the appropriation of a capitalist economy that allows significant amounts of money to be spent to rebuild an identity and heal the imperial wounds that the West, since Kant, has inflicted on Arab/Islamic civilization. Cultural decolonization in the sphere of art and museums does not operate at such a level but in the field of the emerging political society, defined and self-identified through well-thought-out organization.[34] A complex issue that would require a long digression to address here would be the decolonial potentials in the cultural spheres by artists and curators operating away from the capitalist sphere of cultural de-Westernization. To simplify, while the former doesn't call into question the concepts of art and aesthetics, the latter addresses head-on the Eurocentrism of both concepts.[35]

VIII South/North and East/West: The Locations of Border Dwelling and Thinking

So where does this remapping leave us? At the borders: physical, epistemic, ethical, religious, psychological, and aesthetic. Borderlands and borderlines are in the "/" of hemispheric partitions and are also inside each geographic territory. Borderlands are never of equal weight on each side of the line. There is always a power differential: colonial and imperial differences. Modernity/coloniality connects all the borderlands that have been made and remade in the history of the CMP. De-Westernization and decoloniality emerged from destituted territories, from the weaker end of power differentials, be they in the sphere of the state (de-Westernization) or in the cultural sphere (de-Westernization and decoloniality). My argument, as mentioned, is decolonial at two levels: one is the analytics of de-Western responses to and dispute of the CMP, and the other is the pragmatic moving forward of the politics of decolonial investigations. De-Western and decolonial doing and thinking develop inward from the border. Dwelling on the borders creates the conditions for border thinking, doing, and being. Gnoseological and aesthesic reconstitutions are consubstantial

with de-Western and decolonial praxes. Why? First, because you cannot ignore Westernization and re-Westernization because both are omnipresent by
hegemony and domination. Figments of Western cosmology through religion,
science, art, philosophy, and economic and political theories are all over the
world; they are in all of us. Consequently, neither de-Westernization nor decoloniality can ignore Westernization. More so, without Westernization there
would be no need today for either de-Westernization or decoloniality. Both
require border thinking to dispute (de-Westernization) and to delink from
(decoloniality) the rhetoric of modernity and the logic of coloniality. De-
Westernization is not about either submitting or adapting, but of disputing
and delinking. It is about moving in a different direction while recognizing
that different directions cannot be followed simply by forgetting what five
hundred years of Western theological and secular branches of knowledge—the
arts, philosophy, and the sciences, for instance—have achieved in the realms of
education, governmental systems, and economic practices. De-Westernization
is not merely consciously refusing Western ways, but reimagining those ways
within Indigenous frameworks.

De-Westernization cannot be identified with the East, nor decoloniality with the South. They both unfold and propagate in the interstices (the
borderlands and borderlines) of the movable global and hemispheric partitions. Decoloniality, without being named as such back then (see the introduction, section III.3), coexisted with the Westernization of the world (1500–
2000), just as today it coexists with the processes of de-Westernization and
re-Westernization. Decoloniality carries the spatial "de-" from the borders of
global designs; it is the relentless energy of reexisting, reemerging, and remaking, avoiding the unilinear temporal "post-" supplanting the old with the new.

I turn now to decolonial reconstitutions. The next two chapters, 11 and 12,
survey individual thinkers, and chapters 13 and 14 turn to theoretical issues.
Chapter 11 looks into the works of Peruvian thinker and activist José Carlos
Mariátegui. His work is a prelude to Quijano's decolonial thinking. In fact,
Mariátegui is one of the fundamental sources of Quijanos's understanding of
coloniality of power. Because of the question of colonization and land expropriations from the inhabitants of Andean civilization, Mariátegui disobeyed
Marxism, a way of thinking in which the question of the land was peripheral
to the proletarian class and the Industrial Revolution. In chapter 12 I turn to
Afro-Caribbean theorist Sylvia Wynter's tackling of the issue of what it means
to be human—a question that is at once philosophical and political, for the
whole of Western political theory is built on the silent presupposition of actors
and thinkers who are man/human. What today is called "patriarchy" is longer

and larger than Western civilization. What happened in the sixteenth century was a resignification of patriarchy. In that resignification, patriarchy meant masculinity and Christianity (purity of blood) and whiteness (see chapter 1). The fact that females can attain relevant political positions does not change the male dominance of Western political theory. This only shows its flexibility to include females without changing the terms in which political theory was established. Chapter 13 more directly shifts the geography of reasoning and tackles head-on decolonial imperatives of changing the terms of the conversation. In chapter 13 I turn my attention to the geopolitics of knowing, sensing, and believing, examining the parallel between phenomenology and decolonial thinking: which were the needs in each local history that prompted the surfacing of these two schools of thought, one in the context of European modernity and the other in the context of Andean coloniality? Chapter 14 is a crucial chapter of the book as it is entirely about gnoseological and aeshtesic reconstitutions that I outlined in the introduction and acted out through the book. It hints toward the planetary change of epoch (or era) in which the five-hundred-year epoch of changes (of novelty, newness, progress, development) is mutated. The change of epoch (or era) can no longer be understood by adding the prefix "post-," nor can it be captured in a linear arrangement of events: the change of epoch (or era) *is* the advent of the third nomos of the earth.

GEOPOLITICS OF KNOWING, THE QUESTION OF THE HUMAN, AND THE THIRD NOMOS OF THE EARTH

PART IV

11   Mariátegui and Gramsci in "Latin" America

I   Opening

This chapter is based on my response to an invitation to write an article on "Gramsci in Latin América" for a volume titled *Postcolonial Gramsci*.[1] It has been revised and expanded. Two aspects of the invitation and the title prompted my contribution to the proposed volume. One was the postcolonial reading of Gramsci and the other was of Gramsci in Latin America. Since the postcolonial is not part of my agenda, I set aside the first part of the invitation. Moreover, the first issue was related to the second: the interest of Gramsci (whether in translation or in Italian) in Latin America had nothing whatsoever to do with the postcolonial as it was experienced in Asia and Africa during and after the Cold War. Independences and revolutions in South America and the Caribbean (Haiti) were fought around 150 years before Gramsci entered into the Argentinian and Brazilian political and intellectual conversations. The debates at that point were dependency theory and the philosophy and theology of liberation. The postcolonial in Latin America was, and still is (except for a minority of intellectuals who feel comfortable and familiar with Foucault, Derrida, and Lacan), a moot point. Gramsci entered Asian intellectual circles in the UK and the US in the late 1970s and early 1980s, particularly in the sphere of subaltern studies. The "post" in postcolonial presupposes the postmodern, and it came into being in the 1980s, after the publication of François Lyotard's *The Postmodern Condition: A Report on Knowledge* (1979).[2] At that time Gramsci was well established in Argentina in Brazil. It was a pre-postmodern and postcolonial time, so to speak.

When Fredric Jameson published his celebrated *Postmodernism, or the Cultural Logic of Late Capitalism* (1991), postcolonial conversations were already established. Geopolitically and body-politically these two works (Lyotard's and Jameson's) concur on the "post" ethos of modernity. Whether "post" is taken to mean "after" or "something different" is a question of interpretation. What matters is that the prefix "post" signals a fracture of "modernity" within the same cosmology of modernity. Lyotard's book testified by its very existence to how the fracture was felt in Europe, and Jameson's to how it was felt in the US. Jameson expresses his geo-body political sensing of the US by digging into its imaginary of the twentieth century ("there no longer does seem to be any organic relationship between the American history we learn from schoolbooks and the lived experience of the current, multinational, high-rise, stagflation city of the newspapers and of our own everyday life").[3] Lyotard's analysis, by contrast, arose from his lived experience in reconstructed Europe after WWII, the "prologue" to what became the technological revolution and more recently the fourth industrial revolution. Lyotard's disdain for metanarratives of modernity (presumably from 1800 to 1945), based on his own experience of French philosophers, has been captured in his well-known dictum: "Simplifying to the extreme, I define postmodern as incredulity towards metanarratives."[4]

Thus, in the linear history of European thought, the postmodern condition prompted the coexistence of poststructuralism as well as the postcolonial moment. The idea of the postcolonial did not exist before the idea of the postmodern came about. What matters for my argument, deviating from the postcolonial, is that it is *not* derived from the postmodern. As I argued in the introduction to this book, the genealogy of the decolonial erupted during the Cold War, and it had in the Bandung Conference of 1955 an anchor and point of reference. The postcolonial instead found its anchors and points of reference in key figures identified as poststructuralists, including Foucault, Lacan, Derrida, and Gramsci. None of them are relevant for the decoloniality I endorse and practice as it has been construed since the 1990s: as an outcome of the debates on dependency theory and modernization, development, and the theology/philosophy of liberation in South America and the Caribbean since the late 1950s and 1960s; in addition, it has arisen from the fundamental issue of what it means to be human, profusely addressed in the Caribbean in the context of slavery, the Middle Passage, and the plantation system. What I am driving at is a clear distinction between the "post" and the "de," both conceptual and geohistorical. I am underscoring *coexisting options*, entanglements, and power differentials, rather than looking for *what superseded what* in a linear race where the "post" is necessary. Hence, this chapter is about Gramsci and the decolonial in South America and the Caribbean.

While for Lyotard the experience (sensing and knowing) was moored in Europe after the recovery of WWII and the advent of cybernetic and the technological society, and for Jameson it was affixed to the US of the 1950s and 1960s, for Quijano it was the South American Andes and the Third World that made him confront modernity with "coloniality and decoloniality" instead of "postmodernity." My own life trajectory and sensibility is not that of Europe after WWII, nor that of the golden age of the US (1950-1970). As a matter of fact, I left Paris to come to the US in 1973 (the year that Salvador Allende was ousted), when people were living the theatre, so to speak; when French intellectuals began to be translated and published in the US. This again is why, for decolonial thinkers (which I was not at that moment; I was a recent PhD in semiotics and discourse analysis), geo-body politics is crucial for understanding both our local histories as well as others'. I came of intellectual age in the middle of the Cold War as experienced in the Third World with the vibrations of the Cuban Revolution. And the Cold War was not lived (experienced) in the same way in western Europe, the US, and South America. Now, neither Gramsci nor Mariátegui experienced the Cold War. It was the generation after them that did. Consequently, Gramsci's South of Italy and Mariátegui's South American Andes in the 1920s were not just geographical locations on a map in a coeval temporality. Local histories shaped both thinkers, and both thinkers reoriented their received knowledge and subject formation while at the same time transforming their local histories. Geopolitics of knowledge matters, as does the body-politics of knowing and understanding, as I argue in chapter 12. It is in this vein—that of the determinative specificity of local experience—that the following pages were written. Hence, I am here walking the path of the politics of decolonial investigations and gnoseological and aesthesic reconstitutions to understand Mariátegui and Gramsci. Mariátegui was not considered in the postcolonial question of the invitation I received; only "Gramsci in Latin America" was taken into account. To reconstitute, decolonially, the postcolonial readings and uses of Gramsci in South America and the Caribbean (to which I will refer briefly), I needed to introduce Mariátegui and move into a gnoseological and aesthesic argument (on how Mariátegui and Gramsci were not only understood but also sensed), delinking from the epistemology of Western modernity and postmodernity and from the restrictive aesthetics frame in modern European thought.

When you look at the Americas, instead of Asia and Africa, our relations to Europe follow different trajectories than those of the other two continents. The Americas includes the US, which during the struggle for decolonization of the Cold War supported decolonization in Africa and Asia and sustained the foundation of the State of Israel (one year after India's and Pakistan's independence from the UK). At the same time, the US intervened in South America—culturally, diplomatically, and militarily—to contain, if not suppress, the Cuban Revolution, which was the South American/Caribbean parallel to the struggle for decolonization in Asia and Africa. Interestingly enough, the struggle for Cuban independence was termed "revolution," while the independence of India and others after that—including Algeria, South Africa, and the Zapatistas—were identified as decolonial struggles before independence. The independences in the first two cases ended settler colonialism. The second ended apartheid, and the fourth opened a distinctive path within an already existing nation-state. (The Zapatista movement remains a constant set of decolonial processes that started before January of 1994.) January of 1994 was not independence but a declaration of autonomy within the nation-state. Although the US supported decolonization in Asia and Africa in the name of freedom, democracy, and the right to self-determination, it also supported dictatorial regimes in South America and the Caribbean and challenged the outcome of the Cuban Revolution.[5]

In Asia and Africa, decolonization ended settler colonialism from Europe. The Cuban Revolution took over the control of the nation-state to end internal colonialism. Cuba's independence from Spain in 1898 was a transfer of power to the US, the consequence of the Hispano-American war. Moreover, the struggle for autodetermination in Asia and Africa that occupied most of the Cold War happened in the Americas and the Caribbean since the late eighteenth century: the US Revolution (1776), the Haitian Revolution (1804), and several South American countries' independence achieved from 1810 to 1830. Brazil achieved independence later in the nineteenth century, and the Spanish Caribbean has a complicated history that I won't here detail. What matters, though, is that in 1898 Spain lost, in the Hispano-American War, its last colonies, and they were in the Caribbean (Cuba and Puerto Rico). Spain lost also the Philippines, in the Pacific. Three years before, Japan was victorious in the Sino-Japanese war (1895). The consequences were that two new players, the US and Japan, were de facto entering the imperial game in the last decade of the twentieth century; the first occurred within the western European family, while the second introduced a disruption in the history of Western imperial formation. Western imperialisms since 1500 had been white, but the Japanese were, in the eyes of the West, part of the "yellow race." Remember that by the Berlin treatise, European countries distributed among themselves the entire continent of Africa, with the exception of Ethiopia.

What remains from Jean-François Lyotard's *The Postmodern Condition* is his distaste for macro narratives, which he identified with the "the modern condition." I cannot join him in that disdain because I need to decolonially reconstitute what modern macro narratives destituted in order to trace the formation, transformation, and current status of the colonial matrix of power (CMP), which was not visible yet at the time Lyotard wrote the book. But even if it had been, I do not think that it would have been his concern. Nevertheless, it is certainly mine and that of all of those who not only see coloniality but also—and perhaps primarily—sense it. Lyotard was looking at only half the story, which after Hegel's philosophy of history appeared as the totality. And even though he certainly would have been aware of the recent history of French colonialism in Africa and the struggles of decolonization going on at the time of the "postmodern condition," coloniality would not have been necessary, welcome, or hardly sufficient. As the well-known dictum goes, the hunter cannot tell the story as the hunted would tell it. Not that the hunter does not have the right to tell his or her story. He or she doesn't have the right to tell the story or to ignore what is relevant for the hunted, for what we learn from the story of the hunter is about the hunter, not about the hunted. That is one example of the double movement, constitution/destitution (modernity/coloniality). The issue is not, as I am often critiqued for, that western European or Anglo-US scholars and intellectuals should not talk about "coloniality." The question is to what extent each of us senses—feels—coloniality. It is a question of who is talking about what and why. These are basic questions for the politics of decolonial investigations.

Concepts are not floating signifiers of universal scopes that can land wherever and work, detached from the persons, institutions, and societies that need (see chapter 13 and epilogue for more details), create, and use them. They are embedded in the core of lived local histories—whether the local history of western Europe or of the South American Andes—in the memories and sensibilities of living and thinking. That is why geopolitics and body-politics of knowledge are necessary to divest the illusion that concepts created in Europe are relevant for the rest of the world and for non-European praxes of living and thinking.[6] What we are facing here is nothing less than the colonial epistemic and ontological differences, which, by revealing how they work, decolonial thinking contributes to negating and delinking from. If the question "can non-Europeans think?" has been asked, it is because the colonial difference, presupposed in the rhetoric of Western modernity, has doubted or disqualified the ability of non-Europeans to think (see epilogue).

Decolonial macro narratives are unavoidable in advancing gnoseological and aesthesic reconstitutions and bringing to light what modern macro narratives destituted. The macro narratives Lyotard disdained were the narratives of modernity, and I agree with him on this. I do not mean "of modernity" in the sense of the ontological unfolding of universal history. His critique is ingrained in the same frame of mind (sensing, emotioning, and reasoning) as the one he was critiquing. I am not disqualifying Lyotard's critique. I am underscoring the regional value of his argument. Decolonially, macro narratives are necessary and nonnegotiable, for the simple reason that they emerge from the experiences of the destituted, who are experiencing modernity from the exteriority that modernity created.

When it comes to the question of the human in postmodernity, that is, the question of the posthuman, the same decolonial logic applies: neither liberal humanism (Gifford) nor Marxist humanism (Althusser) nor posthumanism, but something else not trapped by the either/or totalizing possibilities. That something else is the exteriority where delinking and reexistence inhabit. It is the place of the decolonial at large because the totality is controlled by modernity/coloniality. What this means is that we must open up the question of the very notion of human and humanism (see chapter 12) beyond the human species, toward Earth and cosmic *vincularidad* (relationality). It is urgent that we delink from the logic of modernity/coloniality (either A or B, either left or right, either me or my enemies, either human or nonhuman, either human or posthuman), which is precisely where Carl Schmitt located the political: the political is about friends and enemies.[7] There is no place for the political beyond that dichotomy. The political, in the politics of decolonial investigations, is not to take side A or B but to delink from the very trap of totalitarian dichotomies. Just as the postmodern celebrated the becoming of a world without borders, populated by fragments and not macro narratives, so the corporations, the banks, and neoliberalism in general were celebrating the same: a borderless world free of macro narratives. Thirty years later, the posthuman and the postanthropocentric overcoming of liberal humanism are celebrated by cheerleaders of the fourth industrial revolution who gather yearly in Davos.[8] With these caveats in mind I approach Mariátegui and Gramsci in South America and the Caribbean.

To focus on Gramsci in "Latin" America without examining the intellectual and political environment in which he was read, translated, used, and discussed would be a sort of un-Gramscian endeavor. As I understand it, Gramsci would not have written about Lenin in Italy without examining the situation there that may or may not have made Lenin relevant. In that regard, and for reasons that will be clarified in the following pages, I start by examining in parallel and in contrast both the Peruvian José Carlos Mariátegui (1894–1930) and the Sardinian Antonio Gramsci (1891–1937). The two great thinkers, who were contemporaries, have been placed in relation several times. The general tendency in these examinations is to underline the influences of Gramsci on Mariátegui. There are a few who have doubts about such an endeavor, although they do not radically contest the idea. The assumption here is that Gramsci could have influenced Mariátegui, never that Mariátegui could have influenced Gramsci. We are, in this assumption, at the core of the geopolitics of knowledge: European thinkers have priority over the rest of the world, even leftist thinkers. And this, of course, is not Gramsci's fault. The underlying presupposition is that "influence" goes from the center to the periphery of the modern/colonial world, never the other way around. I will come back to this issue. In the meantime, I invite you to think about it: they were almost the same age, three years difference. When Mariátegui was in Italy, he was about twenty-four and Gramsci was twenty-seven.

Gramsci was very influential in Argentina and Brazil (particularly after 1960).[9] The young Marxist generation of the era found fresh air in Gramsci's writing as well as the opportunity to break away from the institutional Marxism-Leninism that emanated from Moscow. Later on, we found Gramsci in Mexico (because of the Argentine émigrés in the mid-1970s), and his impact there can be traced today in several places and disciplines. But it is obvious and also necessary to remember that Gramsci was mainly influential within Marxism. For the contemporary debates in Latin America of the 1960s, like dependency theory, the philosophy of liberation, and Indianism (as voiced by the Bolivian Fausto Reinaga), Gramsci was not a necessary reference. If Reinaga had referred to Gramsci, he would have underscored, as he did when confronting Marxist discourse, that Indians were not peasants.[10] "Indians" is a racial/colonial category (crucial for Mariátegui and Quijano, although they are non-Indigenous), while "peasants" is a Marxist category based on social class in Europe after the Industrial Revolution.[11]

In the mid-1970s Jorge Rafael Videla was the architect of terror and of the "dirty war" in Argentina that left over thirty thousand "desaparecidos y desaparecidas" (missing ones). Those who survived migrated, to Spain, France, Venezuela, and many of them to Mexico. A number of presidents followed Videla, from 1981 to 1982, until "the return to democracy" with elected president Raúl Alfonsín. In the mid-1980s, the Argentinian émigrés to Mexico returned to the country—and with them Gramsci. The historical conditions that made Gramsci necessary in the 1960s had radically changed through the turbulence of the 1970s and the return to democracy in the mid-1980s. While postcolonial critiques of colonialism were emerging in the 1980s, in Europe and the US from the pens of Asian immigrants, in South America Gramsci was necessary to continue the rejuvenation of Marxism (controlled by the Communist Party) that had started in the 1960s. But the conditions were different: neoliberalism that was implanted with the coup d'état in Chile in 1973 and the dictatorship of Augusto Pinochet (followed by Rafael Videla in Argentina). But colonialism was neither a political nor an academic concern.

It was taken for granted that in Argentina colonialism ended in 1810, and in most of the rest of South America by the end of the nineteenth century. However, in the mid-1970s and in Mexico, the notion of "internal colonialism" entered the academic, intellectual, and political debates, joining the one on dependency theory. Whereas "decolonization" was the keyword to describe struggles for liberation in Asia and Africa, for the sensibility of the 1960s and 1970s the decolonization in "Latin" America was a moot question. Consequently, when in the 1980s the "postcolonial" moment was introduced in the US both to indicate "after liberation" and simultaneously as a critique of colonialism, in "Latin" America the debate centered on dependency, theology of liberation, internal colonialism, and the Cuban Revolution. Nevertheless, the Cuban Revolution was not framed in the context of similar struggles in Algeria and the decolonization already achieved (cf. India, Indonesia). It was framed in the context of the Cold War, and within that as a confrontation with the US (which of course it was). It was the fear or the excuse of communism that justified the military coup in Chile, the advent of brutal dictatorship in Argentina, and the interstate Operación Cóndor (1969–1981) that terrorized all of South America.[12] While the US was involved in Operación Cóndor, it was supporting decolonization in Africa and Asia in the name of freedom, democracy, modernization, and development.

The relevance of Gramsci in Latin America, before and after the interregnum of dictatorships and Operación Cóndor, was different from the conditions that made him necessary for the foundation of the scholarship that became known as "subaltern studies." This discipline, born in London in the 1970s, was based on the colonial history of India after 1947 and its struggles for the foundation of a nation-state after independence, when South America was under the duress of dictatorship and the lingering of dependency theory debates hung in the air. Aníbal Quijano's work in the 1980s prepared the terrain for the concept of "coloniality," which he launched in 1992. Colonialism was a basic concern for José Carlos Mariátegui, but he was not influential in the 1960s, when Gramsci was adopted by the young Marxist generation. But for Aníbal Quijano, Mariátegui (both were Peruvian, which I mean as a country and a region—the Andes—with a high percentage of Indigenous population) was as relevant as Gramsci was for Ranajit Guha and Indian subaltern studies.[13]

The preceding narrative and the influence of Mariátegui on the thinking of Aníbal Quijano (who was also deeply involved in the dependency theory debates) explain why I deviated from the proposed topic and addressed instead "Gramsci and the decolonial," which puts Gramsci in conversation with decolonial thinking in South/Central America and the Caribbean, a sphere of political and epistemic debate in which Gramsci was not influential. At the same time, however, these conversations were of great import in the region, and mostly unknown or ignored in western Europe.

Gramsci was introduced into left-wing discourse in the early 1960s by the "Latin" (non-Indigenous, non-African) American left.[14] He was a key figure for neither Afro-Caribbean nor Afro-Continental nor Indigenous politically oriented intellectuals. Gramsci was, in short, relevant to left-wing intellectuals of primarily European descent. In that context, he was not related at all, in "Latin" America, to any issues regarding "colonialism." He was first of all a helpful thinker for local Argentinian, Brazilian, and Bolivian Marxists who were detaching themselves from the bureaucracy of the Communist Party and, later on, were entering the debate about the "state" when "modernization and development" (addressed by dependency theory) mutated into "transition to democracy," and the state became the main actor of a new melodrama of "development." "Transition to democracy" was the key expression. The Gramscian left coexisted with, on the one hand, the rehearsal of liberal discourses in the ex-colonies and, on the other, dependency theory and the theology of liberation.[15]

Before the 1980s and the displacement of the debates on the transition to democracy, the left in Argentina and Mexico was divided between supporters of Louis Pierre Althusser and Nicos Poulantzas on the one hand and followers of Gramsci on the other.[16] In Bolivia, it was the period in which René Zavaleta

Mercado was still relying on Gramsci but at the same time was heavily focused on the colonial history of Bolivia that, a few years later, led him to abandon Gramsci and concentrate on theorizing from the history of Bolivia rather than from the debates in the Communist Party or from what Gramsci had to say about the Italian Southern Question.[17] Nevertheless, in Mexico during the last years of his life and while working on the national-popular movement in Bolivia, Zavaleta Mercado (like Mariátegui before him and the Gramscians in Argentina and Brazil) detached himself from Marxism-Leninism, though he kept Marx and Gramsci in his overall original Marxist framework.[18] What characterizes René Zavaleta Mercado's work, like that of Mariátegui and Gramsci, was his originality and his close scrutiny of Bolivian and Latin American sociohistory.[19] In all these debates, colonialism in Argentina and Brazil was out of the question.[20] The idea that colonialism ended mostly in the first half of the nineteenth century with independence from Spain (and later Portugal) was taken for granted. During the years that Gramsci was occupying certain quarters (the 1960s and early 1970s), in another country, Mexico, two influential sociologists—Pablo González Casanova and Rodolfo Stavenhagen—were focusing on "internal colonialism."[21]

Gramsci had entered Latin America as the "savior" of the young leftist generation that was detaching itself from the Communist Party. One could say, approaching Gramsci with regard to colonialism in South America and the Caribbean, that Gramsci's "Southern Question" could be explained through the concept of internal colonialism, but in that case, it would be a Latin American interpretation since the concept did not come from Gramsci himself, and the Southern Question in Italy is, to put it mildly, quite different from the history of the Southern Question in the South American Andes. Internal colonialism was a burning issue in Latin America, as important as the Southern Question in Italy. Decolonially speaking, internal colonialism was bringing forward and preparing the terrain for the advent of the concept of coloniality. If coloniality is the common underlying logic of all Atlantic colonialism, then internal colonialism is a mutation of coloniality: the Spanish colonial settlers were replaced by the native Creole population of European descent. Similar indeed to what happened in Asia and Africa after decolonization, except that the native elites who maintained coloniality in the country were not of European descent. A significant distinction must be made between decolonial struggles in Asia and Africa during the Cold War, the role of Gramsci in subaltern studies, and the national question in Latin America during the Cold War.

The geo-body politics of knowing appears here in full, displacing the assumptions of the universality of knowledge that hold the key to transcendental truths. Southern Italy and the South American Andes, where Gramsci and Mariátegui lived, thought, and acted, were entangled in the colonial matrix of power (CMP) of their time and in their respective settings. Given the meaning of the South, Gramsci in southern Europe and Mariátegui in South America were both struggling with the liberal and Marxist hegemony that they both simultaneously embraced and rejected.

III   Revisiting Mariátegui and Gramsci

As mentioned above, the most obvious place to begin to deal with the Sardinian Gramsci in relation to decolonial thinking is to look at him in tandem with the Andean Peruvian José Carlos Mariátegui. Mariátegui was well acquainted with Marxists of Eastern Europe—Rosa Luxembourg (1871–1919), Georg (György) Lukàcs (1885–1991), and Antonio Labriola (1843–1904)—but Gramsci seems to have been as unknown to Mariátegui as Mariátegui was to Gramsci. Probably, they met when Mariátegui was in Italy, but there is no correspondence to tell us that the meeting was a flashing light for Mariátegui or that Gramsci noticed concerns similar to his own in this young Peruvian intellectual. The influence of Gramsci on Mariátegui seems to have been more wishful thinking on the part of Mariátegui's followers than a historically documented event. What is undeniably true is that both Gramsci and Mariátegui were facing and living parallel "colonial" situations, or, better yet, they were touched by the colonial in their respective local histories: the imperial difference in the South of Europe and the colonial difference in the South American Andes (Peru, Bolivia, Ecuador). Two distinct paths of internal colonialism. But internal colonialism in the history of Europe is not the same as it is in the history of South America. Gramsci's Italy was part of the unfolding of European history from the early city-states of the Italian Renaissance, while the South American Andes at the time of Mariátegui were the outcome of emerging modern/colonial states one century after gaining independence from Spain, coupled with the dense Indigenous history and an Indigenous population that shaped Mariátegui's Marxism.

Gramsci presented the dilemma of the Southern Question in free indirect style and confronted the Southern subaltern with two options: either be with the local elite or be with the workers of the mainland. The colonial question was connected to industrialization and was in turn embedded in the Industrial Revolution. "The dilemma: Are you, poor Sardinian devils, a bloc with the gentry of Sardegna, who have ruined you and who are the local overseers of capitalist exploitation? Or are you a bloc with the revolutionary workers on the mainland, who stand for the abolition of exploitation and emancipation of all who are oppressed? This dilemma was rammed into the heads of those present."[22]

For Mariátegui, the dilemmas arose from the long-lasting colonial legacies and the peculiarity of a nonexisting bourgeoisie in Peru, and, therefore, no proper working class in the sense Gramsci was talking about:

> The agrarian problem is first and foremost the problem of eliminating feudalism in Peru, which should have been done by the democratic-bourgeois regime that followed the War of Independence. But in its one hundred years as a republic, Peru has not had a genuine bourgeois class, a true capitalist class. The old feudal class—camouflaged or disguised as a republican bourgeoisie—has kept its position. The policy of disentitlement, initiated by the War of Independence as a logical consequence of its ideology, did not lead to the development of small property. The old landholding class had not lost its supremacy. The survival of the latifundistas, in practice, preserved the latifundium. Disentitlement struck at the Indian community. During a century of Republican rule, great agricultural property actually has grown stronger and expanded, despite the theoretical liberalism of our constitution and the practical necessities of the development of our capitalist economy.[23]

In sum, the colonial conditions of the rural Italian south and of the industrial north were quite different from the colonial conditions of the ex-colonies in South America, where there was no equivalent to the Italian industrial north. The industrial north of the Americas is literally another story. Conversely, in the Southern Question there is no memory of ancient civilizations dispossessed of their lands and their civilization mutilated as in the Southern American Andes.

Once, in a lecture I mentioned this topic. I was asked during the Q&A period what I thought about the fact that Gramsci may have suffered more in prison under fascism than Mariátegui under internal colonialism. I politely responded that it was a moot point from a political perspective. It may be important in a discussion about Christian institutional morality. The problem is of course not who suffered more (for Indigenous and enslaved Africans and their descendants in the New World suffered, perhaps, more than Gramsci and Mariátegui together), but that Gramsci was in prison because of *fascism* or Mariátegui because of *internal colonialism* and his confrontation with the dictatorship of Augusto B. Leguía. They both were nonetheless targets of the politics of Western modernity and the underlying logic of coloniality: that is the function of destitution. To advance modernity and democracy, if you are on top of institutions that allows you to do that, you have to destitute and eliminate to save capitalism and democracy. The continuity of this principle is obvious today.[24] The problem is that one cannot expect to solve Peruvian problems based on Gramsci's suffering more under fascism than Mariátegui under internal colonialism and Leguía's dictatorship during his early years of critical journalism. But the question reveals how the coloniality of knowing and being in the world infects our emotioning and thinking.

Let's take two parallel instances to illuminate the point I am trying to make. The first deals with the Southern Question and the second with the Indigenous issues. In Italy, given its specific tradition and the singularity of its history, the peasant question manifested itself in two typical and peculiar forms: the Southern Question and the "Vatican Question."[25] For Mariátegui the assumption that the Indian problem is ethnic rather than a consequence of land dispossession is sustained by the most outmoded repertory of imperialist ideas. The concept of inferior races was useful to the western European white man for purposes of expansion and conquest. Mariátegui was not confused by the prevalent rhetoric of modernity of his time, and drastically cut across such naiveté: "To expect that the Indian will be emancipated through a steady crossing of the aboriginal race with white immigrants reflects an anti-sociological naiveté that could only occur to the primitive mentality of an importer of merino sheep. . . . The degeneration of the Peruvian Indian is a cheap invention of the sophists who serve feudal interests."[26] Mariátegui has exposed in his treatment of the "Indian Question" the rhetoric of modernity (civilization and progress) protected by the Peruvian *establishment* and the logic of coloniality that enacted the dispossession of Indian lands. Not by chance Mariátegui is, for Aníbal Quijano, the immediate ancestor for conceptualizing the coloniality of power. Since I am following Quijano's steps, I am not just reporting on Gramsci in "Latin" America from a neutral disciplinary perspective, but in decolonial dialogue with Mariátegui and Gramsci through Quijano's seminal work.

As you can see, Gramsci's local history and Mariátegui's local history are quite far apart although connected by the logic of coloniality: even if they are both walking in the same direction, they have a need to walk parallel roads. Each of them has his own issues to address in his own geo- and body-political locations. To expect that reading Gramsci would help to deal with issues in Peru (or South and Central America or the Caribbean) would be like expecting that reading Mariátegui in Italy would help to address the Southern Question. Of course, Mariátegui could have learned from Gramsci and Gramsci from Mariátegui. But to put Gramsci over Mariátegui would be to reproduce the coloniality of knowledge from the left. The reason that Gramsci is better known than Mariátegui is due to epistemic power differentials and the coloniality of knowledge, of which the left is neither exempt nor innocent. And, of course, this was *not* Gramsci's problem, for he did what he had to do. It is a problem of the "uses" of Gramsci, by the "Latin" American left and by the postcolonial market today.

In any event, what counts is that Mariátegui and Gramsci were radical critics grounded in their own geohistorical and biographical being in the world, confronting the limits of Marxism and their respective abusive states. Mariátegui was facing the lasting legacy of Spanish colonialism, plus the more recent colonialism without colonies (which is just a mutation of coloniality) under British and US economic management. Here is one of the many paragraphs and pages Mariátegui devoted to the issue:

> There is a chapter in the evolution of the Peruvian economy that opens with the discovery of guano and nitrates and closes with the loss of this wealth. . . . These materials, on a remote coast in the South Pacific, were essential to the developments of European or Western industrialism. In addition, unlike other Peruvian products they were not hampered by the rudimentary and primitive state of land transport. Whereas gold, silver, copper, and coal mined from the Andes had to be conveyed great distances over rugged mountain ranges, guano and nitrate deposits lay on the coast within easy reach of the cargo ships.[27]

Both Mariátegui and Gramsci were also facing the quarrel between colonial legacies and the project of nation building. (Italy united in 1861 after being torn apart by Spanish, Austrian, and French colonial expansion in Europe; Peru began the process of nation building in 1821.) Mariátegui lived through the second presidency of the extremely right-wing Augusto B. Leguía (1919–1930) and Gramsci through Benito Mussolini (1925–1943). Both, in their singular local histories, traced parallel trajectories of independent thought, epistemic disobedience confronting the church, and liberal and Marxist doctrines. In this sense they left for us the legacies of the march toward decolonial freedom. Although the term "colonialism" is frequently used in Gramsci's *Notebooks*, it is not one of his keywords. Gramsci has seldom been quoted for having given the term "colonialism" a theoretical meaning, as he is quoted for his concepts of "hegemony" and "subalternity." "Colonialism," however, is one of Mariátegui's key concepts. As a matter of fact, Mariátegui's use of "colonialism" is the forerunner of "coloniality." Colonialism was a historical concern for Gramsci, as is clear when he addresses the Southern Question. But Gramsci's colonial experience was very different from Mariátegui's. Nevertheless, both were touched by coloniality, from which no one could escape in the twentieth century, when the tentacles of progress and civilization were all over the planet. However, an important consideration for both of them was that they were thinkers whose ideas arose from their historical and personal experiences rather than from previous theories or disciplinary requirement. There were both undisciplinary thinkers but of course not undisciplined.

Both Mariátegui and Gramsci were voracious readers; they knew and pondered coexisting theories. Because they grounded their theorizing in their geo- and body-political roots, they remain exemplary intellectual guides, irreducible to one another. As original thinkers, they confronted theories with phenomena to be accounted for, and they challenged existing theories that were derailed by their understanding. Both, in their own local histories and extrapolating from them, confronted the limits of the Marxism of their time as well as the ideas of many others. Thus, while Gramsci provided a wealth of concepts and insights to the renovation of Marxist thinking, Mariátegui provided the conditions for the advent of the concept of coloniality (and hence, decoloniality) and taught us to understand modernity from its receiving end.[28]

IV Reading Gramsci in "Latin" America; Not Reading Mariátegui in Western Europe (and Italy)

There are two common assumptions among scholars and intellectuals who have compared Mariátegui and Gramsci that I would like to call into question here.[29] I already mentioned that Gramsci's influence on Mariátegui is assumed by some, although it is questioned by others. However, no one has even insinuated that Gramsci reframed the Southern Question because he was influenced by Mariátegui's concerns with colonialism in the Andes. The fact that the issue is not raised is a blatant case of the coloniality of knowledge. Influence—in the framework of the coloniality of knowledge—is centrifugal. It goes from Europe to out of Europe; it is never centripetal, like "natural resources" are. Moreover, I have the impression that to enhance Mariátegui's contributions his followers need to postulate or insinuate Gramsci's influence on him, as if Mariátegui cannot stand on his own. Non-Europeans cannot think, as the dictum goes (see epilogue).

To the point: one of the evaluators of this article (who I assume dwelled in the North Atlantic), when it was originally to be published in the volume *Postcolonial Gramsci*, noted that Gramsci, at several opportunities, commented on the situation in South America and on the question of "Latinity." I would respond that in the same fashion Mariátegui has produced countless articles and comments on Europe, on Italy, on the Communist Party, and so on. So, this indeed will be another interesting article to write: what Gramsci had to say about South America and what Mariátegui had to say about Italy, Europe, the European Communist Party, and so on. However, the evaluator's observation did not elaborate on what each author had to say about the country and region of the other. His/her comment was centrifugal. However, to consider only what Gramsci has to say about South America without paying attention to what Mariátegui has to say about Italy and Europe means simply to leave the coloniality of knowledge intact. Such a procedure is obedient to the same self-colonized logic of the South American and Caribbean intellectuals who put Gramsci first and Mariátegui second. My article was (and this chapter is) an effort to shift this colonial geography of reasoning. A probe from the perspective of the politics of decolonial investigations is necessary to delink from colonial epistemic and ontological differences.[30] And a probe from the perspective of gnoseological and aesthesic reconstitutions is necessary to circumscribe the scope of epistemic and aesthetic regulations of knowing and sensing.

Honoring the outside evaluator's comment (with the previous caveat in mind), let's see what Gramsci had to say about Latin America. In his critique of Lamberti Sorrentino's book *Latinitá dell'America*, Gramsci asked, "Are Central and South Americans Latin?" Gramsci asked this question to prepare the Italian reader for his critique of Sorrentino.[31] He was not addressing South and Central Americans, but the Italian readership. The majority of the population of European descent in "Latin" America knows that their languages and cultures are not of German, English, or French descent, but of Italian, Portuguese, and Spanish descent. The social roles of people migrating from the South of Europe and from northwestern (French and Anglo-Saxon) Europe are clearly marked in the literature (novels) from the mid-nineteenth to the first half of the twentieth century. "Latin" in South America meant—at the time the adjective was added to the name of the continent—people of Iberian descent. The French Caribbean was not considered "Latin" American. And contingents of Italian immigrants toward the end of the nineteenth century and after (mainly residing in the Atlantic Coast from Buenos Aires to New York) were not relevant to the previous political decision to call South and Central America "Latin." In the second paragraph of the same entry, Gramsci observes, "Characteristic of South and Central America is a considerable number of Indians who, albeit passively, exercise an influence on the state: it would be useful to have information on the social status of these Indians, on their economic importance, on their role in land ownership and industrial production."[32]

Since Gramsci was addressing Italian readers (and passing over his comment on the passivity of the Indians, which exemplified the landowner myth about the "lazy Indian" in South and Central America), we cannot assume that he was saying this (or that he had anything of interest to say) to Peruvians who were reading Mariátegui or people of other South and Central American countries on the Indian question.[33] Furthermore, in the Italian text, Gramsci's phrase (which Buttigieg translates in the passage quoted above as "Indians") is "Red Skin": "L'America meridionale e centrale è caratterizzata da un numero ragguardevole di pellirossa." This is a noun that in the European tradition goes back to the eighteenth century and identifies all Indigenous people in the Americas, starting with the British colonies and later the US. "Redskin" is also the common vernacular in Hollywood cowboy movies of the twentieth century.

Mariátegui, who died seven years before Gramsci, published *Seven Interpretive Essays*, from which the earlier quotations are drawn, in 1928, and he also wrote many articles that overwhelmingly, indirectly, and without his awareness addressed questions Gramsci was asking in his critique of Sorrentino. This is not, of course, a critique of Gramsci. But we should dismiss any expectation that because Gramsci wrote about South and Central America, what he wrote was relevant for South Americans who were living their own experiences, which were alien to the one Gramsci was living in Italy. As is always the case, what we (all of us) say about event X or person Z is more about ourselves than about X or Z. Who said what, why, and when are basic questions for the politics of decolonial investigations and for gnoseological and aesthesic reconstitutions. Which of course prompts questions to be asked of the observer writing this chapter: a son of Italian immigrants in Argentina who studied philosophy and semiotics.

Now, regarding Gramsci's assessment of South and Central America as well as his assessment of the intellectuals in these locations, his views are certainly very limited. He seems to have in mind "organic intellectuals" and completely bypasses some of his contemporaries, like Mariátegui himself or, from the previous generation, the Cuban José Martí (1853–1895), who died when Gramsci and Mariátegui were children. This is not the place to explore dissident perspectives of not only Creoles (born in Latin America of Spanish descent) and mestizos, but also Indians and Africans in South America. In this regard, Gramsci's views are circumscribed to the European perspective, while Mariátegui offers a corrective to the type of comments that prevail today. The bottom line, however, is not *what* Mariátegui and Gramsci said about the histories and societies of the other, but *why* they said it: what their statements about Europe and South America, respectively, say about themselves. In both cases, what they said, the *enoncé*, was implicated in their own unapologetically original conceptual and political frameworks (their own enunciations). In other words, what Gramsci said about South America and what Mariátegui said about Europe are more relevant to understanding their thoughts than to understanding the issues relevant at the time for Europe or for South America and Central America.

A second reader of my original article pointed out that Gramsci's interest in South America emerged out of an "internationalization of the Southern Question." True. Based on what I just said about the enunciation, it could be surmised that Mariátegui's interest in Europe, Asia, Russia, and Africa was based on his interest in the "internationalization of the Indian Question." And both were right: there are *Souths* all over the globe, as we know today, with popular expressions such as "Global South" and "Global Indigeneity." The same focus held for Mariátegui as well. He has several writings on Europe, on the Italian Communist Party, and on internationalization, and obviously these preoccupations do not arise from the "internationalization of the Southern Question" but from the internationalization of the "Andean Question." I admire Gramsci, but I am not ready to sacrifice the contributions of South American thinkers and fall into an imperialism of the left using Gramsci as a rallying banner. On the other hand, the fact that Gramsci wrote *on* South America and Mariátegui *on* Europe should not make us forget that it is the loci of enunciation rather than the object they talk about that reveals the full meaning of what they say about South America and Europe respectively.

Furthermore, my argument is about the *uses* of Gramsci *in* South America rather than about Gramsci's *interest* in South America. Still, all of this, prompted by a question from one of the evaluators of this article, is a moot point. I was asked to write about the uses of Gramsci in South America and not about what he wrote and/or why he wrote what he wrote about South America. Yet when looking at the biographies of both authors, although they may have met in Italy when Mariátegui was there, nevertheless in 1920 Gramsci was not yet the Gramsci we know today and certainly not the Gramsci of the Southern Question, which he wrote around 1926 when Mariátegui was already back in Peru.[34] Mariátegui's most reliable biographer, Alberto Flores Galindo, in no place in his biography documents a Gramscian influence on Mariátegui.[35]

And a final note that takes us back to the coloniality of knowledge is the possibility that Mariátegui's influence on Gramsci has never been mentioned.

The coloniality of knowledge is tantamount to epistemic racism, from which the Marxist left is not always exempt (see the epilogue).

IV Geopolitics of Knowledge: Mariátegui's "Colonial Question" and Gramsci's "Southern Question" Revisited

IV.1

Where Mariátegui and Gramsci run at the same speed and in the same direction is on the Colonial Question and the Southern Question, respectively. However, their emphasis varies. In Mariátegui's work, colonial legacies in the Andes are as central as hegemony is for Gramsci. If the future for Gramsci was how to build socialist hegemony, for Mariátegui it was how to decolonize and delink from colonial legacies. If at the point that Mariátegui was still thinking within a socialist horizon (even though official Marxists did not recognize him as one of them, for there was no place for land and Indigeneity in Marxism), he was nonetheless walking toward it on a road parallel to Gramsci's. Each of them was facing "similar" historical processes on "different" historical trajectories, but both within the CMP: different local histories within similar global designs. Gramsci frequently reminds the reader that the Southern Question came out of the emerging Italian bourgeoisie, liberating itself from the Bourbon monarchy, unifying Italy, and starting the process of nation-state building while facing the heavy burden of the clergy. This was not a major problem for Mariátegui. Peru did not have the pope, but rather other institutions guiding the structuring of society and of history. For Mariátegui the question of the nation-state (whose rise to prominence started about a century before his active intellectual and political life) was strictly connected to Spanish colonial legacies, and to the insertion—in his time—of the US in South American political life, conflicting with the already established British imperial management (coloniality without settler colonialism) since the second half of the nineteenth century. If Gramsci emphasized the role of the clergy in South America, it was because of his experience in Italy. And although the clergy had and still has a significant presence in South America, it does not permeate society with the same intensity as the papacy in Italy. That was a problem for Gramsci rather than for Mariátegui. Mariátegui had other pressing issues to attend to that were not as relevant for Gramsci. Mariátegui had other enemies: Spanish colonial legacies and secularized Creoles and mestizos, land- and mine-owner elites who implanted internal colonialism in conflictive relations with the church. These, of course, were not problems for Gramsci.

It is not that Mariátegui was oblivious to religion. It is that for him religion had priority over the institutional clergy. He devoted a chapter of his *Seven Interpretive Essays* to "The Religious Factor." The Andean region, and in particular Peru, was where Mariátegui dwelled on the ruins and memories of Tawantinsuyu (Inca's territoriality). For Italy it was Rome and the papacy's religious history. And it is precisely in his historical grounding that Mariátegui begins his chapter on religion (not in Rome): "The Religion of Tawantinsuyu." Cuzco, in the Incanate (the parallel equivalent to the Roman Empire), was the center of the world just as Rome was for the Roman Empire. But the "religions" were different: Rome was the center of enunciation of Christian theology. The Incanate, and Cuzco, was a place that Spanish Christians declared was without religion and managed by the devil, a good justification for transplanting and constituting Spanish religion and government, while simultaneously destituting local government and spiritualities. It was indeed a heavy issue to deal with: to accept Andean spirituality as a religion instead of attributing it to the work of the devil. Relevant for the argument is the trajectory of Catholicism and Christianity during and after independence, and the secular twist taken by the independent governance of Peru. However, and according to the interpretation of Mariátegui by the prominent Peruvian intellectual Flores Galindo (1949–1990), "Perú had a liberal and patriotic clergy from the first day of its revolution. In a few isolated cases, civil liberalism was inflexibly Jacobin, and, in even fewer cases, anti-religious. Most of our liberals came from the Masonic lodges that were so active in preparing the independence, so they almost all professed the deism that made Freemasonry in these Latin countries a kind of spiritual and political substitute for the Reformation."[36]

To speculate about the clergy and secular intellectuals in Latin America from the background of the clergy in Italy may have been significant in Italy, but not in Latin America. All of this happened because of the confusion in Western epistemology of the said with the saying—another reason to move away from it and to work, in emotioning and reasoning, toward gnoseological and aesthesic reconstitutions of epistemology and aesthetics. Although there is of course much more to say about the question of the clergy, the intellectuals, and the local histories of Italy and Peru, I hope these few indications help us to understand that we are facing crossing gazes when Gramsci talks about Latin America and Mariátegui about Italy and Europe.[37] They were both concerned with, and theorizing from, the irreducible differences of their local histories. However, they were located at different points of the colonial matrix of power: Gramsci in the South of Italy, a degraded part of Europe since the pronouncements of Kant and Hegel, while Mariátegui was located in the

Andes and South America, a degraded part of the world in Hegel's philosophy of history. Located at different points of the colonial matrix, Gramsci and Mariátegui were responding from their own locations to the imperial universality of liberalism, Marxism, and Christianity.

IV.2

If we now turn the table around and attempt to understand the Southern Question and Gramsci's take on it from the history of Peru, we would find out that Italy and Peru in the 1920s were going through similar situations at two different ends of the CMP's spectrum: two different manifestations of internal colonialism, one in the very history of Europe's South and the other in the history of European colonial expansion and domination.

Looked at from the standard perspective of Western universal history to which local histories have been appended by Westerners, Italy and Peru have nothing to do with each other. The first was industrial, and the second lay in the confines of the West, a former colony of Spain, with a large "Indian" population, and industrialization not having yet reached it. But if we look at these histories from the perspective of the colonial matrix of power (which I describe in the introduction to this book) that emerged in the sixteenth century and is still alive and well, then Italy and Peru are two clear cases of the rearticulation of intramural imperial (the South of Europe) and extramural colonial (the South of America) differences.[38] If the South of Europe is also a manifestation of internal colonialism, Italy is not a former colony of Europe but, on the contrary, a fundamental piece in the formation of the idea of Europe.

Colonial differences were established vis-à-vis and projected over the non-European population (e.g., Indians and Blacks in the sixteenth century) and vis-à-vis the European population (e.g., Jews and Roma in the same period) as well as destituted regions within a country, like southern Italy. In the eighteenth century, when the control of knowledge, and consequently the management of authority and the economy, moved to the North of Europe (Germany, France, England), a new dimension of the difference appeared: the imperial difference in the history of Europe itself in the eighteen century. The South of Europe lost the clout it had had during the Renaissance (which revalued ancient Greece) and the conquest of America by Spain and Portugal. Furthermore, during the Renaissance the imperial difference was only extramural, projected onto Muslims in the South of Europe—who were expelled from the Iberian Peninsula—and later onto the Ottoman sultanate. I shall remind the reader that colonial and imperial differences are epistemic constructs made possible by the actors, institutions, and languages that control knowledge. In the eighteenth century, English, French, and German took over the management of knowledge, displacing the languages of the (Italian, Spanish, and Portuguese). To control knowledge is more than controlling the content (the enunciated); it is mainly controlling the knowing and the saying, that is, the logic that organizes and manages the content (the enunciation).[39] The idea of the "South of Europe" was put in place in the eighteenth century with all the consequences of its internal structuring that are no doubt in the underground of the European Union. For Gramsci, as a southerner himself, his dwelling in this world was imbued with southern memories and concerns; Mariátegui, on the other hand, was experiencing the legacy of external colonial difference that put him in the very notable situation of being neither European nor Indian, yet still feeling the consequences of the colonial difference.[40]

V   Gramsci in "Latin" America: How the Coloniality of Knowledge Works and Traps Us All

In this section I go forward with the politics of decolonial investigations and with gnoseological reconstitution. I hope the previous sweeping contextualization makes understandable the following question: who introduced Gramsci into "Latin" America, and when and why? Mariátegui and Gramsci were foundational thinkers whose legacies transcended their time and context. Although Gramsci's influence has been wider than Mariátegui's, this disparity is understandable once we know how the CMP works and we understand what colonial epistemic differences mean. When Gramsci entered "Latin" America in the 1960s, those who introduced his ideas respected Mariátegui, but the Andean situation in "Latin" America (of which they themselves were part) was less meaningful than what was happening in Italy and in Europe.[41] Of course, it is still unthinkable that Mariátegui might have entered Italy in the same way: peripheral thinkers are peripheral (see epilogue) and invisible in the European hegemony of discourse (from both right and left). This is why Sartre prefaced Fanon, but it is unthinkable to imagine one of Sartre's books being prefaced by Fanon.

But why was Gramsci introduced into intellectual and political debates, and when, exactly? During my first and second years at the University of Córdoba, Argentina, in 1963, I learned quickly (since I had enrolled in an MA program in philosophy and literature) that there was a new publication being steered by a young generation of Marxist intellectuals, some professors, and public intellectuals with considerable clout at the university, in the intellectual milieu of the city (by then with a population of around six hundred thousand and close to a million today) and in the country. The journal they published was named *Pasado y Presente*. In England, *Past and Present*, under Gramsci's influence, was created in 1952. Ranajit Guha had been in England since 1959, and in 1970 he initiated the Subaltern Studies project. Gramsci was in the air. Soon, after the first issues of *Pasado y Presente* were released in Cordoba, Argentina, I found myself and other students reading Antonio Gramsci. This interest started with the young intellectual dissidents that broke up with the Communist Party shortly after the fall of Juan Domingo Perón in 1955 (notice the coincidence of the year with the Bandung Conference). Curiously and interestingly enough, Gramsci entered Argentina through Córdoba (the second-largest city, very continental) and not through the Atlantic port of Buenos Aires. In Brazil, Gramsci arrived later but under similar circumstances. After the fall of Getulio Vargas in 1964, there was reading and breathing room for a young generation that felt cornered not only by Vargas's dictatorial regime but also by the Communist Party.[42] Gramsci, in other words, was invited to an environment of strong nationalist revival in the early years of the Cold War and the early years of the US's plans for development and modernization of Latin America (note, in this case, my lack of quotation marks or parentheses).

The US program of modernization and development was initiated after Harry Truman's presidential address of 1949, in which he declared that many countries were underdeveloped and needed to be developed. Shortly after Truman's rhetoric, countries to be developed were classified as "Third World" countries. You see how the rhetoric of modernity racializes not only people, but regions and countries. "Development" and "modernization" replaced "progress" and "civilizing missions," the British Empire's rhetoric of modernity. But Gramsci was not referenced (and I do not know if he was read) in the debates on dependency theory, although within the time period that Gramsci was introduced to Latin America, dependency theorists who were also of leftist inclinations had other problems in mind.[43] If anything, "*dependentistas*" were closer to Fanon (*The Wretched of the Earth* was translated into Spanish in 1962), and closer to the struggle for decolonization in Africa than to Gramsci, even if there were differing points of view between Fanon and dependency theorists when it came to the role of the state and racism.[44] Today it could be said that Gramsci's Southern Question implied dependency, but the experience of dependency was lived differently in the South of Italy and South America. As for Mariátegui, he perceived dependency, although he did not have a name for it, which was introduced around twenty years after his death. His words for it were "colonialism" and "racism.|"

Dependency was not a problem of the intramural colonial differences in Europe (the Jewish question, the Roma question) or of the intramural imperial differences, for the South of Europe was a consequence of the intramural imperial difference enacted early on by northern Anglo monarchies (beginning with Elizabeth I of England) that were confronting the Latin Catholic monarchies (Phillip II and Phillip III in Spain). The well-known "Black Legend" was a demonizing strategy (very common today in international politics) of the English monarchy that evinced the intramural imperial difference that would eventually place Anglo-Saxon and Protestant monarchies over Latin Catholic ones in the South.[45] At the same time, the intramural colonial differences were created in Europe in reference to their internal others (e.g., Jews, Roma, refugees). Imperial differences are state imperial politics toward other states that are comparable in many ways but need to degrade. England created the Black Legend to demonize and erode imperial Spain. Colonial differences, at that time, were state politics toward the people of underdeveloped countries. Early on, an extramural imperial difference was traced between Europe and similar civilizations that Europe considered inferior (like the Ottomans). On the other hand, the extramural colonial difference was created to classify first of all Indians and Blacks, and then the people colonized by England and France during the nineteenth century. If you look around, this entire configuration is still alive and well. Italy was placed in the south, but still it was one of Europe's industrial countries, while Brazil, Argentina, Chile, and Peru were not. All these countries were enduring the consequences of being cast and classified by external colonial differences. There was no room for imperial differences: Aztecs, Mayas, and Incas were dismantled as civilizations and their populations mutated into "Indians."

But that was not all. Young Argentinian and Marxist dissidents from the Communist Party (José Aricó, Juan Carlos Portantiero, Oscar del Barco, Héctor Schmucler) introduced Gramsci into the political and intellectual debate, while many other issues were going on concurrently. The introduction of Gramsci into the debate happened more or less at the same time as it occurred in England. But the local histories where quite different. In Argentina, the previous generation was also dissident, and their inspiration to delink from the CMP was an amalgam of Marxism at large and Peronism.[46] They were brilliant analysts of the global economy and the imperial reordering after WWII. For them, as for Mariátegui after WWI, history was a key factor in understanding Argentinian history from the colony to the republic and from the republic to Juan Domingo Perón. These dissidents, who had made their statement since the 1950s after the fall of Perón, were above all nationalists, and their school of thought became known as the " nationalist left."[47] It was at the intersection of two generation of leftist intellectuals that Gramsci entered Argentina. The Gramscian generation was less concerned with Peronism and nationalism than with renovating revolutionary thoughts. Gramsci came in on the same boat, so to speak, as French structuralism and poststructuralism. Gramsci, in other words, was part of a significant renewal of intellectual debate in Europe (Althusserians versus Gramscians) that traveled to Argentina and Brazil, and South America more generally.

European debates were replicated in South America. Althusserians and Gramscians debated with each other and coexisted without dialogue with dependency theorists, liberation theologians, and, in some sense and with a few exceptions (Aricó), the forgetting of Mariátegui. The point being that colonial legacies in South American countries' intellectual traditions, rooted in the history of the region, have to coexist with the importation of the most recent ideas being debated in Europe and the US. The reverse doesn't obtain. The politics of decolonial investigations has here a significant issue to redress, more so because the power differential applies also to the economy, politics, mass media, and education. Fashion applies in political theory and political economy as much as in consumer goods. Coloniality of power operates and molds subjectivities and behaviors across the entire spectrum of intellectual discourse, and impinges on the right, the left, and the center. Gramsci, and European intellectuals in general, did not and do not have to worry about the debates going on in the colonies. Fashion works from center to periphery, not the other way around. (Although it is possible that perhaps in the second decade of the twentieth century, we witnessed a two-way exchange due to the growing influence of de-Westernization and decoloniality; see the epilogue.) Nevertheless, the differential of epistemic power is ingrained in the colonial difference in all its facets and faces. Power differentials cannot be redressed by public policies or military might. They have to be redressed, on the one hand, through gnoseological and aesthesic reconstitutions and, on the other, in ways that make reconstitution desirable and available to all, including actors and governing institutions.

José Aricó, in his classic book on Gramsci in Latin America—a book that is the product of his research, of course, but also of his passionate engagement with Gramsci—devoted a chapter to the following question: "Why Gramsci in Latin América?"[48] Aricó was a public intellectual and activist by today's standards, not an academic. For Aricó, Gramsci entered Argentina at the junction of two key moments: the illusions awakened by the Cuban Revolution in 1959, refurbished in the 1970s, propelled by the crisis of the Cuban Revolution that coincided with the repercussions, in Latin America, of the global turmoil manifested in the global events of 1968. These events included the end of the welfare state and the dawning of a series of dictatorial regimes and acts of state terror (Pinochet in Chile, Videla in Argentina, the infamous "Operación Cóndor," etc.).[49] In short, in the 1970s and 1980s the attention devoted to Gramsci by the Latin American intelligentsia was increasing, and in the context that Aricó describes, the concept of "hegemony" was most helpful.

As the debates in the late 1970s were moving from dependency to the transition to democracy, the question of the state, central for Gramsci in his struggle with fascism, was paralleled in Argentina and in "Latin" America by the rise of dictatorial regimes. On the question of the state, Gramsci offered inspiring alternatives to the indifference of Marxist international thinking. His distinction between civil and political society, next to the idea of hegemony, provided a concept of the state that was alien to orthodox Marxist thinking, which saw in the state a bourgeois institution to be superseded by the dictatorship of the proletariat and the internationalization of the revolution. In South and Central America, the question of the state became a serious concern during the weave of dictatorships in Argentina, Chile, and Brazil. Gramsci provided basic tools to confront dictatorships. The "colonial question" (e.g., coloniality) was forgotten and not related to the weave of dictatorships. In the 1970s Aníbal Quijano was involved in the dependencies debate. When the "transition to democracy" took center stage, Quijano wrote about the "uses" of democracy, rather than the uses of Gramsci. In retrospect, the concept of the coloniality of power that he introduced in 1992 could be prefigured in several of his previous articles, including "Los usos de la democracia burguesa."[50]

However, one of the most interesting aspects of Gramsci's reception, from a decolonial perspective, was his distinction between the "Occident" and "Orient." Bolivian intellectual and activist Fausto Reinaga's *The Indian Revolution* (1969), rooted in Indigenous history, perceived what was more difficult to perceive by non-Indigenous thinkers. His combative style was as original as Mariátegui and Zavaleta Mercado.[51] Born in a rural area, Reinaga was moved by Indigenous dignified anger. Close to Indigenous memories and degraded experiences by Bolivians of European descent (still present in 2020), Western civilization was not a problem for either Mariátegui or Zavaleta Mercado. But it was for Reinaga, who several times assumed himself to be Aymara, an Indian who thinks (see epilogue). Decolonially speaking, the main problem for Reinaga was not so much class struggle or the oppressive state, but Western civilization itself, in which both class struggle and the (modern) state originated. Reinaga addressed and questioned the terms of the conversation, while

Mariátegui and Zavaleta Mercado were critical of the content (state, class struggle). However, since they were addressing issues of the colonial states in "*sociedades abigarradas*" (motley societies), they were dealing with issues quite different from class struggle and the state in western Europe. They both were unmindful of the terms of the conversation and of the underlying logic of coloniality, of which both the state and class struggle were consequences. Reinaga was not. If I am able to perceive and bring to light these distinctions, it is because decolonial political thinking focuses on the invisible logic of the CMP (the underlying structure of Western civilization) that European intellectuals and Latin Americans of European descent couldn't see. Quijano, of course, sensed it in Peru, and he made a move that neither Mariátegui nor Zavaleta was yet able to make: to see the work of the coloniality of power undergirding the political, economic, and cultural events they were analyzing. (I will come back to these issues in chapter 12 and the epilogue.) From Guaman Poma de Ayala to Mahatma Gandhi, from Ottobah Cugoano to Frantz Fanon and the Zapatistas (see the introduction, section III), Western civilization is the main concern from which all the rest is derived. Thus, decolonial political thinking in that genealogy of the praxis of living and thinking always aims to change the terms of the conversation, not only its content. When European thinkers address their own Western civilization, they can do it neither from the embodiment of coloniality and the colonial wounds imposed on the Indigenous population nor from the colonial legacies in which Mariátegui, Zavaleta Mercado, and Fausto Reinaga operated, in spite of the scale of their involvement with the "Indian Question."

But let's return to Gramsci and the Orient/Occident (East/West) question. José Aricó reflects on this point as follows. In the distinction between Orient and Occident that Gramsci introduces in his *Notebooks*, Aricó concludes that "Latin" America belongs, in Gramsci's terms, to the Occident (the West). And indeed the majority of the population, of all the Americas, is of European descent. Not the First Nations and Afro-descendent population. Reflecting also on Juan Carlos Portantiero's seminal book *Los usos de Gramsci* (1977), Aricó accepts that the concept of the Occident is wide enough to include both European countries beyond the core of Europe (like the former Eastern European ones) and non-European countries (like Latin America and the entire continent). For Portantiero Italy, Poland, and Portugal were *estados periféricos* (peripheral states). Portantiero derived, from his reading of Gramsci, reflections on the most industrialized countries in Latin America: Argentina, Brazil, and Mexico. Aricó quotes the following interesting paragraph by Portantiero:

Comparable by their type of development and differing in their irreproducible historical formation, those countries [Italy, Poland, and Portugal] are comparable to Latin America. Latin America is not the "Orient" for it is clear that it has common features with the peripheral West, late in its development. In Latin America, we can see more clearly this "second West" that was formed in Europe toward the end of the nineteenth century. In Latin America, it is the State and politics that model society. But it is a type of State that while attempting to shape a national community cannot achieve the degrees of autonomy and sovereignty of the "Bismarckian" and "Bonapartian" models. In Latin America all the struggles during the nineteenth century were struggles among economically similar groups that fought among themselves for the control of the State. The aim was to control the State to develop the economy in order to promote a more complex structure of social classes.[52]

Portantiero underscored political "dependency" without using the word. Perhaps he did not use it because it was a word in the vocabulary of economic dependency. But dependency runs through the history of coloniality. All colonies and former colonies have been and are dependent until today. Just reading or listening to the news today and paying attention to how the US and the EU relate to the rest of the states, you cannot miss dependency—which is a surface manifestation of coloniality. Hence, Gramsci did not have to worry about dependency. Italy was not a colony of France or England in the same way that Algeria or India was. For Mariátegui, dependency was a part of himself (before dependency theorists made it visible), as it also was for the Gramsci followers like Aricó and Portantiero. For them, internal colonialism was also an alien concept, although internal colonialism was the unavoidable destiny of Argentina after independence in 1810.[53] In this light, Portantiero's quote is interesting for a couple of reasons. First, it addressed the question of interstate relations in the world order (peripheral states), but without taking into account the colonial question (coloniality was not yet known) between modern European peripheral states (Eastern Europe) and the peripheral colonial states in "Latin" America, in Asia, and in Africa, not to mention the "peripheral" state of the Soviet Union in Central Asia.

What Portantiero and Aricó did not "see" was the fundamental reason for the "uses of Gramsci" by Indian subaltern scholarship. The colonial difference was a basic assumption of the subaltern studies project, chiefly by Partha Chatterjee (*The Nation and Its Fragments*, 1993), but it was invisible to Gramsci's follower in Argentina and in Bolivia as well. Zavaleta Mercado's intellectual work (roughly from 1960 to 1984) started from Gramsci and Marxist categories, but he had to deviate from them to account for his crucial concept of "motley society" or *sociedad abigarrada*. However, dependency and internal colonialism, two concepts that were in the air at the time, were keywords in his work. All these concepts came up after Mariátegui's and Gramsci's time, but they are helpful for reflecting in retrospect on the issues that each of them faced in their own eras. For instance, Gramsci could have thought that the Southern Question was a case of internal colonialism. However, it may not have occurred to him, because colonialism was not one of his main concerns. But it was for Mariátegui and later on for Quijano. Similarly, "motley society" would have been an alien concept for Gramsci in Italy and in the European genealogy of thoughts. "Motley society" brought to light, instead, the characteristics of social formations in former colonial countries with majority Indigenous populations. I would guess that "motley society" would be a concept familiar to subaltern studies scholars. And in fact, Chatterjee's elaboration of *The Nation and Its Fragments* points in that direction. For that reason the "colonial difference" is a key concept in his work.[54]

Racism is not taken into consideration in Gramsci's categories of Orient and Occident, which he saw as a way to describe the relations between the state and the civil society. But in Bolivia, civil society becomes motley society, as observed by Zavaleta Mercado, a sociologist of Spanish descent. For Fausto Reinaga, claiming his Aymara identification, "Occident" is racially charged, not just a hemispheric neutral and objective distinction. He made his point forcefully in *América India y Occidente*. Racism was a key concept for Mariátegui as well as for Quijano, who made of racism the spine of the colonial matrix of power. Following up on this genealogy of thoughts, I have connected, in this volume, chapter 1, on racism, with section III, on the geopolitics of hemispheric partition. Racism in America is as pervasive as classism in Europe, and racial distinctions adhere to the categories of Occident and Orient. Lewis R. Gordon told me once, in personal conversation, that Europe smells like class, and the Americas smell like race. In light of all this memorial weight, it should be noted that "the uses of Gramsci in South America" displaced not only Mariátegui from the intellectual scene, but Zavaleta Mercado and Fausto Reinaga as well.

The West, or the "Occidente," understandably was not a central problem for Gramsci, but of course it is for the rest of the planet, where "Occidente" is identified with European expansion and North Atlantic imperial legacies: Hegel's heart of Europe, Gramsci's peripheral Europe, and the "colonial Occident" (America except the US), which was self-described by the Argentine

Bernardo Canal Feijóo as "the confines of the Occident."[55] These Occidents (plural) include both the Occident in which the interconnections between the economy, class structure, and state appear in a more balanced organization and the Occident in which such relations remain in less articulated conditions. The latter were, for Gramsci, the frontier or peripheral states (Poland, Italy, Spain, and Portugal). For the Argentinian left it was important that Gramsci's thought emerged from his living in and observing peripheral Occidental societies. And they concluded that certain Latin American societies where industrialization was advanced, like Argentina, Brazil, and Mexico, were similar to the peripheral societies of Eastern Europe. The historical blindness was remarkable—both for Argentinian and Brazilian followers of Gramsci—for Spain and Portugal are deeply rooted in imperial memories that fell into desuetude (e.g., the intramural imperial difference). Gramsci's analogy is understandable if you suppress race and only pay attention to class. Race, however, is very present in the entire work of José Carlos Mariátegui, so that Gramsci's concept of civil society had to be reworked to account for social organizations in the plurinational Andean region.

Seen from the decolonial perspective argued in this book, Italy, Spain, and Portugal are the roots of European self-proclaimed (imperial) modernity. Portugal-Brazil will need further and specific consideration, and here is not the place to go into that topic. Poland is perhaps the closest parallel to "Latin" America in the sense that since the sixteenth century it has gone through a series of violent colonizations and partitions by the Russian tzarate, the kingdom of Prussia, and the Hapsburg monarchy. For the Gramscian new left, the legacies of the colonial past and the distinction between countries ranked by imperial legacies (Italy, Spain, Portugal) and countries with colonial legacies (Poland, Argentina, Brazil, Mexico) were not as important as they were for the "national left," whose arguments were based in both the history of the nation and the history of imperialism—from Spain and Portugal, to England and France, and ultimately to the US. And they were not important because racism was not taken into consideration. The new left had two foci: to liberate themselves from the Communist Party and to reflect on the state during the era of dictatorship. The national left of the previous generation in Argentina was also formed in contradistinction with the Communist Party, but it has focused on the intersection between national and imperial histories.[56] The new left was more sociologically oriented, less interested in imperial/colonial legacies and national identity.

Gramsci entered "Latin" America perhaps a decade before he made his way into the South Asian subaltern studies historiographical project. However, the emphasis in subaltern studies was different. "Subalternity" was seldom, if ever, an issue in Latin America and certainly not for the new Gramscian left. What caught the attention of both South Asian and Latin American scholars and intellectuals were Gramsci's concepts of "hegemony" and "historical block." However, Latin Americans were more intellectual activists than scholars, while South Asians were more scholars than intellectual activists. Gramsci took both concepts from Georges Sorel to identify the dominant class forms of consent that maintain hegemony through institutions, language, social actors, social relations, and systems of ideas.[57] This difference reveals how Gramsci *was used* in India and how he *was used* in Argentina. South Asian subaltern studies scholars and intellectuals were quick to mutate Gramsci's "subalternity" from the southern European experience to make it work in the colonial experience of India. The colonial context made it necessary to clarify the distinction between hegemony and domination.[58]

"Subaltern subjects" are formed—as is well known—not only by the larger class of deprived, politically marginalized, economically exploited, and subjectively undermined individuals, as Gramsci taught us to see. But in addition to subaltern subjects are the "colonial subjects," and colonial subjects are a different species of subaltern. Colonial subjects are intersected by racism and, therefore, by the extramural colonial difference in its myriad manifestations through times, locations, and changing needs as expressed in the rhetoric of modernity to justify dehumanization and domination. Colonial subjects are specifically those marked by the double-crossing of racism and patriarchy, deepening colonial wounds. These are not central concerns in Gramsci, but they are in Fanon and Mariátegui, grounded in how each of them experienced coloniality. In this regard, subalternity in India is very close to Frantz Fanon's *damnés*, and one could wonder why it was Gramsci and not Fanon who became the point of reference for Asian subaltern studies.[59] A quick answer would be that Fanon was, like Mariátegui, a respected but second-class thinker—a thinker from the colonies (see the epilogue, where I address this issue head on): beyond Gramsci's brilliance, for colonial subjects in peripheral countries (whether India, Argentina, or Brazil), there was the clout of his being a European thinker. Perhaps an added attraction is that he was from the South. Furthermore, in the nineteenth century, Italy belonged to the "peripheral" (i.e., in the South of Europe) modern, capitalist countries of Europe, while India was colonized by the leading European imperial state: Britain.

What is in play here is the intramural colonial difference (Italy, internal colonialism) in which Gramsci is thinking and the extramural colonial difference that lay at the historical foundation of Gandhi, Nehru, and the South

Asian subaltern studies. Here within the framework of internal colonialism was where progressive intellectuals from the ex-colonies looked for their own salvation. They were not looking much into their own past. (This is why Mahatma Gandhi was not embraced in subaltern studies and somehow despised by Guha.)[60] The generation who introduced Gramsci and created *Pasado y Presente* could have named their publication *Amauta* (the journal create by Mariátegui). In Argentina, *Amauta* in Quechua-Aymara languages means "philosopher, man of wisdom." But that name—beyond the fact that it is not in Argentinian and Brazilian memories, languages, and histories—would have been taken as "traditional." Instead, Gramsci was—for the young generation of the new left—a sign of "modernity." In fact, of course, this youthful preference reflected the same ideology of modernity that the US was using to promote its own projects of "development and modernization" (which provoked the critical responses of dependency theory and the theology of liberation): the content was opposed, but the logic was the same. Gnoseological and aesthesic reconstitution, which is what I assume I am doing here, come to the rescue to avoid the "ambuscade" of modern and postmodern frames of mind.

Now the fact that Gramsci entered Argentina through Córdoba and not through Buenos Aires was not insignificant. There is a long history that gave Córdoba its place in Argentina. In 1575, the University of Córdoba was founded. This was a few decades after the creation of the University of Santo Domingo, the University of Mexico, and the University of San Marcos in Lima, and about sixty years before the foundation of Harvard University in 1636. During the nineteenth century Córdoba was a focus of the civil war and the national reorganization beginning in 1862. In 1918, Córdoba was the focus of *reforma universitaria*, or "university reformation," which had an impact all over Spanish America. By the 1960s, Córdoba had become a center of industrial modernization and development. The car industry was responsible for the miracle; Fiat, Kayser, and Renault found their home in Córdoba. And because of that, in 1969 the city witnessed "El Cordobazo": the workers at Kayser, with the support of the student population, literally took over the city. The uprising, which came about a year and a half after the "global 1968" (Beijing, Czechoslovakia, Paris, Mexico), was led not by the Marxist avant-garde but by workers and students in the long tradition of Córdoba University and the shorter tradition of university reformation. The fact, then, that it was in Córdoba where Gramsci found his first shelter in Argentina is indeed quite relevant. It explains in part why Mariátegui was less relevant than Gramsci in this context. A labor force from Argentina's northwest and the adjacent Bolivia migrated to urban centers like Buenos Aires and Córdoba, a process that was initiated and promoted during the first and second presidency of Juan Domingo Perón (1946–1951; 1952–1955). Industrialization transformed Córdoba from a provincial city with visible signs of colonial history into a modern city—nothing less than the center of the car industry in South America. And we all know the meaning the car industries had in the Third World: they carried the promise of entering the thruway to the First World. Thus, Gramsci in Córdoba did not come with the Southern Question, but with the "Northern Question." The industrial environment of Cordoba, where Gramsci found his home in Argentina, was like the Milano of Luchino Visconti's film *Rocco e i suoi fratelli* (1960): the Southern Question in the industrial north.

VI The Garden of Forking Paths

I have already mentioned the national left (*la izquierda nacional*, sometimes also referred to as *el Marxismo nacional*), which made a mark on the political and intellectual debate in Argentina that preceded the advent of the Gramscian left. For the national left history was of the essence. That history was Spanish colonial history followed by the liberal orientation, after independences, that resulted in the founding of colonial nation-states.[61] The national left emerged, indeed, in 1945 when Juan Domingo Perón was rescued from military captivity and became president of Argentina. At that time, a significant number of intellectuals in their thirties (they were born in the first decade of the twentieth century) turned the page and reclaimed Marx independently from Moscow. But, at the same time, they reclaimed a national history narrated from a Marxist perspective and introduced superb analysis of the history of British and US imperialism in America and in Argentina.[62] Contrary to what happened in India, where Marxist canonical narratives were disqualified and superseded in the South Asian subaltern studies guided by Gramsci's vision, the national left in Argentina was not superseded by the Gramscian left that emerged in the early 1960s.[63] They followed parallel and different paths. The splendor of the national left was to absorb Marx and integrate his work into the historical task of building "national consciousness" and making Marxism work from inside the history of former colonialism and current imperial forces.[64] Its misery was to create the conditions for national fundamentalism.

There were other paths unfolding at the time Gramsci entered Latin America in the 1960s. One was the decolonial path opened up (and obviously marginalized) by the Argentine philosopher of German descent Rodolfo Kusch (1920–1979). In the twenty-seven years that elapsed between his first book, *Seducción de la barbarie* (1952), and his last book, *Geocultura del Hombre Americano*

(1979), Kusch's critical and relentless line of demarcation was traced between the right and the left. That is why today it could be said that Kusch was building decolonial arguments without using the term, and it also explains why he was significantly misunderstood and marginalized by the full spectrum of the right and the left. The right was mainly characterized by the urban middle class (wanting to be European) of Buenos Aires and by imperial theories of modernization and development; the left by disengaging from the bureaucracy of the Communist Party. Kusch did not personalize but rather confronted the general principles and assumptions of the Marxist left grounded on his ethnographic work and philosophical reflections on Indigenous and popular thinking in America.[65] Thus, if you are engaged, as Kusch was, in a double critique of the left and the right at their Euro-American point of origination and their route of dispersion in the Americas, and you think from the histories and experiences of the popular (not the subaltern) and the Indigenous, then chances are that among the available options you engage in decolonial thinking, as Kusch did.[66] Kusch was closer to Reinaga than to either the nationalists or the Gramscian left. During the same years, between the late 1950s, when he returned from Paris, and his death in 1994, Fausto Reinaga was also following a parallel trajectory of decolonial thinking based on the memories, categories of thought, and sensibilities of Quechua Aymara histories in the Andean regions. Reinaga was in Paris in the 1950s, when decolonial conversations were in the air and *Presence Africaine* was the journal that agglutinated decolonial conversations in France.

Scholars generally agreed that Gramsci's *Prison Notebooks* marks one of the nodal points of Western Marxism's break with Leninism and the breed of Marxism born of the Bolshevik Revolution. In 2007, the vice president of Bolivia, Álvaro García Linera, assessing the situation of the country, did worry about making clear the distinction between Gramsci on the one hand and Lenin and the Bolshevik Revolution on the other. He wrote, "Any state crisis, then, may be reversible, or it may continue. If the crisis continues a subsequent stage is the catastrophic equilibrium. Lenin spoke of a revolutionary situation, Gramsci of catastrophic equilibrium, both referring to the same phenomenon albeit in distinct languages."[67]

To make this point clear we have to bring racism into the equation, absent in Lenin and Gramsci, and consequently in García Linera. This is not a question of academic debate or scholarly pride. What matters is the correlation between Marxism and ethnicity/racism in America and the Caribbean, which Fausto Reinaga laid bare and Black Caribbean philosophers had as the bases of their reflections, even if they adhered to Marxist legacies. However, it was well felt and known that—in the Caribbean—"Marxist analysis should always be slightly stretched when it comes to colonial issues."[68] García Linera faced a situation in Bolivia that neither Lenin nor Gramsci could have imagined: a country in which 60 percent of the population are the aboriginals of the land, while Marxism is a way of thinking and being that suits people of European descent but not so much Indians and people of African descent because class, in Marxism, silences race/racism. What I am underscoring here are colonial legacies in America, and colonial legacies cannot be dissociated from racism and derived problems and issues alien to those that Lenin and the Bolshevik confronted in Russia, and to those that the Italian Gramsci dealt with. Geo-body politics of knowing and knowledge are fundamental in decolonial thinking as I conceive it, and, of course, for gnoseological reconstitutions in any sphere of knowledge. I am suggesting, consequently, that in spite of the conceptual differences between Lenin and Gramsci, there were more commonalities between Russia and southern Italy at the margin of Europe than between Russia and the Andes of South America. In this land, in all its territory, history, memory, and lived experience, Indians have endured five hundred years of European colonialism, including, of course, Marxism; while in Europe, Russia and especially southern Italy have fallen into the margin of the continent as Hegel perceived in his *Philosophy of History*.

Thus, it is notorious but not surprising that the question of ethnicity and racism, implied in the distinction between Indianism and Marxism, and between Afro-Caribbean thought and Marxism, was absent from the "Latin" American Gramscian left. Who uses Gramsci and reads him? My hypothesis is that in Spanish- and Luso-America, the impact of Gramsci since the 1960s has been felt mainly by a sector of the "Latin" American left, namely, intellectuals of European descent. Gramsci was not adopted by "Indo" Americans or by "Afro" American intellectuals of South and Central America and the Caribbean. There are exceptions for sure, but they are exceptions.

The issues confronted by Indo and Afro intellectuals, scholars, and activists are not the same as those afflicting Euro-descendent activists, scholars, and intellectuals. We are all living in the same world, but we inhabit different corners of the colonial matrix of power. Marxist views cannot be universal; neither for that matter, can liberal, Christian or Islamic views. The decolonial finds its place right there, in the borderlands and borderlines emerging from the clash of abstract universals in their struggle to obtain a universal hegemony. If we are to still use the Gramscian *cosmo-vivencia* (an Indigenous expression meaning "sensing" rather than "viewing" the cosmos), it is necessary to extricate it from the modern political theoretical frame in which it emerged and to bring it to the decolonial horizon. On that horizon, decolonial hegemony will look like pluriversality, like a pluriversal project rather than like the hegemony of one abstract universal. When I say, therefore, that in America Gramsci has been used mainly by the population of European descent but not so much by Indigenous and Black radical thinkers, I have two scenarios in mind. The first involves Fausto Reinaga, the already-mentioned Aymara intellectual and activist. In his book *The Indian Revolution* he stated:

> The manifesto of the Partido Indio de Bolivia (PIB) does not have to be subjected to any model, rule, or logic, formal or intellectual, that governs the political parties of the white-mestizo *"cholaje"* [people of Indian ancestry mixed with other ethnicities, mixed in blood but "white" in mind] of Bolivia and Indoamérica. This is not a manifesto of the social class. It is a manifesto of a race, of a people, of a nation: the manifesto of an entire culture oppressed and silenced. It is not possible to compare with Marx's *Communist Manifesto*. It is not possible to compare because the genial "Moor" did not confront the West (Occident). He confronted the proletarian with the bourgeois class and proposed, within the same Western civilization, the *"intangida"* [incapable of being thought out or realized] communist revolution.[69]

Reinaga assumed an Aymara identity. As such he perceived that a communist revolution within Western civilization could not really be a revolution. Some say he is mestizo. He may have been mestizo in blood, but he was Indian in mind, whereas mestizos in blood are generally white in mind. Mestizos of white mind couldn't accept his Indian identification and accused him of being mestizo and only pretending to be Indian. My point is this: in the preface to his book *The Indian Revolution*, from which the previous quotation is drawn, he is saying that for him the problem is not the struggle between proletariat and bourgeoisie, but rather Western civilization in its entirety (hence "Occident" was a problem, not just a hemispheric description), including the proletarian and bourgeois classes. In other words, proletariat and bourgeoisie are not for him universal concepts. And whether universal history is determined by class struggle is an open question. For Reinaga, as for any decolonial thinkers—not only in America but in the Middle East (or better yet, West Asia), Africa, and Central, East, and Southeast Asia—the problem is not just capitalism but the West, of which both capitalism and Marxism are two important aspects. The problem is the coloniality of power, of which the type of economy described by liberals and Marxists as capitalism is a component, a fundamental one nowadays, but only a component and not the full story.

The second scenario comes from Afro-Caribbean intellectuals and scholars of the past and the present, whether based in the Caribbean or in the US. All are "Fanonians" rather than "Gramscians." (You see my point.) I mentioned before that Lewis Gordon—a philosopher from Jamaica—suggested that Europe smells like class while the Americas smell like race. What did he mean by that? The Europe of the Industrial Revolution and of Marxism is basically "white" Europe.[70] The South of Europe, where mixing bloods and religions could be found, was first "purified" with the expulsion of Jews and Moors at the end of the fifteenth century. Moreover, by the end of the eighteenth century, Enlightenment philosophers were effective in downgrading the southern/Latin region of Europe in such a way that when the question of class began to be formulated, it was formulated in the heart of Europe (England, Germany, and France). That is where ethno-racial conflicts were invisible, because the majority of the population was white and Christian.

Concomitantly, Paget Henry (from Antigua, a Caribbean island) published a landmark book in 2003 that was awarded the first annual Fanon Prize by the Caribbean Philosophical Association in 2004. The title of the book is *Caliban's Reason: Introducing Afro-Caribbean Philosophy*.[71] The chapter before the last is titled "Caribbean Marxism: After the Neoliberal and Linguistic Turn." It contains not one single quote from Gramsci. Certainly, the chapter's focus is "after the neoliberal and linguistic turn," and Gramsci was a strong presence in Latin America in the 1960s when neoliberalism was not yet in the agenda, but apparently, he was not so strong in the Caribbean. Nevertheless, the time period is a factor since Henry devotes a chapter to C. L. R. James (1901–1989), who was ten years younger than Gramsci. To a certain extent James adhered to Marxism until he became disenchanted and wrote *Beyond a Boundary* (1963), a personal and critical narrative of cricket in Jamaica through which he disentangles colonial and racial issues of British imperialism. Curiously, the years surrounding the publication of James's book, in which he distanced himself from Marxism, were the years in which Gramsci was being received by young generations of Marxists, in Argentina and Brazil, who were disenchanted with the Communist Party.

Not quoting Gramsci was not Henry's oversight or careless scholarship, who professed a manifest admiration of Marx's work. It was just that for Black Caribbean intellectuals, Gramsci did not address racial issues, which were as relevant to them as hegemony and "historical block" were for Gramsci. Of course, it was different for Stuart Hall in London, who embraced the European debate on Althusser and Gramsci without abandoning racial issues, which were not relevant for his British colleagues in the cultural studies group. However, although Hall was Caribbean, contrary to Henry he was much more involved in European debates than in Caribbean history. But that is another story, a story in Europe. Certainly, radical Black thinkers of the twentieth century have all been critics of capitalism, like Gramsci, but Marxism doesn't have a monopoly on critiques of capitalism or on visions of the future. Fanon's words in *The Wretched of the Earth* (1961), quoted just above, bear repeating here: "Marxist analysis should always be slightly stretched when it comes to colonial issues."[72]

Last but not least, Anthony Bogues—a Jamaican political theorist—wrote a book about Black radical intellectuals. His line of reasoning is parallel to that of Fanon. Bogues writes, *"Regimes of domination do not rest solely upon economic, political, social and cultural power. They also exist and conduct politics within a field of political and social knowledge,* of ideas that form part of the self- consciousness of all members of society. Given the nature of anti-Black racism and the racialized object (who is human), the Black radical intellectual as critic is first of all engaged with *challenging the knowledge regime of the dominant power"* (emphasis added).[73] This why knowledge is of the essence for the decolonial option and is the target of the politics of decolonial investigations. The economy is not only dispossession and exploitation of labor. The dispossession and exploitation of labor are possible because they are legitimized and subjectivities are manipulated by the control and management of knowledge. Changing the world, as the dictum goes, cannot be advanced if the people inhabiting the world that they/we make do not change. And for that, decolonial ways of thinking and being in the world, of world-making, are unavoidable. It is knowledge and desires that guide a kind of economy that shapes our knowledge and desires. Which means that knowledge doesn't "represent" economic behavior (like exploitation of labor and dispossession of land) but "covers" it up, legitimizes, justifies, and frames its sphere of operation.

It also means that economic regimes of knowledge are what make certain persons more objects and less human, and others more human and privileged. Gramsci was put in prison because of his political ideas involving economic issues, not because of the color of his skin and the meaning of "Blackness" in Western white modernity. I am not saying that one form of violence (either because of ideas or because of skin color or religious belief) deserves more attention or has an epistemic privilege over another. I am saying that for the "Latin" American left that introduced Gramsci, racism was not a problem. Bogues further observes: "We have already noticed that the radical black intellectual is, to use Gramsci's term, an 'organic' intellectual. But he or she is organic with a difference. While in the Gramscian mode radical organic intellectuals provide the missing inventory of the spontaneous philosophy of ordinary people, they do so within a framework and discursive practice that do not call into question their own ontological natures."[74] Understanding the nuances of the colonial matrix of power, how it operates and how knowledge legitimizes and covers up the logic of coloniality, is the fundamental task of the politics of decolonial investigations, to reveal how it works and how to delink. Overcoming the CMP requires a constant understanding of how it works to be able to relinquish (delink) from it.

VII Closing Comments

Exploring the "uses" of Gramsci in "Latin" America allowed me to open up the archive and to follow and weave the colonial signs and threads of a tapestry of South American and Caribbean thought contemporary with and after Gramsci and Mariátegui. This tapestry provides a useful background for the issues I will pursue in the next chapter, learning from the groundbreaking works of Jamaican scholar, activist, and intellectual Sylvia Wynter.

12 **Sylvia Wynter** What Does It Mean to Be Human?

Los seres humanos [anthropos] actuales, somos el presente de una historia de generación y diversificación de linajes por deriva natural en la conservación, por reproducción sistémica, de mundos psíquicos recursivos como ámbitos relacionales y operacionales, en un proceso a la vez de conservación y de transformación del modo Homo sapiens-amans-amans de vivir y habitar biológico-cultural de la unidad ecológica organismo-nicho que generamos e integramos en nuestro vivir-convivir.

We, contemporary human beings, are the present of a history of generation and diversification of lineages by natural drift in the conservation (by systemic regeneration) of recursive psychic worlds as relational and operational spheres, all of which occurred in a process of both conservation and transformation of the *Homo sapiens-amans-amans*'s way of biological-cultural living and inhabiting the ecological unit organism-niche that we generate and integrate in our living-coexisting.—HUMBERTO MATURANA ROMESÍN and XIMENA DÁVILA YÁÑEZ, *El Arbol del Vivir*, 2015, translation mine

I think that the human lineage began in that historical process as a manner of living in the conservation of living in languaging, and that the basic emotion whose conservation made this possible is love. So, I like to call our original ancestor, and the fundamental manner of living still conserved in the present of our lineage, *Homo sapiens-amans amans*. Yet, I also think, that in the long history of our human lineage many branches must have arisen, and are still arising, in which other emotions have become central as guiding emotions in our community living obscuring or replacing love, creating other branching lineages many of which became extinct. I think, for example, that there are two other human forms that are slowly arising in our present, namely *Homo sapiens-amans arrogans,* and *Homo sapiens-amans agressans.*—HUMBERTO MATURANA ROMESÍN, "The Origin and Conservation of Self-Consciousness," 2005

One of the supposed characteristics of primitive peoples was that we could not use our minds or intellects. We could not invent things, we could not create institutions or history, we could not imagine, we could not produce anything of value, we did not know how to use land and other resources from the natural world, we did not practice the "arts" of civilization. *By lacking such virtues we disqualified ourselves, not just from civilization but also from humanity.* In other words, we were not "fully human"; some of us were not even considered partially human.—LINDA TUHIWAI SMITH, "On Being Human," 1999, emphasis added

I Opening

What does it mean to be Human?[1] This is a question that runs parallel to the announcement of the posthuman and the invention of the geological era of the anthropos (the Anthropocene). We who are engaged in this conversation—me writing and you reading—should keep in mind that the name for this created geological era carries the name "anthropos," rather than being the era of the human. That is, the proposed name is not the Humancene but the Anthropocene. One suspects that the species anthropos emerged at some point (dates for the origin vary), while the human *became*: it was an invention of the European Renaissance. See what I mean? The species of living organisms that have walked on the planet for (let's say) four hundred thousand years "became" human when the concept was invented. And the concept was not an innocent and neutral denotation of living organisms walking on their two lower extremities, but it was culturally charged: "human" was identified with "man," another Western invention, to disqualify women, non-Europeans, nonheterosexual people, and non-Christians. For decolonial thinking it is imperative to uncouple the name from the entity or event named. The politics of decolonial investigations should avoid the traps of the content and aim to "redefine" what is human. The target is the enunciation, the terms of the conversation, which invented and used the concept to disqualify lesser humans. The question is when, how, and why some anthropoi (living organisms walking on the two lower extremities) became humans. For while it is clear that as a biological species we are all anthropoi, it is not clear that all anthropoi qualify as humans in the colonial matrix of power. This is precisely the crucial question asked and argued by Sylvia Wynter.

If, then, not all anthropoi of the Anthropocene era are Humans (note here the use of capitalization), then the next question to ask is: what does the post-human mean in the present era? I am playing with "anthropos/anthropoi" (the living, animal organisms we are) and "humanness/human beings" (the organisms that organized themselves by means of the growing complexities of oral/verbal languaging parallel to the use of the hands to build fire and shelter, to hunt, and to expand those capabilities to build computers and atomic bombs). And I use "Human" to refer to an elite of anthropoi that referred to themselves as Humans modeled on Man (following Wynter's argument) and that used "Human/Man" to destitute to lesser status certain humans by creating racial and sexual colonial differences. What would Anthropocene mean when looked at from a decolonial frame?

Let's review the basics. "Cene" is a word-forming element in geology intro-duced by Sir Charles Lyell (1797–1875) from a Latinized form of Greek *kainos*, "new," cognate with the Latin *recens* (see the Online Etymology Dictionary). We know already from previous chapters that "newness" is a keyword in the rhetoric of Western modernity. It may have spread, like a virus, to other lan-guages, but there is no concept of "newness" in Mandarin, Arabic, Aymara, or Bambara, before Western interventions. Contrary to other geological time frames (Oligocene, Pleistocene), it is not clear to me whether the Anthropo-cene (or the "Age of Man" as *Live Science* has it) is chronologically "after" all the geological eras already identified or if it coexists with the latest one, the Holocene.[2] So, then, is the Anthropocene synonymous with the Holocene, or does it coexist with it? In any case, there is a confusion here between the era of the anthropos and the era of man. What would "post" mean in either case? I am not aligning myself with any "post," just mentioning the issue to highlight that there are other trajectories beyond the varieties of the prefix "post." While for modernity/coloniality there is only one time (universal) and it goes from beginning to end, *decolonial* temporalities are *lived* temporalities. The issue is not that there is a four- or five-hour difference between Eastern Standard Time (EST) and Greenwich Mean Time (GMT). The question is that the lived tem-poralities of the colonies are not the same as the lived temporalities of the em-pire. Lived temporalities are not measured by clock temporalities.[3] For those inhabiting decolonial lived temporalities (see Linda T. Smith's epigraph at the beginning of this chapter), the question is whether Indigenous people have their humanity questioned or ignored, and their lived temporalities regulated by universal time. It doesn't matter what time it was in England and what time it was in Aoteaora. The imperial lived temporality in England and for the British settlers in Aoteaora, which they named New Zealand, are not the same as the lived temporality of Maoris whose praxes of living were violently disrupted. Hence, the *time* of the Anthropocene doesn't coincide with the lived temporalities of all the anthropoi on Earth.

Notice, then, that the question "What does it mean to be Human?" is neither a question about the anthropos (a single being or member of a species) nor a question of universal time, but a question about the anthropos that calls *itself* Human/Man, who invented the Anthropocene linear history of the anthropos, and uses its own creation to disqualify anthropoi that are different from *itself* (see the introduction to this volume). The question asks the meaning of "being Human/Man," not of being anthropos, which implies that Human is not an ontological but an epistemological entity. There are no ready-made entities that have come into the world with their own ontological definition. Rather, being Human is the consequence of a sector of the species anthropos defining itself as such. To do so it has been necessary to trace a line between those anthropoi that are considered Human (by self-definition) and those other anthropoi lacking some of the Human qualities. These, again, are the implications of Sylvia Wynter's question (see also chapters 5, 6, 7, and 13). We all come to the world as anthropoi, and we become what in the West was named "human" by living together in languaging and by using our hands. Humanness is basically a *we* not an *I. Homo sapiens amans-amans* in Maturana's words. By the time Human/Man appeared on Earth, communal praxes of living had begun to be destituted by the dominance of *Homo sapiens arrogans* and *agressans*. Communal organizations based on parities, and the complementarity of the two moieties in the parity (e.g., feminine-masculine, sun-moon, day-night), were displaced and parities were transformed in opposite and contradictory directions.

My goal in this chapter is to explore the meaning of being Human at a time when a significant number of anthropoi on the planet are considered not quite Human (due to racism, sexism, nationalism, foreignness, etc., all of which result in the rejection of immigrants and refugees), not equal to the anthropos who invented the Human in his own image. The Anthropocene is also an invention of the Human elite self-defined as such. What would the meaning of "posthuman" be in this context if we started from the difference of living temporalities and, congruent with it, the expulsion of the majority from the category of the Human, so that all were reduced to their/our humanness and, in certain cases, found analogies between certain human beings and the anthropos? The notion of "primitives," invented in Europe in the eighteenth century and used by classic anthropology, is a case in point. Linda T. Smith's epigraph alludes precisely to that. What could the posthuman be in a decolonial frame delinking from the Human? And what would the Anthropocene era be?

It would be helpful to remember, before reading what follows, that all the debates on the posthuman and on postanthropocentrism presuppose the regional cosmology of Man/Human—and its lived temporality—from the Renaissance through the Enlightenment to the postanthropocentric and posthuman debates. Such debates are not relevant in, say, Argentina or Indonesia or South Africa or Uzbekistan; they are basically North Atlantic debates, where GMT is the reference for the planet's time zones grounded in one lived temporality. And if the topics *are* debated in, say, Turkey or South Africa, it would certainly be by a minority who adhere to the lived temporality of the North/West, someone who pays more attention to the conversations in the North Atlantic than to their own lived temporality. Sylvia Wynter's critique of humanism and anthropocentrism (and I follow suit in my argument) is neither posthuman nor postanthropocentric, but an archeology of the Western constitution of the Human/Man and the destitution of lesser humans—an argument that delinks both from the trajectory of humanism and from posthuman anthropocentrism. Or, if you wish, the argument is decolonial in the sense that the question "what does it mean to be Human?" reveals that humanism and anthropocentrism, or posthumanism and postanthropocentrism, are all embedded in the coloniality of knowledge and being. Furthermore, the argument is an archeology of Western civilization and an exercise of the politics of decolonial investigations. Why? Because Wynter asks the questions that posthumanism and/or postanthropocentrism avoids: by accepting that "Human" refers to an existing entity, posthumanism and postanthropocentrism evade asking when the concept came about, where, by whom, and to what purpose. That is why the decolonial inquiry starts by asking these questions: "What does it mean to be Human/Man, for whom, and why?"

II   Sensing, Looking, and Thinking before and after
      the Advent of Man/Human

Following in the footsteps of Frantz Fanon, Humberto Maturana, and Francisco Varela, Sylvia Wynter's works have been pursuing a cognitive and political shift that in this essay I characterize as decolonial. I do not think Wynter would object to that description. However, I am not intending to stamp a label on her, but rather to state that for me, her arguments are decolonial. Why decolonial? Why not postmodern or postcolonial? Because Wynter's work has consistently called into question whether the "post"—in poststructural, post-modern, postcolonial—is a useful conceptual frame. Thus, she puts it aside in order to understand, instead, how particular epistemologies are unthinkable and/or unarticulated within hegemonic Western categories of knowledge and the philosophy of knowing. I would add "posthuman" to the list of her of "posts" being questioned. At stake is experiencing the geopolitical lived temporality of racism and sexism, both nationally and internationally.

Wynter thinks, writes, and speaks (for those of us who have had the pleasure of listening to her) from the body and the sensibility of a Black Caribbean woman. Her erudite discourses are not intra- or transdisciplinary. They are marvelously undisciplinary and epistemically disobedient. She forces you to change the terms of the conversation. Otherwise, you will not understand. You won't be able to enter the conversation until you realize that the terms have changed. Wynter explores the roots and the origin of the concept of Man/Human at the time when a massive slave trade was underway in the Atlantic. Her own geopolitical memories go deep into the Atlantic of the Middle Passage, rather than in the North Atlantic trajectories of Man/Human. She is not looking to change the content of the conversation by adding a prefix within the same cosmology, but to change the terms of the conversation. Changing the terms of the conversation is the goal of gnoseological and aesthesic reconstitutions.

For that reason, Wynter's contribution is not to existing codified knowledge or to some "benevolent" morality defending humanity while hiding racism and sexism to ostensibly promote a sort of universal Humanity. As the dictum goes, "We are all born equal but do not remain equals." Mindful of being a Black woman from the Caribbean (meaning, from the Third World during her formative years), she opted to delink herself from the system of knowledge that disqualifies her from Humanity rather than reclaiming to be recognized as such. Delinking and epistemic disobedience alter one's sensing, one's understanding, and one's being in the world. Paradigmatic changes in science, as earlier argued by Thomas Khun and debated in the 1980s, occur within the same rules of the game that bolster its claims to universality and celebrate change, innovation, and newness.[4] Instead, actively accepting a place in destituted exteriorities (e.g., the lesser humans judged by Man/Human) means to pride the destituted lesser humans, to celebrate dwelling in the borderlands, to refuse being recognized as Man/Human—for it was in the name of the Human that genocides have been committed, and modernity and development defended. Stepping out of the rules of the game and performing epistemic disobedience are the first steps toward reexisting and rebuilding on the destituted rather than just resisting. And here we are again at the heart of the politics of decolonial investigations. Wynter has been showing us the ways.

What Wynter draws from Maturana's insights, in particular his work on autopoiesis, is his biology of cognition, reframing the complementarity—not the opposition—of "sensing" and "knowing." Specifically, Maturana has shown that what you see is not what is but what you see it is. What you sense is correlative to what you see. Hence, aesthesis is not a question of the beautiful and the sublime, but a manifestation of sensing and seeing in your daily personal and professional praxes of living. Or, as Maturana would say, we don't see what there is; we see what we see. His philosophical shift from the philosophy of the mind to the biology of cognition, and from the opposition between biology and culture to the complementarity of cultural biology, are akin to Frantz Fanon's radical shift in the social sciences and the humanities from ontogenesis and phylogenesis to *sociogenesis*. Fanon's distinction between having black skin and being a Negro (sociogenesis) corresponds with Maturana's cultural biology, and Maturana's cultural biology corresponds with Fanon's sociogenesis. Having black skin, or brown, or white, or olive, or any other variation, is a biological surface of the generation and regeneration of the living anthropos. Being a Negro is a cultural classification of an external biological feature of humanness. If you start from the assumption that you do not see what there is but you see what you see, which is an assumption as valid as the one who asserts that you see what there is, the classification is not a representation of what there is but an interpretation of what you see.

Connecting Maturana's neurobiological rendering of cognition and the decolonial thinking that characterizes Sylvia Wynter's work assists us in understanding her relentless (epistemic) disobedience to Western codes of knowledge. Wynter suggests that accepting Western epistemological *principles and rules of knowing* that sustain the idea of the Human and Humanity, an idea created by actors who see themselves as Human and representing Humanity, leave us trapped in a knowledge system. This knowledge system fails to notice that the stories of what it means to be Human—specifically, origin stories that explain who/what we are—are, in fact, narratively constructed by actors who define themselves and identify with the fiction they invented: Human and Humanity. Wynter's sophisticated theoretical and historical explanation of Man1, Man2, etc., and the making of the Human should thus be understood alongside historical and epistemological epochs (medieval, classical) that imagine Human and Humanity through an intelligible cosmogony that requires a juridical-economic colonial presence. Disobeying and delinking open up the possibilities of reexisting, of living otherwise, and vice versa. Reexisting and living otherwise open up the necessity of delinking and disobeying. You cannot think otherwise if your praxis of living is subjected to and obeys the expectations of modernity's storytelling (the rhetoric of modernity) that sets up for you what you should be, what you should think, wear, or eat.

By asking and addressing the question "What does it mean to be Human?" we take the first step toward the gnoseological and aesthesic reconstitution of an ontology removed from its pedestal. The question doesn't ask for a definition of the content (what is Human? what is Humanity?) but asks for whom the concept of the Human came to be, and when and for what purpose. The question questions the enunciation and aims to disclose the *constitutive* stories of Man/Human and the *destitution* to the status of lesser humans (primitives, barbarians, terrorists, gays, Blacks, brown people, Muslims, etc.) of the dispensable and undesirable qualities to preserve the virtuousness of Man/Human.[5] The feeling that Man/Human is an entity that preexists the storytelling that constitutes its ontology prevents us from asking who has been and continues to be destituted in the name of Man/Human. The assumption that the storytelling is about something that exists beyond the story and the storyteller, and that its existence is the horizon to be reached, justifies all Western global designs of salvation, progress, civilization, development, modernization, market democracy, and the like. All these designs are designs of and by Man/Human. If you accept the assumption, you obey the requirement set up by the designs. But if you change the assumption (the terms of the conversation) and start from negating the ontology of Man/Human and obeying its epistemology, then you begin to understand the constitutive aspects of the Western Man/Human and all its implications and consequences in the making and maintaining of the colonial matrix of power (CMP; see introduction, section III.3). The CMP is *his* work, the work sustained by *Homo sapiens arrogans* and *aggresans*. Wynter's work and argument are anchored in the rift that demands changing assumptions and therefore the terms of the conversation. For that reason, the question Wynter asks is not "What is Human?" but "What does it mean to be Human?" The first question keeps you in the system. Asking the second you are already stepping out, dwelling in the borderland of the constituted/destituted and in the terrain of gnoseological and aesthesic reconstitutions. And you are already in the politics of decolonial investigations. Once you change the questions and hence the terms of the conversation, you are engaging in border thinking for the simple reason that you know the assumptions upon which Man/Human was constructed, and you have the experience of the destituted exteriority into which you have been placed because you do not satisfy the requirement to be Man/Human and do not properly fit into its global designs because of your racialized ethnicity, your genderized sexuality, your deviated religiosity, your suspected nationality, or your linguistic accent. Those are the verdicts of "Man/Human as the One who classifies" that Wynter's arguments are unmasking.

Implicitly, Wynter works out her argument in the social sciences and the humanities in tandem with the arguments around cultural biology that Maturana has been advancing since the 1970s in biology and especially neurophysiology. His distinction between the biological and the cultural is not cast from within the modern Western opposition of the cultural versus the biological. Maturana, like Wynter, starts from different assumptions and therefore has been changing the terms from epistemic to gnoseological and aesthesic conversations. For him, the terms "cultural" and "biological" are not opposites in the sense of being distinct from each other. It is the biological (molecular autopoiesis and molecular cognition that humans do not generate) that generates the possibility of the cultural (cultural languaging and cultural uses of hands that molecular autopoiesis made possible and humans manage). *The cultural conceives, describes, and explains the biological, while the biological made possible the cultural in the constant and changing processes of humanness in our praxes of living.* This conceiving, describing, and explaining constitute the biological sciences, which are first of all cultural phenomena and not themselves biological. Once you start from the *cultural* invention of the *biological* foundation of culture, you have stepped outside the code of Western science according to which sciences are nothing more and nothing less than the mirror of nature, and what science does is explain what is already there, in "nature" and in the "universe." Once you take that step you realize that *biological* is not life in itself (bio-) but a discourse about life. It is not what *there is* but what *you see there is*. The ontic (what there is) is always ont*ological*, a discourse about what there is. In this frame, Man/Human is the aberration of modernity and of Western civilization that the politics of decolonial investigations rejects. Maturana showed us the way to delink from the imagery of Western science, while Wynter showed us the path to delink from the imagery of the Western idea that culture is opposite to nature. Both showed us the ways for the necessary and relentless work ahead of gnoseological and aesthesic reconstitutions.

Consequently, "biological" no longer refers to something existing but to the multifarious processes of generation, regeneration, and extinction of living organisms on the planet, offering a window on the constant flows of life. Which means that while "biological" and "cultural" are both Western Man's/Human's concepts (and have been since the European Renaissance, reworking legacies of the Greek and Western Middle Ages), what we should pay attention to—I repeat—is not so much what is being said (the enunciated) but the saying itself (the enunciation): who, when, why, what for is making those distinctions. Science is an activity defined, conceived, and performed by anthropos who in turn have recently invented a new chapter of history: the chapter in which the advent of the anthropos on Earth began to change the planet's environment. The era of the anthropos is the Anthropocene. Eventually, the anthropos, who changed Earth's environment using his/our own hands, arrived at the point where he/we needed and were able to tell the story of how our species changed its environment. In this way, then, the biological is a cultural category and is only made possible by the species of anthropos who culturally created the distinctions between Man/Human and supposedly lesser humans. Pursuing her decolonial politics of scholarship, Wynter's arguments bring to light the cultural dimension of scientific arguments.[6]

It follows from Wynter's argument that we (scholars, intellectuals, scientists) are not taking seriously the idea that evolutionary deselection and biocentricity are *stories of origins with an ontological effect*. COVID-19 is a clear case of evolutionary biological/cultural deselection: the statistics of infections and the death toll are significantly related to poverty. Poverty is a cultural phenomenon; viruses should in general be biological phenomena that, in the human species, impact the cultural milieu. Or they could have a cultural origination (e.g., be lab-made, which is related to the institutional and financial capabilities to produce it) that attack the bio-organism and disrupt its molecular autopoiesis. Put simply: we tend to regard our cosmogonies as natural truth(s) rather than as narratives a community believes. Narratives calcify and beliefs are confused with the ontic existence that the narratives account for. Ontologies (discourses on what there is) are epistemological; they are principles and assumptions upon which narratives—and scientific explanations are narratives—ground other narratives on the ontic. I insist here that one of the beliefs in Western epistemology confuses the explanation or the narration with what is explained and narrated; the ontic is confused with the ontological/epistemological framing of it. That is why "representation" is a key concept in the rhetoric of modernity. This schema self-replicates, as the spread of one belief to other regions of the planet has shown us since the colonization of the Americas. In this way, Wynter's writings on Man/Human and who/what we are serve as a counterpart to Maturana's autopoiesis through Fanon's sociogenesis. The ontological turn in the humanities and the social sciences may have been caught in the epistemic trap of Western modes and principles of knowing, confusing the ontic with the ontological, and assuming that the biological sphere is separated from the cultural sphere. Wynter and Maturana help us to step out of that trap and to work on decolonial gnoseological and aesthesic reconstitutions.

Wynter refuses to embrace the principles sustaining the ontology of Man/ Human in the very act of displaying and dismantling the Western storytelling that constructs it. She argues that our conceptualizations (i.e., those of scholars and intellectuals, who themselves/ourselves are conceptual classes of anthropos) of Man/Human are produced in and by the circularity of the biological/cultural. The problem of the Man/Human is not a problem of ontological identity but the effect of the locus of its *enunciations* (actors, institutions, language) that managed to institute their own universal idea of what is Human and Humanity. The Human is therefore the product of a particular patriarchal epistemology in which Human/Man are indistinguishable. It is embedded in the language. Until recently the general term used to refer to human beings was "Man." When Wynter writes "Human/Man," the mask is detached from the face.[7] One of the tasks of the politics of decolonial investigations is to unveil the fictions of imperial/colonial politics beyond the restricted invention of the individual and Western Christian theology and secular liberalism; hence, Wynter's question, "What does it mean to be Human?," comes to the fore with all the weight that the invention of individual self-interest and Western liberalism carries (even while remaining somewhat hidden; see the introduction, sections III.1 to III.3).

III The Invention of the Human and Its Mutations

Wynter's argument arises from her projection of particular historical and regional moments: the invention of Man1 in the Renaissance (which was a variation of Man0, which originated in the Middle Ages) and its mutation into Man2 (Enlightenment). In none of the coexisting civilizations did such conceptualization exist. That "Human" in Western civilization refers to the image of "Man" is obvious, although dictionaries will tell you that "Man" refers to male and female. If that were the case, why not "Woman" to refer to male and female? Probably because God first created Adam and then Eve. But why did God decide to do it in that order? Probably because the Christian God identifies Himself with males; or vice versa. As Wynter first articulated the thesis in an article published in 2003, Man1 dominates the Western imaginary from the Renaissance to the Enlightenment, Man2 from the Enlightenment until today. In 2017, when I rewrote the article published in 2015 that became this chapter, it was evident that Man3 was on the scene when looking at Man2 in the history of the CMP. Man3 emerges in the interaction of the biological with the technology that biological Man2 was able to build in the Industrial and Technological Revolutions. Similar phenomena motivated the mutation of Man1 into Man2, which imbued the spirit of the European Enlightenment. Cybernetics created the conditions for another mutation, of Man2 into Man3, which motivated the intellectual need to conceive the posthuman, the Anthropocene, and the postnatural (e.g., genetically modified seeds, robotics). Man3 belongs to the same genealogy and corresponds to what in postmodern circles is labeled posthuman, postanthropocentric, and postnature. As in the cases of Man1 and Man2, Man3 is a Janus-faced entity: at once the figure of patriarchy, masculinity, whiteness, and North Atlantic coloniality. However, Man3 has today escaped Frankenstein's lab and got loose. At the same time, because of Man3's technological dimension, Man3 is also the representative of potential postmodern, posthuman, and postanthropocentric liberation. In other words, Man1 and Man2 controlled the enunciation and managed the processes of Westernization; however, and simultaneously, Man3 is under decolonial attack for its already embedded masculinity and whiteness plus its posthuman techno potentials.[8] The triangulation of decoloniality at large, de-Westernization, and re-Westernization coalesce in domestic and interstate conflicts around Man3, the dispute (de-Westernization and re-Westernization) for the control and management of the CMP, and hence the decolonial impetus to delink from the posthuman (see chapter 9).

If a date is required for planting the seeds of Man3 (the posthuman and the postnatural of epistemic and aesthetic re-Westernization), it would be when Norbert Wiener published *Cybernetics or Control and Communication in the Animal and the Machine* (1948). Wiener initiated the conversation on self-regulating machines. The self-regulated machine is not an autopoietic organism. Autopoiesis, Maturana has insisted, is a molecular phenomenon, not a cultural one. Transference to the cultural requires caution rather than easy analogies. Molecular means organisms that were not created by humans. If molecules are created in the lab to create living organisms, it no longer be a biocosmic phenomena but a cultural one, manipulated by autopoietic biocosmic molecular organisms. Molecular biocosmic living organisms regenerate by themselves without need of cultural interventions, although cultural interventions could modify their regeneration (transgenic, for example), but cultural engineered organisms (machines, robotics, AI) created by biocosmic molecular organisms (humans among many other molecular organisms) cannot supplant the biocosmic energies of life on planet Earth. Self-regulated machines, as Wiener characterized them, were created by human beings (autopoietic molecular biocosmic organisms) who emerged in the unknown processes of life in the universe (cosmogonic narratives are to be found in every civilization; in the West religion and science provide two conflicting narratives).[9] *Cybernetics cannot create life;*

they can only create instruments (robotic, AI) or imitate life, like the theatre and epic narrative in Aristotle's *Poetics*. Life that is *poiesis but not autopoiesis*. (It is quite interesting to think about the concept and designation of AI: *artificial* and *intelligence!*)The post (-human, -natural, -anthropocentric) and the cyborg arose at the junction of both the *self-regulating machines* and the *self-generating autopoietic molecular organism*. So far, it is the autopoietic organism that makes and manages the machine, although the machine could alter the biocosmic autopoiesis of molecular organisms. If the day arrives that these relations are inverted, we won't have any concern about climate change, although "cybernetic viruses" are already a "threat to machine security." Machines may be more resilient, and perhaps one day they will be able to decide their own destiny. In the meantime, I find it worthwhile to continue the decolonial path, the praxes of living, thinking, sensing, and reasoning of the molecular biocosmic autopoietic organism that made humanness possible and where the posthuman is meaningless. The gnoseological and aesthesic investigations that bring forth arguments like those by Maturana and Wynter provide us with a caution and a shelter to reject Man/Human and embrace the reconstitution of the biocosmic/cultural humanness and of *Homo sapiens amans amans*.

There is still an important dimension missing from the previous scheme, which was limited to the regional culture of western European storytelling, in all its theological and secular disciplinary dimensions. The missing dimension in the three versions of Man/Human1, 2, and 3 invented by European anthropoi were projected culturally toward anthropoi inhabiting other parts of the planet, speaking other languages, eating different foods, dancing different dances, living in their own ancestral memories. Each model of Man/Human served well the purpose of maintaining the privileges of the anthropoi who projected themselves onto the images of Man1, Man2, and Man3. Wynter's argument (and remember that Man3 is my derivation, not Wynter's) is geo-body political in the sense that it is grounded in her experience of Caribbean histories and her sensing and emotioning as a Black female (i.e., via the formation and transformations of the colonial subject). Man1, Man2, and Man3 did not classify only lesser "Men" but also lesser "Women" in Europe and in the colonies. Sexism in Europe preceded racism and sexism in the colonies.[10] The decolonial ridiculing of the *simulacra* of Man/Human (Lyotard's expression proves to be properly adequate here) fuels the compulsion to reexist in the gnoseological and aesthesic reconstitution of humanness, based on the molecular biocosmic autopoiesis and the consequent biology of cognition. René Descartes is moved away from the center stage and respectfully placed in the storehouse of the great achievement of Western civilization and its idea of modernity.

Once racism and sexism had been implanted in Western epistemology and had succeeded in persisting to this day, Wynter's counterargument reveals—in the act of stating it as well as in the way she states it—the limits of the imperial, racist, and sexist concept of Man1, Man2, and (my addition) Man3. Each version of Man/Human had its critiques and dissents in Europe itself, no doubt. But the intramural critiques cannot be taken as universal; nor can we assume that the obsession for the posthuman in the North Atlantic shall also be the obsession in Latvia and Croatia, in Singapore and South Africa, in Bolivia and Uzbekistan, in Iran and South Africa. The posthuman debate, if it exists in those places, would be limited to a minority eager to disseminate European debates in their own region, or else is limited to some European visitor or migrant eager to disseminate his or her own interests in foreign regions. Coloniality travels in company of the posthuman, certainly. But de-Westernization and decoloniality surge around the world from the global compulsions of modernity and postmodernity.

With this in mind, it could be argued that racism, sexism, and epistemology became part of the package whose point of reference is Man-as-Human, a reference point that corresponds to Wynter's project in her 2003 article "Unsettling the Coloniality of Being"—and across her work—as a move "beyond Man, toward the Human."[11] In my vocabulary, "toward the Human" is expressed as "toward the biocosmic/cultural resurgence and reexistence of humanness." I am not proposing this to correct Wynter but simply to be coherent with my own vocabulary. What Wynter proposes is neither a return to Man1 or Man2 nor the posthuman path; it is the affirmation of the humanness of biocosmic/cultural organisms in languaging and the uses of the hands to create instruments to regulate their/our praxes of living, thinking, doing that are not yet regenerated by the machines themselves. And the day this happens and the machines can conceptualize themselves as *mechanical organisms instead of biocosmic/cultural ones*, it will be a different world in which the self-generating, molecular autopoietic organisms and life on Earth that we know today will either vanish or accept the coexistence of biocosmic/cultural humanness with mechanical organisms. The question at that point would be if mechanical organisms would be complicit with Man1 and Man2 and Man3 to control and dominate, or complicit with biocosmic/cultural humanness to live in harmony and plenitude. In either case, mechanical and technological beings (artificial intelligence) will always remain something made by Man rather than biocosmic molecular organisms created by unknown energies and forces of/in the universe. We do know that Man and biocosmic/cultural humanness can make mechanical organisms and technological beings, and we also know that Man cannot make itself or life on Earth as it was made by the energy and intelligence of what is currently called, in Western vocabulary, the universe.[12]

For Wynter, as well as for many of us following her pathways, the anchor point is not the darker side of the European Enlightenment but the darker side of the European Renaissance: the colonial revolution that established the foundation of the modern/colonial world order with all its consequences, religious, economic, political, aesthetic, epistemic, subjective. The CMP is the regulating mechanism of Westernization, touching all areas of the experience of humans, animals, plants, air, water, food. A regional cosmology (Christianity) established its dominance over the cosmologies that it disavowed in the process of its own global affirmation. Today, the return of the disavowed is manifested in an array of trajectories that I have described as de-Westernization and decoloniality (see introduction), and it is engendering re-Westernizing counterrevolutions. After the failure of neoliberalism to homogenize the world, the long process of Westernization turned into re-Westernization in a desperate effort to retain the privileges acquired by the successful setting up the rhetoric of modernity and the logic of coloniality over five hundred years of Westernization.[13] Posthumanism is constitutive of this counterrevolution.

As far removed as it may seem—as I quickly mentioned above—the question "What does it mean to be Human?" is, on the contrary, a question at the core of the conflicts today between de-Westernization, re-Westernization, and decoloniality (see chapter 9). The horizon of decolonial politics lies beyond choosing between friends and enemies, between right and left, between Republican and Democrat—beyond all the oppositions that no longer pertain in a world order intersected by the energies of de-Westernization, re-Westernization, and decoloniality. Friends and enemies, right and left, good and evil are no longer dyads that you would be able to fit in a triad. Each member of the triad would have two members as enemies, if you would like to put it in Carl Schmitt's terms, and each member has two other members as enemies, *but a different kind* of enemy. The emergence of decoloniality today (but also decolonization during the Cold War) outlasted the possibility of thinking politically in terms of friends and enemies by the installation of a third term coinhabiting with de-Westernization and re-Westernization and delinking from the goals and assumptions that move de-Westernization and re-Westernization. The equilibrium of the dyad is broken because decoloniality is not moved by the same interests that confront de- and re-Westernization.

Consequently, in a triad in which one of the members is not playing according to the rules of the other two, the political conceived in terms of friend and enemy collapses. Or it is valid to decolonially *understand* the confrontation between de- and re-Westernization, but it no longer obtains in the decolonial praxes of living and thinking. If you live and think decolonially, detaching (de-linking) yourself from and simultaneously coexisting with de- and re-Westernization, then you will exit the straitjacket of either A or B (the dyad of the political conceived in terms of friends/enemies) and dwell in the grammar (of decoloniality) that is neither A nor B. Your "enemies" will be both but in different spheres and intensities, and you will exit the failure of Western modernity. And instead of opposing and resisting, the political begins working on delinking from both while engaging in imaginative reexistence, resurgence, and *creative communality*, as Adolfo Albán Achinte would say.[14] This involves using what cannot be avoided and relinquishing the superfluous that traps you in the bubble of modernity, globalization, development (e.g., Do you really need eight hundred TV channels? Do you really need the "new model" of whatever? Do you have to think in terms of either/or?). The triad is the closing of Western binarism, and it is the closing of an epoch and the advent of another epoch in which modern and postmodern frames of mind remain caught in the limits of an epoch that is closing: Westernization from the colonial revolution in the sixteenth century and the opening of Western global designs to its closing by the advent of de-Westernization and decoloniality. The three trajectories are entangled in the coloniality of power and its instrument, the colonial matrix of power.

Look around and concentrate on where coloniality is touching you, affecting your life, most of the time without you noticing it, other times intruding in it, promising to make your life better, and you believing it. The three trajectories I outlined coexist; neither of them is homogenous, but you cannot mistake one for the other, just as you do not mistake Catholic and Protestant or Sunni and Shia. They will coexist for some time, and there will not be one winner that places the other two under its control. Thinking in this way belongs to the previous epoch, the epoch that is closing. There is no longer room for only one global, unipolar, and universal civilization that will eliminate other coexisting ones and will eliminate people's dissent and the will not to be compulsively governed. Re-Westernization is moved by the obsession to maintain Western domination; de-Westernization is moved by the need to delink from Western domination; and decoloniality is moved by the need to delink from both and engage in the preservation of life, rebuilding the communal that Western society dismantled. It is moved by the will to reorient the horizons of the living on Earth, and the will toward gnoseological and aesthetic reconstitution. Epistemic and aesthetic constitution/destitution belongs to the epoch that is closing, the epoch dominated by global designs to Westernize the planet. The dice are cast for the politics of decolonial investigations aiming at the communal horizon of life in harmony with all the living and life on Earth. The politics of decolonial investigations shall contribute to making sense and orienting ourselves in the multipolar world order driven by de-Westernization, and the pluriversal horizon driven by decoloniality at large. The change of epoch that we are experiencing in the present needs a divergent frame of mind. "Futuring" and "defuturing" are interesting verbs that distract you from the work to be done in the present. The future we do not see; it is behind us. We all live in the present with the past in front of us, we see it. The future depends on what we do in the present. The future cannot be defutured, simply because it has not been yet.

Historically, then, for Wynter and for us in the Americas (First Nations, those of European descent, and those of African descent), the year 1492 was the turning point, the colonial revolution, in human history and on planet Earth. But it was also the emergence of decoloniality, as I suggested in the introduction, which commented on the works and deeds of Guaman Poma de Ayala and Quobna Ottobah Cugoano. In the legacy of Cugoano, Sylvia Wynter and many Black intellectuals (such as C. L. R. James, George Lamming, Wilson Harris, Aimé Césaire, Frantz Fanon, and others) draw attention to the significance of plantations and *palenques* and *kilombos*, liberation of the plantation and the creation of counterplantation praxes of living.[15] The fundamental issue underlying this intellectual tradition of rereading European encounters in the Americas is not class or hegemony or subalternity but rather the question "What does it mean to be Human?" Man1 served well to actors and institutions self-identified with Man1's domain: Muslims, Jews, Africans, and "Indians" were all culturally deselected. But this is not all; there was also "Nature," the closest to which were placed Indians and Africans. Those legacies remain alive and well today as has been evident in the debate on Israeli Zionism, anti-Zionism, and anti-Semitism (see chapter 4).

IV Wynter's Epistemic Shift through James's *Counterdoctrine*

After Wynter took from Maturana his radical epistemic shift in the sphere of the sciences, which called into question many of the aims and scaffoldings of philosophy and science, she then turned to C. L. R. James to deal with Man2 and to join James in the same struggle: the Afro-Caribbean epistemic revolution against the Eurocentric concept of Man2 and its role in the construction of racism. But this is a topic for another occasion.

In the previous sections, I discussed Wynter's long, well-researched, and highly insightful articles, a network wherein her ideas and writings are in conversation with one another. It is useful to note here that Wynter doesn't write books. She just thinks and writes and fights her fight. A small revealing detail of decolonial scholarship: you can enter the network by engaging with any of her articles and essays and work your way through it. It is not a linear argument in a well-edited book according to English composition and a publisher's requirements to maintain linear coherence, not to repeat, and flatten every discourse to the same English rules. I could guess today that neither Heidegger's nor Derrida's book manuscripts may have been accepted by English-language publishing companies.

Back to Wynter. Here I'm entering the web of thoughts, through her article on C. L. R. James, "Beyond the Categories of the Master Conception: The Counterdoctrine of Jamesian Poiesis."[16] One of the reasons I am interested in this work is that C. L. R. James—in Wynter's recognition and praise of his thoughts—has been read, particularly in the United States, as primarily a Marxist thinker. This reading was based on his *Notes on Dialectics* (1948) and his *State Capitalism and World Revolution* (1950)—even though his allegiance to Marxism is only partial (see chapter II for the fortunes and misfortunes of Marxism in South America and the Caribbean).[17]

Notice that these two books were published during the same years that Norbert Wiener published *Cybernetics or Control and Communication in the Animal and the Machine* (1948) and his follow-up, forgotten by the scientific community, *The Human Use of Human Beings* (1950). Geo- and body-politics of knowing, sensing, and emotioning cannot be detached from the said knowledge. Power differentials (in this case colonial epistemic differences) made Wiener better known, even if they both wrote in English: Caribbean English has not the same rank as its North Atlantic version.[18] The coincidental chronology is revealing. Wiener saw the danger of what today is labeled "posthuman." After he published his groundbreaking treatise on cybernetics, he sensed the consequences of the techno-instrumental human uses of human beings. Human uses of human beings was not a new concept. What was different augmented the possibilities that techno-instrumentality would allow.[19] He was, so to speak, the generator of Man3 as well as its critic. The posthuman today follows a similar path: it refers to both the splendors and the miseries of technology. We see a similarity when Wynter unravels the complexity of the ways in which James's thought is anchored in the history and experience of the slave trade—and thus the fifteenth and sixteenth centuries—noticing that his sole preoccupation is not with the emergence of the proletarian consciousness (as in Marx) or with cybernetics (as in Wiener) or with the commune or the Coup of 18 Brumaire. Wynter puts it this way:

The starting point for James's displacement/incorporation of the labor conceptual framework is his insistence on the seminal importance of the trade in African slaves. In particular, he wants to end its repression in normative Western conceptual frames. . . . What Wallerstein has called the world system was *constituted* by James as above all a single network of accumulation. This network can be divided into three phases: (1) circulation for accumulation; (2) production for accumulation; and (3) consumption for accumulation. In each of these phases . . . the sources of extractive value . . . [are] different. In the first, it was the African slave, in the second, the working class, and in the third and current phase, it has been the consumer.[20] (Emphasis added.)

These three stages are the core of James's counterdoctrine. Yet his counterdoctrine, Wynter argues, also emerges from his willingness to view and think theoretically and aesthetically *together*. (In the vocabulary I am using here, I would say: "to think gnoseologically and aesthesically together," to remove the sluggishness from "theory" and "aesthetic.") A Jamesian aesthetic and a theoretical doctrine emerge, then, in the questioning of "the dictatorship of the master conceptions of Liberalism and Marxism." To understand the Jamesian doctrine, "it is necessary to look at the semiotic foundations of bourgeois thought, the monarchical system of power it de-legitimated, and the liberal state it helped to establish."[21]

Wynter's analysis of the Jamesian doctrine runs parallel to the arguments advanced by the collective workings of modernity/coloniality/decoloniality, in which this book is inscribed.[22] We have seen different historical trajectories since 1492: the genealogy of the African forced diaspora on the one hand, and the European voluntary diaspora on the other. The differences are not trivial, for belonging to the European diaspora locates one as "almost European," while diasporic Africans are identified as "non-Europeans." These differences, present throughout the Americas and including the Indigenous population, *constitute* the racial logic of the colonial difference. The energy of decolonial thinking and doing is nourished by each of these trajectories in coexistence with the others: First Nations and African diasporas in the Americas respond according to their accumulated ancestral dignified anger. Wynter argues that for conceptual power to be effective, it has to have within it discursive legitimization. As she learned from Michel Foucault, discursive formations go hand in hand with institution building: "Cultural conceptions, encoded in language and other signifying systems, shape the development of political structures and are also shaped by them. *The cultural aspects of power* are as original as the structural aspects; each serve as a code for the other's development. *It is from these elementary cultural conceptions that complex legitimating discourses are constructed*"[23] (emphasis added).

Thus, the complicity between institution building and its legitimizing discourses allowed an "ethno-class" (Wynter's term), the European bourgeoisie, to displace the monarchy and the hegemony of aristocratic classes. This is the constitutive moment of Man2. Wynter explains, "It was not enough to gain politico-economic dominance. It was also necessary to replace the formal monarchical system of signification with a cultural model that 'selected' its values as normative. The elementary cultural conceptions upon which the monarchical system of signification rested can be designated as 'the symbolics of blood.'"[24] Wynter focuses on the paradigmatic change brought about—in the internal history of Europe—by the advent of the bourgeois ethno-classes (Man2), which displaced the monarchy and the church (Man1) and brought into focus the broad spectrum of intellectual, social, and geographic shifts occurring between the European Middle Ages and the Renaissance. These shifts were due, in great part, to the emergence of sixteenth-century Atlantic commercial circuits and the changes this emergence generated in Europe itself. In particular, she underscores the initial (not primitive) moment of capital accumulation, the exploitation of labor, and the initiation of the modern/colonial slave trade in the Atlantic triangle.[25] Here Wynter's argument underscores the massive exploitation of labor in conjunction with the massive appropriation/expropriation (dispossession) of land.

The colonization, expropriation, and violence directed at lands and peoples engendered a new type of economy based on the reinvestments of gains and the impulse to increase production to create and satisfy a global market. In Wynter's analyses, "capitalism" as we know it is revealed to be *one* economic *aspect* of the emerging colonial matrix of power; her analyses, as a result, challenge other approaches that focus solely on the capitalist underpinnings of the slave trade and its accompanying land exploitation. She reveals a more circumscribed role for capitalism, per se by her delineation of features—particularly those brought into view by non-Europeans—that are not driven simply by economic matters but also by cultural practices, social exchanges, and shifts in political allegiances. James was no doubt aware of these other factors, and a purely Marxist reading of his work causes the racial force in his argument to be lost, both because enslaved labor is not proletarian labor and because the enslaved workers in the extended Caribbean plantations before the legal end of slavery were not white and so not the proletarians that Marx saw in Manchester factories in the nineteenth century.

Wynter's analysis thus seeks to think through the nuances of the colonial encounter with and beyond a capitalist frame. Indeed, she reveals that the economy of colonialism alone analytically obscures a much broader narrative of coloniality and encounter. This is the framework that produces her reading of C. L. R. James. She separates James from the coopting of Marxists and describes his thinking by reading his life through a *pieza* conceptual frame.[26] But what is a *pieza* conceptual frame? The *pieza*, Wynter tells us, was the name given by the Portuguese during the slave trade to the African who functioned as the standard measure of the most desirable laborer. The *pieza* "was a man of twenty-five years, approximately, in good health, calculated to give a certain amount of physical labor value against which all others could be measured—with for example, three teenagers equaling one *pieza* and an older man and a woman thrown in a job lot as refuse." Wynter suggests that in the "Jamesian system, the *pieza* becomes an ever-more general category of value, establishing equivalences between a wider variety of oppressed labor power."[27]

The *pieza*, then, can be seen as the anchor, the reference point for a sensibility that emerged in the sixteenth century alongside the conquest of the Caribbean islands, Anahuac, and Tawantinsuyu. It is a measure, furthermore, that did not exist before conquest, and that set in motion a radical shift of economic practices around the planet toward what today we call "capitalism": an economy grounded in accumulation at all cost (war, killing, corruption, exploitation of "nature," i.e., people and Earth both considered "resources"— human and natural). This specific sensibility was the facility through which the ruling class, the merchant class, and conquistadores could build an institution and a legitimating discourse that made certain human lives dispensable vis-à-vis differential categories of value—from the symbolic status of blood (the monarchic moment) to the symbolic status of skin color (the secular moment whose foundation was established in the Spanish colonies in the sixteenth and seventeenth centuries).[28]

The metaphoric and methodological uses of the *pieza* trouble Marxist-oriented analyses that suggest that slavery and racism play a secondary role in the constitution of capitalism. Remembering here Fanon's quote from the previous chapter helps us grasp the inconvenience of the *pieza* metaphor: "This is why Marxist analysis should always be slightly stretched when it comes to addressing the colonial issue."[29] And I would add here, along with Fanon, James, and Wynter, that it should always be stretched *when addressing the colonial matrix of power*. For this reason, Wynter argues that the *pieza* standard requires a repositioning of the mode of production in relation to the mode of domination, a repositioning in which the former becomes a subset of the latter. Connecting this framework to James's theory by noticing that his system is a comment on the significance of the *pieza* allows her to rethink European Marxists' analyses of capitalism. What I am underlining here is that without the focus suggested by Wynter (and Fanon et al.), there is no place outside capitalism from which capitalism can be analyzed. We are saying that you live, experience, enjoy, or suffer capitalism in your geo-body political coordinate; but the same must be said for the colonial matrix of power itself, because capitalism is one of its domains managed by and through the enunciation (the economic domain; see introduction). On this issue Wynter writes, "Economic exploitation only follows on, and does not precede, the mode of domination set in motion by the *imaginaire social* of the bourgeoisie. Consequently, the capitalist mode of production is a subset of the bourgeois mode of accumulation which constitutes the basis of the middle-class hegemony"[30] (emphasis added).

Here is precisely where the Afro-Caribbean analysis set in motion by C. L. R. James joins forces with the modernity/coloniality conceptualization set in motion by Aníbal Quijano. Both are conceptual frameworks as well as emotional flows, and both arise out of their respective local histories in the modern/colonial world order *along with* their broader and unique experience of the colonial wound. A Black in the Caribbean, a mestizo in the Andes, and migrants from European descent are not of the same "rank" in the modern/racial classification, as I mentioned before, yet they/we are sensitive to and aware of the colonial wounds. For Blacks in the Caribbean it is the denigration of the African in the Christian and modern European imaginary; for the First Nations it is the Spanish settlers first and then their heirs that dehumanized them; for immigrants and the population of European descent, is their/our Third World conditions. They/we are cognizant that one does not see and feel capitalism in the same way across time and space and thus across different colonial settings. The posthuman lives in another region, the region of the modern subject. Our region is elsewhere, and is the region of the colonial subject for whom decolonial liberation means healing the wounds felt differently from each of our three entangled histories: those of First Nations, European settlers and their descendants, and the forced migration of enslaved Africans.

Unlike the experience of the posthuman, what you see and feel in each distinctive colonial history is the colonial matrix of power, of which the economy is only one component—albeit today the overarching component. Domination precedes accumulation, and accumulation secures domination, but domination requires a cultural model built through rhetorical narratives on the wonders of modernity, of progress, of development, of growth, of technological innovations, etc., while hiding and enacting, within all the wonders, the logic of coloniality (domination, exploitation, conflicts, and the maintaining of domination and exploitation for accumulation). Modernity, in other words, is constituted by narratives that legitimize domination, exploitation, and war, then and now. Economic coloniality is an outgrowth of the mode of domination; and the mode of domination has been set, transformed, and maintained not by the economy (even if you call it capitalism), but by the desires expressed in the ever-changing rhetoric of modernity and the ever-changing logic of coloniality. The function of the rhetoric of modernity is to shape subjectivities and the belief that constant growth and accumulation are possible, unstoppable, and for the good of everybody. "Capitalism" is an economy of both exploitation and accumulation legitimized by the rhetoric of modernity, which models the subjects being "subjected" to the enchantment of having and possessing. Both modernity and coloniality constitute the colonial matrix of power (CMP). In short, Wynter shows us that the Marxist analysis focuses mainly on economic organization, while the *pieza* example and the colonial matrix focus on the layered workings of a "cultural model" (theological, "scientific," philosophical, aesthetic, religious, subjective) shaping and regulating the desires of Man1, Man2, and Man3. These are now under duress by posthuman arguments (Eurocentered critiques of Eurocentrism) and decolonial arguments (decolonial critiques of Eurocentrism). For Wynter, Quijano, and many Indigenous scholars, activists, and intellectuals through the Americas, dehumanization has been fundamental and still is for capitalism. For the people being dehumanized, a salary increase is necessary under the system, but is far too little for human dignity. The current US government thought at one point that promising the Palestinians and North Koreans to help them develop their country would solve the problem. Many were of the opinion that Palestinians and North Koreans would eat dirt before humiliating themselves by receiving a few dollars.

V   Wynter's Epistemic Shift through Fanon's Sociogenesis

To delink and decolonize means, first, to understand how CMP is controlling all of us, including its creators, managers, and those who dispute its management, and, second, to delink from its tentacles. Hence, the extreme relevance of Wynter's building her genealogy of thought from Fanon to James. In the twenty-first century, taking hold of the state is a dead end. Indigenous people fight for their land. For non-Indigenous people, beyond supporting their arguments and struggles, the main concern is with planet Earth. But of course we cannot take hold of Earth or occupy it as if it were a building. We are on

Earth, and have been since we were born. I list below three settings where we must conduct ourselves as human beings, not as human beings of a particular credo, discipline, or ideological persuasion: one is the state and interstate organizations, signing agreements and holding summits to enunciate their good intentions; the second is the corporations doing what they need to do to obtain "natural resources" of every kind imaginable and to make everything into a commodity (water, air, food, light, energy, etc.); and the third is the narratives legitimizing and critiquing numbers one and two. The decolonial intervenes in the third setting, in the sphere of actors who do not have access to intervene neither on the state nor in the corporations, except manifesting and protesting. For that, there is no need to assume decolonial positions.

In nineteenth-century Europe, when "capitalist" economy reached its high point of hegemony and domination, Darwin explained the achievements of Man2 by means of a biological-evolution narrative. Marx's "social evolution" and "surplus value" unveiled the exploitative bent of Man2, and Freud showed that behind Man2's conscientious subjectivity lay the "unconscious." Evolution, surplus value, and the unconscious became crucial concepts within western European history and sensibility in the *constitution* of Man2. The constitution of Man2 *destituted* and sent to the *exteriority* of the CMP all knowledges that did not fit the epistemic assumptions of Man2, while simultaneously *constituting* its own *interiority*. However, the three conceptual frames of Western knowledge (anchored on the concepts of evolution, exploitation of labor and surplus value, and the unconscious) were firmly embedded in the *constitution of European interiority* (i.e., Eurocentrism and Eurocentric modernity) necessary to destitute European exteriority (coloniality). Eurocentrism in itself is not a sin; all civilizations constitute themselves on the basis of the omphalos syndrome. The sin of Eurocentrism was the aberration: the arrogant pretense to homogenize the planet's human population according to its model and to conceive the harmony of the living as an entity, "nature," reduced to a single noun. When the energy that sustains life on the planet becomes "natural resources," and human beings beyond Man2 are entities who are ontically inferior and rationally deficient, barbarians beyond civilization, underdeveloped beings that need to be developed and terrorists that have to be eliminated by the same sources that created terrorism, then one has a panorama in which, from the right to the left, non-Europeans (and non-Anglo Americans) cannot think (see epilogue).

In building a decolonial genealogy, Fanon's well-known statement, "beside phylogeny and ontogeny stands sociogeny," serves Wynter well.[31] Beginning with it, she unfolds the implications of the sociogenic principle. Notice first, though, that it is through James's and Fanon's colonial subject, and not through Freud's and Marx's modern subjects, that Wynter formulates her arguments. What is sociogenesis and what is a sociogenic principle? In short it is a decolonial concept that confronts and reveals the frontiers of the modern concepts of phylogenesis (Darwin) and ontogenesis (Freud). Sociogenesis uncovers the differential of power embedded in the ranking of languages and knowledges in the modern/colonial world order. Darwin was interested in the biological evolution of the species, so phylogenesis served him well. Freud was not interested in the species but in the individual; therefore ontogenesis was appropriate. Both are modern concepts to explain modern subjectivities and experiences but useless for capturing the experience of the Black colonial subject. Fanon needed a different concept: sociogenesis. In contradistinction with ontogenesis and phylogenesis, sociogenesis is *not an ontological concept* "representing" something that is not the concept itself. Sociogenesis is an epistemological concept (I am here talking the talk of modern epistemology) but *a relational concept*: it is the gaze of the modern subject that *sees* a "Negro" in a person with black skin. Sociogenesis is a powerful concept that discloses how racial and sexual classifications work. Sociogenic classification does not represent what it is, but reveals what the *observer sees and states that it is.* The power of sociogenesis is inherent in its relationality: it is a person's perception of how he/she is seen according to the invisible and taken-for-granted racial (but not only racial) classification established in and by the colonial matrix of power.

Sociogenesis explains that your identity emerges once you realize that you are *seen* by another person and that the other person has been made comfortable by means of a framework of "knowledge" that has secured his or her position in the world at your expense, that you have been classified as socially, culturally, and intellectually beneath the other by someone who lives, knows, and acts within the hegemonic frame of Western knowledge. Fanon knew his skin was black; he did not know he was a "Negro." And he understood that "Negro" is a cultural category in the mind and body of the person classifying and seeing a "Negro" in a person with black skin. He understood that he *was not a Negro, but was seen as a Negro.* Black skin is a feature of the organism, but "Negro" is how Man1 and Man2 ranked lesser humans with African ancestry. A Black body speaking French is not the same as a white body speaking French, even if French is a common language. Fanon knew by experience what an imperial language meant coming from the body of a colonial subject. Fanon told us, "To speak means to be in a position to use a certain syntax, to grasp the morphology of this or that language, but it means above all to assume a culture, to support the weight of a civilization. . . . The Negro of the Antilles will be proportionately whiter—that is, he will be closer to being a real human being—in direct ratio with his mastery of the French language. A man who has a language consequently possesses the world expressed and implied in that language. . . . Mastery of language affords remarkable power."[32]

The paragraph is very explicit and sheds light on what I have been arguing and what Linda T. Smith stated in the epigraph to this chapter: non-Europeans, as seen by Europeans, cannot think. Here Fanon is recognizing the epistemic and ontological colonial difference: the power deriving from mastery of a language and the power differential in a given imperial language between the modern subject (French, white) and the colonial subject (a person with black skin in and from the Caribbean dwelling in France). To speak a language is not only an instrument to communicate but also an instrument to dominate. Science and philosophy, literature and politics, religion and political economy are expressed in modern/imperial languages that conform to regulations about who may enter the conversation, who is entitled (and who is not) to engage in certain topics regarding basic issues of disciplinary praxes. Recall that Western institutional disciplinary knowledge has been built by six modern European imperial languages (one of them being French). Hence, a destituted colonial subject (e.g., the work of the colonial difference), a "Negro" in this case, has two options: either giving up and emptying him-/herself of his/her own being, grounded in his/her praxis of living, or grounding his/her praxis of knowing in his/her praxis of living and becoming a full-fledged decolonial subject who dwells, lives, and thinks in the borderlands and borderlines.

That is why the politics of decolonial investigations is needed to reduce epistemology and aesthetic to their own deserved sizes. This task cannot be achieved through public policies and public marches of protest. It has to be confronted in the terrain of arguments, and arguments need investigations to be effective. Decolonial investigations aim at changing the assumptions of the dominant or hegemonic conversations. And that is what, in my understanding, Wynter is doing and arguing through her decolonial concept of *scientia* (Latin for "knowledge"). Fanon, as well as James and Wynter, recognized that the mastery of a language and the praxis of various related knowledge-making enterprises are governed by rules not always self-evident. Such rules are not self-evident either in a given imperial language itself or in the specific language of a discipline. But the modern disciplines have been formed in the six modern imperial languages (Spanish, Portuguese, Italian, French, English, and German). Doing sociology in Chinese or in French Creole in the Caribbean; doing philosophy in Urdu or Aymara—all remain for local circulation subjected to the epistemic colonial difference. None enters the peer-reviewed sanctions of institutional and international publications. I am not saying that the politics of decolonial investigations should aim to *be recognized*. Not at all. I am claiming the necessity of gnoseological and aesthesic reconstitutions in and out of the imperial disciplinary languages of Western modernity, breaking the code by intervening in the languages in which you have been nurtured. Border thinking proves also to be unavoidable if you do not aim to be recognized but to reexist. In light of Fanon's sociogenesis—in my understanding—Wynter sets up the horizon of meaning for a decolonial *scientia* whose basic task would be to unlearn the disciplines regulated by CMP in order to remake our praxis of living by delinking from Western disciplinary epistemic regulations.

VI   A Decolonial *Scientia* Based on the Sociogenic Principle

Sylvia Wynter extends and enhances Fanon's sociogenic principle by envisioning a *scientia* that explores the coming into being and the consequences of social classifications that divide people and separate "humans" from "nature" (two Western concepts). Wynter has sensed the urgency to delink from epistemology and aesthetics. Her *scientia* runs parallel to my gnoseological and aesthesic reconstitutions. Decolonial *scientia* delinks from the principles and assumptions of modern/colonial sciences grounded on the separation between the knowing subject and the known object. It begins by and from one's personal awareness of her/his place and ranking in the colonial matrix of power; instead of pretending to explore, account for, or explain some kind of "reality" out there, it explores, accounts for, and explains/interprets the hierarchical relations that the modern/colonial sociogenetic classificatory system established (and maintains). The displacement is radical: research is oriented toward the liberation of the actors doing research rather than to the management and control of "reality," including people, which is the overall orientation of modern/colonial sciences. Spelled in the Renaissance manner, Wynter's *scientia* orients the decolonial politics of scholarship and intellectual labor toward understanding and reducing to its own meritorious and local size the Western idea of modern/colonial *science* ranging from Galileo and Newton to Einstein and from Buffon to Linnaeus to Darwin. Let me say at once that I am not denying the achievements of Western science. I am divesting it from the universality of the assumptions that science should proceed on the separation between the knowing subject and the known object, whether the object is out there in "nature" or down here in "society:" the social scientist generally overlooks that he or she is embedded in the society being studied, and the natural scientist overlooks that his/her body is embedded in Earth and the cosmos. Science is a double-edged sword: within the bubble of Western modernity, it introduced a healthy antidote against obscurantism at the same time that it was put at the service of state interests and personal benefits. We have seen this in the US between 2016 and 2020, over climate change and COVID-19. On the other hand, science became an ideological weapon to destitute non-Western knowledges and wisdom. Wynter's *scientia* and Quijano's epistemological reconstitution (which I render here as gnoseological and aesthesic reconstitutions) are two matching decolonial horizons. *Scientia* (plural *scientiae*) legitimizes disavowed reexistence while at the same time uncovering the unintentional consequences of science for colonial subjects and subjectivities.

For this reason, Wynter's work can be posited as a *decolonial scientia* based on Fanon's sociogenic principle. The groundbreaking power of sociogenesis, Wynter argues, arises from Fanon's awareness of reporting, in the *third person*, his own experiences as a *first person* ("Look, a Negro!").[33] The experience he tracks, in other words, is of *being* through the eyes of an imperial *other*— that moment of dwelling on the borderline of the socially deselected, when "evolutionary" sociogenesis separates humans (the lesser ones) from Humans (the ones who classify and set themselves as the standard). Fanon tracks the moment of feeling the pain of the colonial wound that provokes the need for decolonial healing and for dignifying anger (an expression of the Zapatistas). He tracks the moment when he has the *experience* of *knowing* that he is being perceived as not quite human. What does it mean to be human in this scenario, where sociogenesis and the colonial/imperial differences are in constant movement to deselect?

Decolonial scientia is the *scientia* needed—not for progress and development or to find some hidden truth or to innovate within the colonial matrix of power (including, for example, the professional schools that "advance" technology for these purposes or the pharmaceutical and food industries that care more about their profits than the health of their customers). What is needed is *scientia* for liberating the deselected and to halt the modern/colonial processes of inflicting colonial wounds. *Scientia* and *scientiae* are the decolonial horizons of meaning to heal colonial wounds and to regenerate the communal after its dismembering in the processes of the double movement constitution/destitution, of constituting modernity implementing coloniality to destitute. I would add that the horizon of Wynter's *scientia* is the horizon, after Quijano, of gnoseological and aesthesic reconstitutions. The politics of decolonial investigations is common to both, and that is precisely what Wynter has been doing powerfully and relentlessly. We could easily multiply the spheres in which a decolonial *scientia* is needed. Although I do not foresee major university administrators, donors, and boards of trustees supporting any decolonial *scientia*, it doesn't mean that I will drop it. On the contrary, the hegemony claimed by the rhetoric of modernity requires a massive reversal of the politics of knowing, knowledges, and doing research. Who will do that? Scholars, intellectuals, conscientious administrators. Where could it be done? In spaces created for decolonial *scientia* in existing institutions, and in new institutions (workshops, summer schools, pedagogical institutions) created to articulate, enact, and disseminate it.

When it comes to the "Negro problem," Wynter—and before her W. E. B. Du Bois—in arguments pushing forward Fanon's crucial concept of sociogenesis, turns the table around: the problem is projected onto society by the social scientists or the politicians or the media as it was either created by the "Negro" or that exists almost "naturally." The "Negro problem" is not a problem of the Negro (it is rather a white problem with the Negro), but a consequence of sociogenesis at social scale. Seen from the perspective of any of the already established social sciences or humanities, the "Negro problem" would mean not only shattering sociogenesis and maintaining the ontology of society studied by social scientists, but also shattering the subjective presuppositions that guide and motivate Western social scientists (and Western social scientists beyond the West). Decolonial *Scientia* brings to the foreground the hierarchical system of classification in which both decolonial scientists and modern/colonial scientists are trapped. Since we (all on the planet) are implied in the sociogenic principle and classified in/by the colonial matrix of power, our praxis of living has been framed (not determined). Our identity is not what we are, but depends on how and where we have been classified, how we are seen, and how we see what we see. Therefore, the praxis of *scientia* requires the researcher to be aware of his or her sociogenic location in the CMP. Otherwise, sociogenesis and the "Negro problem" will become objects of investigation by someone who places him- or herself outside the sociogenic principle and from that outside "observes," assuming he or she has not been classified. Regarding sociogenesis, however, there is no "outside" for the simple reason that "he" who classifies is embedded in the classification and engaged, aware or not, in maintaining the mechanisms that keep the CMP working. If sociogenesis were to become an *object* of study rather than to serve as *the historical foundation and reconstitution of future global loci of enunciation*, then *scientia* would have been absorbed by the already existing Western hegemonic science. Thus, *scientia* built on the sociogenic principle (in this case the lived experience of the Black man, although this is not the only colonial experience or colonial wound that can sustain the emerging *scientia*) makes clear from the start that the mind/body problem (or the soul/body problem if we take a step back from secularism to Christian theology) *only makes sense in the domain of ontogenesis and phylogenesis.*

Put differently, the sociogenic principle reveals what the ontogenetic and phylogenetic principles hide: that race is not in the body but is built on a social imaginary grounded in colonial differences. Ontogenesis and phylogenesis belong to the epistemic and aesthetic Eurocentered sphere. *Scientia* and *gnoseological and aesthesic reconstitutions* belong to the sphere of the politics of decolonial investigations. Here is where Wynter—following Maturana's archeological exposure of Western science, more specifically of biology—performs the same in the human sciences, through the sociogenic principle. Additionally, the *biological-cultural* in Maturana is of prime relevance for *scientia* and *gnoseological/aesthesic reconstitutions* to find a ground in the hard sciences. After all, what is the sociogenic principle if not a radical delinking from the biology-culture duality (and of course the nature-culture duality as well)? At the same time, Wynter follows Fanon by setting the limits of ontogenesis and phylogenesis: ontogenesis and phylogenesis are categories of the hard sciences (the nomothetic sciences, looking for explanations). Within Western cosmology, the contributions by Sigmund Freud (and then Jacques Lacan) and by Michel Foucault brought significant changes in the sphere of ideographic sciences (looking for meaning rather than explanations).[34] Wynter, Fanon, and Maturana depart from both, the nomothetic and ideographic frames of Western epistemological and hermeneutics. They have been proposing and enacting radical shifts in the terms of the conversations. Which means delinking from the principles and assumptions upon which Western sciences, nomothetic or ideographic, have been established. *Scientia* as proposed by Wynter is neither nomothetic nor ideographic but decolonial, which means that its goal is, among others, to relinquish the principles and assumptions on which Western hard sciences and Western ways of knowing and understanding are based.

Sociogenesis introduces the perspective of the subject that ontogenesis reduces to object, by shifting to the perspective of the colonial subject who was not and is not in the experience of the psychoanalyst as modern subject (Maturana's observer).[35] If pursued further, this path shakes up the very foundation of psychoanalysis: at the moment in which racialized and sexualized subjects (LGTBQ) become psychoanalytic subjects of their own destiny, no longer the object, the masks sexism, racism, and patriarchy fall down.[36] It is from sociogenesis that concepts such as "double consciousness" and "border thinking" come into clear view, both key concepts of the politics of decolonial investigations and reconstitutions. Sociogenesis mobilize that: I am who I am in relation to the other who sees me as such. And in a society structured on racial hierarchies, *becoming* Black is bound up with *being perceived* as Black by a white person (e.g., Fanon understood that he *was* Black, according to the child's and the mother's eyes, in the often-cited scene). At stake here is "l'expérience vécue du Noir" rather than the "fact of Blackness," which was the English translation.[37] This process of being seen and seeing oneself the way one is seen by (racial/sexual) others is sociogenesis or Du Boisian double consciousness. The sociogenic principle is not intended as an object of knowledge in itself, but rather as a locus of enunciation that bonds knowledge with decolonial subjective formations. If modern/imperial epistemology (in its diversity, but always imperial diversity) and *scientia* were spatially, chronologically, and subjectively located vis-à-vis the sociogenic principle, then the project of decolonial *scientia* would emerge and recontextualize our global nodes of space, time, and subjectivity. *Scientia* laid down the path for the politics of decolonial investigations. Recasting these global nodes through sociogeny, we are then able to imagine decolonial *scientia* as follows:

a   Spatially, decolonial *scientia* appears at the borderlands and borderlines (territorial as well as linguistic, subjective, epistemic, ontological) created by the consolidation and expansion of global linear
thinking and the colonial matrix of power. Consequently, decolonial
scientia can literally be taken up all over the globe in parallel to modern science. If coloniality is all over, so must be decolonial *scientia* and
gnoseological/aesthesic reconstitutions. Decolonial *scientia* emerges
from where modern sciences intervened in regions previously
unexploited by the CMP. Decolonial *scientia*'s main goals are to offer
a decolonial option to all of those/us who, one way or another, were
racially and sexually, because of religion or nationality, destitute.
Destitutions provoke reconstitutions. My comments are neither to
critique modern science nor to critique the postmodern critique of
modern sciences.[38] It is building rather than evaluating.

b   Chronologically, *decolonial scientia* regionalizes the history of modern
science and its location within the CMP. The analytics of this history are only in part an archeology or genealogy of its own formation and transformations, bringing to the surface the intended and
unintended consequences of the promised march toward one single
future. The historicity of decolonial *scientia* responds to the outcome
of epistemic colonial differences that secured the totality of knowledge by asserting its universal truth while simultaneously destituting
coexisting gnoseologies, praxis of living and sensing.[39] While in mod-

ern sciences chronology, epistemic breaks, and paradigmatic changes follow one another in a linear chronology, decolonial *scientia* unfolds spatially in many locals and chronologies. Decolonial *scientia* operates on heterogeneous historico-structural nodes and delinks from the tyranny of linear chronologies.[40] Decolonial *scientia* bonds the space of decolonial struggles around the world to the struggles to reassert humanity in the face of exclusions and deprivations, which most recently have taken the form of hostility toward large-scale migrations of the "barbarians" to the "civilized regions."

c   Subjectively, decolonial *scientia* authorizes and promotes the politics and agencies of decolonial subjects that the sociogenic principle relegated to the exteriority of knowing and thinking (see epilogue). The convergence of racism and sexism that sociogenesis discloses reveals that disciplinary regulations prevent the opening to building knowledges and ways of knowing that disobey the management of the hegemonic scientific community. Contrary to male, Christian, and Eurocentric subjects and subjectivities, as well as to female, critical, and/or white counterparts who had significant roles in the structuring of modern/imperial knowledge systems, decolonial subjects are at the border of non-European languages, religions, and gnoseologies. Thus they are among the subjects that have been categorized, through imperial knowledge, as racially subordinate, sexually deviant, economically disadvantaged, and so forth. Decolonial subjects are face-to-face with imperial subjects who, instead of "saving the colonial Other" by some self-initiated actions, turn the plate around and accept the experiences and guidance of decolonial subjects.[41]

Decolonial *scientia* puts forth three types of tasks: first, to reimagine rather than to deny the links between geo-history and knowledge and between biography and knowledge; second, to explore the consequences that Western expansion (today called "globalization") has had and continues to have for the population and the environment (the exploitation of natural resources, for example, as *needed* by imperial economies). These two tasks emphasize the ways in which both particular lands and peoples have been and still are targeted for conversion to Christianity, to civilization, and to development models, and, most recently, for enrollment in the support for "human rights" and "democracy." With these two tasks in mind, it is necessary to look at responses *globally* in order to avoid the imperial and self-misleading trap that focuses primarily on *local* responses to *global* designs. The third task is for decolonial *scientia* to generate world-making and community-building in which life (in general) has priority over economic gains, economic growth, and economic development. This kind of knowledge will subject economic growth to human needs rather than make human needs subservient to economic growth and development.

VII What Is It Like to Be Human? Sociogenesis, Coloniality of Being, and the Politics of Decolonial Investigations

In her rehistorization of the human, Wynter distinguishes between two kinds of histories. One is the history of the emergence and spread on planet Earth of living organisms (and with this flourishing of life, the overrepresentation of Man-as-Human from the European Renaissance to today); that is, the era of the anthropoi or the Anthropocene. The second history is that of the sociohistorical *conditions* that made it possible for the elite (consisting of European men and women) to construct such an idea as "Man-as-Human and posthuman" (i.e., Man3) and to be successful in implementing it. As she notes, the *idea* of Man at a particular moment of world history, the European Renaissance, was also the foundational step for building racism as we sense and know it today (see chapter 1).[42] This rehistorization of the human shifted the geography of reason. Instead of accepting that there is a universal perspective provided by Man's consciousness imploring to be recognized in the house of Humanity, Wynter shifts the perspective to rehistorize what it means to be human, a question that we now understand as being asked from within the framework of sociogenic knowledges and experiences mainly by humans destituted from Humanity.

At this point, it is useful to remember that Wynter points out the misleading translation of one chapter of Fanon's *Black Skin, White Masks* (1952). The chapter in French is titled "L'expérience vécue du Noir." Instead of being translated as "The Lived Experience of Black People," it was translated in a very "scientific" vocabulary: "The *Fact* of Blackness" (emphasis mine). Sociogenesis brings another type of consciousness to the fore: no longer the plain consciousness, without an adjective, of modern territorial subject (e.g., "L'expérience vécue du Blanc"), but the consciousness in and of the borderlands and borderlines: double consciousness that is provoked by the colonial difference. To dwell in the borders means to inhabit the colonial difference from where border thinking emanates. In Wynter's work there is no claim for recognition *within* the hegemonic concept of Humanity but a demand to recognize that the universality of Man/Human is no longer sustainable.[43] For that reason, an important task of decolonial *scientia* is outlining the inventions of

Man/Human (and humanism) and illuminating the who, when, why, what for, and consequences of such invention:

> It is the story in which the idea of humanism, of its decoding since our modes of self-inscription first erupts, where Man and its human Others—that is, Indians, Negros, Natives (and I would add Jews and Muslims)—are first invented. And this history is the history of the expansion of the West from the fifteenth century onwards, and an expansion that is carried out within the terms of its own cultural conception of its own origins. And you see, it is this ethno-culturally coded narrated history that is taught both in a now global academia as well as in all our schools, while it is this history in whose now purely secular terms we are all led to imagine ourselves as Man, as purely biological and economic beings. The *history* for Man, therefore, narrated and existentially lived as if it were the *history-for* the human itself.[44]

Crucial in Wynter's statement is her concept of "history-for." It is through this concept that she is able to show how the local concept of Man/Human and its imperial universality puts out of consideration any other self-conceptualization in languages and civilizations that were not associated with Greek and Latin and thus based in Western Christendom, as Western civilization is. What Wynter calls "human" (without capitals) and the consequent stories of the spread of the human species around the planet from its original sites of becoming—areas in what is now known as Africa—are complemented by Iranian philosopher Ali Shari'ati's assertion that in the Qur'an a distinction is made between *Bashar* (being) and *Ensan* (becoming). In this conceptualization, we (humans without a capital letter) are all *Bashar* (biologically, anthropos); we are collectively that species of living organisms that spread around the planet from time immemorial, thousands of years ago, many centuries before the elite of the European Renaissance classified themselves as Man/Human (culturally, the anthropos becoming Man/Human) and disregarded those who fell outside this category. *Bashar* and *Ensan* are explained by Shari'ati as follows: "The difference between Ensan, Bashar and all the other natural phenomena such as animals, trees, etc., is that all are 'beings' except Ensan who is 'becoming.' . . . But man in the sense of the exalting truth, towards whom we must constantly strive and struggle in becoming, consists of divine characteristics that we must work for as our ideal characteristics. . . . Mind you that becoming Ensan is not a stationary event, rather, it is a perpetual process of becoming and an everlasting evolution towards infinity."[45] Man/Human is reduced to its own size.

I am not offering a Muslim definition as a replacement for Christian humanist definitions. I am noting that humanness is pluriversal and neither

Muslims nor Christians have the right to claim universality beyond the universe of their own conception. And I am further noting that Shari'ati has the same right to be wrong as the European humanists. In other words, I am underscoring that each definition is *truth-for*, arguing pluriversality and thus delinking from the belief and expectation of universality. If an assertion of universality cannot be made from the perspective of *humanitas*, it is because it maintains the point of reference to which to aspire. Decolonial thinking and living are not blueprints to assimilate but to deny the universal pretense of *humanitas*.

The problem Wynter and all of us face is that we—and I mean all of those who are not fully incorporated in the Western construction of Man/Human, that is, all the "we" who do not identify as Human—have been placed outside the category and, furthermore, we do not feel ourselves members of the Human/Man club. It is a club that lives on prejudgements regarding skin color, sexual preferences, non-Western languages, intelligence, (former) Third or Second World people, and any other superficial factor that justifies expelling someone to the exteriority of the enunciation (where the control and management of knowledge and knowing takes place). If this were not the case, I—a South American, Spanish-speaking individual not even residing in Spain, but in the Third World—would not be writing this or any of what I have written since beginning *The Darker Side of the Renaissance* (1995). There is certainly a question of scale to take into account in deselection, and in many ways I have some of the privileges of Man/Human that many other deselected persons do not have. It is possible, we have seen, to belong to a deselected ethnicity and still become president of a state (Barack Obama, Evo Morales), and to be deselected racially or sexually or both, yet still be a Hollywood or popular music star.

This doesn't change the rules of deselection because it doesn't matter what socially deselected individual, region, state, language, or nation hangs over your head if you have been identified in one or more deselected categories. Self-affirmation by individuals and collectives to reexist and recover their lost dignity requires border thinking grounded in border gnoseology. Why? Because you have to affirm yourself in relation to the narratives that deselected you. That is what Fanon did with sociogenesis and Wynter after him; and now I am following in their footsteps with my particular local history and my tracings of the trajectories of immigrant consciousness. We (you, reader, and I) must be ready to go into Wynter's truth-for and its theoretical, political, and ethical implications. As a first step, it is imperative to dig into the Western conditions in which Man/Human emerged. Wynter puts it as follows:

The issue of race as the issue of the Colonial Question, the Nonwhite-Native Question, the Negro Question, yet as one that has hitherto had no name, was and is fundamentally the issue of the genre of human, Man, in its two variants. The clash between Las Casas and Sepulveda was a clash over this issue—the clash as to whether the primary generic identity should continue to be that of Las Casas's theocentric Christian, or that of the newly invented Man of the humanists, as the rational (or *ratiocentric*) political subject of the state. . . . And this clash was to be all the more deep-seated in that the humanists, while going back to the classics and to other pre-Christian sources in order to find a model of being human alternative to the one in whose terms the lay world was necessarily subordinated, had effected their now new conception and its related "formulation of a general order of existence" only by transuming that of the Church's matrix Judeo-Christian conception, thereby carrying over the latter's schematic structure, as well as many of its residual meanings.[46]

Truth-for is the hinge that connects two stories within the racial contours of colonialism: the global story of the human species (the anthropos) and the local story of the European Renaissance Man/Human (Man1, Man2, Man3) that appropriated and universalized the first. The starting assumption in Wynter's thinking is that "every form of life, every living species would now be able to know its reality only in terms of its specific *truth-for.*"[47] This premise already questions the assumption that there is a truth-for someone who can know the truth-for everyone else. For Wynter the premise that every living species has its own truth-for applies to the particular species we are now referring to as humans: the species that can semiotize—that is, translate into audible or visible signs—its own conception of its being as a species and its place among other species:

> For example, before the voyages of the Portuguese and Columbus we can say that all geographies, whatever their great success in serving human needs, had been ethnogeographies—geographical *truth-for* a genre of human. Before Copernicus, the same—all astronomies by means of which humans had regulated and legitimated their societies had been, in their last instance, ethnoastronomies. Before Darwin, again, the same thing. Knowledge of biological forms of life had been, in spite of their great value for human needs, ethnobiologies. And now the rupture with these forms of *truth-for* is going to be made possible only by means of the two intellectual revolutions of humanism, the first which took place in Renaissance Europe, the second which took place at the end of the eighteenth century

in Great Britain. . . . Or to put it more precisely, in our case, an ethno-class or *Western bourgeois form of humanism, whose truth-for at the level of social reality is truth for Man; it cannot be truth for the human.*[48] (Emphasis added.)

VIII Closing Remarks

The main task of Sylvia Wynter during the past forty or more years, at least since the publication of "Ethno or Socio Poetics" (1976), has been to erode the foundation of the Western imperial (racial and patriarchal) concept of Man/Human.[49] Three thinkers who are pillars in her conceptual genealogy of thought are C. L. R. James, Humberto Maturana, and Frantz Fanon. From James, and from the Black and Caribbean intellectual tradition generally, she calls into question the white, post-Renaissance concept of Man/Human. From Maturana, she posits that "creation" of the image of the world is the result of autopoietic (self-generating) processes, and she connects this creation to the work of Frantz Fanon and the recursive constitution of Man-as-Human. From Fanon she gains the concept of sociogenesis. What she proposes, overall, is a shattering of the imperial concept of Humanity based on the ideal of the White Man. She reconceptualizes this ideal not by providing a new definition or image of it, but by changing the question and the terms of the conversations: What does it mean to be Human? Wynter follows this questioning by thinking through that which we have inherited from imperial Europe, the possibilities and limitations of purely Western science and knowledge systems, and how humanness can be recognized as connective and interhuman. From this it is crucial to call into question the right that an ethno-class attributes to itself to "possess" and embody the truth of what Human is and means.

Wynter summarizes this project in a famous phrase: "Towards the Human, after Man."[50] We can add "after anthropocentrism." But the "after" doesn't lead Wynter, or me, to the posthuman and the postanthropocentric. It leads to where we are and will continue to be for a while: to decolonial politics of scholarship and of communal building. Wynter's *scientia* and the politics of decolonial investigations aim to place knowing at the service of reexistence rather than existence at the service of the disciplines. Knowing to live, not living to know. I will come back to this point in the next chapter.

I am now in a position to reformulate the question about the posthuman and the Anthropocene in these ways: Are the posthumans the enunciators of the posthuman? Or is the posthuman an entity detached from the enunciator? Is the enunciator describing his/her (its?) posthumanity? And concurrently, are the scientists who tell the story of the Anthropocene embedded in the story they are telling or outside of it? Are anthropoi themselves the conceptualizers and theoreticians of the Anthropocene? Or are they Humans observing posthuman entities separated from themselves? Are the enunciators of the posthuman themselves posthuman? Are anthropoid scientists postulating the history of the species anthropos on Earth (e.g., the Anthropocene), or are they Humans observing the anthropos and its era, the Anthropocene? These questions change the terms of the conversation and can be formulated from the perspective opened up by the decolonial *scientia* sketched by Wynter when she steps outside the well-guarded territories of modern/colonial sciences, natural and social, and of professional schools. Wynter's move is a reconstitutive move from the exteriority of the CMP; it returns the gaze, looking at the machine of modernity/coloniality working constantly in the double movement of constitution/destitution in which the posthuman and the Anthropocene narratives are trapped. Shifting the geography of knowing, being, and identifying sociogenesis as a modern/colonial tactic of making exteriorities, Wynter has turned the subjects of scientific knowledge into storytellers of modernity/coloniality. Guided by Wynter's *scientia* and Quijano's epistemological reconstitution (which I reworked into decolonial gnoseological and aesthesic reconstitutions), in the next chapter I essay a decolonial reading of Edmund Husserl's phenomenology.

13 Decoloniality and Phenomenology

I The Circumstances

For a long time, I have been interested in Edmund Husserl's *Philosophy as Rigorous Science* (1911) and *The Crisis of European Sciences and Transcendental Phenomenology* (1936). Husserl had a sustained concern with science, but his approach changed from a desire to make philosophy a rigorous science, to confronting the crisis of European sciences, and ultimately to uncovering transcendental consciousness. This trajectory led him to expose, behind the rigor of scientific inquiries, the silenced presence of the "lifeworld."

My early interest in Husserl started when reading *Philosophy as Rigorous Science* as a student of philosophy in Córdoba, Argentina. Later on, during the years spent writing my dissertation in Paris, my research in semiotics and the philosophy of science drove me to *The Crisis of European Sciences*. When I moved to the United States in the mid-1970s, while still in the last stage of writing my dissertation, I ran into Humberto Maturana's *Biology of Cognition* (1970). As a result, when in subsequent years I followed the publications of Humberto Maturana and Francisco Varela, I was ready for the shock and the surprise of encountering Aníbal Quijano's seminal article "Coloniality and Modernity/Rationality" (1992; English translation 2007). "Coloniality" connected all the pieces of a puzzle I had begun to discern. I use the expression "ran into" to describe my encounter with *Biology of Cognition* because the discovery of Maturana and Quijano was serendipitous: I came across Humberto Maturana while looking for a book on cognition by Paul Garvin in the open stacks of the Indiana University library. And I ran into Quijano's essay in a bookstore in Bogotá, Colombia, while looking at the table of new books.[1]

All these works reoriented my praxis of living, that is, my sensing (that something was broadening my horizons), and my reasoning. I began to slide away from thinking within the framework of semiotics and toward the horizons opened up by concepts that were not yet in my vocabulary or my bodily sensibility: biology of cognition, praxis of living, languaging, lifeworld, coloniality, modernity/coloniality, decoloniality. One's sensing changes with one's knowing, and one's knowing reifies or modifies one's sensing. For me all these phenomena and concepts were fluctuating. I began to sense that semiotics was precisely the kind of manifestation of modernity/rationality that Quijano was talking about, complicit with coloniality. Perhaps it was those mutations that made me sensible in the early 1980s to colonialism. It was not an abrupt change of terrain. On the contrary, because I was trained in semiotics and sensitive to signs, I was driven to explore the colonization of languages, the colonization of memories (history), and the colonization of space (cartography).[2]

You may not believe me if I tell you that I still have on my bookshelf the Spanish translation of Husserl's *La filosofía como ciencia estricta* (1961), which I acquired when I was a BA/MA student in Córdoba, Argentina. That this book is still with me, next to other books of philosophy from that time, is a telling sign of how material traces follow someone. I am now rereading the 1962 edition by Editorial Nova, in Buenos Aires, and experiencing again a sensation between incredulity and curiosity. For as we know, according to the story told by Victor Farías (Chile), a former student of Martin Heidegger (Germany), Spanish was not a proper language in which to do philosophy.[3] The same feeling, although expressed in a less accusatory tone, was felt by Spanish philosopher José Ortega y Gasset when, returning to Spain after studying with Husserl, he defined himself as a *philosopher in partibus infidelium*, for at that point he must have felt that doing philosophy in Spain was like doing it, as the Catholics say, "in the lands of the unbelievers," that is, way out of place.[4] I am telling this short story because it made clear to me, in reasoning and sensing, the meaning of the phrases "praxis of living" and "biology of cognition" in Maturana's work and "coloniality of knowledge" in Quijano's work. In short, this personal story of researching, living, sensing, thinking, reasoning, and being in the world while doing what everyone does while living provides the frame in which I here approach decoloniality and phenomenology.

When you change the terrain of sensing and emoting in the process of building rational arguments (oral or written) in a specific language (required by the circumstances), everything depends on where you start.[5] If you start from Husserl's publications and the atmosphere that prompted his arguments, and the publications and the debates and conversations that ensue, you remain caught in the web of Eurocentrism. If you start instead in the former colonies, translating Husserl's book fifty years after its publication, and you are aware of this gap in time and space and make it explicit, you began to swim in the water of the *geopolitics of knowing*, sensing, and believing; the *coloniality of knowledge*; and the *colonial difference*. I start, then, from the translation into Spanish of Husserl's 1911 work, known in Spanish as *La filosofía como ciencia estricta*.

It is not just the abstract and universal arena of ideas that will matter most in the discussion that follows, where Husserl will dominate, but both the praxis of living and my lifeworld, which lured me to Husserl's lifeworld. Sensing and thinking decolonially have driven me to delink from codified knowledges in order to embrace the praxis of living and languaging "in between" national languages (in this case, German, Spanish, and English). I begin, then, with the first paragraph of *La filosofía como ciencia estricta* in the Spanish translation by Elsa Tabernig:

> Desde sus primeros comienzos, la filosofía pretendió ser una ciencia estricta, más aún, la ciencia que satisfaga las necesidades teóricas más profundas y haga posible, desde el punto de vista ético-religioso, una vida regida por normas puramente racionales. Esta pretensión fue sostenida en las diversas épocas de la historia con mayor o menor energía, pero jamás fue abandonada, ni siquiera en momentos en que los intereses y las aptitudes con respecto a la teoría pura parecían debilitarse, o en que los poderes religiosos inhibían la libertad de la investigación.[6]

> From its earliest beginnings, philosophy has claimed to be rigorous science. What is more, it has claimed to be the science that satisfies the loftiest theoretical needs and renders possible, from an ethico-religious point of view, a life regulated by pure rational norms. This claim has been pressed sometimes with more, sometimes with less energy, but it has never been completely abandoned; not even during those times when interest in and capacity for pure theory were in danger of atrophying, or when religious forces restricted freedom of theoretical investigation.[7]

Decolonially read, this paragraph stands out in several respects and sets the tone for the argument that follows. Let us parse it. In the first sentence, Husserl reveals his obsession: establishing philosophy as a strict science. Although in the third sentence he affirms that this claim has been made in different historical periods, it is known that his concept of science comes from Nicolaus Copernicus's and Galileo Galilei's works from the sixteenth and seventeenth centuries, which were consolidated by Isaac Newton's physics in the eighteenth (in *Philosophiae Naturalis Principia Mathematica*). The legacies of astronomy and theoretical physics—two subjects known to Newton as "*Philosophiae Naturalis*"—as well as most other modern Western ideas of science since the eighteenth century, replaced what had previously been the highest frame for the management and control of knowledge: theology. So, in effect, Husserl believes himself entitled to claim, as philosophy itself had done, that philosophy is science.

The path from theological *scientia* (framed in the trivium and the quadrivium) to secular science and philosophy is a foundational trajectory of the coloniality of knowledge.[8] Interpreted from the history of the colonial matrix of power (CMP), this trajectory is foundational for Western modernity.[9] Why? Because when the Renaissance was compounded with European commercial expansion, knowledge and education were piggybacked onto it. The European medieval and Renaissance institution of learning, the university, was transplanted to the New World and then to Asia and Africa. Today, this process has received renewed energy in the United States, which is transplanting universities to the Middle East and to East and South Asia.[10]

This trajectory is constitutive of modernity/coloniality, which means that the constitution of the European praxis of knowing and knowledge (that is, its own conceptualizations and its own enactments of these conceptualizations, i.e., the self-representation of European thinking) was, at the same time, knowingly or not, a downgrading if not an outright disavowal of all the coexisting non-European praxes of knowing and knowledge. Hence the modernity/coloniality of knowledge underscores the power differentials amid the formation and growth of knowledge in Europe and the inattention to or blatant strangling of native knowing and knowledges in the colonies, as well as in non-European civilizations that were not colonized but did not escape coloniality—China, Russia, Japan, the Ottoman sultanate, and so on.

It may sound as if I have lost the gist of my argument. But I have not. I am navigating the geopolitics of knowing, sensing, and believing. Returning to Husserl's quoted paragraph, we find at the surface all the constitutive and underlying assumptions upon which knowledge (*scientia* and science) has been built from the European Renaissance (to which Husserl returned to rebuild) to the Enlightenment (which Husserl critiqued to legitimize his rebuilding of Renaissance *scientia*). What are striking are the foundational assumptions sustaining Husserl's idea of the philosophy of knowledge. Those assumptions leave us—distracted readers—believing that Western knowledge is the final destination and that all other knowledge on the planet, including local histories and non-Western languages, have to catch up or else be left behind. At the time Husserl was writing *La filosofía como ciencia estricta*, it was already taken for granted, especially in the history of German philosophy, that Europe was the spatial center of the planet, that Germany was the center of Europe, and that both were the present in the long trajectory of the Spirit, from the past in China to the present in Europe and Germany, as Hegel outlined in the introduction to his lectures in the philosophy of history.[11] Husserl was thinking in an already *constituted* frame to which he added the spheres of philosophy and science—a frame equivalent to that of Hegel's account of the historical formation of the modern nation-state (the objectivization of Spirit).

Before going further into Husserl's phenomenology, let us pause to consider what I mean by decolonial reading, decoloniality, and decolonial thinking and doing, in the context of both gnoseological and aesthesic reconstitutions (the way) and the politics of decolonial investigations (the horizon) that I am pursuing in this book. Decoloniality (or decolonization as decoloniality) drives us (engaged practitioners) to delink from the narrow history and praxis of Western (i.e., west of Jerusalem) knowledge and brings to the foreground the coexistence (denied by the rhetoric of modernity) of stories, arguments, and *doxa* destituted by Eurocentered languages or taken as objects and/or documents. The linear concept of time (e.g., modernity and tradition) creates mirages in which colonial differences transform differential coexistences into being behind in time (e.g., China and Islam are behind and have to modernize according to the rhetoric of modernity). This is one example of many of how linear timelines serve to arrange the past of all the domains.

It is in this frame of mind that Husserl does not call linear time and specific space (from Greece, north of the Mediterranean, to Germany) into question but, rather, floats on them, assuming the universality of "his" time and space, of "his" lifeworld. He recasts the history of philosophy from the Renaissance, which was a novelty in Continental philosophy (after Descartes, the Renaissance was a superseded chapter of Continental philosophy) to legitimize the claims of his contribution to the *history of philosophy*, which is, indeed, the history of *European* philosophy in the process of constituting itself as *universal* philosophy. Decoloniality, on the other hand, came into being in the

South American Andes at the end of the Cold War. Coloniality is a decolonial concept born in the Third World, and it is the concept that founded decoloniality (i.e., decolonial thinking). Pedagogically speaking—as I pointed out in the introduction to this book—the double relation between coloniality and decoloniality is similar to that between the unconscious and psychoanalysis: the unconscious is a psychoanalytic concept, and psychoanalysis is founded on the unconscious. Analogously, transcendental consciousness is a phenomenological concept, and phenomenology has been bound to the concept of the transcendental consciousness. At stake here is the radical relevance of the geopolitics of knowing, sensing, and believing in decolonial thinking and doing: thinking presupposes praxes of living. AI does not.

In South America, the cultural sphere permeating its inhabitants at the turn of the twentieth century, as well as at the twentieth century's end, was quite different from the predominant cultural sphere permeating the inhabitants of Germany, western Europe, and their neighboring zones of influence. In South America, disregarding the dissimilarities among different countries, there was a sense that in the battle between civilization and barbarism (which was the horizon on which the idea of "Latin" America emerged), civilization was finally victorious.[12] In Europe, on the other hand, World War I had put an end to the illusion of progress and civilization built during the nineteenth century, both for what the reality for Europeans turned out to be, namely, a vision of the barbarism of civilization, and for the political, economic, and cultural repercussions the war had on emerging nation-states that had gained independence from Spain and Portugal and were voluntarily dependent on the United Kingdom and France.[13] The settler colonialism that founded coloniality (i.e., the underlying logic of all modern Western colonialism since 1500) was no longer necessary: the logic of coloniality was and still is at work with or without historical (actually existing) colonialism. The Opium War, for instance, is a case in point: China was not colonized, but it did not escape coloniality. The same could be said about Russia and Japan—although each local history has its peculiar manifestations. The history of South America is the history of native independences from settler colonialism.

Focusing on the coloniality of knowledge brings to the surface the entanglement and power differentials of knowing and knowledge in the colonies, former colonies, and western Europe. During the first half of the twentieth century, continental philosophy, in general, was not a high priority in any of these locations, and phenomenology, in particular, was mostly unknown; when it became influential, and philosophical circles began to be formed in Latin American universities, philosophy came into being with a colonial difference.

The fact that *La filosofía como ciencia estricta* was translated and published in Buenos Aires fifty years after its publication in Germany reveals the time lag between the two ends of the geopolitical spectrum and the power differential manifested in doing philosophy, variously, in Europe, Latin America, Africa, and Asia. All of this is part of the lifeworld (a phenomenological concept) and the praxis of living, thinking, and doing (decolonial concepts) at one or the other end of the spectrum.

In between World War I and World War II, when Husserl was composing *The Crisis of European Sciences and Transcendental Phenomenology: An Introduction to Phenomenological Philosophy* (left unfinished in 1936), South America was experiencing a wave of industrialization that changed its basic agrarian economy to a much more industrial (and urban) one. The labor force required by the emerging dependent industrial economy had stimulated massive migrations from the countryside to the cities and made a more congenial place for European immigration to the Americas between 1880 and World War I. Thinking and intellectual labor in South America (and on the rest of the planet beyond the heart of Hegel's Europe: Germany, France, and the United Kingdom) were, in the first half of the twentieth century, not very troubled by making philosophy a rigorous science.

I will leave the United States aside, but I cannot go on without mentioning the well-known opening paragraph of Alexis de Tocqueville's *Democracy in America*: "I think that in no country in the civilized world is less attention paid to philosophy than in the United States." Written in 1833, when Europe was flourishing with the *philosophes* in France, Kant was leaving his mark in Germany, and Hegel was following suit, the sentence makes evident the fact that in the United States philosophy was at best a secondary concern. There were other pressing concerns that were not those in Europe. Although the second half of the nineteenth and the beginning of the twentieth centuries saw a growing interest in philosophy, "pragmatic" urgencies always encouraged an evasion of philosophy.[14]

It was shortly before and shortly after World War II that original paths of thinking emerged in South America. By "original" I mean, on the one hand, the originality of the literary genre known as the essay. Before the introduction of the social sciences in Latin America, in the 1960s (part of the rhetoric of development and modernization), the essay was the genre par excellence for bringing ideas into the public sphere, exploring both the histories of thought in South America and the present political, economic, and cultural conditions of being and living in America (including the US; see chapter 11). The essay was a manifestation of a specific way of thinking through which the history of thought was explored. On the other hand, it was also by means of the essay that the geopolitical and cultural questions of national, sub-Continental, and Continental identities were explored. Identity was not a problem in European thought. Europeans knew who they were, from the consolidation of Western Christianity since the colonization and conquest of a continent that was renamed America to Hegel. Transcendental issues, such as the ontology of Being, of Time, and of existence (in general), were major concerns. European thinkers did not need to think "Europe." Europe was, they were Europeans, and that was that, all taken for granted. No longer. But the intellectuals of European descent in America (for at that point Indigenous and Afro-descendant thinkers did not participate in the public sphere) could not avoid the question of who they were before thinking about transcendental consciousness, Being, Time, phenomenology, etc. (see epilogue). Geopolitically, in the nineteenth century, identity could not be avoided after independence in the former South American colonies (as with decolonization in Africa and Asia in the second half of the twentieth). A case in point is Edmundo O'Gorman, a philosopher of history and a Mexican of Irish descent. In the 1950s he published two landmark books. Invoking Heidegger's exploration of Being, O'Gorman turned to the "being" of America and concluded that America was not an existing entity to be discovered, since the being of America emerged from its invention. Bringing to light that America was invented and not discovered showed that the very idea of discovery turns out to be a self-serving narrative telling us more about European invention than about invented "America."

By the 1960s, a new question emerged in the already established community of philosophers in South America. This generation, born between 1915 and 1925 and educated between the two world wars, came to prominence in the 1950s and began to ask whether there was any proper philosophy in Latin America. O'Gorman, born in 1906, was at his prime in the 1950s, when the new generation was beginning to leave its mark. Luis Villoro, a Spanish Mexican philosopher born in 1925, addressed at the end of the twentieth century the "problem" of Latin American philosophy that emerged in the1960s, a problem of his generation:[15]

LA POSIBILIDAD DE UNA FILOSOFÍA LATINOAMERICANA
La reflexión filosófica en América Latina se ha puesto en cuestión continuamente a sí misma. En 1842, Juan Bautista Alberdi se planteaba ya el problema de la existencia de una filosofía latinoamericana y creía que ésta podría iniciarse al reflexionar sobre problemas propios del nuevo continente. Desde entonces, muchos pensadores volvieron sobre el mismo

tema: ¿Cómo sería posible una auténtica filosofía latinoamericana? Porque
en nuestros países la filosofía parece tener todos los rasgos de la inauten-
ticidad: falta de originalidad, superficialidad, carencia de continuidad y,
sobre todo, dependencia imitativa de la producción filosófica de otros
países. Al igual que en otros campos de la cultura, la filosofía parece ser, en
América Latina, un reflejo de la actividad que se realiza en las metrópo-
lis culturales. Cobrar conciencia de esta situación, proponer vías para
superarla, ha sido obra de pensadores como Alejandro Korn, José Carlos
Mariátegui, Francisco Romero, Samuel Ramos y Leopoldo Zea.[16]

THE POSSIBILITY OF A LATIN AMERICAN PHILOSOPHY

Philosophical reflection in Latin America has continuously questioned itself. In 1842, Juan Bautista Alberdi was already considering the problem of
the existence of a Latin American philosophy and believed that it could
be initiated by reflecting on problems proper to the new continent. Since
then, many thinkers have returned to the same question: How would an
authentic Latin American philosophy be possible? Because in our countries philosophy seems to have all the features of inauthenticity: lack of
originality, superficiality, lack of continuity, and, above all, imitative dependence on the philosophical production of other countries. As in other
fields of culture, philosophy seems to be, in Latin America, a reflection of
the activity that takes place in the cultural metropolis. To be aware of this
situation, to propose ways to overcome it, has been the work of thinkers
like Alejandro Korn, José Carlos Mariátegui, Francisco Romero, Samuel
Ramos, and Leopoldo Zea. (My translation; emphasis added.)

The question that Villoro asked was prompted by the colonial epistemic difference. You can see it in the work of Argentine political philosopher Juan Bautista
Alberdi (1810–1884). Alberdi wanted a Latin American philosophy, but he did not
ask why it was necessary. He addresses the content and leaves the terms of the
conversations intact. Villoro instead asks how this epistemic dependency can be
overcome. He is aware that the issue is larger than the sphere of philosophy. It is
indeed the epistemic colonial difference that molds all spheres of life (political,
economic, religious, philosophical, scientific, racial, sexual, ethical, etc.) insofar
as such spheres are not just spheres of doing but also spheres of saying, sensing,
and thinking. That is why the essay has been the preferred genre of Latin American thinkers. Every cultural praxis of living among humans (i.e., "handmade"
in the larger sense that all human making is handmade, including robotics and
artificial intelligence) is conceptualized, framed, and defended or contested in
the social as well as in the private sphere. The differences in all spheres between

the discourses managed and controlled by European institutions (starting from the imperial languages in the colonies) have been shaped by European (i.e., embedded in Europe's culture) actors, national languages, and institutions.

That is precisely what Villoro was sensing and expressing in the paragraph quoted above.

III The Advent of *Coloniality* toward the End of the Twentieth Century

In light of the previous geopolitical argument, it is important to remember that Edmund Gustav Albrecht Husserl was born in Prostêjov (1859), a town at that time ruled by the Austro-Hungarian Empire, long before the Czech Republic came into being (1918). But it was in Germany that he became recognized as the founder of the "school of phenomenology" in Continental philosophy. He was compelled, in the spirit of the time and the history of western European philosophy, to engage in a radical critique of historicism and of psychology, arguing that all knowledge can be explained by understanding transcendental consciousness. He was interested not in factual history but in the essential or transcendental consciousness of the lifeworld and historical and scientific knowledge.

Husserl's critique of psychology, which he had confronted to account for transcendental consciousness (a psychological term and phenomenon after all), led him to the conviction that it is possible (and necessary) to postulate a unified philosophy of the sciences by arguing that transcendental consciousness is the limit of all possible knowledge. The obsession with "unified theory" (and Husserl was not the only one, nor the last, to have it) is an obsession of "North Atlantic universal fictions."[17] Affirming the need for a "unified theory" prevents asking the question: why? Who needs it, and what for? The CMP should be understood as the underlying Western presupposition of epistemic gluttony: like the vacuum monster in the film *Yellow Submarine* (directed by George Dunning, 1968), unified theory wants to consume it all. Husserl's work moved from the desire to make phenomenology a rigorous science to an understanding of science in general (and it was to physical science that he primarily turned) as grounded in transcendental consciousness. Furthermore, he was assuming that transcendental consciousness was a universal existent rather than a Eurocentered obsession. Universality and unity are two pillars of the coloniality of knowing and knowledges.

I am recalling some basic issues of Husserl's phenomenology—well known to readers of the *Journal of Speculative Philosophy*, where this essay was originally printed—to buttress my bringing of *coloniality*, and hence *decoloniality*, into the argument. I am now arriving at the crux of the matter. The invention of America (since America did not exist at the time, it could not have been discovered) provided the foundational moment of *epistemic and ontological colonial differences*: the invention of exteriority *within* a unified theory of the planet and the planet's population.[18] Both forms of difference (epistemic and ontological) were postulated without naming them. What was argued by Christians was the need to Christianize the "Indians" and to justify the expropriation of their land. Why? Because they were epistemically and ontologically inferior, ignorant of God, wrongheaded, and they could not govern themselves. That was not just a cultural difference. Rather, there were visible cultural differences hiding the power differentials that constitute epistemic and ontological differences.

The increasingly dominant theological European discourses (a form of storytelling) in all spheres of the social, together with the expanding will for navigation and distant explorations, all supported by the printing press and the publication of books and maps, evince the complicities between the Christian theological mission, the economic interests of entrepreneurs and adventurers, the financial lenders, the political management of non-European Indigenous organizations, and, above all, the increasing management and control of knowledge. This knowledge—institutional, linguistic (European languages dominating over local languages), and subjective (the self-assumed superiority of European actors)—guided and justified the dismantling and replacement of a form of governance among the existing great civilizations of the Americas (Mayas, Aztecs, Incas) by Spanish institutions and justified the expropriation of land, the exploitation of labor, and the accumulation of wealth. Whoever controls and manages meaning (knowledge), also controls and manages money, which together constitute the economic coloniality of capitalism (in the liberal and Marxist vocabulary). The Mayas, Aztecs, and Incas are our Greece and Rome.

It was at this junction that *coloniality* (shorthand for the coloniality of power or the colonial matrix of power) was introduced, in 1990, in South America. While phenomenology, transcendental consciousness, and the lifeworld were concepts that Husserl needed in order to respond to the then current historical and philosophical debates in Europe, for Aníbal Quijano, born in 1928, a Peruvian sociologist who was a teenager when Husserl died, the historical, political, and intellectual debates in South America required a different approach and conceptualization. The pressing issues that fueled Husserl's phenomenology were issues emerging in western Europe after four hundred years of the European accumulation of money and meaning. Husserl was thinking from the heart of Europe (Hegel's expression), while Quijano was dwelling within a world formed by five hundred years of colonial legacies. Coming to terms with the geopolitics of knowing, sensing, and believing was essential for Quijano to understand the structural role of knowledge in the articulation of colonial differences—the expression of power differentials—in all spheres of the world order. For him transcendental consciousness and coloniality have the same status. They are geopolitical and theoretical abstractions needed to understand pressing issues in the lifeworld that generated them.

I am here not so much comparing a Peruvian sociologist in his prime during the fourth quarter of the twentieth century with a German philosopher in his prime during the first quarter of the same century, as I am underscoring the entanglement of modernity/coloniality, an entanglement that generates decoloniality. In other words, decolonial thinking and doing came into being at the moment that it became possible to unmask the complicities of modernity with coloniality (hence, modernity/coloniality). Husserl may not have been aware of it (I believe he almost certainly was not) so he could ignore it, while Quijano could not have ignored it because he and others before were sensing it. His was an awareness of colonial legacies and their trajectories in South America as well as worldwide that triggered the concept of coloniality and the fundamental distinction between colonialism and coloniality. This concept ends up being the anchor and founding stone of a school of thought known under the compound modernity/coloniality as well as modernity/coloniality/decoloniality. I am underlining two distinct lifeworlds, in one of which phenomenology emerges in the heart of Europe, and in the other coloniality emerges in the South American Andes, where the majority of the population are Pueblos Originarios of ancient Andean civilizational descent.

I have just mentioned that coloniality should not be confused with colonialism. "Coloniality" names the underlying logic of all western European colonialism, from the Iberian Peninsula since the sixteenth century, to Holland and Britain since the establishment of the East India Company, to French colonialism since Napoleon, and to the United States since 1945, this last a particular case of coloniality without colonialism. Like Husserl's transcendental consciousness, Sigmund Freud's and Jacques Lacan's unconscious, Karl Marx's surplus value, and Noam Chomsky's deep structures, "coloniality" names something you do not see that operates in what you do see. You do not see coloniality, but the majority of Earth's population do sense it. Coloniality was at its peak in Husserl's time. By 1900 the entire African continent was under the control of western European states. World War I was certainly not unrelated to the intramural conflict of imperial interests. However, in western Europe, coloniality at that time was unthinkable and therefore unsensed, yet it could not be ignored by the African population—a population that had no say in the management, control, creation, and distribution of knowledge. Thus, transcendental consciousness was indirectly, if unwillingly, contributing to a general disregard of colonialism and to hiding an experience of coloniality that nevertheless could not but be a component of Husserl's transcendental consciousness.

The coloniality of knowing and knowledge uncovered precisely regional beliefs in the universality of their fictions. It is not universality per se, or the aim to achieve totality and unification, that constitute the problem, for every cosmogony and cosmology (in their theological, scientific, and philosophical versions) aims at totality. The problem arises when a regional totality becomes totalitarian. "Nothing is less rational, finally," Quijano argued, "than the pretension that the specific cosmic vision of a particular ethnie [i.e., ethnic group, that is, the ethno-European bourgeoisie] should be taken as universal rationality, even if such an ethnie is called Western Europe because this . . . pretend[s] to impose a provincialism as universalism."[19]

The universal pretenses of Western science and philosophy are embedded in Western Christian theology and its secular mutation mainly since the eighteenth century but already at work at the beginning of the seventeenth in Francis Bacon's *Novum Organum* (1620) and a couple of decades later in René Descartes's *Discourse de la method* (1637). Every known non-Western cosmology posits a totality, but for whatever reasons none of the coexisting civilizations on the planet, for thousands of years, were interested or able to intervene in, destitute, and control other civilizations. The crucial concept of coloniality opened up a horizon of understanding and explanation of how the coloniality of knowledge works in all disciplines as well as in the mainstream media and the public sphere.

I have already stated that coloniality is a decolonial concept as much as transcendental consciousness is a phenomenological one. The concept of coloniality brings to light the decolonial approach, just as the approach illuminates the concept. Modernity is not a decolonial concept. It belongs to the European social sciences and humanities (for European they are, created to deal with their own interests and issues), types of storytelling based on assumptions and regulations about story-building that define and defend the contours of Western civilization (the European Union and the United States). However, modernity/coloniality is a decolonial concept. The compound concept undermines, from the lifeworld of colonial legacies, one of the basic assumptions of Western cosmology-philosophy: that concepts denote, that there is a one-to-one correlation between words and things.[20] In every domain of life, since the sixteenth century, Western narratives of the rest of the world, from the Renaissance to the Enlightenment and from both to today, modernity has gone hand in hand with coloniality. There is no modernity without coloniality; hence modernity/coloniality, the foundational step of decolonial thinking and doing, is a decolonial concept. For this reason modernity/coloniality, and the colonial matrix of power, are heterogeneous historic-structural nodes revealing the underlying structure that sustains and governs, in the larger sense of the word, the order of knowledge and the order of being that cannot be captured in the epistemic and aesthetic foundations of Western knowing and sensing.[21]

Before going back to Husserl, let us take another step into the entanglement between modernity/coloniality. The slash that divides and unites the two concepts indicates both the colonial epistemic difference (lesser knowers, knowing, and knowledges) and the ontological difference (lesser beings because lesser knowers). Of course, Husserl's investigation was not directly addressing the inferiority of non-European knowing, thinking, and believing (as Kant did in *Observations on the Feeling of the Beautiful and Sublime*, *Anthropology from a Pragmatic Point of View*, and *Geography*). However, being oblivious to the planetary consequences of European expansion testifies to his disregard for the consequences of Europeans' impact on the lifeworld of the planet in his search for the transcendental European lifeworld.

IV   A Decolonial Take on Husserl's Phenomenology

The task Husserl sets for himself in *The Crisis of European Sciences* is significantly different from the one he undertook in *Philosophy as Rigorous Science*. In *The Crisis*, the goal was no longer that of philosophy becoming a rigorous science but, in fact, to survey the history of modern philosophy since the European Renaissance, which Husserl conceives as the "struggle for the meaning of man."[22] Rightly so—the Renaissance created the image and the idea of Man/Human (see chapter 12 for a discussion of why I capitalize these terms in certain contexts) that became the measuring stick for classifying and ranking lesser men/humans, including European women and the rest of the people on the planet. Man/Human was the point of reference from which to build racism and sexism. Although by "man" Husserl means "human beings," the overall image that comes out of his argument reflects the presupposition of the masculinity of the lifeworld that Husserl inhabited.[23] Prominent European women philosophers were not abundant in philosophical and phenomenological debates. Husserl's destination, in summary, was the understanding of "transcendental consciousness" through the experience of his lifeworld in the sphere of the sciences as well as in, so to speak, everyday life. That was his "object" of investigation (the enunciated and the content of the conversation) and the "objective" of "transcendental phenomenology" (the enunciation or the terms of the conversation).

A crucial moment of his philosophical argument (and for the decolonial one I am myself building) is part III.A, #43, of *The Crisis*, devoted to the *epoché* and the transcendental correlation between world and world consciousness.[24] In this and the following section, Husserl makes a distinction between objective science and science in general, a distinction that brings to light the goal of philosophy struggling to understand the meaning of man. To that end, Husserl introduces the influential concept of lifeworld as a partial problem within the general problem of the objective sciences. This concept calls for a complementary expression, not quite the status of a concept but nevertheless an important expression: life-praxis. The lifeworld is not static; it implies the constant movement of everything done by Man/Human as well as everything that Man/Human did not make but which, on the contrary, made Man (water, air, light, etc.). Whatever cosmological, biological, or theoretical vocabulary you would like to invoke here, the point is that living organisms, a small set of which very recently (more forcefully around 1300 among Western Christians) began to call themselves Man/Human, are part of the lifeworld that Husserl set out to investigate from the Renaissance on. At stake here is the distinction in Greek philosophy between *doxa* and *episteme*. The key insight of Husserl's phenomenology was to realize that objective knowledge of science is grounded in the lifeworld of the scientists, something that the scientists take for granted—hence, the "phenomenological reduction" is necessary to seize and understand the essence of the lifeworld. Gnoseological/aesthesic reconstitutions focus instead on geopolitical praxis of living.

There is here an important disclaimer that Husserl makes to set up the task of the philosopher and "his" (the philosopher's) relation to the lifeworld. He has to suspend and bracket (*epoché*, "bracketing" or "phenomenological *epoché*" or "phenomenological reduction") all sensing and emoting: "Situated *above* his own natural being, and above the natural world . . . —as philosopher, in the uniqueness of his direction and interest— . . . he forbids himself to ask questions which rest upon the ground of the world at hand, questions of being, questions of value, practical questions, about being or not-being, about being valuable, being useful, being beautiful, being good, etc." The task of phenomenological philosophers, then, consists, on the one hand, in detaching themselves from the lifeworld, while recognizing, on the other hand, that the lifeworld in which they are submerged continues to exist. This step is necessary, although it may seem paradoxical to the investigation of the "transcendental correlation between world and world consciousness."[25]

Husserl's urgency to detach himself (as well as the phenomenological philosopher) from the ground of "the world at hand" could be compared with Quijano's urgency to detach ("extricate" is Quijano's term; "delink" is the word I use) himself from the paradigm of rationality/modernity in which Husserl is caught and which includes phenomenology. Quijano writes:

> The critique of the European paradigm of rationality/modernity is indispensable—even more, urgent. But it is doubtful if the criticism consists of a simple negation of all its categories; of the dissolution of reality in discourse; of the pure negation of the idea and the perspective of totality in cognition. It is necessary to *extricate oneself* [cf. delink] from the linkages between rationality/modernity and coloniality, first of all, and definitely from all power which is not constituted by free decisions made by free people. It is the instrumentalization of the reasons for power, of colonial power [i.e., coloniality] in the first place, which produced distorted paradigms of knowledge and spoiled the liberating promises of modernity.[26] (Emphasis added.)

The necessity to extricate oneself from the paradigm of rationality/modernity, which was reformulated in subsequent years as the CMP, and to delink from the CMP, implies a further inevitability to delink from Continental philosophy and phenomenology. This does not mean a "simple negation of all its categories" (a call for fast readers who overlook that *the critique is not of "modernity" in toto but of its aberrations*), as Quijano expresses at the beginning of the quoted paragraph. It means that the problems of Continental philosophy are the problems of Continental western Europe (the "heart of Europe" in Hegel's metaphor), not the problems and issues in need of attention in South America, Southeast and Central Asia, and North and South Africa, in spite of the transplants of Continental philosophy and phenomenology that may be found in any of those locales. The problem beyond Europe is precisely the intrusion (the aberration) of European global designs, in all dimensions, and the devaluation and erasure (destitution) of local histories that do not correspond to the local history of the heart of Europe. The urgencies of most of the planet, beyond the North Atlantic, are related to global coloniality rather than to global modernity, for globalization is the globalization both of modernity and of coloniality—that is, the good, the bad, and the ugly.

I would add that at the other end of the spectrum, a decolonial thinker (instead of a philosopher or phenomenologist) whose prime tasks consist in understanding the historical foundation of the CMP, its transformation, management, and contestation (instead of transcendental consciousness and the lifeworld), and in working on gnoseological and aesthesic reconstitutions, needs to throw her- or himself into the world of colonial epistemic and ontological differences. That is the lifeworld that generates decolonial living, thinking, and doing. I mean this not in Heidegger's sense, where *the* world is *his* sensing and emoting, but rather, thrown into the world of colonial legacies, colonial differences, and colonial wounds. This means to throw oneself into the world of dehumanization in all its dimensions (sexual, racial, linguistic, national, religious, epistemic, ontological). For decolonial thinkers and doers, the awareness of dwelling on the border (rather than dwelling in the territory, where Hegel and Heidegger dwelled), of being thrown, rather than throwing oneself, into colonial differences, is the foundational experience, the essence, to use Husserl's vocabulary, of coloniality and colonial differences. Once decolonial thinkers, beings, and doers find and/or become aware of their place in the colonial matrix of power (next to people experiencing colonial wounds), their awareness will be simultaneous with the urgency to delink from the CMP in order to relink with what the CMP disavows that is relevant to their own being in rebuilding communal islands within and outside societies regulated by the state.

Husserl's constant concern to achieve a rigorous foundation for scientific knowledge is expressed as follows: "Scientific, objective truth is exclusively a matter of establishing what the world, the physical as well as the spiritual world, is in fact. But can the world, and human existence in it, truthfully have a meaning if the sciences recognize as true only what is objectively established in this fashion . . . ? Can we console ourselves with that? Can we live in this world, where historical occurrence is nothing but an unending concatenation of illusory progress and bitter disappointment?"[27] Now we begin to see that it is a question not of denying or ranking but of starting from the entangled coexistence in power differentials, of epistemic and political projects. For Husserl, the question was to maintain the splendors of the scientific procedures of science, while detaching himself from its empirical miseries: science limited to the "factual" dimension of the world. Hence his consistent critique of Cartesian dualism (mind-body), Hume's and Locke's empiricism, and Kant's transcendental idealism, which Husserl replaced with his "transcendental consciousness."

The difference between Husserl and his predecessors is that Husserl's concepts are grounded in an awareness of the lifeworld. By excluding themselves from the history of philosophy in which they are embedded, Husserl argues, other philosophers remain detached from the lifeworld, including the history of philosophy that makes their philosophies possible. Husserl finds his way out of their dilemma by proposing and starting from a new reading of philosophy in the European Renaissance: "It was not always the case," he observes, "that science understood its demand for rigorously grounded truth in the sense of that sort of objectivity which dominates our positive sciences in respect to method and which, having its effects far beyond the sciences themselves, is the basis for the support and wide-spread acceptance of a philosophical and ideological positivism." During the Renaissance, Husserl argues, the specific human questions "were not always banned from the real of science; their intrinsic relationship to all the sciences—even those of which man is not the subject matter, such as the natural sciences—was not left unconsidered."[28] Husserl's reaching out behind the Enlightenment, so to speak (a rare move in the "heart of Europe," where everything—not only philosophy—seems to have gone from Greece to the Enlightenment), and his encounter with the Renaissance at the very beginning of *The Crisis*, lead him to the "lifeworld" that, he noticed, was removed from philosophical reflections from Descartes to Kant. For decolonial thinkers in South America, the Renaissance is unavoidable; it is the darker side of the Renaissance that is *constitutive* of our lifeworld, our praxis of living.[29] That is the modernity/rationality that Quijano experienced.

I pointed out above the differences between colonialism and coloniality. Colonialism is a topic of the social sciences and the humanities. Seen from the colonial histories of South, Central, and North America, political economy, political theory, philosophy, science, and Christian theology are all distinct landscapes of the darker side of the Renaissance. Adam Smith devoted many pages to the topic in his foundational treatise *The Wealth of Nations* (1776), although it is the least-read section in courses and seminars in political science and political economy. Karl Marx, on the contrary, paid much less attention to colonialism, but of course neither of them could think "colonially," for they both were embodied in the modern European lifeworld, not in the colonial lifeworld. They were obviously modern Europeans, not decolonial lifeworld thinkers; they were both backing their enunciations on Greece and Rome, and for them the Atlantic was primarily a site that was contributing to "the wealth of nations" and to "primitive accumulation."[30] Decolonial living and thinking do not start with and could hardly claim Greece and Rome as their/our ancestral grounding. In the Americas, the Atlantic detour of the direct line from Greece-Rome to western Europe, is the grounding of decolonial thinkers from the African diaspora, First Nations, and people of European descent. In this regard, Wynter's ancestry in the Atlantic is different from Quijano's and mine, as it is for the Indigenous decolonial thinkers I will join in the next chapter. Without the Atlantic detour of 250 years (1500–1750), there would not have been a European Enlightenment, an Industrial Revolution, or capitalism. Husserl and his predecessors were facing southeast (toward Greece and Rome), their backs toward the Atlantic that nourished the European lifeworld but not their thinking.

Husserl was, however, aware of the blindness of his predecessors and contemporary scientists to their own lifeworld, at the same time as he himself was blind to the fact that the lifeworld he was invoking was neither universal nor global. Rather, it was the lifeworld of European history imaginatively transplanted, since the Renaissance, thanks to Europe's colonial expansion. Manifestly, the lifeworld in the colonies was not the lifeworld Husserl was experiencing in Freiburg. His blindness to the limits of his own lifeworld was a consequence of his taking for granted assumptions in his lifeworld about the universality of philosophy and of transcendental consciousness. In short, his blindness was a consequence of Eurocentrism. The geopolitics of knowing, sensing, and believing was erased. One of the few moments in which his erasure of geopolitics is implied comes in a couple of paragraphs where he reflects on non-European civilizations. Asking "how the lifeworld, after the *epoché* of the objective sciences, can become the subject matter of a science," he confronts the situation in which "we are thrown into an alien social sphere, that of the Negroes in the Congo, Chinese peasants, etc., [when] we discover that their truths, the facts that for them are fixed, generally verified and verifiable, are by no means the same as ours."[31]

So far, so good for Husserl. This awareness may incline Husserl's reader to celebrate his generous mind. But remember that he is in search of universal truth within transcendental consciousness. His blind spot appears in the following sentences: "But if we set up the goal of a truth about the object which is *unconditionally valid for all subjects*, beginning with that on which normal Europeans, *normal Hindus, Chinese*, etc. agree in spite of all relativity—beginning, that is, with what *makes objects of the life-world common to all, identifiable for them and for us* (even though conceptions of them may differ), such as spatial shape, motion, sense-quality, and the like—*then we are on the way to objective science*"[32] (emphasis added). Here we see Husserl's assumption that all these various groups—"normal Hindus, Chinese, etc."—will agree once we stipulate that the relevant opinions within the groups are the opinions of *normal* members of the group. And of course, their normality should consist in them sharing the views of Europeans. Husserl was founding an objective science of transcendental consciousness. What for? To correct previous shortcomings and to advance toward attaining truth, one could answer. But "What for? To what purpose?" will be addressed below.

The paragraph just quoted sets up Husserl's later distinction between the *objective-logical a priori* and the *a priori of the lifeworld*. The coloniality of knowledge comes out loud and clear in this distinction when we read the paragraph decolonially. First is its assertion that something can be unconditionally valid for all "normal" Europeans, Hindus, Chinese, and so on. (The people of the Congo do not appear in this catalogue of the "normal" except, perhaps, as "etc.") What Husserl is doing here is denying (by ignoring) that Chinese, Hindus, and Congolese have their own ways of thinking and doing, their own praxes of living in their lifeworld, in which their thinking about their praxis has nothing to do with the history of European philosophy of which Husserl is so well aware.[33] What he is saying tells us more about Europeans than about people of the Congo. Husserl failed to recognize the diversity of "the a priori of the lifeworld" on the planet that he perceived as managed and controlled by the "objective-logical knowledge a priori," which is his and Continental philosophy's problem. His recognizing "their" lifeworld is at the same time denying "their own" thinking about it, for the lifeworld he presumes for them is not an ontic but an ontological entity: created by philosophical phenomenology.

V   Modernity/Coloniality and the Decolonial Question of Knowledge

When Quijano underscored the relevance of knowledge and highlighted "rationality" in the title of his article "Coloniality and Modernity/Rationality," he was already deviating from the Eurocentric critique of the modern sciences and of modernity. His critique of modernity and rationality was extramural in the sense that it emerged and unfolded in European exteriority, sensing the borderland lifeworld. "Exteriority"(see introduction, section III.3) is not the ontic outside Europe, but the outside built into the process of building European "interiority." Exteriority is not ontic; it is ontological: storytelling about the outside, the epistemic invention (storytelling) of an ontic "outside." If it were an ontic "outside," it could not be controlled and managed. So it has to be constructed as an "exteriority" to legitimize its devaluation and legitimize its management by global designs (conversion, progress, civilization, development). That is what Eurocentrism means, decolonially speaking. It is a question not of geography but of the epistemological *constitutions* of colonial ontologies (e.g., the coloniality of knowledge and colonial differences).

Quijano was critiquing not just the content but the basic assumptions (i.e., the terms) that grounded the content of this knowledge and provided a foundation for the generation of "new" knowledge—the battle horse of the idea of modernity, since the "New World" entered the European vocabulary in the last decade of the fifteenth century. He changed the terms of the conversation that, until the late 1980s, had dominated the debate on decolonization by mutating—although neither rejecting nor negating—decolonization into decoloniality. There are indeed two manifestations in different historical contexts. The context of decolonization (roughly 1947–1979) was liberal economy versus state communism. The context—in the 1990s—of decoloniality was neoliberalism and the incipient signs of de-Westernization. As a result, the goal of decoloniality was no longer to send the settlers home so that the natives might build their own nation-state, but rather to undertake *epistemic reconstitution*— that is, precisely to change the terms (assumptions and rules) of the conversation rather than just the content, which were the splendors and miseries of decolonization.[34]

Let us take a minute to review the basic points of Quijano's argument. Remember, he was trained not as a philosopher but as a sociologist. Remember also that I am not restricting myself to disciplinary boundaries but addressing issues concerning the geopolitics of knowing and of knowledge. Decoloniality is neither a "field of study" nor a "discipline" but a way of being in the world, interrogating the structures of knowledge and of knowing that we encounter when we are thrown into the world. In the first place, Quijano observes, the assumption that the "subject" is "a category referring to the isolated individual— because the subject constitutes itself in itself and for itself, in its discourse and in its capacity of reflection" should be questioned and rejected.[35] The difference between Quijano's and the postmodern critiques of modernity is obvious in this statement: postmodernity does not question the unique consciousness and personal experience that constitute the subject. Like Husserl's phenomenology, postmodern thinkers dwell in the European lifeworld. Postmodernity has questioned, although it was already challenged by Marx and the Frankfurt school, the idea that the subject is independent of the object to which it is related. Quijano brings this relationality into preeminence: human beings are not isolated anthropoi; the subject cannot be an isolated consciousness but is a consciousness that arises and is formed in relation with other subjects. In African philosophy there is a term that captures this idea with all its consequences: *Ubuntu*.[36]

What are Quijano's problems with the basic assumptions of Western epistemology when he questions modernity/rationality? First is the concept of the "individual and individualistic character of the 'subject' which like every half-truth falsifies the problem by denying inter-subjectivity and social totality to the production sites of knowledge."[37] *Ubuntu relationality* disparages the *ontology of the individual. Gnoseology and aesthesis are built on relationality, while epistemology and aesthetics are built on ontology.* Second is the notion that the known "object" is incompatible with the results of current scientific research, according to which the object's "properties" are modes and times of a given field of relations. The consequences are that once the ontological assumptions about conceiving objects as constituted by their properties are removed and replaced by assumptions that "objects" (material or digital) are constituted by their relationality with their cosmic and cultural web, an ontology of individuals loses its allure and vanishes behind relations among human beings and on the cosmic living Earth. Consequently, the separation between subject and object can no longer be maintained in decolonial thinking. Gnoseological/aesthesic reconstitutions are founded on relations rather than on an individualistic ontology. Relationality is not limited to the field of objects but is also the energy that relates subjects and objects.[38] This argument, derived from Quijano, leads to the following conclusion: "The subject is the bearer of 'reason' while the 'object' is not only external to it, but different [in] nature. In fact, it is 'nature.'"[39] It may seem that Quijano's critique was already at work in Europe; however, there is a radical difference, the difference of the lifeworld and the geopolitics of knowing, sensing, and believing: what Quijano is underlining is that non-European people and regions were made "known (to be) object," and once they were considered objects to be known, they were *destituted* as knowing subject, their knowledge reduced to anthropological facts and their making as objects to be collected in European museums (see chapter 14). Quijano's arguments aim at restituting the destituted rather than at being "objective and scientific" within the limited scope of Western rationality. His goal, in other words, was the reconstitution of knowing, knowledge, and (decolonial) subject formation through dispelling the assumptions (terms of the conversation) that sustain the edifice of European knowledge. His was not that of disputing the truth of the argument and offering "a better version" of whatever was the case, but rather delinking and remaking the terms and regulations of the conversations. The Western obsession with controlling *the* truth (for which management of a unified theory is needed) is the Trojan horse of the coloniality of knowledge.

It is understandable, Quijano continues, that the idea of the individual "subject" was necessary to create the idea of emancipation, in Europe, from monarchic and religious structures of government. For the emerging ethno-class, the bourgeoisie, a person who was subjected to God and the monarch, needed to be liberated, and to be liberated meant to empower himself (for him the individual was and is) as an independent, self-interested person, competitive and egotistic. That was a basic assumption of enlightened emancipation. The coming into being of a European ethno-class (the bourgeoisie) implied to sideline God, the monarchy, and the papacy and to place reason and the individual on top of the pyramid. And they did. But to do so it was necessary and fundamental that knowledge be founded under different assumptions. It was an intramural change in the content of the conversation, not the terms. Secularism was the consequence.

What Quijano identified as the basic assumption of modern Western epistemology, the subject-object distinction, was indeed an epistemic revolution in Europe from Bacon and Descartes on. While Husserl himself was critical of his own European legacy, and his analytics of the crisis of European sciences led him to the search for transcendental consciousness and the lifeworld, which no doubt was a significant turn in the history of Western philosophy and of the philosophy of science, for Quijano the urgencies were different but related. The analytics of the coloniality of power (the colonial matrix of power) and, more specifically, the coloniality of knowledge (which included the analytics of science and Continental philosophy) led him to delink ("extricate oneself") from epistemic Eurocentrism. Delinking was and still is one side of the issue. The other—and here is the main goal of decoloniality—is *gnoseological and aesthesic reconstitution*. Thus formulated, decoloniality no longer remains within the frame of political decolonization during the Cold War. Decoloniality "as decolonization" means gnoseological/aesthesic reconstitutions, while the horizon of decolonization during the Cold War was meant to build native nation-states.

VI Closing and Opening

I arrived at the end of the journey that started with my reencountering Husserl after encountering Quijano, but I had to forgo further exploration of the meaning of the lifeworld, looking into Humberto Maturana's biology of cognition and praxis of living and into Hans Jonas's philosophy of life. Jonas, a former disciple of Edmund Husserl, deviated from Husserl's teaching because of the abstractedness of "transcendental consciousness." He was instead attracted to Heidegger's "existential" concerns. But when Jonas, a Jew, saw Heidegger accepting the rectorate of the University of Freiburg, compounded by Jonas's own personal experiences with the Nazi regime, he turned away from Heidegger to follow his own learning and experience and to explore the phenomenon of life. Working conceptually between Husserl's phenomenology and Hei-degger's "formal existentialism" (the term Jonas used to explain to himself why Heidegger's existentialism led him to join National Socialism), Jonas was led to elaborate an existential explanation of the phenomenon of life, which he published in 1966.[40] Humberto Maturana's *Biology of Cognition* was published in 1970. I doubt that Maturana, at that point, could have read Jonas's book. Maturana, who is profiled sometimes as a second-generation cybernetician, was working between biology and cybernetics.[41]

I will not go into any detail about what the biology of cognition (which I addressed in the previous chapter) and the phenomenology of life have to do with decoloniality. But I will give you a hint. I would say that Maturana's biology of cognition accounts for the emergence of living organisms on the planet and for the emergence of a species of living organism that, through the use of hands and engaging in languaging, was able to coordinate complex behavior and to tell stories about the origin of the cosmos and of the spe-cies of living organisms, sharing the story of creation and of themselves. The lifeworld is one of many concepts referring to the common lived praxis of all autopoietic organisms on Earth. Many because lifeworlds on the planet are not artificially made, and they regenerate autopoietically—it doesn't matter where and when. Regarding Jonas, who detached himself from Husserl first and Heidegger second, he carried the traces of what he was detaching himself from (as is always unavoidable and which could be turned into a strength rather than into lamenting critique). In the preface to *The Phenomenon of Life*, Jonas tells us that life "offers an 'existential' interpretation of biological facts"—which means that life is explained by the life itself of a species or liv-ing organisms, including the human species. In the introduction, he adds the following: "A philosophy of life comprises the philosophy of the organism and the philosophy of the mind."[42] Thus, Jonas offers a philosophical and exis-tential interpretation of biological information, or "facts," while Maturana offers a biological interpretation of cultural "facts," including science and philosophy. Hence, while Jonas changes the *content* of the conversation within Continental philosophy, Maturana has changed the *terms* of the conversation in the wide sphere of knowledge. By offering a biological account of cogni-tion, languaging, and humanness, Maturana has done in the "natural sciences" what decoloniality is attempting to do in the "human sciences" (i.e., social sciences and the humanities, including art and literature). But this is a topic for another essay.

In the next chapter, the final one, I concentrate on the variegated manifesta-tions of gnoseological and aesthesic reconstitutions within the wide spectrum of de-Westernization and decoloniality. Both carry the signs of a change of epoch, rather than of an epoch of changes. The cycle of Westernization of knowledge, politics, economy, subjectivity, is closing due to the irreversible processes of reconstitution of the interstate world order and of the people taking their/our destinies in their/our own hands. I return to Carl Schmitt's first and second nomos of the Earth, the subject of part III of this book. The cycle between 1500 and 2000 was the epoch of the second nomos, of global linear thinking, of unipolarity and universality. The emerging epoch, which I call "the third nomos of the Earth," is becoming the epoch of border thinking, multipolarity, and pluriversality.

The Rise of the Third Nomos of the Earth

Un nuevo sol y una nueva expresión en el lenguaje de la vida donde la empatía por el otro o el bien colectivo sustituye al individualismo egoísta.

Donde los bolivianos nos miramos todos iguales y sabemos que unidos valemos más, estamos en tiempos de volver a ser Jiwasa, no soy yo, somos nosotros.

Jiwasa es la muerte del egocentrismo, Jiwasa es la muerte del antropocentrismo y es la muerte del teologocentrismo.

Estamos en tiempo de volver a ser Iyambae, es un código que lo han protegido nuestros hermanos guaraníes, y Iyambae es igual a persona que no tiene dueño, nadie en este mundo tiene que sentirse dueño de nadie y de nada.

A new sun and a new expression in the language of life where empathy for the other or the collective good replaces selfish individualism.

Where Bolivians all look at each other the same and we know that united we are worth more, we are in times of being *jiwasa* again, it is not me, it is us.

Jiwasa is the death of egocentrism. *Jiwasa* is the death of anthropocentrism and it is the death of theologocentrism.

We are in time to be *Iyambae* again, it is a code that our Guarani brothers have protected, and *Iyambae* is the same as a person who has no owner, nobody in this world has to feel like the owner of anyone and nothing.
—DAVID CHOQUEHUANCA, AYMARA, vice president of Bolivia, Inaugural Discourse, La Paz, November 8, 2020, translation mine

NO·MOS *(n)*

1 a law, convention, or custom governing human conduct

2 (Greek mythology) the daemon of laws and ordinance

NO'M'IC *(a)*

customary; ordinary—applied to the usual English spelling, in distinction
from strictly phonetic methods

AN·O·MIE OR AN·O·MY *(n)*

1 social instability caused by erosion of standards and values

2 alienation and purposelessness experienced by a person or a class as a result
   of a lack of standards, values, or ideals: *"We must now brace ourselves for disqui-
   sitions on peer pressure, adolescent anomie and rage" (Charles Krauthammer)*

RE·SUR·GENCE *(n)*

a continuing after interruption; a renewal

RE·STI·TU·TION *(n)*

early 14c., from Old French *restitution* or directly from Latin *restitutionem*
(nominative *restitutio*) "a restoring," noun of action from past participle
stem of *restituere* "set up again, restore, rebuild, replace, revive, reinstate, re-
establish," from *re-* "again" (see **re-**) + *statuere* "to set up," from PIE root *sta-
"to stand, make or be firm"

RE·CON·STI·TU·TION *(n)*

from *re-* "back, again" + *constitute* (v.); the action of building something up
again; the action of changing the form and organization of an institution

I   The Issues: Anomie/Nomos and Land/Earth

This chapter concentrates on decoloniality, slightly touching on de-
Westernization (see chapters 9 and 10), and reviews and explores in more detail
the concepts of nomos and Earth analyzed in my foreword to *The Anomie of the
Earth: Politics and Autonomy in Europe and the Americas*.[1] In rewriting this chapter
I paralleled Carl Schmitt's "second nomos of the earth" (see below) to Anibal
Quijano's "colonial matrix of power (CMP). My intention is not to supplant or
supersede the former by the latter. That would be a modern not a decolonial
way of reasoning. I want to underscore their coexistence, the geo- and body-
politics of knowing what the two narratives evince, an issue I explored in the
previous chapter by paralleling Husserl's phenomenology with Quijano's coloniality. I argued that we, on the planet, are experiencing a change of epoch (no

longer an epoch of changes), a change of epoch that—we will see below—cannot be accounted for by the advent of a "new nomos" (Schmitt's expression) within the same epoch of the "second nomos." The *transition* metaphor corresponds to the era of the second nomos. The advent of the third nomos is an *explosion* rather than a transition in which de-Westernization, re-Westernization, and decoloniality would coexist for some time. Re-Westernization could be seen as a transition within the second nomos. But de-Westernization and decoloniality are something else: they come out of *reconstitutions* rather than transition. The global turmoil we are all experiencing on the planet cannot be captured by either "newness" within the same, a fixed frame of mind, or an unaltered epoch that only admits changes within its changes that are conveniently accounted for by adding the prefix "post-." What is closing is the epoch of the second nomos, unipolarity in international relations and the hegemony/dominance of Western modernity. Its main features are (a) the interstate disputes over the control and management of the CMP (de-Westernization) and the opening to multipolarity, and (b) the negation and delinking from the CMP (decoloniality) and the opening to pluriversality in the sphere of knowing and knowledges (gnoseology) and subjectivities (aesthesis). Both coexist with re-Westernization, the efforts to maintain unipolarity in international relations and universality in the sphere of knowing, knowledge, and subjectivity (coloniality of power, the CMP). Time is diversifying; post-X is out of place in the change of epoch. The post-X remains functional in the epoch of change to maintain re-Westernization in the sphere of knowledge and knowing (epistemology) and aesthetics (subjectivity).

I start from "anomie" and "Earth," highlighted in the title of the book, *The Anomie of the Earth*. In the alteration of nomos, or the lack of it, anomie implies disorder ("entropy" in the cyber vocabulary), a loss of regulation and equilibrium. The breakdown of harmony between human and life on Earth is today expressed in concerns about "climate change" and "ecological crisis." I interpret "anomie," consequently, as manifestations of the failure of what Carl Schmitt described as the second nomos of the earth (see chapter 9 and section II, below, for more details on this). Schmitt located the advent of the second nomos around 1500; it was spirited by "global linear thinking" that mapped the planets by means of cartography and international law. Schmitt acknowledged that the advent of the second nomos was Eurocentered: descriptively, not evaluative, built to satisfy European's interests. From the perspective and interests of Tawantinsuyu, the territory of Inca civilization in the Andean region of South America, it was a *pachakuti*. The meaning of *pachakuti* is complex, but in this context it could be rendered as follows: *pacha* means land, earth, cosmos, epoch, time (their time, according to their calendar, not European time). *Kuti* means a sudden loss of equilibrium, a radical alteration of sensing and understanding *pacha*. In Spanish, translated into English, the expression was "the world (*pacha*) turned upside-down (*kuti*)." Consequently, the set of events that in the sixteenth century surprised both the migrant Europeans, on the one hand, and people inhabiting the territories of Incas, Mayas, and Aztecs (to name the better-known civilizations), on the other, had distinct meanings and, above all, consequences. For Europeans it was the initial and triumphal moment of the *constitution* of Western civilization, whose first steps were taken in Europe starting in the fourteenth century—constitution simultaneous with *destitution*, experienced by the destituted as *pachakuti*. For Quijano it was the initial moment of both the promise of modernity (salvation) and the logic of coloniality (the colonial difference justifying expropriation, dispossession, exploitation, and devaluation of knowledges, knowing, and subjectivities).

Schmitt was perceiving only one side: the advent of the second nomos. Guaman Poma de Ayala, in experiencing the events (see introduction, section III.3), was perceiving the *pachakuti*. Quijano, dwelling in the ruins of Tawantinsuyu, was sensing *pachakuti* (through Mariátegui) in the history of his country, although he was not of Incan descent. Historical awareness is unavoidable for every person concerned with justice rather than with progress and development. Schmitt framed the foundation and trajectory of international law and global linear thinking; Quijano framed the foundation of coloniality, the underside of modernity, and the trajectory of the CMP and of heterogenous historic-structural thinking, which, in my own interpretation, presupposes border thinking. While Schmitt could ignore coloniality, Quijano couldn't avoid or ignore modernity. His response was decoloniality/decolonization as epistemological reconstitution, which I render here as gnoseological (knowing) and aesthesic (sensing) reconstitutions. "Decolonization" refers to a specific activation of decolonial thinking and doing and responding to decolonization. "Decoloniality" responds to coloniality and addresses the logic undergirding such and such event at such and such moment and place.

The open questions are what did Schmitt learn from the trajectory of the second nomos and global linear thinking about the present state of the world order (in the decade of the 1950s), and what were his scenarios for the future. And, concurrently, what did Quijano learn from the trajectory of the CMP about his present (the 1990s, when he launched the concept) and the first two decades of the twenty-first century, when he was reflecting on the radical transformation of the CMP, which he described as changing "historical horizons of meaning" and I am rendering in this chapter and this book as a change of era and the third nomos of the Earth. For his part, Schmitt imagined that one of three possible scenarios would arise from the closing of the second nomos. He did not name it the "the third nomos of the Earth" but "the new nomos of the Earth." Not surprisingly, he could only imagine one of three possibilities because he took for granted that there is only one linear time in history, the universal linear time of the first and second nomoi that would continue in the new one. "Newness" is the keyword in the constitution of the CMP, from the "discovery of the New World" to the celebration of the "new Tesla" that displaced the "new Toyota," the "new iPhone" that displaced the "new cell phone," or "new ideas" sold as "innovation."

Schmitt derived the third nomos from the linear history he built: the first nomos, the second nomos, and the new nomos. He took for granted that the new nomos would be one more change in the totality of the same frame: the Eurocentered (his own word) nomos of the Earth. He said it without equivocation: "There always has been some kind of *nomos* of the earth. In all the ages of mankind the earth has been appropriated, divided, and cultivated. But before the age of the great discoveries, before the sixteenth century of our system of dating, men had no global concept of the planet in which they lived."[2] For Schmitt, the Eurocentered second nomos closed at the end of WWI. The Russian Revolution put an end to it. Consequently, Schmitt saw that the new nomos would be one of three possibilities, one that the Soviet Union would be victorious. He was writing about these scenarios in 1955. He saw the following three possibilities:

a   Of the two contenders in the Cold War, one would be victorious and so would enforce the final unity of the world. Notice that the myth of the "end of history" is a myth within the frame of an expected unity (see the previous chapter for the myth of a unified theory in philosophy and science).

b   The balance of the previous nomos led by England would be maintained. He saw, in the middle of the twentieth century, that only the US could play the role of arbiter of the global order, which was the case until the US became the sheriff after the end of the Soviet Union.

c   Several independent *Großeräume* (large spaces) or blocs could precipitate a new world order. This is what we have today in the emerging multipolar world order. However, there is more than meets the eye.

Let me clarify before pursuing the issue further that Schmitt's analysis in my arguments is not a theoretical guide but a *European document*, a brilliant European narrative but a document nonetheless. I am not thinking from Schmitt but from Quijano. After Quijano, I have another story to tell and another scenario for the emerging change of era and for the third nomos of the earth. My story begins with the advent of the colonial matrix of power (the CMP), rather than with the second nomos of the Earth. I do not intent to supplant Schmitt's narrative, but to put another option on the table, the decolonial option. I cannot supplant his narrative because I cannot, or I do not want to, tell another narrative from the same locus of enunciation. The decolonial is another option at the edges, the borderlands, the exteriority of the conceptual frame of Schmitt's (and the entire frame of modernity/rationality). My narrative is told from (not about) the colonial history of the Americas and the history of the CMP, not from that of the second nomos, that is, the modern history of Europe since the Renaissance.

II The Advent of Global Linear Thinking and the Second Nomos of the Earth

Global linear thinking, in Carl Schmitt's work, and consequently in the emergence of the second nomos of the Earth, is historically located in the sixteenth century, when Western Christianity and then later a secular Europe intruded on one point of the polycentric first nomos in the "New World." Incas and Aztecs did not know that they were part of the first nomos and that the Hispanic invasions would be one event inaugurating the second nomos. In Schmitt's conception, the first nomos of the Earth, before 1500, consisted of coexisting, in conflict or collaboration, territorial organizations, none of which impinged on all others. There were conflicts, of course, and invasions, and taking over, but not a single civilization intruded and centralized their management. The advent of the second nomos inaugurated the first civilization, Western civilization, which would, over the next five hundred years, intervene in all coexisting civilizations in America, Asia, and Africa. Theology and international law were the two prime structures of knowledge that regulated, justified, and legitimized expansion—the first to conquer souls, the second to appropriate territories. Schmitt's frank statement that global linear thinking, grounded in international law—both of which laid the historical foundation of the second nomos—are Eurocentered (simply meaning, in his own rendering, "centered around European interests") is half the story—half, that is, of the self-fashioned story of modernity that constitutes its own rhetoric (e.g., discourses and narratives legitimizing the enunciations that enunciate "modernity"). The other half is the hidden logic of coloniality acted out by global linear thinking and the constitution of the second nomos. The logic of coloniality is not verbalized; it is enacted and justified by the rhetoric of modernity. It is not Western epistemology and the rhetoric of modernity that uncover coloniality, but decolonial border thinking in the processes of gnoseological and aesthesic reconstitutions. Thus, the anomie of the Earth today is the moment of disintegration of the second nomos, whose signs are manifested in the chaos of the global political and economic disorder and in the loss of balance between the human species and its own source of biotic living, which, in the human semiotic system of the West, was reduced to an entity that can be controlled and exploited: nature. Schmitt himself, foreseeing the disintegration of the second nomos in 1955, wrote a few pages announcing "The New *Nomos* of the Earth," which I have analyzed elsewhere.[3]

If the second nomos and global linear thinking contributed to the making and the unfolding of the rhetoric of modernity and to enacting the logic of coloniality, then the anomie of the Earth is a consequence of, and an opportunity for, decolonial reexistence and resurgence of the emerging global political society, by which I mean the political organization of actors that are neither NGOs nor the state itself (considering that NGOs are typically aligned with domestic or interstate politics). Reexisting and reemerging (I will come back to these concepts) are the horizons of decolonial politics at large, not only state politics but the basic politics demanded by the praxis of living and especially of living within the CMP. Reexisting and reemerging mean the affirmation of the communal subject that the cosmology of modernity "subjected" to the individual subject of society—isolated and pushed to compete and to succeed. The legacies of decolonial politics cannot be found in Greece and Rome; they are to be found in the Americas, first enacted by colonized Indigenous people and enslaved Africans (Guamán Poma de Ayala, Ottobah Cugoano, Túpac Katari) and then manifested in Asia (Mahatma Gandhi) and Africa (Patrice Lumumba, Amílcar Cabral). For many of us who are neither Indigenous nor of African descent in the Americas, nor grounded in their decolonial thinking and praxes of living, our own histories of people of European descent (Creoles, mestizos/as, or immigrants) who live the colonial legacies outside Europe belong to particular trajectories of borderlines (global linear thinking) and borderlands. Our own experiences (i.e., those of people of European descent outside Europe) of colonial legacies and coloniality place us, on the one hand, in the privileges we have vis-à-vis the Indigenous and Afro-descendant population and, on the other, vis-à-vis the racialized imaginary of Europe and Anglo-America, we are placed in the subaltern location of South America, Central America, and the Caribbean.[4] The task of decolonial politics and epistemic reconstitution—at the intersection of privileges and deficiencies—requires disobedience to the ontologies built in an imaginary of Western epistemology and allegiance to destituted gnoseologies, in the Americas and around the planet.[5]

II.1 Sovereignty and Autonomy: The Breakdown of the Second Nomos of the Earth

To properly understand the global dimension of the disintegration of the second nomos of the Earth, it would be helpful to understand Carl Schmitt's trick.[6] The nomos addressed in the volume *The Anomie of the Earth*, for which I wrote the foreword (which is here being expanded), is indeed Schmitt's second nomos. Which means, obviously, that for him there was a first nomos. The first nomos was indeed a plurality of nomoi. Before 1500, interpreting Schmitt's chronology decolonially, all socio-cultural-economic configurations that today we call "civilizations" (ancient China, India, Persia, the Kingdom of Africa, Mayas, Incas, and Aztecs) built themselves in the process of building their own nomos. That is to say, building their own territoriality—their own eco-nomos grounded in their own cosmology. There was no need for everyone to drink from the fountains of Greco-Roman and Christian cosmogonies. For my argument in this book, to trace the scope of decolonial politics and gnoseological reconstitutions, I will concentrate on the nomos of the ancient civilizations of what became known as "America." The presence of the fourth continent in the consciousness of European men of letters is a landmark of Schmitt's second nomos: "The *first nomos* of the earth was destroyed about 500 years ago [that is, by 1500], when the great oceans of the world were opened up. The earth was circumnavigated; America, a completely new, unknown, not even suspected continent was discovered."[7]

The key point for my argument is this: "America, a completely new, unknown, not even suspected continent was discovered." The statement is proverbial: America was not known to many people, but for different reasons. Even the people inhabiting Mapugundun, Anahuac, Turtle Island, Tawantinsuyu of Abya Yala did not know that they were inhabiting "America"—simply because America did not exist yet, and consequently, something that doesn't exist cannot be discovered. In 1504 of the Christian era, a German cartographer, Martin Waldseemüller, honored Amerigo Vespucci by giving his name to a continent that was named differently by the people inhabiting it. Which doesn't mean that a continent was already America before being named America by a European cartographer! As for the Europeans themselves, before they realized that Columbus and Vespucci were navigating the coasts of an enormous land mass, the planet was divided into Asia, Africa, and Europe (see chapter 10). Mayas, Aztecs, and Incas did not know they lived in America, in the same way that Asians did not know they lived in Asia until Christians told them so. What the Indigenous populations in the Andes and Mesoamerica knew was that they were living in Tawantinsuyu, Anahuac, and Yóok'ol kaab. At that point in history, what is today Europe was then Western Christendom, and it was part of the first nomos. The second nomos emerged, then, when a group of Indigenous people of Western Christendom/Europe bumped into the land of Indigenous people of *Ayiti* (the Indigenous name of the island that was renamed Dominica by the Spaniards and Saint Domingue by the French). Bottom line: at the moment of what Europeans called "the discovery of America," and more recently Latin American philosophers of history have rebaptized "the invention of America," everyone on planet Earth was living under what Schmitt described as the first nomos.

The change of epoch that the advent of the second nomos of the Earth announced was the *colonial revolution*, heralded, in the sixteenth century, by the opening of the Atlantic circuits, the unprecedented navigation and commerce occurring around the planet, and, above all, an unprecedented change of consciousness that affected, in different scales and lived experience, the entire planet. In Tawantinsuyu (the territory under Incan management) and the Quechua language, the expression, described above, was *pachakuti*. For the inhabitants of Europe it was a *New World*. In Tawantinsuyu they had to reorganize and accommodate their ancestral world-sense in coexistence with people and institutions whose ancestrality was alien to them. And vice versa: for Spaniards, Quechua and Aymara ancestrality was alien to them. For Spaniards and other Western Christians, it was also a shock, but a positive shock. They called it triumphally "the discovery of a New World" (later on called America).

Five hundred years later, the German jurist, political theorist, and member of the Nazi party Carl Schmitt recognized (like his predecessors Franciscode Gómara, Adam Smith, Karl Marx, and Sigmund Freud, on whom I've commented in the introduction to this volume) that the unprecedented historical events propelled by the Atlantic commercial circuits comprised the advent of the second nomos of the Earth (see chapter 8 for more details). The change of nomos, the displacement of the first by the advent of the second, was no doubt a change of epoch. For Peruvian sociologist, thinker, and activist Aníbal Quijano, the same set of events was the signpost and dawn of the colonial matrix of power, which had no precedent before the sixteenth century anywhere on the planet. It was no doubt a change of epoch (see introduction, section II, on other perceptions of the events). However, while it was recognized widely that in the sixteenth century in the Atlantic a change of epoch was established, the meaning was not the same for everybody concerned.

In this chapter, and in the book, the stories I tell are framed around the advent of the CMP. Now, the advent of the CMP is—as I argue in the introduction—a decolonial concept. Which means that the *colonial* matrix of power is the enunciated, the said, that presupposes a *decolonial* enunciation, the enunciation, the saying. What does this mean? In the introduction, section III, the level of the *enunciated* (the domains, the content) was distinguished from the level of the *enunciation* (the saying that establishes and regulates the domains and the content of the conversations). Both levels conform to the CMP, the constant movement of constitution/destitution, and the changing rhetoric of modernity to legitimize the logic of coloniality (modernity/coloniality). I have also argued that the fundamental decolonial move is the delinking from the CMP's enunciation. Hence, the gnoseological and aesthesic reconstitutions I have been arguing for mean building a decolonial locus of enunciation in which we are able to live and think while disobeying the enunciation of modernity/coloniality that regulates all of us (including the managers of the CMP—e.g., officers of the state, bank CEOs, religious actors, officials of museums and universities, etc.). The specific moves of disobeying and delinking are the stepping stones to entering the realm of gnoseological and aesthesic reconstitutions. The common expression "decolonizing knowledge (the university, the museum, etc.)" starts from disobeying and delinking to be able to reexist, reemerge, and resurge. Reconstitutions of knowing and sensing are paramount and begin in each of us. No pretense of "decolonizing X" makes sense if the subject pronouncing and acting on such a statement remains a modern subject and maintains a subjectivity that, consequently, would confront the content and the domains while living intact the principles and assumptions that sustain the CMP's enunciation.

So the second nomos inaugurates a planetary European narrative, a narrative that became hegemonic and was consolidated by Hegel's lesson in the philosophy of history delivered sometime between 1822 and 1830. Schmitt rehearsed the frame of this narrative, starting in 1500, and connected it with international law (*ius publicum Europaeum*). The "discovery" that inaugurated the second nomos inaugurated at the same time the legal and symbolic European appropriation of the planet supported by European cartography (see chapters 8, 9, and 10). The first nomos in Schmitt's narrative vanished (but only in his narrative, not in the narratives of the people whom Schmitt saw as inhabiting the first nomos) as it was absorbed into a growing Eurocentric narrative of the second nomos:

A *second nomos* of the earth arose from these discoveries of land and sea. The discoveries were not invited. They were made without visas issued by the discovered peoples. The discoverers were Europeans, who appropriated, divided, and utilized the planet. Thus, the second *nomos* of the earth became Eurocentric. The newly discovered continent of America was first utilized in the form of colonies. The Asian landmasses could not be appropriated in the same way. The Eurocentric structure of *nomos* extended only partially, as open land-appropriations, and otherwise in the form of protectorates, leases, trade agreements, and spheres of interest; in short, in a more elastic form of utilization. Only in the 19th century did the land-appropriating European powers divide up Africa.[8]

Let's parse the first sentence of the above extract in the old discourse-analysis way. It is a revealing sentence: the second nomos is a European invention. I do not dispute that assertion. In the next two lines Schmitt insightfully realized that the second nomos arose out of an invasion. The following line reveals his good intentions and his blindness as he uses the word "discoverers" instead of "invaders": land "appropriation" is also land dispossession. Schmitt is betraying a classic blind spot: what was not known to Europeans was supposed to be not existing and "unknown" to everybody else, including the people inhabiting the land Europeans did not know about. Furthermore, we see that Schmitt is already a victim of the idea that what Europeans appropriated were empty lands. For this reason, the language hides from him that these "appropriations" were "dispossessions"—legalized-theological dispossessions that started with the (in)famous *Requerimiento* and continued with international law.[9]

Then came Asia. Neither Russia nor China were dispossessed. They were disrupted but not colonized like India after the colonization of Aztecs, Mayas, and Incas. After 1884 Africa was possessed by European states. All that effort is the work of the second nomos. But what happened to the first nomos? Schmitt is already into the magic effect of linear time, and he thinks of the first nomos as one, not as many, and as in the past. And that is what I am contesting in this chapter. It is obvious that the nomoi of Incas and Aztecs, of Russian and Chinese, of Indians and Africans were not one. Each civilization had its own nomos. But by making them one, Schmitt operates on the already established idea of a single linear timeline, the linear time of European history as narrated by Europeans. This is Schmitt's trick. It is the same logic that made of people in the "discovered" land "Indians" and of African people "Black." To manage and dominate, you have to homogenize. This is the logic of coloniality manifested in the homogenous naming of the rhetoric of modernity.

Schmitt's trick consists in this: when the second nomos of the Earth materialized, what happened to the diversity of the first nomos? It became one and was superseded in the European imaginary of linear time. All the planet belonged to the first and only nomos, on top of which the second nomos was mounted and continued the supposed unilinearity of the first. However, decolonial analytics of the logic of coloniality brings to light that the multiplicity of the first nomos *was never superseded by the second nomos.* That is why today we are witnessing the resurgence of the many civilizational variants of laws, customs, economies, and other social constructions that previously constituted the many forms of life all over the planet. What I hope to accomplish in my work is to bring to wider attention this variegated resurgence.

II.2 The Change of Era and the Advent of the Third Nomos of the Earth: De-Westernization and Decoloniality

The point I am driving at is the retelling of Schmitt's narrative of the first and second nomoi in the coexisting narrative of the CMP. For Schmitt the first nomos encompassed a plurality of nomoi, while the second nomos shattered all of them and constituted itself as the *only* nomos regulating the Earth. In the narrative of the CMP the advent of the second nomos was a change of epoch and the historical foundation of the double movement of constitution/destitution. And here is the difference between Schmitt's narrative and the narrative of the CMP: while for Schmitt "first and second" implies a linear narrative of supersession in the linear "advance" of history, in the narrative of the CMP the constitution of the second nomos destitutes but does not eliminate the existence of the plurality of nomoi. And this is why today, both in the sphere of states and in the sphere of the people (e.g., the political society), reexistence, reemergence, and resurgence are the forces and energies of the first nomos mutating into the third entangled with the second. The epoch of the second nomos shatters. But the second nomos did not vanish. The *advent of the third nomos* marks a change of era, no longer an epoch of changes. In it:

1 Unipolarity is confronted by multipolarity. Multipolarity obtains in the sphere of de-Westernization of interstate relations. Both coexist.
2 Universality is confronted by pluriversality. Pluriversality obtains in the sphere of knowledge and of the people (the political society) decolonially taking their/our destinies in their/our own hands. Both coexist.

Both cases presuppose delinking from the CMP and engaging in gnoseological and aesthesic reconstitutions. The politics of decolonial investigations affects both de-Westernization (e.g., in international relations and international law) and decoloniality (in education, scholarship, reconstitution of the communal, art, etc.) differently. The plurality of nomoi resurging in the third nomos erupts from gnoseological and aesthesic reconstitutions, restituting what the second nomos and, more fully, the colonial matrix of power destituted. However, the second nomos doesn't go away with the advent of the third nomos. All of us on the planet today inhabit the globalization of the second nomos. However, the quantitative majority of people are also inhabiting the first nomos, which was destituted but never destroyed, and are today resurging from the long night shadows of the second nomos. Inhabiting the lands and the memories of the first nomos at the same time as one lives through the invasions of the second nomos in all areas of experience means inhabiting the borderland of the third nomos—that is, the resurgence of the first in coexistence with the second. Linear time is sidelined by the reemergence of the multiplicity of nomoi's local times. Western time becomes one among the many. In the sphere of decoloniality, reemergence means pluriversality; in the sphere of state de-Westernization, reemergence means multipolarity.

The complementarity of nomoi and times relative to each nomos means that the second nomos becomes one among the many in the third nomos of the Earth. The prefix "post-" remains meaningful for the second nomos, but is irrelevant for any of the third nomoi that don't conceive of time as unilinear. The crucial point is this: the eruption of the third nomos inaugurates the change of era that reduces to its own size the supposed universality of linear time. Schmitt's trick (unconscious, I truly believe) consisted of two moves. The first was to cast the plurality of cultures and civilizations in terms of one nomos (the first) and to see them as precursors of his idea of the second nomos. To understand the trick, we should start from a different premise: that there is no *ontic* first or second nomos. Both were *ontological* results of Schmitt's narrative based on the emergence of international law in the *ius publicum Europaeum*. International law was not written in planetary ontology inscribed during the creation of the universe, but the reverse: international law (narratives, arguments, epistemology) created the ontology of the planet according to the global order of the *ius publicum Europaeum*. That is what Schmitt states when saying that international law was Eurocentered: centered on the interests of European imperial monarchies and, later, on the interests of secular bourgeois nation-states in Europe and native elites in the colonies after independence.

Schmitt's second move (unconsciously, I believe) consisted of converting the plurality of nomoi in the first nomos into a singular one and then placing it *before* the second nomos. I said "unconscious" because of the taken-for-granted idea that history is universal and unilinear. By so doing, Schmitt reinforced the belief, which emerged in the eighteenth century, that the "primitives," in his unilinear unfolding of history, were the precursors of the modern. In reality it was only after the invention of the idea of modernity that primitives were imagined in order to trace a fictional, universal line between the first and the second nomoi. Today this powerful fiction is cracking at its foundations, and the signs are already seen in the awakening and resurgence of an overwhelming majority of people who have been placed beyond the lines of the second nomos and its internal family feuds (e.g., Western Hemisphere, South of Europe). But let's stay within the boundaries of the Western Hemisphere.[10]

Often and increasingly, Pueblos Originarios (aboriginals, natives, Indigenous people) are reported as being heroes of resistance against corporations. The award-winning film *Avatar*, the first movie ever to earn over $2 billion worldwide in the initial year of its release, became an emblem of such resistance.[11] A group of Shuar people from the Ecuadorian Amazon went to Quito in three buses to watch *Avatar*. When interviewed later, they said they all recognized the film as their history, not as our story.[12] Our story has been blocked and retold by non-Indigenous scholars and journalists. One of the signs of the third nomos and the change of era is that Indigenous scholars are slowly but relentlessly occupying chairs at the same table with Anglo-American and western European scholars and journalists.

Let's start by listening to a two-minute video by Richard Twiss, a Lakota-American, titled "A Theology of Manifest Destiny" (see the URL provided in the notes). In it he tells us that for Pueblos Originarios, the Manifest Destiny was the legitimization of destitutions, dispossessions, and the alteration of their praxes of living.[13] George Tinker, a Native American theologian of liberation, in the opening of his book *Spirit and Resistance: Political Theology and American Indian Liberation*, tells the story of the United States purchasing enormous amounts of Osage land from the French. Tinker writes, "In 1803 the United States purchased the entirety of Osage land—from France. It had to do with something called the Louisiana Purchase and something having to do with some obscure European legal doctrine called 'the right of discovery.' What it ever had to do with the Osage people, who were never privy to this doctrine or included in the negotiation leading to the purchase, is still a mystery. It was nevertheless a powerful intellectual idea, mere words that, in a sense, enabled Mr. Jefferson to double the size of his country overnight."[14] Up to today, Tinker ponders, the Osage do not understand how their land was purchased by the US from France.

The stories of Twiss and Tinker help us understand the *Requerimiento* from the Indigenous perspective. Twiss and Tinker do not refer to the *Requerimiento*; it is implied in their story of land expropriation and treatises, the strategies of the settlers, who were British and of British descent. Tinker's story takes place in 1803, almost four hundred years after the *Requerimiento* was read to Indigenous people, who did not understand Spanish; it told them that they were under the rule of the king of Spain and the Catholic church. The rhetoric of modernity had changed (the first was in Spanish the other in English), the actors had changed, but the logic of coloniality remained intact. By 1803, it was no longer God's design in the pens of Spaniards guiding the *Requerimiento*, but God's design in the pens of the Anglo-Americans' Manifest Destiny, which was enacted in the name of the nation-state. (The phrase wasn't coined until a few decades later, but the idea was certainly operational in the early 1800s.) Bartolomé de Las Casas, who vehemently protested the *Requerimiento* and put all his energy into a defense of "the Indians," never had the delicacy to invite "Indians" to help establish his arguments. In both these instances, there was an unspoken collusion among white men (theologians defending a doctrine of just war, or a single theologian, Las Casas, defending the Indians and promoting their conversion), and there was an exclusive agreement between Frenchmen and American men in the Louisiana Purchase.

Tinker's narrative and argument are a consequence of the first internal scramble, among Western states (France and the US), for control of the second nomos of the Earth. The first nomos, or nomoi if you wish, of Osage and Lakota nations was overruled, destituted in the constitution of the CMP. The Monroe Doctrine and the idea of the Western Hemisphere as a preserve of the United States put a halt to the initial European imperial impulse to possess and dispossess and transferred European hegemony to the United States. The conception of the Western Hemisphere, interestingly enough, was an idea born in the Americas (although America was thought to be equivalent to the US). Europe was the West, but the Americas were not counted in that West. The Western Hemisphere thus placed an imaginary line in the Atlantic that claimed the rights of "Americans" to the lands contained within the hemisphere. Here an explicit demand for an auto-nomos (within the second nomos, for the destitution of the first nomos continued) Western Hemisphere also established a nonexplicit line demarcating the North of the Western Hemisphere from the South (Central America, including Mexico, the Caribbean, and South America). Now you can play with the South of the North (see chapter 10). This was a demarcation in the Americas that was already prefigured in Europe, when France and England took over Spain and Portugal in planetary land and sea, and Germany took over the intellectual legacies of the Italian Renaissance. Hence, the "South of Europe" became a symbolic construction that created the intramural imperial difference. Thus, in the Americas, the struggle to recover the land is common to all Pueblos Originarios/Native Americans/First Nations, but the various arguments and specific claims are tied up with the specific local histories of whichever European imperial state (Spain, Portugal, France, England, Holland) shaped their destiny. That struggle has a name today: resurgence.

We should give Schmitt the credit he deserves, that of honestly mapping the second nomos of the Earth and explaining how crucial international law was and is in establishing, transforming, and maintaining it. The Western Hemisphere was the first scramble among peers; the partition of Africa at the Berlin Conference of 1884 the second. All this occurred within the boundaries of re-noming and accommodating new players within the same family that was managing the colonial matrix of power.

III Multipolarity and Pluriversality: Reemerging Cosmologies from the Polycentric First Nomos

The previous section was guided by departing (delinking) from Schmitt's second nomos. This section will be guided by departing from James Lovelock's *Gaia: A New Look at Life on Earth* (1979). Why I am addressing Gaia in connection to nomos will become clear below. Lovelock tells the story of how first he realizes that life on Earth could be explained by looking at its parts, as well as at the sum of them, with information provided by chemists and physicists. He realized that Earth was something other than the sum of its parts, something other than what was accepted in Western epistemology. So he needed a name for this entity, and he found Gaia, which is the name of the Greek Earth goddess (also known as Gaea), from which the sciences of geography and geology derive their names. "Earth," then, is more than the land and water masses we see on the map. It includes the biosphere and the atmosphere, and of course their interaction with the cosmos, especially the sun and the moon. Lovelock explains that the conditions for life on the planet did not preexist the emergence of life, but the emergence of life created the conditions of both its emergence and its survival. I am describing something known today by people educated in Western epistemology. Indigenous people have known it for centuries, without knowing the Greeks. In the South American Andes the word was *pacha*. *"Pacha"* is a complex word that encompasses the cosmic energy that comes from the sky and the telluric force that comes from earth. *Pacha +* *mama*, mother earth, generates life and maintains life.

I want to stress two points from Lovelock's *discovery*, so to speak, that Gaia is a living organism. Better stated, it is life that makes Gaia what it is. Gaia did not preexist life; life is constitutive of Gaia. The first of these two points is that what Lovelock *discovered* was that which his own ancestors in the Western sciences *ignored* and *silenced* (destituted): the foundation of Indigenous cosmologies took for granted that Earth (Pachamama) is a living organism and that we (human animals) make up a very small proportion of living organisms on the planet and in the universe. The invention of "nature" (a crucial concept in coloniality) reduced the splendorous complexity and diversity of living lives on the planet to one simple object, *nature*, and nature was the opposite of what Men/Humans do, which is *culture*. Man/Human became more and more identified with culture and distant from nature. Climate change is one of many consequences.

But, what is the "something other" that Gaia is? Lovelock describes it as the self-regulating organism we (all living organisms, including human animals) live in, and which strives to exist, whether or not a species' existence is purposeful and goal seeking, as it is in us humans. What is the purpose of living for nonhuman organisms other than just living? Lovelock uncovered living life for Western-formatted minds, which was well known for centuries before the advent of Western knowledge (theological and secular) ignored it and built itself on the belief of Western truth without parentheses. He writes, "Life has not adapted to an inert world determined by the dead hand of chemistry and physics. We live in a world that has been built by *our ancestors*, ancient and modern, and which is continuously maintained by all things alive today. Organisms are adapting in a world whose material state is determined by the activities of their neighbors. This means that changing the environment is part of the game. To think otherwise would require that evolution be a game with rules like cricket or baseball—one in which the rules forbade environmental change"[15] (emphasis added).

"Our ancestors" is ambiguous. On the one hand, it seems to refer to the ancestors of the human species and to the living life itself, to the life that creates organisms that inhabit and are inhabited by life; that is Gaia. But on the other hand, "our ancestors" are the Greek ancestors who named Gaia, the planet, inhabited by many other people and languages. For Aymaras it was *pacha*, for example. It doesn't refer to any species in particular but to the energy that made possible all species in the animal, vegetable, and mineral kingdoms, to use an old and simple metaphor. For Chinese it was *tianxia* (All under heaven): "*Tianxia*, a dense concept referring to 'the world', has three meanings: 1) the earth or all lands under the sky; 2) a common choice made by all peoples in the world, or a universal agreement in the 'hearts' of all people; and 3) a political system for the world with a global institution to ensure universal order. With the concept of *tianxia*, therefore, the world is understood as consisting of the physical world (land), the psychological world (the general sentiment of peoples) and the institutional world."[16] In the restricted sense of the word, Lovelock's ancestors are not the ancestors of most Africans, Asians, or First Nations of the Americas. And they are my mediated ancestors through the colonial education I received in Argentina and that keeps me trapped in a restricted ancestry from which I have been working to delink. Delinking doesn't mean eradicating, but reducing these influences to their own size and moving away, in the reemerging pluriverse, from what I learned from my ancestries.

The second point I want to stress is Lovelock's anecdote of how he found that Gaia properly named the self-regulating, not purposeful nor goal-seeking, organism that brought life to Earth. The anecdote describes the idea as coming from a friend and writer in his neighborhood. Had Lovelock had an Aymara friend and writer, I am sure that this friend would have suggested "Pachamama" instead of "Gaia." And I am sure that it could have been the same if Lovelock had been talking with a Chinese or Bambara speaker, just to mention a few more. They would have offered him the word of their languages. But they had been destituted in the processes of constituting the coloniality of knowledge—more specifically, the colonial matrix of thoughts, as Charles Esche, whom I mentioned in the introduction, calls it. The point is that every known civilization coexisting in the first nomos of the Earth created expressions to name what "Gaia" and "Pachamama" mean for Greeks and Aymara, respectively. Furthermore, the words "Gaia," "*tianxia*," and "Pachamama" were devised to name the cosmic and telluric energies of life-forming on the planet, including the species of animal that invents concepts to describe the cosmic and earthly energies of life. Nonhuman animals do not have a name for the place they inhabit, but certainly they have a sense of themselves in their dwelling place, the niche of their life-forming and survival.

Here I am assuming a correspondence between the first nomos of the Earth and the "cosmology" or "*cosmo-vivencia*" (as Aymara intellectuals would refer to their sense of *pacha*, the cosmos) of each culture or civilization; and that is the reason why I brough Lovelock into the conversation. The world order before 1500 was composed of many nomoi, and it was polycentric in both senses, auto-nomic (a self-made nomos) and cosmologic. But then at some point among the many histories of the polycentric planetary world order, one local history emerged (Western Christianity, which mutated into Western civilization) and began—by 1500—to establish itself while at the same time encroaching on other civilizations. The second nomos originated and became monocentric. In the process, a double movement was at work: building its own interiority by expelling to the exteriority praxes of living and knowing that did not fit with the design of its interiority. (That is the double movement of constitution/destitution.) Hence, global designs emerged from this double process of securing the territoriality (material, visual, and conceptual) of Western civilization and expelling to its exteriority what did not fit in the interiority but still had to be under its control and management. The exteriority was invented to remain under management and regulations. That was one of the fundamental strategies of the second nomos. "Cosmology" is one dimension of this: a Christian God overruled the Andean *pacha* and Mesoamerican Teotl, as well as Chinese, Indian, and African cosmogonies and cosmologies. While the Christian God, *pacha*, *tianxia*, and Teotl are the anchors in each cosmology's narratives of the creation of everything and narratives of the ethnicity to which the narrators belong, the Christian God had masculine features while Teotl, *pacha*, and *tianxia* implied the complementary energies that congealed to create the entities and relations populating the world. Dual complementary energies are infused in every living organism destined to regenerate the species. These complementary energies are what in a Western vocabulary would be called the feminine and the masculine. There is a reason why *pacha* and Teotl were the origination and incarnation of the energies that we name masculine and feminine, and the reason is that life itself, to be regenerated, needs both energies, at least for all the organisms that storytellers of the cosmologies in question might encounter during their life spans. Water and air and fire and land are living organisms as well, but their cycles of existence follow a different pattern from those of other living organisms, whose only life cycle was observed by storytellers of the creation of the world and of themselves, be the stories ancient or modern, like the so-called Big Bang Theory.

Contrary to modern sciences, in storytelling about the creation of the world and of the human species (that is, storytelling in which masculine and feminine appear as divided, not as complementary), what counts are not the individual organisms in which the masculine and the feminine are incarnated, but the energy that continues beyond the birth and death of those organisms. Living organisms, in other words, are means by which the energy of life continues: singular organisms have a beginning and an end. Now, if the current ecological excesses of human "culture" since the Industrial Revolution extinguishes current living conditions, it doesn't mean that life on Earth will end because "humans" are no longer here. Transient living organisms, the human species included, are just that: transient. We come and go, life continues. What matters is life, not us. Living with the awareness of transientness would help to blow down the egos that the Western premium for individualism has installed in the minds of many.

It would be too presumptuous, arrogant, and individualistic (i.e., informed by the Western ego) to think that we, humans, are important, and that life is at our service. Indeed, we are at the service of life. It would be too anthropocentric to think that the biosphere needs "us." *We, human beings, are being used by living energies to maintain life on Earth and to maintain Gaia/Pachamama's life, not the other way around.* Western anthropocentrism was the negation, in the constitution of the colonial matrix of power, of *cosmo-vivencias* in which the anthropos (the storyteller) was not the center of the world (the anthropocentric, inverted analogy of the Copernican revolution), but one small eruption of living energies. Consequently, the difference between nature on the one hand and Gaia and *pacha* on the other is that "nature" names an overall entity that can be investigated by knowing subjects separated from it. Nature contributed to the emergence of anthropocentrism, while in Gaia and *pacha* the anthropos was not the center; it just was. Instead, if you think about it from the assumptions of Gaia and *pacha*, you realize that the knowing subject is indeed a component of the object to be known, and that Gaia and *pacha* are the creative and sustaining forces, the energies, while nature is what has been created by the energies that inhabit nature itself.

Nature was a concept already established in Christian theology when Spaniards invaded Tawantinsuyu, Anahuac, and Abya Yala. In the European Renaissance (fourteenth century), the conception of "nature" was introduced to Western vocabulary. It was derived from the Latin *natus* (birth), the creation of the universe. As such, the noun refers to the restorative energy of life—not to an entity, but to the energy of living. It refers to all of what human beings cannot do (even with artificial intelligence): "'The universe,' literally 'birth,' from *natus*, 'born,' past participle of *nasci* 'to be born,' from the PIE [proto-Indo-European] root *gene-* 'give birth, beget.' By mid-14c. as 'the forces or processes of the material world; that which produces living things and maintains order.' From late 14c. as 'creation, the universe'; also 'heredity, birth, hereditary circumstance; essential qualities, inherent constitution, innate disposition' (as in human nature); also 'nature personified, Mother Nature.'"[17]

At that point *pacha, natura, tianxia* all had equivalent meaning. Why was "nature" awarded the gold medal and the equivalent expressions destituted and, following European invasions, supplanted? If *natura* means live and members of the human species are born (*natus*), that means all humans, not only Men/Humans, can *cultivate* (as in agri-culture); so *cultura* became distinguished from *natura*. But from the Renaissance to the Enlightenment the original meaning of *nature* was forgotten. The original meaning (birth, give birth) was forgotten. Instead of referring to creation it referred to the created, to entities; the verb became a noun, and the phrase "natural resources" consolidated it. What is meaningful in Western epistemology doesn't have to be meaningful for all other coexisting civilizations. Decolonial gnoseological reconstitutions, then, start with decolonial epistemic reduction, uncoupling words, nature, and culture from the presupposed ontologies they name. They are useful inventions of praxes of living and not universal representations of "realities."

Fascinated by the New World's nature, the Jesuit priest José de Acosta composed a philosophical and ethnographic argument to account for the people and land unknown to European Christians. The title is telling for the purpose of my argument here: *Natural and Moral History of the Indies* (1589).[18] For him, "nature" encompassed all the visible signs of creation, and so knowing and understanding "nature" meant knowing and admiring its creator. It was the mode of the time to read the planet in a semiotic vein. Both Galileo Galilei (1564-1642) and José de Acosta (1539-1600) read the "book of nature" as a sign system. Galileo was secular and read the book of nature; Acosta was Jesuit and saw in the signs of the planet and the universe the greatness of its creator. The metaphor of the book came from the European Middle Ages. For Acosta, it came from the Bible. A few decades later, Francis Bacon (1561-1626) changed direction and inaugurated the distancing of nature (the invented ontological entity) from the living organisms that conceived the concept of nature (the invented epistemic entity).[19] From then on, via the work of Copernicus and his contemporary Galileo, the road to Newton and Kant was paved. And with it, the wall between nature and humans arose. That is the legacy that Lovelock had to surmount by displacing nature and reintroducing Gaia into the picture. In a way, what Lovelock did was to reverse a Western conception of the life of the macroorganism, Gaia, and transform it into the life of living organisms that tell stories about the creation of the world and ourselves. For non-European and Indigenous genealogies of thoughts, the situation was and is radically different. Lovelock was working within his own Western history of ideas, or archeology of ideas if you prefer. He revamped his own *premodern ancestry*—that is, premodern Europe—Greek and Latin cosmologies that since the Renaissance had been the foundation of Western civilization, through the language of science as it had unfolded in the West since Francis Bacon's *New Organon*. On the contrary, New World civilizations *were not premodern; they were, and continue to be, nonmodern*. Premodern is a modern concept. Nonmodern is a decolonial concept negating the idea of the premodern. The negation leads and is a consequence of gnoseological and aesthesic reconstitutions, and both are the work of the decolonial politics of investigations and argumentations. For non-European and Indigenous thinkers, the problem was and is the perception that their own cosmologies (or cosmogonies, as they usually say it), languages, thinking, and histories of thought—which conceived of flows and interconnectivity between all living organisms—were disavowed by the concepts of two opposed entities, nature versus culture. Since Indigenous people were seen by Europeans as barbarians, they were seen as people without culture. When, in the West, Galileo pronounced his enduring metaphor, "the book of nature," he was affirming the role of scientists as having the same authority as the clergy.[20] For theologians like Acosta, to understand nature was to understand its creator; for Galileo, to understand nature was like understanding words and paragraphs in a book. But for non-Europeans and Indigenous people, if they knew about it, all of that was irrelevant: it was a family feud among Europeans. It only acquired relevance when the European family feuds began to encroach and be imposed on them.[21] Today, the irrelevance of the legacies of such North Atlantic family feuds could be better understood, from a Native American perspective, in the powerful and sarcastic arguments of Osage thinker and activist Vine Deloria Jr., author of *Evolution, Creationism and Other Modern Myths*.[22]

The following paragraphs from *Vivir Bien/Buen Vivir*, by Aymara intellectual and activist Fernando Huanacuni Mamani, resonate with much Indigenous storytelling around the planet, unveiling the assumptions upon which Bacon provided a "new interpretation of nature."[23] And when I say "storytelling," I am saying that Western theories, scientific or philosophic, are also stories we live with (I will come back to this point). Huanacuni Mamani states:

1 The fundamental right to the West is the right to life and liberty, but when a Western human being refers to the term "life" he is referring exclusively to human life because he considers many beings, organic and inorganic, as inferior. So he does not feel obliged to respect life of neither the former nor the latter. In addition, a Western human being in his individualistic, disintegrated and exclusionary cosmovision conceives

[human] life as something isolated from nature. Under this logic the West promotes only the welfare of the human beings. But it is more: *it promotes the welfare of only some human beings* focusing only on economic development and therefore disregarding essential realities of life.

2 Western civilization sustains the idea of the individual that emerged from a cosmovision detaching human species from Nature and by doing so it introduced the misunderstanding of the dynamics of life. It is the culture of death that conceives also the superiority of one person over another, that has generated a culture of use and abuse, exploitation, racism, accumulation and the violence of disposable relations; that has generated the suffering of many generations and the deterioration of Mother Earth.[24] (Translation mine; emphasis added.)

Huanacuni Mamani does not write, and doesn't intend to write, academic prose. His is Indigenous cosmology in action and could hardly be corrected by Western scientific research, unless Western scientists can demonstrate that Indigenous thinkers are wrong in their beliefs, an argument that will be discounted as outside empirical confirmation. Huanacuni Mamani's prose could only be corrected by someone holding scientific or postmodern beliefs in one particular reality and a belief that science is the only way to know it; it could only be disputed by someone who holds truth without parentheses and does not admit any other truth on a given topic beyond his or her own. That is precisely what early missionaries thought about *machis, tlamatinimes,* and *amautas* (persons of wisdom in Mapudungun, Nahuatl, and Quechua-Aymara, respectively). Mamani's book is already in its sixth edition (2016). The first edition was printed in 2010. As is apparent, the language is different from Lovelock's but the conception is similar: life is larger than the totality of organisms, including living organisms that are named human (*humano, essere umano, humaine, mensch*) in Western languages. This is a far cry from Acosta and Bacon, who were writing at the moment of consolidation of the colonial matrix of power and the beginning of its first transformation. The theocentric conception of "nature" in Acosta is displaced by the secular and anthropocentric version of Frances Bacon's. To repeat, for Acosta, understanding and knowing "nature" means knowing and understanding its creator, while for Bacon "nature" is to be understood as existing at the service of man, as I have explained elsewhere.[25] Inorganic organisms (e.g., those without nervous systems, like rocks, water, and wind) are not lifeless. "Inorganic" in Indigenous cosmologies doesn't mean inert. Rocks participate in the universe's energies just as any organism going through the cycle of life does, beginning to end.[26] The prison house of Western vocabulary makes it difficult to talk about issues that are instead easy to address in Indigenous languages from Mapugundun to Nishnaabeg, going through Aymara, Tojolabal, and Osage.

Life on the planet does not converse in the sense that Humberto Maturana gives to conversation over communication.[27] Conversation is the path to education, while communication and transmission of information is more relevant to schooling: one teaches and the other learn what the one is teaching. Communication and transmission of information impoverish the flows and energies of living, which conversation (face to face, not Facebook) endorses and promotes. But life energy in itself, on the planet and in the biosphere (not to say in the universe), consists in the flow of the living, as Indigenous thought has it, existing in the contents and the changing present of living life. However, self-named humans (us) seem to be the only animals who can constantly expand the coordinates of their/our praxes of living. That means we can invent theories (like this one, or Marxism, or quantum mechanics, or new materialism) to explain our praxis of living and the biosphere and the Earth we are living on; we can invent a vocabulary for "matter" as something outside of us and call it "nature," to hide and make sense of the unrepresentable energies of living. However, neither "matter" nor "nature" have any meaning in languages and civilizations in which what counts are relations and not entities. In such languages ontology is unthinkable, for relations are not entities; rather, relations flow between and around entities.

To bring the point back home: (1) Lovelock (along with posthuman theories and new materialism arguments) is changing the contents of the conversation within the Western concept of Human/Humanism and nature (e.g., anthropocentrism); (2) Human/Humanism (anthropocentrism) involved assumptions and arguments that devise and enact global designs to Westernize the planet; (3) these circumstances required non-European Indigenous people—whose memories did not go back to Greece and to Gaia but instead went back to *pacha* and other equivalent concepts in various non-European languages—to confront Western Human/Humanism and nature from non-Western memories. This situation extends today to Lovelock, posthumanism, and new materialism in the sense that while these arguments may be in agreement with the limits of anthropocentrism, they provide no way out of the Western way, constantly recycling their own past. Hence, they reproduce the Eurocentric enunciations caught in the universal presupposition of matter (and not flows, for example) and the unilinear concept of time.[28] Pluriversality offers a decolonial way out, and pluriversality cannot, by definition, be reduced to one single perspective, for then it would be universalism. This amounts to a version of what happened with multiculturalism: multiculturalism has been allowed and even promoted so long as it doesn't disturb the terms of the conversation, which is managed and controlled by the state. Pluriversality presupposes that the argument starts from some place other than from refashioning the content of the Western traditions while maintaining the management of the enunciation. Starting from what has been denied and silenced by Western epistemology is the beginning of any epistemic restitution.

IV Denaming/Renaming and Denoming/Renoming

Nature is a concept of the second nomos of the Earth that destituted similar ones, like *pacha* and *tianxia*, belonging to the first nomoi of the Earth. From Tawantinsuyu to Anahuac to "Turtle Island" (the original Anishinaabek name for North America)—all were renamed Indias Occidentales, New World, America. The second nomos not only renamed but also and fundamentally "renomed" the continent in the very act of renaming: the New World and America were integrated into the second nomos. The nomos of America, for instance, is quite different from the existing nomoi of Tawantinsuyu, Anahuac, Abya-Yala, Turtle Island. The second nomos of the Earth meant Western Christianity and then secular Europe intruding, encroaching, appropriating land, and destituting knowledge and world-sense: communal organizations where humans integrated themselves to the Earth and cosmos were replaced by a society limited to human beings in relation to God, first, and then to Reason after the Enlightenment. The results of global linear thinking violated and devalued the meanings of existing cosmologies and praxes of living. In time, the same happened to the rest of the planet. The 2015 "Rhodes Must Fall" movement in South Africa (directed specifically and symbolically at a statue commemorating Cecil Rhodes) was for that locality a sign of the beginning of resurgence, reexistence, and therefore "denoming" by renaming. These acts presuppose border thinking and praxis, for in order to make Rhodes fall it is first necessary to acknowledge the existence that Rhodes repressed. Disrespecting the visible symbols of the colonial matrix of power is a sign of gnoseological and aesthesic disobedience, a sign of delinking, of opening to gnoseological and aesthesic reconstitutions. The wave initiated with "Rhodes Must Fall" extended to Europe and to the US after the killing of George Floyd.

Denaming and denoming are today urgent tasks of gnoseological and aesthesic reconstitutions. Both operations presuppose rebuilding ways of knowing, knowledges (gnoseology), and sensibilities associated with destituted praxes of living (aesthesis). The narratives that justified Western renaming and renoming are falling in desuetude all over the planet, including in the former western Europe and the US. These are the signs of the third nomos of the Earth arising. For that reason, denaming and denoming lead to reexistence and to gnoseological and aesthesic reconstitutions. Slogans and public policies are not enough to accomplish this task, a task that needs strong arguments next to labor, whatever labor is required according to the tasks; and arguments need to be supported by investigations. The task requires not only bringing down the Rhodes statues (a physical praxis) but also having the knowledge and advancing the arguments that pertain to how Rhodes was set up in the first place, including which narratives justified his monument, why his time ran out, and why he should be demoted. His was the time of the expanding universality of the second nomos. Narratives of and for the third nomos are emerging, and the politics of decolonial investigations are required to delink from the traps and regulations of the second nomos.

Denoming and denaming the second nomos is a self-assigned project for de-Westernization and decoloniality, no matter how far apart their goals may be in other domains.[29] We, the planetary population, are entering a third state, *the third nomos of the Earth*. This chapter was written before COVID-19 and the parallel economic and financial crisis, which is radicalizing the close of an epoch (that of the second nomos) and accelerating the change of epoch (the advent of the third nomos). The third nomos shall not be imagined as a synthesis of the first and the second, in textbook Hegelian dialectics. It is, on the contrary, the resurgence of what preceded the universality of the second nomos: the polycentricity of the first nomos. The preceding polycentricity is today being rearticulated in two diverse trajectories: the multipolar interstate world order (where Europe and then the US were the regents of the planet) and subjectivities (de-Western subjects); and the pluriversality of thought and subjectivities (decolonial subjects). These are the two main trajectories forming the third nomos of the Earth.

Because of the multiple trajectories, both multipolar and pluriversal, the third nomos of the Earth cannot be conceptualized as a post–second nomos for the simple reason that conceptualizing it as such would mean maintaining the global time of re-Westernization, unipolarity in the world order, and the universality of modern Western thought. Consequently, the posthuman will remain within the confines and extension of the second nomos, (re)Westernization with its global designs, disrupted by de-Westernization and decoloniality. In the way of gnoseological and aesthesic reconstitutions, which do *not describe* the third nomos but *are part of it*, I would say that the third nomos of the Earth is what emerges from the irrepressible explosion of the second nomos, from which de-Westernization (multipolarity in the interstate system) and decoloniality (pluriversality in the autonomos organization of political society) have arisen. Further, COVID-19 evinced the desperation of NATO countries to contain the consequences of that explosion. The third nomos is the plurality that consists of the coexistence of three trajectories for human civilization: Western civilization, the reemergence of non-Western civilizations (de-Westernization), and the reexistence of the global pluriversality (decoloniality). Re-Westernization has mutated from the triumphal and revolutionary mode of Westernizing the world into a violent counterreformation.

Denoming and denaming are processes of gnoseological and aesthesic reconstitutions, then, involving processes of erasing the dominating and manipulative regulations of the second nomos. De-Westernization, as its prefix indicates, enacts an interstate politics of denoming, and China's One Belt, One Road Initiative is a colossal project of denoming, renaming, and reorienting. History is moving from East to West, but not as Hegel imagined it. The Asian Infrastructure Investment Bank is another case. The US was not invited to either of these enterprises. On the other hand, the US under Barack Obama organized the TPP (Trans-Pacific Partnership), and China was not invited. The New Development Bank (NDB), originally the BRICS Bank, is a third case in point. This denoming implies gnoseological and aesthesic reconstitutions: such projects could not be envisioned from the narrow frame of Western epistemology and aesthetics. The NDB is cutting across continental and hemispheric divides, indeed, across all well-organized planetary partitions existing under the second nomos. The BRICS countries are in East Asia (China), South Asia (India), North Asia (Russia), Africa (South Africa), and South America (Brazil). (See chapters 8 and 9 for more on Westernization, the second nomos, and continental partitioning.)

The wide-ranging efforts of these initiatives create not only economic and political problems for the global designs of re-Westernizers who intend to contain them, but also problems of knowledge, knowing, and subjectivities. It is at this level that Western interpreters have more difficulties understanding, and it is precisely the gnoseological and aesthesic innovations that are the most distinctive de-Western movers toward the third nomos of the Earth. Capitalist economy is global, but knowing (gnoseology) and subjectivities (aesthesis) are not. The second nomos at this point can neither be avoided nor erased. But it is being reduced to its own size as a *member* of a multipolarity, no longer the regent and sheriff. The multiplicity of the first nomoi that were not killed but destituted and marginalized is now a piñata of earlier civilizations with the potential to burst open in who-knows-what altered forms. The second nomos is being overcome by a third nomos that is neither a *synthesis* nor a *post* nor an entirely *new nomos* in the sense of being a linear progression from the second to the third, although this is apparently what re-Westernization is intended to do: enable things to change in order to remain the same. But apparently it is too late for this.

Overcoming the second nomos is not a matter of enacting good liberal public policies or exploiting goodwill from the writers of *Foreign Affairs*. It needs knowledge and arguments built on border epistemology and border doing—like the One Belt, One Road Initiative for de-Westernization, or the Zapatistas for decoloniality. The type of knowledge necessary for denoming is not the type emanating from the very entities that were created by actors and institutions established and maintained by the second nomos. Neither Saul of Tarsus (Saint Paul) nor Baruch Spinoza (a European of Jewish descent) would be relevant for de-Westernizing and decolonial denoming. They do not *represent* the people for whom the history of Europe/Christianity is either irrelevant or secondary. For people of European descent in South America or in the non-European countries of the British Commonwealth (e.g., Ireland until 1949), depending on the position these people occupy in the social structure, they might join any of the three trajectories. If one of them were to opt for de-Westernization or decoloniality, it would mean that one has recognized colonial difference, for there is no imperial difference when former colonies became modern/colonial states, be these states Australia or Argentina. To make a claim for universal humanity disregarding colonial and imperial differences would be to endorse liberal morality or neoliberal re-Westernization. When, for instance, Indigenous philosophies emphasize the brotherhood of all life on Earth, including humans, they are not imperial in the sense that they would preach or force their views on the rest of the humanity, as Christianity, liberal morality, and neoliberal re-Westernization imply.

Decolonial denoming, denaming, and reconstituting are the trajectories I endorse and engage in. For that, I need the analytics of coexisting trajectories (the de-Westernization and re-Westernization that I can neither endorse nor ignore). Decolonial resurgences and reexistences demand reconstitutions of knowledges (gnoseology) and praxes of living (aesthesis) that emerge from communal memories that were not built on the ideological principle of compulsory social and economic "change" and "progress" within the historical horizon of the second nomos of the Earth. Nothing remains as it is in the unfolding of living, but "change" and "progress" are, however, designs to *control and manage the uncontrollable flows of life on Earth, including the human species*. It is precisely the civilization that was built on the foundations of the second nomos and the idea of "newness" (e.g., New World, new credit card, new iPhone, new

Toyota, new Tesla) that has capitalized on change, progress, development, and newness (innovation). Thus the urgent need for prefixes—post-, neo-, new—to maintain and control the second nomos of the Earth. The ideology is clear on close inspection: if you "control" change, progress, and development, you control the destiny of a wishful unipolar planetary civilization, and you hide and repress the fact that "change" always happened whether you wanted it or not. And if you enrolled yourself in the "post" and in the "new," you are ahead; you are not falling behind; you move with the times, but your subjectivity is controlled by your anxiety over falling out or behind.

Let's concentrate now on decolonial involvements and commitments in the advent of the third nomos of the Earth—coexisting, I remind you, with de- and re-Westernization.

V   Gnoseological and Aesthesic Reconstitutions

The background for this section is three autonomic organizations that could not have been what they are without disobeying all the domains of the CMP and above all its controlling and managing enunciation. The first, historically, is what Haitian sociologist and decolonial thinker Jean Casimir describes as "la beauté du peuple souverains" (the beauty of the sovereign people) of Haiti; the second are the Zapatistas, which the eminent Mexican sociologist Pablo González describes as "networks of resistance and autonomy"; and the third is Rojava, theoretically oriented by Abdullah Öcalan in his series of "manifesto(s) for a democratic civilization" and properly rendered by interdisciplinary thinkers, activists, and community organizers working toward an alternative to the nation-states, as Pinar Dinc argues (see also chapter 4).[30] These three cases form the background of this section and chapter, but my analysis points toward understanding the will to heal, liberate, and reconstitute the destituted in a way that is meaningful to "us" (whoever is in the "us") today, in the present.

V.1

Denoming, renaming, and resurgences are gnoseological, ethical, and political processes to supersede and delink from the tyranny of the second nomos. This vision is extremely clear already and also provides the energy, the joy, the enthusiasm, and the motivation for the emerging political society that we have witnessed increasing because of COVID-19 and in spite of it. Consider, for example, elections in Chile and Bolivia, the first to redraft the constitution written in the era of Augusto Pinochet, the second to reelect and reinstall the MAS (Marcha hacia el socialismo) that was destituted for a year by a Christian, corporate, legal, and military coup. I will focus here on (and learn from) Pueblos Originarios/Native Americans/First Nations/Aboriginals—from the Americas to New Zealand and Australia, from Asia to Africa. I am not an anthropologist who intends to "study and report what they do." Following in their steps, in this chapter I work on gnoseological and aesthesic reconstitution of hegemonic and dominant knowledge, on regulations of knowing and sensing. Rodolfo Kusch's concern was Indigenous and popular thinking that called into question his own thinking as a trained philosopher and his own sensing as a middle class Argentine and an immigrant of German descent.[31]

I found Leanne Simpson's work—and especially *Dancing on Our Turtle's Back: Stories of Nishnaabeg Re-Creation, Resurgence, and New Emergence*—an unmistakable sign of Indigenous resurgence on par with Frantz Fanon, Steve Biko, and W. E. B. Du Bois for Black consciousness; with Gloria Anzaldúa for Chicana/Latina consciousness; and with Rodolfo Kusch for immigrant consciousness.[32] These are my references for gnoseological and aesthesic reconstitutions, displacing the canon of Western thought that become an "object of study" and no longer the "epistemic and aesthetics guideline" to know, sense, and be in the world. Sure, there are prominent dissenting thinkers in Western modernity, *within the second nomos of the Earth*. I respect them and join them in solidarity, but their problems are not my problems (see chapters 12 and 13). Indigenous and popular thinking in the Americas, following Kusch's teachings, permeates and informs, for various reasons, my emotioning and my reasoning. There are various issues in Simpson's work that I would like to underscore as unmistakable signs of gnoseological and aesthesic reconstitutions arising from the experience of border dwelling and the enactment of border thinking. All of them point toward the origination of pluriversality. Border dwelling and thinking, pluriversality, and the third nomos of the Earth shall be seen as gnoseological and aesthesic reconstitutions in the making. I will begin with four passages extracted from two chapters of Simpson's book, respectively titled "Nishnaabeg's Resurgence: Stories from Within" and "Theorizing Resurgence from within Nishnaabeg Thought."

> [1] Building diverse, *nation-culture-based resurgences* means significantly re-investing in our own ways of being, regenerating our political and intellectual traditions; articulating and living our legal systems, language learning, ceremonial and spiritual pursuits; creating and using our artistic

and performance-based traditions. All of this requires—as individuals and collectives—to diagnose, interrogate and eviscerate the insidious nature of conquest, empire, and imperial thought in every aspect of our lives.

[2] *Western theory*, whether based in post-colonial, critical or even liberation strains of thought, has been exceptional in diagnosing, revealing and even interrogating colonialism. . . . Yet western theories of liberation have for the most part failed to resonate with the vast majority of Indigenous People, scholars or artists. In particular, western-based social movement theory has failed to recognize the broader contextualization of resistance within Indigenous thought, while also ignoring the contestation of colonialism as a starting point. . . . Indigenous thought . . . not only maps a way out of colonial thinking by confirming Indigenous life-ways or alternative ways of being in the world. Ultimately Indigenous theory seeks to dismantle colonialism while simultaneously building a renaissance of Mino bimaadiziwin.[33]

Mino bimaadiziwin means, like *Sumak kawsay* (Ecuadorian Kichwa) and *Suma qamaña* (Bolivian Aymara), to live in harmony and plenitude—not in competition, and without anxiety about what the CMP expects you to be and do and how to live. Therefore, the goals of communal life are not development, accumulation, having more. Those are ideals for the *social* among humans, not for *communal* horizons of life in harmony with all organisms on Earth, including humans. It requires working to live, not surrendering to the CMP and living to work. Working to live requires the constant work required to keep life in balance among humans, and also between humans and the rhythms of the universe (seasons; seeding; menstruation; movements of the sun and the moon, of winds and water, of the Earth, etc.).

[3] Part of being Indigenous in the twenty-first century is that regardless of where or how we have grown up, we've all been bathed in a vat of cognitive imperialism, perpetuating *the idea that Indigenous Peoples were not, are not, thinking peoples*, an insidious mechanism to promote neo-assimilation and obfuscate the historic atrocities of colonialism. In both subtle and overt ways, the current generation of Indigenous Peoples has been repeatedly told that individually we are stupid, and that collectively our nations were and are void of higher thoughts [see epilogue to this book]. *This is reinforced when the academic industrial complex*—often propped up by Indian and Northern Affairs Canada (INAC)—promotes colonizing education to our children and youth as the solution to dispossession, poverty, violence

and lack of self-determination over our lives. *Cognitive imperialism also rears its ugly head in every discipline every time a student is told that there is no literature or no thinking available on any given topic from within Indigenous intellectual traditions.*[34] (Emphasis added.)

In my work from *Local Histories/Global Designs* (2000) to *On Decoloniality* (2018), I have been critiqued for my romantic "uses" of the "Indians" and for considering them in the "past." These kinds of critiques come from postmodern and/or Marxist (or both) scholars and intellectuals. I find the critiques revealing in their denial. To accept that "Indians" are thinking endangers their solid basis of critical thought within the second nomos of the Earth. Exteriority shall be maintained so that Eurocentered critiques of Eurocentrism are preserved. That is part of re-Westernization in the sphere of epistemology and aesthetics. And I would add that not only Indigenous people but non-Euro-Anglo Americans in general are dubiously capable of thinking. On this topic I conclude this book, with an epilogue addressing head on what Simpson forcefully brings to light from her own praxes of living, memories, and knowing. We Third World people were also destituted, recognized for our/their cultural but not epistemic competence. "Latin" America has been celebrated for its literature since the 1960s. In the distribution of scientific labor during the Cold War, the Third World produced "culture," not knowledge. Hence, instead of begging to belong and surrender, epistemic and aesthetic disobedience turned us into gnoseological and aesthesic reconstitutions. I am not so concerned with how we dismantle the master's house, but I am very concerned with how we (re)build our own house, or our own houses. And "our" is not one universal; it is the pluriversal beyond global designs. "Our" means whoever feels and acts toward affirming the third nomoi of the Earth. For whatever we want to do in this direction we need to engage simultaneously in gnoseological and aesthesic reconstitutions. Epistemology and aesthetics belong to the second nomos. Our own house cannot be decolonially rebuilt within the frames of epistemic and aesthetic constitution/destitution.

Simpson continues:

[4] Cree scholar, poet and visual artist Neal McLeod has written extensively about the importance of *storytelling*. . . . Neal writes that the process of storytelling within Cree tradition requires storytellers to remember the ancient stories that made their ancestors "the people they were," and that this requires a remembering of language. He also emphasizes that storytellers have a responsibility to the future to imagine a social space that is just and where Cree narratives will flourish. *Storytelling is at its core decolo-*

nizing, because it is a process of remembering, visioning and creating a just reality where Nishnaabeg live as both Nishnaabeg and peoples. Storytelling then becomes a lens through which we can envision our way out of cognitive imperialism, where we can create models and mirrors where none existed, and where we can experience the spaces of freedom and justice. *Storytelling becomes a space where we can escape the gaze and the cage of the Empire, even if it is just for a few minutes.*[35] (Emphasis added.)

The first paragraph is about resurgence; the second is about the limits of Western theory and the potential of Indigenous theories to "simultaneously [build] a renaissance of Mino bimaadiziwin"; the third paragraph is about the belief that Indigenous people (and non-Europeans in general) cannot think; the fourth is about storytelling as theory, which makes us look at Western theories as storytelling endowed with a privileged power differential and the clout that the word "theory" has acquired. The fourth paragraph also offers a highlight of the disintegration of the second nomos of the Earth and decolonial denoming, rebuilding, resurging, and reconstituting the restitution of *Mino bimaadiziwin*. This expression and its equivalents, as mentioned, name *communal* horizons of living in harmony and plenitude, rather than aiming at *social* democracy or development. They are key concepts in the process of epistemic reconstitution and the reemergence of the communal rather than improving "society" or claiming to "go beyond" modernity, Western epistemology, or capitalism. The four paragraphs are a prime enactment of gnoseological and aesthesic reconstitutions and, therefore, an acting out of the politics of decolonial investigations.

Simpson's quoted paragraphs give you an idea of what denoming and epistemic reconstitution means and show that they start from the decoloniality of being. Decoloniality of being, like freedom, cannot be *given* but has to be *taken*. And the acts of decolonial denoming and the politics of decolonial investigations that undergird the four paragraphs are not questions of public policy and swift theories, but arise from persistent ancestrality engaging in life-forming (subjectivities) and thought-forming (knowing and knowledge). It should be understood that reemergences are not promises of a "return" to the "authentic" and "primal" paradise that existed before the second nomos. "Indians" have not been buried in the past; neither are they touristic relics for Western tourists and museums. The third nomos emerges from exteriority, state politics, and political society, in coexistence with efforts to maintain the privileges of the second nomos. Exteriority means border dwelling, and border dwelling generates border thinking and border sensing, which are the trademarks of the third nomos. Territorial thinking (epistemology) and territorial sensing (aesthetics) were trademarks of the second nomos.

V.2

Let's move on to the questions of land, autonomy, and self-governance in the emerging third nomos. One may expect that this step would, ideally, require me to flood the text with quotations, so you can read what Indigenous thinkers have to say and how they say it, if only to dissipate postmodern ideas on indigeneity or the *National Geographic*'s images and stories. But I am not doing ethnography. Rather, I am trying to think gnoseologically and aesthesically and to think in conversation with Indigenous thinkers' own conceptions of knowledges, theory, and storytelling. I would not necessarily be required to make such prefatory statements if I were dealing with European thinkers, for then I would not be expected to do ethnography on, for example, Kant and Hegel. It would be taken for granted that when I engage with them it would be in accordance with the accepted rules of the Western scholarly game. The reasons for these prefatory notes were mentioned by Simpson in the third paragraph above, and I devote the entire epilogue to this issue, which is crucial for the politics of decolonial investigations and gnoseological and aesthesic reconstitutions, both of which require epistemic and aesthetic disobedience and delinking.

Delinking implies epistemic disobedience in political theory in order to open up and affirm decolonial political and aesthesic modes of reexistence. Since I am not doing ethnography, I focus on two cases here: Indigenous epistemology in the South American Andes and in Canadian North America.. Therefore, I will sacrifice the richness of Indigenous thinking all over the world and rely on two examples: Fernando Huanacuni Mamani (Aymara) and Taiaiake Alfred (Kahnawake Mohawk). I highlight their parallel concerns, as well as those of many other Indigenous scholars, artists, activists, elders, and Indigenous people in general, who, aware of their colonial history, are now opting to delink from the state (the visible manifestation of the colonial matrix of power) and to reexist (or if you wish, to resist in order to reexist). My intention here is to consider the views of Indigenous thinkers, as I did with Husserl in the previous chapter, "Decoloniality and Phenomenology." My own thinking follows the lead of Indigenous thinkers, while distancing myself from Western thinkers, in solidarity with their critique of their own modernity, several of whom I was schooled in and who at some point in my life ceased to be relevant. I found in Indigenous thinkers a need (and I see in them my own need) to disobey and delink; I perceived that necessity manifested in their different vocabularies and praxes, which of course are related to each of their local histories. In Canadian North America, the decolonial politics of delinking is enacted by rejecting the state politics of recognition.[36] In the Andes (Bolivia and Ecuador) Indigenous decolonial politics forced into the constitutions of both countries the principle of a "plurinational state." This means that the Indigenous population *doesn't need to be recognized; they are one nation of the state, next to the white and mestizo/a populations.*[37] A second important philosophical and political principle that changes the terms of the conversation is that the *land does not belong to us, to human beings; we belong to the land.* The simplicity of this experience has been destituted by both the myth of private property and the triumph of industrial and technological revolutions, which have separated the human species from its "natural" belonging. But the destructive myth of private property extending to land has been voiced, and properly subdued, by the very Western academy. Karl Marx's critique of capitalism was based on the experience of the Industrial Revolution in Europe. Henry George's critique of capitalism was based on privatizing land, which could not be produced by the Industrial Revolution. Inequality and the exploitation of labor have two different explanations based on the lived experience of capitalism: land possession and dispossession in the Americas as lived by critical Anglo-Americans and by dispossessed First Nations on the one hand, and on the other the Industrial Revolution, one of the consequences of land appropriation and dispossession since the sixteenth century.[38] This means we belong to the life of Gaia/Pachamama, a life that was there before the anthropos era and will continue after each of us, each individual, dies. This principle extends to living life: life does not belong to us; we belong to life; we are its servants helping its continuity. Current debates on the posthuman, postnatural, new materialism (see below) are built on the principles of Western modernity; they change the content but not the underlying terms of the conversation, as I argued earlier; they belong to the episteme of the second nomos.

V.3

In his book *Vivir Bien/Buen Vivir*, Fernando Huanacuni Mamani devotes one section of Chapter Paqallqu (chapter 7) to "Economía Comunitaria Complementaria" (Complementary Communal Economy).[39] Since most of the likely readers of the book are not Aymara speakers or Indigenous by upbringing or education, it is important to remember that "communal" does not mean either "the commons" or the "commonwealth."[40] And it is different from the "social":

the social is circumscribed by human organizations and relations. "Communal" mean relations with the Earth, the cosmos, all living beings, including relations among humans. The constitution of the social destituted the communal to build itself as the dominant force. "Complementary" means "to be in coexistence with." In coexistence with what? With the dominant ideas and praxes of the economy in the South American Andes and in Bolivia in particular. Thus, the communal economy coexists with capitalism, which is the economy for the social that has been dominant in Bolivia and the Andes since the Incanate (the Incan organization) and more so since the European Enlightenment, when the economy was conceptualized according to the interests of liberal and socialist politics and capitalist and communist economies. For communal economies, the priority is living. Living life in harmony and plenitude (*Sumak kawsay*) has priority over capital and labor. It means that in a communal economy, labor is subjected to living rather than living being subjected to increasing wealth, as it would in a capitalist economy, or to the top-down state planning of a socialist organization, or to the state's control of specific sectors of the economy (police, health care, public infrastructure) in a communist economy.

The above outline of the priorities, horizons, and goals of these three types of economies (capitalist, socialist, and communal) are complemented by what Huanacuni Mamani calls "Formas de Organización" (Types of Organization). "Society" is the term for the predominant type of organization for both capitalist and socialist political philosophies. For Indigenous civilizations in the South American Andes, the "communal" is the *ayllu*, the unit equivalent to the Greek *oikos* (house, family). The overall supracommunal organization of the ancient Inca civilization was Tawantinsuyu. (*Tawantin* means a group of four, and *suyu* the organization within each group.) Each group consisted of *ayllus*, then *markas* that interconnected the *ayllus*, and finally the *suyu*. The *suyu* was constituted, in other words, of *ayllus* and *markas*.

Not every Indigenous civilization will have this organization. I mention them because restitution of the destituted doesn't restore the past as it was, but reconstitutes the communal today as it coexists with the social. The social cannot be eliminated in a short time, which doesn't prevent the need to reconstitute the communal by all of us according to our memories, possibilities, and potentials, for the social cannot be reformed. To decolonize the social means to delink from it and build the communal. Rebuilding the communal for non-Indigenous people doesn't mean rebuilding the Indigenous communal, but building the communal guided by the models of Indigenous communalities. What is important are *the principles* of the "communal," based on a type of economy whose priorities, horizons, and goals differ, once again, from those of capitalist and socialist economies. Capitalist societies are formed by two groups: one consisting of the privileged, wealthy minority and the sectors at its service, and the other comprising various layers of the majority of exploited and excluded people. A socialist organization, at least in theory, is "conformed" (i.e., formed together) by all human beings. In the communal organization, life, of humans and the planet, has priority over everything else.

There is much more to say about this type of economy and its interrelations with other aspects of the communal such as education, health, food, and an ancestral legal system.[41] I turn to Huanacuni Mamani, from whom I learned some basic principles of communal economies, and quote from him:

> Complementary communal economy will help us (Indigenous nations) permanently; it is a commitment to life or, rather, to the principles of life. One feature of communal enterprises, is the rotation of responsibilities; in this way all assume some responsibility and comply with the community.[42] Under this form of social organization every entrepreneurial venture should have as a premise the caring for life. Only what is beneficial to the community shall be preserved; whatever is constructive will be preserved and what is destructive will be eliminated. In communal complementary economic policies of Good Living [*Sumak kawsay*], states must project and undertake a modified structure of relationship, above all of "helping" [meaning not interfering with] people to organize in terms of reciprocity and complementarity, without subordination.[43]

The crucial point is the shift in the geography of emotioning and reasoning, to one in which we embody the basic principle that we all belong to the land and to Earth, and that we, as a species, belong to cosmic life. Even if a minute sector of life can be *imitated and reproduced, what can be reproduced by science and technology is the **content** of life, never the enunciation of life: the cosmic energies that generate the very scientists and technicians that imitate and reproduce the content of life*. Bodies, all kinds of living bodies, can be technologically modified, sure, whether through transgenic seeds or artificial organs, but the reverse (a machine infused with animal organs) is improbable. For science and technology to be at the service of life, communal economies are necessary. While capitalism reigns, science and technology will be at the service of domination, increasing wealth and professional benefits. Of course, it is doubtful that technology will solve the problems affecting life on the planet today if technology continues to operate on the principle that everything in Gaia/Pachamama is at our disposal and that our goal is not only to dominate living life (e.g., nature) but to increase our wealth and our created artifacts (including androids). Here is a paragraph where Huanacuni Mamani makes this point:

> From the concept that we are children of Mother Earth [Pachamama] are derived several teachings: one of them is that our relationship with the earth is precisely that, a relationship. It is not about negotiating rights in exchange for responsibilities. In a relationship with Mother Earth, responsibilities are already implied. Therefore, it is necessary to differentiate terms, concepts, and/or categories. When we talk about the relationship with Mother Earth, we do not talk about "owning the land," since we belong to it. So, far from claiming a right to property, what we should understand is the importance of restoring the "Right of Relationship" with Mother Earth.[44]

Learning from Indigenous philosophy (as my generation in Argentina learned from Greek, medieval, and modern European philosophy), as Huanacuni Mamani argues in chapter 7, made me realize that shifting the terms of the conversation requires locating ourselves at the receiving end of colonial (epistemic and ontological) differences and understanding and shifting to gnoseological and aesthesic reconstitutions. To do so, I argue that the politics of decolonial investigations is a must. We cannot achieve reconstitution if we remain within the conceptual web, presuppositions, and subjectivities shaped by Western epistemology and aesthetics. From there it is possible to perceive the limits and limitations of "human" rights (chapter 13), centered not only on the anthropos but also on one (unipolar in the sphere of interstate relations; universal in the sphere of social belief) conception of rights (since the sixteenth century, as discussed in chapter 5), fashioned and managed by Man/Human.[45] We will encounter in Gerald Taiaiake Alfred principles and arguments similar to Huanacuni Mamani's.

V.4

The impulse behind Gerald Taiaiake Alfred's arguments is similar to that behind Mamani's. Among other specific features, Huanacuni Mamani names the chapters of his book *Vivir Bien/Buen Vivir* using Aymara numbers, the meaning of which in Aymara cosmology carries the memories of his ancestors. Alfred organizes his arguments following the structure of present-day Kahnawake Mohawk ceremonies, which carry the memories and spirits of his ancestors. What follows is my argument arranged to converse with Taiaiake Alfred's argument in his book *Peace, Power, Righteousness: An Indigenous Manifesto.* He begins the section "First Words" with this paragraph: "The ritual of condolence is an ancient and sacred custom among my people, the Rotihoshhonni. In its structure, words, and deep meaning, this ceremony is an expression of the transformative power inherent in many healing traditions. For this reason, I have chosen condolence as the metaphorical frame work for my own thought on the state of Native America and the crucial role of indigenous tradition in alleviating the grief and discontent that permeates our existence."[46]

This quotation exemplifies a decisive move in the politics of scholarship and its stretch to the public sphere. Both Taiaiake Alfred and Huanacuni Mamani are making strong statements by highlighting Indigenous concepts, ideas, emotions. Their gnoseological and aesthesic reconstitutions cannot avoid the coexistence of Western epistemology, but at the same time they do not surrender to it. Rather, they bring forward their ancestrality instead of conceding to Western ancestrality, which is not theirs but was imposed upon them. *Ancestrality (the ground of being and enunciating) cannot be transferred.* Only the content can: knowledge can be transferred, but not knowing. For these reasons, both Taiaiake Alfred and Huanacuni Mamani cannot avoid border thinking: their arguments emerge from their praxes of living and their experiences in the ongoing flow of daily life filled with the teachings of their ancestors and the life in their languaging. At the same time, their enunciation is confronted with the dominant knowledge of the state and of state institutions. They both live and think in the ground of their ancestrality surrounded by the knowledge of the state and of state institutions (education), grounded in Western ancestrality.

The politics of decolonial investigations is fueled by the will to heal colonial wounds (see also Lorena Cabnal, in the introduction, section III.3) and the will to reexist while shaking up the mental and social slavery and disregarding where we all (classified and classifiers) have been located in the colonial matrix of power (CMP). But while for some the will is to dominate and to be a slave of their own will to dominate, for the majority of human beings the will is the will to live and to reexist. There is always a dignified rage that goes together with the processes of healing.[47] When it comes to the question of the form of governance, we see that the form of governance emerging from reexistence and healing cannot be based on Western political theories from Plato and Aristotle and their successors. Neither can it be based on Confucian political constitutionalism.[48] I mention the Confucian option to dispel the taken-for-granted idea that political theories (theories about the organization of the social, i.e., the *polis* in Greek) arise only out of the traditions of Greek philosophy. I also wish to remind ourselves of the coexistence of options in the global order, those options running parallel to the ones that Huanacuni Mamani analyzes in the Bolivians' complementary communal economy. Taiaiake Alfred's decolonial politics of governance similarly tracks with Huanacuni Mamani's (and vice versa). Here is another passage from *Peace, Power, Righteousness*: "The imposition of Western governance structures and the denial of indigenous ones continue to have profoundly harmful effects on indigenous people. Land, culture and government are inseparable in traditional philosophies; each depends on the others, and this means that the denial of one aspect precludes recovery for the whole. Without a value system that takes traditional teachings as the basis for government and politics, the recovery will be never complete."[49]

When it comes to the reconstitution (gnoseological and aesthesic) of governance, an Indigenous decolonial politics of investigations that claims autonomy does not mean that the entirety of Canada or Bolivia should be subjected to Indigenous forms of governance. That is the political cuckoo of liberal and neoliberal arguments. On the contrary, the claims hold *that the settlers in Canada, and the descendants of the settlers in Bolivia, do not have the right to impose* their "national" autonomy on other nations within the same state (Canada or Bolivia in this case). The concept of the "plurinational state" in Bolivia's and Ecuador's constitutions addresses these issues. That is, a settler-state's governance should not be foisted on people who do not want to submit to laws that emanated from the settlers' skin and spirit (e.g., subjectivity) that dispossessed First Nations from the land and destituted them as lesser human beings (see chapter 12). That is why for Indigenous and non-Indigenous intellectuals, gnoseological and aesthesic reconstitutions are a must, and the decolonial politics of investigations needs to delink from epistemological and aesthetic restrictions and limitations. Which means that in Bolivia and Canada (and many other "national" states), the Indigenous population doesn't have *to be subjected* to the Bolivian or Canadian national state but has the right to *participate in and be part of the governance*. "Plurinational state" simply means that there is not one single nation that belongs to the state and rules its governance, but that the "state" shall be ruled and governed by the plurality of nations. Gnoseological and aesthesic reconstitutions of governance at this moment have to work, on the one hand, toward the auto-nomos (i.e., the autonomy) of Indigenous nations, and have to deal, on the other, with pressure from the state to prevent their autonomy. It is, de facto, a situation of border dwelling and border thinking, of the coming forward of the decolonial pluriversality and the third nomos of the Earth; the modern (in the North Atlantic), the colonial/modern (in the former colonies), and the idea of one nation/one state belong to the epoch of the second nomos of the earth. The third nomos is already announcing a change of epoch that cannot be subsumed under the frame of an epoch of changes, where newness within the same reigns.

How would this be possible? The idea and effectuation of one nation/ one state (the nation-state) destituted the possibilities that today the plurinational state is paving. But the plurinational state is inconceivable within the frame of the political theory that effectuated the nation-state. Hence, the plurinational-state implies gnoseological and aesthesic reconstitutions. However, there is another problem associated with the constitution of the plurinational state (both the written constitution and the administrative framework of the state form of governance): capitalist and/or socialist economies prevent complementary communal economies from existing. Now, the principles of reciprocity in which communal economies are organized must not be interpreted in the same terms as Western liberal or socialist concepts of economy, that is, as economies of growth to increase wealth or to increase distribution. Huanacuni Mamani reports, "All forms of relationship in the *ayllu* like in the ancient Greek *oykos*, both referring to home and non-Christian family as the basic unit of communal organization, must be in permanent balance and harmony with everything, because when these rules are broken the consequences are for everyone. Within the *ayllu* there is no place for the term 'resource' since if everything lives, what exists are beings and not objects, and the human being is not the only parameter of creation. . . . In the *ayllu*, we do not seek to dominate anything, we seek to relate to ourselves under the principle and awareness of the *ayni* (reciprocity, the energy that flows between all forms of existence)."[50]

There is more to it than this. There is the whole mode of existing and praxis of living. This is why reemerging from colonial depletion is the first principle of gnoseological and aesthesic reconstitution of the economy. Friends and enemies (if you would like to conceive the political in those terms) are subordinated to reexistence. If Schmitt thought of friend and enemy as the way to conceive the political, it is because in Germany (and in western Europe) reexistence was not a problem he had to deal with.[51] They were, they exist, they think. The political is not a question for Indigenous reconstitution of the *ayllu*'s economy, but it is when it comes to confronting the settler-state that prevents them from gaining their autonomy. And it may also infiltrate the minds of people in the *ayllu*. Beyond the friend/enemy concept of the political, the majority of the population that has been destituted from Western political theory does not have to think about the political (organization of the *polis*, which is equivalent to the *suyu* (group of *ayllu*s or *ayllukuna*). In this respect Taiaiake Alfred has something to say that reinforces the inevitability of border thinking in every sphere of gnoseological and aesthesic reconstitution:

"Native American community today is framed by two value systems that are fundamentally opposed. One, still rooted in traditional teaching, structures social and cultural relations; the other, imposed by the colonial state, structures politics. This disunity is the fundamental cause of factionalism in Native communities, and it contributes significantly to the alienation that plagues them. What those who seek to understand and remedy the problems that flow from it often don't realize is that this separation was deliberate."[52]

Friend/enemy is the political structure within the settler-state in Canada and all other former colonies. However, the settlers' colonial states were founded on internal colonialism and dependency from the metropole as an extension of European imperial nation-state formation. Hence, if friend/enemy defines the political for European nation-states, it is the political only for the settler nation/state, not for the Indigenous population, who have a different agenda: to delink, rebuild, reemerge. Therefore, the politics of decolonial investigations proves to be crucial in dispelling the idea that the political (the principles of knowing and sensing in the organization of living together) be limited to friend/enemy.[53] For that reason, the state politics of recognition in Canada is radically rejected by Indigenous thinkers and activists.[54]

Friends and enemies, in Schmitt's concept of the political, serve well to help us understand domestic state and interstate politics (e.g., the "allies" of re-Westernization and de-Westernization). Decolonial politics is, however, opening up a different scenario in the history of the European nation-state precisely because decolonial politics is not grounded in European political theories. It is the work toward gnoseological reconstitutions of the political that nourishes decolonial politics. The settler's nation-state in the former colonies followed the model of Western political theories, shattering Indigenous millenarian governance. This is one of the main reasons for the failures of the modern/colonial nation-state to achieve autonomy. In Europe it was possible to operate with the idea that one nation corresponds to one state. The ethnic diversity in the colonies made it difficult to identify one nation with one state, due to the presence of Indigenous nations (also called tribes). Taiaiake Alfred phrases these issues as follows: "The imposition of Western governance structures and the denial of indigenous ones continue to have profoundly harmful effects on indigenous people. Land, culture and government are inseparable in traditional philosophies; each depends on the others, and this means that the denial of one aspect precludes recovery for the whole. Without a value system that takes traditional teachings as the basis for government and politics, the recovery will never be complete."[55]

In a plurinational state, the goal is to coordinate the autonomous governance of each nation with the overarching entity we call the state proper (here, the plurinational state). The US, for instance, is a composite of states, but each state is governed by people of the same "nation." The US is so far a plurination but a monostate: the state is controlled by one ethnicity—that is, one nation, the Anglo-American nation. It is possible to imagine a future in which the US becomes a plurinational state in which today's ethnic minorities might govern autonomous states and have a say in the United Plurinational States of North America. The rules of the game have to change; the terms of the conversation have to change. A top-down governing body must give way to a horizontal configuration of governances. This would involve an overarching administration with coordinating functions only, not one or two financial or military "elites" deciding for all. The Zapatistas' decolonial politics, for example, is expressed in a single political principal: "To rule and obey at the same time."[56] The failure of the bourgeois model of the nation-state has reached its limits, as can be seen everywhere, and it is being debated.[57] No doubt the idea of a domestic plurinational state would impinge on the global inter-pluri-state system. This topic requires a lengthier treatment. I am mentioning it to consider seriously that there is no need to remain attached to the idea that one nation/one state (i.e., the nation-state) should be the universal and eternal form of governance. Suffice it to say here that the multipolar world order in the making would require both de-Westernization and decoloniality to overcome both the monopolar existing world order and the mononational existing nation-state. What is crucial is the following: a plurinational state is *not* a decolonial goal, but a contribution that decolonial thinking can make to change the "content" of Western political theory. The decolonial global in governance should be *auto-nomic* organizations of communal praxes of living that, currently, would coexist with the nation-state and that, eventually, would lead to forms of governance at the service of life and to end a form of governance that life must serve. The Zapatistas, once again, offer one example among many minor organizations of people who have realized that the state is not at their service, but at the service of corporations and investors.

Returning to the domestic aspects of governance and the issues of domestic plurinational states: justice at the service of people instead of people justifying judicial systems is of prime concern. For Huanacuni Mamani, justice should be placed in the politics of the "rights to relation," an expression that highlights a fundamental principle of Indigenous cosmologies. It is not a cosmology based on entities and matter, but on flow, flux, and energetic relations, of all what there is, including the relations that interconnect what there is. This principle sounds strange to modern Western subjects used to seeing "things" not "relations." But think about this: Immanuel Kant built a solid social architecture based on what Isaac Newton identified as the laws of nature. Well, think about the communal that cannot be built on the *laws* (τοῦ νόμου, *tou nómou*) of nature but has been built and is reemerging on the *flux* of Pachamama. In the ancient Greek vocabulary, justice would be what accords with the *law* of the cosmos. In Aymara vocabulary and philosophy, justice materializes in *harmony and balance* among persons and between persons and all the living. Extractivism alters the harmony and the balance; it cannot be a just activity, for it disturbs the harmony among people and in the niches that makes life sustainable. The fundamental "law" (if law is a proper concept in this context) of *pacha* is equilibrium and harmony; that injunction has been destituted by settlers' interferences. As brutal as the Aztecs' sacrifices may look today, they were done to maintain the equilibrium of Teotl (Náhuatl for "cosmos," meaning that Teotl is the creator of the cosmos, just as the cosmos is the creator of Teotl). Obviously, Aztec civilization was not "perfect," but neither is Western civilization. However, the first was disrupted and destituted, while Western civilization constituted itself by destitution and continued transforming and updating itself. I am just underscoring that each civilization conceives and executes its rights and wrongs based on its own cosmogonies, cosmologies, and praxes of living. Is this cultural relativism? Perhaps. But who has the right to interfere? *Who has the right to intervene while at the same time preventing intervention in their/our own affairs?* One answer may be: the actors that belong to the civilization that created the concept of "cultural relativism." Huanacuni Mamani writes:

> When we speak of the relationship with Mother Earth we do not speak of being "owners of the earth," since we belong to her. Far from claiming a property right, what we should understand is the importance of reestablishing the "Right of Relationship" with Mother Earth. . . .
>
> In the West, ordinary justice grants the right to property to someone when they obtain a title; but in the Ancestral Community Legal System, by principle, no one owns the land, but we have the "right of relationship." This right emerges when we live together in the place, we generate life relationships and we fulfill the roles and responsibilities within the community.[58]

In rejecting anthropocentrism, Taiaiake Alfred's arguments and Mamani's words coincide with the arguments of posthumanism and new materialism, but the arguments are made in different terrains and across colonial epistemic and ontological differences.[59] The proponents of posthumanism and new materialism are fighting their own shadows, the shadows that destituted what Indigenous thinkers (above all the Elders) always knew. Indigenous thinkers do not need posthumanism because they were never considered humans, and they do not need new materialism because materialism is not in their ancestrality. Their cosmology, distinct from Western cosmology in which new materialism is embedded, is not an accumulation of *atomic and cellular entities* but the constant *flows of relational life* and existence. What matters is that decolonial Indigeneity, in its own praxes of living and thinking, was—since 1500—a constant delinking from Western materialism and anthropocentrism (humanism). Consequently, posthumanism and new materialism are not issues that torment them. There is no room, then, for posthumanism from the experience of someone who has been left in the exteriority of the human, and there is no room for new materialism for the person who inhabits a world populated with relations rather than with object and matter. Both posthumanism and new materialism are transdisciplinary projects that remain within the Western secular and scientific assumptions about materiality derived from modern Western sciences and universality. I am not saying that Indigenous conceptions are "better" or "preferable." They are options, like posthumanism and new materialism. I am saying simply that they coexist. The Indigenous option is contributing to the making of the third nomos of the Earth. New materialism and posthumanism are contributing to maintaining the second nomos of the Earth. Similar considerations should be made about Western liberal *environmental or ecological humanism*. They remain within the critical sphere of the second nomos. Ecological humanism changes the content, not the terms, of the conversation in the interiority of the CMP.

Indigenous arguments change the terms of the conversations. They dispute the assumptions and principles upon which the CMP has been built. And they do it through meticulous gnoseological and aesthesic reconstitutions. Taiaiake Alfred enumerates some of the difficulties and challenges implied by gnoseological and aesthesic reconstitutions: "Most non-indigenous people have always seen indigenous people in problematic terms: as obstacles to the progress of civilization, wards of the Crown, relics of savagery, the dregs of modern society, criminals and terrorists. Over the centuries, indigenous people themselves have consistently defended their nationhood as best they could. . . . It would be a tragedy if generations of Native people should have suffered and sacrificed to preserve what is most essential to their nations' survival only to see it given away in exchange for the status of a third-order government within a European-American economic and political system."[60] Indigenous decolonial politics is not only about resistance but about rebuilding on the assumptions and principles of their own cosmologies, where humanism and materialism are absent. They are changing the terms of the conversation, reconstituting their own enunciation, and contributing to the advent of the third nomos of the earth (see introduction, section III.3).

V.5

The overall goal of the decolonial Indigenous politics of knowing and knowledge has been articulated in expressions such Sumak kawsay (in Tawantinsuyu) and Mino bimaadiziwin (in Turtle Island). The reenchantment of the world is on the way. These are two expressions for harmony, balance, and plenitude among many that Huanacuni Mamani cites from various Indigenous languages throughout the Americas. Not democracy, but harmony and plenitude. Not a universal model of democracy that serves limited local elites, but local variations and manifestations of the same principles. To understand the meaning of Sumak kawsay, Huanacuni Mamani (corroborated by many Indigenous leaders and intellectuals) states that it is necessary to understand the world-sense and world-conception of the ancestors, the living memory that cannot be captured by any digital archive. Digital archives are a new manifestation of the coloniality of knowledge, erasing, destituting, and silencing living memories, a lived archive, and lived ancestry. How did our elders and ancestors, he asks, understand and express (via storytelling) their general idea of the world and of life on Earth?

Huanacuni Mamani starts by explaining the meaning of pacha (which I described in general terms earlier). Everything has been created, he states, by two complementary forces: energy (Pachacamac), the cosmic force that comes down from the sky, and Pachamama, the telluric force of land or Earth. (PA means "two," and CHAMA means "force or energy.") These two forces converge in the generation and regeneration of living life; at the same time, they generate and regenerate themselves in the process. This means that there is no abstract entity that created the world and human beings, and that remains separate from the creation. Now if you give names to the two forces and say one is masculine and the other feminine, you will understand that the feminine and the masculine are in all of us. They are complementary, not opposite, and are independent from the Western association of the first with "woman" and the second with "man." So everybody (animal, plant, human) is at once feminine and masculine. And they are not opposed by complementary energies of life-making and life-regeneration (ayni in Aymara). Briefly, two forces, cosmic and telluric, converge to generate and regenerate life.[61]

If ontology (metaphysics, or the study of being) were thinkable in Aymara or Quechua, it would not focus on entities as beings, even less on Being (in Heidegger's sense), but on relations. An ontology of relations would be wrongly named because ontology hides relationality. To focus on relations—those which interrelate and interconnect all dimensions of existence—is quite different from focusing on the interconnected entities themselves. To focus on energies and the flow of life is quite different from focusing on matter and the law of the cosmos, or on the meaning of Being that makes beings understood. It is also important here to note, as Taiaiake Alfred describes, that the decolonial Indigenous political points toward communal resurgence, plenitude, and harmony as conceived and pursued starting from this conception of the generation and regeneration of life. Hence, there is no conflict between the creationism and evolutionism such as the conflict that torments theological and secular scientific minds in the West and wherever else Western cosmology has been accepted. Once you dwell in this conception you dwell on the border, for your cosmology has to be articulated in coexistence with the mononational state in which specific Indigenous projects are thought out and implemented.

In the last chapter of *Dancing on Our Turtle's Back*, titled "Shi-Kiin: New Worlds," Leanne Simpson offers another path toward changing the terms of the conversation and enacting *Mino bimaadiziwin*.[62] She tells the story of a conversation, held in a classroom, between a Nishnaabeg elder (Robin Green-ba) and a scientist from the Indigenous Environmental Resources of Winnipeg about sustainable development. At some point Leanne asks Robin if there is an expression in the Nishnaabeg language equivalent to "sustainable development." The answer, as you can imagine if you have followed my argument, is no. He told the class that thinking in terms of sustainable development is backward, that we should be doing the opposite. Leanne says, "He explained that what makes sense from a Nishnaabeg perspective is that humans should be taking as little as possible, giving up as much as possible, to promote sustainability and promote Mino bimaadiziwin in the coming generations. He felt that we should be as gentle as possible with our Mother, and that we should be taking the bare minimum to ensure our survival. He talked about how we need to manage ourselves so that *life can promote more life*."[63]

VI Concluding Remarks

The long voyage through gnoseological and aesthesic reconstitutions, border thinking, and the third nomos of the Earth is arriving at its point of destination. Facing the danger of climate change, the violence of state policies, and interstate wars led today by the conflict between de-Westernizing delinking and re-Westernizing efforts to contain and prevent it, one could keep on hoping that goodwill and technology will solve our problems. It is too late to hold that kind of hope, which relies on the goodwill of governing actors and institutions that are themselves trapped in the colonial matrix of power (CMP). The will to dominate and control a planet with almost eight billion people has become unmanageable, a dream that was possible to maintain during the epoch of the second nomos. Changes of name in state governance; interstate institutions like the International Monetary Fund and the World Bank; efforts to re-Westernize the world order by domination—these are contributing to the ill-being of all, exemplified by the desperation of actors running institutions that are out of place. An irrepressible energy propels the eruption of the third nomos of the Earth, in the wide array of both state-led de-Westernization projects and people-led decolonial projects; cosmopolitics is displacing geopolitics.

Epilogue Yes, We Can: Border Thinking, Pluriversality, and Colonial Differentials

La Europa que consideró que su destino, el destino de sus hombres, era hacer de su humanismo el arquetipo a alcanzar por todo ente que se le pudiese asemejar; esta Europa, lo mismo la cristiana que la moderna, al trascender los linderos de su geografía y tropezar con otros entes que parecían ser hombres, exigió a éstos que justificasen su supuesta humanidad.—LEOPOLDO ZEA, *La filosofía americana como filosofía sin más,* 1969

The free-thinker's and artist's functions are not to remove the contradictions and discrepancies that exist in the heart of a society, but to enter them into the feeling and consciousness of the society. . . . Contradictions must enter subjectivity in order to cause movement. This is why poverty does not cause movement, it is the feeling of poverty that does. . . . One of the ways to enter contradiction and positive realities into the consciousness of the present generation is to seek help from those who have covered this route already. That is, instead of studying Marx, Sartre, Heidegger and so forth (which have nothing to do with our condition anyway) we need to find out what Fanon, Mawloud, Yassin, Radhakrishnan (former Indian Prime Minister and philosopher), the thinkers of Chad, the Congo and so forth have said. —ALI SHARI'ATI, "The Mission of a Free Thinker," 1970–1971

A free-thinker's function is not to lead society. . . . The most worthless elements for leading people are free-thinkers. . . . Free-thinkers have been the worst disaster for revolution.—ALI SHARI'ATI, "The Mission of a Free Thinker," 1970–1971

Q. So, you are proposing a theory.

A. No, I am not a theory maker. Whoever makes up theory is only good for universities.

Q. Europeans have reached a progressive thinking stage, why are they behaving this way?

A. I think they are biased. They believe in their own superiority, and have created a type of thinking atmosphere, called "egocentrism" which is self-centeredness. An egocentric individual doesn't count others as human beings. This philosophy has existed in the West since ancient Greece. . . .

Q. In the case of African thinkers, he despised so much that it helped him to gain consciousness. But being despised is not true in our case. Is it?

A. *It is not true that we are not being despised. The fact is that we are not aware that we are being despised.*

—ALI SHARI'ATI, "The Mission of a Free Thinker," 1970–1971, emphasis added

We have a history of people putting Maori under a microscope in the same way a scientist looks at an insect. The ones doing the looking are giving themselves the power to define.

—MERATA MITA, quoted by LINDA TUHIWAI SMITH, "Colonizing Knowledges," in *Decolonizing Methodologies: Research and Indigenous Peoples* (1999)

I   Preliminaries: The Scope of the Issue

This epilogue has a story, and the story—not only the argument—serves well the purpose of an epilogue to the politics of decolonial investigation, the title of this volume. It all started in December 2012, prompted by Santiago Zabala's panegyric of Slavoj Žižek that appeared on Al Jazeera, titled "Slavoj Žižek and the Role of the Philosopher," and was expanded by the intervention of Iranian intellectual Hamid Dabashi's essay titled "Can Non-Europeans Think?"[1] Because the issue highlighted by Dabashi's question has been hanging over the heads of many Latin American intellectuals since the 1960s—as Leopoldo Zea's epigraph above testifies—and because it was certainly felt in my emotioning (in my blood and my skin), I was pleased to find out that someone from Iran was having similar concerns, and so I entered the conversation.[2]

Dabashi's question—"Can non-Europeans think?"—captures in a few words an ongoing history of dismissal (as Ali Shari'ati has it in the above epigraphs and also as underscored by Leopoldo Zea) that began in the sixteenth century. Dismissal is a light form of destitution secured by epistemology and aesthetics. Gnoseological and aesthesic reconstitution means to reclaim what has been destituted by the rhetoric of modernity and its praxical (from "praxis," not from "practice") consequences: the intellectual arrogance of the majority of North Atlantic scholars, intellectuals, artists, journalists—briefly, all of whom work in the spheres of knowledge and aesthetics. The bottom line is that for the majority of Europeans, non-Europeans are lesser humans and are rationally deficient; therefore, it is questionable, although not said, whether non-Europeans can think according to the European standards for thinking. But that is not the point; the point is that non-European scientists, scholars, intellectuals, and journalists *do not have to obey European standards*. For the good of the many, *the politics of decolonial investigations proposes just that: to disobey and delink*. The assumption that non-Europeans cannot think also implies that knowledge-making is the task of European thinkers. For that reason, it is generally assumed that persons from non-European regions of the planet have wanted and still want to study in Europe, and now also in the US. It is also the reason why, in the sixteenth and seventeenth centuries, European-style universities were created in the New World, and why at the end of the twentieth century and the beginning of the twenty-first, US universities are being transplanted into Asia and the Middle East.[3] That is, *they/we* cannot think. More precisely, non-European Christians are unable to think like European Christians. Which is perfectly all right, and it was accepted, even by non-Europeans, that *they/we* were deficient thinkers.

Universality outplayed pluriversality; the advent of the European second nomos of the Earth in 1500 concealed the multiplicity of existing nomoi that Carl Schmitt located as the first nomos of the Earth (that is, the world order before 1500). And nomoi imply knowing, sensing, understanding, believing, and living accordingly. The multiplicity of existing nomoi was concealed and destituted by the advent of the second nomos, but not killed. And that is the situation today: the resurgence (restitution) of the earliest nomoi (a diversity of them, not only one) after five hundred years of destitution. Restitution is not a physical operation; it is a gnoseological and aesthesic one. The resurgences (not going back) of the first nomoi today are irreversible. That is what ancestrality means, ancestrality overcoming history. Resurgences and reexistences (not returns) are manifested in two wide and diverse trajectories: (1) de-Westernization and multipolarity, and (2) decoloniality and pluriversality. The point now is not only that non-Europeans can think; it is that if their/our thinking is going to be truly theirs/ours, it has to be disobedient. Without disobedient thought, there would be neither de-Westernization and multipolarity nor decoloniality and pluriversality. If both trajectories are possible, it is because border thinking (border epistemology) has erupted and can no longer be controlled. In large measure, the political, military, and economic turmoil in the world order is due to de-Westernization; in the sphere of thought it is due to decoloniality. Briefly, Dabashi's question "can non-Europeans think?" pulls the mask off universal belief and the supposed benefits of homogeneity, and indirectly opens up the task for the decolonial politics of investigations, thinking beyond Western research regulations managed by granting institutions and promoted by universities and museum administrations.

The Black person, Frantz Fanon writes, is not ontologically Black; he/she is Black in front of a white person.[4] He/she is a "Noire," which for the white gaze is much more than having black skin. Here, ontology is displaced by the experience of the colonial difference that Fanon renders as sociogenesis. Fanon identified a phenomenon that extends to all non-white people, and this phenomenon is a psychological and epistemic one rather than a biological or a purely chromatic one. Third World intellectuals unconsciously and sometimes consciously classified, sociogenetically speaking, from the First World, although "Third World" has been assumed by politically engaged intellectuals, scholars, artists, and activists as a place of pride rather than one of humiliation.

From the First World's perspective, the Third World's thinking is local; at best, it is of interest to First World anthropologists, bankers, corporations, Western nation-states, and a few others. If sociogenesis is the experience of living under the colonial difference, then dwelling in the colonial difference means dwelling on the borderlines and borderlands, "being seen as." Exteriority means that you are seen in the border by someone who is in the territory: "Look mom, a Negro." The awareness of "being seen as" is a *relational* experience, not an *ontological* one. In this case you are in the border zones (two sides of the border separated and connected by power differentials) between a white and Black person, seen and decided on in white territory. So the decolonial question is not about locations in the Third World or the Global South but on the border zone, dwelling in the colonial difference. Whether you are in the West and the North or in the East and the South, the power differential that unites and divides the two sides of the border cannot be avoided whether you are aware of it or not. If you dwell on the despised side of the border, border dwelling becomes the condition of border thinking and border thinking the gnoseological and aesthesic mover of decoloniality. If you dwell *in* the territory, you would like to preserve epistemology and aesthetics. Hence, it is not so much the Global South or the Third World that matters but the border zone that mutates from a place of humiliation to a place of pride and reexistence, reclaiming, and restituting. That is the trust of decolonial reconstitutions and therefore of decolonial politics. If you are there and do not want to be there, then you have to choose between two options: to accept in resignation what you have been told you are, strive for recognition, and obey the epistemic and aesthetic regulations; or to reject recognition and strive for gnoseological and aesthesic reconstitutions.[5]

Reconstitutions demand delinking. You cannot reconstitute gnoseologically and aesthesically if you do not disobey and remain within the spider web of epistemology and aesthetics; that is, within the colonial matrix of power (CMP). Reconstitution means delinking to reexist. And that is the path that Fanon showed us: once you become aware that you are what you are sociogenetically, you inhabit the border, your existence is on the border. Now the task is to convert, sociogenetically, existence into reexistence. And that is another aspect of the path that Fanon showed us. There cannot be only a single mode of reexistence. The many disavowed local histories, memories, and forms of existence that characterized the first nomos are multiple and complex. As a result, decolonial reexistences that delink from modern/colonial universality and emerge from multiple actualizations of colonial differences will also be multiple and pluriversal. They enunciate the pluriversal.

As I have said throughout this book, the major task of the politics of decolonial investigations—its "raison d'être"—is to change the terms in which the conversations on knowing, understanding, and existing take place, rather than to change their content (ontology) while preserving their terms. And changing the terms means to change the questions upon which Western knowledge and regulation of knowing are founded and to engage in epistemic reconstitution. De-Westernization—which is very important in blocking neoliberal homogenization—is changing the content but not the terms of the conversations: a capitalist economy is common to de- and re-Westernization. And by changing the content, it is disputing the control of the CMP; it is not questioning its existence. De-Westernization changes the content in that it delinks from the monopoly of Western universals and rebuilds in the present, reconstituting and restituting the praxes of living and thinking and the relevance of destituted languages and currencies, while restoring living memories that the making of the CMP and the imperial difference cast out from "history." It became possible by appropriating the economy of accumulation (capitalism) but rejecting its ideologies: liberalism and neoliberalism. This is one of the explanations for the present turmoil, which is not a second Cold War; the confrontation between de-Westernization and re-Westernization is significantly different from the confrontation between (neo)liberalism and socialism/communism, two Western systems of ideas. De-Westernization, instead, brings forward modes of existence that have been disavowed and concealed by the success of Westernization across the planet and that re-Westernization would like to continue. This was the meaning of Fukuyama's "the end of history."

De-Westernizing projects aim at preserving their pasts, secured by economic (capitalist) affirmation. Paradoxical as it may seem, it was the appropriation of the economy of accumulation (capitalism) but the rejection of its foundational ideologies (mercantilism, liberalism, neoliberalism) that allowed China to stand on its own and to reclaim Confucius instead of Aristotle, while people are rejoining Buddhism.[6] Buddhism is closer to home than Christianity. And while there are people who join Buddhism in western Europe and the US, what happens in these cases is that the route of dispersion expands from the point of origination. Christianity is a West Asian religion, but it had been reoriented toward the West when Rome became the hub instead of Constantinople. And Buddhism, as far as I know, did not originate in Paris or London during the European Middle Ages, or in Greece or Rome. There is no determinism here. Memories are attached to places, rituals, buildings, languages— in the same way that Westernization and re-Westernization want to preserve the West's historical foundation and its valued legacies. There is not one and only one cosmogonic and/or historical foundation that is universally valid for all; there is not one set of values, principles, and regulations of knowing and sensing that is valid for all. These are the issues behind Dabashi's question, to which I will now add: "Can non-European think and sense?" According to Immanuel Kant, the answer is no, as he stated in *Observations on the Feeling of the Beautiful and Sublime* (1764). Since then epistemology and aesthetics have been set up and regulated by Western actors and institutions, so it did not need to be said all the time. It became a presupposition and a prejudgement. It may be that two or more civilizations share similar values, but the universes of meaning in which those values make sense are not the same. If Confucius, Aristotle, and Jesus have some elements in common, none of the three universes of meaning (Confucianism, Greek philosophy, or Christianity)—and no actor professing their beliefs and no institutions under their command—has the right to privilege its universality over the others. One of the crucial aftermaths of pluriversality is reducing North Atlantic universals to their own size; therefore, Western scholars, journalists, intellectuals, and scientists are losing their privileges to discuss and decide what is good or bad beyond their own domestic concerns. The confrontation is above all a confrontation of knowledge, for after all, economies, politics, and armies are supported by principles of knowledge, investigation, and argumentation, beyond the technicalities of economic transactions, political administrations, and military actions.[7]

I am black; I am in total fusion with the world, in sympathetic affinity with the earth, losing my id in the heart of the cosmos—and the white man, however intelligent he may be, is incapable of understanding Louis Armstrong or songs from the Congo. I am black, not because of a curse, but because my skin has been able to capture all the cosmic effluvia. I am truly a drop of sun under the earth.—FRANTZ FANON, *Black Skin, White Masks*

As long as the black man is among his own, he will have no occasion, except in minor internal conflicts to experience his being through others. There is of course the momentum of "being for others," of which Hegel speaks, but every ontology is made unattainable in a colonized [and civilized] society. It would seem that this fact has not been given sufficient attention by those who have discussed the question. In the Weltanschauung of a colonized people there is an impurity, *a flaw that outlaws any ontological explanation.* Someone may object that this is the case with every individual, but such an objection merely conceals a basic problem. *Ontology—once it is finally admitted as leaving existence by the wayside—does not permit us to understand the being of the black man. For not only must the black man be black; he must be black in relation to the white man.*—FRANTZ FANON, *Black Skin, White Masks*, emphasis added

Fanon's statements in the epigraphs above highlight two crucial basics of this chapter. The first is *vincularidad* ("linking"), a Spanish word used by Indigenous thinkers in the Andes to underscore the interrelations of all living organisms on the planet and their energy in common with the cosmos—life in itself, so to speak. *Vincularidad* is what modernity/coloniality erased with the invention of two separate entities: Man/Human and Nature (see introduction, section III, and chapter 12 for an explanation of the contexts within which these words are capitalized). That separation established the path of modernity/postmodernity and of human/posthuman: the invention of the self, taken to be the "essence" of Man/Human. The separation was a pillar in the advent and formation of the second nomos of the Earth (chapter 14). As far as we know, this separation did not exist in the polycentricity and multiplicity of the first nomos. Fanon makes that energy reemerge to reexist. If decolonial politics is the politics of reconstitution and reexistence, here is a manifestation from which we who feel touched by coloniality at the receiving end can learn to delink from the modern/self and relink with the energy of the cosmos: *vincularidad* with all the living, not only the limited sphere of the human species, shall be restituted in the search to live in harmony and plenitude, and for that, gnoseological/aesthesic reconstitutions are necessary to pulverize and overcome all colonial epistemic/aesthetic differences.

We are not all Blacks, and so the colonial difference is felt and played out differently. Fanon himself let us know this by referring to Jean-Paul Sartre's statement on the Jewish questions in his book *Anti-Semite and Jew*: "They (the Jews) have allowed themselves to be poisoned by the stereotype that others have of them, and they live in fear that their acts will correspond to their stereotype. . . . *We may say that their conduct is perpetually over-determined from inside*."[8] Fanon adds, "He (the Jew) is a white man, and, apart from some rather debatable characteristics, he can sometimes go unnoticed. . . . Granted, the Jews are harassed—what am I thinking of? They are hunted down, exterminated, cremated. . . . The Jew is disliked from the moment he is tracked down. But in my case, everything takes on a *new* guise. I am given no chance. *I am over-determined from without*. I am the slave not of the 'idea' that others have of me but of my own appearance."[9]

Decolonization today means something different from what Fanon was referring to in the early 1950s in France and then in Algeria. Africa was not colonized in the sixteenth century, as it was after the Berlin Conference of 1884. Between the sixteenth and the eighteenth centuries, Africa provided enslaved human beings for labor in the New World. What Fanon senses is the persistence of the colonial difference inflicted on enslaved Black Africans since that time. And that is what he is telling us by saying that he rejects all immunization of the emotions (i.e., not rejecting the emotions per se, but rejecting immunization against experiencing them): "Some identify with ancestors of mine who had been enslaved or lynched; I decided to accept this. It was on the universal level of the intellect that I understood this inner kinship." Historical ancestry does not count as much for him as the historical persistence of the colonial difference, epistemic and ontological: "And then the occasion arose when I had to meet the white man's eyes. . . . In the white world the man of color encounters difficulties in the development of his bodily schema. Consciousness of the body is solely a negating activity. It is a third-person consciousness."[10]

To feel that one inhabits colonial differences, to sense coloniality in our bodies (which includes the brain), it is not necessary to be colonized. Jews were not colonized, but they did not escape coloniality—historically following their expulsion from the Iberian Peninsula after 1492 (see chapters 3 and 4). Enslaved Africans during the colonial period were not colonized in the manner that Aztecs, Incas, and Mayas were colonized. But they all endured coloniality in different modalities. The Chinese have not been colonized in the same way that India was, but they did not escape coloniality. The Opium Wars encroached on their destiny. China's responses to coloniality engendered Sun-yat Sen; India's responses generated Mahatma Gandhi: two non-Europeans who could think and sense. Settler European colonialism in Africa was deployed in earnest after the Berlin Conference and the Scramble for Africa, 1885–1914. However, in all these cases coloniality was at work. Coloniality doesn't need colonialism, although the concept is derived from colonialism. Concomitantly, the colonial difference manifests itself in many guises and is enacted with more or less force depending on the appearance and/or the local histories of the people affected. The equivalent settler colonialism today means to be subjected to the colonial difference, to be considered epistemically deficient and ontologically inferior. Beyond the scales of coloniality, the main issue remains and is expressed in the second quote of Fanon's that appears below the subhead to this section: "*Ontology—once it is finally admitted as leaving existence by the wayside—does not permit us to understand the being of the black man. For not only must the black man be black; he must be black in relation to the white man.*"

Fanon is teaching all of us who feel intruded on by colonial difference and who know explicitly or implicitly that non-Euro-Americans are deficient and inferior (cannot think and sense properly)—that is what "underdeveloped" means, and also "emergent economies." The prison house of Western epistemic assumptions is ontology and not *vincularidad*. Once you pay attention to *vincularidad*, you began to become aware of three crucial *existential* dimensions that reveal precisely why Fanon is telling us that *ontology* leaves *existence* by the wayside:

a   Ontology stresses entities (thus the invention of Nature to kill living energies) rather than *vincularidad* (relations).
b   Coloniality blocks holistic *vincularity* (relations) and replaces it with power relations dictated by the colonial matrix of power.
c   To reexist, it is absolutely necessary not to expect recognition (see chapter II), but to affirm with pride what for modernity/coloniality is considered a deficiency: "When I should have been begged, implored, I was denied the slightest recognition. I resolved, since it was impossible for me to get away from an *inborn complex* to assert myself as a BLACK MAN. Since the other hesitated to recognize me, there remained only one solution: to make myself known."[11]

This is a robust affirmation of reexistence turning the colonial difference upside down, enacting gnoseological and aesthesic reconstitution. This is why recognition remains a state's moral intention, as Glen Coulthard convincingly argued (see chapter 14). Recognition from those from whom you do not want to lose privilege is a way to turn the colonial difference upside down. Asking the question "can non-Europeans think?" is tantamount to asking, "Can non-Europeans exist?" Insofar as ontology is protected by Western epistemology, ontology will cast existence to the wayside and keep colonial difference alive. I paraphrase Fanon to frame the following argument: "Since the other hesitates to recognize non-European thinkers as equal, there remains only one solution: to make ourselves known." Making ourselves known means to *recognize* that modernity/coloniality is upon us but that at the same time we have recourse to revamp what modernity/coloniality has denied: modernity/coloniality destitution ignites the energy of restitution. To do so we need to engage in border thinking. *It will not be possible, without border gnoseology, for us to be what we want to be, having recourse only to the epistemology that questioned our existence.* To reexist means to deny the denial of the deficiencies that the values of modernity bestowed upon the dehumanized population. Border thinking and border epistemology (at this point epistemology mutates into gnoseology) are the necessary moves for decolonial healings.[12] And given the multiplicity of experiences upon which colonial differences have inflicted wounds, there cannot be one universal remedy, one blueprint of border thinking. Border thinking implies the pluriversal.

III   The Issues and Their Consequences

III.1

The previous sections provided a background to better grasp the meanings implied in Dabashi's question. The variations in and different intensities of experiencing colonial *differences* engender varieties and different intensities of colonial *wounds*. Colonial wounds require decolonial healings, and decolonial healings are personal/communal processes of liberation, of delinking from the CMP as it touches us in our personal experiences. Decolonial healing is in "us" rather than in the individual "I," the isolated and self-sufficient ego. In that sense, each of us is responsible, communally, for our own decolonial healing and liberation. Fanon revealed a healing path for everyone wounded by colonial differences: delinking from the effects of Man/Human managing and making himself visible in the CMP. Delinking means to reject the imposed destitution of yourself and to assume with pride what the colonial difference attempts to impinge on you—that is, to engage in decolonial political restitution of your "envisioned self," to use Steve Biko's expression, and in the words of Lorena Cabnal, to engage in cosmic-political healing (see introduction, section III.3). Healing follows the trajectories of reemergence and reexistence manifested today in the state politics of de-Westernization and decoloniality by and for the emerging political society. Both trajectories operate in parallel spheres of life, the former in that of the state and interstate relations, and the latter in that of the politicization of civil society and the emerging global political society. This argument departs from the legacies of Plato's *pharmacon* (poison or remedy) recast in postmodern Continental philosophy.[13] It starts from someplace else, from the colonial wound (poison) enacting decolonial healing (remedy).

I entered the conversation—as I mentioned above—because Dabashi's questions actualized a long history of epistemic colonial differences. Neither Dabashi nor I am European (and non-Europeans are, as we know, an enormous variety of people in terms of ethnicity, sexuality, religions, languages, memories, poetry, ways of living and conducting themselves/ourselves, dressing, eating), and this variety is one reason Dabashi's question can be asked and pursued on many fronts. In spite of national, regional, linguistic, and religious differences between Dabashi and me, we have one thing in common. We are Third World intellectuals, heretofore non-Europeans. Persians are indigenous to their land, with their own memories, languages, and territoriality, whereas in the diverse countries of South and Central America, as well as in the Caribbean islands, a sector of the population is descended from Europeans of various stages and periods, from the earlier "conquistadores" and settlers (mainly Spanish and Portuguese), to the late nineteenth-century massive immigration (mainly Italians on the continent). "Of European descent" means marginal Europeans with a variety of privileges. And it is also the population (to which I belong) that displaced Indigenous and African descendants.

Dabashi's question echoes a similar one asked some fourteen years before by the Singaporean (a non-European, of course) thinker, intellectual, and philosopher Kishore Mahbubani when he asked *Can Asians Think?* (1998).[14] The issue highlighted by Dabashi was not a personal one, as I understood it when I entered the conversation, but a systemic and long-standing issue now surfacing. And, more interesting, it was an issue that could not have not occurred to Continental philosophers to ask. Why indeed would they if it was presupposed that that was the case? Continental philosophers have their own, and for them more pressing, issues, and thinking is taken for granted in their being, as stamped by Descartes when he stated that because he thinks, he is. Decolonially speaking, the formulation leaves out and in silence a vast rest of humanity.

The decolonial assertion shall be indeed: I am where I think, which means I am in the exteriority, and it is in the borderlines of exteriority that I think.[15]

The similarity between the questions asked by two non-European intellectuals—one based in the US and involved in Middle Eastern politics, the other in Singapore and involved in high diplomacy—should not be taken lightly. It is not trivial because epistemic racism impacts social and institutional spheres. Both questions indeed unveil the fact that racism as we still sense it today infects epistemology and aesthetics, hidden beneath the naturalization of certain ways of thinking and knowledge-making that are given the name Eurocentrism. Racism is not a question of one's blood type (the Christian criterion used in sixteenth-century Spain to distinguish Christians from Moors and Jews in Europe) or the color of one's skin (Africans and peoples of the New World civilizations; see chapter 1). It consists in devaluing the humanity of certain people by dismissing it or devaluing it (even when not intentional) while highlighting and extolling European philosophy, assuming it to be universal. Though it may be global, because it rides along on imperial expansion, it certainly cannot be universal. Racism is a classification, and classification is an epistemic maneuver rather than an ontological reality that embodies the essence of the classification. It is a system of classification enacted by actors, institutions, and categories of thought that enjoy the privilege of being hegemonic or dominant, and that imposes itself as ontological truth reinforced by "scientific" research.

Mahbubani's book was published in 1998. It was reprinted three times in the following years, and saw second and third editions up to 2007. Who was reading the book and debating this issue? I did not find the book quoted in academic publications I read and workshops and conferences I attended. Not only that, when I asked friends and colleagues if they knew or had read Mahbubani's book, they responded blankly before saying no and then asking who Mahbubani was. Since Mahbubani is a diplomat and a public figure in international diplomacy, I suspect that his readers belong to that world and to that of the media anchors who interview him. I also suspect that many scholars would be suspicious of an Asian thinker playing with philosophy and the silences of history and asking such an uncomfortable question.

The question Dabashi and Mahbubani raised is not whether non-Europeans can *do philosophy*, but whether they/we can *think*.[16] Philosophy is a regional and historical endeavor (see chapter 13). Whether we can engage in philosophy or not is irrelevant. But, if we cannot think, that would be serious! Thinking is a common feature of living organisms endowed with nervous systems. That includes humans (and certainly Europeans). What all human beings do is not philosophy, which is not a necessity, but thinking, which is unavoidable. Institutional theory and philosophy are not necessary for living. Greeks named philosophy their way of thinking and suggested regulations to do it properly. This is of course understandable, but it is an aberration to project a regional definition of a regional way of thinking as a universal standard by which to judge and classify.

In consequence, what Dabashi, Mahbubani, and I (among others) are doing is delinking from the "disciplinarity" of philosophy, and from disciplinary racial and gender normativity.[17] It is common to be informed that such and such person was denied tenure because of hidden ethnic or gender reasons. Disciplinary normativity operates on an assumed geopolitics of knowledge. In the 1970s, it was common among Africans and Latin American scholars trained in philosophy to ask whether one could properly talk about philosophy in Africa or in Latin America. A similar problem was faced by Spanish philosopher José Ortega y Gasset at the beginning of the twentieth century. He returned to Spain after studying philology and philosophy in Germany and defined himself as "philosopher *in partibus infidelium*" (in the lands of unbelievers). He must have had an instinctive understanding of what Hegel meant when he referred to "the heart of Europe." Ortega y Gasset could have joined us in this conversation by asking, "Can Spaniards think?" His writings are "indisciplinary" in the strict sense that philology and philosophy require. But I would venture that they are "un-disciplinary" as well. For he was a thinker engaged in epistemic disobedience, a practice that is growing around the world, including in western Europe and the US.[18]

The question asked in the 1970s—whether philosophy was a legitimate endeavor in Africa and in Latin America–was left behind. The following generation trained in philosophy took a different attitude. Nigerian philosopher Emmanuel Chukwudi Eze published a groundbreaking article in 1997 titled "The Color of Reason: The Idea of 'Race' in Kant's Anthropology."[19] Eze inverted canonical approaches to Kant's oeuvre. Instead of starting from Kant's major works and leaving aside his minor texts (*Anthropology from a Pragmatic Point of View* and *Geography*), Eze saw in Kant's minor works the racial prejudices embedded in his monumental philosophy. Philosophy turned out to be not only a discipline for theoretical thought and argument (and love of wisdom) but also a tool to *disqualify* (that is, to disavow in the act of classifying those people who do not conform to Western conceptions of philosophers and to philosophy's rational demands).

Racial classification is an epistemic creation rather than a scientific description and/or representation of what is. The correlation between race and intelligence is an illusion based on beliefs that locate intelligence in one race: the race that created the idea of racism and the correlation between race and intelligence. It is not the color of one's skin that matters, but one's deviation from Western rationality (modernity/rationality was Quijano's formula) that Western Man has created built on his belief system. This is why now asking whether Asians or non-Europeans can think is relevant at the same time that it is necessary. Not, of course, for non-Europeans, bur for Euro-Americans who still believe so. Christian theology and secular philosophy and science constructed a system of classification of people and regions of the world that still govern us and shape debate by informing the presuppositions that underlie systems of knowledge.[20] The reasons for the emergence of new disciplinary formations beginning in the US in the 1970s are to be found in the intellectual world's liberation from the epistemic racial and sexual classifications of over five hundred years of Western epistemic hegemony. People of color and of nonheteronormative sexual preferences were able to think for themselves and were no longer simply the object of study by white heterosexuals. They could also reflect on the fact that they were considered people to be studied.

Classifications are cultural constructions by biological organisms making distinctions. Making distinctions is an operation that all living organisms enact in their/our praxes of living. If living is knowing and knowing implies thinking, it is because knowing and thinking are embedded in the cultural praxis of living, and the cultural praxis of living needs classification and organization. But when classification is coupled with the coloniality of knowledge, it becomes a pernicious tool, for it carries the seeds of ranking. Carl Linnaeus (1707–1778) in science and Immanuel Kant (1724–1804) in philosophy were the two architects of the mutation from theological to secular classification. Secular philosophy and science displaced Christian theology as the preferred epistemic normativity. English, French, and German thinkers, philosophers, and scientists became the gatekeepers (willingly or not) and regulators of classificatory thought. The eighteenth century was the moment in which Asians entered the Western philosophical picture in earnest. Orientalism was a classification and ranking: the colonial differential at work. Orientalism was nothing but that: knowers and thinkers (philosophers) walking hand in hand with philologists "studying" the Orient. The arrogance of epistemic power mutated from Renaissance Christian men of letters and missionaries to secular philologists and philosophers who could think and in their thinking could cast doubts on other human beings who did not think according to assumptions about the Orient and regulations of thinking.

That is how racial classifications made inroads into epistemology and aesthetics and established hierarchies of forms of knowing, knowledge, taste, and the greatness of individual artistry ("genius," to use Kant's word). Classifications and hierarchies are built and carried out by actors installed in institutions that they themselves have created or from which they have earned—"inherited" is often more truthful than "earned"—the right to classify and rank. Values are infused in differences. Hence, the making of colonial and imperial differences are rooted in the CMP's enunciation. Such actors and institutions legitimize the zero point of epistemology as the word of God (Christian theology) or the word of Reason (secular philosophy and science). He who does the classifying classifies himself among the classified (the enunciated), but he remains the only one who classifies among all those being classified. This is a powerful trick that, like any magic trick, the audience does not see as such but as something that just happens. Those who are classified as less human do not have much say in their classification (except to dissent), while those who classify always place themselves at the top of the classification. Darwin was right to observe that skin color is irrelevant in the *classification* of races.

Yet in spite of that, it is a dominant factor in the public sphere. It arises perhaps from Kant's ethno-racial tetragon according to which the Yellow race inhabits Asia, the Black race Africa, the Red (Native American) race America (which for Kant was just the British colonies), and the white race Europe. Following Linnaeus's scheme of classification, which was basically descriptive, Kant added a ranking and connected racism with geopolitics.[21] The trick is that the classification is enacted on the basis of the exclusive privilege of the white race, whose actors and institutions were located in Europe, their languages and categories of thought derived from Greek and Latin, inscribed in the formation of the six modern/colonial European languages: Italian, Spanish, and Portuguese (dominant during the Renaissance), and German, English, and French (dominant since the Enlightenment). I feel that Hamid Dabashi reacted not to Zabala's first paragraph in itself but to the many disavowals that the paragraph elicited. My sense is that if the paragraph had been slightly different, Dabashi would not have engaged in the debate, and neither would I. Had Zabala written something like "Žižek is the most important philosopher in Continental Philosophy," Dabashi may not have paid any attention to it. However, *the problem would have persisted*. Because the problem was not the paragraph per se, but what it elicited, which of course long preceded and went far beyond the paragraph.

III.2

Let us further elaborate on the long-standing philosophical assumptions of the complicities between Western modern epistemology (I underscore that epistemology is not universal) and racism, which are highlighted in Mahbubani's and Dabashi's titles. Frantz Fanon sensed and understood it: "It is clear that what divides this world is first and foremost what species, what race one belongs to. In the colonies, the economic infrastructure is also a superstructure. The cause is effect: you are rich because you are white; you are white because you are rich."[22] Most rational, scientific arguments about race are based on nonrational assumptions. It is assumed that race is ontological (e.g., there are races) and that science describes what it is and how races differ in their levels of intelligence.

One could translate Fanon's unveiling of the hidden principles of racial socioeconomic classification into epistemic and ontological ones: "You do philosophy because you are white"; "you are white because you do [European] philosophy"—where "whiteness" and "doing philosophy" stand for the ontological dimensions of the person. Behind the person is not just a skin color but also a language operating on principles and assumptions of knowledge. That is, there is an epistemology at work that transforms "black skin" into "Negro," and "Negro" is much more than skin color. The same applies to "thinking." Fanon again perceived this in 1952 when he wrote that to speak (and I believe that he implied also to write) a language is not just to master a grammar and a vocabulary but to carry the weight of a civilization.[23] He perceived that racism was not only a question of the color of one's skin but of language, and therefore of categories of thought that have established a hierarchy of languages in relation to reliable knowledges.

If according to racial classifications one (person) is epistemically and ontologically inferior (or suspect), one cannot think (that is, one can, but one is not believable), and one does not belong to the club of "universal" genealogy grounded in the Greek and Latin languages that mutated into the six modern/ colonial European languages. Persian doesn't belong to that genealogy. And Spanish missed the train of the second era of modernity in the eighteenth century. In addition, Spanish has been further devalued as a Third World language of Spanish America. Therefore, if one wishes to join the club of Continental philosophy and one's language is Persian, Latin American Spanish, Urdu, Aymara, or Bambara, or even a civilizational language like Mandarin, Russian, or Turkish, one must learn the *languages* of secular philosophy (German and French, mainly). At this point we can take the argument a step further: if one speaks and writes in Spanish, one has trouble aspiring to become a philosopher. That is what motivated the Chilean Victor Farías to write his book on Heidegger. As Farías relates in his preface, Heidegger informed him that Spanish was not a language of philosophy, something José Ortega y Gasset understood at the beginning of the twentieth century. Ortega y Gasset's declaration that he was himself a philosopher *in partibus infidelium* was a response elicited by feeling the intramural imperial epistemic difference: after studying in Germany in the 1920s and then returning to Spain and writing in Spanish, he knew that he could not be a *philosopher proper*.[24] The South of Europe had been considered suspect in terms of rationality by Enlightenment philosophers, chiefly Kant and Hegel.

Robert Bernasconi, trained in Continental philosophy, has reflected on the challenges that African philosophy poses to Continental philosophy: "Western philosophy traps African philosophy in a double bind: either African philosophy is so similar to Western philosophy that it makes no distinctive contribution and effectively disappears; or it is so different that its credentials to be genuine philosophy will always be in doubt."[25] Bernasconi has made an important move within Continental philosophy conversations. However, his move could be pushed beyond the regional discipline of Continental philosophy and branched into other parts of the world's modes of thinking. Therefore we could change the direction of the questions and ask to what extent non-European ways of thinking in non-European languages challenge Continental philosophy. I am not faulting Bernasconi for not asking that question. The question asked by Dabashi, "can non-Europeans think?," addresses the silence revealed in Bernasconi's observation in his role as a Continental philosopher. This may not be the type of question one has to ask in order to be the most important (European) philosopher alive, as Zabala argues that Žižek is.

Mahbubani, with no connection to Dabashi or Bernasconi (as far as I know), but attuned to Eurocentrism in his own experience in Southeast Asia, points toward other possibilities. Imagine, he suggests, if he were to ask, "Can Europeans think?" The answer to this question would be one of surprise. Who could doubt that Europeans can think? Indeed, a non-European person who asks, "Can Europeans think?" would most likely be regarded by a European as a racist. But if an Asian person asks, "Can Africans think?," many Europeans would, unfortunately, not dissent, based on Hume's (in)famous dictum, repeated by Kant, that Africans cannot think. Kant challenges his readers: "To cite a single example in which a Negro has shown talents, and asserts that among the hundreds of thousands of blacks who are transported elsewhere from their countries *although many of them have even been set free*, still not a single one was ever found who presented anything great in art or science or any other praise-worthy quality, even though among the whites some continually rise aloft from the lowest rabble, and through superior gifts earn respect in the world."[26] Small wonder that Nigerian philosopher Emmanuel Chukwudi Eze unveiled Kant's epistemic racism.

III.3

Mahbubani, as his position in government indicates, thinks "from above"—but he thinks from the *exteriority* of the above. He is a thinker of de-Westernization as Samuel Huntington, for example, is a thinker of re-Westernization. If you are not interested in the processes of thinking from above, whether radical or organic or re-Western (like Huntington, Kissinger, or Brzezinski), and of de-Westernization, you can skip this section. However, decoloniality coexists today, and it will coexist for a few more decades. Hence, decoloniality cannot be thought about and acted upon as if it were the only option moving the world order and the everyday life of billions of people. Back to Mahbubani. In the preface to the second edition of *Can Asians Think?*, he writes:

> The title chosen for this volume of essays—"Can Asians Think?"—is not accidental. It represents essentially two questions folded into one. The first, addressed to my fellow Asians, reads as "Can you think? If you can, why have Asian societies lost a thousand years and slipped far behind the European societies that they were far ahead of at the turn of the last millennium?"
>
> The second question, addressed primarily to my friends in the West [remember, Mahbubani is a diplomat], is "Can Asians think for themselves?" We live in an essentially unbalanced world. The flow of ideas, reflecting 500 years of Western domination of the globe, remains a one-way street—from the West to the East. Most Westerners cannot see that they have arrogated to themselves the moral high ground from which they lecture the world. The rest of the world can see this.[27]

Since the term "the West" is often used, let's pause to clarify it. First, as I explained in chapter 10, north of the Mediterranean Sea, "the West" refers to the area west of Jerusalem, where Western Christians dwell, before that territory became better known as Europe. South of the Mediterranean, the word used is "Maghreb," which means west of Mecca and Medina. But of course, neither Mahbubani nor I refer to Maghreb when we use the term "the West."

Second, by "the West" neither I nor probably he means Romania, the former Yugoslavia, Poland, or Latvia. What constitutes the West more than geography is a linguistic family, a belief system, and an epistemology. It is constituted by the six modern European and imperial languages (to repeat): Italian, Spanish, and Portuguese, which were dominant during the Renaissance, and English, French, and German, which have been dominant since the Enlightenment. The latter states and languages form the "heart of Europe," in Hegel's expression, but they are also held by Kant to be the three states with the highest degree of civilization. Thus "the West" is shorthand for "Western civilization."

Now that we've cleared up what "the West" means, let's stay with Mahbubani for one more paragraph.[28] He continues: "Similarly, Western intellectuals are convinced that their minds and cultures are open, self-critical and—in contrast to ossified Asian minds and cultures—have no 'sacred cows.' The most shocking discovery of my adult life was the realization that 'sacred cows' also exist in the Western mind. During the period of Western triumphalism that followed the end of the Cold War, a huge bubble of moral pretentiousness enveloped the Western intellectual universe."[29] Coloniality, not just colonization, has a long history and a wide range. What might connect Mahbubani with a Mexican ethno-historian of the second half of the twentieth century? When in the 1950s Miguel León-Portilla published *La filosofía Náhuatl* (1958), translated as *Aztec Thought and Culture*, he was harshly attacked.[30] How could he dare not just to believe but to state outright that philosophy was practiced by the Aztecs in the Náhuatl language? How could he dare to think that "Indians" could have philosophy? The critique came not from Continental philosophers, who did not care much about these debates in the New World, but from Eurocentric philosophers in Mexico—imperial collaborationists and defenders of philosophical universality (which means universality as interpreted by regional European philosophy).

Let us consider a more recent example of the way epistemic Eurocentrism works within the unconscious of even prominent European philosophers. Slavoj Žižek was invited to speak at the Seminarios Internacionales de la Vicepresidencia del Estado Plurinacional de Bolivia, led by Álvaro García Linera, in 2011. The title of his speech was "¿Es posible pensar un cambio radical hoy?"—"Is it possible to think a radical change today?"[31] At one point Žižek examines the proposal of John Holloway, an Irish-born lawyer and sociologist of Marxist tendency, based in Puebla (Mexico), to "change the world without taking power."[32] By "without taking power" Holloway means without the "taking of the state" by a revolutionary movement. Holloway based his arguments on the

Zapatistas' uprising. His interpretation of the Zapatistas' goals and orientation is not necessarily that of the Zapatistas. Žižek starts by discussing and debunking Holloway's proposals, and then brings the Zapatistas and Subcomandante Marcos into the conversation. He introduces one of his frequent jokes, one he apparently learned from his friends in Mexico. He said they told him that they don't use the title "Subcomandante Marcos" anymore but rather Subcomediante (Subcomedian) Marcos. I surmise that Žižek's Mexican friends were Marxists. Marxists have a problem with Marcos because he had detached himself from Marxism shortly after arriving in Chiapas, in the 1980s, and immersed himself in Indigenous philosophy and politics—or, if you will, political philosophy.[33]

I don't know about you, but I consider the act of debunking one's opponent, in public, with a joke that carries epistemic racial overtones, quite uncalled for. Had the joke been made to an audience in Britain or Austria, it might have been uncontroversial, assuming that the audience agreed with the perspective of the joke. The joke elicited laughs in the Bolivian audience, the members of which were not visible but one could imagine were supporters of Evo Morales's presidency. But telling that joke in Bolivia, a self-proclaimed state promoting "communal socialism" (whether the claim is actualized is another matter; here I am interested only in the claim itself), and which has the majority of the Indigenous population behind it, certainly showed a lack of tact (and perhaps sureness of touch). Furthermore, the event had been organized by then vice president Álvaro García Linera. The reader should know or remember that Subcomandante Marcos refused President Evo Morales's invitation to attend his inauguration. Far from being a *comediante*, Marcos is an intellectual who converted from Marxism to Indianism (Indigenous people thinking about themselves and the world, much in the same way that Marxism allows people to think about themselves and the world). Marcos joined an existing Indigenous organization in the Mayan area of southern Mexico.[34] Certainly he masqueraded with his outfits, watch, pipes, gun, and so on. But this was just a different sort of masquerade from that practiced by current kings and queens, secular presidents and vice presidents, unless we believe that these others are not staged and only the public persona of Subcomandante Marcos is. An urban Marxist intellectual, Rafael Guillén (trained in philosophy at university) went to the South of Mexico to teach Indians that they were oppressed and had to liberate themselves, only to discover that Indians have known for five hundred years, and without reading Marx, that they were oppressed and have not stopped fighting for their survival and a new existence. Far from being a *comediante*, Marcos (now Subcomandante Galeano) has the openness and courage both to perceive the limits of Marxism and to recognize the potential of decoloniality. This is the kind of philosophy and thinking that one finds among non-European thinkers and philosophers.

Žižek's comment on Subcomandante Marcos reminds me of what I have heard on several occasions in different countries from people who attended his talks. These things have been said in private, in the same way that I imagine Žižek heard about Subcomandante Marcos in private conversations with his Mexican friends. Many different people have observed that Žižek is a clown, in French a *bouffon*. But I do not recall anyone saying this in public. It has remained in the realm of private conversation until this moment. I am now making it public to counterbalance Žižek's uncalled-for comment on Subcomandante Marcos.[35] And, parallel to this, to challenge his dictatorial inclination to confront with insults those who doubt or express indifference to his reputation as the most important (European) philosopher alive, even though this status is irrelevant to non-European thinkers who do not worship Continental philosophy. The general issue of epistemic colonial differences touches all of us in different ways. We respond to it accordingly.[36]

In a sense, I am following Chandra Muzaffar's recommendation regarding *Charlie Hebdo*'s freedom-of-expression insults. There is no reason to kill someone who insults you, believing that what this someone did was a legitimate freedom of expression. Someone who insults on the basis of such a belief is a victim of the arrogance of power and the privileges of a presumed "neutral," or "objective," epistemology. Muzaffar correctly understood the situation, and stated, "One should respond to satirical cartoons with cartoons and other works of art that expose the prejudice and bigotry of the cartoonists and editors of Charlie Hebdo. *One should use the Charlie Hebdo cartoons as a platform to educate and raise the awareness of the French public about what the Quran actually teaches and who the Prophet really was and the sort of noble values that distinguished his life and struggle*"[37] (emphasis added). This is why the politics of decolonial investigations is a must.

We (non-European intellectuals, including Muzaffar) should use racist jokes and insults (to paraphrase Muzaffar) as a platform to educate and raise the awareness of the European public about colonial epistemic differences and decolonial thinking. This is the spirit in which non-European thinkers and philosophers are, and should be, responding to European arrogance from the right and from the left. We are no longer silent, nor asking for recognition; this should be clear by now. As First Nations intellectuals, thinkers, artists, and activists of Canada insist, recognition is to be wholly rejected.[38] At stake are the affirmation and reemergence of the communal (rather than the commons

and the common good). This is one of the paths that we non-European thinkers are following.

III.4

Let's go back to Bernasconi's question, which helps our understanding of how
the epistemic and ontological colonial difference works to promote philosophy
as a superior and standard way of thinking. What kind of challenge does Continental philosophy pose to non-European thinkers, philosophers and nonphi-
losophers alike? The decolonial question would be: How should or how did
non-European thinkers respond to the challenge? My argument throughout
this book, and certainly before, is through delinking and epistemic disobedience, without which gnoseological and aesthesic reconstitutions are unvi-
able.[39] There is a significant precedent in the decolonial genealogy of thought
established by Mohandas Gandhi, which I highlighted in the introduction to
this volume (section III). The call to disobedience is the call to nonsubmission,
to affirmation, to the denial of destitution and the recovery of the destituted.
Not going back to the past but bringing the destituted back, rebuilding autonomy and self-determination in *exteriority* without requesting to be recognized
by actors, institutions, and rules of the CMP. It was nothing less than what is at
stake in Dabashi's and Mahbubani's question: can non-Europeans think? It is
that question also that calls for the politics of decolonial investigations.

Now I turn to a philosophical disobedience and the reconstitution of
grounded thinking by examining the work of an Argentine philosopher of
German descent, Rodolfo Gunther Kusch (1922–1979), who was trained in philosophy at the University of Buenos Aires. He struggled during his entire life
with this question, which was not formulated as such during his time, but the
question asked today helps us understand what Kusch was struggling for and
why he changed direction and disobeyed the disciplinary regulations in which
he was schooled. Kusch disobeyed and changed direction. And he paid the
consequences. Expelled from his teaching position in Buenos Aires, he landed
in Catamarca, in the Northwest of Argentina. And expelled from there, he
ended his life in a small town in the Jujuy province, bordering with Bolivia.
The most elaborate of his works is *El pensamiento indígena y popular en América*
(Indigenous and popular thinking in America; 1970). The first chapter is titled
"El pensamiento Americano" (Thinking in America). In its opening sentences
Kusch confronts Continental philosophy's challenges to Argentinian (and
South American) philosophers head-on. Kusch points out that in America
there is an official way of doing philosophy and a personal way of doing it. The

first, learned at the university, consists basically of a European set of problems and issues translated into philosophical language. The second is implicit in the way of life and the thinking on city streets and in the countryside alike, as well as at home; it parallels and coexists with the official way of doing philosophy at university and is grounded in issues and problems in the Americas, rather than in learning about European issues, problems, and ways of thinking. Kusch stresses that it is not a matter of rejecting Continental philosophy, but of looking for what, a few years later, he called "pensamiento propio": losing the fear of thinking on one's own, fear instilled by the force of colonial epistemic and ontological differences.

The colonized person, we know, more often than not assumes that she or he belongs to the ontology in which she or he has been classified. That is how the colonial difference works. But once you "see" the trick, you delink and start thinking on your own rather than translating European problems into the language of philosophy as taught in America (or Asia or Africa).

These are Kusch's teaching legacies. By "pensamiento propio" he means the freedom "to appropriate" what you need from Continental philosophy (in this case) instead of being appropriated by it. That move implies that you delink from the official ways and expectations of doing philosophy. Delinking implies epistemic disobedience. And that was Kusch's response to the challenge of Continental philosophy to Third World philosophers. Yet to do what he proposes—he recognizes—is not an easy task: "But this is what is so weighty. In order to carry out such a conceptualization, it is necessary not just to know philosophy, but above all—and this is very important—to face reality abiding a degree of distortion few can sustain. To investigate daily life in order to translate it into thinking is a dangerous venture, since it is necessary, particularly here in America, to make the grave mistake of contradicting the frameworks to which we are attached."[40]

Kusch confronts Heidegger's *Dasein* (Being; better yet, being in the world, a human awareness of its own existence) and then departs from it. Thinking in Aymara and Aymara thought do not fit with thinking in German and German philosophical thought. Kusch opted for disobeying philosophy and attending to Indigenous and popular thinking, with all the epistemic and political consequences that disobedience entailed. By disobeying, Kusch found the path to the gnoseological and aesthesic reconstitutions that he carried consistently through his life. He asks what the meaning of *Dasein* could be in America, given that it was a concept nourished and propelled by the German language and by a certain ethos of the German middle class between the two wars. From that question Kusch derives the conviction that thinking may be a universal activity of all living organisms endowed with a nervous system, but that thinking organisms do so in their own niche, involving memories, languages, and sociohistorical tensions and dissatisfactions. Heidegger's experience, which led to his conceiving of *Dasein*, is quite alien to the American one. Consequently, how could the purported universality of Being be accepted? Kusch realized also that the Argentinian middle class lived in a parallel universe of meaning but in sociohistorical conditions that were extremely different from those experienced by the German middle class. Kusch's intellectual life began in the last years of the first presidency of Juan Domingo Perón, a so-called "populist" leader. Kusch wrote *Indigenous and Popular Thinking in América* between the fall and the return of Perón.

From his early work in the 1950s (at the time Fanon was fighting his fight in France), Kusch turned his back on his social roots and shifted his gaze toward Indigenous culture. It was not his intention to describe the life of Indigenous people, as anthropologists do, but to understand the logic of their thinking, as philosophers do when studying other philosophers. Not an easy task since he had to deal with the baggage of Continental philosophy learned at the university. Here again one experiences the epistemic colonial difference and is reminded of the question Bernasconi did not (could not?) ask: What challenges are thrown to Continental philosophy by thinking beyond the line that connects ancient Greece and Rome with the heart of Europe? Global linear thinking left a legacy beyond international law that crosses over all disciplinary formations, for colonial differences are everywhere, and a way to overcome them is to first understand how they work. Acting on them requires gnoseological and aesthesic reconstitutions. They cannot be overcome by public policy. They have to be addressed in the sphere of knowledge, which is what I believe I am doing. The praxis of living within the cultural consequences of global linear thinking (beyond the molecular autopoiesis of our bodies) guides and blinds us to the praxis of thinking that philosophy can neither regulate nor control. Consequently, to do philosophy in the colonies (and former colonies) following Kusch's guidance, one has two options: either to join a branch of Continental philosophy (science, psychoanalysis, sociology, etc.), which is equivalent to a branch of McDonald's (scale is not being considered in this analogy), or to delink and engage in *pensamiento propio*.[41] In the former colonies, that is the awakening, the awareness of border dwelling, of border thinking. Briefly, the awareness and the need, as Kusch, thus of abandon philosophy and engage in gnoseological and aesthesic reconstitutions.

For example, Kusch found that in the Aymara language, the word *utcatha* has certain parallels with *Dasein*, a word that Heidegger picked up from popular German. Through *utcatha*, Kusch unfolds a complex universe of meaning that allows him to work through his understanding of Indigenous ways of thinking—which simultaneously requires delinking from Continental philosophy to reconstitute ways of thinking in America that have been transmitted through generations in parallel to the teaching of philosophy, in Spanish, at the transplanted European-style universities. In this process, the issue is not to *reject* Continental philosophy but, on the contrary, to know it in order to *delink* from it. Otherwise, what would you delink from if you do not know what you have to delink from? That is, to undermine the CMP and by the same token to undermine those of its epistemic classifications that operate not by empirical description but by unconscious or conscious silences. With this process, Kusch finds out first that the Aymara word *utcatha* has several meanings, all of which are associated with the type of experience that Heidegger was exploring through the word *Dasein*. But the Aymara people did not need and of course did not read Heidegger. It is safe to suppose that not only German languages make it possible to reflect on human existence and the life of the cosmos. Kusch understood this and connected the meaning of an Aymara word with Indigenous people's expressions of their sense and understanding of themselves on planet Earth. He realized that in Aymara ways of thinking and being in the world, a "passive" attitude has been used to justify "white" middle-class perceptions of "Indians'" laziness.

Yet Kusch saw something else in what was defined as "passiveness" and the refusal to engage in white people's idea of work. What appeared—from the perspective of modernity and modernization and the distorted perceptions of the urban middle class—to be passiveness and laziness was for Kusch an "active passiveness" and a refusal to sell one's labor and change one's way of life to satisfy the requirements of Western development and modernization, which, at that moment, were already the US's project. Kusch reconstituted the epistemic concept of "work" and turned it into a gnoseological concept honoring the Aymara ways of thinking. He created the concept of *estar siendo*, taking advantage of the distinction between the verbs *ser* and *estar* in Spanish, a distinction that has no equivalent in other Western languages (Italian, *essere-essere*; German, *sein-sein*; French, *être-être*; English, *to be-to be*). Kusch's groundbreaking untranslatable category *estar siendo* denotes an active passiveness that refuses, rejects, *and negates* the expectation to join and act on the storytelling of modernity and modernization. *Estar siendo* is an affirmation of what the modernity of *Dasein* wants to eliminate or incorporate into being: a sense of its "thereness" in the processes of becoming. The relationality of *estar siendo* encompasses the constant flux of the cosmos, indicating the movements of a verb irreducible to a noun: Being. *Estar siendo* expresses a beyond to being, a more cosmic sense of belonging to a beyond not circumscribed by immediate surroundings: *vincularidad* (relationality) is unharmonious with Being. In this it is a negation of *Dasein* and one that affirms the embeddedness of Aymara (and many other Indigenous languages) within the constant flux of the cosmos. Being belongs to a cosmology where the noun is embedded with the materiality of the cosmos. Hence, "ontology" refers to entities, not to relations. From this active passiveness and an assumption of unboundedness to the flux of existence emerged the revolutionary, philosophical, and political idea of the *Suma Qamaña* and *Sumak Kawsay* recently inscribed in the constitutions of Bolivia and Ecuador.

IV. Closing Remarks: Epilogue and Book

IV.1

I shall outline some of the ethical, philosophical, epistemological, aesthesic, and political issues that this debate has brought into the open. It is crucial in order to understand and engage in the politics of decolonial investigation to propel epistemic/aesthesic reconstitutions. Certainly, we can and do think, but the point is not just thinking, but what we do with our thinking. Knowledge is what thinking "produces," be it a philosophical concept, a Turing machine, a nuclear bomb, or digital objects. Whatever we do with our hands—always in relation to others and to the modulations of our daily living, our memories and desires—is always connected with our thinking. Making visible and audible signs, and organizing them in clusters of meaning, we human beings name religion, philosophy, cosmogony, science, art, politics, economy, car industry, or pottery store—all of which requires labor. Labor—whether it is the labor of the slave or the labor of the master who has to keep his plantation going, whether it is the labor of the factory owner or of the CEO of a corporation or of the waged labor employees—all requires thinking. Thinking could be the solitary, silent, inert stillness of a living organism (the "body" in common parlance), but that is not common. None of these creations would exist in our world if it were not for thinking and working collectively, for better or worse, to control and dominate, to obey or disobey, or just to exist according to the circumstances. The latter is not a common option among human beings. Samuel Beckett's *The Unnamable* (1953) captured this possible but improbable situation. All this to say that the task of the politics of decolonial investigations should be directed to understanding the CMP: the constituted knowledge (the enunciated), the constituting knowing (the enunciation), and the simultaneous destitutions of coexisting knowledges and knowing. If non-Europeans were destituted for their capacity to think, as the CMP requires, the responses are not to play the same game to demonstrate that yes, we can, but to engage in reconstitutions of the destituted. Decolonial investigations are responses calling for epistemic and aesthetic disobedience, independent thoughts, and decolonial freedom. What the politics of decolonial investigations is not is to search for a "decolonial universal model" to the satisfaction of all. Pluriversality cannot be a global, even less a universal, design. However, decolonial investigations, as I have argued in this book, aim to be a mover and a strong participant in the change of era we on the planet are experiencing in the twenty-first century, propelled by *multipolarity* in the sphere of the interstate global order, delinking from *unipolarity* and *universality* in the sphere of political society, and breaking the chains and the regulations of *universal* knowledge and knowing and aesthetics and sensing. Hence, gnoseological and aesthesic reconstitution is the proposal I have made, joining the larger praxis of decolonial knowing and sensing that has been at work since the second half of the twentieth century.

The politics of decolonial investigations is a terrain in which decoloniality could today be effective, in and beyond the academe. If the coloniality of knowledge is managing people's subjectivity and sensibility, slogans and manifestations will not be sufficient. The situation that Frantz Fanon so courageously and insightfully confronted and fought in Algeria and in Ghana, and the vibrant pages he left for all of us, has dramatically changed. Decolonial politics is a particular way of doing politics in your everyday life and your professional life, whether you are in the academy or in any other domain where investigations are required to sustain and advance your arguments. Decoloniality is an option, an option that did not exist conceptually as such before the second half of the twentieth century; and decolonial investigations are a task and an orientation within the option. Decolonization, Fanon stated, "is the veritable creation of *new men* [sic]. But this creation owes nothing of its legitimacy to any supernatural power; the 'thing' which has been colonized becomes man [sic] during the same process by which it frees itself"[42] (emphasis added).

IV.2

I close the book and the epilogue by outlining some of the issues prompted by the questions asked by Mahbubani and Dabashi, which run parallel to Sylvia Wynter's question: what does it mean to be Human? I hope also that these closing words contribute to understand the meaning and scope of the politics of decolonial investigations and of gnoseological and aesthesic reconstitutions.

The goal enunciated by Fanon—the coming of a new humanity—requires us to free ourselves from the nonhuman conditions in which racial and sexual lines have been drawn in the making of the unipolar world order. Sixty years after Fanon wrote, not only did colonization and decolonization mutate into coloniality and decoloniality (see introduction), but so also did the idea Fanon may have had of what "a new humanity" might mean. In an earlier chapter I outlined what we might call decolonial paths to delink from the modern/colonial hegemonic idea of Man/Human, arguing that Man and Human are concepts, not "reality." There are not ontic Humans on the planet. But, yes, there are anthropoi who conceive of themselves as Humans and assigned themselves the task of judging who is Human and who is not.

Sixty years after Fanon, dissatisfaction within the cosmology of modernity has led postmodern thinkers to argue for the coming into being of the posthuman. The posthuman intertwines humans (anthropos) with intelligent technology that is created by humans (anthropos) themselves, and it projects a future state of humanity in which information technology transforms us into automata-like humanoids. Under the circumstances, Sartre's view of the Jews and Fanon's of the Blacks should be reassessed in relation to the posthuman (Man3, chapter 12). The decolonial human should not be confused with either the posthuman or the postcolonial. Why? Because the decolonial is addressing the enunciation of the CMP and calling into question who is the human that is speaking and defining the Human, while the posthuman (including the cyborg) and the postcolonial call into question the content, that is, the already-established definition of what is Human. The decolonial question is, instead, "What does it mean to be Human?," bringing to the foreground the destitutions (racial, sexual, religious, linguistic, economic, political, etc.) that were and are enacted in the name of Human and Humanity.

The unquestioned enthusiasm for technology in concepts of the posthuman and postnature make them compatible with re-Westernizing global designs. Both "posts" question the modern concepts of human and of nature, but they remain within the overall cosmology that invented the concepts of human and nature. The terms of epistemological conversations are not questioned in these "new" cosmologies, only their intramural content.[43] Similar observations could be made about the New Materialism.[44] New Materialism detaches itself from postmodernity. "New" displaces and replaces the prefix "post" and tackles the "two cultures" (the sciences and the humanities) and struggles to undo oppositional dichotomies like nature versus culture or man versus woman, etc. The adjective "new" places the project squarely in the modernity/postmodernity frame of mind, where "newness" and "post" are the prefixes to announce a change in the content of the conversation while leaving the terms untouched. "Materialism," on the other hand, is not a question of ontology but rather celebrates it. Consistent with the efforts of the practitioners of New Materialism to blur the distinction between the two cultures and dichotomic oppositions, they see ontology and epistemology as entangled, which is concurrent with my own view of the matter. However, the practitioners of New Materialism and decolonial thinkers arrive at similar conclusions and urgencies from different routes. Our starting point is not the genealogy of Western physics and Western scientists but Indigenous philosophies in which dichotomies never existed and in which "nature" is a strange concept because relationality is not with an entity, "nature," which in the West is opposed to "culture." Rather, relationality is everything in the universe and in daily life; it includes relations with water, wind, light, Earth, river, mountains, etc. Black Foot thinker Lloyd Little Bear has made the point succinctly in one of his short talks on "Indigenous knowledges and Western sciences."[45]

The "ontology of relations" argued by Karen Barad runs parallel to *vincularidad* (the state of being linked with all the living) in Indigenous millenarian cosmology.[46] Still, *vincularidad* is not matter, not ontology, but movement, flow (*ollin* in Náhuatl).[47] And it has been always like that, from before Western interventions. So restitution of the destituted is of the essence to avoid the re-Westernization of ontology under the banner of relations. Needless to say, it is not a question of either/or, but of and/and; not a question of a "new" universality but the opening to pluriversality or the coexistence of *vincularidad* with the ontology of relations. On the other hand, Barad's argument also runs parallel to Édouard Glissant's "poetics of relation."[48] In these three cases we see the distinctive universes of meanings in which the concepts of "relations/relationality" acquire their meaning. And we see also that while dichotomies are a problem for Western thinkers, they have never been a problem for Indigenous and Afro-genealogies of thoughts and praxes of living—not until "Western science" told them that the world is based on dichotomies and that dichotomies have to be dismantled.[49] But there is more. Although "science" today is said not to be Western but global, the epistemic power differential could only be ignored by someone who believes in the universality of the Western concept, history, and practice of science. African thinker Paulin J. Hountondji asked in the 1990s a question that goes right to the point I am making in this chapter:

It seems urgent to me that the scientists in Africa, and perhaps generally in the Third World, question themselves on the meaning of their practice as scientists, its real function in the economy of the entirety of scholarship, its place in the process of production of knowledge on a world-wide basis. . . .

Scientific activity in the Third World seems to be characterized, globally, by its position of dependency. This dependency is of the same nature than that of economic activity.[50]

You may argue that "poetics" and "ontology" are both words from ancient Greek. But the problem is not so much the meaning of the two words in Greece when Aristotle was able to write about both poetics and metaphysics (which New Materialism revamps), but that Glissant's poetics of relations is grounded on the history of Atlantic slavery rather than on the physics pioneered by European scientists such as Bohr, Einstein, and Heisenberg.

Underscoring the parallels is important because in New Materialism and decoloniality (in terms of both Indigenous *vincularidad* and Afro-Caribbean poetics of relations), rivers and mountains, stars and water, air and atoms, molecules and the sun and the moon, the cat and the tiger—all are inter- and intra-*vinculados* (linked). The parallels reside in the fact that while New Materialism arrives at this conclusion in its critique of its practitioners' European ancestors, Indigenous philosophy did not arrive at this conclusion. It has been their way of thinking and being in the world for centuries and is now reemerging. For that reason, *vincularidad* and the poetics of relations are not "new"; they are manifestations of decolonial reexistence and reemergence (see chapter 13). As such, they are the continuation of a long-lasting confrontation whose object is to survive slavery, to survive colonization, and to overcome the conscious and unconscious, explicit and implicit, belief that non-Europeans cannot think or that what they think is of limited relevance. Decolonial and border thinking in the Americas and the Caribbean doesn't arrive at conclusions similar to those of New Materialism and doesn't correct its European ancestors, but we—non-Indigenous—have been learning from Indigenous philosophy and cosmology (rather than Greek thinkers) that the universe is not conceived as *matter* but as *flow and vincularidad*. Quantum mechanics could not have arisen in Indigenous cosmologies: flow and *vincularidad* do not invite geometry and mathematics. Gnoseological and aesthesic reconstitution is the unavoidable remaking of the hermeneutics/epistemology that seeps like a polluted stream through European thinking, from the theological to the secular.

The decolonial focus on *vincularidad* and the poetics of relations through multiple histories and trajectories (see chapter 13) leaves ontology by the wayside (a Fanon ipse dixit) and distances itself from what seem to be mutations of modernity/coloniality in the vocabulary and the arguments regarding the posthuman and postnature. Decolonial, posthuman, New Materialism are distinct options. Posthuman and decolonial-human arguments (chapter 12) run parallel—the first questioning the liberal notion of human and humanism originating with the European Renaissance; the second questioning the concept of Man/Human in Western civilization that now includes the posthuman and posthumanism. Decolonially I would ask, when confronting posthuman and postnature arguments (as well as postdevelopment and other existing or would-be "posts"), how many of the almost eight billion people on the planet will merge with machines, will differentiate themselves from nature, and will see themselves cut off from the cosmos and separated from the living? Or will they/many of us extinguish? Because life preexisted and made possible the postmodern *biology* explicit in Nickolas Rose's concept of "the politics of life itself," the decolonial question addresses the postmodern "political politics of life itself."[51] While recognizing these concerns of a numerical minority in the industrial states that promote them, with research grants and other means, the decolonial politics of investigations delinks from the biotechnological arguments that allow people more freedom to take care of themselves through health insurance—arguments that blend well with the market ideology of transforming health care into consumerism.[52] The decolonial politics of investigations instead joins the care for life that was destituted by modernity/coloniality, the knowledge and knowing that come from "life itself" on Earth and in the cosmos, and that made it possible for the human species to survive and expand for thousands if not millions of years. Freeing ourselves from the classification bequeathed to us requires that we break with the unipolar idea of knowledge, which in the decolonial vocabulary translates into Eurocentric epistemic universality. Decolonial horizons drive us toward epistemic pluriversality. Or, if one wishes to maintain some kind of universality, one might refer to *pluriversality as a universal project* (in which Western universality will remain a regional belief): the will to reexist and to uncover the harmony of plurilanguaging love.[53]

Notes

Preface

1 I borrow the expression from Partha Chatterjee to underscore the sector of civil society whose members, beyond casting votes at the proper time, take matters into their own hands not expecting that the government, banks, or corporations will do good for them/us. Decoloniality, at large and in the particular mode I argue here, cannot be an academic project of the civil society. That's even more true when you assume that the decolonial is already an option to join political society. See Partha Chatterjee, *Lineages of Political Society* (New York: Columbia University Press, 2011).

2 Several years ago, I dealt with this issue but was unable to find a way out of "epistemology." I used the concepts in two ways, in the standard modern meaning of the concept while addressing decolonial issues with the same word. It was recently that I found in gnoseology a way out of epistemology. So the title today would be, "Decolonizing Western Epistemology/Building Decolonial Gnoseologies." The article in question is Walter D. Mignolo, "Decolonizing Western Epistemology/Building Decolonial Epistemologies," in *Decolonizing Epistemologies: Latina/Latino Theology and Philosophy*, ed. Ada María Isasi Díaz and Eduardo Mendieta (New York: Fordham University Press, 2012), 19–43.

3 Mike Ennis, "Historicizing Nahua Utopias" (PhD diss., Duke University, 2006). See also Silver Moon and Mike Ennis, "The View of the Empire from the Altepetl: Nahua Historical and Global Imagination," in *Rereading the Black Legend: The Discourses of Religious and Racial Differences in the Renaissance Empires*, ed. Margaret R. Greer, Walter D. Mignolo, and Maureen Quilligan (Chicago: University of Chicago Press, 2007), 150–66.

4 W. E. B. Du Bois, *The Negro Problem* (New York: Humanity Books, 2003 [1898]); Lewis Gordon, "What Does It Mean to Be a Problem?," in *Existentia Africana: Understanding Africana Existential Thought* (London: Routledge, 2000), 62–95.

5 Henry George, *Progress and Poverty* (New York: Cosimo, 2005 [1879]).

6 For a collection of Aníbal Quijano's essays from after he introduced "coloniality" and conceived decolonial horizons as "epistemic reconstitutions" and subjective delinking, see Walter D. Mignolo, ed., *Aníbal Quijano: Ensayos en torno a la colonialidad del poder* (Buenos Aires: Ediciones del Signo, 2019).

7 Erick Gloeckner, "Workplace Investigation Tips from Sherlock Holmes," Nonprofit Risk Management Center, accessed October 1, 2020, https://nonprofitrisk .org/resources/e-news/workplace-investigation-tips-from-sherlock-holmes/. See also Darrin, "Seven Investigation Strategies from Sherlock Holmes," North American Investigations, September 13, 2013, https://pvteyes.com/7-investigation -strategies-sherlock-holmes/.

8 Walter D. Mignolo and Rolando Vázquez, "Decolonial AestheSis: Colonial Wounds/Decolonial Healings," *Social Text: Periscope*, July 15, 2013, https:// socialtextjournal.org/periscope_article/decolonial-aesthesis-colonial -woundsdecolonial-healings/; Walter D. Mignolo, "Reconstitución epistémico/estética: La aesthesis decolonial una década después," *Calle 14: Revista de investigación en el campo del arte* 14, no. 25 (2019): 15–32.

9 Miguel León-Portilla, *Aztecs Thought and Culture* (Norman: University of Oklahoma Press, 1990); James Maffie, "Aztec Philosophy," *Internet Encyclopedia of Philosophy*, accessed May 31, 2020, https://www.iep.utm.edu/aztec/; L. Sebastian Purcel, "Eudaimonia and Neltiliztli: Aristotle and the Aztecs on the Good Life," *Hispanic/Latino Issues in Philosophy Newsletter* 10, no. 2 (Spring 2017): 10–19. For similar arguments on technological thoughts and cosmology in China, see Yuk Hui, *The Question Concerning Technology in China: An Essay in Cosmotechnics* (Windsor Quarry, UK: Urbanomic, 2016). For southern Africa, see Clapperton Chakanetsa Mavhunga, ed., *What Do Science, Technology and Innovation Mean from Africa?* (Boston: MIT Press, 2017); Mogobe B. Ramose, *African Philosophy through Ubuntu* (Harare, ZW: Mond Books, 1999); Fainos Mangena, "Hunhu/Ubuntu in the Traditional Thought of Southern Africa," *Internet Encyclopedia of Philosophy*, accessed May 26, 2020, https://www.iep.utm.edu/hunhu/?fbclid=IwAR2Clka7Ac UN5s8AlMUdb6gG9rQHgLLx9TE0018_SEXlZ5qn-khUWL37wQE; Mohammed Abed al-Jabri, *The Formation of the Arab Reason: Texts, Traditions and the Construction of Modernity in the Arab World*, trans. Center of Arab Unity Studies (London: I. B. Tauris, 2011 [1988]).

10 See Mignolo and Vázquez, "Decolonial AestheSis."

11 For my previous elaboration on gnoseological and aesthesic reconstitutions, see Mignolo, "Reconstitutción epistemémitco/estética."

12 Walter D. Mignolo, "Who Speaks for the 'Human' in Human Rights?," in *Human Rights from the Third World Perspective*, ed. Jose-Manuel Barreto (London: Cambridge Scholars Publishing, 2015), 44–65.

13 Walter D. Mignolo, "Decolonial Body-Geo Politics at Large," in *Decolonizing Sexualities: Transnational Perspectives, Critical Interventions*, ed. Sandeep Bakshi, Suhraiya Jivraj, and Silvia Posocco (Oxford: Counterpress, 2016), vii–xviii.

14 Paget Henry, *Caliban's Reason: Introducing Caribbean Philosophy* (London: Routledge, 2000); Antony Bogues, *Black Prophet, Black Heretics: Radical Political Intellectuals* (London: Routledge, 2003); Jean Casimir, *Une lecture décoloniale de l'histoire des Haïtienne: Du Traité de Ryswick à l'Occupaton Américaine (1697–1915)*, preface by Walter D. Mignolo, afterword by Michel Hector (Port-au-Prince: L'Impremeur S. A., 2018) (English translation: *The Haitians: A Decolonial History* [Chapel Hill: University of North Carolina Press, 2020]); Louis R. Gordon, *What Fanon Said: A Philosophical Introduction to His Life and Thought* (New York: Fordham University, 2015).

15 Moulay Driss El Maarouf, Taieb Belghazi, and Farouk El Maarouf, "COVID-19: A Critical Ontology of the Present," *Educational Philosophy and Theory* (April 26, 2020), https://www.tandfonline.com/doi/full/10.1080/00131857.2020.1757426.

Introduction

1 "Our first objective is to prevent the re-emergence of a new rival, either on the territory of the former Soviet Union or elsewhere, that poses a threat on the order of that posed formerly by the Soviet Union. This is a dominant consideration underlying the new regional defense strategy and requires that we endeavor to prevent any hostile power from dominating a region whose resources would, under consolidated control, be sufficient to generate global power. These regions include western Europe, East Asia, the territory of the former Soviet Union, and Southwest Asia." Excerpts from the Pentagon's plan after the collapse of the Soviet Union: "Prevent the Re-Emergence of a New Rival," *New York Times*, March 8, 1992, https://www.nytimes.com/1992/03/08/world/excerpts-from-pentagon-s-plan -prevent-the-re-emergence-of-a-new-rival.html.

2 J. William Fulbright, *The Arrogance of Power* (New York: Random House, 1967).

3 Aníbal Quijano, "Coloniality and Modernity/Rationality," *Cultural Studies* 21, no. 2 (2007 [1992]), 177.

4 Nelson Maldonado-Torres, "The Coloniality of Being: Contributions to the History of a Concept," *Cultural Studies* 21, no. 2–3 (2007): 240–70.

5 See Walter D. Mignolo and Rolando Vazquez, "Decolonial AestheSis: Colonial Wounds/Decolonial Healings," *Social Text Periscope*, July 15, 2013, https://socialtextjournal.org/periscope_article/decolonial-aesthesis-colonial -woundsdecolonial-healings/. See also Walter D. Mignolo, "Reconstitución epistémica/estética: La aesthesis decolonial una década después," *Calle 14: Revista de Investigación en el campo del arte* 14, no. 25 (2010): 14–32.

6 I am borrowing this concept from Partha Chatterjee, *Lineages of Political Society: Studies in Postcolonial Democracy* (New York: Columbia University Press, 2011).

7 A vigorous decolonial current of thought in Eastern Europe is underway. See, for instance, Ovidiu Tichindeleanu, "Decolonial AestheSis in Eastern Europe:

Potential Paths of Liberation," in *Social Text: Periscope*, ed. Walter D. Mignolo and Rolando Vásquez, July 15, 2013, https://socialtextjournal.org/periscope _article/decolonial-aesthesis-in-eastern-europe-potential-paths-of-liberation /, and "Towards a Critical Theory of Postcomunism: Beyond Anticommunism in Romania," *Radical Philosophy*, January/February 2010, https://www .radicalphilosophy.com/article/towards-a-critical-theory-of-postcommunism; Manuela Boatcă, "Multiple Europes and the Politics of Difference Within," *Worlds and Knowledges Otherwise*, Spring 2013, Center for Global Studies, Duke University, https://www.radicalphilosophy.com/article/towards-a-critical-theory -of-postcommunism; Polina Manolova, Katarina Kusic, and Philipp Lottholtz, "Decolonial Theory and Practice in Southeast Europe," special issue, *dVERSIA Magazine*, March 2019, https://issuu.com/dversiamagazine/docs/dversia-special -issie-decolonial-th.

8 Chatterjee, *Lineages of Political Society*.

9 See Walter D. Mignolo, "Sustainable Development or Sustainable Economies? Ideas towards Living in Harmony and Plenitude," *Socioscapes: International Journal of Societies, Politics and Cultures* 1, no. 1 (2020): 48–65.

10 Oswald Spengler, *Man and Technics: A Contribution to a Philosophy of Life*, trans. Charles Francis Atkinson and Michael Putman (London: Artktos Media, 2015 [1932]).

11 Walter D. Mignolo, "The Geopolitics of Sensing and Knowing: On (De) Coloniality, Border Thinking and Epistemic Disobedience," *Confero* 1, no. 1 (2013): 129–50, DOI: 10.3384/confer.2001-4562.13v1iii129.

12 Aníbal Quijano, "Coloniality and Modernity/Rationality," English translation in *Cultural Studies* 21, no. 2–3 (2007 [1992]): 168–78, DOI: 10.1080/09502380601164353. For related information about Quijano's work on coloniality/decoloniality, see a collection of his articles in Walter D. Mignolo, ed., *Aníbal Quijano: Ensayos en torno a la colonialidad del poder* (Buenos Aires: Ediciones del Signo, 2019); and also Walter D. Mignolo and Catherine E. Walsh, *On Decoloniality: Concepts, Analytics, Praxis* (Durham, NC: Duke University Press, 2018).

13 I address some of these issues in previous publications. See Walter D. Mignolo, "The Role of the Humanities in the Corporate University," *PMLA* 115, no. 5 (2000): 1238–45, DOI: 10.2307/463306; Walter Mignolo, "Globalization and the Geopolitics of Knowledge: The Role of the Humanities in the Corporate University," in *The American-Style University at Large: Transplants, Outposts and the Globalization of Higher Education*, ed. Kathryn L. Kleypas and James I. McDougall (Lanham, MD: Lexington Books, 2011), 3–40.

14 Lourdes Godinez Leal, "Lorena Cabnal: Defensora del cuerpo-tierra de las mujeres," *CN cimacnoticias*, October 2015, https://cimacnoticias.com.mx/noticia /lorena-cabnal-defensora-del-cuerpo-tierra-de-las-mujeres/; Gabriela Gonzáles Ortuño, "Los feminismos afros en Latinoamérica y el Caribe, tradiciones disidentes: Del pensamiento anticolonial a la defensa de la tierra," *Investigaciones Feministas* 9, no. 2 (December 2018): 239–54, DOI: 10.5209/INFE.58936; Feminismo Comunitario del Abya Yala, "Manifiesto sobre el golpe de estado y las elec-

ciones generales en Bolivia," *Prensa Comunitaria*, December 2019, https://www
.feminismocomunitario.com/.

15 Walter D. Mignolo, *Local Histories/Global Designs: Coloniality, Subaltern Knowledges, and Border Thinking*, 2nd ed. (Princeton, NJ: Princeton University Press, 2012 [2000]).

16 Mignolo, "Globalization and the Geopolitics of Knowledge."

17 Aníbal Quijano, "Colonialidad del poder y subjetividad en America Latina," *Contextualizaciones Latinoamericanas* 3, no. 5 (2015): 1–13.

18 Lee Kuan Yew, interview on *Meet the Press*, October 22, 1967, video, https://www
.youtube.com/watch?v=VexrmTacOAA.

19 Mark R. Thompson, "Why Deng Xiaoping and China Could Never Truly Understand Singapore," *News Lens*, February 2020, https://international.thenewslens
.com/article/114061. See also Lee Kuan Yew, "The Future of China," interview in *Lee Kuan Yew: The Grand Master's Insights on China, the United States, and the World*, ed. Graham Allyson and Robert D. Blackwill with Ali Wayne (Cambridge, MA: MIT Press, 2012), 1–18.

20 "Hybrid warfare is an emerging, but ill-defined notion in conflict studies. It refers to the use of unconventional methods as part of a multi-domain warfighting approach. These methods aim to disrupt and disable an opponent's actions without engaging in open hostilities." "Explainer: What Is 'Hybrid Warfare and What Is Meant by the 'Gray Zone,'" *The Conversation*, June 17, 2019, https://
theconversation.com/explainer-what-is-hybrid-warfare-and-what-is-meant-by-the
-grey-zone-118841.

21 Margaret E. Greer, Walter D. Mignolo, and Maureen Quilligan, eds., *Rereading the Black Legend: The Discourses of Religion and Racial Difference in the Renaissance Empires* (Chicago: University of Chicago Press, 2007).

22 Francisco López de Gómara, *Historia general de las Indias* (Caracas: Biblioteca Ayacucho, 1965 [1553]), 14.

23 Adam Smith, *An Inquiry into the Nature and Causes of the Wealth of Nations* (Chicago: University of Chicago Press, 1976 [1776]), 141.

24 Nelson Maldonado-Torres, "The Topology of Being and the Geopolitics of Knowledge," *City* 8, no. 1 (2004): 29–56, DOI: 10.1080/1360481042000199787.

25 Just two examples: Leanne Betasamosake Simpson (Mississauga Nishnaabeg), *Dancing on Our Turtle's Back: Stories of Nishnaabeg Re-Creation, Resurgence, and a New Emergence* (Winnipeg, MB: Arbeiter Ring Publishing, 2011), and Fernando Huanacuni Mamani (Aymara), *Vivir Bien/Buen Vivir: Filosofía, políticas, estrategias y experiencias de los pueblos ancestrales*, 6th ed. (La Paz: Instituto International de Integración, 2015).

26 Karl Marx, *Capital*, vol. 1, trans. Ben Fowkes and David Fernbach (London: Penguin Classics, 1976 [1867]), 915–16.

27 "Barbarian located in space": Walter D. Mignolo "(De)Coloniality at Large: Time and the Colonial Difference," in *The Darker Side of Western Modernity: Global Futures, Decolonial Options* (Durham, NC: Duke University Press, 2011), 149–80.

28 See also Eric Williams, *Capitalism and Slavery* (Chapel Hill: University of North Carolina Press, 1994 [1944]).

29 Aníbal Quijano and Immanuel Wallerstein, "Americanity as a Concept or the Americas in the Modern/World System," *International Social Science Journal* 34, no. 4 (1992): 549–57.

30 Quijano, "Coloniality and Modernity/Rationality," 16.

31 It became obvious to him after two decades of participation in dependency theory debates. For readers not familiar with the dependency debate, the bibliography is extensive. Here is a useful summary: Vincent Ferraro, "Dependency Theory: An Introduction," in *The Development Economics Reader*, ed. Giorgio Secondi (London: Routledge, 2008), 58–64, https://www.mtholyoke.edu/acad /intrel/depend.htm.

32 Oswald Spengler, *The Decline of the West: Form and Actuality* (vol. 1, 1918) and *Perspective of World History* (vol. 2, 1922) (London: Oxford Paperback, 2013).

33 Sigmund Freud, *Civilization and Its Discontents*, trans. James Strachey (New York: W. W. Norton, 2010 [1930]), 58–60.

34 James Maffie, "Aztec Philosophy," *Internet Encyclopedia of Philosophy*, esp. section 3.a, "How Can Humans Maintain Their Balance on the Slippery Earth?," https://iep.utm.edu/aztec/#SH3a. On this topic see also the classic study by Miguel León-Portilla, *Aztec Thought and Culture: A Study of the Ancient Nahuatl Mind*, trans. Jack Emory Davis (Norman: University of Oklahoma Press, 1990 [1963]), and also James Maffie, *Aztec Philosophy: Understanding a World in Motion* (Boulder: University Press of Colorado, 2014).

35 Sebastian Purcell, "What the Aztecs Can Teach Us about Happiness and the Good Life," *AEON Newsletter*, accessed December 20, 2020, https://aeon.co/ideas /what-the-aztecs-can-teach-us-about-happiness-and-the-good-life. For a more detailed analysis see Sebastian Purcell, "Eudaimonia and Neltiliztli: Aristotle and the Aztecs on the Good Life," *APA Newsletter on Hispanic/Latino Issues in Philosophy* 16, no. 2 (Spring 2017): 10–21.

36 Lorena Cabnal, "TZK' AT, Red de Sanadoras Ancestrales del Feminismo Comunitario desde Iximulew-Guatemala," *Ecología Política*, January 10, 2018, https://www .ecologiapolitica.info/?p=10247.

37 In the following sections I explore in more detail the issues I addressed in chapter 6 of Mignolo and Walsh, *On Decoloniality*.

38 See Mignolo, *Local Histories/Global Designs*. Facing the issue of translating "patrón colonial de poder," Quijano's expression, it was my sense that "matrix" would more effectively than "pattern" render the idea that Quijano expressed with "patrón." However, the patriarchal dimension implied in "patron" was lost and has to be added and remembered when we use "matrix." On the other hand, "matrix" has several meanings. The one that interests me here is the composite "management structure/frame of mind": a frame of mind that built, transformed, and managed the CMP at the same time that the management structure shapes the frame of mind of the managers and the managed. For this sense of "matrix," see Christopher A. Bartlett and Sumantra Thoshal, "Matrix Management: Not a

Structure, a Frame of Mind," *Harvard Business Review*, July–August 1990, accessed June 1, 2020, https://hbr.org/1990/07/matrix-management-not-a-structure-a -frame-of-mind. Metaphorically the CMP could be seen in parallel with the film *The Matrix*, directed by Lilly Wachowski and Lana Wachowski, 1999.

39 Aníbal Quijano, "Colonialidad del poder y clasificación social," in *Cuestiones y Horizontes: De la dependencia histórico-estructural a la colonialidad/descolonialidad del poder* (Buenos Aires: CLACSO, 2014), 289.

40 Aníbal Quijano, "Coloniality of Power, Eurocentrism and Social Classification," trans. Michel Ennis, in *Coloniality at Large: Latin America and the Postcolonial Debate*, ed. Mabel Moraña, Enrique Dussel, and Carlos A. Jáuregui (Durham, NC: Duke University Press, 2008), 193.

41 Aníbal Quijano, "Coloniality of Power, Eurocentrism and Social Classification."

42 Aníbal Quijano, "Coloniality of Power, Eurocentrism and Social Classification."

43 Aníbal Quijano, "Coloniality and Modernity/Rationality."

44 Among the many who have followed up on Quijano's seedings are Catherine Walsh, Edgardo Lander, María Lugones, Rita Segato, Zulma Palermo, María Eugenia Borsani, Adolfo Albán-Achinte, Pedro Pabl Gómez, Julio Mejía Navarrete, Nelson Maldonado-Torres, Pablo Quintero, Jean Casimir, Roberto Espinosa, Boris Marañon Pimentel, César Germaná. And among the younger generation joining the project are Madina V. Tlostanova, Alanna Lockward (1961–2019), Rolando Vázquez, Ovidiu Tichindeleanu, Raúl Moarquech Ferrera-Balanquet, Barbara Aguer, and Facundo Giuliano. Beyond the wider and growing recognition of Quijano's work, I have mentioned a few names whose work follows up on or explicitly recognizes their debt to Quijano's work and that I have been in contact with and have worked with.

45 Thomas Piketty has amassed an impressive amount of data to account for the mutually constitutive forces of capitalism/inequality. See especially *Capital and Ideology*, trans. Arthur Goldhammer (Cambridge, MA: Harvard University Press, 2020). What Quijano articulated was the formation of a structure of management and mindset that began to be formed in the sixteenth century in the Atlantic, involving western Europe, Africa, and what became the Americas. Hence, modernity/coloniality is the decolonial version of capital/inequality: in the same way that there is no modernity without coloniality, there cannot be capitalism without inequality. The idea was brilliantly argued in the nineteenth century by US thinker Henry George in his classic and often forgotten book *Progress and Poverty* (1879). That is, progress/modernity and poverty/coloniality.

46 Maurits Cornelis Escher, *Drawing Hands*, lithograph, 1948, reproduced February 15, 2018, https://moa.byu.edu/m-c-eschers-drawing-hands/.

47 The basic philosophy of the geopolitical distributions of languages and meaning has been outlined in Walter D. Mignolo, "Globalization/Mundialization: Civilization Processes and the Relocation of Languages and Knowledges," in *Local Histories, Global Designs*, 278–313.

48 Walter D. Mignolo, "Globalization and the Geopolitics of Knowledge: The Role of the Humanities in the Corporate University," in *The American-Style Univer-*

sity at Large: Transplants, Outposts, and the Globalization of Higher Education, ed. Kathyn L. Kleypas and James I. Mc. Dougall (Lanham, MD: Lexington Books, 2012), 3–40.

49 Quijano, "Coloniality and Modernity/Rationality," 177.

50 Definition of "gnosis," Online Etymology Dictionary, accessed August 11, 2020, https://www.etymonline.com/word/gnosis.

51 Walter D. Mignolo, "On Gnosis and the Imaginary of the Modern/Colonial World System," in *Local Histories/Global Designs*, 3–48.

52 Valentine Y. Mudimbe, *The Invention of Africa: Gnosis, Philosophy, and the Order of Knowledge* (Bloomington: Indiana University Press, 1988).

53 Maldonado-Torres, " On the Coloniality of Being."

54 Definition of "aesthetic," *Online Etymology Dictionary*, accessed December 20, 2020, https://www.etymonline.com/search?q=aesthetic.

55 Immanuel Kant, *Observations on the Feeling of the Beautiful and Sublime*, ed. Patrick Frierson and Paul Guyer (Cambridge, UK: Cambridge Texts in the History of Philosophy, 2011 [1794]); Immanuel Kant, *Critique of Judgement* (Cambridge, MA: Hackett Classics, 1987 [1820]); G. W. F. Hegel, *Introduction to Aesthetics* (Oxford, UK: Oxford University Press, 1979 [1820]).

56 Guaman Poma de Ayala, *El primer nueva corónica y buen gobierno*, trans. Rolena Adorno, John V. Murra, y Jorge L. Urioste (Mexico City: Fondo de Cultura Económica, 1980). See also the digital edition produced by the Royal Library of Copenhagen, accessed May 15, 2020, http://www5.kb.dk/permalink/2006/poma /info/en/frontpage.htm.

57 I am borrowing the concept of "grounded normativity" from Glen Coulthard and Leanne Betasamosake Simpson, "Grounded Normativity/Place-Based Solidarity," *American Quarterly* 68, no. 2 (2016): 249–55.

58 Coulthard and Simpson, "Grounded Normativity."

59 Jean Casimir, *Une lecture décoloniale de l'histoire des Haïtienne: Du Traité de Ryswick à l'Occupaton Américaine (1697–1915)* (Port-au-Prince: L'Impremeur S. A., 2018), https://lenouvelliste.com/article/187914/jean-casimir-propose-une-lecture -decoloniale-de-lhistoire-des-haitiens. English translation: *The Haitians: A Decolonial History* (Chapel Hill: University of North Carolina Press, 2020)

60 Enlace Zapatista, http://enlacezapatista.ezln.org.mx/.

61 Mohandas Gandhi, *Gandhi: "Hind Swaraj" and Other Writings*, ed. Anthony J. Parel (Cambridge, UK: Cambridge University Press, 1997 [1909]), 44–45, 47.

62 Ajay Skaria, "Gandhi's Radical Conservatism," *Seminar* 662 (2014): 31.

63 Mark Thomson, *Gandhi and His Ashrams* (Bombay: Popular Prakashan, 1993).

64 Ajay Skaria, "Gandi's Politics: Liberalism and the Question of *Ashram*," *South Atlantic Quarterly* 101, no. 4 (2002): 955–86.

65 Walter D. Mignolo, "The Zapatistas' Theoretical Revolution: Its Historical, Ethical and Political Consequences," in *The Darker Side of Western Modernity: Global Futures, Decolonial Options* (Durham, NC: Duke University Press, 2011), 213–51; Jean Casimir, *The Haitians: A Decolonial History*, trans. Laurent Dubois, foreword by Walter D. Mignolo (Chapel Hill: University of North Carolina Press, 2020).

66 Nina Pacari, "Ecuador Taking on the Neolibral Agenda," *NACLA Report on the Americas* 29, no. 5 (1996), 23–32; Félix Patzi Paco, *Sistema comunal: Una propuesta alternativa al sistema libera para salir de la colonialidad y del liberalismo* (La Paz, Bolivia: Comunidad de Estudios Alternativas [CEA], 2004); Simón Yampara, "Territorio, cosmovisión el/la qamaña y el buen vivir," Revista Inti Pacha 1/7, La Paz, Bolivia: Ediciones Qamañpacha de la Fundación "Suma Qamaña," Instituto Tecnológico de Investigación Indi Andino, 2005; Luis Macas, "Interview with CONAIE's Luis Macas: 'We Want a Total Transformation,'" NACLA *Report on the Americas,* September 2007, https://nacla.org/news/2007/8/24/interview-conaies-luis-macas-%E2%80%9Cwe -want-total-transformation; Huanacuni Mamani, *Vivir Bien/Buen Vivir.*

67 D'Arcy Ishpeming'enzaabid Rheault Bizhiw, *Anishinaabe Mino-Bimaadiziwin (The Way of a Good Life): An Examination of Anishinaabe Philosophy, Ethics and Traditional Knowledge* (Peterborough, ON: Debwewin Press, 1999).

68 Mogobe B. Ramose, "The Philosophy of Ubuntu and Ubuntu as Philosophy," in *Philosophy from Africa: A Text with Readings,* ed. P. H. Coetzee and A. P. J. Roux (Oxford, UK: Oxford University Press, 2002), 230–37.

69 Mimerose P. Beaubrun, *Nan Dòmi: An Initiate's Journey into Haitian Voudou,* trans. D. J. Walker (San Francisco: City Lights Books, 2013).

70 Sylvia Wynter, "Towards the Sociogenic Principle: Fanon, the Puzzle of Conscious Experience, of 'Identity' and What it's Like to be 'Black,'" in *National Identities and Sociopolitical Changes in Latin America,* ed. Mercedes F. Durán-Cogan and Antonio Gómez-Moriana (London: Routledge, 2001), 30–66.

71 Louis R. Gordon, "What Does It Mean to Be a Problem? W. E. B. Dubois and the Study of the Black Folk," in *Existentia Africana: Understanding Africana Existential Thought* (London: Routledge, 2000), 62–95.

72 Maldonado-Torres, "The Topology of Being and the Geopolitics of Knowledge."

73 Frantz Fanon, *The Wretched of the Earth,* trans. Richard Philcox (New York: Grove Press, 2004 [1961]).

74 Frantz Fanon, *Black Skin, White Masks,* trans. Richard Philcox, rev. ed. (New York: Grove Press, 2008 [1952]), 35.

75 Fanon, *The Wretched of the Earth,* 235–40.

76 Gloria Anzaldúa, *Borderlands/La Frontera: The New Mestiza* (San Francisco: Aunt Lute Books, 2007 [1987]), 25.

77 Anzaldúa, *Borderlands/La Frontera,* 60–61.

78 José de Sousa Silva, "Una época de cambios o un cambio de época? Elementos de referencia para interpretar las contradicciones del momento actual," Boletín ICCI "RIMAY," April 2001, http://icci.nativeweb.org/boletin/25/souza.html.

79 Joe Biden's presidential acceptance speech, November 7, 2020, video, https://www.youtube.com/watch?v=kIMhZcyrbrQ.

80 Collectif, "Les manifest des 100," *Le Monde,* November 2, 2020; Alana Lentin and cosignatories, "Open Letter : The Threat of Academic Authoritarianism— International Solidarity with Antiracist Academics in France," Open Democracy, November 5, 2020, https://manifestedes90.wixsite.com/monsite. On the museum front, here is one reference among many: MTL Collective, "From Institutional

Critique to Institutional Liberation? A Decolonial Perspective on the Crisis of Contemporary Art," *October* 165 (2018): 192–227.

81 Juan Donoso Cortés, *Essays on Catholicism, Liberalism and Socialism: Considered in Their Fundamental Principles* (London: Forgotten Books, 2017 [1852]).

82 Eric Miller, "The Radical Rise of Liberation Theology: An Interview with Calles Barger," *Religion and Politics*, September 25, 2018, https://religionandpolitics.org /2018/09/25/the-radical-rise-of-liberation-theology-an-interview-with-lilian-calles -barger/.

83 Quijano, "Coloniality and Modernity/Rationality." And Aníbal Quijano, "América Latina: Hacia un nuevo sentido histórico," *Cátedra Indígena Intercultural*, April 2015, http://www.reduii.org/cii/?q=node/47.

84 "China's Partnership Diplomacy and Successful Implementation of the BRI," *Belt and Road News*, March 27, 2020, https://www.beltandroad.news/2020/03/27/chinas -partnership-diplomacy-successful-implementation-of-the-bri/.

85 Carl Schmitt, *The Concept of the Political* (Chicago: University Chicago University Press, 2007 [1932]).

86 Michel-Rolph Trouillot, "North Atlantic Universals: Universal Fictions, 1492–1945," *South Atlantic Quarterly* 101, no. 4 (2002): 839–58.

87 Constance Classen, *The Museum of the Senses: Experiencing Art Collections* (London: Bloomsbury Academic, 2017).

88 Website of Enlace Zapatista, accessed December 20, 2020, https://enlacezapatista .ezln.org.mx/. See particularly Subcomandante Insurgente Galeano's latest reflections, dated October 2020, where we see gnoseological and aesthesic reconstitutions at work. See also, from former Subcomandante Marcos, the notable essays on the fourth world war, "La cuarta guerra mundial," *Inmotion Magazine*, October 26, 2001, https://inmotionmagazine.com/auto/cuarta.html. See also, concomitant with the argument I am making, Mignolo, "The Zapatistas' Theoretical Revolution."

89 "The International Peasants' Voice," La Vía Campesina, accessed October 15, 2020, https://viacampesina.org/en/international-peasants-voice/. See also *Food Sovereignty Now! A Guide to Food Sovereignty*, European Coordination Via Campesina, 2018, https://viacampesina.org/en/wp-content/uploads/sites/2/2018/02/Food -Sovereignty-A-guide-Low-Res-Vresion.pdf.

90 See the web page of the Global University for Sustainability, accessed October 13, 2020, https://our-global-u.org/oguorg/about-us/. See her work on YouTube here, accessed October 15, 2020, www.youtube.com/channel/UClIP6qH6BInA9 _nIsUAYcMw?feature=emb_ch_name_ex.

One. Racism as We Sense It Today

1 "The Incanate in the Andes and the Tlatoanate in the Valley of Mexico": Coloniality of knowledge is manifested in the imposition of Western vocabulary to homogenize and appropriate the meaning of non-Western knowledges and languages. Generally, the domains of the Aztecs and the Incas are called "empires." Well, the rulers were not emperors but Incas in one case and Tlatoani in the

other. Imagine if we started calling Julius Caesar Tlatoani or Inca? The same goes for the Ottoman ruler. The ruler was a sultan, not an emperor; hence the Ottoman sultanate. Imagine again that someone called Julius Caesar a sultan. What would your reaction be?

2 *Online Etymological Dictionary*, accessed September 24, 2020, https://www.etymonline.com/search?q=indigenous.

3 For an argument on the human as an overrepresentation of man, see Sylvia Wynter, "Unsettling the Coloniality of Being/Power/Truth/Freedom: Towards the Human, after Man, Its Overrepresentation: An Argument," *New Centennial Review* 3, no. 3 (2003): 257–337.

4 Margaret R. Greer, Walter D. Mignolo, and Maureen Quilligan, *Rereading the Black Legend. The Discourse of Religious and Racial Difference in the Renaissance Empires.* Chicago: The University of Chicago Press, 2008.

5 Emily C. Bartels writes, "In 1596, Queen Elizabeth issued an 'open letter' to the Lord Mayor of London, announcing that 'there are of late divers blackamoors brought into this realm, of which kind of people there are already here to manie,' and ordering that they be deported from the country." One week later, she reiterated her "good plea sure to have those kind of people sent out of the land" and commissioned the merchant Casper van Senden to "take up" certain "blackamoors here in this realm and to transport them into Spain and Portugal." Finally, in 1601, she complained again about the "great numbers of Negars and Blackamoors which (as she is informed) are crept into this realm," defamed them as "infidels, having no understanding of Christ or his Gospel," and, one last time, authorized their "deportation." "Too Many Blackamoors: Deportation, Discrimination, and Elizabeth I," SEL: *Studies in English Literature 1500–1900* 46, no. 2 (2006): 305, DOI: 10.1353/ sel.2006.0012.

6 Racism as an epistemological and ontological construction of imperial knowledge (Christian theology and secular egology—i.e., secular philosophy and secular science) has been argued in several places after Aníbal Quijano's seminal works on "coloniality of power." Racism has been construed as an epistemic projection over bodies, regions, languages, religions, and, in general, everything that needed to be destituted in the constitution of Western civilization, Western modernity, and the underlying structure, the CMP. This has been accomplished by devaluing non-Western people in relation to the human ideal in both the European Renaissance and European Enlightenment (e.g., in the *Declaration of the Rights of Man and of the Citizen*; see chapter 7).

7 Eric Williams made this observation in the 1940s: "Here, then, is the origin of Negro slavery. The reason was economic, not racial; it had to do not with the color of the laborer, but the cheapness of labor." *Capitalism and Slavery* (Chapel Hill: University of North Carolina Press, 1994 [1944]). Notice that he says "Negro slavery" and not "slavery." It is not Greek slavery that counts today as racism, but the historical foundation of the colonial matrix of power.

8 For the historical foundation of capitalism as a consequence of the conquest of America, see Aníbal Quijano and Immanuel Wallerstein, "Americanity as a

Concept, or the Americas in the Modern/World System," *International Social Science Journal* 34, no. 4 (1992): 549–57, and also Aníbal Quijano, "Coloniality and Modernity/Rationality," English translation in *Cultural Studies* 21, no. 2–3 (2007 [1992]): 168–78, DOI: 10.1080/09502380601164353. For the Atlantic commercial circuits as a sequitur of the previous two articles, see Walter D. Mignolo *Local Histories/Global Designs: Coloniality, Subaltern Knowledges, and Border Thinking*, 2nd ed. (Princeton, NJ: Princeton University Press, 2012 [2000]).

9 Although Jews, like Indians and Blacks, were classified through colonial difference (internal for Jews), Muslims were classified according to the external imperial difference: no Christian was unaware of the ancient Islamic caliphate and the then-current Ottoman sultanate. Think of the Chinese and Japanese today: no Westerner is unaware that they may be "yellow" according to the Linnaeus and Kantian classifications but are not at the same level as Indians, Blacks, and Jews. See Greer, Mignolo, and Quilligan, *Rereading the Black Legend*.

10 I introduced the term "egology" in 2007. "Theology" subsumed a conceptual frame (-*logy*) centered on God (*theo*), but in light of the displacement of God in favor of the individual that emerged in the European Renaissance and was consolidated in the eighteenth century, *theo* was displaced by *ego*, hence "theology" was displaced by "egology." See also Walter D. Mignolo, "Delinking: The Rhetoric of Modernity, the Logic of Coloniality and the Grammar of De-coloniality," *Cultural Studies* 21, no. 2 (2007): 449–514, DOI: 10.1080/09502380601162647. (The revised French translation, "La désobéissance épistemique: Réthorique de la modernité, logique de la colonialité et grammaire de la décolonialité," trans. Yasmine Jouhari and Marc Maesschalk [Amsterdam: Peter Lang, 2015]). On "egology" see Larry Siedentop, *Inventing the Individual: The Origins of Western Liberalism* (London: Allen Lane Publishers, 2014).

11 I have addressed these questions in more detail in my essay "On Comparison: Who Is Comparing What and Why?," in *Comparison: Theories, Approaches, Uses*, ed. Rita Felski and Susan Friedman (Baltimore: Johns Hopkins University Press, 2013), 99–119.

12 Aníbal Quijano, "Coloniality of Power, Eurocentrism, and Social Classification," in *Coloniality at Large: Latin America and the Postcolonial Debate*, ed. Mabel Moraña, Enrique Dussel, and Carlos A. Jáuregui (Durham, NC: Duke University Press, 2008), 182–83.

13 Greer, Mignolo, and Quilligan, *Rereading the Black Legend*.

14 For a detailed exploration of "blood" in the Western Christian imaginary, see Gil Anidjar, *Blood: A Critique of Christianity* (New York: Columbia University Press, 2014).

15 "Logically and historically race was an epistemic category to legitimize *racism*": This idea is further developed in Greer, Mignolo, and Quilligan, *Rereading the Black Legend*.

16 I deal with the connections between Islamophobia and Hispanophobia in chapter 2.

17 By "modern/colonial," I refer to the philosophical and political European concept of modernity, countered by dissenting histories that place coloniality as the missing half of the story; by "imperial/colonial," I refer to both sides of the equation between imperial and colonial. Although modern imperialism (i.e., Western

capitalist empires) without colonies have been in place since the nineteenth century (e.g., England in South America, and England and the United States in China since the Opium War), there is no capitalist Western empire without coloniality. Thus, by "imperial/colonial" I mean imperiality/coloniality. Which means that imperial/colonial have been specifically Western historical configurations since 1500—for example, imperial/colonial Spain, England, France, the Netherlands—while imperiality/coloniality refers to the common structure underlying all of them. Furthermore, neither expression refers to, say, China, the Incas, the Ottomans, or the Persians. The CMP is a Western invention and has been managed by the West since 1500. However, the situation is changing. See chapters 8, 9, and 10.

18 "May have mixed blood but no Indigenous political spirituality": George E. Tinker, *Spirit and Resistance: Political Theology and American Indian Liberation* (Minneapolis: Fortress Press, 2004). On the question of mestizaje from a decolonial perspective, see Javier Sanjinés, "Foundational Essays as 'Mestizo-Criollo Acts': The Bolivian Case," *Latin American and Caribbean Ethnic Studies* 11 (2016), 266–86. See also his book, *Mestizaje Upside Down: Aesthetic, Politics in Modern Bolivia* (Pittsburgh: University of Pittsburgh Press, 2004).

19 I have addressed these issues in "Decolonial Body-Geo-Politics at Large," foreword to *Decolonizing Sexualities: Transnational Perspectives, Critical Interventions*, ed. Sandeep Bakshi, Suhraiya Jivraj, and Silvia Posocco (Oxford, UK: Counterpress, 2016), vii–xviii. https://criticallegalthinking.com/2016/11/03/decolonizing-sexualities -foreward-walter-mignolo/.

20 Racism is basically a construction of a dominant (imperial) discourse. What happens when the racialized person disengages from the will to be racially true? Frantz Fanon's concept of the sociogenic principle is expanded by Sylvia Wynter, "Towards the Sociogenic Principle: Fanon, the Puzzle of Conscious Experience, of 'Identity,' and What It's Like to Be 'Black,'" in *National Identities and Sociopolitical Changes in Latin America*, ed. Mercedes F. Durán-Cogan and Antonio Gómez-Moriana (London: Routledge, 2001), 30–66.

Two. Islamophobia/Hispanophobia

1 Samuel Huntington, *The Clash of Civilizations and the Remaking of the World Order* (New York: Simon and Schuster, 1996), and "The Hispanic Challenge," *Foreign Policy* 141 (March 2004): 30.

2 "The United States has found it exceedingly difficult to define its 'national interests' in the absence of Soviet Power. That we do not know how to think about what follows the US-Soviet confrontation is clear from the continued references to the 'post-Cold War period.'" Condoleezza Rice, "Campaign 2000: Promoting the National Interest," *Foreign Affairs*, January/February 2000, https://www .foreignaffairs.com/ articles/2000-01-01/campaign-2000-promoting-national -interest.

3 On "the particularities of Islamophobia in the Russian Federation," see Madina Tlostanova, "Life in Samarkand: Caucasus and Central Asia vis-a-vis Russia, the

West and Islam," *Human Architecture* 5, no. 1 (2006): 105–16. Also relevant for my argument is her "Post-Socialist Eurasia in Civilization of Fear: Another Christianity and Another Islam," in *Hégémonie et Civilisation de la Peur*, 9éme Colloque International, Academie de la Latinité, Alexandria, April 13–17, 2004, textes de reference edité par Candido Méndes (Rio de Janeiro: Unesco/Universidad Cándido Méndes, 2004), 389–412. Much of what I say here about the histories and cultures of Russia/Soviet Union, its colonies, and its relationships with Western capitalist empires, I owe to other publications by and personal conversations with Madina V. Tlostanova.

4 Kenneth E. Bailey, *Jesus through Middle Eastern Eyes: Cultural Studies in the Gospel* (New York: IVP Academic Press, 2008).

5 Robert Lelham, *Through the Western Eyes: Eastern Orthodoxy: A Reformed Perspective* (Tain, Scotland: Christian Focus Publications, 2010).

6 Gil Anidjar, *The Jew, the Arab: A History of the Enemy* (Stanford, CA: Stanford University Press, 2003).

7 Arthur Kemp, *March of the Titans: The Complete History of the White Race* (Burlington: Ostara Publications, 2011), 171.

8 Tariq Ali, *Shadows of the Pomegranate Tree* (London: Verso, 1992), 244.

9 See Madina Tlostanova, "Between the Soviet/Russian Dependencies: Neoliberal Delusions, De-Westernizing Options and Decolonial Drives," *Cultural Dynamics* 27, no. 2 (2015): 267–83, DOI: 10.1177/0921374015585230. The history of China presents a similar scenario, except it is also a civilization that was disrupted in the Opium War. Recovery and resurgence, throughout the long nineteenth century and up until today, place the entire configuration (culture, politics, economy) in a double bind: dependency on the US in tension with the task of rebuilding while confronting the difficulties of containment. See, for instance, Kishore Mahbubani, "Is China Expansionist?," in *Has China Won? The Chinese Challenge to American Primacy* (New York: Public Affairs, 2020), 79–104. Mahbubani is the only analyst of the global scene that I know who is familiar with the histories and entanglements of East Asia, Europe, and the US. His skin (let's put it that way) has been soaked in East, South, and Southeast Asia. That makes his work different from similar analyses published by Western politicians, scholars, and journalists. Mahbubani is constantly exploring the imperial difference, although he doesn't employ the term. It is my decolonial reading of his de-Western arguments.

10 The "fundamental fear" we are witnessing and experiencing today is the latest manifestation of the five-hundred-year-old logic of coloniality: defending the sites of power in the discourses of Christianity and the Western countries. On the current production of fear, see Bobby S. Sayyid, *A Fundamental Fear: Eurocentrism and the Emergence of Islamism* (London: Zed Books, 1997), and Corey Robin, *Fear: The History of a Political Idea* (London: Oxford, 2004).

11 Margaret R. Greer, Walter D. Mignolo, and Maureen Quilligan, eds., *Rereading the Black Legend: The Discourses of Racial and Religious Differences in the Renaissance Empires* (Chicago: University of Chicago Press, 2007).

12 Philip C. Almond, "In Spite of Their Differences, Jews, Christians and Muslims Worship the Same God," *The Conversation*, September 5, 2017, https://theconversation.com/in-spite-of-their-differences-jews-christians-and-muslims-worship-the-same-god-83102.

13 Gil Anidjar, *Blood: A Critique of Christianity* (New York: Columbia University Press, 2014).

14 Aníbal Quijano's foundational essay on the coloniality of power is "Colonialidad y modernidad/racionalidad," in *Los conquistados* (Bogotá: Tercer Mundo Editores, 1992), 439–48. An English translation can be found in "Coloniality and Modernity/Rationality," in *Globalizations and Modernities*, ed. Goran Therborn (Stockholm: Forskningsgrådsnämnden, 1999). For an Afro-Caribbean perspective on the significance of events, see Sylvia Wynter, "1492: A 'New World' View," in *Race, Discourse and the Americas: A New World View*, ed. Vera Lawrence and Rex Nettleford (Washington, DC: Smithsonian Institution Press, 1995), 5–57.

15 To understand the northern European "feelings" toward Spaniards and Arabs, it would suffice to read section IV of Immanuel Kant's *Observations on the Feeling of the Beautiful and Sublime*, ed. Patrick Frierson and Paul Guyer (Cambridge, UK: Cambridge University Press, 2011 [1764]).

16 The point I am underscoring here comes to light when reading, back to back, Jean-Jacques Rousseau, *The Social Contract* (London: Penguin, 2004 [1762]), and Charles W. Mills, *The Racial Contract* (Ithaca, NY: Cornell University Press, 1997).

17 The definition of "race" as used in sixteenth-century Spanish can be found in the dictionary by Sebastián de Covarrubias Horozco, *Tesoro de la lengua castellana o Española*, ed. Ignacio Arellano and Rafael Zafra (Madrid: Iberoamericana Vervuert, 2006 [1611]).

18 Barbara Fuchs, "The Spanish Race," in Greer, Mignolo, and Quilligan, *Rereading the Black* Legend, 88–98. In England, and in Shakespeare, the meaning of "Moor" was far from precise. See Emily C. Bartels's "Making More of the Moor: Aaron, Othello, and Renaissance Refashionings of Race" *Shakespeare Quarterly* 41, no. 4 (1990): 433–52, DOI: 10.2307/2870775. See also Ella Shohat, "The Specter of the Blackamoor," *The Comparatist* 42 (2018): 158–88.

19 Alonso de Sandoval, a Creole in the viceroyalty of Nueva Granada (today Colombia and Venezuela), during the first half of the seventeenth century published *De instauranda Aethiopium Salute: Naturaleza, policia sagrada i profana, costumbres i ritos, disciplina i catechismo evangelico de todos etiopes* (1627, 1647). I owe this information to Eduardo Restrepo. For a general overview of Sandoval's treatise, see Juliana Beatriz Almedia de Souza, "Las Casas, Alonso de Sandoval and the Defence of Black Slavery," *Topoi: Revista de Histórica* 2 (2006), http://socialsciences.scielo.org/scielo.php?script=sci_arttext&pid=S1518-33192006000200004.

20 Theo- and ego-politics of knowledge (the two basic frames of the epistemic rhetoric of modernity and the epistemic logic of coloniality), as affirmations of Western epistemology and disaffirmations of non-Western knowledge, are explained in my article "Delinking: The Rhetoric of Modernity, the Logic of Coloniality and the Grammar of De-coloniality," *Cultural Studies* 21, no. 2 (2007): 449–514, doi

.org/10.1080/09502380601162647. Revised editions were translated into German, Swedish, Rumanian, Spanish, and French.

21 Emmanuel Chukwudi Eze, "The Color of Reason: The Idea of 'Race' in Kant's Anthropology," in *Postcolonial African Philosophy: A Critical Reader* (London: Wiley-Blackwell, 1997), 103–40.

22 Bartolomé de Las Casas, *Brevísima descripción de la destrucción de las Indias* (1552), ed. José Miguel Martínez Torrejón, accessed December 22, 2020, http://www.cervantesvirtual.com/obra-visor/brevsima-relacin-de-la-destruccin-de-las-indias-0/html/847e3bed-827e-4ca7-bb80-fdcde7ac955e_18.html. There are many translations with title variations and adaptations based on the politics of the editor to emphasize how barbaric the Spanish were and how civilized the British and Dutch were. See, for example, Roberto Valdeón, "Tears of the Indian and the Power of Translation: John Phillips' Version of *Brevísima relación de la destrucción de las Indias*," *Bulletin of Spanish Studies* 89, no. 6 (2012): 839–58.

23 Bartolomé de Las Casas, *Apologética Historia Sumaria* (Madrid: Alianza Editorial, 1992 [1536]), chapters CCLXIV, CCLXV, CCLSVI, and CCLVII.

24 Aimé Césaire, *Discours sur le colonialisme* (1955). A new edition, followed by *Discours sur la négritude*, was published by Présence Africaine, Paris, in 2004, 36.

25 The nineteenth ecumenical council opened at Trent on December 13, 1545, and closed there on December 4, 1563. Its main object was the definitive determination of the doctrines of the church in answer to the heresies of the Protestants; a further object was the execution of a thorough reform of the inner life of the church by removing the numerous abuses that had developed therein.

26 See Quobna Ottobah Cugoano, *Thoughts and Sentiments on the Evil of Slavery* (London: Penguin Classics, 1999 [1787]).

27 William H. Prescott, *History of the Conquest of Mexico and of the Conquest of Peru* (New York: Random House, 1956 [1843, 1847]).

28 For a more detailed exploration of this idea, see my essay "Coloniality at Large: The Western Hemisphere in the Colonial Horizon of Modernity," *New Centennial Review* 1, no. 2 (2001): 19–54, https://www.jstor.org/stable /41949278.

29 G. W. F. Hegel. *The Philosophy of History*, trans. J. Sibree (New York: Prometheus Books, 1991 [1822]), 102.

30 Gloria Anzaldúa, *Borderlands/La Frontera: The New Mestiza* (San Francisco: Aunt Lute Books, 2007 [1987]), 99.

31 *Romanus Pontifex* (Granting the Portuguese a perpetual monopoly in trade with Africa), January 8, 1455, Papal Encyclicals Online, accessed September 30, 2020, https://www.papalencyclicals.net/nichol05/romanus-pontifex.htm.

32 Angela Weiler, "Introduction: The *Requerimiento* (1513)," Open Anthology of Earlier American Literature, accessed May 5, 2020, https://press.rebus.community /openamlit/chapter/the-requerimiento/.

33 It should be remembered that in the sixteenth century all four continents were interconnected physically and economically in European consciousness, and have been entangled, until today, in the popular and scientific cartographic imaginary. Globalism, at the time, was driven by the global designs of Western

Christian and Spanish monarchs. First it was Britain and then the US in the ensuing five hundred years of Western globalism. Schmitt captured the radical change in his conception of the "second nomos of the Earth." Carl Schmitt, *Les nomos de la terre dans le droit des gens du jus publicum Europeaum*, translated from German to French by Lilyane Deroche Gurcel (Paris: Presses Universitaires de France, 1988 [1950]).

34 It is interesting to note that a sector of the progressive and Marxist left is now taking Schmitt's book as the bible of the forgotten part of the modern/colonial world, Spain. But, still, this is half the story, the one told from the perspective of modernity. Schmitt should not be read today without acknowledging the imperial and racist dimensions of international law. One could imagine that if a person and scholar (whether or not trained in Western universities) takes seriously the inscription on his or her African body and the geopolitics behind the inscription, s/he wouldn't need to read Schmitt to understand that international law and land have gone hand in hand in the modern/colonial formation of capitalism since the sixteenth century. See Siba N'Zatioula Grovogui, *Sovereigns, Quasi Sovereigns, and Africans* (Minneapolis: University of Minnesota Press, 1996).

35 See Elvira Vilches, *New World Gold* (Chicago: University of Chicago Press, 2010); Peter Gordon and Juan José Morales, *The Silver Way: China, Spanish America and the Birth of Globalization, 1515–1865* (London: Penguin Special, 2017).

36 On reciprocity: The Quechua concept of *ayni*, or reciprocity, still exists today. A more encompassing description is relationality of all the cosmos, or *pacha* (kosmos). I refer also to reciprocity, a type of labor based on working to live rather than living to work, as it developed under economic coloniality, from forced slavery to waged labor. When someone needs something and calls for help, the compensation is not with money but with a similar kind of work. Ayni forms of exchange are called *faena* (tasks), which are complemented with *mita* (taking turns) in helping one another (not competing).

37 The history of the *Requerimiento* is not just past history. It is very present. See, for instance, Steven Newcomb, "Why the Papal Bull Claiming Dominion over Non-Christian Lands Still Matters," *Indian Country Today*, August 2013, https://indiancountrytoday.com/archive/why-papal-bull-claiming-dominion-over-non-christian-lands-still-matters-HKRuUqe_5kCiOS52QpZCEg.

38 Rice, "Campaign 2000."

39 Juan de Vallejo, *Memorial de la vida de Fray Francisco Jiménez de Cisneros*, ed. Antonio de la Torre y del Cerro (Madrid: Centro de Estudios Históricos, 1913), 35. A modernized transcription by Daniel Einsenberg:

> Para desarraigarles del todo de la sobredicha su perversa y mala secta, les mandó a los dichos alfaquís tomar todos sus alcoranes y todos los otros libros particulares, cuantos se pudieron haber, los cuales fueron más de 4 ó 5 mil volúmenes, entre grandes y pequeños, y hacer muy grandes fuegos y quemarlos todos; en que había entre ellos infinitos que las encuadernaciones que tenían de plata y otras cosas moriscas, puestas en ellos, valían 8 y

10 ducados, y otros de allí abajo. Y aunque algunos hacían mancilla para los tomar y aprovecharse de los pergaminos y papel y encuadernaciones, su señoría reverendísima mandó expresamente que no se tomase ni ninguno lo hiciese. Y así se quemaron todos, sin quedar memoria, como dicho es, excepto los libros de medicina, que había muchos y se hallaron, que éstos mandó que se quedasen; de los cuales su señoría mandó traer bien 30 ó 40 volúmenes de libros, y están hoy en día puestos en la librería de su insigne colegio y universidad de Alcalá, y otros muchos añafiles y trompeticas que están en la su iglesia de San Ildefonso, puestos, en memoria, donde su señoría reverendísima está sepultado.

Daniel Eisenberg, "Cisneros y la Quema de los Manuscritos Granadinos," *Ballandalus*, July 1, 2013, https://ballandalus.wordpress.com/2013/07/01/cisneros-y-la-quema-de-los-manuscritos-granadinos-by-daniel-eisenberg/. See also Meagan O'Halley, "Placing Islam: Alternative Visions of the Morisco Expulsion and Spanish-Muslim Christian Relations in the Sixteenth Century" (PhD diss., Duke University, 2013), chapter 1, http://dukespace.lib.duke.edu/dspace/bitstream/handle/10161/7193/OHalley_duke_0066D_11863.pdf?sequence=1.

40 David Hollinger, *Post-Ethnic America: Beyond Multiculturalism*, 2nd ed. (New York: Basic Books, 2006 [1996]).

41 Rice, "Campaign 2000."

42 W. D. Hurton, "The Military-Industrial Complex Revisited," in *Global Focus: US Foreign Policy at the Turn of the Millennium*, ed. M. Hoey and T. Barry (New York: St. Martin Press, 2000), 21–43.

43 Resources for exploring both topics are enormous and include bibliographies, videographies, and webpages, as well as the decolonial organizations described in the previous paragraph. Here are some examples: Islamic Human Rights Commission, *Islamophobia, Diversity and the Crisis of Democracy*, video, September 17, 2014, https://www.youtube.com/watch?v=MziMD2dHyU4; Bobby S. Sayyid, *Recalling the Caliphate: Decolonisation and World Order* (London: Hurst and Co., 2014); Emma Pérez, *The Decolonial Imaginary: Writing Chicanas into History* (Bloomington: Indiana University Press, 1999); Monica Hanna, Jennifer Hartog Vargas, José David Saldívar, eds., *Junot Díaz and the Decolonial Imagination* (Durham, NC: Duke University Press, 2016).

Three. Dispensable and Bare Lives

1 Racism is not a question of knowing but of sensing. However, sensing is related to and managed by knowledge. Think about how racism has "manifested" in the US in the past decade. On a larger scale, and connected with the impact of linear global thinking every day, the control and management of knowledge and ways of knowing imply control and management of the senses, of sensibility, of aesthesis. On this topic see Constance Classen, *A Cultural History of the Senses in the Age of Empire* (London: Bloomsbury Academic, 2018).

2 Leroy Little Bear, "Indigenous Knowledge and Western Sciences," Banff Center Talk, January 14, 2015, https://www.youtube.com/watch?v=gJSJ28eEUjI; Humberto R. Maturana, "Reality: The Search for Objectivity or the Quest for a Compelling Argument," *Irish Journal of Psychology* 9, no. 1 (1988): 25–82, DOI: 10.1080/03033910.1988.10557705.

3 This chapter was rewritten after spending two years at the Decolonial Summer School in Middelburg, Netherlands, which I codesigned and cotaught with Rolando Vázquez. In 2010 and 2011 we explored "Coloniality, Slavery and the Holocaust," https://h-net.msu.edu/cgi-bin/logbrowse.pl?trx=vx&list=H -Ideas&month=1103&week=b&msg=XsfWXbvQrfLXho53Ic42jg&user=&pw=. We did not *compare* slavery and the Holocaust but we asked instead what place each event has been assigned in the colonial matrix of power (CMP) and how they came to be as a consequence of the logic of racial classification that surfaced in the late fifteenth and the sixteenth centuries and resulted in the expulsion of the Jews from the Iberian Peninsula and the massive trade of African human beings in the Atlantic. Finding the hidden logic connecting the two events, 450 years apart, was an effort to change the terms of the conversation and to illuminate the logic of coloniality hidden underneath the rhetoric of modernity.

4 The controversial issue of whether or not Elizabeth I deported "blackamoors" is evidence that "Blacks" and "Moors" were a concern of the British and Spanish, and part of the history of the Black Legend (see chapter 1). On "deportation," see Emily C. Bartels, "Too Many Blackamoors: Deportation, Discrimination, and Elizabeth I," *SEL: Studies in English Literature 1500–1900* 46, no. 2 (2006): 305–22, DOI: 10.1353/ sel.2006.0012.

5 Margaret R. Greer, Walter D. Mignolo, and Maureen Quilligan, eds., *Rereading the Black Legend: The Discourses of Religious and Racial Difference in the Renaissance Empires* (Chicago: University of Chicago Press, 2007); see also chapter 2 in this volume.

6 Bartels, "Too Many Blackamoors," points out that in 1596 Queen Elizabeth issued an "open letter" to the Lord Mayor of London, announcing that "there are of late divers Blackamoors brought into this realm, of which kind of people there are already here to many," and they could have been Muslim or not in Europe and Africa. As a consequence, when "African Blacks" were enslaved and transported to the New World, they were severed from their respective African kingdoms and found themselves with diverse languages, diverse systems of belief, and diverse memories. In retrospect, the racial matrix (and the historical foundation of racism as we know it today) is a combination of two structures, one religious and one secular. Christian theology and European egology (in the sense suggested by René Descartes and Immanuel Kant) both provided a frame for racial classification and management of the population. Let's imagine two triangles (see the illustrations in chapter 1 of this book). One of them has Christian theology/Christians at the apex of the triangle and Islamic Theology/Muslims/Moors and Jewish Theology/ Jews at the two ends of the base. "Moriscos" and "conversos," along the legs of the triangle, designate the "religious mestizaje," the mixing of Christian and Moorish blood on the one hand and Christian and Jewish blood on the other. This was

clear in the Iberian Peninsula or, if you wish, in the heart of the emerging empire. In the colonies, the situation was different since there was no religion of the book and therefore no order that "blackamoors" be deported from the country. Shortly after, Queen Elizabeth reiterated her "good pleasure to have those kind of people sent out of the land" and commissioned the merchant Casper van Senden to "take up" certain "Blackamoors here in this realme and to transport them into Spain and Portugall." Finally, in 1601, she complained again about the "great numbers of *Negers* and Blackamoors which "are crept into this realm." She defamed them as "infidels, having no understanding of Christ or his Gospel," and, one last time, authorized their deportation.

7 For an elaboration of these two concepts, see Walter D. Mignolo, "Epistemic Disobedience, Independent Thought, and Decolonial Freedom," *Theory, Culture and Society* 26, no. 7–8 (2009): 159–81, DOI: 10.1177/0263276409349275.

8 Maturana, "Reality."

9 This idea is further developed in the introduction and epilogue of this book, and illustrated by several of the articles contained in Greer, Mignolo, and Quilligan, eds., *Rereading the Black Legend*.

10 See chapter 2 of this book for more on these issues.

11 By "modern/colonial" I refer to the decolonial perspective opened up by Aníbal Quijano, who brought forward the missing half of the story wherein "modernity" appears as a totality by ignoring that there is no modernity without coloniality. Moreover, when I say "imperial/colonial" I refer to both sides of the equation, the metropolis and its colonial dominion. However, imperialism without settler colonies and modern imperialism (i.e., Western capitalist empires) without colonies have been in place since the nineteenth century (e.g., England in South America, and England and the US in China since the Opium Wars); there are no Western capitalist empires without coloniality. Thus, by "imperial/colonial" I also mean "imperiality/coloniality." Lucy Mayblin, "Modernity/Coloniality," Global Social Theory, accessed May 5, 2020, https://globalsocialtheory.org/concepts/colonialitymodernity.

12 Walter D. Mignolo, "Delinking," *Cultural Studies* 21, no. 2 (2007): 449–514. For a revised version in French, see *La désobéissance épistémique: Rhétorique de la modernité, logique de la colonialité et grammaire de la décolonialité*, trans. Yasmine Jouhari and Marc Maesschalck (Amsterdam: Peter Lang, 2015).

13 Among the profuse literature on the historical aspects of the event, one book stands out for my argument: Zygmunt Bauman, *Modernity and the Holocaust* (Ithaca, NY: Cornell University Press, 1989). Bauman's argument is sociological and addresses the shortcomings of sociology in understanding the event. For my argument, I retain the (rhetoric of) modernity that justified (following the logic of coloniality) the Holocaust.

14 Guy Taylor, "Netanyahu Slams Kerry for Insisting that Israel Can Be Jewish or Democratic, Not Both," *Washington Times*, December 28, 2016, http://www.washingtontimes.com/news/2016/dec/28/john-kerry-israel-can-be-jewish-or-democratic-not-/.

15 Quobna Ottobah Cugoano, *Thoughts and Sentiments on the Evil of Slavery* (London: Penguin Classics, 1999 [1787]), 85.

16 And it would be necessary to remember here the conceptual arguments and the genealogy of the decolonial thoughts of Mahatma Gandhi, Frantz Fanon, Patrice Lumumba, Steve Biko, and Amílcar Cabral (see the introduction to this book).

17 Eric Williams, *Capitalism and Slavery* (Chapel Hill: University of North Carolina Press, 1994 [1944]), 32.

18 Robert Mitchel and Catherine Waldby, *Tissue Economies: Blood, Organs, and Cell Lines in Late Capitalism* (Durham, NC: Duke University Press, 2006). The obvious connections between enslaved Africans in the early imperial/colonial Atlantic period and enslaved and exploited women today have made even the editorial page of the *New York Times*. See Bob Hebert, "Today's Hidden Slave Trade," *New York Times*, October 2007, https://www.nytimes.com/2007/10/27/opinion/27herbert.html.

19 "Economic and Financial Indicators: Poverty," *The Economist*, April 19, 2007, https://www.economist.com/economic-and-financial-indicators/2007/04/19/poverty. A good account of the "invention of economic poverty" (different from the religious sense of "poverty of spirit") was provided by Karl Polanyi, *The Great Transformation: The Political and Economic Origins of Our Time* (Boston: Beacon Press, 1944), 35–58.

20 Ankie Hoogvelt, *Globalization and the Postcolonial World: The New Political Economy and Development* (Baltimore: Johns Hopkins University Press, 1997), xii.

21 Henry George, *Progress and Poverty, An Inquiry into the Cause of Industrial Depressions and of Increase of Want with Increase of Wealth: The Remedy* (New York: Robert Schalkenbach Foundation, 1997 [1879]).

22 Charles Duhigg, "At Many Homes, More Profit and Less Nursing," *New York Times*, September 23, 2007, https://www.nytimes.com/2007/09/23/business/23nursing.html. To what extent Obamacare changed this habit requires another investigation.

23 Andrew Ward, "Bush Digs in over Healthcare Bill," *Financial Times*, September 21, 2007, https://www.ft.com/content/a3a9fc76-71e5-11dc-8960-0000779fd2ac.

24 Norbert Wiener, *The Human Uses of Human Beings* (New York: Houghton Mifflin Harcourt, 1950). Wiener's intuition is at full speed today, and the spirit of economic coloniality (benefits first, lives second) is also expanding. See Frank Schirrmacher, *Ego: The Game of Life* (London: Polity Press, 2015).

25 See Bauman, *Modernity and the Holocaust*, chapter 3.

26 Hannah Arendt, *The Origins of Totalitarianism* (New York: Harcourt Brace, 1976 [1948]), 297.

27 Arendt, *The Origins of Totalitarianism*, 295.

28 Aimé Césaire, *Discourse on Colonialism*, trans. Joan Pinkham (New York: Monthly Review, 1972 [1955]), 36. At the time of Césaire's writing, the Herero genocide was not known publicly. It has been exposed during the past couple of decades. See Andre Vitcheck, "Namibia: Germany's African Holocaust," *Global Research*, September 23, 2014, http://www.globalresearch.ca/namibia-germanys-african-holocaust/5403852; see also the brilliant documentary film by director Jean-Marie Tenó, *Le malentendu colonial* (Colonial misunderstanding), 73:00, Cameroon, 2004.

29 Khatija Bibi Khan, "The Kaiser's Holocaust: The Coloniality of German's Forgotten Genocide of the Nama and the Herero in Namibia," *African Identities* 10, no. 3 (2012), 211–20.

30 Claudia Koonz, *The Nazi Conscience* (Cambridge, MA: Belknap Press, 2003), 11–12.

31 Lewis Gordon, "What Does It Mean to Be a Problem? W. E. B. Dubois and the Study of the Black Folk," in *Existentia Africana: Understanding Africana Existential Thought* (London: Routledge, 2000), 62–95.

32 Arendt, *The Origins of Totalitarianism*, 291.

33 Arendt, *The Origins of Totalitarianism*, 292.

34 Kelly Oliver, *Technologies of Life and Death: From Cloning to Capital Punishment* (New York: Fordham University Press, 2013).

35 Richard W. Rahn, "Financial Fascism," April 28, 2010, reprinted by the Cato Institute, https://www.cato.org/publications/commentary/financial-fascism. See also Thomas J. DiLorenzo, "Economic Fascism," Foundation for Economic Education, June 1994.

36 Arendt, *The Origins of Totalitarianism*, 293.

37 Walter D. Mignolo, "The Darker Side of the Enlightenment: A Decolonial Reading of Kant's Geography," in *The Darker Side of Western Modernity: Global Futures, Decolonial Options* (Durham, NC: Duke University Press, 2011), 181–212.

38 The point was forcefully made by Franz Hinkelammert after the invasion of Kosovo. See his article "The Hidden Logic of Modernity: Locke and the Inversion of Human Rights," *World and Knowledges Otherwise* 1, no. 1 (2004): 1–27.

39 Arendt, *The Origins of Totalitarianism*, 293.

40 Arendt, *The Origins of Totalitarianism*, 297.

41 Both quotes from Arendt, *The Origins of Totalitarianism*, 297. On Giorgio Agamben, see Eva Plonowska Ziarek, "Bare Life," in *Impasses of the Post-Global: Theory in the Era of Climate Change*, vol. 2, ed. Henry Sussman (Ann Arbor, MI: Open Humanities Press, 2012), 194–211.

42 Both quotes from Arendt, *The Origins of Totalitarianism*, 297.

43 As a significant aside we should remember former US president Ronald Reagan's (in)famous 1987 speech in Berlin in which he admonished the leader of the Soviet Union, Mikhail Gorbachev, "Mr. Gorbachev, tear down this wall!!" Yet, today, the "wall" shall be rebuilt!

44 Arendt, *The Origins of Totalitarianism*, 297.

45 Walter D. Mignolo, "I Am Where I Do: Remapping the Order of Knowledge," in *The Darker Side of Western Modernity*, 77–118.

46 Francisco de Vitoria, *Relectio de Indis, o libertad de los Indios*, bilingual critical edition by L. Pereña and J. M. Perez Prendes, introductory studies by V. Beltrán de Herrera et al. (Madrid: Consejo Superior de Investigaciones Científicas, 1967 [1539]). For more detail see Antony Anghie, *Imperialism, Sovereignty and the Making of International Law* (Cambridge, UK: Cambridge University Press, 2005).

47 György E. Szönyi, "Broadening Horizons of Renaissance Humanism from the Antiquity to the New World," *Primerjalna književnost* 41, no. 2 (2018): 5–34.

48 For a revision of the debate and the continuity of the issues debated then with the war on terror being enacted now, see Daniel R. Brunstetter and Dana Zartner, "Just War against Barbarians: Revisiting the Valladolid Debates between Sepúlveda and Las Casas," *Political Studies* 59, no. 3 (2010): 733–52.

49 See Donoso Cortés, *Essays on Catholicism, Liberalism and Socialism: Considered in Their Fundamental Principles* (London: Forgotten Books, 2017 [1852]).

50 On this topic, it is good to remember once in a while the classic article by Carl E. Pletsch, "The Three Worlds, or the Division of Social Scientific Labor, circa 1950–1975," *Comparative Studies in Society and History* 23, no. 4 (1981): 565–90.

51 Siba N'Zatioula Grovogui, *Sovereigns, Quasi Sovereigns, and Africans: Race and Self-Determination in International Law* (Minneapolis: University of Minnesota Press, 1996), 65.

52 The role of Christianity in the formation of the CMP could be inferred from Michael Prior's study *The Bible and Colonialism: A Moral Critique* (London: Sheffield Academic Press, 1997).

53 Tomoko Masuzawa, *The Invention of World Religion* (Chicago: University of Chicago Press, 2005), part I.

54 American Israel Public Affairs Committee (AIPAC), "Our Mission," accessed August 15, 2020, https://www.aipac.org/.

Four. Decolonizing the Nation-State

1 Gianni Vattimo and Michael Marder, eds., *Deconstructing Zionism: A Critique of Political Metaphysics* (London: Bloomsbury Academic, 2013).

2 This chapter follows up on Aníbal Quijano's seminal essay "Estado-nación, ciudadanía y democracia," in *Democracia para una nueva sociedad (modelo para armar)*, ed. Helena González and Heidful Schmidt (Caracas: Nueva Sociedad, 1997), 139–52.

3 I am grateful to Santiago Slabodsky not only for reading this piece and making recommendations, but also for engaging in a discussion of his recommendations. I am also grateful to him for over ten years of conversation on Zionism, Judaism, anti-Semitism, and decolonial thinking, as well as for letting me read his chapter on Theodor Herzl from *Decolonial Judaism* before it was published.

4 Marc Ellis, *Judaism Does Not Equal Israel* (New York: The New Press, 2009).

5 I qualify "modernity" as "Western" because "modernity" is not the ontic outcome of universal history, but the Western/European selection and interpretation of the unaccountable flow of human deeds all over the planet in different temporalities. Decolonially speaking, "modernity" is the name projected in and by Western narratives across the planet to affirm its own *constitution* as the center of space and the present time while destituting, by the same token, all of what is considered to be in the margins and in the past. Modernity is a concept built on the colonization of space (we are the center and you are the margin) and of time (we are the present and you are the past). Modernity is constituted by a heterogeneous set of self-fashioned narratives (e.g., see the level of the enunciation in the introduction to this book) by European actors running institutions of global relevance,

educational systems, theories of the social, cultural, and natural worlds, etc.—all based in knowledge sanctioned by European languages, while narrating their own achievements and legitimizing dispossession, overrule, and invasion.

6 Theodor Herzl, *The Jewish State*, trans. Sylvie D'Avigdor (New York: American Zionist Emergency Council, 1946 [1896]), reproduced at Jewish Virtual Library, accessed August 23, 2020, www.jewishvirtuallibrary.org/jsource/Zionism/herzl2 .html. When Herzl wrote his programmatic text, he had fully embraced the rhetoric of modernity, but from a subaltern position: there was no state yet where he could see the consequences of the implementation of his ideas. A case for reflection: projects of liberation from a subaltern position are just that—projects. We could cite many cases, like Vladimir Lenin's writings before the Russian Revolution and the advent of the Soviet Union. Lenin fully endorsed the rhetoric of modernity from a Marxist, rather than a liberal, point of view. See Nikolai Ssorin-Chaikov, "Modernity and Time," in *Two Lenins: A Brief Anthropology of Time* (Chicago: Hau Books, 2017), 121–131, accessed May 26, 2020, https://haubooks.org /wp-content/uploads/2017/02/978-0-9973675-3-9-text.pdf.

7 Michael Prior, *The Bible and Colonialism: A Moral Critique* (London: Sheffield Academic Press, 1997).

8 In this vein, see Santiago Slabodsky, *Decolonial Judaism: Triumphal Failures of Barbaric Thinking* (New York: Palgrave, 2014).

9 Regarding the term "patria": In English, "patriot" is defined as someone who would die for his "country." In French and Spanish, the term is used to indicate someone who would die for his *patrie* or his *patria*.

10 To follow my argument, it would help here to recall a memorable statement by Joe Biden quoted in the previous chapter: "To be Zionist, it is not necessary to be Jewish." ShalomTV, excerpt from interview with Joe Biden, March 6, 2013, accessed May 5, 2020, video, https://www.youtube.com/watch?v=Uo-UXZ-1ups.

11 Ellis, *Judaism Does Not Equal Israel*, ix.

12 Desmond Tutu, "Foreword," in Ellis, *Judaism Does Not Equal Israel*, vii–viii.

13 Giulio Meotti, "Tutu's War on Israel, Jews," *Y-Net Magazine*, August 11, 2011, http:// www.ynetnews.com/articles/0,7340,L-4107913,00.html.

14 Alan M. Dershowitz, "Bishop Tutu Is No Saint When It Comes to Jews," Gatestone Institute, International Policy Council, December 20, 2010, http:// www.gatestoneinstitute.org/1742/bishop-tutu-is-no-saint-when-it-comes-to-jews; Robert Fine, "Blame Games Won't Lead Us to Peace," *Mail and Guardian*, October 2010, https://mg.co.za/article/2010-10-08-blame-game-wont-lead-us-to-peace/.

15 Jewish Virtual Library, "The Six-Day War: Background and Overview (June 5–10, 1967)," accessed May 5, 2020, https://www.jewishvirtuallibrary.org/background -and-overview-six-day-war.

16 An interesting effort in this direction is the book by Roxanne L. Euben, *Enemy in the Mirror: Islamic Fundamentalism and the Limits of Modern Rationalism: A Work of Comparative Political Theory* (Princeton, NJ: Princeton University Press, 1999).

17 When describing communities of faith, here is not the place to go into the communities of belief in Asia (Confucianism, Buddhism), in Africa, and in the great

civilizations of Tawantinsuyu and Anahuac (Incas, Mayas, and Aztecs), but they shall be kept in mind in the larger picture of religions, ethics, and spirituality destituted by Western Christianity.

18 By 1900, when political Zionism emerged, the major European centers of Jewish population were Russia (3 million-plus) and the Austro-Hungarian Empire (1.2 million-plus). In the US, the Jewish population was about 1.5 million. By 1942, the main concentration of Jews was in central Europe. Jewish Virtual Library, "Modern Jewish History: Distribution of the Jews in the World (1942)," https://www .jewishvirtuallibrary.org/distribution-of-the-jews-in-the-world-1942. If cultural Zionism had its point of origination in Russia and Poland, political Zionism emerged in central Europe, where the winds of the West were blowing strong: the Austro-Hungarian Empire collapsed in 1918.

19 Franz Hinkelammert, "The Hidden Logic of Modernity: Locke and the Inversion of Human Rights," *World and Knowledges Otherwise* 1, no. 1 (2004): 1–27.

20 On the engineering aspect of Nazi genocide, see Zygmunt Bauman, *Modernity and the Holocaust* (Ithaca, NY: Cornell University Press, 1989). On the "yellow peril," see Gregory Blue, "Gobineau on China: Race Theory, the 'Yellow Peril' and the Critique of Modernity," *Journal of World History* 10, no. 1 (1999): 93–139, DOI: 10.1353/ jwh.2005.0003.

21 See Benedict Anderson, *Imagined Communities: Reflections on the Origins and Spread of Nationalism*, rev. ed. (London: Verso, 2016); Sara Castro-Kláren and John Chastin, *Beyond Imagined Communities: Reading and Writing the Nation in Nineteenth Century Latin America* (Washington, DC: Woodrow Wilson Center, 2003). For Canada, see Glean Sean Coulthard, *Red Skin, White Masks: Rejecting the Colonial Politics of Recognition* (Minneapolis: University of Minnesota Press, 2014). In India the story is different still. See Partha Chatterjee, *The Nation and Its Fragments: Colonial and Postcolonial Histories* (Princeton, NJ: Princeton University Press, 1993).

22 Odin Ávila Rojas, "La experiencia Zapatista: Análisis sobre sus prácticas democráticas," *Revista de Ciencias Sociales* 31, no. 42 (2018, 195–211); Walter D. Mignolo and Rolando Vázquez, "Mexico's Indigenous Congress: Decolonising Politics," Al Jazeera, September 27, 2017, https://www.aljazeera.com/opinions/2017/9/27/mexicos -indigenous-congress-decolonising-politics/. See also Bobby S. Sayyid, *Recalling the Caliphate: Decolonisation and the World Order* (London: Hurst and Co., 2014).

23 Catherine Walsh, "The Plurinational and Intercultural State: Decolonization and State Re-founding in Ecuador," *RUDN Journal of Philosophy* 1 (2012) 103–15.

24 For a detailed account, see Michael Prior, *Zionism and the State of Israel: A Moral Inquiry* (London: Routledge, 1999).

25 A recent detailed and insightful account is available in David Nirenberg, *Anti-Judaism: The Western Tradition* (Chicago: University of Chicago Press, 2013), 13–47, 217–68.

26 An account of the racial formation in the sixteenth century, as we know it today, could be found in Margaret Greer, Walter Mignolo, and Maureen Quilligan, eds., *Rereading the Black Legend: The Discourse of Religious and Racial Difference in the Renaissance Empire* (Chicago: University of Chicago Press, 2008).

27 Regarding my use of the term "shahanate": As I have touched on in previous chapters, the shah was not an emperor; he was a shah—in the same way that an emperor was not a shah. Consequently, Persia was not an empire but a shahanate, in the same way that Rome was not a shahanate but an empire. If we fail to make these distinctions across time and space, we remain trapped in the colonial and imperial difference of imagining that all socio-economic-cultural organizations that in the West are conceptualized as empires derive from Julius Caesar and are modeled on the Roman Empire. If we step out—delink—from the cognitive imperial dream, then the Roman Empire could just as correctly be called the Roman sultanate or the Roman Incanate, for example.

28 "Pre-State Israel: The Sykes-Picot Agreement (1916)," Jewish Virtual Library, accessed September 30, 2020, https://www.jewishvirtuallibrary.org/the-sykes-picot -agreement-1916.

29 Robert Melson, Introduction, "The Armenian Genocide: Selected Articles from *Holocaust and Genocide Studies*," Oxford Academic, accessed December 29, 2020, https://academic.oup.com/DocumentLibrary/HGS/Melson_Introduction.pdf.

30 Sun Yat-sen, *The Three Principles of the People*, trans. Frank W. Price (London: Soul Care Publishing, 2011 [1924]). Sun Yat-sen embraced nationalism in a double critique of the Qin Dynasty and of foreign imperialism (which at that time was only Western—the agents of the Opium Wars). Democracy and socialism did not have for Sun Yat-sen the same meaning that they did in the West. Both were useful to the "three principles of the people." Critics of this work abound. I am only interested in the impact of nationalism (of the people) that in China opened up the search for the state (a form of governance). The trajectory is known from the split of Mao Zedong and Chiang Kai-shek over the correct interpretation of *The Three Principles*, the governance of Mao Zedong, the opening of Deng Xiaoping, and the history since then to Xi Jinping. In terms of the nation-state, it could not be avoided totally, but China did not fall into the trap of a universal form of nation-state and the universality of democracy, which, of course, is a fundamental component in the rhetoric of "democratic nation-states."

31 Toby Dodge, *Inventing Iraq: The Failure of Nation Building and a Future Denied* (New York: Columbia University Press, 2003).

32 Walter D. Mignolo, "Citizenship, Knowledge and the Limits of Humanity," *American Literary History* 18, no. 2 (2006): 312–31.

33 Conrad Cherry, *God's New Israel: Religious Interpretations of American Destiny* (Chapel Hill: University of North Carolina Press, 1998); Prior, *The Bible and Colonialism*.

34 Desmond Tutu, "Israel Liberate Yourself by Liberating Palestine," *Popular Resistance*, August 20, 2014, https://popularresistance.org/desmond-tutu-israel-liberate -yourselves-by-liberating-palestine/.

35 Karen B. Brodkin Sacks, *How Jews Became White Folks and What That Says about Race in America* (New Brunswick, NJ: Rutgers University Press, 1998), 79–96.

36 Michael Brenner, *Zionism: A Brief History*, trans. Shelley L. Frisch (Princeton, NJ: Marku and Wienner, 2003). However, from a decolonial perspective, "international nationalism" is not a paradox but a historical consequence of decolonial

struggles in Asia and Africa (Bandung Conference, 1955) and in nonaligned countries elsewhere (Non-Aligned Movement Conference, Belgrade, 1961). Still, the directionality of these projects is not congruent: decolonial struggles were directed toward ending Western imperial control of their territories and toward building their own states, while Zionism moved in the reverse direction, wishing to gain a territory and build a state with the support of imperial forces.

37 "*Requerimiento*, 1510 (Requirement: Pronouncement to be Read by Spanish Conquerors to Defeated Indians)," National Humanities Center, accessed September 30, 2020, https://nationalhumanitiescenter.org/pds/amerbegin/contact/text7/requirement.pdf.

38 Carl Schmitt, *The Nomos of the Earth in the International Law of the Jus Publicum Europaeum*, trans. G. L. Ulmen (New York: Telos Press, 2006 [1950]). For the CMP as the grounding of Western civilization, see Walter D. Mignolo, *The Darker Side of Western Modernity: Global Futures, Decolonial Options* (Durham, NC: Duke University Press, 2011).

39 Patrick Gathara, "Berlin 1884: Remembering the Conference That Divided Africa," Al Jazeera, November 15, 2019, https://www.aljazeera.com/opinions/2019/11/15/berlin-1884-remembering-the-conference-that-divided-africa/.

40 Antony Anghie, *Imperialism, Sovereignty and the Making of International Law* (Cambridge, UK: Cambridge University Press, 2007); Sba N'Zatioula Grovogui, *Sovereigns, Quasi-Sovereigns, and Africans: Race and Self-Determination in International Law* (Minneapolis: University of Minnesota Press, 2005).

41 Herzl, *The Jewish State*.

42 Herzl, *The Jewish State*.

43 Slabodsky, *Decolonial Judaism*.

44 Berdal Aral, "The Idea of Human Rights as Perceived in the Ottoman Empire," *Human Rights Quarterly* 26, no. 2 (2004): 454–82. Notice that the Ottoman sultanate was not an empire (see discussion above), a simple example of the omnipresence of coloniality of knowledge.

45 It is noteworthy, for example, that in President Barack Obama's speech on the occasion of the ten-year anniversary of the invasion of Iraq, he spelled out in great detail the cost of human lives—not only in terms of the dead but also in the personal psychological consequences for the soldiers and their families, the physical and mental wounds that will be with them for the rest of their lives. Yet he mentioned only the lives of US citizens and passed over in silence the hundred thousand–plus Iraqi lives lost, the destruction of the country's infrastructure, and the disaggregation of the Iraqi state's social fabric.

46 Steve Holland, "Trump to Host Israel-United Arab Emirates Deal-Signing Ceremony on September 15," Reuters, September 15, 2020, https://www.reuters.com/article/israel-emirates-usa-int/trump-to-host-israel-united-arab-emirates-deal-signing-ceremony-on-september-15-idUSKBN25Z2VY.

47 Michael Martinez, "5 Things to Know about Obama's First Presidential Visit to Israel," CNN, March 20, 2013, http://www.cnn.com/2013/03/20/politics/obama-mideast-five-things/.

48 The "Middle East" was a Western/US invention at a time when the Industrial
    Revolution brought about the need for "natural resources" (oil) and oil was dis-
    covered in the region. It was US naval officer Alfred T. Mahan that baptized the
    region in 1902. See chapters 8 and 10 of this book.
49 John Wojcik, "More than Meets the Eye behind the Iran Sanctions," *People's
    World*, December 6, 2016, https://www.peoplesworld.org/article/more-than-meets
    -the-eye-behind-the-iran-sanctions.

Five. The Many Faces of Cosmo-polis

1 Manfred B. Steger, *Globalism: The New Market Ideology* (London: Rowman and
   Littlefield, 2001).
2 Peimin Ni, "The Silk Order: A Philosophical Perspective," DOC Research Institute, March 26, 2018, https://doc-research.org/2018/03/silk-order-philosophical
   -perspective/. Ni offers a de-Westernizing perspective. For a defensive re-
   Westernizing perspective, see Tim Winter, "Silk Roads and Cultural Routes,"
   E-flux Architecture, accessed September 30, 2020, https://www.e-flux.com
   /architecture/new-silk-roads/313107/silk-roads-and-cultural-routes/.
3 The need to expand Christianity was at work before the "discovery" of America. At that time, the only possible expansion was toward the East. Portugal was
   navigating the Mediterranean and the Atlantic to the south and into the Indian
   Ocean. Castile had yet to emerge. Columbus, Italian himself, was well aware of
   these "rumors." For the seed of the Christian global designs that materialized in
   the Atlantic in the sixteenth century, see Francis M. Rogers, "The Council of
   Florence and the Portuguese Princess," in *The Quest for Eastern Christians: Travels
   and Rumors in the Age of Discovery* (Minneapolis: University of Minnesota Press,
   1962), 50–70.
4 See, for example, Seldon Pollock, "Cosmopolitanism and the Vernacular in History," *Public Culture* 12, no. 3 (2000): 15–54.
5 Immanuel Kant, "What Is Enlightenment?," website of Columbia University,
   orig. pub. 1784, accessed June 1, 2020, http://www.columbia.edu/acis/ets/CCREAD
   /etscc/kant.html.
6 Charles Taylor, "The Politics of Recognition," in *Multiculturalism: Examining the
   Politics of Recognition*, ed. A. Gutmann (Princeton, NJ: Princeton University Press,
   1992), 25–73; Jurgen Habermas, *The Inclusion of the Other: Studies in Political Theory*,
   ed. Ciaran Cronin and Pablo de Greiff (Boston: MIT Press, 1998).
7 This argument is being forcefully made by First Nations scholars in Canada. See
   Glen Coulthard, *Red Skin, White Masks: Rejecting the Colonial Politics of Recognition*
   (Minneapolis: University of Minnesota Press, 2014); Leanne Betasamosake Simpson, *As We Have Always Done: Indigenous Freedom from Radical Resistance* (Minneapolis: University of Minnesota Press, 2015).
8 See Taiaiake Alfred, *Wasáse: Indigenous Pathways of Action and Freedom* (Toronto:
   University of Toronto Press, 2009), and *Peace, Power, Righteousness: An Indigenous
   Manifesto* (New York: Oxford University Press, 2009); Leanne Simpson, *Dancing

on Our Turtle's Back: Stories of Nishnaabeg Re-Creation, Resurgence, and New Emergence (Winnipeg, MB: Arbeiter Ring Publishing, 2011).

9 For (modern) critical cosmopolitanism, see Gerard Delanty, "The Cosmopolitan Imagination: Critical Cosmopolitanism and Social Theory," *British Journal of Sociology* 57, no. 1 (2006): 25–47.

10 In this section I am following Aníbal Quijano's concept and argument. See "Heterogeneidad histórico structural," *IV Encuentro de la Cátedra América Latina*, Rio de Janeiro, Brazil, video October 22, 2013, https://www.youtube.com/watch ?v=NXrD1_gTbNQ. See also Walter D. Mignolo, "Cosmopolitan Localisms: Overcoming Colonial and Imperial Differences," in *The Darker Side of Western Modernity: Global Futures, Decolonial Options* (Durham, NC: Duke University Press, 2011), 252–94.

11 Walter D. Mignolo, "(De)Coloniality at Large: Time and the Colonial Difference," in *The Darker Side of Western Modernity*, 149–80.

12 See Bernt Reiter, ed., *Constructing the Pluriverse: The Geopolitics of Knowledge* (Durham, NC: Duke University Press, 2018).

13 Karen Tumulty, "How Donald Trump Came Up with 'Make America Great Again,'" *Washington Post*, January 18, 2017, https://www.washingtonpost.com /politics/how-donald-trump-came-up-with-make-america-great-again/2017/01/17 /fb6acf5e-dbf7-11e6-ad42-f3375f271c9c_story.html.

14 Xi Jinping, "President Jinping's Speech to Davos in Full," World Economic Forum, January 17, 2017, https://www.weforum.org/agenda/2017/01/full-text-of -xi-jinping-keynote-at-the-world-economic-forum. For more details on this topic, see Liu Ming, "Xi Jinping's Vision of a Community with a Shared Future for Humankind," in Ren Xiao and Liu Ming, *Chinese Perspectives on International Relations for the Jinping Era*, National Bureau of Asian Research, Special Report #85, June 2020, https://www.nbr.org/wp-content/uploads/pdfs/publications/sr85 _chineseperspectives_jun2020.pdf.

15 May Sim, "A Confucian Approach to Human Rights," *History of Philosophy Quarterly* 21, no. 4 (2004): 337–56.

16 Joseph Höffner, *La ética colonial española del siglo de oro: Cristianismo y dignidad humana*, translated into Spanish by Franscisco de Asis Caballero (Madrid: Ediciones de Cultura Hispánica, 1957 [1947]): 289–335; Julia Kristeva, *Strangers to Ourselves*, trans. L. S. Roudiez (New York: Columbia University Press, 1991), 127–68; David Held, *Democracy and the Global Order* (Stanford, CA: Stanford University Press, 1995), 48–99.

17 Lewis R. Gordon, *Fanon and the Crisis of European Man: An Essay on Philosophy and the Human Sciences* (New York: Routledge, 1995).

18 Michel-Rolph Trouillot, *Silencing the Past: Power and the Production of History* (Boston: Beacon Press, 1995), 75.

19 D. Ramos et al., *La ética en la conquista de América* (Madrid: Consejo Superior de Investigaciones Científicas y Técnicas, 1984).

20 Francisco de Vitoria, *Relectio de Indis, o libertad de los Indios*, bilingual critical edition by L. Pereña and J. M. Perez Prendes, introductory studies by V. Beltrán de

Heredia et al. (Madrid: Consejo Superior de Investigaciones Científicas, 1967 [1539]).

21 De Vitoria's notion of a "natural right" is not quite like Kant's "natural law," which indirectly obscured the question of "the other" that more recently became Jürgen Habermas's concern (see Habermas, *The Inclusion of the Other*).

22 For further details on the idea of human rights, see Walter D. Mignolo, "Who Speaks for the 'Human' in Human Rights?," in Barreto, ed., *Human Rights from the Third World Perspective*, 44–65.

23 Jürgen Habermas's reflections on the nation-state are a centrifugal analysis: from Europe toward Asia and Africa, projecting European categories over memories and organizations alien to the regional memories and praxes of living that call for the need of the nation-state in Europe. I cannot start an analysis of the nation-state from Europe. I start from the moment of the revolutions in the Americas (the Anglo-US Revolution and the Haitian Revolution) and of the independences in Luso-Spanish America. Habermas sees modernity; I see coloniality. Habermas, *The Inclusion of the Other*. As for Kymlicka, his arguments take a liberal position that confronts the critique of liberalism advanced by feminists, Marxists, and communitarians. My argument is neither of those. Rather it addresses the decolonial and the decolonial question regarding liberalism, which is that since its advent it has been a major force of coloniality. Here again, I start from the consequences of liberalism in the colonies wrought by local actors who increased the repression of Indigenous and Afro-South-Central American and Caribbean people. See Will Kymlica, *Liberalism, Community and Culture* (Oxford, UK: Clarendon Press, 1989). As for the liberal take on "minority rights," I side with the "minority activists and intellectuals" claiming their own rights: that is, decolonial politics confronting liberal politics. See Will Kymlicka, *Multicultural Citizenship: A Liberal Theory of Minority Rights* (Oxford, UK: Clarendon Press, 1995). As for "minorities" arguing their own rights, see Coulthard, *Red Skin, White Masks*.

24 McCarthy, "On Reconciling Cosmopolitan Unity and National Diversity."

25 I am here repeating a well-known story (Ernest Cassirer, *The Myth of the State*. New Haven: Yale University Press, 1951 [1932]) and displacing it with a reading that takes the perspective of the "Man of Color" rather than the perspective of the "White Man's Burden" (Gordon, *Fanon and the Crisis of European Man*). What for the white man is a burden for a man of color is a Calvary. Once again, half the story is discernible: the rhetoric of modernity (white man's burden) hiding the logic of coloniality (the man of color's Calvary).

26 "The philosophical invention of the South of Europe (Kant, Hegel)": The situation is repeated in the media. Western media are widely read, and they report one side. See, for example, Jon Sharman, "Chinese State Media Tells Donald Trump's Team to 'Prepare for Military Clash,'" *The Independent*, January 13, 2017, http://www .independent.co.uk/news/world/asia/rex-tillerson-south-china-sea-state-media -prepare-military-clash-donald-trump-global-times-a7525061.html. Chinese media like *Global Times* has less impact on Western readers, although it is published in

English; see "Is Tillerson's Bluster Just a Bluff for Senate?," *Global Times*, January 13, 2017, http://www.globaltimes.cn/content/1028568.shtml. On the invention of the Orient, see Edward Said, *Orientalism* (London: Pantheon Books, 1978).

27 Antonello Gerbi, *La disputa del Nuevo Mundo: Storia di una polemica, 1750-1900*, trans. Antonio Alatorre (Mexico City: Fondo de Cultura Económica, 1982 [1955]); Walter D. Mignolo, *Local Histories/Global Designs: Coloniality, Subaltern Knowledges, and Border Thinking*, 2nd ed. (Princeton, NJ: Princeton University Press, 2012 [2000]), 49-90.

28 Janet Abu-Lughod, *Before European Hegemony: The World System A.D. 1250-1350* (New York: Oxford University Press, 1982); Fernand Braudel, *Afterthoughts on Material Civilization and Capitalism* (Baltimore: Johns Hopkins University Press, 1979); Giovanni Arrighi, *The Long Twentieth Century* (London: Verso, 1994); Enrique Dussel, *Ética de la liberación en la edad de la globalización y de la exclusión* (Mexico City: Universidad Autónoma Nacional de México, 1998), 3-31; Mignolo, *Local Histories/ Global Designs*, 3-48.

29 On "nature and natural history," see Gerbi, *La disputa del Nuevo Mundo*.

30 Immanuel Kant, *The Metaphysics of Morals*, ed. and trans. Mary Gregor (Cambridge, UK: Cambridge University Press, 1996 [1785]), and "Perpetual Peace," in *Kant on History*, ed. Lewis White Beck, trans. Lewis White Beck, Robert E. Anchor, and Emil L. Fackenheim (Englewood Cliffs, NJ: Macmillan, 1963 [1795]), 85-136. See also McCarthy, "On Reconciling Cosmopolitan Unity and National Diversity."

31 Frederick P. Van De Pitte, introduction to Immanuel Kant, *Anthropology from a Pragmatic Point of View*, trans. Victor Lyle Dowdell (Carbondale: Southern Illinois University Press, 1996 [1797]).

32 Emmanuel Chukwudi Eze, "The Color of Reason: The Idea of 'Race' in Kant's Anthropology," in *Postcolonial African Philosophy: A Critical Reader*, ed. E. C. Eze (London: Wiley-Blackwell, 1997), 103-40; Tsenay Serequeberhan, "The Critique of Eurocentrism and the Practice of African Philosophy," in Eze, ed., *Postcolonial African Philosophy*, 141-61; Enrique Dussel, "Eurocentrism and Modernity (Introduction to the Frankfurt Lectures)," in *Postmodernism in Latin America*, ed. J. Beverley, J. Oviedo, and M. Arona (Durham, NC: Duke University Press, 1995), 65-76; Enrique Dussel, *Ética de la liberación en la edad de la globalización y de la exclusión*, 129-62.

33 Enrique Dussel, "Eurocentrism and Modernity," 66.

34 Enrique Dussel, *Filosofia de la liberación*, Red de Bibliotecas Virtuales CLASCO (Consejo Latinoamericano de Ciencías Sociales), orig. pub. 1996 [1977], accessed August 25, 2020, http://biblioteca.clacso.edu.ar/clacso/otros/20120227024607/filosofia.pdf.

35 Walter D. Mignolo, "The Darker Side of the Enlightenment: A Decolonial Reading of Kant's Geography," in *The Darker Side of Western Modernity*, 181-212.

36 Enrique Dussel, "Eurocentrism and Modernity," 68.

37 Eze, "The Color of Reason," 117-19.

38 Gerbi, *La disputa del Nuevo Mundo*, 414-18.

39 Kant, *Anthropology from a Pragmatic Point of View*.

40 Mary Gregor, "Kant on 'Natural Rights,'" in *Kant and Political Philosophy*, ed. R. Beiner and W. J. Booth (New Haven, CT: Yale University Press, 1993), 50–75.

41 Kant, "Perpetual Peace," para. no. 344.

42 Kant, *Anthropology from a Pragmatic Point of View*, 226.

43 Syed Farid Alatas, *Applying Ibn Khaldūn: The Recovery of a Lost Tradition in Sociology* (Abingdon, UK: Routledge, 2014), 31

44 Kant, *Anthropology from a Pragmatic Point of View*, 231–32.

45 G. W. F. Hegel, *The Philosophy of History*, trans. J. Sibree (New York: Dover, 1956 [1822]), 102.

46 Immanuel Kant, "Perpetual Peace," 121, n. 62.

47 Micheline R. Ishay, ed., "United Nations Universal Declaration of Human Rights (1948)," in *The Human Rights Reader* (New York: Routledge, 1997); Susan Koshy, "From Cold War to Trade War: Neocolonialism and Human Rights," *Social Text* 58 (1999): 1–32, http://www.jstor.org/stable/466713.

48 Chakravarthu Raghavan, *Recolonization: GATT, the Uruguayan Round, and the Third World* (London: Zed, 1990), 20–30.

49 Howard Tolley Jr., *The U.N. Commission on Human Rights* (Boulder, CO: Westview Press, 1987).

50 Milton Friedman, with the assistance of Rose Friedman, *Capitalism and Freedom* (Chicago: University of Chicago Press, 1962).

51 F. A. Hayek, *The Road to Serfdom*, ed. Milton Friedman (Chicago: University of Chicago Press, 1994 [1944]); Friedman, *Capitalism and Freedom*; Zbigniew Brzezinski, *Between Two Ages: America's Role in the Technetronic Era* (New York: Viking, 1970); Richard Cooper, ed., *Towards a Renovated International System: A Report of the Trilateral Integrators Task Force to the Trilateral Commission* (New York: Trilateral Commission, 1973). On the dissenting side, see Senator J. William Fulbright, *The Arrogance of Power* (New York: Random House, 1967). And for the dissenting side from the Third World, see Dominican former president and writer Juan Bosch, *Pentagonism: A Substitute for Imperialism*, trans. Helen R. Lane (New York: Grove Press, 1968).

52 Celso Furtado, *El desarrollo económico: Un mito* (Mexico City: Fondo de Cultura Económica, 1974).

53 In 1973, David Rockefeller, then CEO of Chase Manhattan Bank, initiated the Trilateral Commission. President Jimmy Carter's national security adviser, Zbigniew Brzezinski, was its main ideologue.

54 Brzezinski, *Between Two Ages*, 8.

55 Abdullahi An-Na'im, "What Do We Mean By Universal?," *Index of Censorship* 4, no. 5 (September 1994): 120–27. An-Na'im's observation at this point could be applied to de Vitoria, Kant, and *The Universal Declaration of Human Rights*.

56 An-Na'im, "What Do We Mean By Universal?"

57 Samuel Huntington, *The Clash of Civilizations and the Remaking of the World Order* (New York: Simon and Schuster, 1996).

58 Mignolo, *Local Histories/Global Designs*.

59 Nicholas Dirks, "Introduction: Colonialism and Culture," in Colonialism and Culture, ed. Nicholas B. Dirks (Ann Arbor: University of Michigan Press, 1992), 1–26.

60 Sandeep Bakshi, Suhraiya Jivraj, and Silvia Posocco, *Decolonizing Sexualities: Transnational Perspectives, Critical Interventions* (Oxford, UK: Counterpress, 2016).

61 See Robert Kagan, *The Jungle Grows Back: America and Our Imperiled World* (New York: Knopf, 2018), and Kishore Mahbubani, *Has the West Lost It? A Provocation* (London: Penguin, 2018).

62 See, for instance, S. Sayyid, *Recalling the Caliphate: Decolonisation and World Order* (London: Hurst and Co., 2014), chap. 5; Yan Xuetong, *Ancient Chinese Thought, Modern Chinese Power* (Princeton, NJ: Princeton University Press, 2011); Jian Qing, *A Confuciant Constitutional Order: How China's Ancient Past Can Shape Its Political Future*, trans. Edmund Ryden, ed. Daniel A. Bell and Ruiping Fan (Princeton, NJ: Princeton University Press, 2013).

63 See, for instance, Mogobe B. Ramose, "The Death of Democracy and the Resurrection of Timocracy," *Journal of Moral Education* 39, no. 3 (2010): 291–303; Mogobe B. Ramose, "To Whom Does the Land Belong? Mogobe Bernard Ramose Talks to Derek Hook," *Psychology in Society* 50 (2016): 64–68, DOI: 10.17159/2309-8708/2016/n50a5; Aníbal Quijano, "'Bien vivir': Entre el 'desarrollo' y la des/colonialidad del poder," in *Ecuador Debate: Acerca del Buen Vivir*, Quito: Centro Andino de Acción Popular CAAP 84 (2011): 77–87; Walter D. Mignolo, "Democracia liberal, camino de la autoridad humana y transición al vivir bien," Sociedad y Estado, Brasilia, January/April 2014, https://www.scielo.br/scielo.php?script=sci_arttext&pid=S0102-69922014000100003.

64 Let's take just one example: India, which inherited (for better or worse) the British form of governance. A recent article published in *Foreign Policy* deploys a surprising analysis of the cost of democracy in India (a big country in terms of voters to convince!). Abheek Bhattacharya, "India's $7 Billion Election," *Foreign Policy*, April 23, 2019.

65 A brilliant example, although others can also be found among the Indigenous Zapatistas, is Leanne Simpson's *Dancing on Our Turtle's Back*. She thinks with a Nishnaabeg vocabulary and cosmology, and she states at the beginning of her book that our theories are storytelling. She uses the word "theory" but looks at it as a form of storytelling that theory was supposed to "supersede" and "overcome." See also, from the Bolivian Andes, Fernando Huanacuni Mamani, *Buen Vivir/Vivir Bien: Filosofía, políticas, estrategias y experiencias regionales Andinas* (Lima: Coordinadora Andina de Organizaciones Indigenas, 2010). I will return to these issues in chapter 13.

66 Slavoj Žižek, "A Leftist Plea for 'Eurocentrism,'" *Critical Inquiry* 24, no. 4 (1998): 1009.

67 Žižek, "A Leftist Plea for 'Eurocentrism.'"

68 "Relativism," *Stanford Encyclopedia of Philosophy*, first pub. September 11, 2015, https://plato.stanford.edu/entries/relativism/#WhaRel.

69 Here I am following up on the distinctions made in the introduction to my book *The Darker Side of Western Modernity* and on Humberto Maturana's formulation between truth without parentheses and truth in parentheses. The distinction could

be extended to the idea of the universal. Since "universality" is a strong concept in the Western sphere of knowledge, it cannot be ignored, but there is no need either to accept as it is. Hence, the distinctions I am proposing. This distinction also runs parallel to Aníbal Quijano's distinction between totality and totalitarian totality. Every cosmology, Quijano stated, takes totality for granted. But a totalitarian totality is a project that purports to manage, control, and devalue other cosmologies. Decolonial totalities are in parentheses while modern/colonial totalities (to which modern and modern critical cosmopolitanisms belong) are formulated as totalities without parentheses—that is, as the one and only cosmopolitanism.

70 On "North Atlantic universal fictions," see Michel-Rolph Trouillot, "North Atlantic Universals: Analytical Fictions, 1492–1945," *South Atlantic Quarterly* 101, no. 4 (Fall 2002): 839–58.

Six. Cosmopolitanism and the Decolonial Option

The first version of this essay was presented as the opening lecture for the project Multiple Trajectories, Critical Interrogations, led by Kamari Clarke, Ariana Hernández-Reguant, and Moira Fradinger at Yale University (November 2, 2008), under the title "Decolonial Cosmopolitanism between Theology and the Spirit of Global Capitalism."

1 Serge Latouche, *L' Occidentalization du Monde: Essays sur la signification, la portée et les limites de l'uniformation planetaire* (Paris: Maspero, 1989).

2 Fuyuki Kurasawa, "Cosmopolitanism from Below: Alternative Globalization and the Creation of Solidarity without Bonds," *Archives of European Sociology* 45, no. 2 (2004): 233–55. See also the web page of the Grass Roots Global Justice Alliance: http://ggjalliance.org/worldsocialforums.

3 Immanuel Kant, *Anthropology from a Pragmatic Point of View*, trans. Victor Lyle Dowdell (Carbondale: Southern Illinois University Press, 1996 [1798]), 235.

4 Kant, *Anthropology from a Pragmatic Point of View*, 249.

5 Denghua Zhang, "The Concept of 'Community of Common Destiny' in China's Diplomacy: Meaning, Motives and Implications," *Asia and Pacific Studies* 5, no. 2 (2018): 196–207; Jacob Mardell, "The 'Community of Common Destiny' in Xi Jinping's New Era," *The Diplomat*, October 25, 2017, https://thediplomat.com/2017/10/the-community-of-common-destiny-in-xi-jinpings-new-era/; Liza Tobn, "Xi's Vision for Transforming Global Governance: A Strategic Challenge for Washinton and Its Allies," *Texas National Security Review* 2, no. 1 (2018), https://tnsr.org/2018/11/xis-vision-for-transforming-global-governance-a-strategic-challenge-for-washington-and-its-allies/.

6 Xiang Bo, "Backgrounder: Xi Jinping's Thoughts on Socialism with Chinese Characteristics for a New Era," NPC and CPPCC, Annual Sessions 2018, March 17, 2018, http://www.xinhuanet.com/english/2018-03/17/c_137046261.htm.

7 Pope Francis, "Encyclical Letter *Fratelli Tutti* of the Holy Father Francis on Fraternity and Social Friendship," October 3, 2020, http://w2.vatican.va/content

/francesco/en/encyclicals/documents/papa-francesco_20201003_enciclica-fratelli
-tutti.html.

8 John Letzing, "Here Is the Pope's Prescription for Resetting the Global Economy
in Response to COVID-19," World Economic Forum, October 9, 2020, https://www
.weforum.org/agenda/2020/10/here-s-the-pope-s-prescription-for-resetting-the
-global-economy-in-response-to-covid-19/.

9 Peimin Ni, "The Silk Order: A Philosophical Perspective," DOC Research Institute, March 26, 2018, https://doc-research.org/2018/03/silk-order-philosophical
-perspective/.

10 An argument in favor of the civilizational state can be found in Zhang Weiwei,
The China Wave: Rise of a Civilizational State (Hackensack, NJ: World Century
Publishing, 2011). A counterargument can be found in Christopher Coker, *The Rise
of the Civilizational State* (Cambridge, UK: Polity Press, 2019).

11 Kant, *Anthropology from a Pragmatic Point of View*, 248.

12 Peter H. Wilson, "The Causes of the Thirty Years' War, 1618–48," *English Historical
Review*, 123, no. 502 (2008): 554–86.

13 Stephen Toulmin, *Cosmopolis: The Hidden Agenda of Modernity* (New York: Free
Press, 1990), 128.

14 Holland had a flourishing commercial interregnum in the seventeenth century,
but Dutch is not one of the top ten languages in terms of number of speakers.
Portuguese is in seventh place, above Italian and French and below Arabic and
Bengali.

15 Toulmin, *Cosmopolis*, 133.

16 Toulmin, *Cosmopolis*, 133.

17 Toulmin, *Cosmopolis*, 133.

18 See Kwame Anthony Appiah, *Cosmopolitanism: Ethics in a World of Strangers* (New
York: W. W. Norton, 2006). The crimes of coloniality are often covered in velvet
and shoveled out of the public eye, as can be perceived in this beautifully written
and well-advertised essay.

19 Guaman Poma de Ayala's work, finished in 1615, was presumably composed
over a period of two decades. See Felipe Guaman Poma de Ayala, *El primer nueva
corónica y buen gobierno*, trans. Rolena Adorno, John V. Murra, and Jorge L. Urioste
(Mexico City: Fondo de Cultura Económica, 1980 [1615]).

20 For a simple description from an Andean perspective, see Anonymous, "Southern Cross: Our Wheel of Life in Heavens," Los Bosques.net, accessed September 30, 2020, https://www.losbosques.net/southern-cross-our-wheel-of-life-in
-heavens/.

21 Josef Eastermann, *Filosofía Andina: Sabiduría Indígena Para un Mundo Nuevo* (La Paz:
Editorial ISEAT, 2006). Eastermann is a Swiss theologian, based in La Paz, who
works closely with Aymara thinkers on the topic of the daily life of Aymaras. See
also the other half of the story, told by Aymara intellectual Fernando Huanacuni
Mamani, *Bien vivir, Buen vivir: Filosofía, políticas, estrategias y experiencias regionales Andinas* (Lima: Coordinadora Andina de Organizaciones Indigenas, 2010), discussed
in chapter 14 of this book.

22 Notice that when I say *"pacha*-sophy" instead of "philo-sophy," I am engaging in border thinking. The difficulty is that in this field of knowledge, Western vocabulary is hegemonic—local and global at the same time. The first step is to denaturalize it, to "steal" the word for "-sophy" and to attribute it to *"pacha"* and in the movement to destitute "philo-" and so to reconstitute *pacha*-sophy. Border thinking begins at this moment and is tantamount to sensing and dwelling on the border. The decolonial work begins by reducing the impact of Western knowledge; to "decolonize knowledge" (a common expression nowadays) involves the meticulous and relentless work of eroding the hegemony by depriving Western epistemic vocabulary of its unwarranted universality. This is a task of decolonial politics.

23 "What Is Good Governance?," United Nations Economic and Social Commission for Asia and the Pacific, July 10, 2009, https://www.unescap.org/sites/default /files/good-governance.pdf. The article states that the notions of good and bad governance are increasingly being used in the development literature. Needeless to say this is a modern criterion of good governance that implies the logic of coloniality. Which is not the same as the idea of good government found in the work of Guaman Poma de Ayala between 1580 and 1616, or that of the Zapatistas in the twentieth century, or that of Indigenous Canadian thinkers and activists more recently. There is no single idea and enactment of good governance. It depends on the goals: good governance for whom and for what?

24 For Indigenous scholars, intellectuals, and activists in Canada thinking about Indigenous governance vis-à-vis the settler nation-state, see Alfred Taiaiake, *Peace, Power, Righteousness: An Indigenous Manifesto* (New York: Oxford University Press, 2009) and *Wasáse: Indigenous Pathways of Action and Freedom* (Toronto: University of Toronto Press, 2009). See also Glen Sean Coulthard, *Red Skin, White Masks: Rejecting the Colonial Politics of Recognition* (Minneapolis: University of Minnesota Press, 2014).

25 Antony Anghie, "Francisco de Vitoria and the Colonial Origins of International Law," in *Laws of the Postcolonial*, ed. E. Darian-Smith and P. Fitzpatrick (Ann Arbor: University of Michigan Press, 1999), 102.

26 Condoleezza Rice, "Rethinking the National Interest: American Realism for a New World," *Foreign Affairs*, July–August 2008, https://www .foreignaffairs.com/articles/2008-06-01/rethinking-national-interest, and "Campaign 2000: Promoting the National Interests," *Foreign Affairs*, January/February 2000, https://www.foreignaffairs.com/articles/2000-01-01/ campaign-2000-promoting-national-interest.

27 Anghie, "Francisco de Vitoria and the Colonial Origins of International Law," 103.

28 Manfred Steger, "Ideologies of Globalization," *Journal of Political Ideologies* 10, no. 1 (2005): 12.

29 A recent op-ed by Parag Khanna tells the story clearly and succinctly: "No Longer in Thrall to Western Democracy, Asia Turns to Technocrats for Answers," *Global-is-Asian*, January 10, 2017, https://lkyspp.nus.edu.sg/gia/article/no-longer-in -thrall-to-western-democracy-asia-turns-to-technocrats-for-answers.

30 Number 2 is the artificial intelligence and companion of *Homo economicus*: "In 1952, only 2 percent of the articles in the main economics journal in the USA contained mathematical formulae. By the end of the century, when *Homo economicus* became Number 2 and stepped up to rule the world, it was felt necessary to recall a time when there was economics without mathematics. It was just a period after mathematics. It may be hard for younger economists to imagine, but until nearly midcentury it was not unusual for theorists using material techniques to begin with a substantial apology, explaining that this approach need not assume that humans are automatons deprived of free will." Frank Schirrmacher, *Ego: The Game of Life* (New York: Polity Press, 2015), 59.

31 "Being" is translated into Spanish as either *ser* or *estar*. In this case I mean *estar*. For an elaboration on these concepts, see Rodolfo Kusch, *El pensamiento indígena y popular en América* (Indigenous and Popular Thinking in America), trans. Joshua M. Price and María Lugones (Durham, NC: Duke University Press, 2010 [1970]).

32 Partha Chatterjee, *The Politics of the Governed: Reflections on Popular Politics in Most of the World* (New York: Columbia University Press, 2004), 27–52.

33 Walter D. Mignolo, "The De-colonial Option and the Meaning of Identity in Politics," *Anales Instituto Ibero Americano: Nueva Epoca* 9/10 (2007): 43–72.

34 Just remember that Norbert Wiener's *Cybernetics or Control and Communication in the Animal and the Machine* (Cambridge, MA: MIT Press, 1948), was published just after the end of WWII. It was the blueprint for Number 2. Wiener realized the risk of his proposal, and two years later he published *The Human Use of Human Beings* (New York: Houghton Mifflin Harcourt, 1950). The scientific community celebrated the first work and discredited the second, arguing that Wiener was a terrific scientist but not a humanist. Wiener was announcing, in his language, the potentials of artificial intelligence to shift the logic of coloniality under a renovated rhetoric of modernity. And the unfolding of events in the second half of the twentieth century proved him right.

35 Frantz Fanon, *The Wretched of the Earth*, trans. Richard Philcox (New York: Grove Press, 2004 [1961]), 209–10.

36 Taiaiake, *Peace, Power, Righteousness*, 30.

Seven. From "Human" to "Living" Rights

1 Edmundo O'Gorman, *La invención de América: El universalismo en la cultura occidental* (Mexico City: Universidad Autónoma de México, 1958); Serge Latouche, *L' Occidentalization du monde: Essays sur la signification, la portée et les limites de l' uniformation du monde* (Paris: Maspero, 1989).

2 The theologian of liberation Franz J. Hinkelammert called attention to this blind spot after the NATO intervention in Kosovo in "The Hidden Logic of Modernity: Locke and the Inversion of Human Rights," *World and Knowledges Otherwise* 1, no. 1 (2004): 1–27.

3 José-Manuel Barreto, ed., *Human Rights from a Third World Perspective* (Newcastle, UK: Cambridge Scholars Publishing, 2013).

4 Nikolai Karkov and Zhivka Vallavicharska, "Rethinking East-European Socialism: Notes toward an Anti-Capitalist Methodology," *International Journal of Postcolonial Studies* 20, no. 6 (2018): 185–213.

5 Henry George, *Progress and Poverty* (New York: Cosimo, 2005 [1879]).

6 I have explored this issue in Walter D. Mignolo, "Who Speaks for the 'Human' in Human Rights?," in Barreto, ed., *Human Rights from a Third World Perspective*, 44–65.

7 Eric Posner, "The Case against Human Rights," *The Guardian*, December 2014, https://www.theguardian.com/news/2014/dec/04/-sp-case-against-human-rights.

8 The Eleanor Roosevelt speech "The Struggle for Human Rights" can be found at the website American Rhetoric: Top 100 Speeches, accessed August 29, 2020, http://www.americanrhetoric.com/speeches/eleanorroosevelt.htm.

9 Rady Ananda, "More Problems with Glyphosate: Rice Growers Sound Alarm," *Food Freedom*, May 2011, http://foodfreedom.wordpress.com/tag/andres-carrasco/. See also Marcela Valente, "Argentina: Poison from the Sky," *Global Issues*, December 2011, http://www.globalissues.org/news/2011/12/09/12171; Alejandra Paganelli et al., "Glyphosate-Based Herbicides Produce Teratogenic Effects on Vertebrates by Impairing Retinoic Acid Signaling," *Chemical Research in Toxicology: ACS Publications*, October 2010, https://pubs.acs.org/doi/abs/10.1021/tx1001749. Furthermore, there is the problem of open-pit mining, the problems and consequences of which have already been covered, in Spanish and English, mainly in blogs and elsewhere on the web. Little, as expected, is found in the mainstream media. One example is María Trigona, "Resisting Mining: Brutal Repression and Uprising in Argentina," *Upside Down World*, February 23, 2010, http://upsidedownworld.org/main/argentina-archives-32/2376-resisting-mining-brutal-repression-and-uprising-in-argentina. The health consequences of this type of mining (where you see that bodies of living organisms are "nature") are also being well documented. Representatives of the state, and of course corporation leaders, argue the benefits for "development." See Sharon Pratt, "Open Cast Mining 'Affects Child Health,'" BBC, December 2, 1999, accessed September 25, 2020, http://news.bbc.co.uk/2/hi/health/546685.stm. A search will demonstrate that the locations of such mines are nowhere in western Europe, the US, or Canada. A cautionary note: I am not advocating for stopping mining, but for being aware of the consequences of mining in a capitalist society that sacralizes gold and also created the need for metal, such as coltan, for cell phones, iPads, and other technological gadgets. All of this is also well documented. If you have not been following these violations of the rights of the particular species we call human, this is a good place to start: Pulitzer Center, "In Focus: Congo's Bloody Coltan," featured on *Foreign Exchange with Fareed Zakaria*, 2006, video, 4:36, http://www.youtube.com/watch?v=3OWj1ZGn4uM; Pan Afrikan, "Congo 20 Million Dead the Role US and Its Allies Played," July 1, 2011, video, http://www.youtube.com/watch?feature=endscreen&v=8YPldzhAKgk&NR=1.

10 This call has been forcefully made in Lucía Gorricho, "Lectura de la Sentencia, Juicio Ético a las Transnacionales," November 5, 2011, video, https://www.youtube.com/watch?v=VLS8gCFZTEQ.

11 Margaret Greer, Walter Mignolo, and Maureen Quilligan, eds., *Rereading the Black Legend: The Discourse of Race and Religion in the Renaissance Empires* (Chicago: University of Chicago Press, 2008).

12 Walter D. Mignolo, "Racism and Human Rights," *Bolivia Changes*, June 2008. http://boliviachanges.blogspot.com/2008/06/racism-and-human-rights.html. There is no other explanation, in my understanding, beyond racism for the series of events perpetrated by US soldiers in Afghanistan in which they burned copies of the Koran, urinated on dead Afghan bodies, and massacred civilians without any reason. The politics of human rights falls very short when violations are perpetrated by citizens of the country that champions human rights and assigns itself the role of watchman over global human rights. See "Los talibanes juran vengar la matanza de Kandahar," *El País Internacional*, March 2012, http://internacional.elpais.com/internacional/2012/03/12/actualidad/1331538127_294245.html.

13 Hinkelammert, "The Hidden Logic of Modernity."

14 Steve Chovanec, "Syria's 'Moderate Terrorists' Supported by the CIA: Media Disinformation," Centre de recherche sur la mondialisation, March 26, 2016, https://www.mondialisation.ca/syrias-moderate-terroristsh-supported-by-the-the-cia-media-disinformation/5515957. Regarding the term "moderate terrorists": the rhetoric of modernity has no limit in its chameleonic adaptation to justify the unjustifiable.

15 On violations of human rights under Barack Obama's administration, see Keneth Roth, "Barack Obama's Shaky Legacy on Human Rights," Human Rights Watch (originally published in *Foreign Policy*), January 2017, https://www.hrw.org/news/2017/01/09/barack-obamas-shaky-legacy-human-rights; on violations under Donald Trump's administration, see "United States Events of 2018," Human Rights Watch, accessed May 6, 2020, https://www.hrw.org/world-report/2019/country-chapters/united-states.

16 Costas Douzinas, "The Paradoxes of Human Rights," in *Human Rights and Empire: The Political Philosophy of Cosmopolitanism* (Oxford, UK: Routledge-Cavendish, 2007), part I; Makau Mutua, *Human Rights: A Political and Cultural Critique* (Philadelphia: University of Pennsylvania Press, 2008); Lynn Hunt, "The Paradoxical Origins of Human Rights," and Jeffrey N. Wasserstrom, "The Chinese Revolution and Contemporary Paradoxes," both in *Human Rights and Revolutions*, ed. Jeffrey N. Wasserstrom et al. (Lanham, MD: Rowman and Littlefield, 2007), 3–21 and 22–46; Oliver Mendelsohn and Upendra Baxi, eds., *The Rights of the Subordinated Peoples* (Delhi: Oxford India Paperbacks, 1994).

17 For an elaborated argument on the privileges of the human vis-à-vis humans detached from nature by blocking the body's relationality with life on earth (bio-logical) and the relationality of the body with the cosmos (cosmo-logical), see Walter D. Mignolo, "The Invention of the 'Human' and the Three Pillars of the Colonial Matrix of Power (Racism, Sexism, and Nature)," in *On Decoloniality: Concepts, Analysis, Praxis*, Catherine E. Walsh and Walter D. Mignolo (Durham, NC: Duke University Press, 2018), 153–76.

18 Regarding immigration: the logic of in-migration control is extended to emerging economies. Now that the EU and the US are short of job offerings, Brazil is facing immigration problems. The logic is the same: qualified migrants have a much better chance of obtaining a visa than poor people and less qualified people, who are running away from the poverty of their own country. The conflict is between ethics and politics, between who is considered "human" (because they are valuable to the economy of the country) and who is considered "less human/anthropos" (and therefore can be dispensed with). See Marcia Carmo, "Racismo é um problema econômico, diz diretor de agência antipobreza da ONU," BBC News/Brasil, June 2, 2019, https://www.bbc.com/portuguese/brasil -48424611.

19 José Manuel Barreto, "Imperialism and Decolonization as Scenarios of Human Rights History," in Barreto, ed., *Human Rights from a Third World Perspective*, 140–71. See also Mutua, *Human Rights*.

20 Anna Grear, "Challenging Corporate 'Humanity': Legal Disembodiment, Embodiment and Human Rights," *Human Rights Law Review* 7, no. 3 (2007): 1–33. Now China is facing a problem similar to that of Third World countries. China is rich in natural resources, and corporations desperate to make money are invading these well-endowed territories. See Liu Ying, "Further Opening-Up to Protect Free Trade," *China Daily*, December 2019, https://global.chinadaily.com.cn/a /201912/17/WS5df818b0a310cf3e3557e825.html, and Douzinas, *Human Rights and Empire*. As for development, "living rights or life rights" calls for *sustainable economies* rather than *sustainable development*. On this, see Walter D. Mignolo, "Sustainable Development or Sustainable Economies?," *Socioscapes: International Journal of Societies, Politics and Cultures* 1, no. 1 (2020): 48–65.

21 There was slavery before then, but none of the slaves were regarded as commodities because a capitalist economy did not exist in the region. The commodification of human life is a constitutive part of the foundation of capitalist economy in the sixteenth century. Commodification of life doesn't only mean that people are bought and sold. It means that like any other commodity, when the use of a commodity reaches the end of its useful life, they are dispensed with as a disposable object. See Eric Williams, *Capitalism and Slavery* (Chapel Hill: University of North Carolina Press, 1994 [1944]).

22 See the gold mine Yanacocha, in Peru. The mining company Newmont Corporation introduces itself this way: "In 2007, Newmont became the first gold company selected to be part of the Dow Jones Sustainability World Index." "About Us," Newmont Corporation, accessed May 25, 2020, https://www.newmont.com/about -us/default.aspx. Newmont is located in Cajamarca, which, curiously enough, was the place where Francisco Pizarro captured Atahualpa Inca, ensuring the conquest of Tawantinsuyu and enabling the beginning of mining in the modern/colonial world. This was when international law and *ius gentium* were being elaborated in Salamanca by Francisco de Vitoria. An explanation of the damages and consequences of open-pit mining can be found at "Peru: Documental explica daños provocados por la minería del oro en Cajamarca" (Peru: An explanation of

the damages of open-pit gold mining in Cajamarca), Servindi.org, March 20 2012, http://servindi.org/actualidad/61541.

23 See "Argentina, Buenos Aires: Se inicia el juicio ètico popular a las transnacionales," BioDiversidad, October 27, 2011, http://www.biodiversidadla.org/Noticias/Argentina _Buenos_Aires_se_inicia_el_Juicio_etico_popular_a_las_transnacionales .

24 My note. Whoever has read Nikolas Rose, *The Politics of Life Itself: Biomedicine, Power and Subjectivity in the Twenty-First Century* (Princeton, NJ: Princeton University Press, 2006), may find this statement either out of place or really appropriate with regard to time. The vision of "life in itself" couldn't be farther apart from the views of the JETC: the politics of life itself aims to prolong life with its back to the corporation's politics of "death in itself."

25 Gorricho, "Lectura de la Sentencia, Juicio Ético a las Transnacionales."

26 "On average, gold mining today produces seventy tons of waste for every ounce of gold, while also consuming and polluting massive amounts of water. An estimated 50 percent of these mining operations occur on native lands. For many Indigenous peoples, who often rely on their environment for food and necessities, mining threatens not only their livelihood, but also their spirituality and traditional way of life." "Barrick's Dirty Secrets: Communities Respond to Gold Mining's Impacts Worldwide," Corpwatch, May 1, 2007, http://www.corpwatch .org/article.php?id=14466. One of the largest transnational corporations in search of gold is Barrick Gold, from Canada.

27 Gnoseological and aesthesic reconstitution today is larger than its decolonial versions. For general investigations on reconstitution of knowing and sensing, see Kongjian Yu, "Green Infrastructure through the Revival of Ancient Wisdom," American Academy of Art and Sciences, Bulletin, Summer 2017, https://www .amacad.org/news/green-infrastructure-through-revival-ancient-wisdom, and Khazamula J. Maluleka, "Indigenous African Philosophy of Ubuntu as a Foundation for a Conducive Environment for Culturally Responsive Teaching and Learning in South Africa," International Conference on New Trends in Teaching and Education, Barcelona, Spain, September 5–7, 2019, https://www.dpublication .com/wp-content/uploads/2019/09/19-5299.pdf; for these trends in South America, see Unai Villalba, "*Buen Vivir* vs. Development: A Paradigm Shift in the Andes?," *Third World Quarterly* 34, no. 8 (2013): 1427–42.

28 Hans-Peter Dürr, J. Daniel Dahm, and Rudolf Prinz zur Lippe, "Potsdam 'Denkschrift' 2005," Federal Ministry of Education and Research of Germany, October 2005, https://one88hiq.files.wordpress.com/2014/02/postdamer-denkschrift _en.pdf. (For the condensed version known as the "Potsdam Manifesto 2005," go to http://www.gcn.de/download/manifesto_en.pdf.) See also Bertrand Russell and Albert Einstein, "Russell-Einstein Manifesto," Atomic Heritage Foundation, July 9, 1955, accessed May 6, 2020, https://www.atomicheritage.org/key -documents/russell-einstein-manifesto.

29 "Two outcomes of the European Enlightenment": See my book *The Darker Side of Western Modernity: Global Futures, Decolonial Options* (Durham, NC: Duke University Press, 2011).

30 The collapse of the Soviet Union weakened the argument for national interests and national defense. Before 9/11, the promotion of "national interests" alerted us to the need to invent a new enemy to legitimize claims of national security. Condoleezza Rice, "Campaign 2000: Promoting the National Interest," *Foreign Affairs*, January/February 2000, https://www.foreignaffairs.com/articles/2000-01-01/campaign-2000-promoting-national-interest.

31 Dürr, Dahm, and zur Lippe, "Potsdam 'Denkschrift' 2005."

32 Regarding the Congo: "The moral righteousness with which the West often approaches the problems in the DRC conveniently overlooks the global contours of its economic exploitation. In reality, a deep restructuring of the political and economic systems is necessary, changes that are likely not possible on merely a national level but would require the participation of Western nations as well." Sarah van Beurden, "A New Congo Crisis?," *Origins: Current Events in Historical Perspective* 11, no. 4 (January 2018), http://origins.osu.edu/article/new-congo-crisis.

33 Russell and Einstein, "Russell-Einstein Manifesto."

34 Hinkelammert, "The Hidden Logic of Modernity."

35 Charles Esche, "Separation: In Conversation with Charles Esche," in *Permanent Temporariness*, ed. Sandi Hilal and Alessandro Petti (Amsterdam: Idea Books, 2019), 45–52. In this conversation Esche evaluates decolonization and demodernity, the latter as a possibility for western Europe. (A separate version of the conversation can be found here: http://www.decolonizing.ps/site/wp-content/uploads/2019/01/in-conversation-with-Charles-Esche.pdf.)

36 I write "scientific" because Western science is just that, Western, not universal. Today Western codified knowledge has been accepted but is increasingly questioned—not in its regional value but in its universal pretense. See Walter Mignolo, "The Splendors and Miseries of 'Science': Coloniality, Geopolitics of Knowledge and Epistemic Pluriversality," in *Cognitive Justice in a Global World: Prudent Knowledges for a Decent Life*, ed. Boaventura de Sousa Santos (Lanham, MD: Lexington Books, 2007), 375–96. See also Walter Mignolo, "Prophets Facing Sidewise: The Geopolitics of Knowledge and the Colonial Difference," *Social Epistemology* 19, no. 1 (2005): 111–27, DOI: 10.1080/ 02691720500084325.

37 *The Guardian* reported in April of 2011 that Bolivia was set to pass the world's first laws granting all nature equal rights with humans. John Vidal, "Bolivia Enshrines Natural World's Rights with Equal Status for Mother Earth," *The Guardian*, April 10, 2011, http://www.guardian.co.uk/environment/2011/apr/10/bolivia-enshrines-natural-worlds-rights. "The law of Mother Earth, now agreed by politicians as well as grassroots social groups, redefines the country's rich mineral deposits as 'blessings.' These laws are expected to lead to radical new conservation measures and social/political interventions to reduce pollution and control industry." Susan AKA Peacefull, "UN Treaty: Mother Earth Has a Right to Life," *WorldPeacefull* (blog), April 2011, http://wpas.worldpeacefull.com/2011/04/un-treaty-mother-earth-has-a-right-to-life/.

38 Dürr, Dahm, and zur Lippe, "Potsdam 'Denkschrift' 2005."

39 Dürr, Dahm, and zur Lippe, "Potsdam 'Denkschrift' 2005."

40 Dürr, Dahm, and zur Lippe, "Potsdam 'Denkschrift' 2005."

41 See Friends of the Congo, *Crisis in the Congo: Uncovering the Truth,* June 18, 2011, video, http://www.youtube.com/watch?v=vLV9szEu9Ag.

42 See Ramón Grosfóguel, "Human Rights and Anti-Semitism after GAZA," *Human Architecture: Journal of the Sociology of Self-Knowledge* 7 (Spring 2009): 89–102.

43 Life rights should, let me repeat, not be limited to human rights in the political sphere, but should address the life-rights violations that threaten the lives of entire communities by outright genocide or indirectly by the pesticide, cyanide, and mercury used in agriculture and mining to advance "development." Control of weapons of mass destruction should be a concern of life rights. For Noam Chomsky it makes good sense to talk Iran into signing a treatise of nonproliferation, together with India, Pakistan, and Israel, who are supported by the US and have never signed any nonproliferation agreements. See Noam Chomsky, "'Losing' the World: American Decline in Perspective," Al Jazeera, February 2012, http://www .aljazeera.com/indepth/opinion/2012/02/2012215773268827.html. That was in 2012. President Trump changed the scenario.

44 For the recent Dakota Indigenous protests over pipeline access, see Justin Worland, "What to Know about the Dakota Access Pipeline Protests," *Time,* October 28, 2016, http://time.com/4548566/dakota-access-pipeline-standing -rock-sioux/.

45 The original in Spanish reads as follows: "A más de 500 años de colonización y recolonización del continente, este Tribunal sostiene que no es lo mismo vivir 'de' la naturaleza que vivir 'con' y 'en' la Naturaleza. Sin embargo, en defensa de los cometidos insaciables de las empresas transnacionales, y en un marco de profundización de la lógica capitalista y de expansión de las fronteras de explotación, se destruye el medio ambiente y se tiende a acabar a pueblos enteros, a comunidades indígenas y criollas campesinas que hoy parecen ser consideradas 'poblaciones sobrantes' de la sociedad." Gorricho, "Lectura de la Sentencia, Juicio Ético a las Transnacionales."

46 Richard Wright, *The Color Curtain: A Report on the Bandung Conference* (Jackson: University Press of Mississippi, 1996 [1956]).

47 See Mignolo, "The Splendors and Miseries of 'Science.'"

48 The original in Spanish: "Este Tribunal Ético Popular considera que no es posible enjuiciar a las transnacionales sin hacerlo, simultáneamente, al llamado 'modelo de desarrollo' y al sistema capitalista, patriarcal y racista que lo ha generado, lo reproduce y lo extiende en torno a un sujeto central que es el hombre blanco, burgués, propietario, heterosexual, occidental y Cristiano." Colectivo Anselmo Lorenzo, "Sentencia del Tribual del Juicio Ético a las Transnacionales," *Boletin Informativo,* November 13, 2011, http://www.bolinf.es/wp/sentencia-del-tribunal -del-juicio-etico-a-las-transnacionales/#.X3KSMFkpDjA.

49 Martin Heidegger, "The Question Concerning Technology," in *Basic Writings,* ed. David Farrell Krell (New York: Harper, 2008), 307–42.

1 Walter D. Mignolo, "Coloniality at Large: The Western Hemisphere in the Colonial Horizon of Modernity," *New Centennial Review* 1, no. 2 (2001): 19–54, https://www.jstor.org/stable /41949278.

2 Kwan-Hsing Chen, *Asia as Method: Toward Deimperialization* (Durham, NC: Duke University Press, 2010); Kishore Mahbubani, *Can Asians Think?* (London: Times Edition, 2009 [1998]); Kishore Mahbubani, *Has the West Lost It?* (London: Penguin, 2018).

3 Walter D. Mignolo, "Spirit Out of Bounds Returns to the East: The Closing of the Social Sciences and the Opening of Independent Thought," *Current Sociology* 61, no. 4 (2014): 584–602.

4 Waler D. Mignolo, "Geopolitics of Sensing and Knowing," *Confero* 1, no. 1 (2013): 129–50, DOI: 10.3384/confer.2001-4562.13viii129.

5 Kishore Mahbubani, *The New Asian Hemisphere: The Irresistible Shift of Global Power to the East* (New York: Public Affairs, 2008).

6 "Treaty between Spain and Portugal Concluded at Tordesilla, June 7, 1494," Avalon Project: Documents in Law, History, and Diplomacy, Yale Law School, Lillian Goldman Law Library, accessed May 8, 2020, https://avalon.law.yale.edu/15th _century/mod001.asp.

7 Richard Twiss, "A Theology of Manifest Destiny," March 7, 2008, video, 2:47, https://www.youtube.com/watch?v=4mEkMyiKNWo.

8 John Cary's map of the two hemispheres (London, first printed 1816) summarizes the cartographic imaginary since the second half of the seventeenth century: John Cary, *World and Four Continents* (map), 1827, "Cary's New Map of the Eastern and Western Hemisphere, containing the whole of the New Discoveries, and every Improvement to the Present time, 1827," accessed September 28, 2020, https://www .crouchrarebooks.com/maps/view/cary-john-world-and-four-continents.

9 See Carl Schmitt, "The Western Hemisphere," in *The Nomos of the Earth in the International Law of the Jus Publicum Europaeum*, trans. G. L. Ulmen (New York: Telos Press, 2006 [1950]), 281–94.

10 Theodore Roosevelt, "Annual Message to Congress for 1904," House Records HR 58A-K2, Center for Legislative Archives, National Archives, accessed May 25, 2020, http://www.ourdocuments.gov/doc.php?flash=true&doc=56.

11 For more on Manifest Destiny, see Anders Stephanson, *Manifest Destiny: American Expansion and the Empire of Rights* (New York: Hills and Wang, 1996).

12 More details on this point can be found in Walter D. Mignolo, "The Moveable Center: Ethnicity, Geometric Projections and Coexisting Territorialities," in *The Darker Side of the Renaissance: Literacy, Territoriality, and Colonization*, 2nd ed. (Ann Arbor: University of Michigan Press, 2012 [1995]), 219–58.

13 At the time I was editing the original version of this chapter (2012), the news reported one of the most evident (and distressing) moves to regain and maintain US leadership and the unipolar world order: President Barack Obama announcing plans to invade Syria, seeking support from Congress only after his decision, and bypassing the United Nations. This constitutes an effort to maintain the

leadership of Northern Hemispheric America. Under these circumstances, who is theorizing the studies of hemispheric America and what for? See Ben Rhodes, "Syrian 'Red Line' Crisis," *The Atlantic*, June 3, 2018, https://www.theatlantic.com /international/archive/2018/06/inside-the-white-house-during-the-syrian-red -line-crisis/561887/.

14 Deborah Bonella, "Is Latin America's Turn to the Right Waning?," OZY, October 26, 2019, https://www.ozy.com/around-the-world/is-latin-americas-turn-to -the-right-waning/225265/.

15 Xi Jinping, "President Jinping's Speech to Davos in Full," World Economic Forum, January 17, 2017, https://www.weforum.org/agenda/2017/01/full-text-of-xi -jinping-keynote-at-the-world-economic-forum.

16 For Russia's geopolitical configuration and the Caucasus (South) in the global picture, see Madina Tlostanova, "The South of the Poor North: Caucasus Subjectivity and the Complex of Secondary 'Australism,'" in "The Global South and World Dis/Order," ed. Caroline Levander and Walter D. Mignolo, special issue: *Global South* 5, no. 1 (2011): 66–84.

17 For the distinction between "Occident" and "the West" see Joschka Fischer, "Is This the End of the West?," World Economic Forum, December 7, 2016, https:// www.weforum.org/agenda/2016/12/is-this-the-end-of-the-west-asks-joschka -fischer.

18 Hillary Clinton, "America's Pacific Century," *Foreign Policy*, October 11, 2011, https://foreignpolicy.com/2011/10/11/americas-pacific-century/.

19 Luis Bilbao, "Alianza del Pacífico: Obama pesca en el Sur," *América Latina en Movimiento,* February 7, 2013, https://www.alainet.org/es/active/65333.

20 President Barack Obama strongly supported and praised the Pacific Alliance in South America, an alliance formed by the right-wing presidents of the moment. The Pacific Alliance in South America was a key player in Barack Obama's project of the Trans-Pacific Partnership to contain China. See William Finnegan, "Why Does Obama Want This Trade Deal So Badly?," *New Yorker*, June 11, 2015, https:// www.newyorker.com/news/daily-comment/why-does-obama-want-the-trans -pacific-partnership-so-badly.

21 Lewis R. Gordon, *Disciplinary Decadence: Living Thoughts in Trying Times* (London: Routledge, 2007).

22 In their path-breaking article, Quijano and Imanuel Wallerstein connected the invention of America with the formation of the colonial matrix of power (Quijano's formulation): "Americanity as a Concept or the Americans in the Modern/World System," *International Social Science Journal* 34, no. 4 (1992): 549–57. Notice that "modern/world system" is Wallerstein's concept. "Modern-colonial world system" it is not Wallerstein's concept; it has been conceived by and since Quijano's work.

23 Schmitt, *The Nomos of the Earth*, 86–100.

24 I explore in more detail the issues of human subjectivity and the invention of "nature" in chapter 3 of the book I coauthored with Catherine Walsh: *On Decoloniality: Concepts, Analytics, Praxis* (Durham, NC: Duke University Press, 2018).

25 "Territorial Disputes in the South China Sea," Council on Foreign Relations, Global Conflict Tracker, September 24, 2020, https://www.cfr.org/global-conflict -tracker/conflict/territorial-disputes-south-china-sea.

26 Max Horkheimer, "Traditional and Critical Theory," in *Critical Theory: Selected Essays*, trans. Matthew J. O'Connell (New York: Continuum 1975 [1937]), 188–243.

27 The entire argument of my book *The Darker Side of the Renaissance* has been guided by these principles.

28 Walter D. Mignolo, *The Idea of Latin America* (London: Wiley-Blackwell Manifestos, 2005).

29 Definition of "hemisphere," *Online Etymology Dictionary*, accessed January 3, 2021, https://www.etymonline.com/word/hemisphere.

30 "The Global North/South Divide," Royal Geographical Society, accessed May 25, 2020, https://www.rgs.org/CMSPages/GetFile.aspx?nodeguid=9c1ce781-9117-4741 -afoa-a6a8b75f32b4&lang=en-GB.

31 See Madina Tlostanova, "The South of the Poor North: Caucasus Subjectivity and the Complex of Secondary 'Australism,'" in "The Global South and World Dis/Order," ed. Caroline Levander and Walter Mignolo, special issue: *Global South* 5, no. 1 (2011): 66–84.

32 Jack Keilo, "Jerusalem at the Very Center of the World, Bünting's Map and Social Construction," Centres and Centralities, August 2013, updated July 3, 2016, https://centrici.hypotheses.org/215.

33 For more on Mercator, see Marc Vis, "History of the Mercator Projection" (undergraduate thesis, University of Utrecht, 2018).

34 On the meaning of Ortelius's map, see especially chapter 5 of my book *The Darker Side of the Renaissance*.

35 Fernand Braudel, *The Mediterranean and the Mediterranean World in the Age of Philip II*, trans. Siân Reynolds (Berkeley: University of California Press, 1995 [1949]).

36 "Obama announced it in Japan in 2009": Mark E. Manyin, coordinator, *Pivot to the Pacific? The Obama Administration's "Rebalancing" Toward Asia*, Congressional Research Service, March 28, 2012, https://fas.org/sgp/crs/natsec/R42448.pdf. See also Aaron Mehta, "'Pivot to the Pacific' Is Over, Senior U.S. Diplomat Says," *Defense News*, March 14, 2017, https://www.defensenews.com/pentagon/2017/03/14/pivot -to-the-pacific-is-over-senior-u-s-diplomat-says/.

37 "Israel miembro de la Alianza del Pacífico" (Israel joins Pacific Alliance), Embassy of Israel, Dominican Republic, December 2, 2014, https://embassies.gov.il /santo-domingo/NewsAndEvents/Pages/ISRAEL-ACEPTADO-COMO-PAIS -OBSERVADOR-EN-ALIANZA-DEL-PACIFICO.aspx.

38 Walter D. Mignolo, "Venezuela: The Symptoms of Multipolarity," DOC Research Institute, January 29, 2019, https://doc-research.org/2019/01/venezuela-symptoms -multipolarity/.

39 Walter D. Mignolo, "The Logic of the In-Visible: Decolonial Reflections on the Change of Epoch," *Theory, Culture and Society* 37, no. 7/8 (December 2020), https:// journals.sagepub.com/doi/10.1177/0263276420957741.

1 Kishore Mahbubani, *The New Asian Hemisphere: The Irresistible Shift of Global Power to the East* (New York: Public Affairs, 2008).

2 Serge Latouche, *L'occidentalization du monde* (Paris: Maspero, 1989), locates the origin of Westernization around the mid-seventeenth century. It is the limited European view of modern/colonial history.

3 Kishore Mahbubani, "Peeling Away the Western Veneer," *New Perspective Quarterly* 30, no. 4 (2013): 87–91.

4 Kishore Mahbubani, *Has the West Lost It? A Provocation* (London: Penguin, 2018).

5 S. Rajaratnam, *The Prophetic and the Political: Selected Speeches and Writings*, ed. Chan Heng Chee and Obaid ul Haq (Singapore: Graham Brash, 1987).

6 Lee Kuan Yew, interview on *Meet the Press*, October 22, 1967, video, https://www.youtube.com/watch?v=VexrmTacOAA; see also Lee Kuan Yew, "The Future of China," interview in *Lee Kuan Yew: The Grand Master's Insights on China, the United States, and the World*, ed. Graham Allison and Robert D. Blackwill with Ali Wayne (Cambridge, MA: MIT Press, 2012), 1–18.

7 Wang Hui's four volumes tracing the history of Chinese thought give you an idea of what I am talking about. Wang Hui, *China from Empire to Nation-State*, trans. Michael Gibbs Hill (Cambridge, MA: Harvard University Press, 2014). For a quick view, see "The Liberation of the Object and the Interrogation of Modernity: Rethinking *The Rise of Chinese Thought*," *Modern China* 34, no. 1 (2008): 114–40, and "A Dialogue on *The Rise of Modern Chinese Thought: Liberating the Object and an Inquiry into the Modern*," *Positions: Asia Critique* 20, no. 1 (2012): 287–306. The subtitle announces border thinking.

8 Sukarno, "Opening Address Given by Sukarno (Bandung, 18 April 1955)," CVCE.eu, accessed September 30, 2020, https://www.cvce.eu/en/obj/opening_address_given _by_sukarno_bandung_18_april_1955-en-88d3f71c-c9f9-415a-b397-b27b8581a4f5 .html.

9 Iran and Saudi Arabia, for example, were under dynastic rulers. For the rest of the countries present at the conference, see "Final Comuniqué of the Asian Conference of Bandung (April 1955)," CVCE.eu, accessed January 4, 2021, https:// www.cvce.eu/en/obj/final_communique_of_the_asian_african_conference_of _bandung_24_april_1955-en-676237bd-72f7-471f-949a-88b6ae513585.html.

10 Walter D. Mignolo, "Re:emerging, Decentering and Delinking: Shifting the Geographies of Sensing, Believing and Knowing," *Ibraaz: Contermporary Visual Culture in North Africa and the Middle East*, May 8, 2013, https://www.ibraaz.org/essays/59. More recently, the politics of cultural de-Westernization have continued. See Mylène Ferrand Lointier, "Yuko Hasegawa: 'New Sensorium—Exiting from the Failures of Modernization,'" *Seismopolite: Journal of Art and Politics*, August 2016, http://www.seismopolite.com/yuko-hasegawa-new-sensorium-exiting-from-the -failures-of-modernization.

11 Syed Muhammad Naquib Al-Attas, *Islam and Secularism* (Lahore: Suhail Academy, 1978), 133–68.

12 Mahbubani, *The New Asian Hemisphere*, 127–74.

13 Walter D. Mignolo, "The Role of the BRICS Countries in the Becoming World Order," in *Humanity and Difference in the Global Age* (Beijing: Académie de la Latinité, 2012), http://alati.com.br/fr/publicacoes/humanity-and-difference-in -the-global-age/. Walter D. Mignolo, "Neither Capitalism, nor Communism but Decolonization, Part I," *Critical Legal Studies: Law and the Political*, March 21, 2012, http://criticallegalthinking.com/2012/03/21/neither-capitalism-nor-communism -but-decolonization-an-interview-with-walter-mignolo/.

14 J. William Fulbright, *The Arrogance of Power* (New York: Random House, 1967). In the same vein, Juan Bosch, *Pentagonism: A Substitute for Imperialism* (New York: Grove Press, 1968). Bosch follows up on Fulbright, addressing US foreign policy in the Caribbean and Latin America.

15 For more details, see Yanis Varoufakis, "The Global Plan," in *The Global Minotaur* (London: Zed Books, 2011), 93, 94. "For the first time since the rise of capitalism, all the world's trade relied on a single currency (the dollar) and was financed on a single epicenter (Wall Street). . . . Washington since 1932 realized that history had presented them with a remarkable opportunity: to erect a post-war global order that would cast American hegemony in stainless steel" (57). This unfolding is parallel and complementary to the arrogance of power and to "pentagonism."

16 Palash Ghosh, "BRICS Summit-Delhi Declaration," *International Business Times*, March 29, 2012, http://www.ibtimes.com/articles/321440/20120329/brics-delhi -declaration-russia-china-india-brazil.htm; "Fourth BRICS Summit: Delhi Declaration," University of Toronto, BRICS Information Centre, March 29, 2012, http://www.brics.utoronto.ca/docs/120329-delhi-declaration.html. In 2016 Mahbubani coauthored an article with Larry Summers, "The Fusion of Civiliza- tions: The Case for Global Optimism," *Foreign Affairs*, May/June 2016, https://www .foreignaffairs.com/articles/2016-04-18/fusion-civilizations, which echoes Mah- bubani's book *The Great Convergence: Asia, the West and the Logic of One World* (New York: Public Affairs, 2014). Summers's and Mahabubani's views run parallel with a gap: Summers is a territorial thinker; East Asia is an object of study. Mahbubani is a de-Western, decolonial thinker.

17 Syed Farid Alatas, "The Islamization of Knowledge: Interview with Farid Alatas," *Religioscope* 2 (January 2008), http://religion.info/english/interviews/article_358 .shtml.

18 Al-Attas, "The Dewesternization of Knowledge," in *Islam and Secularism*, 133.

19 Hans M. Weerstra, "De-Westernizing the Gospel: The Recovery of Biblical Worldview," *International Journal of Frontier Missions* 16, no. 3 (Fall 1999): 129–34; E. Randolph Richard and Brandon J. O'Brien, *Misreading Scripture with Western Eyes: Removing Cultural Blinders to Better Understand the Bible* (London: IVP Books, 2012).

20 Rufus Burrow Jr., "Toward Womanist Theology and Ethics," *Journal of Feminist Studies and Religion* 15, no. 1 (Spring 1999): 77–95; George E. Tinker, *Spirit and Resis- tance: Political Theology and American Indian Liberation* (Minneapolis, MN: Fortress Press, 2004). It should be noted that "political theology" has nothing whatsoever to do with Carl Schmitt's book of a similar title. James H. Cone, *Black Theology of Liberation* (New York: Orbis Books, 1970).

21 The expression "weapon of the people" is from Jean Casimir. See his *Une lecture décoloniale de l'histoire des haïtiens: Du Traité de Ryswick à l'occupation américaine (1697–1915)* (Port au Prince: L'Imprimeur, 2018). English translation: *The Haitians: A Decolonial History*, trans. Laurent Dubois, fwd. Walter D. Mignolo (Chapel Hill: University of North Carolina Press, 2020).

22 "The Bull Inter Caera (Alexander VI), May 4, 1493," NativeWeb.org, accessed May 8, 2020, https://tainowoman.com/about/the-tie-system/the-inter-caetera -bull-1493-and-el-requerimiento-of-charles-i-1514/. The few that claim to be of Taino and Arawak descent (the natives that lived in the islands before the Spanish intrusion, without passports) are correcting this and many other historical aberrations still interpreted as human progress in bringing Christianity and Western civilization to the "Americas."

23 This legacy is precisely what Kishore Mahbubani addresses in one of his early books. See Suzy Hansen, "Can Asians Think?," *Salon*, March 26, 2002, http://www .salon.com/2002/03/25/asians/.

24 Law Wing Sang, *Collaborative Colonial Power: The Making of the Hong Kong Chinese* (Hong Kong: Hong Kong University Press, 2009). See also Peter d'Errico, "'Collaborative Colonialism': A Way to Analyze Native/Non-native Relations," *Indian Country Today*, May 10, 2017, https://indiancountrytoday.com/archive /collaborative-colonialism-a-way-to-analyze-native-non-native-relations-9_JBS _CkToasH56sAHJflA.

25 Pablo Peralta M., "Bolivia's CONAMAQ (Consejo Nacional de Ayllus y Markas del Qullasuyu) Indigenous Movement," *Upside Down World*, May 2014, http:// upsidedownworld.org/archives/bolivia/bolivias-conamaq-indigenous-movement -we-will-not-sell-ourselves-to-any-government-or-political-party/.

26 See Walter D. Mignolo, "The Communal and the Decolonial," *Turbulence*, 2010, http://www.turbulence.org.uk/index.html@p=391.html.

27 "American Leadership in the World," The Record: White House Archives, President Barack Obama, 2009–2016, accessed May 8, 2020, https:// obamawhitehouse.archives.gov/the-record/foreign-policy. Mahbubani and Summers, "The Fusion of Civilizations." This is not the occasion to comment on the shift in Mahbubani's argument. I refer to questions raised by Stephen M. Walt, "The (Con)Fusion of Civilizations," *Foreign Affairs*, May 4, 2016, http:// foreignpolicy.com/2016/05/04/the-confusion-of-civilizations-larry-summers -enlightenment/.

28 Kishore Mahbubani, "Western Dominance Is an Historical Aberration," interview by Ankita Mukhopadhyay, *The Fair Observer*, October 23, 2019, https://www .fairobserver.com/region/asia_pacific/us-uk-china-india-east-west-dominance -balance-power-news-16251/.

29 Diego A. Manrique, "Los dilemas del filántropo Bono," *El Pais*, September 20, 2010, https://elpais.com/diario/2010/09/20/cultura/1284933606_850215.html.

30 Walter D. Mignolo, "Bono contra China," Personal blog, Internet Archive, November 1, 2007, https://web.archive.org/web/20071210093257 /http://waltermignolo.com/2007/11/01/bono-contra-china/.

31 Partha Chatterjee, "Talking about Our Modernity in Two Languages," in *A Possible India: Essays in Political Criticism* (Calcutta: Oxford University Press, 1998), 263–285.

Ten. The South of the North and the West of the East

EPIGRAPH: Quoted by Osamah F. Khalil, "The Crossroads of the World: U.S. and British Foreign Policy Doctrines and the Construct of the Middle East, 1902–2007," 2014.

1 According to WIKI 2: Wikipedia Republished, the expression "Global South" is attributed to Carl Oglesby, a US teacher and activist, in an article published in the journal *Commonweal* devoted to the Vietnam War and published in 1969. WIKI 2, s.v. "Global South," last modified December 23, 2020, https://wiki2.org/en/Global_South.

2 Franco Cassano, *Southern Thoughts and Other Essays* (New York: Fordham University Press, 2012); Roberto M. Dainotto, "Does Europe Have a South? An Essay on Borders," in "The Global South and World Dis/Order," ed. Caroline Levander and Walter D. Mignolo, special issue: *Global South* 5, no. 1 (2011): 37–50; Madina Tlostanova, "The South of the Poor North: Caucasus Subjectivity and the Complex of Secondary 'Australism,'" in Levander and Mignolo, "The Global South and World Dis/Order," 66–87; Boaventura de Sousa Santos, ed., *Epistemologies of the South: Justice against Epistemicide* (London: Routledge, 2014).

3 Raewyn Connell, *Southern Theory: Social Sciences and the Global Dynamics of Knowledge* (Sydney: Allen and Unwin, 2008); Raewyn Connell and Nour Dados, "Where in the World Does Neoliberalism Come From?," *Theory and Society* 43 (2014): 117; Jean and John Commaroff, *Theory from the South, or, How Euro-America Is Evolving toward Africa* (Boulder, CO: Paradigm, 2012); Sabelo J. Ndlovu-Gatsheni, *Epistemic Freedom in Africa: Deprovincialization and Decolonization* (London: Routledge, 2018).

4 Madina Tlostanova, "Between the Russian/Soviet Dependencies, Neoliberal Delusions, Dewesternizing Options, and Decolonial Drives," *Cultural Dynamics* 27, no. 2 (July 1, 2015): 267–83, DOI: 10.1177/0921374015585230; "The South of the Poor North"; "Life in Samarkand: Caucasus and Central Asia vis-à-vis Russia, the West and Islam," *Human Architecture* 5, no. 1 (2006): 105–16; *What Does It Mean to Be Post-Soviet? Decolonial Art from the Ruins of the Soviet Empire* (Durham, NC: Duke University Press, 2018); Walter D. Mignolo and Madina V. Tlostanova, *Learning to Unlearn: Decolonial Reflections from Eurasia and the Americas* (Columbus: Ohio State University Press, 2012).

5 The Program in Latino/a Studies in the Global South at Duke University has inserted itself in the larger scenes of dividing global linear thinking (see below for this expression).

6 Kuan-Hsing Chen, *Asia as Method: Toward Deimperialization* (Durham, NC: Duke University Press, 2010).

7 Carl E. Pletsch, "The Three Worlds, or the Division of Social Scientific Labor, circa 1950–1975," *Comparative Studies in Society and History* 23, no. 4 (1981): 565–90, https://www.jstor.org/stable/178394.

8 The ethnological and historical foundation of modern/colonial Western knowledge has been powerfully documented and argued by Anthony Pagden in his classic book *The Fall of Natural Man: The American Indian and the Origins of Comparative Ethnology* (Cambridge, UK: Cambridge University Press, 1982), https://academic.oup.com/ahr/article-abstract/88/4/1114/113467?redirectedFrom=fulltext. See particularly chapters 6, 7, and 8 on Bartolomé de Las Casas, Josè de Acosta, and Joseph Francois Lafitau.

9 Chen, *Asia as Method.*

10 I have been making this argument through the years. See, for instance, *Local Histories/Global Designs: Coloniality, Subaltern Knowledges, and Border Thinking,* 2nd ed. (Princeton, NJ: Princeton University Press, 2012 [2000]), and "Epistemic Disobedience, Independent Thought, and Decolonial Freedom," *Theory, Culture and Society* 26, no. 7–8 (2009): 159–81, DOI: 10.1177/0263276409349275. See also Walter D. Mignolo and Madina V. Tlostanova, "Theorizing from the Borders: Shifting to Geo- and Body-Politics of Knowledge," *European Journal of Social Theory* 9, no. 2 (2006): 205–21, DOI: 10.1177/1368431006063333.

11 My reflections on the amalgamation of languaging and the use of hands owes a debt to Humberto Maturana, "Biology of Language: The Epistemology of Reality," in *Psychology and Biology of Language and Thought: Essays in Honor of Eric Lenneberg,* ed. George A. Miller and Elizabeth Lenneberg (New York: Academic Press, 1978), 27–63, and André Leroi-Gourhan, *Le geste et la parole* (Paris: Albin Michel, 1964).

12 Walter D. Mignolo, "The Global South and World Dis/Order," *Journal of Anthropological Research* 67, no. 2 (2011): 165–88, https://www.journals.uchicago.edu/doi/10.3998/jar.0521004.0067.202. See also Levander and Mignolo, "The Global South and World Dis/Order."

13 Carl Schmitt, *The Nomos of the Earth in the International Law of the Jus Publicum Europaeum,* trans. G. L. Ulmen (New York: Telos Press, 2006 [1950]). For my take on it, check out Walter D. Mignolo, "From the Global Linear Thinking to a Multipolar World," *Radio Papesse,* May 2015, https://www.radiopapesse.org/en/archive/interviews/walter-mignolo-from-the-global-linear-thinking-to-a-multipolar-world.

14 Cartography and the colonization of space (or cartographic coloniality) was explored in chapters 5 and 6 of my book *The Darker Side of the Renaissance: Literacy, Territoriality, and Colonization* (Ann Arbor: University of Michigan Press, 2012 [1995]).

15 Elizabeth Hill Boone and Walter D. Mignolo, *Writing without Words: Alternative Literacies in Mesoamerica and the Andes* (Durham, NC: Duke University Press, 1994).

16 InterCP International, "Introducing the Maghreb Window: The Land Where the Sun Sets, the End of the Earth," *Global Alliance Newsletter,* May 2014, http://www.intercp.org/2014/05/introducing-the-maghreb-window-the-land-where-the-sun-sets-the-end-of-the-earth/.

17 Osamah F. Khalil, "The Crossroads of the World: U.S. and British Foreign Policy Doctrines and the Construct of the Middle East, 1902–2007," *Diplomatic History* 38, no. 2 (2014): 299–344.

18 Richard Beck, "Why Are We in the Middle East?," *n+1 Magazine*, Fall 2016, https://nplusonemag.com/issue-26/reviews/why-are-we-in-the-middle-east/.

19 "The Global North/South Divide," Royal Geographical Society, accessed May 25, 2020, https://www.rgs.org/CMSPages/GetFile.aspx?nodeguid=9c1ce781-9117-4741-af0a-a6a8b75f32b4&lang=en-GB.

20 I am referring here to the classical debate in analytical philosophy prompted by Willard Van Orman Quine's article "On What There Is," *Review of Metaphysics* 2, no. 5 (1948): 21–38.

21 Tlostanova, "The South of the Poor North."

22 At that time, no one had a clear vision of the position and form of the Indias Occidentales landmasses, but figures 10.3 and 10.4 illustrate what the Treaty of Tordesillas accomplished. The Spanish mapping of "Indias del Poniente" unfolded after the treaty. "Poniente" means "where the sun sets." The observer is located in Spain. See the detailed cartographic account by Ricardo Padrón, *The Indies of the Setting Sun: How Early Modern Spain Mapped the Far East and the Transpacific West* (Chicago: University of Chicago Press, 2020). Considering this account, "Orientalism" was the outcome of the ascendant northern Europeans looking East, while for Spanish cartographers, Orientalism and Occidentalism were two extremes of the empire. French, British, and German intellectuals could not have been concerned with Occidentalism, for their monarchies were overwhelmed by Spain and Portugal in the New World.

23 By 1530, although no one at the time had the image of Earth that we have today, the planet as mapped by the pope and the crowns of the Iberian Peninsula looked more or less as shown in figures 10.3 and 10.4 in this chapter.

24 Chen Hong, "On Matteo Rici's Interpretations of Chinese Culture," *Coalabah* 16 (2015): 87–100, https://revistes.ub.edu/index.php/coolabah/article/view/15426; Florin-Stefan Morar, "The Westerner: Matteo Ricci's World Map and the Quanderies on the European Identity in the Late Ming Dynasty," *Journal of Jesuit Studies* 6, no. 1 (2019): 14–30, https://brill.com/view/journals/jjs/6/1/article-p14_14.xml?language=en.

25 I explored this issue in detail in chapter 5 of *The Darker Side of the Renaissance*, and I examined the implications of the nomos of the Earth in chapter 2 of *The Darker Side of Western Modernity: Global Futures, Decolonial Options* (Durham, NC: Duke University Press, 2011).

26 Beyond the already classic and monumental (multivolume) book *The History of Cartography*, published by the University of Chicago Press, two more recent and specific histories of cartography are, from the Spanish perspective (that is, the South of Europe), Ricardo Padrón, *The Spacious Word: Cartography, Literature, and Empire in Early Modern Spain* (Chicago: University of Chicago Press, 2004), and, from the British perspective (that is, the North of Europe), the also excellent Jerry Brotton, *A History of the World in 12 Maps* (New York: Viking, 2013).

27 Ehiedu E. G. Iweriebor, "The Colonization of Africa," *Africana Age*, Schomburg Center for Research in Black Culture, New York Public Library, accessed May 26, 2020, https://wayback.archive-it.org/11788/20200107232503/http://exhibitions.nypl.org/africanaage/index2.html; see also Walter D. Mignolo, "Bono contra China," personal blog, Internet Archive, November 1, 2007, https://web.archive.org/web/20071210093257/http://waltermignolo.com/2007/11/01/bono-contra-china/.

28 See Madina Tlostanova, "Internal Colonization: Russia's Imperial Experience (Book Review)," *Postcolonial Europe*, May 2014, http://www.postcolonial-europe.eu/reviews/166-book-review-internal-colonization-russias-imperial-experience-.html.

29 Samuel P. Huntington, *The Clash of Civilizations and the Remaking of the World Order* (New York: Simon and Schuster, 1996). See also "First, Second and Third World," Nations Online Project, accessed Sept 30, 2020, https://www.nationsonline.org/oneworld/third_world_countries.htm.

30 See Walter D. Mignolo, "Re:Emerging, Decentering and Delinking: Shifting the Geographies of Sensing, Believing and Knowing," *Ibraaz: Contemporary Visual Culture in North Africa and the Middle East*, May 8, 2013, https://www.ibraaz.org/essays/59/.

31 The inversion of Aristotelian cause-effect logic by the logic of coloniality was disclosed by Frantz Fanon: "You are rich because you are white, you are white because you are rich." See *The Wretched of the Earth*, trans. Richard Philcox (New York: Grove Press, 2004 [1961]), 5.

32 Alexandra Peers, "Qatar Purchases Cézanne's *The Card Players* for More than $250 Million, Highest Price Ever for a Work of Art," *Vanity Fair*, February 2, 2012, http://www.vanityfair.com/culture/2012/02/qatar-buys-cézanne-card-players-201202; Robin Progrebin, "Qatar Redrawing the Art Scene," *Gulf News*, July 27, 2013; "With Annual Acquisition Budget of $1 Billion a Year, Shaikha Al Mayassa is Creating a First Class Contemporary Collection," *Gulf News*, July 27, 2013.

33 Sheikha Al Mayassa, "Globalizing the Local," TEDWomen 2010, accessed September 30, 2020, https://www.ted.com/talks/sheikha_al_mayassa_globalizing_the_local_localizing_the_global/transcript?language=en.

34 "Emerging political society": Partha Chatterjee, "On Civil and Political Society in Postcolonial Democracies," *Notes on Scholarly Books* (blog), May 2009, http://notesonscholarlybooks.blogspot.com/2009/05/partha-chatterjee-on-civil-and.html.

35 See the dossier by Walter D. Mignolo and Rolando Vázquez, "Decolonial AestheSis: Colonial Wounds/Decolonial Healings," *Social Text: Periscope*, July 15, 2013, https://socialtextjournal.org/periscope_article/decolonial-aesthesis-colonial-woundsdecolonial-healings/.

Eleven. Mariátegui and Gramsci in "Latin" America

1 Srivastava, Neelam, and Baidik Bhattacharya, eds., *The Postcolonial Gramsci* (London: Routledge, 2011). I use quotation marks for "Latin" America because, as I have argued in *The Idea of Latin America* (London: Wiley-Blackwell Manifestos, 2005), "Latin America" is not a subcontinent but a political project. It is the

political project of the sector of the population of European descent that has controlled the state, the economy, and education since the respective independence of the newly formed countries starting at the beginning of the nineteenth century. Such political projects sidelined the Indigenous and Afro-descendant sectors of the population. Decolonial politics today is emerging from these sectors.

2 Jean-François Lyotard, *La condition postmoderne* (Paris: Les Éditions de Minuit, 1979). A decade later Fredric Jameson published in the US his celebrated *Postmodernism, or the Cultural Logic of Late Capitalism* (Durham, NC: Duke University Press, 1991).

3 Jameson, *Postmodernism*, 22.

4 Lyotard, *La condition postmoderne*, xxiv.

5 An important scheme of the history of US foreign politics in South/Central America and the Caribbean is provided by Juan Bosch, former Dominican Republic democratic president (who lasted only a few months in power after being elected). See his *Pentagonism: A Substitute for Imperialism* (New York: Grove Press, 1968; Spanish ed. 1967).

6 See, for example, the arguments by Iranian theologian and intellectual Ali Shari'ati and Caribbean sociologist and thinker Loyd Best. Ali Shari'ati, *Man and Islam* (Baltimore: Islamic Publications International, 1977); "Man and Islam: 'The Free Man and Freedom of Man,'" Iran Chamber Society, accessed September 6, 2020, http://www.iranchamber.com/personalities/ashariati/works/free_man _freedom_man.php. Lloyd Best, "Independent Thoughts and Caribbean Freedom: Thirty Years Later," *Caribbean Quarterly* 43, no. 1/2 (March–June 1997): 16–24, https://www.jstor.org/stable/40653983.

7 See Charles E. Frye, "Carl Schmitt's Concept of the Political," *Journal of Politics* 28, no. 4 (November 1966): 818–30.

8 Klaus Schwab, *The Fourth Industrial Revolution* (Davos, Switz.: Currency Publisher, 2017), 97–115. See also the web page https://www.weforum.org/agenda/2016/01/the -fourth-industrial-revolution-what-it-means-and-how-to-respond/.

9 For the "arrival" of Gramsci in Brazil in the 1960s, see Lincoln Secco, *A recepção de Gramsci no Brasil* (São Paulo: Cortez, 2002). In Argentina, see José M. Casco, "El Gramsci de Portantiero: Cultura, política e intelectuales en la argentina de postguerra," *Acta Sociológia* 68 (2015): 71–93.

10 Fausto Reinaga, *La revolución India* (La Paz: Partido Indio de Bolivia, 1969), https:// elcondortk.blogspot.com/2018/09/la-revolucion-india-de-fausto-reinaga.html.

11 A recently published article refreshes the reading of Gramsci in "Latin" America and takes issue with the state politics of Evo Morales and García Linera. It was García Linera rather than Morales who brought Gramsci into state politics, through the fundamental work of Zavaleta Mercado between the late 1960s and the 1980s, which I examine in this chapter. See Michela Coletta and Malayna Raftopoulos, "Latin America Readings of Gramsci and the Bolivian Indigenous National State," *Latin American and Caribbean Ethnic Studies*, Taylor and Francis Online, August 10, 2020, https://www.tandfonline.com/doi/full/10.1080/17442222 .2020.1805845?scroll=top&needAccess=true.

12 Giles Tremlett, "Operation Condor: The Cold War Conspiracy That Terrorized South America," *The Guardian*, September 3, 2020, https://www.theguardian.com/news/2020/sep/03/operation-condor-the-illegal-state-network-that-terrorised-south-america.

13 See Walter D. Mignolo, "Coloniality of Power and Subalternity," in *The Latin American Subaltern Studies Reader*, ed. Ileana Rodriguez (Durham, NC: Duke University Press, 2001), 224–44.

14 Fausto Reinaga, who self-identified as *qheswaymaras* (of Aymara and Quechua descent), was a prolific writer and intense activist. He confronted Indianism with Occidentalism, which includes the non-Indigenous population in Bolivia, whether liberal or Marxist. Although he was aligned with Marxism in the 1950s, in his seminal book *La revolución India* he connects Marxism with Occidentalism. Frantz Fanon was, for Reinaga, understandably, an ally and inspiration; both addressed Third World politics in general and, in particular, racism based on their respective local histories. As for Gramsci's presence in Afro-Caribbean politics and philosophy, it seems to be absent. See the chapter titled "Caribbean Marxism: After the Neoliberal and Linguistic Turn" in Paget Henry, *Caliban's Reason: Introducing Afro-Caribbean Philosophy* (London: Routledge, 2000), 221–246. Although the chapter focuses on recent years, it is preceded by a contextualization going back to the 1960s. Furthermore, from what I know of the very creative and politically influential Caribbean New World project, Gramsci did not have much to offer to it. For a great profile of this group and its achievements, see Brian Meeks and Norman Girvan, eds., *Caribbean Reasonings: The Thought of New World, the Quest for Decolonisation* (Kingston, JM: Ian Randle Publishers, 2010).

15 For the "transition to democracy," see Guillermo O'Donnell and Philippe C. Schmitter, *Transitions from Authoritarian Rules: Tentative Conclusions about Uncertain Democracies* (Baltimore: Johns Hopkins University Press, 2013); Hernán Pablo Toppi, "Guillermo O'Donnell y su aporte al desarrollo de la democracia en América Latina desde la tercera ola·de democratización," *Revista del Instituto de Ciencias Jurídicas de Puebloa* 12, no. 42 (2018): 9–28; José Nun, *La situación de los sectores populares en el prodeso argentine de transición hacia la democracia* (Buenos Aires: Centro Latinoamericano para el Análisis de la democracia, 1988). Nun distinguished "liberal democracy" from "democratic liberalism" to avoid the imperial bent associated with the former expression.

16 Nicos Poulantzas, *Las clases sociales en el capitalismo actual*, 10th ed. (Mexico City: Siglo Veintiuno Editores, 1977).

17 René Zavaleta Mercado, *Lo nacional-popular en Bolivia* (La Paz: Los Amigos del Libro, 1986). See also Luis H. Antezana, *Dos conceptos en la obra de René Zavaleta Mercado: Formación abigarrada y democracia como autodeterminación* (College Park, MD: Latin American Studies Center Series 1, 1991).

18 "National-popular" is René Zavaleta Mercado's concept indicating that the national is not entirely popular, but the popular is a sector of the national. See *Lo nacional-popular en Bolivia*, specifically chapter xviii, "La estructura explicativa de lo nacional-popular en Bolivia."

19 On the work of René Zavaleta Mercado, see Luis Antezana, *La diversidad social en Zavaleta Mercado* (La Paz: Centro Boliviano de Estudios Multidisciplinarios, 1991); Luis Tapia, *La producción del conocimiento local: Historia y política en la obra de René Zavaleta Mercado* (La Paz: Universidad Mayor de San Andrés, 2002). In reality, Tapia's book is mostly, and rightly so, about "the local production of knowledge" rather than "the production of local knowledge." This is precisely the point I am underlining here on Gramsci and Mariátegui; they are engaged in the local production of knowledge rather than in the production of local knowledge.

20 See an updated review in Anne Freeland, "The Gramscian Turn: Readings from Brazil, Argentina and Bolivia, *A Contracorriente* 11, no. 2 (2014): 278-301.

21 Pablo González Casanova, "Colonialismo interno (una redefinición)," in *La teoría marxista hoy*, ed. A. Boron, J. Amadeo, and S. González (Buenos Aires: Consejo Latinoamericano de Ciencias Sociales [CLASCO], 2006), 409-34; Adriana Chazarreta, "La propuesta analítica de Rodolfo Stavenhagen," *Prácticas de oficio, investigación y reflexión en ciencias sociales* 6 (August 2010), https://static.ides.org.ar /archivo/www/2012/04/artic123.pdf.

22 Antonio Gramsci, *The Southern Question* (Montreal: Guernica Editions, 2006), 38.

23 José Carlos Mariátegui, *Seven Interpretative Essays on Peruvian Reality* (Austin: University of Texas Press, 1971 [1928]), 41.

24 Fascism in Europe and internal colonialism in South America at the time were two faces of modernity. Barbarism, in other words, is the hidden side of civilization, not its opposite. On this topic see Eric Hobsbawm, "Barbarism: A User's Guide," *New Left Review* 1, no. 206 (1994): 44-54.

25 Gramsci, *The Southern Question*, 32.

26 Mariátegui, *Seven Interpretative Essays on Peruvian Reality*, 25.

27 Mariátegui, *Seven Interpretative Essays on Peruvian Reality*, 33.

28 Aníbal Quijano, "Colonialidad y Modernidad/Racionalidad," in *Los conquistados: 1492 y la población indígena* (Bogotá: Tercer Mundo Editores, 1992), 11-20. Although the concept was already circulating at the end of the 1980s, the first printed version was in 1992. For an updated version of this article in English, see Quijano, "Coloniality and Modernity/Rationality," in *Cultural Studies* 21, no. 2-3 (2007 [1992]): 168-78, DOI: 10.1080/09502380601164353.

29 See, for instance, Joaquin Santana, "Gramsci y Mariátegui," Centro de Estudios Miguel Enríquez, Archivo Chile, 2003-2006, accessed May 6, 2020, https://static.ides.org.ar/archivo/www/2012/04/artic123.pdf. Santana is professor of philosophy at the Universidad of Habana, Cuba. Notice that Gramsci comes first; it is not "Mariátegui and Gramsci" but the other way around. The title of this chapter confronts this long-lasting self-colonized mentality in South America. See also Osvaldo Fernández-Díaz, "Gramsci y Mariátegui frente a la ortodoxia," *Nueva Sociedad* 115 (1991): 135-44. The author is a Chilean professor at Paris Nanterre University. Again, the title of this article rehearses Eurocentrism from the left.

30 I have explored in several places the question of "Latinity," notably in *The Idea of Latin America*. It was very well known and debated among intellectuals from the right and from the left that "Latinity" was mainly a French imperial export and an import of the right-wing South American elite.

31 Antonio Gramsci, *Prison Notebooks*, trans. and ed. Joseph A. Buttigieg, vol. 2 (New York: Columbia University Press, 2011), 11. Gramsci's text in Italian can be found in *I Quaderni di Cacere*, accessed January 6, 2021, https://quadernidelcarcere .wordpress.com.

32 Gramsci, *Prison Notebooks*, 11.

33 The myth of the Indian's passivity was widespread among the population of European descent in South America. But not only in South America, it was global. See, for instance, for Southeast Asia, Syed Hussein Alatas, *The Myth of the Lazy Native: A Study of the Image of the Malays, Filipinos and Javanese from the 16th to the 20th Century and Its Function in the Ideology of Colonial Capitalism* (London: Frank Casa and Co., 1977).

34 David Forgacs, "Some Aspects of the Southern Question," in *The Antonio Gramsci Reader: Selected Writings 1916-1935* (New York: New York University Press, 2000), 171-85.

35 Alberto Flores Galindo, *La agonía de Mariátegui: La polémica con la Komintern* (Lima: Centro de Estudios y Promoción del Desarrollo, 1980), 20-21.

36 Manuel Burga and Alberto Flores Galindo, "Apogeo y crisis de la República Aristocrática," in Alberto Flores Galindo, *Obras Completas* (Lima: Fundación Andina, 1994 [1980]), 145-46.

37 For more on the expression "crossing gazes," see Walter D. Mignolo, "Crossing Gazes and the Silence of the 'Indians': Theodor De Bry and Guamán Poma de Ayala," *Journal of Medieval and Early Modern Studies* 41, no. 1 (2011): 173-223, DOI: 10.1215/10829636-2010-016.

38 For a more detailed explanation, see Marina Gržinić and Walter Mignolo, "De-Linking Epistemology from Capital and Pluri-Versality: A Conversation, Part I," *Reartikulacija* 4 (2008): 20-22.

39 I have elaborated on the geopolitics of knowledge in several places. See, for instance, chapter 2 of *Local Histories/Global Designs*, 2nd ed. (Princeton, NJ: Princeton University Press, 2012 [2000]). See also "Geopolitics of Knowledge and the Colonial Difference," *South Atlantic Quarterly* 101, no. 1 (Winter 2002): 57-96, DOI: 10.1215/00382876-101-1-57.

40 I have dealt with the distinction between "living" and "dwelling" on several occasions. The most recent is in Walter D. Mignolo, "I Am Where I Do," in *The Darker Side of Western Modernity: Global Futures, Decolonial Options* (Durham, NC: Duke University Press, 2011), 77-117.

41 Antonio Gramsci's translations appeared in Argentina toward the end of the 1950s and the beginning of the1960s: *El materialismo y la filosofía de Benedetto Croce* (Buenos Aires: Editorial Lautaro, 1958); *Introducción a la filosofía de la praxis*, selected and translated by J. Solé-Tura (Barcelona: Ediciones Península, 1970); *Los intelectuales y la organización de la cultura* (Buenos Aires: Ediciones Lautaro, 1960); *Notas*

sobre Maquiavelo, sobre política y sobre el estado moderno (Buenos Aires: Nueva Visión, 1973).

42 See Secco, *A recepção de Gramsci no Brasil.*

43 In retrospect, the connections are being made. However, the essays provide a Gramscian reading of the Third World from the First World. And coloniality continues on all fronts, the right, the left, and the center. See William Robinson, "A Gramscian Reading of Latin American Development" (book review), *Latin American Perspectives* 42, no. 1 (2015): 101–2.

44 David L. Blaney, "Reconceptualizing Autonomy: The Difference Dependency Theory Makes," *Review of International Political Economy* 3, no. 3 (1995): 459–97.

45 See Margaret R. Greer, Walter D. Mignolo, and Maureen Quilligan, eds., *Rereading the Black Legend: The Discourses of Religious and Racial Difference in the Renaissance Empires* (Chicago: University of Chicago Press, 2008).

46 Verónica Herrera, "The Persistence of Peronism," *Berkeley Review of Latin American Studies,* Spring 2007, http://clas.berkeley.edu/research/argentina-persistence -peronism.

47 One of the most prolific writers of the national left (delinking from the Communist Party) was Juan José Hernández Arregui (1913–1974). Among his most relevant books: *Imperialismo y cultura* (Buenos Aires: Editorial Amerindia, 1957); *La formación de la conciencia nacional* (Buenos Aires: Ediciones Hachea, 1960); *Nacionalismo y liberación* (Buenos Aires: Peña Lillo Ediciones, 2004 [1969]). Notice that the national left was active during the years that Gramsci was being translated and incorporated into the Gramscian left—two different lefts, indeed: the Euro-oriented and the nationalist.

48 José Aricó, *La cola del diablo: Itinerario de Gramsci en América Latina* (Buenos Aires: Puntosur, 1988), 34ff.

49 For more on Operation Condor, see "Operation Condor, 1968–1989," National Security Archive, accessed May 26, 2020, https://nsarchive.gwu.edu/events /operation-condor-1968-1989.

50 Aníbal Quijano, "Los usos de la democracia burguesa," in *Sociedad y Política*, reprinted in Aníbal Quijano, *Cuestiones y horizontes: Antología Esencial* (Buenos Aires: CLACSO, 2014), 245–69.

51 Reinaga, *La revolución India.*

52 Juan Carlos Portantiero, *Los usos de Gramsci* (Mexico City: Folio, 1987), 93.

53 Cristobal Kay, "Reflections on the Latin American Contribution to Development Theory," *Development and Change* 22 (1991): 31–68.

54 Partha Chatterjee, *The Nation and Its Fragments: Colonial and Postcolonial Histories* (Princeton, NJ: Princeton University Press, 1993), 14–34; Mignolo, "Geopolitics of Knowledge and the Colonial Difference."

55 See Bernardo Canal Feijóo, *El extremo occidente* (Buenos Aires: Editorial Sudamericana, 1954). The concern with being labeled "peripheral" was very pronounced in the 1950s.

56 Zulma Palermo, ed., *Pensamiento Argentino y opción descolonial*, 2nd ed. (Buenos Aires: Ediciones del Signo, 2016).

57 Ernesto Laclau left Argentina during the years that Gramsci was introduced there, and he returned Gramsci to Europe, so to speak. See Benjamin Bertram, "New Reflections on the 'Revolutionary' Politics of Ernesto Laclau and Chantal Mouffe," *boundary 2* 22, no. 3 (Autumn 1995): 81–110.

58 See Ranajit Guha, *Dominance without Hegemony* (Boston: Harvard University Press, 1997). The uses of Gramsci by Guha and the South Asian subaltern studies collective are radically different from the uses of Gramsci by the new left in Latin America. The contention for dominance between the two groups studied by Guha (the British colonial elite and the local Indian elite) was no longer comparable with the situation in South and Central America, where countries obtained "independence" in the first half of the nineteenth century.

59 See Walter D. Mignolo, "Coloniality of Power and Subalternity," in *The Latin American Subaltern Studies Reader*, ed. Ileana Rodriguez (Durham, NC: Duke University Press, 2001), 224–44; Walter D. Mignolo, "On Subaltern and Other Agencies," *Postcolonial Studies* 8, no. 4 (2005): 381–407.

60 Interestingly enough, Guha critiqued Gandhi for his shortcomings in front of the masses, while Partha Chatterjee and Ashis Nandy highly praise Gandhi for his overall decolonial (my word, not theirs) project and his confrontation with Western civilization. See Partha Chatterjee, "Modernity and Indian Nationalism," in *India Revisited: Conversation on Contemporary India*, ed. Ramin Jahanbegloo (Oxford, UK: Oxford University Press, 2008), 45–50; Ashis Nandy, "Gandhi and the Indian Identity," in Jahanbegloo, *India Revisited*, 51–58. For Gramsci, Western civilization was not a concern (nor for Marx): they were living and thinking within it. For Reinaga and Gandhi, and for Mariátegui, Western civilization was a problem because it embraced capitalism. For Marx and Gramsci, capitalism was a problem, not Western civilization. For Guha, see the section on Gandhi in *Dominance without Hegemony*. See also the interviews with Partha Chatterjee and Ashis Nandy in Jahanbegloo, *India Revisited*.

61 I say "colonial nation-states" for the simple reason that their historical foundations in America, Africa, and Asia (after World War II) differ from the historical foundation of "modern nation-states" in Europe after the French Revolution. The French Revolution was not a revolution against imperial domination; on the contrary, it opened ways to new forms of imperialism. Italy, to a minor degree, was on the same path. Italy's colonies were not on the same scale as France's and England's, but the colonial mentality (and frustrations) were there. We should remember that fascism, Nazism, and Francoism materialized in countries that remain on the margins of "the core of Europe": Spain lost all its colonies in 1898, and Italy's and Germany's colonial possessions were of a comparatively minor scale. Gramsci was living and thinking in that tradition and with those memories, while Mariátegui was aligned with the nationalist left in the colonial history of Spanish America and in a region with a high density of Indigenous population. And, of course, the subaltern studies South Asia group were still thinking within a colonial situation that not only was different from South America, but was radically different from Italy. The introduction of Gramsci in Spanish America (and in

Brazil) allowed his followers to cut the strings with the "populism" of the national left and focus instead on the theoretical aspects of class struggles within the capitalist logic: capitalist bourgeoisie against the working class. The nationalist left was fully aware of the racial aspects of colonial histories; the Gramscians were not.

62 Among the many books published on these issues, see Arregui, *Imperialismo y Cultura* and *La formación de la conciencia nacional*; Jorge Abelardo Ramos (1921–1994), *Ejército y semicolonia* (Buenos Aires: Editorial Sudestada, 1968), and *El marxismo de Indias* (Buenos Aires: Biblioteca Universal Planeta, 1972); Arturo Jauretche (1901–1974), *Ejército y política* (Buenos Aires: Peña Lillo, 1958), *Política y economía* (Buenos Aires: Peña Lillo, 1977), and *Los profetas del odio y la yapa: La colonización pedagógica* (Buenos Aires: Peña Lillo, 1975).

63 On the South Asian subaltern studies project, see the classical debate between Gyan Prakash and O'Hanlon and Washbrook, in Prakash, "Can the 'Subaltern' Ride? A Reply to O'Hanlon and Washbrook," *Comparative Studies in Society and History* 34, no. 1 (1992): 168–84.

64 For a recent reevaluation of this trajectory, see Palermo, *Pensamiento Argentino y opción descolonial.*

65 Rodolfo Kusch, *Indigenous and Popular Thinking in América*, trans. María Lugones and Joshua M. Price (Durham, NC: Duke University Press, 2010 [1970]). See the review by Rocío Quispe-Agnoli, *Hispanic Review* 79, no. 4 (Autumn 2011): 667–70. DOI: 10.1353/hir.2011.0056.

66 See Kusch, *Indigenous and Popular Thinking in América.*

67 Álvaro García Linera, "Catastrophic Equilibrium and Point of Bifurcation," MR Online, June 22, 2008, https://mronline.org/2008/06/22/catastrophic-equilibrium-and-point-of-bifurcation/.

68 Frantz Fanon, *The Wretched of the Earth*, trans. Richard Philcox (New York: Grove Press, 2004 [1961]), 5.

69 Reinaga, *La revolución India*, 1969, 382; my own translation. Notice that for Reinaga there is no "Latin" America—the America to which people of European descent belong—but rather there is "Indo" America, the America of the Indigenous today, named Abya-Yala by Indigenous people themselves. See Emilio del Valle Escalante, "For Abya-Yala to Live the Americas Must Die: Towards a Trans-Hemispheric Indigeneity," *Native Americans and Indigenous Studies* 5, no. 1 (2018): 42–68. This article was published simultaneously in Maya-Quiché and Spanish.

70 See Lewis Gordon, "What Does It Mean to Be a Problem? W. E. B. Dubois and the Study of the Black Folk," in *Existentia Africana* (London: Routledge, 2000), 65.

71 See Henry, *Caliban's Reason.*

72 Fanon, *The Wretched of the Earth*, 5.

73 Anthony Bogues, *Black Heretics, Black Prophets: Radical Political Intellectuals* (London: Routledge, 2003), 70.

74 Bogues, *Black Heretics, Black Prophets*, 71.

Twelve. Sylvia Wynter

FIRST EPIGRAPH: For readers not familiar with Maturana's work I would like to underscore two points relevant to my argument: (1) The biological-cultural conception of living organisms facilitates an understanding of the prejudgement and the charged cultural construction of the very concept of the human and the dehumanization enacted by the creators and defenders of a concept shaped according to their (male) image. (2) Maturana's introduction of the descriptor "*Homo sapiens-amans-amans*" summarizes his conceptualization of humanness, before Man1 and Man2 were culturally constructed to the benefit of some: "What is special about us human beings is that we are animals that are the present of a lineage of bipedal primates that followed an evolutionary path of transformation and change centered around the conservation of a loving manner of living in the intimacy of sharing food, tenderness, and collaboration"; that is, the fact that we, as a species, are still alive today and are—in general—born in an atmosphere of care (increasingly broken up by the growing inequality and consequent devastation of communal relations replaced by selfishness and competition, discrimination and oppression, to which replacement the self-constitution of Man1 and Man2 have greatly contributed).

1 I capitalize "Human" and "Man" in certain specific cases to underline the terms' fictional dimension, which is built on the biological ontology of the *Homo sapiens*. The word "human" in all lowercase letters refers to a variety of racialized lesser beings; hence, "human" is also a cultural fiction invented from the perspective of the Humans who control discursive meaning in the public sphere.

2 Mary Bagley, "Holocene Epoch: The Age of Man," *LiveScience*, March 27, 2013, http://www.livescience.com/28219-holocene-epoch.html.

3 See my chapter "(De)Coloniality at Large: Time and the Colonial Difference," in *The Darker Side of Western Modernity* (Durham, NC: Duke University Press, 2011), 149–80.

4 See Thomas Kuhn, *The Structure of Scientific Revolutions* (Chicago: University of Chicago Press, 1962).

5 See in this regard the compelling arguments by Gloria Wekker, *White Innocence: The Paradoxes of Colonialism and Race* (Durham, NC: Duke University Press, 2016).

6 Sandra Harding, ed. *The Postcolonial Science and Technology Studies* (Durham, NC: Duke University Press, 2011); Walter D. Mignolo, "The Splendors and Miseries of 'Science': Coloniality, Geopolitics of Knowledge, and Epistemic Pluriversality," in *Cognitive Justice in a Global World: Prudent Knowledges for a Decent Life*, ed. Boaventura de Sousa Santos, (Lanham, MD: Lexington Books, 2007), 375–96; Walter D. Mignolo, "Prophets Facing Side Wise: The Geopolitics of Knowledge and the Colonial Difference," *Social Epistemology* 19, no. 1 (2005): 111–27.

7 Larry Siedentop, *Inventing the Individual: The Origins of Western Liberalism* (London: Allen Lane Publishers, 2014).

8 Alexander G. Weheliye, *Habeas Viscus: Racializing Assemblages, Biopolitics and Black Feminist Theories of the Human* (Durham, NC: Duke University Press, 2014).

9 Vine Deloria Jr., *Evolution, Creationism and Other Modern Myths* (Ann Arbor, MI: Fulcrum Publishing, 2004). "Cosmology and Theology," *Stanford Encyclopedia of Philosophy*, rev. April 5, 2017, https://plato.stanford.edu/entries/cosmology -theology/.

10 For more on sexism in Europe, see Sylvia Federici, *Caliban and the Witch: Women, the Body and Primitive Accumulation* (Brooklyn, NY: Autonomedia, 2004).

11 Sylvia Wynter, "Unsettling the Coloniality of Being/Power/Truth/Freedom: Towards the Human, after Man, Its Overrepresentation: An Argument," *New Centennial Review* 3, no. 3 (2003): 257–337.

12 Maria Dada, "Yuk Hui, 'On the Existence of Digital Objects,'" *Theory, Culture and Society*, March 23, 2018, https://www.theoryculturesociety.org/blog/review-yuk -hui-on-the-existence-of-digital-objects.

13 Walter D. Mignolo, "Delinking: The Rhetoric of Modernity, the Logic of Co-loniality and the Grammar of De-coloniality," *Cultural Studies* 21, no. 2 (2007): 449–514, DOI: doi.org/10.1080/09502380601162647.

14 Adolfo Albán Achinte, *Prácticas creativas de re-existencia: Más allá del arte . . . el mundo de lo sensible* (Buenos Aires: Ediciones del Signo, 2018).

15 Jean Casimir, "The Counter-Plantation System," Magistral Class, Middelburg De-colonial Summer School, June 2018, https://vimeo.com/346377343; Jean Casimir, *The Haitians: A Decolonial History*, trans. Laurent Dubois, fwd. Walter D. Mignolo (Chapel Hill, NC: University of North Carolina Press, 2020).

16 Sylvia Wynter, "Beyond the Categories of the Master Conception: The Counter-doctrine of the Jamesian Poiesis," in *C. L. R. James's Caribbean*, ed. Paget Henry and Paul Buhle (Durham, NC: Duke University Press, 1992), 63–91.

17 C. L. R. James, *Notes on Dialectics: Hegel, Marx and Lenin* (Westport, CT: Lawrence Hill, 1969); C. L. R. James, *State Capitalism and World Revolution*, written in col-laboration with Raya Dunayevskaya and Grace Lee (Chicago: Charles H. Kerr Publishing, 1986). It would be helpful in this context for the reader to remember Antonio Gramsci's work (see chapter 11). It is clear that the problems James and Gramsci have with Marxism—rather than with Marx—are related to their respec-tive embodied histories: a white from southern Italy who writes about "the South-ern Question" and a Black Caribbean for whom "the Human Question" and racism are of primary concern. Both kinds of experience were off the Marxists' radar.

18 Jamaican-American writer and essayist Michelle Cliff sensed and knew this very well. In 1982 she published a memorable piece, "If I Could Write This in Fire, I Would Write This in Fire," in *Home Girls: A Black Feminist Anthology*, ed. Barbara Smith (New York: Kitchen Table: Women of Color Press, 1982), 15–30.

19 In the past few years a paragraph by Carl Sagan (from his book published in 1995, *Demon Haunted-World: Science as a Candle in the Dark*) has invaded social media. Sagan was witnessing what Wiener feared:

> Science is more than a body of knowledge; it is a way of thinking. I have a foreboding of an America in my children's or grandchildren's time—when the United States is a service and information economy; when nearly all the

key manufacturing industries have slipped away to other countries; when awesome technological powers are in the hands of a very few, and no one representing the public interest can even grasp the issues; when the people have lost the ability to set their own agendas or knowledgeably question those in authority; when, clutching our crystals and nervously consulting our horoscopes, our critical faculties in decline, unable to distinguish between what feels good and what's true, we slide, almost without noticing, back into superstition and darkness.

The paragraph can be found all over, including here: https://paleofuture.gizmodo .com/yes-the-eerie-carl-sagan-prediction-thats-going-viral-1791502520.

20 Wynter, "Beyond the Categories of the Master Conception," 81–82.

21 Wynter, "Beyond the Categories of the Master Conception," 65.

22 For an overview, see Walter D. Mignolo and Arturo Escobar, eds., *Globalization and the Decolonial Option* (London: Routledge, 2009).

23 Wynter, "Beyond the Categories of the Master Conception," 65.

24 Wynter, "Beyond the Categories of the Master Conception," 65.

25 Walter D. Mignolo, *Local Histories/Global Designs: Coloniality, Subaltern Knowledges, and Border Thinking*, 2nd ed. (Princeton, NJ: Princeton University Press , 2012 [2000]).

26 Scott McLemee and Paul Le Blanc, eds., *C. L. R. James and Revolutionary Marxism: Selected Writing 1939–1949* (Amherst, MA: Humanity Books, 1993); Wynter, "Beyond the Categories of the Master Conception," 73.

27 Wynter, "Beyond the Categories of the Master Conception," 81.

28 Santiago Castro-Gómez, *La Hybris del Punto Cero: Ciencia, raza e ilustración en la Nueva Granada (1750–1816)* (Bogotá: Editorial Javeriana, 2005); Walter D. Mignolo, *The Idea of Latin America* (London: Wiley-Blackwell Manifestos, 2005), chap. 2.

29 Frantz Fanon, *The Wretched of the Earth*, trans. Richard Philcox (New York: Grove Press, 2004 [1961]).

30 Wynter, "Beyond the Categories of the Master Conception," 81.

31 Frantz Fanon, *Black Skin, White Masks*, trans. Richard Philcox, rev. ed. (New York: Grove Press, 2008 [1952], 11.

32 Fanon, *Black Skin, White Masks*, 17–18.

33 Fanon, *Black Skin, White Masks*, 109.

34 Michel Foucault, "Nietzsche, Freud, Marx," in *Nietzsche, Cahiers du Royaumont* (Paris: Les Éditions de Minuit, 1964), 183–200.

35 Fanon was clear about this in North Africa, where he had to confront the "trauma" of Berbers and Arabs. Rather than trauma, what Fanon was confronting were colonial wounds. Trauma and colonial wounds have distinctive personal and historical configurations. Traumas are sort of modern wounds, the individual altered in his or her own territory; colonial wounds are the consequences of racial/sexual dehumanization. Race is not a feature of trauma, but it is the essential feature of colonial wounds. Fanon may not have had that concept, but he realized the fracture between psychiatry and psychoanalysis in Vienna and Paris (Fanon

knew the first publications of Lacan, although the Lacan we know today is the later one). See Fanon, "Colonial War and Mental Disorders," in *The Wretched of the Earth*, 181–234. My own work was with South American psychoanalysts who were trained in France in the Lacanian School and who recognized that they too are colonial subjects. At that moment, psychoanalysis joined the decolonial option. See Walter D. Mignolo, *Hacer, pensar y vivir la decolonialidad: Textos reunidos y presentados por comunidad psicoanalítica/pensamiento decolonial* (Mexico City: Borde Sur y Ediciones Navarra, 2016).

36 In France, Paul B. Preciado has made the case speaking from the sexualized transsexual body. See Mathilde Girard, "Ce que Paul B. Preciado fait à la psychanalyse," *AOC*, October 1, 2020, https://aoc.media/opinion/2020/01/09/ce-que -paul-b-preciado-fait-a-la-psychanalyse/. In Latin America, the call into question came from the decolonial/racial end. See María Amelia Castañola and Mauricio González (coordinators), *Decolonialidad y psicoanálisis* (Mexico City: Colección Borde Sur y Ediciones Navarra, 2017).

37 Frantz Fanon, "L'expérience vécue du Noir," *Esprit: Nouvelle Série* 179, no. 5 (1951): 657–79.

38 See a preview of these ideas in Walter D. Mignolo, "Prophets Facing Sidewise," *Social Epistemology* 19, no. 1 (2005): 111–27, DOI: 10.1080/ 02691720500084325.

39 See Walter D. Mignolo, "(De)Coloniality at Large: Time and the Colonial Difference," in *The Darker Side of Western Modernity: Global Futures, Decolonial Options* (Durham, NC: Duke University Press, 2011), 149–80.

40 "Operates on heterogeneous historico-structural nodes": Emanuel Barrera Calderón and María Florencia Valinotto, "La heterogeneidad histórico-estructural en América Latina: Diálogos con Marx," *Nómadas* 48 (April 2018): 49–63.

41 Conceptual epistemic-political doing (e.g., praxes such as writing, organizations, workshops, art exhibits, etc.) in this domain are present in overwhelming numbers in the sphere of racism and sexism. I mention my take on it in relation to the argument I am unfolding here. Some of the relevant arguments are addressed in more detail in my preface, "Decolonial Body-Geo Politics at Large," in *Decolonizing Sexualities: Transnational Perspectives, Critical Interventions*, ed. Sandeep Bakshi, Suhraiya Jivraj, and Silvia Posocco (Oxford, UK: Counterpress, 2016), vii–xviii.

42 See "Racism as We Sense It Today," chapter 1 of this book.

43 Recognition is out of the question for decolonial *scientia*. For similar arguments by Indigenous Canadian scholars, intellectuals, and activists, see Glen Coulthard, *Red Skin, White Masks: Rejecting the Colonial Politics of Recognition* (Minneapolis: University of Minnesota Press, 2014).

44 David Scott, "The Re-enchantment of Humanism: An Interview with Sylvia Wynter," *Small Axe* 8 (September 2000): 119–207.

45 Ali Shari'ati, "Modern Man and His Prisons," in *Man and Islam* (North Haledon, NJ: Islamic Publications International, 2006 [1976]), 47. See also Mahbi Abedi and Mehdi Abedi, "The Architect of the 1979 Islamic Revolution," *Iranian Studies* 19, no. 3/4 (1986): 229–34.

46 Wynter, "Unsettling the Coloniality of Being," 288.

47 Scott, "The Re-enchantment of Humanism," 196.
48 Scott, "The Re-enchantment of Humanism," 196.
49 Sylvia Wynter, "Ethno or Socio Poetics," *Alcheringa* 2 (1976): 78–94.
50 Taken from the subtitle of Wynter's article "Unsettling the Coloniality of Being."

Thirteen. Decoloniality and Phenomenology

1 Humberto Maturana, *Biology of Cognition: Biological Computer Laboratory Research* (Urbana: University of Illinois Press, 1970); Humberto Maturana and Francisco Varela, *The Tree of Knowledge: The Biological Roots of Human Understanding* (Boston: New Science Library, 1987); Aníbal Quijano, "Colonialidad y Modernidad/Racionalidad," in *Los conquistados: 1492 y la población indígena* (Bogotá: Tercer Mundo Editores, 1992), 439–48; Paul L. Garvin, ed., *Cognition: A Multiple View* (New York: Spartan Books, 1970).

2 Walter D. Mignolo, *The Darker Side of the Renaissance: Literacy, Territoriality, and Colonization*, 2nd ed. (Ann Arbor: University of Michigan Press, 2012 [1995]).

3 Victor Farías, *Heidegger et le nazisme* (Paris: Verdier, 1987). For an explanation of the affair, see Tom Rockmore, "Heidegger after Farias," *History of Philosophy Quarterly* 8, no. 1 (1991): 81–102. Rockmore, following Farías, interprets the links with National Socialism in Heidegger's vision of the German historical destiny, the German spirit, and the superiority of German language. In this interpretation, Heidegger's racism is embedded in his philosophical thoughts and surfaces in his political commitments.

4 See Jesús Ruiz Fernández, "La idea de filosofía en José Ortega y Gasset," Departamento de Filosofía, Universidad Complutense de Madrid, E-Prints Complutense, 2009, http://eprints.ucm.ed/9522/.

5 Due to space limitations, I will not deal with Afro-Caribbean philosophy and thought, which have much to offer in understanding the work of colonial epistemic differences. For insightful arguments, see Paget Henry, *Caliban's Reason: Introducing Afro-Caribbean Philosophy* (London: Routledge, 2000), and Lewis R. Gordon, *Existentia Africana: Understanding Africana Existential Thought* (London: Routledge, 2000).

6 Edmund Husserl, *La filosofía como ciencia estricta*, trans. Elsa Tabernig (Buenos Aires: Editorial Nova, 1962), 7. See also Edmund Husserl, *The Crisis of European Sciences and Transcendental Phenomenology: An Introduction to Phenomenological Philosophy*, trans. David Carr (Evanston: Northwestern University Press, 1970 [1936]).

7 Edmund Husserl, *Philosopy as Rigorous Science*, trans. and intro. by Quentin Lauer (New York: Harper and Row, 1965 [1911]), 71.

8 "Framed in the trivium and the quadrivium": James J. Murphy, ed., *Three Medieval Rhetorical Arts* (Berkeley: University of California Press, 1971).

9 Walter D. Mignolo, "The Splendors and Miseries of 'Science': Coloniality, Geopolitics of Knowledge, and Epistemic Pluriversality," in *Cognitive Justice in a Global World: Prudent Knowledge for a Decent Life*, ed. Boaventura de Sousa Santos (Lanham, MD: Rowman and Littlefield, 2007), 353–73. See also my article "Prophets

Facing Sidewise: The Geopolitics of Knowledge and the Colonial Difference," *Social Epistemology* 19, no. 1 (2005): 111–27, DOI: 10.1080/ 02691720500084325. For a detailed description of the colonial matrix of power, see the introduction to this volume.

10 See also Walter Mignolo, "Globalization and the Geopolitics of Knowledge. The Role of the Humanities in the Corporate University," in *The American-Style University at Large: Transplants, Outposts, and the Globalization of Higher Education*, ed. Kathryn L. Kleypas and James I. McDougall (Lanham, MD: Lexington Books, 2012), 3–40.

11 G. W. F. Hegel, *The Philosophy of History*, trans. J. Sibree, prefaces by J. Sibree and Charles Hegel (Ontario: Batoche Books, 2001), 96–127.

12 For more on "Latin" America, see Walter D. Mignolo, *The Idea of Latin America* (London: Wiley-Blackwell Manifestos, 2005).

13 On barbarism and civilization, see Eric Hobsbawn, "Barbarism: A User's Guide," *New Left Review* I, no. 206 (1994): 44–54.

14 Alexis de Tocqueville, *Democracy in America* (Chicago: University of Chicago Press, 2002 [1833]), bk. 2, chap. 1. No one has yet traced, to my knowledge, the evasions *in* American philosophy as does Cornel West, *The American Evasion of Philosophy: A Genealogy of Pragmatism* (Madison: University of Wisconsin Press, 1989).

15 It became common practice to refer to "Latin" America after the 1960s. Juan Bautista Alberdi in the middle of the nineteenth century could not have referred to "Latin" America because "Latin" America did not yet exist. See Mignolo, *The Idea of Latin America*.

16 Luis Villoro, "La posibilidad de una filosofía latinoamericana," in *México entre libros: Pensadores del siglo XX* (Mexico City: El Colegio Nacional/Fondo de Cultura Económica, 1995), 90–118, at 95.

17 Michel-Rolph Trouillot, "North Atlantic Universals: Analytical Fictions, 1492–1945," *South Atlantic Quarterly* 101, no. 4 (2002): 839–58, at 848.

18 For more on "the invention of America," see Edmundo O'Gorman, *La invención de América: Investigacíon acerca de la estructura histórica del Nuevo Mundo y del sentido de su devenir* (Mexico City: Universidad Nacional de México, 1958); English translation: *The Invention of America: An Inquiry into the Historical Nature of the New World and the Meaning of Its History* (Bloomington: Indiana University Press, 1961).

19 Aníbal Quijano, "Coloniality and Modernity/Rationality," English translation in *Cultural Studies* 21, nos. 2–3 (2007 [1992]): 168–78, at 175, DOI: 10.1080/09502380601164353.

20 Michel Foucault, *Les mots et les choses* (Paris: Gallimard, 1966).

21 For a detailed description, see Walter D. Mignolo, "Global Coloniality and the World Disorder: Decoloniality after Decolonization and De-Westernization after the Cold War," reprinted in *The Courage of Hope: A World Beyond Global Disorder*, ed. Fred Dallmayr and Edward Demenchonok (Cambridge, UK: Cambridge Scholars Publishing, 2017), 90–117.

22 Husserl, *The Crisis of European Sciences and Transcendental Phenomenology*, 14.

23 Husserl, *The Crisis of European Sciences and Transcendental Phenomenology*, 122.

24 Husserl, *The Crisis of European Sciences and Transcendental Phenomenology*, 151ff.

25 Husserl, *The Crisis of European Sciences and Transcendental Phenomenology*, 152, 151.

26 Quijano, "Coloniality and Modernity/Rationality," 177.

27 Husserl, *The Crisis of European Sciences and Transcendental Phenomenology*, 6–7.

28 Husserl, *The Crisis of European Sciences and Transcendental Phenomenology*, 7.

29 Mignolo, *The Darker Side of the Renaissance*.

30 Adam Smith, "On the Colonies" and "The Mercantile System," in *An Inquiry into the Nature and Causes of the Wealth of Nations* (1776), vol. 2, bk. 4, chaps. 7–8, Library of Economics and Liberty, accessed May 26, 2020, http://www.econlib.org/library/Smith/smWN.html. For a decolonial reading of the Smith sections on colonialism, see Walter D. Mignolo, "Second Thoughts on *The Darker Side of the Renaissance*," in Mignolo, *The Darker Side of the Renaissance*, 427–63.

31 Husserl, *The Crisis of European Sciences and Transcendental Phenomenology*, 137, 139.

32 Husserl, *The Crisis of European Sciences and Transcendental Phenomenology*, 139.

33 Building on Gloria Wekker's general argument in her *White Innocence: Paradoxes of Colonialism and Race* (Durham, NC: Duke University Press, 2016), one could make this equation: "white ignorance legitimizes white innocence." I owe this formulation to Manuela Boatcă.

34 Tunisian writer Hélé Béji, dividing her time between Tunisia and Paris, participated in the struggles for liberartion of Tunisia. Here she offers self-reflections several decades later: Hélé Béji, *Nous, décolonisés* (Paris: Aerea, 2008).

35 Quijano, "Coloniality and Modernity/Rationality," 172. Postmodern debates at the end of the twentieth century did not radically question the privilege of the individual. It is in recent debates on the posthuman that Continental philosophy has begun to pay attention to relationality. See Ceder Simon, "Cutting through Water: Towards a Post-human Theory of Educational Relationality" (PhD diss., Lund University, 2016). Relationality in Quijano, as well as in millenarian Indigenous philosophy in the Americas, is as fundamental as ontology in Western metaphysics. Indigenous philosophy does not see objects but, rather, relations. Humberto Maturana arrived at the same conclusion many years ago, precisely through explaining the biology of cognition and the origin of living organisms, to which Human/Man is a latecomer. See Simón Aymara Yampara Huarachi, "Cosmovivencia Andina: Vivir y convivir en armonía integral—Suma Qamaña," *Bolivian Studies Journal* 18 (2011): 1–22. As for Maturana, relationality is embedded in the structural coupling between organism and niche, in structural coupling between living organisms, in languaging, and in the biology of cognition. See Maturana and Varela, *The Tree of Knowledge*, chaps. 9–10.

36 James Ogude, Steve Paulson, and Anne Strainchamps, "I Am Because You Are: An Interview with James Ogude," CHC Ideas, June 21, 2019, https://chcinetwork.org/ideas/i-am-because-you-are-an-interview-with-james-ogude.

37 Quijano, "Coloniality and Modernity/Rationality," 172.

38 This was the crucial point that Max Horkheimer made in his classic "Traditional and Critical Theory," in *Critical Theory: Selected Essays*, trans. Matthew J. O'Connell (New York: Continuum, 1975 [1937]), 188–243.

39 Quijano, "Coloniality and Modernity/Rationality," 173.

40 Hans Jonas, *The Phenomenon of Life: Towards a Philosophical Biology* (New York: Harper and Row, 1966).

41 In the 1960s Maturana was researching, with colleagues in the United States, vision in frogs and pigeons. This investigation led him to turn around the belief previously held in Western civilization (from common knowledge to the natural sciences and philosophy) that the images of the world enter through the eyes and are communicated to the brain. Maturana reversed this by arguing and showing that it is the nervous system that "creates" an image of what we see. His well-known dictum: "We do not see what there is, we see what we see." The question of "what there is" occupied analytic philosophy for a long while. See Willard Van Orman Quine, "On What There Is," *Review of Metaphysics* 2, no. 5 (1948): 21–38. The first article I know of where Maturana devised the fundamental explanation of the emergence of living organisms on Earth, the ideas that would be encapsulated in the concept of molecular autopoiesis, is from 1974: Humberto Maturana, "The Organization of the Living: A Theory of the Living Organization," reprinted in *International Journal of Human-Computer Studies* 51 (1999): 149–68.

42 Jonas, *The Phenomenon of Life*, i.

Fourteen. **The Rise of the Third Nomos of the Earth**

EPIGRAPHS: Choquehuanca quoted in La *Razón*, November 8, 2020, https://www.la-razon.com/nacional/2020/11/08/lea-el-discurso-completo-de-la-posesion-del-vicepresidente-david-choquehuanca/. The first four definitions are from *MacMillan Dictionary* online, https://dictionary.cambridge.org/dictionary/english/anomie. The next definition is from *Online Etymology Dictionary*, https://www.etymonline.com/. The last definition is from *Lexico: The US Dictionary*, https://www.lexico.com/en/definition/reconstitution.

1 Federico Luisetti, John Pickles, Wilso Kayser, eds. *The Anomie of the Earth: Philosophy, Politics, and Autonomy of the Earth in Europe and the Americas.* Durham, NC: Duke University Press, 2015.

2 Carl Schmitt, "The New *Nomos* of the Earth," in *The Nomos of the Earth in the International Law of the Jus Publicum Europaeum*, trans. and annot. G. L. Ulmen (New York: Telos Press, 2006 [1950]), 351–55.

3 Schmitt, "The New *Nomos* of the Earth." I have elaborated on this topic in *The Darker Side of Western Modernity: Global Futures, Decolonial Options* (Durham, NC: Duke University Press, 2011), chap. 1, 27–76.

4 Ralph Bauer and José Antonio Mazotti, *Creole Subjects in Colonial American Identities* (Chapel Hill: University of North Carolina Press, 2009); "El Camino de los Inmigrantes," Argentina.gob.ar, accessed, October 1 2020, https://www.argentina.gob.ar/interior/migraciones/museo/el-camino-de-los-inmigrantes.

5 Gloria Wekker, *White Innocence: Paradoxes of Colonialism and Race* (Durham, NC: Duke University Press, 2016). The argument focusses on the Netherlands. However, it highlights indirectly the blindness (perverse or ignorant) underlying the entire

spectrum of Western epistemology and the subject formation of the white population from family to higher education, from the media to art and literature. The second nomos of the Earth mapped the planet geopolitically at the same time that it encircled the imaginary of people building and living under the second nomos. If I and many others referred to in this chapter are able to make this kind of argument, it is because the second nomos is disintegrating in all domains—knowledge above all.

6   I unfolded this argument in chapters 2 and 3 of *The Darker Side of Western Modernity*.

7   Schmitt, "The New *Nomos* of the Earth," 351.

8   Schmitt, "The New *Nomos* of the Earth," 352.

9   The text of *Requerimiento* can be read here: Juan Lopéz de Palacios Rubios, *El Requerimiento (1513)*, Encyclopedia Virginia, March 18, 2013, https://www .encyclopediavirginia.org/El_Requerimiento_by_Juan_Lopez_de_Palacios _Rubios_1513.

10 For more details on the idea of the Western Hemisphere in relation to this argument, see Walter D. Mignolo, "Coloniality at Large: The Western Hemisphere in the Colonial Horizon of Modernity," *New Centennial Review* 1 , no. 2 (2001): 19–54, https://www.jstor.org/stable /41949278. See also chapters 8 and 10 of this book.

11 Esme E. Deprez, "'Avatar' Tops Box Office, Passes $2 Billion Worldwide," Bloomberg, January 31, 2010, https://www.bloomberg.com/news/articles/2010-01-31/ -avatar-tops-box-office-passes-2-billion-worldwide.

12 Jeremy Hance, "La verdadera historia de Avatar: Los pueblos indígenas en la lucha para salvar sus hogares en la selva de la explotación de las Corporaciones," *Mongabay Latam*, January 4, 2010, https://es.mongabay.com/2010/01/la-verdadera -historia-de-avatar-los-pueblos-indigenas-en-la-lucha-para-salvar-sus-hogares-en -la-selva-de-la-explotacion-por-las-corporaciones/.

13 Richard Twiss, "A Theology of Manifest Destiny," March 7, 2008, video, 2:47, https://www.youtube.com/watch?v=4mEkMyIKNWo. For more details on the topic see Richard Twiss, *Rescuing the Gospel from the Cowboys: A Native American Expression of the Jesus Way* (London: InterVarsity Press, 2015).

14 George E. Tinker, *Spirit and Resistance: Political Theology and American Indian Liberation* (Minneapolis: Fortress Press, 2004), ix.

15 James Lovelock, *Gaia: A New Look at Life on Earth* (Oxford, UK: Oxford University Press, 1979), 33.

16 Zhang Feng, "The *Tianxia* System: World Order in a Chinese Utopia," *China Heritage Quarterly*, March 2010, http://www.chinaheritagequarterly.org/tien-hsia .php?searchterm=021_utopia.inc&issue=021.

17 "Nature," *Online Etymology Dictionary*, accessed January 11, 2021, https://www .etymonline.com/search?q=nature.

18 José de Acosta, *Natural and Moral History of the Indies*, ed. Jane E. Mangan, trans. Frances López-Morillas, pref. and comment. Walter D. Mignolo (Durham, NC: Duke University Press, 2002 [1589]).

19 Francis Bacon, *The New Organon; or, True Directions Concerning the Interpretation of Nature* (*Novum Organum*), ed. Lisa Jardine and Michael Silverthorne (Cambridge, UK: Cambridge University Press, 2000 [1620]).

20 Robert P. Crease, "The Critical Point: The Book of Nature," *Physics World* (December 2006): 16, http://www.robertpcrease.com/wp-content/uploads/2014/09/PW-Dec-2006-Book-of-Nature.pdf.

21 On this point see the classic book by Antonello Gerbi, *La disputa del Nuovo Mondo: Storia di una polemica, 1750–1900*, trans. Antonio Alatorre (Mexico City: Fondo de Cultura Económica, 1982 [1955]).

22 Vine Deloria Jr., *Evolution, Creationism and Other Modern Myths* (Ann Arbor, MI: Fulcrum Publishing, 2004).

23 Fernando Huanacuni Mamani, *Vivir Bien/Buen Vivir: Filosofía, políticas, estrategias y experiencias regionales* (Lima: Coordinadora Andina de Organizaciones, 2010).

24 Huanacuni Mamani, *Vivir Bien/Buen Vivir*, 163–64.

25 See Acosta, *Natural and Moral History of the Indies*, "Introduction," xvii–xxvii, and "Commentaries," 451–518.

26 The struggle of "new materialism" is embedded in the western European tradition of binary oppositions. Beyond Europe this is not a praxis. As we see in this chapter, Indigenous philosophies or cosmogonies do not have that problem, because for them the universe and life on Earth are in constant flow, there is no place to fix the opposition, and duality is never oppositional but complementary. There is no day without night, no happiness without sadness, no masculine without feminine, and so forth. Time is movement, not a linear display of binary oppositions. But after all, both are limited to the western European frame of thoughts. See Rick Dolphhijn and Iris van der Tuin, *New Materialism: Interviews and Cartographies* (Ann Arbor, MI: Open Humanities Press, 2012).

27 Humberto Maturana and Ximena Paz Dávila, "Education as Viewed from the Biological Matrix of Human Existence," *Towards Life-Knowledge*, orig. pub. 2006, reproduced January 13, 2018, https://bsahely.com/2018/01/13/education-as-viewed-from-the-biological-matrix-of-human-existence-2006-by-humberto-maturana-and-ximena-paz-davila/.

28 For an uncompromised demythification of Western universal time, see Mark Rifkin, *Beyond Settler Time: Temporal Sovereignty and Indigenous Self-Determination* (Durham, NC: Duke University Press, 2017).

29 Some examples: decolonially, in South Africa, "Rhodes must fall," mentioned just above. Another example is the long-lasting arguments and organizations of Indigenous people aimed at recovering expropriated land. De-Westernization: Russian control of Crimea to stop Western expansion toward the East. Cultural de-Westernization is explicit in the Sharjah Biennial 11, as argued in Walter D. Mignolo, "Re:emerging, Decentering and Delinking: Shifting the Geographies of Sensing, Believing and Knowing," *Ibraaz: Contemporary Visual Culture in North Africa and the Middle East*, May 8, 2013, https://www.ibraaz.org/essays/59. On the museum, see Walter D. Mignolo, "Enacting the Archive, De-centering the Muses: The Museum of Islamic Art in Doha and the Museum of Asian Civilizations in Singapore," *Ibraaz: Contemporary Visual Culture in North Africa and the Middle East*, November 6, 2013, https://www.ibraaz.org/essays/77. The fact that de-Westernization is a growing political, economic, and cultural orientation

doesn't mean that it is a promise for a glorious future or a waiting room for paradise. It simply means that it is and has been forced by Westernization and re-Westernization (see chapter 9).

30 Jean Casimir, *The Haitians: A Decolonial History* (Chapel Hill: University of North Carolina Press, 2020); Pablo González Casanova, "The Zapatistas 'Caracoles': Networks of Resistance and Autonomy," *Socialism and Democracy* 19, no. 3 (2005): 79–92; Abdullah Öcalan, *The Sociology of Freedom: Manifesto of the Democratic Civilization*, vol. 3 (Oakland, CA: PM Press, 2020); Pinar Dinc, "The Kurdish Movement and the Democratic Federation of Northern Syria: An Alternative to the (Nation-)State Model?," *Journal of Balkan and Near Eastern Studies* 22, no. 1 (2020): 47–67, https://www.tandfonline.com/doi/pdf/10.1080/19448953.2020.1715669 ?needAccess=true.

31 Rodolfo Kusch, *Indigenous and Popular Thinking in América*, trans. María Lugones and Joshua M. Price (Durham, NC: Duke University Press, 2010 [1970]).

32 Leanne Betasamosake Simpson, *Dancing on our Turtle's Back: Stories of Nishnaabeg Re-Creation, Resurgence, and a New Emergence* (Winnipeg, MB: Arbeiter Ring Publishing, 2011).

33 Simpson, *Dancing on our Turtle's Back*, 17–18, 31–32. See also D'Arcy Rheault, *Anishinaabe Mino-Bimaadiziwin: The Way of a Good Life* (Peterborough, ON: Debwewin Press, 1999).

34 Simpson, *Dancing on our Turtle's Back*, 32.

35 Simpson, *Dancing on our Turtle's Back*, 34–35. See also Neal McLeod, *Cree Narrative Memory: From Treaties to Contemporary Times* (Vancouver, BC: Purich Publishing, 2009).

36 See the argument built on this issue by Glen Sean Coulthard, *Red Skin, White Masks: Rejecting Colonial Politics of Recognition* (Minneapolis: University of Minnesota Press, 2014).

37 Itzamná Ollantay, "Estado nación y estado plurinacional," *Telesurtv.net* (blog), June 16, 2016, http://www.telesurtv.net/bloggers/Estado-Nacion-y-Estado -Plurinacional-20160616-0001.html.

38 Henry George, *Progress and Poverty* (New York: Cosimo, 2005 [1879]).

39 The chapters in his book are presented with their numbers in alphabetic writing. "Paqallqu" is "chapter 7" in Aymara. We will see below that Taiaiake Alfred deploys a similar strategy in the organization of his argument.

40 See Walter D. Mignolo, "The Communal and the Decolonial," *Turbulence: Ideas in Movement*, 2010, http://turbulence.org.uk/turbulence-5/decolonial/.

41 Marcelo Fernandez Osco, *La ley del Ayllu: Práctica de jach'a justicia y jisk'a justicia (justicia mayor y justicia menor) en la comunidades aymaras*, La Paz: PIEB, 2000.

42 The Zapatistas have a decolonial political theory, expressed in a single phrase, to underscore this principle: "To govern and to obey at the same time." It means that whoever rules is at the service of the community; the community is not at the service of the ruler. This principle cannot obtain in either capitalist or socialist socioeconomic organizations.

43 Huanacuni Mamani, *Vivir Bien/Buen Vivir*, 153.

44 Huanacuni Mamani, *Vivir Bien/Buen Vivir*, 163.

45 See Walter D. Mignolo and Catherine E. Walsh, *On Decoloniality: Concepts, Analytics, Praxis* (Durham, NC: Duke University Press, 2018), chap. 8.

46 Gerald Taiaiake Alfred, *Peace, Power, Righteousness: An Indigenous Manifesto* (New York: Oxford University Press, 2009), 8.

47 "Primer Festival Mundial de la Digna Rabia," *Enlace Zapatista*, January 2009, http://enlacezapatista.ezln.org.mx/2010/01/24/primer-festival-mundial-de-la-digna-rabia/.

48 Bui Ngoc Son, *Confucian Constitutionalism in East Asia* (London: Routledge, 2016).

49 Taiaiake Alfred, *Peace, Power, Righteousness*, 16.

50 Huanacuni Mamani, *Vivir Bien/Buen Vivir*, 148.

51 Carl Schmitt, *The Concept of the Political* (Munich: Duncker and Humblot, 1932).

52 Taiaiake Alfred, *Peace, Power, Righteousness*, 25.

53 See George E. Tinker, *Spirit and Resistance: Political Theology and American Indian Liberation* (Minneapolis, MN: Fortress Press, 2004).

54 Coulthard, *Red Skin, White Masks*.

55 Taiaiake Alfred, *Peace, Power, Righteousness*, 35–36.

56 Walter D. Mignolo and Rolando Vázquez, " Mexico's Indigenous Congress: Decolonising Politics," Al Jazeera, September 27, 2017, https://www.aljazeera.com/indepth/opinion/mexico-indigenous-congress-decolonising-politics-170926093051780.html.

57 For one example among many outlining the crisis of the current nation-state, see Rana Dasgupta, "The Demise of the Nation State," *The Guardian*, April 5, 2018, https://www.theguardian.com/news/2018/apr/05/demise-of-the-nation-state-rana-dasgupta: "The most momentous development of our era, precisely, is the waning of the nation state: its inability to withstand countervailing 21st-century forces, and its calamitous loss of influence over human circumstance." For the idea of the plurinational state, see Catherine Walsh, "Afro and Indigenous Life-Visions in/and Politics: (De)colonial Perspectives in Bolivia and Ecuador," *Bolivian Studies Journal* 18 (2011): 49–69, DOI: 10.5195/bsj. 2011.43.

58 Huanacuni Mamani, *Vivir Bien/Buen Vivir*, 67.

59 On new materialism, see Rick Dolphijn and Iris van der Tuin, *New Materialism: Interviews and Cartographies* (Ann Arbor, MI: Open Humanities Press, 2012).

60 Taiaiake Alfred, *Peace, Power, Righteousness*, 121.

61 Huanacuni Mamani, *Vivir Bien/Buen Vivir*, 199.

62 "Theorizing Resurgence from within Nishnaabeg Thought," in Simpson, *Dancing on our Turtle's Back*, 31–47. The equivalent forces are from Gzhwe Mnidoo.

63 Simpson, *Dancing on our Turtle's Back*, 141.

Epilogue: Yes, We Can

EPIGRAPHS: Leopoldo Zea, *La filosofía latinoamericana como filosofía sin más* (Mexico City: UNAM, 1969); Ali Shari'ati, "The Mission of a Free Thinker," in *Man and Islam*, trans. F. Marjani (North Heldon, NJ: Islamic Publications International,

1981), 112, 110; Linda Tuhiwai Smith, "Colonizing Knowledges," in *Decolonizing Methodologies: Research and Indigenous People* (London: Zed Books, 1999).

1 Santiago Zabala, "Slavoj Žižek and the Role of the Philosopher," Al Jazeera, December 25, 2012, https://www.aljazeera.com/indepth/opinion/2012/12 /20121224122215406939.html; Hamid Dabashi, "Can Non-Europeans Think?," Al Jazeera, January 15, 2013, https://www.aljazeera.com/indepth/opinion/2013/01 /201311414142638797542.html.

2 Here is my entry into the conversation: Walter D. Mignolo, "Yes, We Can: Non-European Thinkers and Philosophers," Al Jazeera, February 19, 2013, https:// www.aljazeera.com/indepth/opinion/2013/02/20132672747320891.html.

3 Walter D. Mignolo, "Globalization and the Geopolitics of Knowledge: The Role of the Humanities in the Corporate University," in *The American-Style University at Large: Transplants, Outposts, and the Globalization of Higher Education*, ed. Kathryn L. Kleypas and James I. McDougall (Lanham, MD : Lexington Books, 2012), 3–40.

4 Frantz Fanon, "L'expérience vécue du Noir," chapter 5 in *Peau noire, masques blancs* (Paris: Maspero, 1952), 109–40. I quote here the French edition because the English translation of the chapter title misses the point. It is translated as "The Fact of Blackness." Notice that "fact" comes from a very American mindset. In Fanon it is experience, lived experience, which cannot be reduced to "fact."

5 See Glen Sean Coulthard, *Red Skin, White Masks: Rejecting the Colonial Politics of Recognition* (Minneapolis: University of Minnesota Press, 2014).

6 Yang Siqi, "Life in Purgatory: Buddhism Is Growing in China, but Remains in Legal Limbo," *Time*, March 16, 2016, https://time.com/4260593/china-buddhism -religion-religious-freedom/.

7 Confucius's reemergence in today's China has been widely addressed in the past decade. For more recent explorations, see Paula Marantz Cohen, "Confucianism in China Today," *American Scholar*, October 4, 2012, https://theamericanscholar .org/confucianism-in-china-today/#.XZauZZNKi3U; Peimin Ni, "The Silk Order: A Philosophical Perspective," DOC Research Institute, March 26, 2018, https://doc-research.org/2018/03/silk-order-philosophical-perspective/. Confucian reemergence is a strong pillar of epistemic and political de-Westernization—that is, stopping the neoliberal project of homogenizing the planet under Western global designs, from the cycle of Westernization (1500–2000, under theological, liberal, and Marxist designs) to neoliberal re-Westernization (2000 forward). However, neoliberal re-Westernization has been restricted to the West's area of influence. De-Westernization blocked the project. Singaporean thinker Kishore Mahbubani has been a strong intellectual and political voice on these issues. See, for instance, "The Dangers of Democratic Delusions," Mahubani.net, March 26, 2009, http://mahbubani.net/articles%20by%20dean/The%20dangers%20of%20 Democratic.pdf. See also Andrew Lathman, "The Confucian Continuities of Chinese Geopolitical Discourse," in *Chinese World: Multiple Temporalities and Transformations* (Saint Paul, MN: Macalester College, 2007), 243–51.

8 Frantz Fanon, *Black Skin, White Masks*, trans. Richard Philcox, rev. ed. (New York: Grove Press, 2008 [1952]), 115. In the same vein, Jews of consciousness (to use Mark

Ellis's expression; see chapters 3 and 4) have been making parallel arguments, grounded in both Jews' memories and Jews' histories, when they are confronted with the Zionist state. See, for instance, Santiago Slabodsky, *Decolonial Judaism: Triumphal Failures of Barbaric Thinking* (New York: Palgrave Macmillan, 2014). See also Reyes Mate, *Memory of the West: The Contemporaneity of Forgotten Jewish Thinkers*, trans. John R. Welch (Amsterdam: Rodopi, 1994).

9 Fanon, *Black Skin, White Masks*, 115–16.

10 Fanon, *Black Skin, White Masks*, 113, 110.

11 Fanon, *Black Skin, White Masks*, 115.

12 Walter D. Mignolo. "Decolonial Geo-Body-Politics at Large: Foreword to *Decolonizing Sexualities*," *Critical Legal Thinking*, November 3, 2016, https://criticallegalthinking.com/2016/11/03/decolonizing-sexualities-foreward-walter-mignolo/. See also Rolando Vázquez Melken and Rosa Wevers, "Decolonial Aesthesis and the Museum: An Interview with Rolando Vázquez," *Stedelijk Studies*, accessed September 30, 2020, https://stedelijkstudies.com/journal/decolonial-aesthesis-and-the-museum/ for more on this concept. The alternative to "healing" would be a "cure," as in the psychoanalytic cure. However, there are radical differences between the goals of a psychoanalytic cure and those of decolonial healing. See Walter D. Mignolo, *Hacer, pensar y vivir la decolonialidad: Textos reunidos y presentados por comunidad psicoanalítica/pensamiento decolonial* (Mexico City: Borde Sur y Ediciones Navarra, 2016). See also Walter D. Mignolo and Rolando Vázquez, "Decolonial AestheSis: Colonial Wounds, Decolonial Healings," *Social Text Periscope*, July 15, 2013, https://socialtextjournal.org/ periscope_article/decolonial-aesthesis-colonial-woundsdecolonial-healings/.

13 Gerasimos Kakoliris, "The 'Undecidable' Pharmakon: Derrida's Reading of Plato's Phaedrus," ResearchGate, January 2013, https://www.researchgate.net/publication/282648428_The_Undecidable_Pharmakon_Derrida's_Reading_of_Plato's_Phaedrus.

14 Kishore Mahbubani, *Can Asians Think? Understanding the Divide between East and West* (Hanover NH: Steerforth Press, 2001 [1998]).

15 Walter D. Mignolo, "I Am Where I Think: Epistemology and the Colonial Difference," *Journal of Latin American Cultural Studies* 8, no. 2 (1999): 235–45, DOI: 10.1080/13569329909361962.

16 This is not the place to engage in a decolonial exploration of Martin Heidegger's "What Calls for Thinking?," in *Basic Writings*, ed. David Farrell Krell (New York: Harper, 1977 [1954]), 341–68. For a descriptive analysis, see Brent Dean Robbins, "Joyful Thinking-Thanking: A Reading of Heidegger's 'What Is Called Thinking?,'" *Janus Head* 13, no. 2 (Fall 2014): 13–21. Heidegger's question is bidirectional: in one direction it asks what kind of activity is called thinking; the other asks what provokes and demands someone to think. For living organisms, thinking is living and living is thinking, although not all living organisms engage in languaging to be aware of, name, and reflect on the activity called "thinking." Thinking is one crucial aspect of the praxis of living, without which the organism will die as a result of its incapacity to establish its niche and distinguish between what is

beneficial and detrimental for the praxis of its life. Decolonial thinking emerges late in the history of the human species, when certain praxes of living are described in the narratives of modernity/coloniality that engendered decoloniality and decolonial thinking.

17 Bringing race into philosophy is not a concern of Continental philosophy. There is no reason for it to be, for philosophy is assumed (by its practitioners) to be universal and disembodied. Furthermore, if the question of race is brought into Continental philosophy, it would have to be recognized that philosophy is complicit with the making of the epistemic difference. On this, see Lucius T. Outlaw Jr., *On Race and Philosophy* (London: Routledge, 1996).

18 Walter D. Mignolo, "Epistemic Disobedience, Independent Thought and Decolonial Freedom," *Theory, Culture and Society* 26, no. 7–8 (2009): 159–81, DOI: 10.1177/0263276409349275.

19 Emmanuel Chukwudi Eze, "The Color of Reason: The Idea of 'Race' in Kant's Anthropology," in *Postcolonial African Philosophy: A Critical Reader*, ed. E. C. Eze (London: Wiley-Blackwell, 1997), 103–31.

20 Aníbal Quijano, "Coloniality of Power, Eurocentrism, and Social Classification," trans. Michael Ennis, in *Coloniality at Large: Latin America and the Postcolonial Debate*, ed. Mabel Moraña, Enrique D. Dussel, and Carlos A. Jáuregui (Durham NC: Duke University Press, 2008 [Spanish ed. 2000]), 181–224.

21 See Eze, "The Color of Reason."

22 Frantz Fanon, *Les damnés de la terre* (Paris: Maspero, 1961), 65.

23 Frantz Fanon, *Peau noire, masques blancs*.

24 Victor Farías, *Heidegger and Nazism* (Philadelphia: Temple University Press, 1991). For Ortega y Gasset, see Jesús Ruiz Fernández, "La idea de filosofía en José Ortega y Gasset," Departamento de Filosofía, Universidad Complutense de Madrid, E-Prints Complutense, 2009, http://eprints.ucm.es/9522/1/T31067.pdf.

25 Robert Bernasconi, "African Philosophy's Challenge to Continental Philosophy," in Eze, ed., *Postcolonial African Philosophy*, 183–96.

26 Immanuel Kant, *Beobachtungen über das Gefühl des Schönen und Erhabenen* (Observations on the Feeling of the Beautiful and Sublime), trans. John T. Goldthwait, 2nd ed. (Berkeley: University of California Press, 2003 [1764]), 11.

27 Mahbubani, *Can Asians Think?*, 9.

28 I recommend one of his earlier articles in this vein, an invited lecture at the BBC in 2000, collected in *Can Asians Think?*, 47–67.

29 Mahbubani, *Can Asians Think?*, 9.

30 Miguel León-Portilla, *Aztec Thought and Culture: A Study of the Ancient Náhuatl Mind*, trans. Jack Emory Davis (Norman: University of Oklahoma Press, 1990 [1963]).

31 Álvaro García Linera and Slavoj Žižek, "¿Es posible pensar un cambio radical hoy?," November 11, 2014, video, https://www.youtube.com/watch?v=YoQEi4rOVRU.

32 Linera and Žižek, "¿Es posible pensar un cambio radical hoy?," min. 46.

33 Walter Mignolo, "The Zapatistas' Theoretical Revolution: Its Historical, Ethical and Political Consequences," in *The Darker Side of Western Modernity: Global*

Futures, Decolonial Options, ed. Walter D. Mignolo (Durham, NC: Duke University Press, 2011), 213–51.

34 See Mignolo, "The Zapatistas' Theoretical Revolution."

35 Linera and Žižek, "¿Es possible pensar un cambio radical hoy?"

36 Bernasconi, "African Philosophy's Challenge to Continental Philosophy."

37 Chandra Muzaffar, "Paris—A Dastardly Act of Terror: The Case for an Independent Investigation," *Global Research*, January 11, 2015, www.globalresearch.ca/paris-a-dastardly-act-of-terror-the-case-for-an-independent-investigation/5423889.

38 Leanne Betasamosake Simpson, *Dancing on our Turtle's Back: Stories of Nishnaabeg Re-Ccreation, Resurgence, and New Emergence* (Winnipeg, MB: Arbeiter Ring Publishing, 2011). Simpson observes, in a groundbreaking chapter, that storytelling is "our way of theorizing." Substitute "philosophizing" for "theorizing" and you will get the picture. See also Coulthard, *Red Skin, White Masks*.

39 Walter D. Mignolo, "Epistemic Disobedience, Independent Thought, and Decolonial Freedom," *Theory, Culture, and Society* 26, no. 7–8 (2009): 159–81; Addety Pérez Miles, "Unbound Philosophies and Histories: Epistemic Disobedience in Latin American Contemporary Art," *International Encyclopedia of Art and Design Education*, August 14, 2018, https://onlinelibrary.wiley.com/doi/abs/10.1002/9781118978061.ead039.

40 Rodolfo Kusch, *Indigenous and Popular Thinking in América*, trans. María Lugones and Joshua Price, intro. Walter Mignolo (Durham NC: Duke University Press, 2010 [1970]), 2.

41 Walter D. Mignolo, *Local Histories, Global Designs: Coloniality, Subaltern Knowledges and Border Thinking*, 2nd ed. (Princeton, NJ: Princeton University Press, 2012 [2000]).

42 Fanon, *Les damnés de la terre*, 28.

43 See N. Katherine Hayles, *How We Became Posthuman: Virtual Bodies in Cybernetics, Literature, and Informatics* (Chicago: University of Chicago Press, 1999). As the dictum goes, I do not see myself in this "we"; Cary Wolfe, *Before the Law: Humans and Other Animals in Biopolitical Frame* (Chicago: University of Chicago Press, 2012). It is a good argument for the insiders of modernity; the argument takes a different path among Indigenous thinkers and activists. Rosi Braidotti, *The Posthuman* (Cambridge, UK: Polity Press, 2013).

44 See Diana Coole and Samantha Frost, eds., *New Materialism: Ontology, Agency, and Politics* (Durham, NC: Duke University Press, 2010); Rick Dolphijn and Iris van der Tuin, *New Materialism: Interviews and Cartographies* (Ann Arbor, MI: Open Humanities Press, 2012), http://openhumanitiespress.org/books/download/Dolphijn-van-der-Tuin_2013_New-Materialism.pdf. The arguments on the posthuman and the new materialism seem to continue the North Atlantic divide that we have seen in Jean-François Lyotard and Fredric Jameson on postmodernity. Here are two connections: postmodernity celebrated a world without borders and so did neoliberalism; the posthuman and postnature celebrate the radical transformation brought by technology, and so does the new face of neoliberalism. See, for instance, the book by the creator and manager of Davos Forum, Klaus Schwab, *The Fourth Industrial Revolution* (Geneva: World Economic Forum, 2016).

45 Leroy Little Bear, "Indigenous Knowledge and Western Science," Banff Center Talk, January 14, 2015, video, 21:32, https://www.youtube.com/watch?v=gJSJ28eEUjI.

46 Rick Dolphjin and Iris van der Tuin, "Interview with Karen Barad," in Dolphjin and van der Tuin, *New Materialism*, 48–70.

47 "*Yóllotl* (corazón), es un derivado de la misma raíz que *ollin* (movimiento), lo que deja entrever la más fundamental concepción náhuatl de la vida: yoliliztli; y del corazón: yóllotl, como movimiento, tendencia." English translation, "*Yóllotl* (heart), is a derivative of the same root as *ollin* (movement), which shows the most basic Náhuatl conception of life: *yoliliztli*; and of the heart: *yóllotl*, as movement, tendency." Miguel León-Portilla, *La filosofía Náhuatl: Estudiada en sus fuentes* (Mexico City: Fondo de Cultura Económica, 1958).

48 Édouard Glissant, *Poetics of Relation*, trans. Betsy Wing (Ann Arbor: University of Michigan Press, 1997 [1990]), 131–210.

49 Mogobe Ramose, *African Philosophy through Ubuntu* (Harare, ZW: Mond Books, 1999).

50 Paulin J. Hountondji, "Recapturing," in *The Surreptitious Speech: Présence Africaine and the Politics of Otherness, 1947-1987*, ed. V. Y. Mudimbe (Chicago: University of Chicago Press, 1992), 238–48. See also Sandra Harding, *Is Science Multicultural? Postcolonialism, Feminism and Epistemologies* (Bloomington: Indiana University Press, 1988), and my own "The Splendors and Miseries of 'Science': Colonialty, Geopolitics of Knowledge, and Epistemic Pluriversality," in *Cognitive Justice in the Global World*, ed. Boaventura de Sousa Santos (Lanham, MD: Lexington Books, 2007), 353–73.

51 Nikolas Rose, *The Politics of Life Itself: Biomedicine, Power, and Subjectivity in the Twenty-First Century* (Princeton, NJ: Princeton University Press, 2007); Kaushik Sunder Rajan, *Biocapital: The Constitution of Postgenomic Life* (Durham, NC: Duke University Press, 2006).

52 An early examination of Rose's arguments from a decolonial perspective can be found in Walter D. Mignolo, "Regeneración y reciclaje: Descolonizar la ciencia y la bio-tecnología para liberar la vida," in *Rastros y rostros de la biopolítica*, ed. Ignacio Mendiola Gonzalo (Barcelona: Anthropos, 2009), 181–200.

53 In the sense sketched in the introduction to this book.

Bibliography

Abed al-Jabri, Mohammed. *The Formation of the Arab Reason: Texts, Traditions and the Construction of Modernity in the Arab World*. Translated by the Center of Arab Unity Studies. London: I. B. Tauris Publishers, 2011 [1988].

Abedi, Mahbi, and Mehdi Abedi, "The Architect of the 1979 Islamic Revolution." *Iranian Studies* 19, no. 3/4, (1986): 229–34.

Abu-Lughod, Janet L. *Before European Hegemony: The World System A.D. 1250–1350*. New York: Oxford University Press, 1982.

Achinte, Adolfo Albán. *Prácticas creativas de re-existencia: Más allá del arte . . . el mundo de lo sensible*. Buenos Aires: Ediciones del Signo, 2018.

Acosta, José de. *Natural and Moral History of the Indies*. Edited by Jane E. Mangan. Translated by Frances López-Morillas. Preface and commentary by Walter D. Mignolo. Durham, NC: Duke University Press, 2002 [1589].

Alatas, Syed Farid. *Applying Ibn Khaldūn: The Recovery of a Lost Tradition in Sociology*. Abingdon, UK: Routledge, 2014.

Alatas, Syed Farid. "Research: The Islamization of Knowledge: Interview with Farid Alatas." *Religioscope* 2 (January 2008). http://religion.info/english/interviews /article_358.shtml.

Alatas, Syed Hussein. *The Myth of the Lazy Native: A Study of the Image of the Malays, Filipinos and Javanese from the 16th to the 20th Century and Its Function in the Ideology of Colonial Capitalism*. London: Frank Casa and Co., 1977.

Al-Attas, Syed Muhammad Naquib. *Islam and Secularism*. Lahore: Suhail Academy, 1978.

Alcoff, Linda Martín. "Mignolo's Epistemology of Coloniality." *New Centennial Review* 7, no. 3 (Winter 2007), 79–101.

Alfred, Taiaiake. *Peace, Power, Righteousness: An Indigenous Manifesto*. New York: Oxford University Press, 2009.

Alfred, Taiaiake. *Wasáse: Indigenous Pathways of Action and Freedom*. Toronto: University of Toronto Press, 2009.

Ali, Tariq. *Shadows of the Pomegranate Tree*. London: Verso, 1992.

Al Mayassa, Sheikha. "Globalizing the Local." TEDWomen 2010, accessed September 30, 2020. https://www.ted.com/talks/sheikha_al_mayassa_globalizing_the _local_localizing_the_global/transcript?language=en.

Almond, Philip C. "In Spite of Their Differences, Jews, Christians and Muslims Worship the Same God." *The Conversation*. September 5, 2017. https://theconversation .com/in-spite-of-their-differences-jews-christians-and-muslims-worship-the-same -god-83102.

"American Leadership in the World." *The Record: White House Archives, President Barack Obama, 2009–2016*, accessed May 8, 2020. https://obamawhitehouse.archives.gov /the-record/foreign-policy.

Ananda, Rady. "More Problems with Glyphosate: Rice Growers Sound Alarm." *Food Freedom* (blog). May 2011. http://foodfreedom.wordpress.com/tag/andres -carrasco/.

Anderson, Benedict. *Imagined Communities: Reflections on the Origins and Spread of Nationalism*. Rev. ed. London: Verso, 2016.

Anghie, Antony. "Francisco de Vitoria and the Colonial Origins of International Law." In *Laws of the Postcolonial*, edited by E. Darian-Smith and P. Fitzpatrick, 89–108. Ann Arbor: University of Michigan Press, 1999.

Anghie, Antony. *Imperialism, Sovereignty and the Making of International Law*. Cambridge, UK: Cambridge University Press, 2005.

Anidjar, Gil. *Blood: A Critique of Christianity (Religion, Culture, and Public Life)*. New York: Columbia University Press, 2014.

Anidjar, Gil. *The Jew, the Arab: A History of the Enemy*. Stanford, CA: Stanford University Press, 2003.

An-Na'im, Abdullahi. "What Do We Mean by Universal?" *Index of Censorship* 4, no. 5 (September 1994): 120–27.

Anonymous. "Southern Cross: Our Wheel of Life in Heavens." Los Bosques.net, accessed September 30, 2020. https://www.losbosques.net/southern-cross-our-wheel -of-life-in-heavens/.

Antezana, Luis H. *Dos conceptos en la obra de René Zavaleta Mercado: Formación abigarrada y democracia como autodeterminación*. College Park, MD: Latin American Studies Center Series 1, 1991.

Antezana, Luis H. *La diversidad social en Zavaleta Mercado*. La Paz: Centro Boliviano de Estudios Multidisciplinarios, 1991.

Anzaldúa, Gloria. *Borderlands/La Frontera: The New Mestiza*. San Francisco: Aunt Lute Books, 2007 [1987].

Appiah, Kwame Anthony. *Cosmopolitanism: Ethics in a World of Strangers*. New York: W. W. Norton, 2006.

Aral, Berdal. "The Idea of Human Rights as Perceived in the Ottoman Empire." *Human Rights Quarterly* 26, no. 2 (2004): 454–82.

Arendt, Hannah. *The Origins of Totalitarianism*. New edition with added prefaces. New York: Harcourt Brace, 1976 [1948].

"Argentina, Buenos Aires: Se inicia el Juicio ético popular a las transnacionales." Biodiversidad.org, October 27, 2011. http://www.biodiversidadla. org/Noticias/Argentina_Buenos_Aires_se_ inicia_el_Juicio_etico_popular_a_las_transnacionales.

Aricó, José. *La cola del diablo: Itinerario de Gramsci en América Latina*. Buenos Aires: Puntosur, 1988.

Arrighi, Giovanni. *The Long Twentieth Century: Money, Power and the Origins of Our Times*. London: Verso, 1994.

"The Asian-African (Bandung) Conference: Fact and Fiction." *Black Past*, August 8, 2017. https://www.black past.org/global-african-history/perspectives-global -african-history/asian-african-bandung-conference-fact-and-fiction/.

Astorga Poblete, Daniel. "Tlacauthli, altepetl y tlalli: Conceptos básicos de estructuración del espacio, territorio y tierra en el México pre-colombino." PhD diss., Duke University, 2015. https://www.researchgate.net/publication/324269952 _Tlacauhtli _altepetl_y_tlalli_Conceptos_basicos_de_estructuracion_del_espacio_territorio_y_tierra_ en_el_Mexico_pre-colombino.

Bacon, Francis. *The New Organon; or, True Directions Concerning the Interpretation of Nature (Novum Organum)*. Edited by Lisa Jardine and Michael Silverthorne. Cambridge, UK: Cambridge University Press, 2000 [1620].

Bagley, Mary. "Holocene Epoch: The Age of Man." *LiveScience*, March 27, 2013. http://www.livescience.com/28219-holocene-epoch.html.

Bailey, Kenneth E. *Jesus through Middle Eastern Eyes: Cultural Studies in the Gospel*. New York: IVP Academic Press, 2008.

Bakshi, Sandeep, Suhraiya Jivraj, and Silvia Posocco, eds. *Decolonizing Sexualities: Transnational Perspectives, Critical Interventions*. Oxford, UK: Counterpress, 2016.

Balakian, Peter. "Raphael Lemkin, Cultural Destruction, and the Armenian Genocide." In *The Armenian Genocide: Selected Articles from Holocaust and Genocide Studies*, edited by Robert Melson. Oxford Academic: *Holocaust and Genocide Studies* 27, no. 1 (2013): 57–89. DOI: 10.1093/hgs/dct001.

Ball, Joshua. "The Early Stages of a Multipolar World Order." *Global Security Review*, June 10, 2019. https://globalsecurityreview.com/the-early-stages-of-a-multipolar -world-order/.

Barreto, José Manuel. "Conquest, Independence and Decolonisation." In Barreto, ed., *Human Rights from a Third World Perspective*.

Barreto, José Manuel, ed. *Human Rights from a Third World Perspective: Critique, History and International Law*. Newcastle, UK: Cambridge Scholars Publishing 2013.

Barreto, José Manuel. "Imperialism and Decolonization as Scenarios of Human Rights History." In Barreto, ed., *Human Rights from a Third World Perspective*, 140–71.

"Barrick's Dirty Secrets: Communities Respond to Gold Mining's Impacts Worldwide." *Corpwatch*, May 1, 2007. https://corpwatch.org/article.php?id=14466.

Bartels, Emily C. "Making More of the Moor: Aaron, Othello, and Renaissance Refashionings of Race." *Shakespeare Quarterly* 41, no. 4 (1990): 433–54. DOI: 10.2307/2870775.

Bartels, Emily C. "Too Many Blackamoors: Deportation, Discrimination, and Elizabeth I." *SEL: Studies in English Literature 1500–1900* 46, no. 2 (2006): 305–22. DOI: 10.1353/ sel.2006.0012.

Bartlett, Christopher A., and Sumantra Ghoshal. "Matrix Management: Not a Structure, a Frame of Mind." *Harvard Business Review*, July–August 1990. Accessed June 1, 2020. https://hbr.org/1990/07/matrix-management-not-a-structure-a -frame-of-mind.

Beaubrun, Mimerose P. *Nan Dòmi: An Initiate's Journey into Haitian Voudou.* Translated by D. J. Walker with a preface by Madison Smartt Bell. San Francisco: City Lights Books, 2013 [2010].

Bauer, Ralph, and José Antonio Mazotti. *Creole Subjects in Colonial American Identities.* Chapel Hill: University of North Carolina Press, 2009.

Bauman, Zygmunt. *Modernity and the Holocaust.* Ithaca, NY: Cornell University Press, 1989.

Beck, Richard. "Why Are We in the Middle East?" *n+1 Magazine*, Fall 2016. https:// nplusonemag.com/issue-26/reviews/why-are-we-in-the-middle-east/.

Béji, Hélé. *Nous, décolonisés.* Paris: Aerea, 2008.

Bernasconi, Robert. "African Philosophy's Challenge to Continental Philosophy." In Eze, *Postcolonial African Philosophy*, 183–96.

Bertram, Benjamin. "New Reflections on the 'Revolutionary' Politics of Ernesto Laclau and Chantal Mouffe." *boundary 2* 22, no. 3 (Autumn 1995): 81–110.

Best, Lloyd. "Independent Thoughts and Carribean Freedom: Thirty Years Later." *Carribean Quarterly* 43, no. 1/2 (March–June 1997): 16–24. https://www.jstor.org /stable/40653983.

Bhambra, Gurminder K. "Postcolonial and Decolonial Dialogues." *Postcolonial Studies* 17, no. 2 (2014): 115–21. DOI: 10.1080/13688790.2014.966414.

Bhattacharya, Abheek. "India's $7 Billion Election." *Foreign Policy*, April 23, 2019.

Biagini, Hugo E., and Arturo A. Roig. *El pensamiento alternativo en Argentina.* Buenos Aires: Editorial Biblos, Tomo I, 2004.

Biden, Joe. Presidential acceptance speech. November 7, 2020. Video. https://www .youtube.com/watch?v=k1MhZcyrbrQ.

Biello, David. "Mass Deaths in America Start New CO_2 Epoch." *Scientific American*, March 2015. https://www.scientificamerican.com/article/mass-deaths-in-americas -start-new-co2-epoch/.

Bilbao, Luis. "Alianza del Pacífico: Obama pesca en el Sur." *América Latina en Movimiento*, Febuary 7, 2013. https://www.alainet.org/es/active/65333.

Blaney, David L. "Reconceptualizing Autonomy: The Difference Dependency Theory Makes." *Review of International Political Economy* 3, no. 3 (1995): 459–97.

Blue, Gregory. "Gobineau on China: Race Theory, the 'Yellow Peril' and the Critique of Modernity." *Journal of World History* 10, no. 1 (1999): 93–139. DOI: 10.1353/ jwh.2005.0003.

Bo, Xiang. "Backgrounder: Xi Jingping's Thoughts on Socialism with Chinese Characteristics for a New Era." NPC and CPPCC, Annual Sessions 2018, March 17, 2018. http://www.xinhuanet.com/english/2018-03/17/c_137046261.htm.

Boatcă, Manuela. "Multiple Europes and the Politics of Difference Within." *Worlds and Knowledges Otherwise*, Spring 2013, Center for Global Studies, Duke University, https://www.radicalphilosophy.com/article/towards-a-critical-theory-of-postcommunism.

Bogues, Antony. *Black Heretics, Black Prophets: Radical Political Intellectuals*. London: Routledge, 2003.

Bond, Peter. "Maturana, Technology, and Art: Is a Biology of Technology Possible?" *Cybernetics and Human Knowing* 2, no. 2 (2004): 1–22.

Bonello, Deborah. "Is Latin America's Turn to the Right Waning?" OZY, October 26, 2019. https://www.ozy.com/around-the-world/is-latin-americas-turn-to-the-right-waning/225265/.

Boone, Elizabeth Hill, and Walter D. Mignolo. *Writing without Words: Alternative Literacies in Mesoamerica and the Andes*. Durham, NC: Duke University Press, 1994.

Bosch, Juan. *Pentagonism: A Substitute for Imperialism*. Translated by Helen R. Lane. New York: Grove Press, 1968. Spanish ed. 1967.

Braidotti, Rosi. *The Posthuman*. Cambridge, UK: Polity Press, 2013.

Braudel, Fernand. *Afterthoughts on Material Civilization and Capitalism*. Baltimore: Johns Hopkins University Press, 1979.

Braudel, Fernand. *The Mediterranean and the Mediterranean World in the Age of Philip II*. Translated by Siân Reynolds. Berkeley: University of California Press, 1995 [1949].

Brenner, Michael. *Zionism: A Brief History*. Translated by Shelley L. Frisch. Princeton, NJ: Marku and Wienner, 2003.

Brodkin Sacks, Karen B. *How Jews Became White Folks and What That Says about Race in America*. New Brunswick, NJ: Rutgers University Press, 1998.

Brotton, Jerry. *A History of the World in 12 Maps*. New York: Viking, 2013.

Brunstetter, Daniel R., and Dana Zartner. "Just War against Barbarians: Revisiting the Valladolid Debates between Sepúlveda and Las Casas." *Political Studies* 59, no. 3 (2010): 733–52. DOI:10.1111%2Fj.1467-9248.2010.00857.x.

Brzezinski, Zbigniew. *Between Two Ages: America's Role in the Technetronic Era*. New York: Viking, 1970.

"The Bull Inter Caera (Alexander VI), May 4, 1493." NativeWeb.org. Accessed May 8, 2020. https://tainowoman.com/about/the-tie-system/the-inter-caetera-bull-1493-and-el-requerimiento-of-charles-i-1514/.

Burga, Manuel, and Alberto Flores Galindo. "Apogeo y crisis de la República Aristocrática." In Alberto Flores Galindo, *Obras Completas*, 145–46. Lima, Peru: Fundación Andina, 1994 [1980].

Burrow, Rufus, Jr. "Toward Womanist Theology and Ethics." *Journal of Feminist Studies in Religion* 15, no. 1 (Spring 1999): 77–95.

Cabnal, Lorena. "TZK'AT, Red de Sanadoras Ancestrales del Feminismo Comunitario desde Iximulew-Guatemala." *Ecología Política*, January 10, 2018. https://www.ecologia politica .info/?p=10247.

Caldéron, Emanuel Barrera, and María Florencia Valinotti. "La heterogeneidad histórico-estructural en América Latina: Diálogos con Marx." *Nómadas* 48 (April 2018): 49–63.

"El Camino de los Inmigrantes." Argentina.gob.ar, accessed October 1, 2020. https://www.argentina.gob.ar/interior/migraciones/museo/el-camino-de-los-inmigrantes.

Canal Feijóo, Bernardo. *El extremo occidente.* Buenos Aires: Editorial Sudamericana, 1954.

Carmo, Marcia. "Racismo é um problema econômico, diz diretor de agência antipobreza da ONU." BBC News/Brasil, June 2, 2019. https://www.bbc.com/portuguese/brasil-48424611.

Cary, John. *World and Four Continents* (map). "Cary's New Map of the Eastern and Western Hemisphere, containing the whole of the New Discoveries, and every Improvement to the Present time, 1827." Accessed September 28, 2020. https://www.crouchrarebooks.com/maps/view/cary-john-world-and-four-continents.

Casanova, Pablo González. "The Zapatistas 'Caracoles': Networks of Resistance and Autonomy." *Socialism and Democracy* 19, no. 3 (2005): 79–92.

Casco, José M. "El Gramsci de Portantiero: Cultura, política e intelectuales en la argentina de post-guerra." *Acta Sociológica* 68 (2015): 71–93.

Casimir, Jean. "The Counter-Plantation System." Magistral Class, Middelburg Decolonial Summer School, June 2018. https://vimeo.com/346377343.

Casimir, Jean. *The Haitians: A Decolonial History.* Translated by Laurent Dubois. Foreword by Walter D. Mignolo. Chapel Hill: University of North Carolina Press, 2020.

Casimir, Jean. *Une lecture décoloniale de l'histoire des haïtiens: Du Traité de Ryswick à l'occupation américaine (1697–1915).* Preface by Walter D. Mignolo. Afterword by Michel Hector. Port-au-Prince: L'Imprimeur, 2018.

Cassirer, Ernst Alfred. *The Myth of the State.* New Haven, CT: Yale University Press, 1951 [1932].

Cassano, Franco. *Southern Thoughts and Other Essays.* New York: Fordham University Press, 2012.

Castañeda, Jorge G. "Latin America's Left Turn: There Is More than One Pink Tide." *Foreign Affairs,* May/June 2006. https://www.foreignaffairs.com/articles/south-america/2006-05-01/latin-americas-left-turn.

Castañola, María Amelia, and Mauricio González, coordinators. *Decolonialidad y psicoanálisis.* Mexico City: Colección Borde Sur y Ediciones Navarra, 2017.

Castro-Gómez, Santiago. *La Hybris del Punto Cero: Ciencia, raza e ilustración en la Nueva Granada (1750–1816).* Bogotá: Editorial Javeriana, 2005.

Castro-Gómez, Santiago. "The Missing Chapter of Empire," *Cultural Studies* 21, no. 2–3 (2007): 428–48.

Castro-Kláren, Sara, and John Chastin. *Beyond Imagined Communities: Reading and Writing the Nation in Nineteenth Century Latin America.* Washington, DC: Woodrow Wilson Center, 2003.

Césaire, Aimé. *Discourse on Colonialism.* Translated by Joan Pinkham. New York: Monthly Review, 1972 [1955].

Césaire, Aimé. *Discours sur le colonialisme*. Paris: Présence Africaine, 2004 [1955].

Chatterjee, Partha. *Lineages of Political Society: Studies in Postcolonial Democracy*. New York: Columbia University Press, 2011.

Chatterjee, Partha. "Modernity and Indian Nationalism." In Jahanbegloo, *India Revisited*, 45–50.

Chatterjee, Partha. *The Nation and Its Fragments: Colonial and Postcolonial Histories*. Princeton, NJ: Princeton University Press, 1993.

Chatterjee, Partha. "On Civil and Political Society in Postcolonial Democracies." *Notes on Scholarly Books* (blog), May 2009. http://notesonscholarlybooks.blogspot .com/2009/05/partha-chatterjee-on-civil-and.html.

Chatterjee, Partha. *The Politics of the Governed: Reflections on Popular Politics in Most of the World*. New York: Columbia University Press, 2004.

Chatterjee, Partha. "Talking about Our Modernity in Two Languages." In *A Possible India: Essays in Political Criticism*, 263–285. Calcutta: Oxford University Press, 1998.

Chazarreta, Adriana. "La propuesta analítica de Rodolfo Stavenhagen." *Prácticas de oficio, investigación y reflexión en ciencias sociales* 6 (August 2010). https://static.ides .org.ar/archivo/www/2012/04/artic123.pdf.

Chen, Kuan-Hsing. *Asia as Method: Toward Deimperialization*. Durham, NC: Duke University Press, 2010.

Cherry, Conrad. *God's New Israel: Religious Interpretations of American Destiny*. Chapel Hill: University of North Carolina Press, 1998.

Chomsky, Noam. "'Losing' the World: American Decline in Perspective." Al Jazeera, February 15, 2012. https://www.aljazeera.com/indepth/opinion/2012/02 /2012215773268827.html.

Chovanec, Steve. "Syria's 'Moderate Terrorists' Supported by the CIA: Media Disinformation." Centre de recherche sur la mondialisation, March 26, 2016. https://www .mondialisation.ca/syrias-moderate-terrorists-supported-by-the-the-cia-media -disinformation/5515957.

Classen, Constance. *A Cultural History of the Senses in the Age of Empire*. London: Bloomsbury Academic, 2018.

Classen, Constance. *The Museum of the Senses: Experiencing Art Collections*. London: Bloomsbury Academic, 2017.

Cliff, Michelle. "If I Could Write This in Fire, I Would Write This in Fire." In *Home Girls: A Black Feminist Anthology*, edited by Barbara Smith, 15–30. New York: Kitchen Table: Women of Color Press, 1982.

Clinton, Hillary. "America's Pacific Century." *Foreign Policy*, October 11, 2011. https:// foreignpolicy.com/2011/10/11/americas-pacific-century/.

Cohen, Paula Marantz. "Confucianism in China Today." *American Scholar*, October 4, 2012. https://theamericanscholar.org/confucianism-in-china-today/# .XZauZZNKi3U.

Coker, Christopher. *The Rise of the Civilizational State*. Cambridge, UK: Polity Press, 2019.

Colectivo Anselmo Lorenzo. "Sentencia del Tribunal del Juicio Ético a las Transnacionales." *Boletín Informativo*, November 13, 2011. http://www.bolinf.es/wp/sentencia -del-tribunal-del-juicio-etico-a-las-transnacionales/#.X73VCV57mPR.

Coletta, Michela, and Malayna Raftopoulos, "Latin American Readings of Gramsci and the Bolivian Indigenous Nationalist State." *Latin American and Caribbean Ethnic Studies*. Taylor and Francis Online, August 10, 2020. https://www.tandfonline.com/doi/full/10.1080/17442222.2020.1805845?scroll=top&needAccess=true.

Commaroff, Jean and John. *Theory from the South, or, How Euro-America Is Evolving toward Africa*. Boulder, CO: Paradigm, 2012.

Cone, James H. *Black Theology of Liberation*. New York: Orbis Books, 1970.

Connell, Raewyn. *Southern Theory: Social Science and the Global Dynamics of Knowledge*. Sydney: Allen and Unwin, 2008.

Connell, Raewyn, and Nour Dados. "Where in the World Does Neoliberalism Come From?" *Theory and Society* 43 (2014): 117.

Coole, Diana, and Samantha Frost, eds. *New Materialism: Ontology, Agency, and Politics*. Durham, NC: Duke University Press, 2010.

Cooper, Richard, ed. *Towards a Renovated International System: A Report of the Trilateral Integrators Task Force to the Trilateral Commission*. New York: Trilateral Commission, 1973.

Cortés, Juan Donoso. *Essays on Catholicism, Liberalism and Socialism: Considered in Their Fundamental Principles*. London: Forgotten Books, 2017 [1852].

"Cosmology and Theology." *Stanford Encyclopedia of Philosophy*, revised April 5, 2017. https://plato.stanford.edu/entries/cosmology-theology/.

Coulthard, Glen Sean. *Red Skin, White Masks: Rejecting the Colonial Politics of Recognition*. Minneapolis: University of Minnesota Press, 2014.

Coulthard, Glen, and Leanne Betasamosake Simpson. "Grounded Normativity/Place-Based Solidarity." *American Quarterly* 68, no. 2 (2016): 249–55.

Covarrubias Horozco, Sebastián de. *Tesoro de la lengua castellana o Española*. Edited and illustrated by Ignacio Arellano and Rafael Zafra. Madrid: Iberoamericana Vervuert, 2006 [1611].

Crease, Robert P. "Critical Point: The Book of Nature." *Physics World* (December 2006): 16. www.robertpcrease.com/wp-content/uploads/2014/09/PW-Dec-2006-Book-of-Nature.pdf.

Cristobal, Kay. "Reflections on the Latin American Contribution to Development Theory." *Development and Change* 22 (1991): 31–68.

Cugoano, Quobna Ottobah. *Thoughts and Sentiments on the Evil of Slavery*. London: Penguin Classics, 1999 [1787].

Dabashi, Hamid. "Can Non-Europeans Think?" Al Jazeera, January 15, 2013. https://www.aljazeera.com/indepth/opinion/2013/01/20131142638797542.html.

Dabashi, Hamid. "To Protect the Revolution, Overcome the False Secular-Islamist Divide." Al Jazeera, December 2, 2012. https://www.aljazeera.com/indepth/opinion/2012/12/201212815384368495.html.

Dada, Maria. "Yuk Hui, 'On the Existence of Digital Objects.'" *Theory, Culture and Society*, March 23, 2018. https://www.theoryculturesociety.org/blog/review-yuk-hui-on-the-existence-of-digital-objects.

Dainotto, Roberto M. "Does Europe Have a South? An Essay on Borders." In Levander and Mignolo, "The Global South and World Dis/Order," 37–50.

Darrin. "Seven Investigation Strategies from Sherlock Holmes." *North American Investigations* (blog), September 13, 2013. https://pvteyes.com/7-investigation-strategies-sherlock-holmes/.

Dasgupta, Rana. "The Demise of the Nation State." *The Guardian*, April 5, 2018. https://www.theguardian.com/news/2018/apr/05/demise-of-the-nation-state-rana-dasgupta.

de Gómara, Francisco López. *Historia general de las Indias*. Caracas: Biblioteca Ayacucho, 1965 [1553].

Delanty, Gerard. "The Cosmopolitan Imagination: Critical Cosmopolitanism and Social Theory." *British Journal of Sociology* 57, no. 1 (2006): 25–47.

Deloria, Vine, Jr. *Evolution, Creationism and Other Modern Myths*. Ann Arbor, MI: Fulcrum Publishing, 2004.

Deprez, Esme E. "'Avatar' Tops Box Office, Passes $2 Billion Worldwide." Bloomberg, January 31, 2010. https://www.bloomberg.com/news/articles/2010-01-31/-avatar-tops-box-office-passes-2-billion-worldwide.

d'Errico, Peter. "'Collaborative Colonialism': A Way to Analyze Native/Non-native Relations." *Indian Country Today*, May 10, 2017. https://indiancountrytoday.com/archive/collab orative-colonialism-a-way-to-analyze-native-non-native-relations-9_JBS_CkToasH56s AHJflA.

Dershowitz, Alan M. "Bishop Tutu Is No Saint When It Comes to Jews." Gatestone Institute, International Policy Council, December 20, 2010. http://www.gatestoneinstitute.org/ 1742/bishop-tutu-is-no-saint-when-it-comes-to-jews.

de Sousa Santos, Boaventura, ed. *Cognitive Justice in a Global World: Prudent Knowledges for a Decent Life*. Lahnam, MD: Lexington Books, 2007.

de Sousa Santos, Boaventura, ed. *Epistemologies of the South: Justice against Epistemicide*. London: Routledge, 2014.

de Sousa Silva, José. "Una época de cambios o un cambio de época? Elementos de referencia para interpretar las contradicciones del momento actual," Boletín ICCI "RIMAY," April 2001, http://icci.nativeweb.org/boletin/25/souza.html.

Di-Capua, Yoav. *No Exit: Arab Existentialism, Jean Paul-Sartre and Decolonization*. Chicago: University of Chicago Press, 2018.

DiLorenzo, Thomas J. "Economic Fascism." Foundation for Economic Education, June 1, 1994. https://fee.org/articles/economic-fascism/.

Dinc, Pinar. "The Kurdish Movement and the Democratic Federation of Northern Syria: An Alternative to the (Nation-)State Model?" *Journal of Balkan and Near Eastern Studies* 22, no. 1 (2020): 47–67. https://www.tandfonline.com/doi/pdf/10.1080/19448953.2020.1715669?needAccess=true.

Dirks, Nicholas. "Introduction: Colonialism and Culture." In *Colonialism and Culture*, edited by Nicholas B. Dirks, 1–26. Ann Arbor: University of Michigan Press, 1992.

Dodge, Toby. *Inventing Iraq: The Failure of Nation Building and a Future Denied*. New York: Columbia University Press, 2003.

Dolphijn, Rick, and Iris van der Tuin. "Interview with Karen Barad." In Dolphijn and van der Tuin, *New Materialism*, 48–70.

Dolphijn, Rick, and Iris van der Tuin. *New Materialism: Interviews and Cartographies.* Ann Arbor, MI: Open Humanities Press, 2012.

Dorato, Mauro. "Why Is the Language of Nature Mathematical?" In *Galileo and the Renaissance Scientific Discourse: First Roma Workshop on Past and Present Perceptions of Science,* edited by Giovanni Antonini and Aldo Altamore, 65–67. Rome: Edizione Nuova Cultura, 2009.

Douzinas, Costas. *Human Rights and Empire: The Political Philosophy of Cosmopolitanism.* Oxford, UK: Routledge-Cavendish, 2007.

Douzinas, Costas. "The Paradoxes of Human Rights." Part I of *Human Rights and Empire.*

Du Bois, W. E. B. *The Negro Problem.* New York: Humanity Books, 2003 [1898].

Duhigg, Charles. "At Many Homes, More Profit and Less Nursing." *New York Times,* September 23, 2007. https://www.nytimes.com/2007/09/23/business/23nursing .html.

Dürr, Hans-Peter, J. Daniel Dahm, and Rudolf Prinz zur Lippe. "Postdam 'Denkschrift' 2005." Federal Ministry of Education and Research of Germany, October 2005. https://one88hiq.files.wordpress.com/2014/02/postdamer-denkschrift _en.pdf.

Dussel, Enrique. *Ética de la liberación en la edad de la globalización y de la exclusión.* Mexico City: Universidad Autónoma Nacional de México, 1998.

Dussel, Enrique. "Eurocentrism and Modernity (Introduction to the Frankfurt Lectures)." In *Postmodernism in Latin America,* edited by J. Beverley, J. Oviedo, and M. Arona, 65–76. Durham, NC: Duke University Press, 1995.

Dussel, Enrique. *Filosofía de la liberación.* Red de Bibliotecas Virtuales CLASCO (Consejo Latinoamericano de Ciencias Sociales), orig. pub. 1996 [1977], accessed August 25, 2020, http://biblioteca.clacso.edu.ar/clacso/otros/20120227024607 /filosofia.pdf.

Eastermann, Josef. *Filosofía Andina: Sabiduría Indígena Para un Mundo Nuevo.* La Paz: Editorial ISEAT, 2006.

"Economic and Financial Indicators: Poverty." *The Economist,* April 19, 2007. https:// www.nytimes.com/2007/10/27/opinion/27herbert.html.

Eisenberg, Daniel. "Cisneros y la Quema de los Manuscritos Granadinos." *Ballandalus,* July 1, 2013. https://ballandalus.wordpress.com/2013/07/01/cisneros-y-la-quema-de -los-manuscritos-granadinos-by-daniel-eisenberg/.

Ellis, Marc. *Judaism Does Not Equal Israel: The Rebirth of the Jewish Prophetic.* Foreword by Desmond Tutu. New York: New Press, 2009.

El Maarouf, Moulay Driss, Taieb Belghazi, and Farouk El Maarouf. "COVID-19: A Critical Ontology of the Present." *Educational Philosophy and Theory,* April 26, 2020. https://www.tandfonline.com/doi/full/10.1080/00131857.2020.1757426.

Enlace Zapatista. http://enlacezapatista.ezln.org.mx/. Accessed December 20, 2020.

Ennis, Mike. "Historicizing Nahua Utopias." PhD diss., Duke University, 2006.

Erazo, Paúl Mena. "La mayor organización indígena de Ecuador se moviliza contra Correa." *El País,* March 3, 2012. https://elpais.com/internacional/2012/03/08 /actualidad/ 1331190707_452752.html.

Escalante, Emilio del Valle. "For Abya-Yala to Live the Americas Must Die: Towards a Trans-Hemispheric Indigeneity." *Native Americans and Indigenous Studies* 5, no. 1 (2018): 42–68.

Esche, Charles. "Separation: In Conversation with Charles Esche." In *Permanent Temporariness*, edited by Sandi Hilal and Alessandro Petti, 45–52. Amsterdam: Idea Books, 2019.

Escher, Maurits Cornelius. *Drawing Hands*. Lithograph, 1948. Reproduced February 15, 2018. https://moa.byu.edu/m-c-eschers-drawing-hands/.

Escobar, Arturo. "Worlds and Knowledges Otherwise: The Latin American Modernity/Coloniality Research Program." *Cultural Studies* 21, no. 2–3 (2007): 179–210.

Euben, Roxanne L. *Enemy in the Mirror: Islamic Fundamentalism and the Limits of Modern Rationalism: A Work of Comparative Political Theory*. Princeton, NJ: Princeton University Press, 1999.

"Explainer: What Is 'Hybrid Warfare' and What Is Meant by the 'Grey Zone'?" *The Conversation*, June 17, 2019. https://theconversation.com/explainer-what-is-hybrid -warfare-and-what-is-meant-by-the-grey-zone-118841.

Eze, Emmanuel Chukwudi. "The Color of Reason: The Idea of 'Race' in Kant's Anthropology." In Eze, *Postcolonial African Philosophy*, 103–40.

Eze, Emmanuel Chukwudi, ed. *Postcolonial African Philosophy: A Critical Reader*. London: Wiley-Blackwell, 1997.

Fanon, Frantz. *Black Skin, White Masks*. Translated by Richard Philcox. Rev. ed. New York: Grove Press, 2008 [1952].

Fanon, Frantz. *Les damnés de la terre*. Paris: Maspero, 1961.

Fanon, Frantz. "L'expérience vécue du Noir." *Esprit: Nouvelle Série* 179, no. 5 (1951): 657–79.

Fanon, Frantz. "L'expérience vécue du Noir." In *Peau noire, masques blancs*, 109–40. Paris: Maspero, 1952.

Fanon, Frantz. *The Wretched of the Earth*. Translated by Richard Philcox. New York: Grove Press, 2004 [1961].

Farías, Victor. *Heidegger and Nazism*. Philadelphia: Temple University Press, 1991.

Farías, Victor. *Heidegger et le nazisme*. Paris: Verdier, 1987.

Federici, Sylvia. *Caliban and the Witch: Women, the Body and Primitive Accumulation*. Brooklyn, NY: Autonomedia, 2004.

Felski, Rita, and Susan Friedman, eds. *Comparison: Theories, Approaches, Uses*. Baltimore: Johns Hopkins University Press, 2013.

Feminismo Comunitario del Abya Yala, "Manifiesto sobre el golpe de estado y las elecciones generales en Bolivia." *Prensa Comunitaria*, December 22, 2019. https:// www.feminismo comunitario.com/.

Feng, Zhang. "The *Tianxia* System: World Order in a Chinese Utopia." *China Heritage Quarterly*, March 2010. http://www.chinaheritagequarterly.org/tien-hsia.php ?searchterm=021_utopia.inc&issue=021.

Fernández, Jesús Ruiz. "La idea de filosofía en José Ortega y Gasset." Departamento de Filosofía, Universidad Complutense de Madrid, E-Prints Complutense, 2009. http://eprints.ucm.ed/9522/.

Fernández-Díaz, Osvaldo. "Gramsci y Mariátegui: Frente a la ortodoxia." *Nueva Sociedad* 115 (1991): 135–44.

Ferraro, Vincent. "Dependency Theory: An Introduction." In *The Development Economics Reader*, edited by Giorgio Secondi, 58–64. London: Routledge, 2008. https://www.mtholyoke.edu/acad/intrel/depend.htm.

"Final Communiqué of the Asian Conference of Bandung (April 1955)." CVCE.eu, accessed January 4, 2021. https://www.cvce.eu/en/obj/final_communique_of_the _asian_african_conference_of_bandung_24_april_1955-en-676237bd-72f7-471f -949a-88b6ae513585.html.

Fine, Robert. "Blame Games Won't Lead Us to Peace." *Mail and Guardian* October 8, 2010. https://mg.co.za/article/2010-10-08-blame-game-wont-lead-us-to-peace/.

Finnegan, William. "Why Does Obama Want This Trade Deal So Badly?" *New Yorker*, June 11, 2015. https://www.newyorker.com/news/daily-comment/why-does-obama -want-the-trans-pacific-partnership-so-badly.

"First, Second and Third World." Nations Online Project, accessed Sept 30, 2020. https://www.nationsonline.org/oneworld/third_world_countries.htm.

Fischer, Joschka. "Is This the End of the West?" World Economic Forum, December 7, 2016. https://www.weforum.org/agenda/2016/12/is-this-the-end-of-the-west-asks -joschka-fischer.

Flores Galindo, Alberto. *La agonía de Mariátegui: La polémica con la Komintern*. Lima: Centro de Estudios y Promoción del Desarrollo, 1980.

Food Sovereignty Now! A Guide to Food Sovereignty. European Coordination Via Campesina, 2018. https://viacampesina.org/en/wp-content/uploads/sites/2/2018/02/Food -Sovereignty-A-guide-Low-Res-Vresion.pdf.

Forgacs, David. "Some Aspects of the Southern Question." In *The Antonio Gramsci Reader: Selected Writings 1916–1935*, 171–85. New York: New York University Press, 2000.

Foucault, Michel. *Les mots et les choses*. Paris: Gallimard, 1966.

Foucault, Michel. "Nietzsche, Freud, Marx." In *Nietzsche: Cahiers du Royaumont*, 183–200. Paris: Les Éditions de Minuit, 1964.

"Fourth BRICS Summit: Delhi Declaration," University of Toronto, BRICS Information Centre, March 29, 2012, http://www.brics.utoronto.ca/docs/120329-delhi -declaration.html.

Freeland, Anne. "The Gramscian Turn: Readings from Brazil, Argentina and Bolivia." *A Contracorriente* 11, no. 2 (2014): 278–301.

Friedman, Milton, with the assistance of Rose Friedman. *Capitalism and Freedom*. Chicago: University of Chicago Press, 1962.

Friends of the Congo. *Crisis in the Congo: Uncovering the Truth*. June 18, 2011. Video. https://www.youtube.com/watch?v=vLV9szEu9Ag.

Freud, Sigmund. *Civilization and Its Discontents*. Translated by James Strachey. New York: W. W. Norton, 2010 [1930].

Frye, Charles E. "Carl Schmitt's Concept of the Political." *Journal of Politics* 28, no. 4 (November 1966): 818–30.

Fuchs, Barbara. "The Spanish Race." In Greer, Mignolo, and Quilligan, *Rereading the Black Legend*, 88–98.

Fulbright, J. William. *The Arrogance of Power*. New York: Random House, 1967.

"Full Video: China's Grand Military Parade Celebration." CCTV English, September 7, 2015. Video, 1:40. https://www.youtube.com/watch?v=JzrpCC7XmyE.

Furtado, Celso. *El desarrollo económico: Un mito*. Mexico City: Fondo de Cultura Económica, 1974.

Gandhi, Mohandas. *Gandhi: "Hind Swaraj" and Other Writings*. Edited by Anthony J. Parel. Cambridge, UK: Cambridge University Press, 1997 [1909].

García Linera, Álvaro. "Catastrophic Equilibrium and Point of Bifurcation." MR Online, June 22, 2008. https://mronline.org/2008/06/22/catastrophic-equilibrium -and-point-of-bifurcation/.

García Linera, Álvaro, and Slavoj Žižek. "¿Es possible pensar un cambio radical hoy?" November 11, 2014. Video. https://www.youtube.com/watch?v=YoQEi4rOVRU.

Garvin, Paul L., ed., *Cognition: A Multiple View*. New York: Spartan Books, 1970.

Gathara, Patrick. "Berlin 1884: Remembering the Conference That Divided Africa." Al Jazeera, November 15, 2019. https://www.aljazeera.com/opinions/2019/11/15/berlin -1884-remembering-the-conference-that-divided-africa/.

George, Henry. *Progress and Poverty*. New York: Cosimo, 2005 [1879].

George, Henry. *Progress and Poverty: An Inquiry into the Cause of Industrial Depressions and of Increase of Want with Increase of Wealth: The Remedy*. New York: Robert Schalken-bach Foundation, 1997 [1879].

Gerbi, Antonello. *La disputa del Nuevo Mundo: Storia di una polemica, 1750–1900*. Trans-lated by Antonio Alatorre. Mexico City: Fondo de Cultura Económica, 1982 [1955].

Ghosh, Palash. "BRICS Summit-Delhi Declaration." *International Business Times*, March 29, 2012. http://www.ibtimes.com/articles/321440/20120329/brics-delhi -declaration-russia-china-india-brazil.htm (accessed May 8, 2020).

Girard, Mathilde. "Ce que Paul B. Preciado fait à la psychanalyse." *AOC*, October 1, 2020. https://aoc.media/opinion/2020/01/09/ce-que-paul-b-preciado-fait-a-la -psychanalyse/.

Glissant, Édouard. *Poetics of Relation*. Translated by Betsy Wing. Ann Arbor: Univer-sity of Michigan Press, 1997 [1990].

"The Global North/South Divide." Royal Geographical Society. Ac-cessed May 25, 2020. https://www.rgs.org/ CMSPages/GetFile. aspx?nodeguid=9c1ce781–9117–4741-af0a-a6a8b75f32b4&lang=en-GB.

Gloeckner, Erin. "Workplace Investigation Tips from Sherlock Holmes." Risk Manage-ment Center, accessed May 24, 2020. https://nonprofitrisk.org/resources/e-news /workplace-investigation-tips-from-sherlock-holmes/.

Goldsman, Florencia. "Lorena Cabnal: 'Recupero la alegría sin perder la indignación, como un acto emancipatorio y vital.'" *Pikara Online Magazine*, November 13, 2019. https://www.pikaramagazine.com/2019/11/lorena-cabnal-recupero-la-alegria-sin -perder-la-indignacion-como-un-acto-emancipatorio-y-vital/

González Casanova, Pablo. "Colonialismo interno (una redefinición)." In *La teoría marxista hoy*, edited by A. Boron, J. Amadeo, and S. González, 409–34. Buenos Aires: CLASCO, 2006.

Gordon, Lewis R. *Disciplinary Decadence: Living Thoughts in Trying Times.* London: Routledge, 2007.

Gordon, Lewis R. *Existentia Africana: Understanding Africana Existential Thought.* London: Routledge, 2000.

Gordon, Lewis R. *Fanon and the Crisis of European Man: An Essay on Philosophy and the Human Sciences.* New York: Routledge, 1995.

Gordon, Lewis R. "Sartre and Fanon on Embodied Bad Faith." In *Sartre on the Body: Philosophers in Depth*, edited by Katherine J. Morris, 183–99. London: Palgrave Macmillan, 2010.

Gordon, Lewis R. "What Does It Mean to Be a Problem? W. E. B. Du Bois and the Study of the Black Folk." In Gordon, *Existentia Africana: Understanding Africana Existential Thought*, 62–95. London: Routledge, 2000.

Gordon, Lewis R. *What Fanon Said: A Philosophical Introduction to His Life and Thought.* New York: Fordham University Press, 2015.

Gordon, Peter, and Juan José Morales. *The Silver Way: China, Spanish America and the Birth of Globalization, 1515–1865.* London: Penguin Special, 2017.

Gorricho, Lucía. "Lectura de la sentencia Juicio Etico a las Transnacionales." November 5, 2011. Video. https://www.youtube.com/watch?v=VLS8gCFZTEQ.

Gramsci, Antonio. "Un examen de la situación italiana." Discusión preliminar presentado en la reunión del Comité Directivo del Partido Comunista, *Rinascita*, April 14, 1967, 21–22.

Gramsci, Antonio. *Los intelectuales y la organización de la cultura.* Buenos Aires: Ediciones Lautaro, 1960.

Gramsci, Antonio. *Introducción a la filosofía de la praxis.* Selected and translated by J. Solé-Tura. Barcelona: Ediciones Península, 1970.

Gramsci, Antonio. *El materialismo y la filosofía de Benedetto Croce.* Buenos Aires: Editorial Lautaro, 1958.

Gramsci, Antonio. *Notas sobre Maquiavelo, sobre política y sobre el estado moderno.* Buenos Aires: Nueva Visión, 1973.

Gramsci, Antonio. *Prison Notebooks.* Translated and edited by Joseph A. Buttigieg, vol. 2. New York: Columbia University Press, 2011.

Gramsci, Antonio. *Quaderni del Cacere (Quattro Volumi).* WordPress, accessed January 6, 2021. https://quadernidelcarcere.wordpress.com.

Gramsci, Antonio. *The Southern Question.* Translated by Pasquale Verdicchio. Montreal: Guernica Editions, 2006.

"La gran emigración europea durante el siglo XIX y principios del siglo XX." *Documentalium* (blog). September 15, 2015. https://www.documentalium.com/2015/09/la -gran-emigracion-europea-durante-el.html.

Grear, Anna. "Challenging Corporate 'Humanity': Legal Disembodiment, Embodiment and Human Rights." *Human Rights Law Review* 7, no. 3 (2007): 1–33.

Greer, Margaret R., Walter D. Mignolo, and Maureen Quilligan, eds. *Rereading the Black Legend: The Discourses of Religious and Racial Difference in the Renaissance Empires*. Chicago: University of Chicago Press, 2008.

Gregor, Mary. "Kant on 'Natural Rights.'" In *Kant and Political Philosophy*, edited by R. Beiner and W. J. Booth, 50–75. New Haven, CT: Yale University Press, 1993.

Grosfóguel, Ramón. "Human Rights and Anti-Semitism after Gaza." *Human Architecture: Journal of the Sociology of Self-Knowledge* 7 (Spring 2009): 89–102.

Grovogui, Siba N'Zatioula. *Sovereigns, Quasi Sovereigns, and Africans: Race and Self-Determination in International Law*. Minneapolis: University of Minnesota Press, 1996.

Gržinić, Marina, and Walter Mignolo. "De-Linking Epistemology from Capital and Pluri-Versality: A Conversation, Part I." *Reartikulacija* 4 (2008): 20–22.

Guaman Poma de Ayala, Felipe. *El primer nueva corónica y buen gobierno*. Digital facsimile and transcript. Royal Library of Copenhagen, Denmark, orig. pub. 1615, accessed June 1, 2020. http://www5.kb.dk/permalink/2006/poma/ info/en/frontpage.htm.

Guaman Poma de Ayala, Felipe. *El primer nueva corónica y buen gobierno*. Translated by Rolena Adorno, John V. Murra, and Jorge L. Urioste. Mexico City: Fondo de Cultura Económica, 1980 [1615].

Guha, Ranajit. *Dominance without Hegemony*. Boston: Harvard University Press, 1997.

Habermas, Jürgen. *The Inclusion of the Other: Studies in Political Theory*. Edited by Ciaran Cronin and Pablo De Greiff. Boston: MIT Press, 1998.

Hance, Jeremy. "La verdadera historia de Avatar: Los Pueblos Indígenas en la lucha para salvar sus hogares en la selva de la explotación de las Corporaciones." *Mongabay Latam*, January 4, 2010. https://es.mongabay.com/2010/01/la-verdadera -historia-de-avatar-los-pueblos-indigenas-en-la-lucha-para-salvar-sus-hogares-en -la-selva-de-la-explotacion-por-las-corporaciones/.

Hanna, Monica, Jennifer Hartog Vargas, José David Saldívar, eds. *Junot Díaz and the Decolonial Imagination*. Durham, NC: Duke University Press, 2016.

Hansen, Suzy. "Can Asians Think?" *Salon*, March 26, 2002. https://www.salon.com /2002/03/25/asians/.

Harding, Sandra. *Is Science Multicultural? Postcolonialism, Feminism and Epistemologies*. Bloomington: Indiana University Press, 1988.

Harding, Sandra, editor. *The Postcolonial Science and Technology Studies*. Durham, NC: Duke University Press, 2011.

Hayek, F. A. *The Road to Serfdom*. Edited by Milton Friedman. Chicago: University of Chicago Press, 1994 [1944].

Hayles, N. Katherine. *How We Became Posthuman: Virtual Bodies in Cybernetics, Literature, and Informatics*. Chicago: University of Chicago Press, 1999.

Hegel, Georg Wilhelm Friedrich. *Introduction to Aesthetics: Being the Introduction to the Berlin Aesthetics Lectures of the 1820s*. Translated by T. M. Knox. Oxford, UK: Oxford University Press, 1979.

Hegel, Georg Wilhelm Friedrich. *Introductory Lectures on Aesthetics*. Translated by Bernard Bosanquet. Edited by Michael Inwood. London: Penguin Classics, 1993.

Hegel, Georg Wilhelm Friedrich. *The Philosophy of History*. Translated by J. Sibree. Prefaces by J. Sibree and Charles Hegel. New York: Dover, 1956 [1822].

Hegel, Georg Wilhelm Friedrich. *The Philosophy of History*. Translated by J. Sibree. New York: Prometheus Books, 1991 [1822], 102.

Heidegger, Martin. "The Question Concerning Technology." In *Basic Writings*, edited by David Farrell Krell, 307–42. New York: Harper, 2008.

Heidegger, Martin. "What Calls for Thinking?" In *Basic Writings*, edited by David Farell Krell, 341–68. New York: Harper, 1977 [1954].

Held, David. *Democracy and the Global Order: From the Modern State to Cosmopolitan Governance*. Stanford, CA: Stanford University Press, 1995.

Henry, Paget. *Caliban's Reason: Introducing Afro-Caribbean Philosophy*. London: Routledge, 2000.

Henry, Paget, and Paul Buhle, eds. *C. L. R. James's Caribbean*. Durham, NC: Duke University Press, 1992.

Herbert, Bob. "Today's Hidden Slave Trade." *New York Times*, October 27, 2007. https://www.nytimes.com/2007/10/27/opinion/27herbert.html.

Hernández Arregui, Juan José. *La formación de la conciencia nacional*. Buenos Aires: Ediciones Hachea, 1960.

Hernández Arregui, Juan José. *Imperialismo y cultura*. Buenos Aires: Editorial Amerindia, 1957.

Hernández Arregui, Juan José. *Nacionalismo y liberación*. Buenos Aires: Peña Lillo Ediciones, 2004 [1969].

Herrera, Verónica. "The Persistence of Peronism." *Berkeley Review of Latin American Studies*, Spring 2007. http://clas.berkeley.edu/research/argentina-persistence-peronism.

Herzl, Theodor. *The Jewish State*. Translated by Sylvie D'Avigdor. New York: American Zionist Emergency Council, 1946 [1896]. Reproduced at Jewish Virtual Library. Accessed August 23, 2020. www.jewishvirtuallibrary.org/jsource/Zionism/herzl2.html.

Herzl, Theodor. *Der Judenstaat: Versuch einer modernen Lösung der Judenfrage* ("The Jewish State: Proposal of a Modern Solution for the Jewish Question"). Leipzig: M. Breitenstein's Verlags-Buchhandlung, February 14, 1896.

Hinkelammert, Franz. "The Hidden Logic of Modernity: Locke and the Inversion of Human Rights." *World and Knowledges Otherwise* 1, no. 1 (2004): 1–27.

Hobsbawn, Eric. "Barbarism: A User's Guide." *New Left Review* 1, no. 206 (1994): 44–54.

Höffner, Joseph. *La ética colonial española del siglo de oro: Cristianismo y dignidad humana*. Translated into Spanish by Franscisco de Asis Caballero. Madrid: Ediciones de Cultura Hispánica, 1957 [1947]: 289–335.

Hollinger, David. *Post-Ethnic America. Beyond Multiculturalism*. 2nd ed. New York: Basic Books, 2006 [1996].

Hong, Chen. "On Matteo Ricci's Interpretations of Chinese Culture." *Coolabah* 16 (2015): 87–100. https://revistes.ub.edu/index.php/coolabah/article/view/15426.

Hoogvelt, Ankie. *Globalization and the Postcolonial World: The New Political Economy and Development*. Baltimore: Johns Hopkins University Press, 1997.

Horkheimer, Max. "Traditional and Critical Theory." In *Critical Theory: Selected Essays*, translated by Matthew J. O'Connell, 188–243. New York: Continuum, 1975 [1937].

Hountondji, Paulin J. "Recapturing." In *The Surreptitious Speech: Présence Africaine and the Politics of Otherness, 1947–1987*, ed. V. Y. Mudimbe, 238–48. Chicago: University of Chicago Press, 1992.

Huanacuni Mamani, Fernando. *Vivir Bien/Buen Vivir: Filosofía, políticas, estrategias y experiencias regionales Andinas*. Lima: Coordinadora Andina de Organizaciones Indígenas, 2010.

Huanacuni Mamani, Fernando. *Vivir Bien/Buen Vivir: Filosofía, políticas, estrategias y experiencias de los pueblos ancestrales*. 6th ed. La Paz: Instituto International de Integración, 2015.

Hui, Wang. *China from Empire to Nation-State*. Translated by Michael Gibbs Hill. Cambridge, MA: Harvard University Press, 2014.

Hui, Wang. "A Dialogue on *The Rise of Modern Chinese Thought*: Liberating the Object and an Inquiry into the Modern." *Positions: Asia Critique* 20, no. 1 (2012): 287–306.

Hui, Wang. "The Liberation of the Object and the Interrogation of Modernity: Rethinking *The Rise of Chinese Thought*." *Modern China* 34, no. 1 (2008): 114–40.

Hui, Yuk. *The Question Concerning Technology in China: An Essay in Cosmotechnics*. Windsor Quarry, UK: Urbanomic, 2016.

Hunt, Lynn. "The Paradoxical Origins of Human Rights." In Wasserstrom et al., eds., *Human Rights and Revolutions*, 3–21.

Huntington, Samuel. *The Clash of Civilizations and the Remaking of the World Order*. New York: Simon and Schuster, 1996.

Huntington, Samuel. "The Hispanic Challenge." *Foreign Policy* 141 (March 2004): 30.

Hurton, W. D. "The Military-Industrial Complex Revisited." In *Global Focus: U.S. Foreign Policy at the Turn of the Millennium*, edited by M. Hoey and T. Barry. New York: St. Martin's Press, 2000.

Husserl, Edmund. *The Crisis of European Sciences and Transcendental Phenomenology: An Introduction to Phenomenological Philosophy*. Translated by David Carr. Evanston, IL: Northwestern University Press, 1970 [1936].

Husserl, Edmund. *La filosofía como ciencia estricta*. Translated by Elsa Tabernig. Buenos Aires: Editorial Nova, 1962.

Husserl, Edmund. *Philosophy as Rigorous Science*. Translated and introduction by Quentin Lauer. New York: Harper and Row, 1965 [1911].

InterCP International. "Introducing the Maghreb Window: The Land Where the Sun Sets, the End of the Earth." *Global Alliance Newsletter*, May 2014, http://www.intercp.org/2014/05/introducing-the-maghreb-window-the-land-where-the-sun-sets-the-end-of-the-earth/.

"The International Peasants' Voice." La Vía Campesina, accessed October 15, 2020. https://viacampesina.org/en/international-peasants-voice/.

Ishay, Micheline R., ed. "United Nations Universal Declaration of Human Rights (1948)." In *The Human Rights Reader*. New York: Routledge, 1997.

Islamic Human Rights Commission (IHRCtv). *Islamophobia, Diversity and the Crisis of Democracy*. September 17, 2014. Video, 1:05:59. https://www.youtube.com/ watch?v=MziMD2dHyU4.

"Israel miembro en Alianza del Pacífico" (Israel joins Pacific Alliance). Embassy of Israel, Dominican Republic, December 2, 2014. https://embassies.gov.il /santo domingo/NewsAndEvents/Pages/ISRAEL-ACEPTADO-COMO-PAIS-OBSERVADOR-EN-ALIANZA-DEL-PACIFICO.aspx.

"Is Tillerson's Bluster Just a Bluff for Senate?" *Global Times*, January 13, 2017. http:// www.globaltimes.cn/content/1028568.shtml.

Iweriebor, Ehiedu E. G. "The Colonization of Africa." *Africana Age*. Schomburg Center for Research in Black Culture. New York Public Library, accessed May 26, 2020. https://wayback.archive-it.org/11788/20200107232503/http://exhibitions.nypl.org /africanaage/index2.html.

Jahanbegloo, Ramin, ed. *India Revisited: Conversations on Contemporary India*. Oxford, UK: Oxford University Press, 2008.

James, C. L. R. *Notes on Dialectics: Hegel, Marx, Lenin*. Westport, CT: Lawrence Hill, 1969.

James, C. L. R. *State Capitalism and World Revolution*. Written in collaboration with Raya Dunayevskaya and Grace Lee. Chicago: Charles H. Kerr Publishing, 1986.

James, C. L. R. *State Capitalism and World Revolution*. Charles H. Kerr Library, 2013.

Jameson, Fredric. *Postmodernism, or the Cultural Logic of Late Capitalism*. Durham, NC: Duke University Press, 1991.

Jauretche, Arturo. *Ejército y política*. Buenos Aires: Peña Lillo, 1958.

Jauretche, Arturo. *Política y economía*. Buenos Aires: Peña Lillo, 1977.

Jauretche, Arturo. *Los profetas del odio y la yapa: La colonización pedagógica*. Buenos Aires: Peña Lillo, 1975.

Jewish Virtual Library. "Modern Jewish History: Distribution of the Jews in the World (1942)." Accessed May 26, 2020. https://www.jewishvirtuallibrary.org/distribution -of-the-jews-in-the-world-1942.

Jewish Virtual Library. "The Six-Day War: Background and Overview (June 5–10, 1967)." Accessed May 5, 2020. https://www.jewishvirtuallibrary.org/background -and-overview-six-day-war.

Jinping, Xi. "President Jinping's Speech to Davos in Full." World Economic Forum, January 17, 2017. https://www.weforum.org/agenda/2017/01/full-text-of-xi-jinping -keynote-at-the-world-economic-forum.

Jonas, Hans. *The Phenomenon of Life: Towards a Philosophical Biology*. New York: Harper and Row, 1966.

Kagan, Robert. *The Jungle Grows Back: America and Our Imperiled World*. New York: Knopf, 2018.

Kakoliris, Gerasimos. "The 'Undecidable' Pharmakon: Derrida's Reading of Plato's Phaedrus." ResearchGate. January 2013. https://www.researchgate.net/publication /282648428_The_Undecidable_Pharmakon_Derrida's_Reading_of_Plato's _Phaedrus.

Kant, Immanuel. *Anthropology from a Pragmatic Point of View*. Translated by Victor Lyle Dowdell. Carbondale: Southern Illinois University Press, 1996 [1797].

Kant, Immanuel. *Beobachtungen über das Gefühl des Schönen und Erhabenen* (Observations on the Feeling of the Beautiful and Sublime). Translated by John T. Goldthwait. 2nd ed. Berkeley: University of California Press, 2003 [1764].

Kant, Immanuel. *Critique of Judgement* (Kritik der Urteilskraft). Translated by Werner S. Pluhar. Cambridge, MA: Hackett Classics, 1987 [1820].

Kant, Immanuel. *The Metaphysics of Morals*. Edited and translated by Mary Gregor. Cambridge, UK: Cambridge University Press, 1996 [1785].

Kant, Immanuel *Observations on the Feeling of the Beautiful and Sublime*. Ed. Patrick Frierson and Paul Guyer. Cambridge, UK: Cambridge Texts in the History of Philosophy, 2011 [1764].

Kant, Immanuel. "Perpetual Peace." In *Kant: On History*, edited by Lewis White Beck, translated by Lewis White Beck, Robert E. Anchor, and Emil L. Fackenheim, 85–136. Englewood Cliffs, NJ: Macmillan, 1963 [1795].

Kant, Immanuel. "What Is Enlightenment?" Website of Columbia University, orig. pub. 1784, accessed June 1, 2020. http://www.columbia.edu/acis/ets/CCREAD /etscc/kant.html.

Kapoor, Ilan. "Žižek, Antagonism and Politics Now: Three Recent Controversies." *International Journal of Žižek Studies* 12, no. 1 (2018).

Kapron, Benjamin. "Cacophonous Settler Grounded Normativity." Master's thesis, York University, 2016. https://fes.yorku.ca/wp-content/uploads/2018/08 /outstanding_papers_Kapron_B.pdf.

Karkov, Nikolai, and Zhivka Vallavicharska. "Rethinking East-European Socialism: Notes toward an Anti-Capitalist Methodology." *International Journal of Postcolonial Studies* 20, no. 6 (2018): 185–213.

Kassam, Ashifa. "Spain's Podemos Inspired by Syriza's Victory in Greek Elections." *The Guardian*, January 26, 2015. https://www.theguardian. com/world/2015/jan/26/ spain-podemos-syriza-victory-greek-elections.

Kebede, Messay. "Ethnic Politics and Individual Rights. An Alternative Vision for Ethiopia." ECADF (*Ethiopian News and Views*), October 30, 2013. http://ecadforum .com/2013/10/30/ethnic-politics-and-individual-rights/.

Keilo, Jack. "Jerusalem at the Very Centre of the World, Bunting's Map and Social Construction." Centres and Centralities, August 12, 2013, updated July 3, 2016. https://centrici.hypotheses.org/215.

Kemp, Arthur. Map, "The Six Hundred Year White Reconquest of Spain and Portugal." In *March of the Titans: The Complete History of the White Race*, 171. Burlington: Ostara Publications, 2011.

Khalil, Osamah F. "The Crossroads of the World: U.S. and British Foreign Policy Doctrines and the Construct of the Middle East, 1902–2007." *Diplomatic History* 38, no. 2 (April 2014): 299–344. DOI: 10.1093/dh/dht092.

Khan, Khatija Bibi. "The Kaiser's Holocaust: The Coloniality of German's Forgotten Genocide of the Nama and the Herero in Namibia." *African Identities* 10, no. 3 (2012): 211–20.

Khanna, Parag. "No Longer in Thrall to Western Democracy, Asia Turns to Technocrats for Answers." *Global-is-Asian*, January 10, 2017. https://lkyspp.nus.edu.sg/gia
/article/no-longer-in-thrall-to-western-democracy-asia-turns-to-technocrats-for
-answers.

Koonz, Claudia. *The Nazi Conscience*. Cambridge, MA: Belknap Press, 2003.

Koshy, Susan. "From Cold War to Trade War: Neocolonialism and Human Rights."
Social Text 58 (1999): 1–32. http://www.jstor.org/stable/466713.

Kristeva, Julia. *Strangers to Ourselves*. Translated by L. S. Roudiez. New York: Columbia
University Press, 1991.

Kuhn, Thomas. *The Structure of Scientific Revolutions*. Chicago: University of Chicago
Press, 1962.

Kurasawa, Fuyuki. "Cosmopolitanism from Below: Alternative Globalization and
the Creation of Solidarity without Bonds." *Archives of European Sociology* 45, no. 2
(2004): 233–55.

Kusch, Rodolfo. *Indigenous and Popular Thinking in América*. Translated by María
Lugones and Joshua M. Price. Introduction by Walter D. Mignolo. Durham, NC:
Duke University Press, 2010 [1970].

Kymlicka, Will. *Liberalism, Community and Culture*. Oxford, UK: Clarendon Press,
1989.

Kymlicka, Will. *Multicultural Citizenship: A Liberal Theory of Minority Rights*. Oxford, UK:
Clarendon Press, 1995.

Las Casas, Bartolomé de. *Apologética Historia Sumaria*. Madrid: Alianza Editorial, 1992
[1536].

Las Casas, Bartolomé de. *Brevísma relación de la destruición de las Indias* (1552). Edited
by José Miguel Martínez Torrejón. Accessed December 22, 2020. http://www
.cervantesvirtual.com/obra-visor/brevisima-relacin-de-la-destruccin-de-las-indias
-0/html/847e3bed-827e-4ca7-bb80-fdcde7ac955e_18.html.

Las Casas, Bartolomé de. *The Spanish Colonie, or Briefe Chronicle of the Acts and Gestes of
the Spaniardes in the West Indies, Called the Newe World, for the Space of Xl. Yeeres: Written in the Castilian Tongue by the Reuerend Bishop Bartholomew De Las Cases or Casaus,
a Friar of the Order of S. Dominicke. And Nowe First Translated into English, by M. M. S.*
London: By Thomas Dawson for William Brome, 1583.

Lathman, Andrew. "The Confucian Continuities of Chinese Geopolitical Discourse."
In *Chinese World: Multiple Temporalities and Transformations*, 243–51. Saint Paul, MN:
Macalester College, 2007.

Latouche, Serge. *L'occidentalization du monde: Essays sur la signification, la portée et les
limites de l'uniformation planetaire*. Paris: Maspero, 1989.

Latouche, Serge. *The Westernization of the World: Significance, Scope and Limits of the Drive
toward Global Uniformity*. New York: Polity Press, 1996.

Lawrence, Vera, and Rex Nettleford, eds. *Race, Discourse and the Americas: A New World
View*. Washington, DC: Smithsonian Institution Press, 1995.

Leal, Lourdes Godinez. "Lorena Cabnal: Defensora del cuerpo-tierra de las mujeres."
CN cimacnoticias, October 22, 2015. https://cimacnoticias.com.mx/noticia/lorena
-cabnal-defensora-del-cuerpo-tierra-de-las-mujeres/.

Lelham, Robert. *Through the Western Eyes: Eastern Orthodoxy: A Reformed Perspective.* Tain, Scotland: Christian Focus Publications, 2010.

Lentin, Alana, and cosignatories. "Open Letter : The Threat of Academic Authoritarianism—International Solidarity with Antiracist Academics in France." Open Democracy, November 5, 2020. https://manifestedes90.wixsite .com/monsite.

Leroi-Gourhan, André. *Le geste et la parole.* Paris: Albin Michel, 1964.

León-Portilla, Miguel. *Aztec Thought and Culture: A Study of the Ancient Nahuatl Mind.* Translated by Jack Emory Davis. Norman: University of Oklahoma Press, 1990 [1963].

León-Portilla, Miguel. *La filosofía Náhuatl: Estudiada en sus fuentes.* Mexico City: Fondo de Cultura Económica, 1958.

Letzing, John. "Here Is the Pope's Prescription for Resetting the Global Economy in Response to COVID-19." *World Economic Forum,* October 9, 2020. https://www .weforum.org/agenda/2020/10/here-s-the-pope-s-prescription-for-resetting-the -global-economy-in-response-to-covid-19/.

Levander, Caroline, and Walter Mignolo, eds. "The Global South and World Dis/Order." Special issue, *Global South* 5, no. 1 (2011). https://www.jstor.org /stable/10.2979/globalsouth .5.1.1?seq=1#page_scan_tab_contents.

Little Bear, Leroy. "Indigenous Knowledge and Western Science." Banff Center Talk, January 14, 2015. Video, 21:32. https://www.youtube.com/watch?v=gJSJ28eEUjI.

Little Bear, Leroy. "Little Bear Offers a Different View of Science." Website of Arizona State University. 2011. https://asunow.asu.edu/content/qa-little-bear-offers -different-view-science.

Lointier, Mylène Ferrand. "Yuko Hasegawa: 'New Sensorium—Exiting from the Failures of Modernization.'" *Seismopolite: Journal of Art and Politics,* August 2016. http://www.seismopolite.com/yuko-hasegawa-new-sensorium-exiting-from-the -failures-of-modernization.

"Los talibanes juran vengar la matanza de Kandahar." *El País Internacional,* March 2012. https://elpais.com/internacional/2012/03/12/actualidad/1331538127_294245.html.

Lovelock, James. *Gaia: A New Look at Life on Earth.* Oxford, UK: Oxford University Press, 1979.

Lu, Caitlin. "Matteo Ricci and the Jesuit Mission in China, 1583–1610." In *The Concord Review,* 2011. http://www.tcr.org/tcr/essays/EP_TCR_21_3_Sp11_Matteo%20Ricci .pdf.

Luisetti, Federico, John Pickles, and Wilson Kayer, eds. *The Anomie of the Earth: Philosophy, Politics, and Autonomy of the Earth in Europe and Latin America.* Durham, NC: Duke University Press, 2015.

Lyotard, Jean-François. *La condition postmoderne: Rapport sur le savoir.* Paris: Les Éditions de Minuit, 1979.

Macas, Luis. "Interview with CONAIE's Luis Macas: 'We Want a Total Transformation.'" NACLA *Report on the Americas,* September 17, 2007. https://nacla.org /news/2007/8/24/interview-conaies-luis-macas-%E2%80%9Cwe-want-total -transformation.

Mahbubani, Kishore. *Can Asians Think? Understanding the Divide between East and West.* Hanover, NH: Steerforth Press, 2001 [1998].

Mahbubani, Kishore. *Can Asians Think? Understanding the Divide between East and West.* London: Times Edition, 2009 [1998].

Mahbubani, Kishore. "The Dangers of Democratic Delusions." Mahubani.net, March 26, 2009. http://mahbubani.net/articles%20by%20dean/The%20dangers%20of%20Democratic.pdf.

Mahbubani, Kishore. *The Great Convergence: Asia, the West and the Logic of One World.* New York: Public Affairs, 2014.

Mahbubani, Kishore. *Has the West Lost It? A Provocation.* London: Penguin, 2018.

Mahbubani, Kishore. "Is China Expansionist?" In *Has China Won?* New York: Public Affairs, 2020, 79–104.

Mahbubani, Kishore. *The New Asian Hemisphere: The Irresistible Shift of Global Power to the East.* New York: Public Affairs, 2008.

Mahbubani, Kishore. "Peeling Away the Western Veneer." *New Perspective Quarterly* 30, no. 4 (2013): 87–91.

Mahbubani, Kishore. "Western Dominance Is an Historical Aberration." Interview by Ankita Mukhopadhyay. *The Fair Observer*, October 23, 2019. https://www.fairobserver.com/region/asia_pacific/us-uk-china-india-east-west-dominance-balance-power-news-16251/.

Mahbubani, Kishore, and Larry Summers. "The Fusion of Civilizations: The Case for Global Optimism." *Foreign Affairs*, May/June 2016. https://www.foreignaffairs.com/articles/016-04-18/fusion-civilizations.

Maffie, James. "Aztec Philosophy." *Internet Encyclopedia of Philosophy.* Accessed May 31, 2020. https://www.iep.utm.edu/aztec/.

Maffie, James. *Aztec Philosophy: Understanding a World in Motion.* Boulder: University Press of Colorado, 2014.

Maldonado-Torres, Nelson. "On the Coloniality of Being: Contributions to the History of a Concept." *Cultural Studies* 21, no. 2–3 (2007): 240–70. DOI: 10.1080/09502380601162548.

Maldonado-Torres, Nelson. "The Topology of Being and the Geopolitics of Knowledge." *City* 8, no. 1 (2004): 29–56. DOI: 10.1080/1360481042000199787.

Maluleka, Khazamula J. "Indigenous African Philosophy of Ubuntu as a Foundation for a Conducive Environment for Culturally Responsive Teaching and Learning in South Africa." International Conference on New Trends in Teaching and Education. Barcelona, Spain, September 5–7, 2019, https://www.dpublication.com/wp-content/uploads/2019/09/19-5299.pdf.

Mangena, Fainos. "Hunhu/Ubuntu in the Traditional Thought of Southern Africa." *Internet Encyclopedia of Philosophy*, accessed May 26, 2020. https://www.iep.utm.edu/hunhu/?fbclid=IwAR2Clka 7AcUN5s8AlMUdb6gG9rQHgLLx9 TE0018_SEXlZ5qn-khUWL37wQE.

Manolova, Polina, Katarina Kusic, and Philipp Lottholtz, eds. "Decolonial Theory and Practice in Southeast Europe." Special issue, *dVERSIA Magazine*, March 2019, https://issuu.com/dversiamagazine/docs/dversia-special-issie-decolonial-th.

Manrique, Diego A. "Los dilemas del filántropo Bono." *El País*, September 20, 2010. https://elpais.com/diario/2010/09/20/cultura/1284933606_850215.html.

Manyin, Mark E., coordinator. *Pivot to the Pacific? The Obama Administration's "Rebalancing" Toward Asia*. Congressional Research Service, March 28, 2012. https://fas.org/sgp/crs/natsec/R42448.pdf.

Mardell, Jacob. "The 'Community of Common Destiny' in Xi Jingping's New Era." *The Diplomat*, October 25, 2017. https://thediplomat.com/2017/10/the-community-of-common-destiny-in-xi-jinpings-new-era/.

Mariátegui, José Carlos. *Seven Interpretative Essays on Peruvian Reality*. Translated by Jorge Basadre. Austin: University of Texas Press, 1971 [1928].

Martinez, Michael. "5 things to Know about Obama's First Presidential Visit to Israel." CNN, March 20, 2013. https://www.cnn.com/2013/03/20/politics/obama-mideast-five-things/.

Marx, Karl. *Capital: A Critique of Political Economy*, vol. 1. Translated by Ben Fowkes and David Fernbach. London: Penguin Classics, 1976 [1867].

Masuzawa, Tomoko. *The Invention of World Religions: Or, How European Universalism Was Preserved in the Language of Pluralism*. Chicago: University of Chicago Press, 2005.

Mate, Reyes. *Memory of the West: The Contemporaneity of Forgotten Jewish Thinkers*. Translated by John R. Welch. Amsterdam: Rodopi, 2004.

Maturana, Humberto. *Biology of Cognition: Biological Computer Laboratory Research*. Urbana: University of Illinois Press, 1970.

Maturana, Humberto. "Biology of Language: The Epistemology of Reality." In *Psychology and Biology of Language and Thought: Essays in Honor of Eric Lenneberg*, edited by George A. Miller and Elizabeth Lenneberg, 27–63. New York: Academic Press, 1978.

Maturana, Humberto. "Human Beings versus Machines? Or Machines as Instruments of Human Design?" *TechnoMorfica*, 1997, accessed January 12, 2021. https://v2.nl/archive/articles/metadesign.

Maturana, Humberto R. "Ontology of Observing: The Biological Foundations of Self Consciousness and the Physical Domain of Existence." In *Conference Workbook for "Texts in Cybernetic Theory": An In-Depth Exploration of the Thought of Humberto R. Maturana, William T. Powers, and Ernst von Glasersfeld: A Conference of the American Society for Cybernetics, October 13–23, 1988, Felton, California*, edited by R. E. Donaldson, 67–53. Washington, DC: American Society for Cybernetics, 1988. Accessed May 28, 2020. https://pdfs.semanticscholar.org/b197/549e065158d8102ca973ae705ad8f0082e14.pdf.

Maturana, Humberto R. "The Organization of the Living: A Theory of the Living Organization." Reprinted in *International Journal of Human-Computer Studies* 51, no. 2 (1999): 149–68. https://doi.org/10.1006/ijhc.1974.0304.

Maturana, Humberto R. "Reality: The Search for Objectivity or the Quest for a Compelling Argument," *Irish Journal of Psychology* 9, no. 1 (1988): 25–82. DOI: 10.1080/03033910.1988.10557705.

Maturana, Humberto, and Ximena Paz Dávila. "Education as Viewed from the Biological Matrix of Human Existence." *Towards Life-Knowledge*. Orig. pub. 2006.

Reproduced January 13, 2018. https://bsahely.com/2018/01/13/education-as-viewed
-from-the-biological-matrix-of-human-existence-2006-by-humberto-maturana
-and-ximena-paz-davila/.

Maturana, Humberto, and Francisco Varela. *The Tree of Knowledge: The Biological Roots of Human Understanding.* Boston: New Science Library, 1987.

Maturana Romesín, Humberto. "The Origin and Conservation of Self-Consciousness." *Kybernetics* 34, no. 1/2 (2005): 54–88.

Maturana Romesín, Humberto, and Ximena Dávila Yáñez. *El Arbol del vivir.* Santiago de Chile: MVP Editores-Escuela Matriztica, 2015.

Mavhunga, Clapperton Chakanetsa, ed. *What Do Science, Technology and Innovation Mean from Africa?* Boston: MIT Press, 2017.

Mayblin, Lucy. "Modernity/Coloniality." Global Social Theory, accessed May 5, 2020. https://globalsocialtheory.org/concepts/colonialitymodernity/.

McCarthy, Thomas. "On Reconciling Cosmopolitan Unity and National Diversity." *Public Culture* 11 (1999): 175–208.

McEwan, Ian. *Machines Like Me.* London: Nan A. Talese, 2019.

McKittrick, Katherine, ed. *Sylvia Wynter: On Being Human as Praxis.* Durham, NC: Duke University Press, 2015.

McLemee, Scott, and Paul Le Blanc, eds. *C. L. R. James and Revolutionary Marxism: Selected Writing 1939–1949.* Amherst, MA: Humanity Books, 1993.

McLeod, Neal. *Cree Narrative Memory: From Treaties to Contemporary Times.* Saskatoon, SK: Purich Publishing, 2009.

Meeks, Brian, and Norman Girvan, eds. *Caribbean Reasonings: The Thought of New World, the Quest for Decolonisation.* Kingston, JM: Ian Randle Publishers, 2010.

Mehta, Aaron. "'Pivot to the Pacific' Is Over, Senior U.S. Diplomat Says." *Defense News,* March 14, 2017. https://www.defensenews.com/pentagon/2017/03/14/pivot-to-the -pacific-is-over-senior-u-s-diplomat-says/.

Melson, Robert. Introduction, "The Armenian Genocide: Selected Articles from *Holocaust and Genocide Studies.*" Oxford Academic, accessed December 29, 2020. https://academic.oup.com/DocumentLibrary/HGS/Melson_Introduction.pdf.

Mendelsohn, Oliver, and Upendra Baxi, eds. *The Rights of the Subordinated Peoples.* Delhi: Oxford India Paperbacks, 1994.

Meotti, Giulio. "Tutu's War on Israel, Jews." *Y-Net Magazine,* August 11, 2011. http:// www.ynet news.com/articles/0,7340,L-4107913,00.html.

Mignolo, Walter D., ed. *Aníbal Quijano: Ensayos en torno a la colonialidad del poder.* Buenos Aires: Ediciones del Signo, 2019.

Mignolo, Walter D. "Bono contra China." Personal blog, Internet Archive, November 1, 2007. https://web.archive.org/web/2007121009327/http://walter mignolo .com/2007/11/01/bon o-contra-china/.

Mignolo, Walter D. "Border Thinking and Decolonial Cosmopolitanism: Overcoming Colonial/Imperial Differences." In *Routledge International Handbook of International Studies,* edited by Gerard Delanty. London: Routledge, 2018.

Mignolo, Walter D. "Border Thinking, Decolonial Cosmopolitanism and Dialogues among Civilizations." In *The Ashgate Research Companion on Cosmopolitanism,* edited by Maria Rovisco and Magdalena Nowicka, 329–48. Farnham, UK: Ashgate Publishing, 2011.

Mignolo, Walter D. "Citizenship, Knowledge and the Limits of Humanity." *American Literary History* 18, no. 2 (2006) 312–31.

Mignolo, Walter D. "Coloniality at Large: The Western Hemisphere in the Colonial Horizon of Modernity." *New Centennial Review* 1, no. 2 (2001): 19–54. https://www.jstor .org/stable /41949278.

Mignolo, Walter D. "Coloniality of Power and Subalternity." In *The Latin American Subaltern Studies Reader*, edited by Ileana Rodriguez, 224–44. Durham, NC: Duke University Press, 2001.

Mignolo, Walter D. "The Communal and the Decolonial." *Turbulence*, 2010. http:// turbulence.org.uk/turbulence-5/decolonial/.

Mignolo, Walter D. "Cosmopolitan Localisms: Overcoming Colonial and Imperial Differences." In Mignolo, *The Darker Side of Western Modernity*, 252–94.

Mignolo, Walter D. "Crossing Gazes and the Silence of the 'Indians': Theodor De Bry and Guamán Poma de Ayala." *Journal of Medieval and Early Modern Studies* 41, no. 1 (2011): 173–223. DOI: 10.1215/10829636-2010-016.

Mignolo, Walter D. "The Darker Side of the Enlightenment: A Decolonial Reading of Kant's Geography." In Mignolo, *The Darker Side of Western Modernity*, 181–212.

Mignolo, Walter D. *The Darker Side of the Renaissance: Literacy, Territoriality, and Colonization*. 2nd ed. Ann Arbor: University of Michigan Press, 2012 [1995].

Mignolo, Walter D. *The Darker Side of Western Modernity: Global Futures, Decolonial Options*. Durham, NC: Duke University Press, 2011.

Mignolo, Walter D. "Decolonial Body-Geo-Politics at Large: Foreword to *Decolonizing Sexualities*." *Critical Legal Thinking*, November 3, 2016. https://criticallegalthinking .com/2016/11/03/decolonizing-sexualities-foreward-walter-mignolo/.

Mignolo, Walter D. "Decolonial Body-Geo Politics at Large." Foreword to *Decolonizing Sexualities: Transnational Perspectives, Critical Interventions*, edited by Sandeep Bakshi, Suhraiya Jivraj, and Silvia Posocco, vii–xviii. Oxford, UK: Counterpress, 2016.

Mignolo, Walter D. "(De)Coloniality at Large: Time and the Colonial Difference." In Mignolo, *The Darker Side of Western Modernity*, 149–80.

Mignolo, Walter D. "The De-colonial Option and the Meaning of Identity in Politics." *Anales Instituto Ibero Americano: Anales Nueva Epoca* 9–10 (2007): 43–72.

Mignolo, Walter D. "Decolonizing Western Epistemology/Building Decolonial Epistemologies." In *Decolonizing Epistemologies: Latina/Latino Theology and Philosophy*, edited by Ada María Isasi Díaz and Eduardo Mendieta, 19–43. New York: Fordham University Press, 2012.

Mignolo, Walter D. "Delinking: The Rhetoric of Modernity, the Logic of Coloniality and the Grammar of De-coloniality." *Cultural Studies* 21, no. 2 (2007): 449–514. DOI: doi.org/10.1080/09502380601162647.

Mignolo, Walter D. "Democracia liberal, camino de la autoridad humana y transición al vivir bien." Sociedade e Estado, Brasília, Jan./Apr. 2014. https://www.scielo.br /scielo.php?script=sci_arttext&pid=S0102-69922014000100003.

Mignolo, Walter D. "Enacting the Archive, De-centering the Muses: The Museum of Islamic Art in Doha and the Museum of Asian Civilizations in Singapore." *Ibraaz: Contemporary Visual Culture in North Africa and the Middle East*, November 6, 2013, https://www.ibraaz.org/essays/77.

Mignolo, Walter D. "Epistemic Disobedience, Independent Thought, and Decolonial Freedom." *Theory, Culture, and Society* 26, no. 7–8 (2009): 159–81. DOI: 10.1177/0263276409349275.

Mignolo, Walter D. "From the Global Linear Thinking to a Multipolar World." *Radio Papesse*, May 2015. https://www.radiopapesse.org/en/archive/interviews/walter -mignolo-from-the-global-linear-thinking-to-a-multipolar-world.

Mignolo, Walter D. "Geopolitics of Knowledge and the Colonial Difference." *South Atlantic Quarterly* 101, no. 1 (Winter 2002): 57–96. DOI: 10.1215/00382876-101-1-57.

Mignolo, Walter D. "Geopolitics of Sensing and Knowing: On (De)coloniality, Border Thinking and Epistemic Disobedience." *Confero* 1, no. 1 (2013): 129–50. DOI: 10.3384/confer.2001-4562.13v1ii129.

Mignolo, Walter D. "Global Coloniality and the World Disorder: Decoloniality after Decolonization and De-Westernization after the Cold War." Reprinted in *A World Beyond Global Disorder: The Courage to Hope*, edited by Fred Dallmayr and Edward Demenchonok, 90–117. Cambridge, UK: Cambridge Scholars Publishing, 2017.

Mignolo, Walter. "Globalization and the Geopolitics of Knowledge: The Role of the Humanities in the Corporate University." In *The American-Style University at Large: Transplants, Outposts, and the Globalization of Higher Education*, edited by Kathryn L. Kleypas and James I. McDougall, 3–40. Lanham, MD: Lexington Books, 2012.

Mignolo, Walter D. "Globalization and the Geopolitics of Knowledge: The Role of the Humanities in the Corporate University." *Nepantla: Views from South* 4, no. 1 (2000): 97–119. https://www.muse.jhu.edu/article/40206.

Mignolo, Walter D. "Globalization/Mundialization: Civilization Processes and the Relocation of Languages and Knowledges." In *Local Histories/Global Designs*, 278–313.

Mignolo, Walter D. "The Global South and World Dis/Order." *Journal of Anthropological Research* 67, no. 2 (2011): 165–88. https://www.journals.uchicago.edu/doi/10.3998 /jar.0521004.0067.202.

Mignolo, Walter D. "Habitar las fronteras: Psicoanálisis, geo-historicidad de los cuerpos y decolonialidad." In Mignolo, *Hacer, pensar y vivir la decolonialidad*, 31–39.

Mignolo, Walter D. *Hacer, pensar y vivir la decolonialidad: Textos reunidos y presentados por comunidad psicoanalítica/pensamiento decolonial*. Mexico City: Borde Sur y Ediciones Navarra, 2016.

Mignolo, Walter D. "I Am Where I Do: Remapping the Order of Knowledge." In Mignolo, *The Darker Side of Western Modernity*, 77–117.

Mignolo, Walter D. "I Am Where I Think: Epistemology and the Colonial Difference." *Journal of Latin American Cultural Studies* 8, no. 2 (1999): 235–45. DOI: 10.1080/13569329909361962.

Mignolo, Walter D. *The Idea of Latin America*. London: Wiley-Blackwell Manifestos, 2005.

Mignolo, Walter D. "Interview with Walter Mignolo/Part 1: Activism and Trajectory." *E-International Relations*, January 17, 2017. https://www.e-ir.info/2017/01/17/interview-walter-mignolopart-1-activism-and-trajectory/.

Mignolo, Walter D. "Interview with Walter Mignolo/Part 2: Key Concepts." *E-International Relations*. January 21, 2017. https://www.e-ir.info/2017/01/21/interview-walter-mignolopart-2-key-concepts/.

Mignolo, Walter D. "The Invention of the 'Human' and the Three Pillars of the Colonial Matrix of Power (Racism, Sexism, and Nature)." In Mignolo and Walsh, *On Decoloniality*, 153–76.

Mignolo, Walter D. "Islamophobia/Hispanophobia: The (Re)configuration of the Racial Imperial/Colonial Matrix." *Human Architecture* 5, no. 1 (2006): 13–28. https://scholarworks.umb.edu/humanarchitecture/vol5/iss1/3.

Mignolo, Walter D. *La désobéissance épistémique: Rhétorique de la modernité, logique de la colonialité et grammaire de la décolonialité.* Translated by Yasmine Jouhari and Marc Maesschalk. Amsterdam: Peter Lang, 2015.

Mignolo, Walter D. *Local Histories/Global Designs: Coloniality, Subaltern Knowledges, and Border Thinking.* 2nd ed. Princeton, NJ: Princeton University Press, 2012 [2000].

Mignolo, Walter D. "The Logic of the In-Visible: Decolonial Reflections on the Change of Epoch." *Theory, Culture and Society* 37, no. 7/8 (December 2020). https://journals.sagepub.com/doi/10.1177/0263276420957741.

Mignolo, Walter D. "Modernity and Decoloniality." Oxford Bibliography Online, 2011. http://www.oxfordbibliographies.com/view/document/obo-9780199766581/obo-9780199766581-0017.xml.

Mignolo, Walter D. "The Moveable Center: Ethnicity, Geometric Projections and Co-existing Territorialities." In *The Darker Side of the Renaissance: Literacy, Territoriality, and Colonization*, 2nd ed. (Ann Arbor: University of Michigan Press, 2012 [1995]), 219–58.

Mignolo, Walter D. "Neither Capitalism, nor Communism but Decolonization, Part I." *Critical Legal Studies: Law and the Political*, March 21, 2012. http://criticallegalthinking.com/2012/03/21/neither-capitalism-nor-communism-but-decolonization-an-interview-with-walter-mignolo.

Mignolo, Walter D. "The North of the South and the West of the East." *Ibraaz: Contemporary Visual Culture in North Africa and the Middle East*, November 6, 2014. https://www.ibraaz.org/essays/108/.

Mignolo, Walter D. "On Comparison: Who Is Comparing What and Why?" In Felski and Friedman, *Comparison: Theories, Approaches, Uses.*

Mignolo, Walter D. "On Gnosis and the Imaginary of the Modern/Colonial World System." In Mignolo, *Local Histories/Global Designs*, 3–48.

Mignolo, Walter D. "On Subaltern and Other Agencies." *Postcolonial Studies* 8, no. 4 (2005): 381–407.

Mignolo, Walter D. "Prophets Facing Sidewise: The Geopolitics of Knowledge and the Colonial Difference." *Social Epistemology* 19, no. 1 (2005): 111–27. DOI: 10.1080/02691720500084325.

Mignolo, Walter D. "Racism and Human Rights." *Bolivia Changes* (blog), June 6, 2008. http://boliviachanges.blogspot.com/2008/06/racism-and-human-rights.html.

Mignolo, Walter D. "Reconstitución epistémica/estética: La aesthesis decolonial una década después." *Calle 14: Revista de investigación en el campo del arte* 14, no. 25 (2019): 14–32, DOI: 10.14483/21450706.14132.

Mignolo, Walter D. "Re:emerging, Decentering and Delinking: Shifting the Geographies of Sensing, Believing and Knowing." *Ibraaz: Contemporary Visual Culture in North Africa and the Middle East*, May 8, 2013. https://www.ibraaz.org/essays/59.

Mignolo, Walter D. "Regeneración y reciclaje: Descolonizar la ciencia y la biotecnología para liberar la vida." In *Rastros y rostros de la biopolítica*, edited by Ignacio Mendiola Gonzalo, 181–200. Barcelona: Anthropos, 2009.

Mignolo, Walter D. "The Role of the BRICS Countries in the Becoming World Order." In *Humanity and Difference in the Global Age*. Beijing: Académie de la Latinité, 2012. http://alati.com.br/fr/publicacoes/humanity-and-difference-in-the-global-age/.

Mignolo, Walter D. "The Role of the Humanities in the Corporate University," *PMLA* 115, no. 5 (October 2000): 1238–45. DOI: 10.2307/463306.

Mignolo, Walter D. "Second Thoughts on *The Darker Side of the Renaissance*." In Mignolo, *The Darker Side of the Renaissance*, 427–63.

Mignolo, Walter D. "Spirit Out of Bounds Returns to the East: The Closing of the Social Sciences and the Opening of Independent Thought." *Current Sociology* 61, no. 4 (2014): 584–602.

Mignolo, Walter D. "The Splendors and Miseries of 'Science': Coloniality, Geopolitics of Knowledge, and Epistemic Pluriversality." In *Cognitive Justice in a Global World: Prudent Knowledges for a Decent Life*, edited by Boaventura de Sousa Santos, 375–96. Lanham, MD: Lexington Books, 2007.

Mignolo, Walter D. "Sustainable Development or Sustainable Economies?" *Socioscapes: International Journal of Societies, Politics and Cultures* 1, no. 1 (2020): 48–65.

Mignolo, Walter D. "Venezuela: The Symptoms of Multipolarity." DOC Research Institute, January 29, 2019. https://doc-research.org/2019/01/venezuela-symptoms-multipolarity/.

Mignolo, Walter D. "Who Speaks for the 'Human' in Human Rights?" In Barreto, *Human Rights from a Third World Perspective*, 44–65.

Mignolo, Walter D. "Yes, We Can: Non-European Thinkers and Philosophers." Al Jazeera, February 19, 2013. https://www.aljazeera.com/indepth/opinion /2013/02 /20132672747320891.html.

Mignolo, Walter D. "The Zapatistas' Theoretical Revolution: Its Historical, Ethical and Political Consequences." In Mignolo, *The Darker Side of Western Modernity*, 213–51.

Mignolo, Walter D., and Arturo Escobar, eds. *Globalization and the Decolonial Option*. London: Routledge, 2009.

Mignolo, Walter D., and Michelle K. "Decolonial Aesthesis: From Singapore, to Cambridge, to Duke University." *Social Text: Periscope*, July 2013. http:// socialtextjournal.org/periscope_article/decolonial-aesthesis-from-singapore-to -cambridge-to-duke-university/.

Mignolo, Walter D., and Madina V. Tlostanova. *Learning to Unlearn: Decolonial Reflections from Eurasia and the Americas.* Columbus: Ohio State University Press, 2012.

Mignolo, Walter D., and Madina V. Tlostanova. "Theorizing from the Borders: Shifting to Geo-and Body-Politics of Knowledge." *European Journal of Social Theory* 9, no. 2 (2006): 205–21. DOI: 10.1177/1368431006063333.

Mignolo, Walter D., and Rolando Vázquez. "Decolonial AestheSis: Colonial Wounds/ Decolonial Healings." *Social Text: Periscope,* July 15, 2013, https://socialtextjournal .org/ periscope_article/decolonial-aesthesis-colonial-woundsdecolonial-healings/.

Mignolo, Walter D., and Rolando Vázquez. "Mexico's Indigenous Congress: Decolonising Politics." Al Jazeera, September 27, 2017. https://www.aljazeera.com/indepth /opinion/mexico-indigenous-congress-decolonising-politics-170926093051780 .html.

Mignolo, Walter D., and Catherine E. Walsh. *On Decoloniality: Concepts, Analytics, Praxis.* Durham, NC: Duke University Press, 2018.

Miller, Eric. "The Radical Rise of Liberation Theology: An Interview with Calles Barger." *Religion and Politics,* September 25, 2018. https://religionandpolitics.org /2018/09/25/the-radical-rise-of-liberation-theology-an-interview-with-lilian-calles -barger/.

Mills, Charles W. *The Racial Contract.* Ithaca, NY: Cornell University Press, 1997.

Ming, Liu. "Xi Jingping's Vision of a Community with a Shared Future for Humankind." In Ren Xiao and Liu Ming, *Chinese Perspective on International Relations for the Jinping Era.* National Bureau of Asian Research, Special Report #85, June 2020 https://www.nbr.org/wp-content/uploads/pdfs/publications/sr85 _chineseperspectives_jun2020.pdf.

Mitchel, Robert, and Catherine Waldby. *Tissue Economies: Blood, Organs, and Cell Lines in Late Capitalism.* Durham, NC: Duke University Press, 2006.

Moon, Silver, and Mike Ennis. "The View of the Empire from the Altepetl: Nahua Historical and Global Imagination." In Greer, Mignolo, and Quilligan, *Rereading the Black Legend,* 150–66.

Morar, Florin-Stefan. "The Westerner: Matteo Ricci's World Map and the Quandaries on the European Identity in the Late Ming Dynasty." *Journal of Jesuit Studies* 6, no. 1 (2019): 14–30. https://brill.com/view/journals/jjs/6/1/article-p14_14.xml ?language=en.

MTL Collective. "From Institutional Critique to Institutional Liberation? A Decolonial Perspective on the Crisis of Contemporary Art." *October* 165 (2018): 192–227.

Mudimbe, V. Y. *The Invention of Africa: Gnosis, Philosophy, and the Order of Knowledge.* Bloomington: Indiana University Press, 1988.

Murphy, James J., ed. *Three Medieval Rhetorical Arts.* Berkeley: University of California Press, 1971.

Mutua, Makau. *Human Rights: A Political and Cultural Critique.* Philadelphia: University of Pennsylvania Press, 2008.

Muzaffar, Chandra. "Paris—A Dastardly Act of Terror: The Case for an Independent Investigation." *Global Research,* January 11, 2015. www.globalresearch.ca/paris-a -dastardly-act-of-terror-the-case-for-an-independent-investigation/5423889.

Nandy, Ashis. "Gandhi and the Indian Identity." In Jahanbegloo, *India Revisited*, 51–58.

Ndlovu-Gatsheni, Sabelo J. *Epistemic Freedom in Africa: Deprovincialization and Decolonization*. London: Routledge, 2018.

Newcomb, Steven. "Why the Papal Bull Claiming Dominion over Non-Christian Lands Still Matters." *Indian Country Today*. August 2013. https://indiancountrytoday.com/archive/why-papal-bull-claiming-dominion-over-non-christian-lands-still-matters-HKRuUqe_5kCiOS52QpZCEg.

Ni, Peimin. "The Silk Order: A Philosophical Perspective." DOC Research Institute, March 26, 2018. https://doc-research.org/2018/03/silk-order-philosophical-perspective/.

Nirenberg, David. *Anti-Judaism: The Western Tradition*. Chicago: University of Chicago Press, 2013.

Novak, Matt. "Yes, the Eerie Carl Sagan Prediction That's Going Viral Is Real." Gizmodo, January 23, 2017. https://paleofuture.gizmodo.com/yes-the-eerie-carl-sagan-prediction-thats-going-viral-1791502520.

Nun, José. *La situación de los sectores populares en el prodeso argentine de transición hacia la democracia*. Buenos Aires: Centro Latinoamericano para el Análisis de la democracia, 1988.

Öcalan, Abdullah. *The Sociology of Freedom: Manifesto of the Democratic Civilization*, vol. 3. Oakland, CA: PM Press, 2020.

O'Donnell, Guillermo, and Philippe C. Schmitter. *Transitions from Authoritarian Rule: Tentative Conclusions about Uncertain Democracies*. Baltimore: Johns Hopkins University Press, 2013.

O'Gorman, Edmundo. *La invención de América: El universalismo en la cultura occidental*. Mexico City: Universidad Autónoma de México, 1958.

O'Gorman, Edmundo. *La invención de América: Investigación acerca de la estructura histórica del Nuevo Mundo y del sentido de su devenir*. Mexico City: Universidad Nacional de México, 1958. English translation: *The Invention of America: An Inquiry into the Historical Nature of the New World and the Meaning of Its History*. Bloomington: Indiana University Press, 1961.

Ogude, James, Steve Paulson, and Anne Strainchamps. "I Am Because You Are: An Interview with James Ogude." CHC Ideas, June 21, 2019. https://chcinetwork.org/ideas/i-am-because-you-are-an-interview-with-james-ogude.

O'Halley, Meagan. "Placing Islam: Alternative Visions of the Morisco Expulsion and Spanish-Muslim Christian Relations in the Sixteenth Century." PhD diss., Duke University, 2013. http://dukespace.lib.duke.edu/dspace/bitstream/handle/10161/7193/OHalley_duke_0066D_11863.pdf?sequence=1.

Oliver, Kelly. *Technologies of Life and Death: From Cloning to Capital Punishment*. New York: Fordham University Press, 2013.

Ollantay, Itzamná. "Estado nación y estado plurinacional." *Telesurtv.net* (blog), June 16, 2016. https://www.telesurtv.net/bloggers/Estado-Nacion-y-Estado-Plurinacional-20160616-0001.html.

"Operation Condor, 1968–1989." National Security Archive, accessed May 26, 2020. https://nsarchive.gwu.edu/ events/operation-condor-1968–1989.

Ortuño, Gabriela Gonzáles. "Los feminismos afro en Latinoamérica y el Caribe, tradiciones disidentes: Del pensamiento anticolonial a la defensa de la tierra." *Investigaciones Feministas* 9, no. 2 (December 2018): 239–54. DOI: 10.5209/INFE.58936.

Osco, Marcelo Fernandez. *La ley del Ayllu: Práctica de jach'a justicia y jisk'a justicia (justicia mayor y justicia menor) en la comunidades aymaras.* La Paz: PIEB, 2000.

Outlaw, Lucius T., Jr. *On Race and Philosophy.* London: Routledge, 1996.

Ouviña, Hernán. "René Zavaleta, frecuentador de Gramsci." In *René Zavaleta Mercado: Pensamiento crítico y marxismo abigarrado,* 29–76. Buenos Aires: Facultad de Ciencias Sociales, 3, 2016.

Pacari, Nina. "Ecuador Taking on the Neoliberal Agenda." *NACLA Report on the Americas* 29, no. 5 (1996): 23–32. DOI: 10.1080/10714839.1996.11722889.

Padrón, Ricardo. *The Indies of the Setting Sun: How Early Modern Spain Mapped the Far East and the Transpacific West.* Chicago: University of Chicago Press, 2020.

Padrón, Ricardo. *The Spacious Word: Cartography, Literature and the Empire in Early Modern Spain.* Chicago: University of Chicago Press, 2004.

Paganelli, Alejandra, Victoria Gnazzo, Helena Acosta, Silvia L. López, and Andres E. Carrasco. "Glyphosate-Based Herbicides Produce Teratogenic Effects on Vertebrates by Impairing Retinoic Acid Signaling." *Chemical Research in Toxicology: ACS Publications,* October 2010. https://pubs.acs.org/doi/abs/10.1021/tx1001749.

Pagden, Anthony. *The Fall of Natural Man: The American Indian and the Origins of Comparative Ethnology.* Cambridge, UK: Cambridge University Press, 1982. https://academic.oup.com/ahr/article-abstract/88/4/1114/113467?redirectedFrom=fulltext.

Palacios Rubios, Juan Lopéz de. *El Requerimiento (1513).* Encyclopedia Virginia, March 18, 2013. https://www.encyclopediavirginia.org/El_Requerimiento_by_Juan_Lopez_de_Palacios_Rubios_1513.

Palermo, Zulma, ed. *Pensamiento Argentino y opción descolonial,* 2nd ed. Buenos Aires: Ediciones del Signo, 2016.

Pan Afrikan. "Congo 20 Million Dead the Role US and Its Allies Played." July 1, 2011. Video. https://www.youtube.com/watch?feature=endscreen&v=8YPldzhAKgk&NR=1.

Patzi Paco, Félix. *Sistema comunal: Una propuesta alternativa al sistema liberal: una discusión teórica para salir de la colonialidad y del liberalismo.* La Paz: Comunidad de Estudios Alternativas (CEA), 2004.

Peers, Alexandra. "Qatar Purchases Cézanne's *The Card Players* for More than $250 Million, Highest Price Ever for a Work of Art." *Vanity Fair,* February 2, 2012. http://www.vanityfair.com/culture/2012/02/qatar-buys-cezanne-card-players-201202.

Peralta M., Pablo. "Bolivia's CONAMAQ (Consejo Nacional de Ayllus y Markas del Qollasuyu) Indigenous Movement." *Upside Down World,* May 2014. http://upsidedownworld.org/ archives/bolivia/bolivias-conamaq-indigenous-movement-we-will-not-sell-ourselves-to-any-government-or-political-party/.

Pérez, Emma. *The Decolonial Imaginary: Writing Chicanas into History.* Bloomington: Indiana University Press, 1999.

Pérez Luño, Antonio-Enrique. *La polémica sobre el Nuevo Mundo: Los clásicos españoles de la Filosofía del Derecho*. Madrid: Editiorial Trotta, 1992.

Pérez Miles, Addety. "Unbound Philosophies and Histories: Epistemic Disobedience in Latin American Contemporary Art." *International Encyclopedia of Art and Design Education*, August 14, 2018. https://onlinelibrary.wiley.com/doi/abs/10.1002/9781118978061.ead039.

"Perú: Documental explica daños provocados por la minería del oro en Cajamarca" (Peru: An explanation of the damages of open-pit gold mining in Cajamarca). Servindi.org, March 20, 2012. http://www.servindi.org/actualidad/61541.

Piketty, Thomas. *Capital and Ideology*. Translated by Arthur Goldhammer. Cambridge, MA: Harvard University Press, 2020.

Pletsch, Carl E. "The Three Worlds, or the Division of Social Scientific Labor, circa 1950–1975." *Comparative Studies in Society and History* 23, no. 4 (October 1981): 565–90. https://www.jstor.org/stable/178394.

Polanyi, Karl. *The Great Transformation: The Political and Economic Origins of Our Time*. Boston: Beacon Press, 1944.

Pollock, Seldon. "Cosmopolitanism and the Vernacular in History." *Public Culture* 12, no. 3 (September 2000): 15–54.

Pope Francis. "Encyclical Letter *Fratelli Tutti* of the Holy Father Francis on Fraternity and Social Friendship." October 3, 2020. http://w2.vatican.va/content/francesco/en/encyclicals/documents/papa-francesco_20201003_enciclica-fratelli-tutti.html.

Portantiero, Juan Carlos. *Los usos de Gramsci*. Mexico City: Folio, 1987.

Posner, Eric. "The Case against Human Rights." *The Guardian*, December 4, 2014. https://www.theguardian.com/news/2014/dec/04/-sp-case-against-human-rights.

Poulantzas, Nicos. *Las clases sociales en el capitalismo actual*. 10th ed. Mexico City: Siglo Veintiuno Editores, 1977.

Prakash, Gyan. "Can the 'Subaltern' Ride? A Reply to O'Hanlon and Washbrook." *Comparative Studies in Society and History* 34, no. 1 (1992): 168–84.

Pratt, Sharon. "Open Cast Mining 'Affects Child Health.'" BBC, December 2, 1999, accessed September 25, 2020. http://news.bbc.co.uk/2/hi/health/546685.stm.

Prescott, William H. *History of the Conquest of Mexico and of the Conquest of Peru*. New York: Random House, 1956 [1843, 1847].

"Pre-State Israel: The Sykes-Picot Agreement (1916)." Jewish Virtual Library, accessed September 30, 2020. https://www.jewishvirtuallibrary.org/the-sykes-picot-agreement-1916.

"Primer Festival Mundial de la Digna Rabia." *Enlace Zapatista*, January 2009. http://enlacezapatista.ezln.org.mx/2010/01/24/primer-festival-mundial-de-la-digna-rabia/.

Prior, Michael. *The Bible and Colonialism: A Moral Critique*. London: Sheffield Academic Press, 1997.

Prior, Michael. *Zionism and the State of Israel: A Moral Inquiry*. London: Routledge, 1999.

Pulitzer Center. "In Focus: Congo's Bloody Coltan." Featured on *Foreign Exchange with Fareed Zakaria*, 2006. Video, 4:36. https://www.youtube.com /watch?v=3OWj1ZGn4uM.

Purcell, L. Sebastian. "Eudaimonia and Neltiliztli: Aristotle and the Aztecs on the Good Life." *APA Newsletter on Hispanic/Latino Issues in Philosophy* 16, no. 2 (Spring 2017): 10–21.

Purcell, Sebastian. "What the Aztecs Can Teach Us about Happiness and the Good Life." *AEON Newsletter*, accessed December 20, 2020, https://aeon.co/ideas/what -the-aztecs-can-teach-us-about-happiness-and-the-good-life.

Qing, Jian. *A Confucian Constitutional Order: How China's Ancient Past Can Shape Its Political Future*. Translated by Edmund Ryden, edited by Daniel A. Bell and Ruiping Fan. Princeton, NJ: Princeton University Press, 2013.

Quijano, Aníbal. "América Latina: Hacia un nuevo sentido historico." *Cátedra Indígena Intercultural* (blog), April 2015, 21–44. http://anibalquijano.blogspot.com/2016/01 /2010-america-latina-hacia-un-nuevo.html.

Quijano, Aníbal. "'Bien vivir': Entre el 'desarrollo' y la des/colonialidad del poder." In *Ecuador Debate: Acerca del Buen Vivir*. Quito: Centro Andino de Acción Popular, CAAP 84, (2011): 77–87.

Quijano, Aníbal. "Colonialidad del poder y clasificación social." In *Cuestiones y Horizontes: De la dependencia histórico-estructural a la colonialidad/descolonialidad del poder*. Buenos Aires: CLACSO, 2014.

Quijano, Aníbal. "Colonialidad del poder y clasificación social." Festschrift for Immanuel Wallerstein. *Journal of World-Systems Research* 6, no. 2 (Autumn/Winter 2000): 342–88.

Quijano, Aníbal. "Colonialidad del poder y subjetividad en América Latina." *Contextualizaciones Latinoamericanas* 3, no. 5 (July/December 2011): 1–13.

Quijano, Aníbal. "Colonialidad y modernidad/racionalidad." In *Los conquistados: 1492 y la población indígena*, 439–48. Bogotá: Tercer Mundo Editores, 1992.

Quijano, Aníbal. "Coloniality and Modernity/Rationality." English translation in *Cultural Studies* 21, no. 2–3 (2007 [1992]): 168–78. DOI: 10.1080/09502380601164353.

Quijano, Aníbal. "Coloniality and Modernity/Rationality." In *Globalizations and Modernities: Experiences and Perspectives of Europe and Latin America*, edited by Göran Therborn and coeditor Lise-Lotte Wallenius with English-language supervisor Jan Teeland, 11–20. Stockholm: Forskningsrådsnämnden, 1999.

Quijano, Aníbal. "Coloniality of Power, Eurocentrism and Latin America." *Nepantla: Views from South* 1 no. 3 (2000): 533–80.

Quijano, Aníbal. "Coloniality of Power, Eurocentrism, and Social Classification." Translated by Michael Ennis. In *Coloniality at Large: Latin America and the Postcolonial Debate*, edited by Mabel Moraña, Enrique D. Dussel, and Carlos A. Jáuregui, 181–224. Durham, NC: Duke University Press, 2008.

Quijano, Aníbal. "Estado-nación, ciudadanía y democracia." In *Democracia para una nueva sociedad (modelo para armar)*. Edited by Helena González and Heidulf Schmidt. Caracas: Nueva Sociedad, 1997, 139–52.

Quijano, Aníbal. "Heterogeneidad histórico-estructural." *IV Encuentro de la Cátedra América Latina*, Rio de Janeiro, Brazil, October 22, 2013. Video. https://www .youtube.com/watch?v=NXrDı_gTbNQ.

Quijano, Aníbal. "Los usos de la democracia burguesa." In *Sociedad y Política*. Reprinted in Aníbal Quijano, *Cuestiones y horizontes: Antología Esencial*, 245–69. Buenos Aires: CLACSO, 2014.

Quine, Willard Van Orman. "On What There Is." *Review of Metaphysics* 2, no. 5 (1948): 21–38.

Quispe-Agnoli, Rocío. Review of *Indigenous and Popular Thinking in America*, by Rodolfo Kusch, translated by María Lugones and Joshua M. Price. *Hispanic Review* 79, no. 4 (Autumn 2011): 667–70. DOI: 10.1353/hir.2011.0056.

Raghavan, Chakravarthi. *Recolonization: GATT, the Uruguayan Round, and the Third World*. London: Zed, 1990.

Rahn, Richard W. "Financial Fascism." April 28, 2010. Reprinted by the Cato Institute. https://www.cato.org/publications/commentary/financial-fascism.

Rajan, Kaushik Sunder. *Biocapital: The Constitution of Postgenomic Life*. Durham, NC: Duke University Press, 2006.

Rajaratnam, S. *The Prophetic and the Political: Selected Speeches and Writings*. Edited by Chan Heng Chee and Obaid ul Haq. Singapore: Graham Brash, 1987.

Ramos, D., A. García, I. Pérez, M. Lucena, J. González, V. Abril, L. Pereña, R. Hernández, J. Brufau, C. Bacieron, J. Barrientos, A. Rodríguez, P. Cerezo, P. Borges, and G. Lohmann. *La ética en la conquista de América*. Madrid: Consejo Superior de Investigaciones Científicas y Técnicas, 1984.

Ramos, Jorge Abelardo. *Ejército y semicolonia*. Buenos Aires: Editorial Sudestada, 1968.

Ramos, Jorge Abelardo. *El marxismo de Indias*. Buenos Aires: Biblioteca Universal Planeta, 1972.

Ramose, Mogobe B. *African Philosophy through Ubuntu*. Harare, ZW: Mond Books, 1999.

Ramose, Mogobe B. "The Death of Democracy and the Resurrection of Timocracy." *Journal of Moral Education* 39, no. 3 (2010): 291–303.

Ramose, Mogobe B. "The Philosophy of Ubuntu and Ubuntu as a Philosophy." In *Philosophy from Africa: A Text with Readings*, edited by Pieter Hendrik Coetzee and A. P. J. Roux, 230–37. Oxford, UK: Oxford University Press, 2002.

Ramose, Mogobe B. "To Whom Does the Land Belong? Mogobe Bernard Ramose Talks to Derek Hook." *Psychology in Society* 50 (2016): 64–68. DOI: 10.17159/2309-8708/2016/n50a5.

"Reconstitution." Lexico, accessed May 10, 2020. https://www.lexico. com/en/ definition/reconstitution.

Reinaga, Fausto. *La revolución India*. La Paz: Partido de Bolivia, 1969. https://elcondortk .blogspot.com/2018/09/la-revolucion-india-de-fausto-reinaga.html.

Reiter, Bernd, ed. *Constructing the Pluriverse: The Geopolitics of Knowledge*. Durham, NC: Duke University Press, 2018.

"*Requerimiento*, 1510 (Requirement: Pronouncement to be Read by Spanish Conquerors to Defeated Indians)." National Humanities Center Resource, accessed September 30, 2020. https://nationalhumanitiescenter.org/pds/amerbegin/contact/text7/requirement.pdf.

Rheault, D'Arcy Ishpeming'enzaabid. *Anishinaabe Mino-Bimaadiziwin (The Way of a Good Life): An Examination of Anishinaabe Philosophy, Ethics and Traditional Knowledge.* Peterborough, ON: Debwewin Press, 1999.

Rhodes, Ben. "Syrian 'Red Line' Crisis." *The Atlantic*, June 3, 2018. https://www.theatlantic.com/international/archive/2018/06/inside-the-white-house-during-the-syrian-red-line-crisis/561887/.

Rice, Condoleezza. "Campaign 2000: Promoting the National Interest." *Foreign Affairs*, January/February 2000. https://www.foreignaffairs.com/articles/2000-01-01/campaign-2000-promoting-national-interest.

Rice, Condoleezza. "Rethinking the National Interest: American Realism for a New World." *Foreign Affairs*, July/August 2008. https://www.foreignaffairs.com/articles/2008-06-01/rethinking-national-interest.

Richard, E. Randolph, and Brandon J. O'Brien. *Misreading Scripture with Western Eyes: Removing Cultural Blinders to Better Understand the Bible.* London: IVP Books, 2012.

Rifkin, Mark. *Beyond Settler Time: Temporal Sovereignty and Indigenous Self-Determination.* Durham, NC: Duke University Press, 2017.

Robbins, Brent Dean. "Joyful Thinking-Thanking: A Reading of Heidegger's 'What Is Called Thinking?'" *Janus Head* 13, no. 2 (Fall 2014): 13–21.

Robin, Corey. *Fear: The History of a Political Idea.* London: Oxford University Press, 2004.

Robinson, William. "A Gramscian Reading of Latin American Development" (book review). *Latin American Perspectives* 42, no. 1 (2015): 101–2.

Rockmore, Tom. "Heidegger after Farias." *History of Philosophy Quarterly* 8, no. 1 (1991): 81–102.

Rogers, Francis M. "The Council of Florence and the Portuguese Princes." In *The Quest for Eastern Christians: Travels and Rumor in the Age of Discovery*, 50–70. Minneapolis: University of Minnesota Press, 1962. https://muse.jhu.edu/book/32291.

Rojas, Odin Ávila. "La experiencia Zapatista: Análisis sobre sus prácticas democráticas." *Revista de Ciencias Sociales* 31, no 42. (2018): 195–211.

Roosevelt, Eleanor. "The Struggle for Human Rights." *American Rhetoric: Top100 Speeches*, accessed August 29, 2020. http://www.americanrhetoric.com/speeches/eleanorroosevelt.htm.

Roosevelt, Theodore. "Annual Message to Congress for 1904." House Records HR 58A-K2. Center for Legislative Archives, National Archives. Accessed May 25, 2020. http://www.ourdocuments.gov/doc.php?flash=true &doc=56.

Rose, Nikolas. *The Politics of Life Itself: Biomedicine, Power and Subjectivity in the Twenty-First Century.* Princeton, NJ: Princeton University Press, 2007.

Rošker, Jana. "Epistemology in Chinese Philosophy." *Stanford Encyclopedia of Philosophy*, Fall 2018. https://plato.stanford.edu/archives/fall2018/entries/chinese-epistemology/.

Roth, Kenneth. "Barack Obama's Shaky Legacy on Human Rights." Human Rights Watch (originally published in *Foreign Policy*), January 9, 2017. https://www.hrw .org/news/2017/01/09/barack-obamas-shaky-legacy-human-rights.

Rousseau, Jean-Jacques. *The Social Contract*. London: Penguin Press, 2004 [1762].

Russell, Bertrand, and Albert Einstein. "Russell-Einstein Manifesto." Atomic Heritage Foundation, July 9, 1955, accessed May 6, 2020. https://www.atomicheritage.org /key-documents/russell-einstein-manifesto.

Said, Edward W. *Orientalism*. London: Pantheon Books, 1978.

Saliba, George. *Islamic Science and the Making of the European Renaissance*. Boston: MIT Press, 2007.

Sang, Law Wing. *Collaborative Colonial Power: The Making of the Hong Kong Chinese*. Hong Kong: Hong Kong University Press, 2009.

Sanjinés, Javier. "Foundational Essays as 'Mestizo-Criollo Acts': The Bolivian Case." *Latin American and Caribbean Ethnic Studies* 11 (2016): 266–86.

Sanjinés, Javier. *Mestizaje Upside Down: Aesthetic, Politics in Modern Bolivia*. Pittsburgh, PA: University of Pittsburgh Press, 2004.

Santa Maria, Fernandez de. *The Discovery of America and the School of Salamanca*. Cambridge, UK: Cambridge University Press, 1977.

Santana, Joaquin. "Gramsci y Mariátegui." Centro de Estudios Miguel Enríquez, Archivo Chile, 2003–2006, accessed May 6, 2020. https://static.ides.org.ar/archivo /www/2012/04/artic123.pdf.

Sayyid, Bobby S. *A Fundamental Fear: Eurocentrism and the Emergence of Islamism*. London: Zed Books, 1997.

Sayyid, Bobby S. *Recalling the Caliphate: Decolonisation and the World Order*. London: Hurst and Co., 2014.

Schirrmacher, Frank. *Ego: The Game of Life*. New York: Polity Press, 2015.

Schmitt, Carl. *The Concept of the Political*. Munich: Duncker and Humblot, 1932.

Schmitt, Carl. *The Concept of the Political*. Chicago: University of Chicago University Press, 2007 [1932].

Schmitt, Carl. "The New Nomos of the Earth." In *The Nomos of the Earth in the International Law of the Jus Publicum Europaeum*, 351–55.

Schmitt, Carl. *Le Nomos de la terre dans le droit des gens du jus publicum Europaeum*. Translated from German to French by Lilyane Deroche Gurcel. Paris: Presses Universitaires de France, 1988 [1950].

Schmitt, Carl. *The Nomos of the Earth in the International Law of the Jus Publicum Europaeum*. Translated by G. L. Ulmen. New York: Telos Press, 2006 [1950].

Schmitt, Carl. "The Western Hemisphere." In *The Nomos of the Earth in the International Law of the Jus Publicum Europaeum*, 281–94.

Schwab, Klaus. *The Fourth Industrial Revolution*. Davos: Currency Publisher, 2017. https://www.weforum.org/agenda/2016/01/the-fourth-industrial-revolution-what -it-means-and-how-to-respond/.

Schwab, Klaus. *The Fourth Industrial Revolution*. Geneva: World Economic Forum, 2016.

Scott, David. "The Re-enchantment of Humanism: An Interview with Sylvia Wynter." *Small Axe* 8 (September 2000): 119–207.

Secco, Lincoln. *A recepção de Gramsci no Brasil*. São Paulo: Cortez, 2002.

Serequeberhan, Tsenay. "The Critique of Eurocentrism." In Eze, *Postcolonial African Philosophy*, 141–61.

ShalomTV, excerpt from interview with Joe Biden, March 6, 2013. Accessed May 5, 2020. Video. https://www.youtube.com/watch?v=Uo-UXZ-1ups.

Shari'ati, Ali. *Man and Islam*. Baltimore: Islamic Publications International, 1977.

Shari'ati, Ali. *Man and Islam*. Translated by F. Marjani. North Heldon, NJ: Islamic Publications International, 2006 [1976].

Shari'ati, Ali. "Man and Islam: 'The Free Man and Freedom of Man.'" Iran Chamber Society, accessed September 6, 2020. http://www.iranchamber.com/personalities /ashariati/works/free_man_freedom_man.php.

Shari'ati, Ali. "Modern Man and His Prisons." In Shari'ati, *Man and Islam*, 2006 edition, 47.

Sharman, Jon. "Chinese State Media Tells Donald Trump's Team to 'Prepare for Military Clash.'" *The Independent*, January 13, 2017. https://www.independent. co .uk/news/world/asia/rex-tillerson-south-china-sea-state-media-prepare-military -clash-donald-trump-global-times-a7525061.html.

Shohat, Ella. "The Specter of the Blackamoor." *The Comparatist* 42 (2018): 158–88.

Siedentop, Larry. *Inventing the Individual: The Origins of Western Liberalism*. London: Allen Lane Publishers, 2014.

Sim, May. "A Confucian Approach to Human Rights." *History of Philosophy Quarterly* 21, no. 4 (2004): 337–56.

Simon, Ceder. "Cutting through Water: Towards a Post-human Theory of Educational Relationality." PhD diss., Lund University, 2016.

Simpson, Leanne Betasamosake. *As We Have Always Done: Indigenous Freedom from Radical Resistance*. Minneapolis: University of Minnesota Press, 2015.

Simpson, Leanne Betasamosake. *Dancing on Our Turtle's Back: Stories of Nishnaabeg Re-Creation, Resurgence, and a New Emergence*. Winnipeg, MB: Arbeiter Ring Publishing, 2011.

Siqi, Yang. "Life in Purgatory: Buddhism Is Growing in China, but Remains in Legal Limbo." *Time*, March 16, 2016. https://time.com/4260593/china-buddhism-religion -religious-freedom/.

Skaria, Ajay. "Gandhi's Politics: Liberalism and the Question of Ashram." *South Atlantic Quarterly* 101, no. 4 (2002): 955–86. DOI: 10.1215/00382876-101-4-955.

Skaria, Ajay. "Gandhi's Radical Conservatism." *Seminar* 662 (October 2014): 30–35.

Slabodsky, Santiago. *Decolonial Judaism: Triumphal Failures of Barbaric Thinking*. New York: Palgrave McMilllian, 2014.

Smith, Adam. *An Inquiry into the Nature and Causes of the Wealth of Nations*. Chicago: University of Chicago Press, 1976 [1776].

Smith, Linda Tuhiwai. "Colonizing Knowledges." In *Decolonizing Methodologies*.

Smith, Linda Tuhiwai. *Decolonizing Methodologies: Research and Indigenous People*. London: Zed Books, 1999.

Smith, Linda Tuhiwai. "On Being Human." In *Decolonizing Methodologies*.

Snaza, Nathan, and Aparna Mishra Tarc. "'To Wake Up Our Minds': The Re-Enchantment of Praxis in Sylvia Wynter." *Curriculum Inquiry* 49, no. 1 (2019): 1–6.

Son, Bui Ngoc. *Confucian Constitutionalism in East Asia*. London: Routledge, 2016.

Sotelo Valencia, Adrián. "La Teoría Marxista de la Dependencia (TMD) en la actualidad." *Direito e Praxis: Revista* 9, no. 3, 1677–1693 (2018). DOI: 10.1590/2179-8966/2018/36562.

Souza, Juliana Beatriz Almeida de. "Las Casas: Alonso de Sandoval and the Defence of Black Slavery." *Topoi: Revista de Histórica* 2 (2006). http://socialsciences.scielo.org/scielo.php?script=sci_arttext&pid=S1518-33192006000200004.

Spengler, Oswald. *The Decline of the West: Form and Actuality* (vol. 1, 1918) and *Perspective of World History* (vol. 2, 1922). London: Oxford Paperback, 2013.

Spengler, Oswald. *Man and Technics: A Contribution to a Philosophy of Life*. Translated by Charles Francis Atkinson and Michael Putman. London: Artktos Media, 2015 [1932].

Srivastava, Neelam, and Baidik Bhattacharya, eds. *The Postcolonial Gramsci*. London: Routledge, 2011.

Ssorin-Chaikov, Nikolai. "Modernity and Time." In *Two Lenins: A Brief Anthropology of Time*, 121–31. Chicago: Hau Books, 2017.

Steger, Manfred B. *Globalism: The New Market Ideology*. London: Rowman and Littlefield, 2001.

Steger, Manfred. "Ideologies of Globalization." *Journal of Political Ideologies* 10, no. 1 (2005): 12.

Stephanson, Anders. *Manifest Destiny: American Expansion and the Empire of Right*. New York: Hill and Wang, 1996.

Subcomandante Marcos, "La cuarta guerra mundial." *Inmotion Magazine*, October 26, 2001. https://inmotionmagazine.com/auto/cuarta.html.

Sukarno. "Opening Address Given by Sukarno (Bandung, 18 April 1955)." CVCE.eu, accessed September 30, 2020. https://www.cvce.eu/en/obj/opening_address_given_by_sukarno_bandung_18_april_1955-en-88d3f71c-c9f9-415a-b397-b27b8581a4f5.html.

Susan AKA Peacefull. "UN Treaty: Mother Earth Has a Right to Life." *WorldPeacefull* (blog), April 15, 2011. https://wpas.worldpeacefull.com/2011/04/un-treaty-mother-earth-has-a-right-to-life/.

Szönyi, György E. "Broadening Horizons of Renaissance Humanism from the Antiquity to the New World." *Primerjalna književnost* 41, no. 2 (July 2018): 5–34.

Tapia, Luis. *La producción del conocimiento local: Historia y política en la obra de René Zavaleta Mercado*. La Paz: Universidad Mayor de San Andrés, 2002.

Tapia Mealla, Luis. *La estructura explicativa de lo nacional-popular en Bolivia*. Bueno Aires: Biblioteca CLACSO, 2002. https://core.ac.uk/download/pdf/35176389.pdf.

Taylor, Charles. "The Politics of Recognition." In *Multiculturalism: Examining the Politics of Recognition*, edited by A. Gutmann, 25–73. Princeton, NJ: Princeton University Press, 1992.

Taylor, Guy. "Netanyahu Slams Kerry for Insisting Israel Can Be Jewish or Democratic—Not Both." *Washington Times*, December 28, 2016. http://www.washingtontimes.com/news/ 2016/dec/28/john-kerry-israel-can-be-jewish-or-democratic-not-/.

Tenó, Jean-Marie, dir. *Le malentendu colonial* (Colonial misunderstanding). Documentary film, 73:00, Cameroon, 2004.

"Territorial Disputes in the South China Sea." Council on Foreign Relations, Global Conflct Tracker, September 24, 2020. https://www.cfr.org/global-conflict-tracker/conflict/territorial-disputes-south-china-sea.

Thomson, Mark. *Gandhi and His Ashrams*. Bombay: Popular Prakashan, 1993.

Thompson, Mark R. "Why Deng Xiaoping and China Could Never Truly Understand Singapore." *News Lens*, February 2020. https://international.thenewslens.com/article/114061.

Tichindeleanu, Ovidiu. "Decolonial AestheSis in Eastern Europe: Potential Paths of Liberation." *Social Text: Periscope*, July 15, 2013. https://socialtextjournal.org/periscope_article/decolonial-aesthesis-in-eastern-europe-potential-paths-of-liberation/.

Tichindeleanu, Ovidiu. "Towards a Critical Theory of Postcommunism: Beyond Anticommunism in Romania." *Radical Philosophy*, January/February 2010. https://www.radicalphilosophy.com/article/towards-a-critical-theory-of-postcommunism.

Tinker, George E. *Spirit and Resistance: Political Theology and American Indian Liberation*. Minneapolis, MN: Fortress Press, 2004.

Tlostanova, Madina. "Between the Russian/Soviet Dependencies: Neoliberal Delusions, Dewesternizing Options, and Decolonial Drives." *Cultural Dynamics* 27, no. 2 (July 1, 2015): 267–83. DOI: 10.1177/0921374015585230.

Tlostanova, Madina. "Internal Colonization: Russia's Imperial Experience (Book Review)." *Postcolonial Europe*, May 10, 2014. http://www.postcolonial-europe.eu/reviews/166-book-review-internal-colonization-russias-imperial-experience-.html.

Tlostanova, Madina. "Life in Samarkand: Caucasus and Central Asia vis-à-vis Russia, the West, and Islam." *Human Architecture* 5, no. 1 (Fall 2006): 105–16.

Tlostanova, Madina. "Post-Socialist Eurasia in Civilization of Fear: Another Christianity and Another Islam." In *Hegémonie et Civilisation de la Peur*, 9éme Colloque International, Academie de la Latinité, Alexandria, April 13–17, 2004. Textes de reference edité par Cândido Mendes (Rio de Janeiro: UNESCO/Universidade Cândido Mendes, 2004), 389–412.

Tlostanova, Madina. "The South of the Poor North: Caucasus Subjectivity and the Complex of Secondary 'Australism.'" In Levander and Mignolo, "The Global South and World Dis/Order," 66–84.

Tlostanova, Madina. *What Does It Mean to Be Post-Soviet? Decolonial Art from the Ruins of the Soviet Empire*. Durham, NC: Duke University Press, 2018.

Tobn, Liza. "Xi's Vision for Transforming Global Governance: A Strategic Challenge for Washington and Its Allies." *Texas National Security Review* 2, no. 1 (2018). https://tnsr.org/2018/11/xis-vision-for-transforming-global-governance-a-strategic-challenge-for-washington-and-its-allies/.

Tocqueville, Alexis de. *Democracy in America*. Chicago: University of Chicago Press, 2002 [1833].

Tolley, Howard, Jr. *The U.N. Commission on Human Rights*. Boulder, CO: Westview Press, 1987.

Toppi, Hernán Pablo. "Guillermo O'Donnell y su aporte al desarrollo de la democracia en América Latina desde la tercera ola de democratización." *Revista del Instituto de Ciencias Jurídicas de Puebloa* 12, no. 42 (2018): 9–28.

Toulmin, Stephen. *Cosmopolis: The Hidden Agenda of Modernity*. New York: Free Press, 1990.

"Treaty between Spain and Portugal Concluded at Tordesillas, June 7, 1494." Avalon Project: Documents in Law, History, and Diplomacy, Yale Law School, Lillian Goldman Law Library, accessed May 8, 2020. https://avalon.law.yale.edu/15th_century/mod001.asp.

Tremlett, Giles. "Operation Condor: The Cold War Conspiracy That Terrorized South America." *The Guardian*, September 3, 2020. https://www.theguardian.com/news/2020/sep/03/operation-condor-the-illegal-state-network-that-terrorised-south-america.

Trigona, María. "Resisting Mining: Brutal Repression and Uprising in Argentina." *Upside Down World*, February 23, 2010. http://upsidedownworld.org/main/argentina-archives-32/2376 resisting-mining-brutal-repression-and-uprising-in-argentina.

Trouillot, Michel-Rolph. "North Atlantic Universals: Analytical Fictions, 1492–1945." *South Atlantic Quarterly* 101, no. 4 (2002): 839–58.

Trouillot, Michel-Rolph. *Silencing the Past: Power and the Production of History*. Boston: Beacon Press, 1995.

Tuck, Eva, and K. Wayne Yang, "Decolonization Is Not a Metaphor." *Decolonization: Indigeneity, Education and Society* 1, no. 1 (2012): 1–40. https://jps.library.utoronto.ca/index.php/des/article/view/18630.

Tumulty, Karen. "How Donald Trump Came Up with 'Make America Great Again.'" *Washington Post*, January 18, 2017. https://www.washingtonpost.com/politics/how-donald-trump-came-up-with-make-america-great-again/2017/01/17/fb6acf5e-dbf7-11e6-ad42-f3375f271c9c_story.html.

Tutu, Desmond. "Foreword." In Ellis, *Judaism Does Not Equal Israel*, vii–viii.

Tutu, Desmond. "Israel Liberate Yourself by Liberating Palestine." *Popular Resistance*, August 20, 2014. https://popularresistance.org/desmond-tutu-israel-liberate-yourselves-by-liberating-palestine/.

Twining, William, ed. *Human Rights, Southern Voices: Francis Deng, Abdullahi An-Na'im, Yash Ghai and Upendra Baxi*. Cambridge, UK: Cambridge University Press, 2009.

Twiss, Richard. *Rescuing the Gospel from the Cowboys: A Native American Expression of the Jesus Way*. London: InterVarsity Press, 2015.

Twiss, Richard, "A Theology of Manifest Destiny." March 7, 2008. Video, 2:47. https://www.youtube.com/watch?v=4mEkMy1KNW0.

"United States Events of 2018." Human Rights Watch, accessed May 6, 2020. https://www.hrw.org/world-report/2019/country-chapters/united-states.

Valdeón, Roberto A. "Tears of the Indian and the Power of Translation: John Phillips' Version of *Brevísima relación de la destrucción de las Indias*." *Bulletin of Spanish Studies* 89, no. 6 (2012): 839–58.

Valente, Marcela. "Argentina: Poison from the Sky." *Global Issues*, December 9, 2011. http://www.globalissues.org/news/2011/12/09/12171.

Vallejo, Juan de. *Memorial de la vida de Fray Francisco Jiménez de Cisneros*. Edited by Antonio de la Torre y del Cerro. Madrid: Centro de Estudios Históricos, 1913.

Van Beurden, Sarah. "A New Congo Crisis?" *Origins: Current Events in Historical Perspective* 11, no. 4, January 2018. http://origins.osu.edu/article/new-congo-crisis.

Van De Pitte, Frederick P. Introduction to *Anthropology from a Pragmatic Point of View*, by Immanuel Kant, translated by Victor Lyle Dowdell. Carbondale: Southern Illinois University Press, 1996.

Van Orman Quine, Willard. "On What There Is." *Review of Metaphysics* 2, no. 5 (1948): 21–38.

Varoufakis, Yanis. "The Global Plan." In *The Global Minotaur*. London: Zed Books, 2011.

Vattimo, Gianni, and Michael Marder, eds. *Deconstructing Zionism: A Critique of Political Metaphysics*. London: Bloomsbury Academic, 2013.

Vázquez Melken, Rolando, and Rosa Wevers. "Decolonial Aesthesis and the Museum: An Interview with Rolando Vázquez." *Stedelijk Studies*, accessed September 30, 2020. https://stedelijkstudies.com/journal/decolonial-aesthesis-and-the-museum/.

Vilches, Elvira. *New World Gold: Cultural Anxiety and Monetary Disorder in Early Modern Spain*. Chicago: University of Chicago Press, 2010.

Villalba, Unai. "*Buen Vivir* vs. Development: A Paradigm Shift in the Andes?" *Third World Quarterly* 34, no. 8 (2013): 1427–42.

Villanueva, Edgar. *Decolonizing Wealth: Indigenous Wisdom to Heal Divides and Restore Balance*. Oakland, CA: Berrett-Koehler Publishers, 2018.

Villoro, Luis. "La posibilidad de una filosofía latinoamericana." In *México entre libros: Pensadores del siglo XX*. Mexico City: El Colegio Nacional/Fondo de Cultura Económica, 1995.

Vis, Marc. "History of the Mercator Projection." Undergraduate thesis, University of Utrecht, 2018.

Vitcheck, Andre. "Namibia: Germany's African Holocaust." *Global Research*, September 23, 2014. http://www.globalresearch.ca/namibia-germanys-african-holocaust/5403852.

Vitoria, Francisco de. *Relectio de Indis, o libertad de los Indios*. Bilingual (Latin and Spanish) critical edition by L. Pereña and J. M. Pérez Prendes. Introductory studies by V. Beltrán de Heredia, R. Agostino Iannarone, T. Urdánoz, A. Truyol, and L. Pereña. Madrid: Consejo Superior de Investigaciones Científicas, 1967 [1539].

Wachowski, Lilly and Lana, dirs. *The Matrix*. Burbank, CA: Warner Home Video, 1999. DVD.

Walsh, Catherine. "Afro and Indigenous Life-Visions in/and Politics: (De)colonial Perspectives in Bolivia and Ecuador." *Bolivian Studies Journal* 18 (2011): 49–69. DOI: 10.5195/bsj.2011.43.

Walsh, Catherine. "Pedagogical Notes from the Decolonial Cracks." *e-misférica* 11 no. 1 (2014). https://hemisphericinstitute.org/en/emisferica-11-1-decolonial-gesture/11-1 -dossier/pedagogical-notes-from-the-decolonial-cracks.html.

Walsh, Catherine. "The Plurinational and Intercultural State: Decolonization and State Re-founding in Ecuador." *RUDN Journal of Philosophy* 1 (2012): 103–15.

Walt, Stephen M. "The (Con)fusion of Civilizations." *Foreign Affairs*, May 4, 2016. http://foreignpolicy.com/2016/05/04/the-confusion-of-civilizations-larry -summers-enlightenment/.

Wanderley, Sergio E. P. V., and Alexandre Faria. "Border Thinking as Historical Decolonial Method: Reframing Dependence Studies to (Re)connect Management and Development." EnANPAD 2013. http://www.anpad.org.br/admin/pdf/2013 _EnANPAD_EOR2021.pdf.

Ward, Andrew. "Bush Digs in over Healthcare Bill." *Financial Times*, October 3, 2007. https://www.ft.com/content/a3a9fc76-71e5-11dc-8960-0000779fd2ac.

Wasserstrom, Jeffrey N. "The Chinese Revolution and Contemporary Paradoxes." In Wasserstrom et al., eds., *Human Rights and Revolutions*, 22–46.

Wasserstrom, Jeffrey N., Greg Grandin, Lynn Hunt, and Marilyn B. Young, eds. *Human Rights and Revolutions*. Lanham, MD: Rowman and Littlefield, 2007.

Weerstra, Hans M. "De-Westernizing the Gospel: The Recovery of Biblical World-view." *International Journal of Frontier Missions* 16, no. 3 (Fall 1999): 129–34.

Weheliye, Alexander G. *Habeas Viscus: Racializing Assemblages, Biopolitics and Black Feminist Theories of the Human*. Durham, NC: Duke University Press, 2014.

Weiler, Angela. "Introduction: The *Requerimiento* (1513)." Open Anthology of Earlier American Literature. Accessed May 5, 2020. https://press.rebus.community /openamlit/chapter/the-requerimiento/.

Weiwei, Zhang. *The China Wave: Rise of a Civilizational State*. Hackensack, NJ: World Century Publishing, 2011.

Wekker, Gloria. *White Innocence: Paradoxes of Colonialism and Race*. Durham, NC: Duke University Press, 2016.

West, Cornel. *The American Evasion of Philosophy: A Genealogy of Pragmatism*. Madison: University of Wisconsin Press, 1989.

"What Is Good Governance?" United Nations Economic and Social Commission for Asia and the Pacific, July 10, 2009. https://www.unescap.org/sites/default/files /good-governance.pdf.

Wiener, Norbert. *Cybernetics or Control and Communication in the Animal and the Machine*. Cambridge, MA: MIT Press, 1948.

Wiener, Norbert. *The Human Use of Human Beings*. New York: Houghton Mifflin Harcourt, 1950.

Williams, Eric. *Capitalism and Slavery*. Chapel Hill: University of North Carolina Press, 1994 [1944].

Wilson, Peter H. "The Causes of the Thirty Years' War, 1618–48." *English Historical Review* 123, no. 502 (2008): 554–86.

Winter, Tim. "Silk Roads and Cultural Routes." E-flux Architecture, accessed September 30, 2020. https://www.e-flux.com/architecture/new-silk-roads/313107/silk-roads-and-cultural-routes/.

Wojcik, John. "More than Meets the Eye behind the Iran Sanctions." *People's World*, December 6, 2016. https://www.peoplesworld.org/article/more-than-meets-the-eye-behind-the-iran-sanctions.

Wolfe, Cary. *Before the Law: Humans and Other Animals in Biopolitical Frame*. Chicago: University of Chicago Press, 2012.

Wolters, Eugene. "Žižek Is Getting His Own Opera(s)." *Critical Theory*, March 15, 2013. http://www.critical-theory.com/zizek-is-getting-his-own-operas/.

Worland, Justin. "What to Know about the Dakota Access Pipeline Protests." *Time*, October 28, 2016. https://time.com/4548566/dakota-access-pipeline-standing-rock-sioux/.

Wright, Emma. "Decolonial Education: Our Collective (Hi)story(ies)." *Pachaysana* (blog), October 5, 2015. https://www.pachaysana.org/single-post/2015/10/05/Decolonial-Education-our-collective-historyies.

Wright, Richard. *The Color Curtain: A Report on the Bandung Conference*. Jackson: University Press of Mississippi, 1996 [1956].

Wynter, Sylvia. "1492: A 'New World' View." In *Race, Discourse and the Americas: A New World View*, edited by Vera Lawrence and Rex Nettleford, 5–57. Washington, DC: Smithsonian Institution Press, 1995.

Wynter, Sylvia. "Beyond the Categories of the Master Conception: The Counterdoctrine of the Jamesian Poiesis." In Henry and Buhle, *C. L. R. James's Caribbean*, 63–91.

Wynter, Sylvia. "Ethno or Socio Poetics." *Alcheringa* 2, (1976): 78–94.

Wynter, Sylvia. "Towards the Sociogenic Principle: Fanon, Identity, the Puzzle of Conscious Experience, and What It Is Like to Be 'Black.'" In *National Identities and Sociopolitical Changes in Latin America*, edited by Mercedes F. Durán-Cogan and Antonio Gómez-Moriana, 30–66. London: Routledge, 2001.

Wynter, Sylvia. "Unsettling the Coloniality of Being/Power/Truth/Freedom: Towards the Human, after Man, Its Overrepresentation: An Argument." *New Centennial Review* 3, no. 3 (2003): 257–337.

Xuetong, Yan. *Ancient Chinese Thought, Modern Chinese Power*. Princeton, NJ: Princeton University Press, 2011.

Yampara Huarachi, Simón. "Comprensión aymara de la tierra-territorio en la cosmovisión andina y su ordenamiento para la/el qamaña." In Yampara Huarachi, Tórrez Eguino, and Mamani Morales, *Uraq-pacha utan utjawi/qamawi: Cosmovisión territorial ecologia y medio ambiente*, 13–44.

Yampara Huarachi, Simón. "Cosmovivencia Andina: Vivir y convivir en armonía integral—Suma Qamaña." *Bolivian Studies Journal* 18 (2011): 1–22.

Yampara Huarachi, Simón, Mario Tórrez Eguino, Saúl Mamani Morales. *Uraq-pacha utan utjawi/qamawi: Cosmovisión territorial ecologia y medio ambiente.* La Paz: Ediciones Qamaña Pacha de la Fundación "Suma Qamaña," Instituto Tecnológico de Investigación Indi Andino, 2005.

Yat-sen, Sun. *The Three Principles of the People.* Translated by Frank W. Price. London: Soul Care Publishing, 2011 [1924].

Yew, Lee Kuan. "The Future of China." Interview in *Lee Kuan Yew: The Grand Master's Insights on China, the United States, and the World,* edited by Graham Allison and Robert D. Blackwill with Ali Wyne, 1–18. Cambridge: MIT Press, 2013.

Yew, Lee Kuan. Interview on *Meet the Press,* October 22, 1967. Video. https://www.youtube.com/watch?v=VexrmTacOAA.

Ying, Liu. "Further Opening-Up to Protect Free Trade." *China Daily,* December 17, 2019. https://global.chinadaily.com.cn/a/201912/17/ WS5df818b0a310cf3e3557e825 .html.

Yu, Kongjian. "Green Infrastructure through the Revival of Ancient Wisdom." American Academy of Art and Sciences, Bulletin, Summer 2017. https://www.amacad .org/news/green-infrastructure-through-revival-ancient-wisdom.

Zabala, Santiago. "Slavoj Žižek and the Role of the Philosopher." Al Jazeera, December 25, 2012. https://www.aljazeera.com/indepth/opinion/2012/12/ 20121224122215406939.html.

Zavaleta Mercado, René. *Lo nacional-popular en Bolivia.* La Paz: Los Amigos del Libro, 1986.

Zea, Leopoldo. *La filosofía latinoamericana como filosofía sin más.* Mexico City: UNAM, 1969.

Zhang, Denghua. "The Concept of 'Community of Common Destiny' in China's Diplomacy: Meaning, Motives and Implications." *Asia and Pacific Studies* 5, no. 2 (2018): 196–207.

Ziarek, Eva Plonowska. "Bare Life." In *Impasses of the Post-Global: Theory in the Era of Climate Change,* vol. 2., edited by Henry Sussman, 194–211. Ann Arbor, MI: Open Humanities Press, 2012.

Žižek, Slavoj. "A Leftist Plea for 'Eurocentrism.'" *Critical Inquiry* 24, no. 4 (1998): 1009.

Žižek, Slavoj. "A Reply to My Critics." *Philosophical Salon.* August 15, 2016. https:// thephilosophical salon.com/a-reply-to-my-critics/.

Index

academia: coloniality of knowledge and, 80–81; decolonialism and, 76–81; Global South conversation and, 350–51; hemispheric partitions conversation and, 298–99; indigenizing of the academy and, 327; politics of scholarship and, 299–310

Acosta, José de, 86

actors, colonial matrix of power and, 47

aesthesic reconstitutions: colonialism and need for, 24; cosmopolitan localism and, 199; defined, xx–xxi; emotional, physical and spiritual recovery and, 32–33; geopolitics and, 63; human rights paradigm and, 264–67; movements of, 56–61; nature rights and human rights and, 262–67

aesthesis: aesthetics *vs.*, xii; healing and reconstitution of, 11–12; reconstitutions and, 55–56

aesthetics: aesthesis *vs.*, xii; coloniality of, x–xi; de-Westernization and, 320–22; etymology of, 55–56; knowledge/ understanding and, 49

Afghanistan, US human rights violations in, 60n12

Africa: cartography and colonization of, 371–73; in Christian cosmology, 88; decolonization in, 15–16, 158–60; dismantled kingdoms in, 165–66; as Global South, 350–54; Haitin Revolution and decoloniality in, 63–65; Indian investment in, 345; international law and colonialism in, 150–52; nation-state formation in, 162; racism and cartography in, 363–70; sustainable knowledge conversation and, 334–39; temporality of history in, 194

African Americans, philosophers as, 292–93

African peoples, in racial hierarchies, 88, 91–93

African philosophy, gnosis and, 54–55

Afro-Caribbean culture: Haitian Revolution and intellectuals from, 63–65; philosophers in, 292–93

Agamben, Giorgio, 143

Akbar, 105

Alatas, Syed Farid, 211

Alexander the VI (Pope), 331, 365, 367

Alfred, Taiaiake, 253

Algeria: Fanon's discussion of, 71–73; as nation-state, 157

Ali, Tariq, 103–4, 126

Alianza del Pacífico, 296, 311

allyu (Andean administration), 43

civil disobedience, Gandhi and, 68–73

civilization: Freud on malaise of, 28–29; invasion and interference with, 354–55

civilizational states, de-Westernization and, 236–37

Civilization and Its Discontents (Freud), 28–31

Civil Rights movement: academic influence of, 302; de-Westernization and, 321–22

The Clash of Civilizations (Huntington), 101, 364

classification, of regions and continents, 282–83

class structure: racism and, 109–12; social classification *vs.*, xvii–xviii, 97–98; social relations in nation-states and, 239–40

Clinton, Hillary, 297–98, 311, 322

Cold War: colonial matrix of power and, 123; decolonization and, 14–18, 28, 64–65, 319–22; human rights during, 213–17; international politics during, 344; Islamophobia in wake of, 100–101; modern/colonial world order after, 194–95; neoliberalism and civilizational resurgences and, 79–81; Third World conversation about, 350–54

collaborative colonialism, 335

colonial difference: Christian narrative of, 128–30; cosmopolitanism and, 219–20; decoloniality and, 474–75, 510, 535; decolonial *scientia* and, 450–51; Fanon on, 445–49, 534, 537–39; hemispheric partitions and, 290; historical evolution of, 37–38; history of, 541, 551; human rights and, 198, 278; intramural and extramural, 88, 115–16, 138–39, 206–18, 241–46, 373–74; modern/colonial world order and, 93–94, 222–23, 385; nation-state and role of, 170–71, 189–90; Orientalism and, 109; philosophy and, 552–55; pluriversality *vs.*, 540; racism as outcome of, 89, 144; in South America, 391, 401–5, 460–69; subaltern studies and, 408–11; Wynter's Human/Man, 422, 438, 452–53

coloniality and colonization: of being, 5; cosmopolitanism and, 240–43; globaliza-

tion and, 247–50; governmentality and, 244–47; hemispheric partitions and, 290–93; human rights and, 255–57, 274–75; immigration and refugeeism and, xviii; Islamophobia and, 100–101; knowledge and logic of, 358; of knowledge and sensing, x–xi, 12–13; legalized land dispossession and, 172–74; nation-state formation and, 162–64; neoliberal market democracy and, 196; Quijano on power and, 7–9, 36, 90–93; racial dispossession and, 157; racism linked to, 93–98, 108–12; Renaissance philosophy and logic of, 201–4; responses to, 78–81; rhetoric of modernity and, 105–7, 154–55; secularization and, 195; sustainable knowledge conversation and, 335–39; Western civilization and, xiii–xiv; Westernization and, 315–16; wounds of, 3–4, 9–12; Zionism and, 155–56

"Coloniality and Modernity/Rationality"(Quijano), 27–28

"Coloniality of Power, Eurocentrism and Social Classification" (Quihano), 36

colonial matrix of power (CMP): actors in, 47; Afro-Caribbean history and, 64–65; Anzaldúa's work and, 74–75; cartography and, 370–73; China's challenge to, 12–13; Cold War and, 123; conservatism and, 77–81; constitutional frame for, 34–51; cosmopolitanism and, 230–32; cosmopolitan localism and, 193–99, 250–52; decoloniality and, 250–52; destitutions and, 51–53; de-Westernization and, xii, 108–12, 195–99, 325–27; disputed control and management of, 324–27; domains of, 36–51; domination/exploitation/conflict triad, 46–47; Enlightenment reconfiguration of, 112–19; ethno-racial pentagon (US) and, 124–26; formation of, 24; geopolitics and, xx–xxi; globalization and, 184–88; hemispheric partitions and, 300–310; history of, 18–19, 195; Holocaust and, 64–65, 115, 132, 145–47, 151–52, 58n3; human rights and, 266–67; immigrants and, 93–98;

colonial matrix of power (*cont.*)
institutions and, 48; international law
and, 147–51; invention of Western hemisphere and, 289–93; Israeli nation-state
and mutation of, 161–64; knowledge
and, 27–28; languages and, 47; linear
global thinking and, 370–73; Mahbubani's de-Westernization discourse and,
341-43; Marxism and, 77–81; modern/
colonial world order and, 21–34, 574n17;
nation-states and, 154–55; racism and,
88–93, 112–19; reconstitutions and, 53–73;
rhetoric of modernity and, 31–32; secular
liberalism and, 77–81; sociogenesis and,
71–73; technics of domination and,
7–8; unconsciousness and, 9; Western
imperialism and, 335–36

Columbus, Christopyer, 87, 111

commodification of life, 133–34; human
rights and, 258–61, 263–67, 602n21

common good/commonwealth, liberial
ideology of, 328–30

communal, ideology of: complementary
communal economy, 517–20; definitions
of, 328–30; in Fanon's decolonial narrative, 72–73; in Indigenous civilizations,
32–33; Indigenous concepts of, 337–39;
relationality and, 52–53

communism, human rights and, 274

community of shared destiny, Xi Jinping's
concept of, 196–97, 235–36, 588n30

Comunidad de Estados Latino-
Americanos y Caribeños (CELAC),
298

The Conflict of the Faculties (Kant), 74

Confucianism: Chinese revamping of, 194,
221, 323; de-Westernization and, 199,
270; economic policy and, 248; universality and, 227

Connell, Raewyn, 350

Consejo Nacional de Ayllus y Markas del
Qullasuyu; (National Council of Ayllus
and Markas of Qullasuyu) (CONAMAQ),
338–39

conservatism: colonial matrix of power
and, 77–81; evolution of, 149

constitution/destitution/reconstitution
triad: colonial matrix of power and,
46–47; de-Westernization and, xii

constitution framework: colonial matrix of
power and, 46–51; cosmopolitanism and,
205–12; destitutions and, 51–53; nature
rights and human rights and, 262–67

contested modernities, de-Westernization
and, 346-48

conversas/os (Jewish converts to Christianity), 91–93, 111, 112–19

conversation(s). *See* enunciation; languages; narrative; national security
rhetoric; peace rhetoric; rhetoric of
modernity; salvation rhetoric

corporations, rights violations by, 258–61,
279–80

Cortés, Hernán, 105

Cosmopolis: The Hidden Agenda of Modernity
(Toulmin), 237–40

cosmopolitanism: Atlantic detour in,
243–47; cultural relativism and human
rights universality and, 216–17; decoloniality and, 232–34; Eurocentrism and,
199–204, 207–12; globalism and globalization and, 184–88; historic-structural
nodes and, 193–99; *Homo economicus* and,
247–50; human rights and, xviii–xix,
198–99, 204–5, 213–17; imperialism and,
240–43; Kant's racial hierarchies and,
234–35; modern/colonial world order
and, 204–12; modernity's hidden agenda
and, 237–40; neoliberal ideology and,
230–32; salvation rhetoric and, 188–93

cosmopolitan localism, 185–88; decoloniality and, 188–93, 250–52; horizontality of,
240–43; human rights and, 198–99; local
histories and, 252–53; pluriversality and,
217–24, 240–43

Council of Trent, 116, 241, 578n25

Covarrubias Horozco, Sebastián de, 110–11,
577n17

COVID-19 pandemic: flux of the present
and, 6; Great Reset initiative and, 236;
political and economic impact of, ix–x,
xxi, 3–4

Creoles, racial hierarchies and, 95–98
Cugoano, Quobnah Ottobah, 26, 61–63;
    Afro-Caribbean history and, 64–65; on
    economics of dispensable lives, 132–36;
    racism challenged by, 118–19; on slavery,
    145–46; on Western imperialism, 116
cultural sphere: de-Westernization and,
    319–22, 325–27; pluriversality and,
    223–24; praxes of living and, 354–58
curanderas/curanderos (healers), Latin
    American preference for, 34
currency policies, de-Westernization and,
    324, 610n15
cybernetics, modern/colonial world order
    and, 249–50, 599n34

Dahm, J. Daniel, 271–73
Dainotto, Roberto, 350
*The Darker Side of the Renaissance: Literacy,
    Territoriality, and Colonization* (Mignolo),
    85–86, 309–10, 316, 321
debates of Valladolid, 148, 201–4
*Declaration of the Rights of Man and of the
    Citizen*, 62, 137, 141, 171; Kantian cos-
    mopolitanism and, 207, 231–32. *See also*
    human rights
Decolonial Judaism (Mate & Slabodsky), 179
decolonization and decoloniality:
    academia and, x–xi, 76–81; Bandung
    Conference and, 316–17; communal
    structure and, 329–30; cosmopolitan-
    ism and, 232–34, 243–47; cosmopolitan
    localism and, 185–93, 197–99, 250–52;
    creation of Israel linked to, 158–60;
    defined, 563n1; destitutions and, 54–55;
    de-Westernization and, 196–99, 320–22,
    326–27, 338–39, 347–48; economy do-
    main of CMP and, 41; Fanon's analysis
    of, 70–73; genealogy of, 56–61; global
    proliferation of, 80–81; hemispheric
    partitions and, 300–310; life and human
    rights and, 271–80; modernity and,
    207–9; nation-states and, 14–15, 28,
    79–81, 155–57, 160–64, 588n36; neoliberal
    governance and, 248–50; options involv-
    ing, 229–32; particular meanings of,

13–14; pluriversality and, 217–24; in post-
    war era, 323; race and racism and, 110–12;
    racism and cartography and, 365–70;
    rejection of recognition and, 243–47;
    trajectory of, xi–xii, 4–6; unconscious-
    ness and, 9. *See also* post-colonialism
Decolonizing the Mind (Ngũgĩ wa
    Thiong'o), 61
Deconstructing Zionism (Mignolo), 154
de Gómara, Francisco López, 22, 28
De l'égalité des races humaines (Firmin), 118
democracy: cosmopolitanism and, 218–24;
    decolonialism and divesting from,
    54–55, 595n64; neoliberal globalism and,
    248–50
Deng Xiaoping, 18–19, 317–18, 588n30
dependency theory: interstate relations
    and, 214–17; nation-state formation and,
    162–64
derecho de gentes, 202–4
destitution framework: colonial matrix of
    power and, 51–53; cosmopolitanism and,
    205–12; in *Hind Swaraj* (Gandhi), 68–73;
    nature rights and human rights and,
    262–67
development politics: cartography and,
    370–73; de-Westernization and, 340–43;
    imperialism and, 323; sustainable knowl-
    edge conversation and, 333–39
de Vitoria, Francisco: cosmopolitanism
    and, 189–93, 201–4, 207, 213, 244–47;
    international law and, 120–21; on *ius
    gentium*, 148–52, 243; multiculturalism
    and, 205; on property rights, 77; World
    War II and work of, 213–14
de-Westernization: Bandung Conference
    and, 17–19, 316–17; in Bolivia, 163; China
    and, 294–95; colonial matrix of power
    and, 195–99; contested modernities and,
    346–48; emergence of, 77–81; globalism
    and, 249–50; hemispheric partition and,
    296–98, 311–12; Mahbubani's discussion
    of, 315–16, 339–43; nation-state formation
    and, 163; neoliberal governance and,
    248–50; political and economic
    initiatives for, 320–22; post-Cold

ethnicity: ethno-racial pentagon (United States) and, 123-26; human rights victims and, 260-61; Jewish identity and, 171-72; racial classifications and ranking of, 97-98, 112-19, 171-72; religious divisions and, 101-3

ethno-racial pentagon (United States), 123-26

Eurocentrism: cosmopolitanism and, 187-88, 199-204, 207-12; human rights paradigm and, 264-67; racism and cartography and, 365

European diaspora: discourse of fear among, 106; racial hierarchies and, 93-98

European egology, racism and, 89, 574n10, 581n6

European politics and economics: colonial self-affirmation of, 24; de-Westernization and, 296-98; divesting knowledge from, 54-55; enunciation of, 49-51; Israeli nation-state formation and, 166-69; nation-state governance and, 154-55; secularism and Zionism and, 164-66, 169-72

European Renaissance: coexisting empires in, 106; globalism during, 186-88; languages of, 47; narratives of Indigenous encounters in, 147; race classification in, 109-10, 117-19; social classification in, 105-6; South/North divide established during, 91-93, 118-19, 246-47; Western civilization and, xiii-xiv

European Union: South/North divide in Europe and, 118-19; territorial politics and, 196

evolutionary drift, postcolonial emergence of, xi-xii

Exortación al Emperador Carlos V para que, hecha la paz, con los príncipes cristianos, haga la Guerra contra los turcos (Sepúlveda), 148

expert knowledge, legality of rights and, 258-61, 277-80

exteriority, colonial matrix of power and, 36

Eze, Emmanuel Chukwudi, 209

Fabian, Johannes, 193-94

Fanon, Frantz: decoloniality and, 319; on decolonization, 64-65, 70-73, 252; on logic of coloniality, 358; on racism, 118; reconstitutions in work of, 33

fear, discourses of: Islamophobia and, 99-101; logic of coloniality and, 576n10; racism and, 106

Firmin, Anténor, 118

First Nations. *See* Indigenous peoples

flows: colonial matrix of power and, 50-51; in Fanon's decolonial narrative, 71-73, 443-44, 449

Floyd, George, 321

food sovereignty, 81

Forum for Inter-American Research (FIAR), 299-300

Foucault, Michel, 113; sustainable knowledge debate and, 334

France, monetary dispute with US, 323-24

Francis (Pope), 235-36

Fratelli Tutti (papal encyclical), 235-37

French colonialism, Haitian Revolution and, 63-65

French Revolution: cosmopolitanism and, 205-12; human rights and, 137, 141-43; nation-state formation and, 156-57, 170, 195; right *vs.* left in, 344

Freud, Sigmund, 9, 28-33, 135

Friedman, Milton, 230-32, 247, 339

Friedman, Frances, 315-16, 344-45

Fulbright, William, 323

Gaius (Roman jurist), 203

Gandhi, Mohandas, 65-73, 119, 261, 347

gender: bodily biological and behavioral factors and, 97-98; hierarchies of colonial difference and, 87-88; Western modernity and logic of, 85-89

geopolitics: cartography and territory and, 359-61; cosmopolitan localism and decoloniality, 250-52; decoloniality and, 161-64; Global South/Eastern Hemisphere and Third World and, 349-54; hemispheric partitions and, 282-83; human rights paradigm and, 264-67;

geopolitics (*cont.*)
  of knowledge, 140–46; racial hierarchies
    and, 93–98; racism and cartography
    and, 363–70
George, Henry, 135
get Australia/New Zealand and Huntington, 372–73
Gironde (France), 344
global health: aesthesic reconstitutions
  and, 32; decoloniality and, 81
globalism: cosmopolitanism and, 184–88;
  European cartographic imaginary and,
  578n33; historical-structural nodes and,
  196–99; pluriversality and decolonialism
  and, 217–24; post–Cold War emergence
  of, 247–50
globalization: China's dominance in, 296;
  globalism and, 247–50; imperial and colonial differences and, 215–17; postmodern ideology and, 230–32
Global North: capitalization of resource
  extraction by, 301–10; cartography and,
  361–63, 370–73; hemispheric partitions
  and, 290; linear global thinking and,
  370–73; Russia's designation as, 351
Global South: cartography and, 361–63,
  370–73; emergence of, xix–xx; hemispheric partitions and, 290, 294–98; linear global thinking and, 370–73; Pacific
  Ocean project of, 297–98; resistance and
  opposition in, 355–58; resource extraction in, 301–10; Third World and, 349–54
Global University for Sustainability, 81
Glorious Revolution (England): human
  rights and, 137, 141–43; nation-state
  formation and, 156–57, 170, 195
gnoseological reconstitutions: border
  gnoseology and decoloniality and,
  332–33; cosmopolitan localism and, 199;
  exploration of, xx–xxi; Fanon's contributions to, 65–73; Gandhi's contributions to, 65–73; geopolitics and, 63; Guaman Poma's decolonialism and, 58–61;
  human rights paradigm and, 264–67;
  knowledge/understanding domain and,
  41–42; movements of, 56–61; nature

rights and human rights and, 262–67;
  racial hierarchies and, 96–98
gnoseology, termonology, 563n2
gnosis, reconstitutions and, 54–55
Gobineau, Comte (Joseph Arthur), 118
Goodman, Nelson, 359
governance: coloniality and, 244–47,
  598n23; communal form of, 329–30,
  337–38; configuration in CMP of, 39–43;
  destitutions and, 51–53; enunciation
  and, 48–51; Guaman Poma's concept
  of, 241–43, 598n23; institutions in, 48;
  knowledge and, 39–40; of nation-states,
  154–55; neoliberal globalism and, 248–50;
  racial hierarchies of, 96–98
Gramsci, Antonio, 350; geopolitics and, xx
Greenwich Meridian, 366–67, 369–70
Grotius, Hugo, 77, 120
grounded normativity, 61–63, 70, 570n57
Grovogui, Siba N'Zatioula, 121, 150–52
Grupo de Lima, 296
Guadalupe-Hidalgo Treaty (1848), 104, 117
Guaidó, Juan, 296
Guaman Poma de Ayala: Afro-Caribbean
  history and, 64–65; Cugoano and,
  62–63; decolonialism of, 58–61; Gandhi
  and, 69; *Nueva corónica y buen gobierno* of,
  241–43; racism challenged by, 118–19

Habana Health Care, 135
Habermas, Jürgen, 205, 207, 334, 592n23
*Habitar la frontera: Sentir y pensar la descolo-
  nialidad, Antología: 1999-2014* (Carballo &
  Herrera Robles), xiv
Haiti, nation-state formation in, 167–68
Haitian Revolution: cosmopolitanism and,
  190–93, 201; decolonial reconstitutions
  and, 63–65
happiness, Freud on pursuit of, 28–31
Hasegawa, Yuko, 320
Has the West Lost It? A Provocation (Mah-
  bubani), 316
Hayek, Fredrich, 247
Hegel, G. F. W., 251; on aesthetics, 55–56;
  cosmopolitanism and, 149, 212, 240; on
  philosophy of history, 117–18, 251, 288

imperial/colonial terminology, 582n11

imperial differences: intramural and extramural, 26–27; Christian-Muslim conflicts and, 115–16; Cold War updating of, 215–17; coloniality and, 165–66; cosmopolitanism and, 189–93; destitutional framework and coloniality and, 206–7; de-Westernization and, 318–19; dispensability of human life and, 138–46; European Union and, 118; Global South/ Eastern Hemisphere conversation and, 350–54; Holocaust and slavery and, 138–46; land dispossession and, 241–43; nation-states and, 114, 207–12; racism and, 109–12; religion and, 114; in Renaissance Europe, 200–204; sovereignty concept and, 246–47

Incanate territories, 105; European encounter with, 147; social classification in, 108

India: British colonialism in, 66–73, 166–69, 195; de-Westernization and, xi–xii, 347–48; hemispheric and inter-American research on, 303–4; independence of, 162; as nation-state, 157; partition of, 168

"Indian doubt" debate, 201–4

Indians. *See* Indigenous peoples

Indias Occidentales: Christian invention of, 357; European creation of, 23–24; racialization of, 122, 365–66; as racialized terminology for America, 122–23; *Requerimiento* and possession of, 331–33; Spanish coloniality and naming of, 132–33, 291

Indias Orientales: Christian invention of, 357; European creation of, 23–24, 291; Middle East in framework of, 132–33; racist cartography of, 365–66

indigeneity and indigenous, concepts of, etymology of, 86–87

Indigenous peoples: aesthesic reconstitutions for, 32–33; communal cosmos among, 241–43; debate on life and human rights and role of, 276; dismantled civilizations of, 165–66; economic

theory and, 43; European narratives of encounters with, 147; genocide of, racism linked to, 108–12; governance structures of, 162–64; indigenization of knowledge by, 327; land dispossession and brutalization of, 119–21, 171–72; nationalist elite statecraft by, 319–22; in racial hierarchies, 91–93; rejection of recognition by, 243–47; religions among, 111–12; rights of, 148; secular Native American thinkers, theology and, 291–93; temporality of history in, 194; unversal property concepts of, 241–43; Westernization framing of, 22–24

Indonesia, Bandung Conference organized by, 319–22

Industrial Revolution, 26, 29; disposability of human beings and, 136; institutions in, 48; nation-state formation and, 170; natural resources concept and, 122–23

The Influence of Sea Power upon History, 1660–1783 (Mahan), 122

injustice, frames of knowledge in challenge to, 13–14

institutions, in colonial matrix of power, 48

Inter-American Development Bank (IDB), 323

Inter Caetera (papal bull), 331

internal colonialism, decolonization and, 157

International Bank for Reconstruction and Development (IBRD), 323

international law: Christianity and, 152–53; coloniality and, 120–21, 147–52, 579n34; hemispheric partitions and, 301–10; historical emergence of, 240–43; origins of, 148–50; Westernization and, 356–58

International Law and Colonialism in Africa (Umozurike), 150–52

International Monetary Fund (IMF): colonial matrix of power and, 108; de-Westernization and, 298, 322–25; economic crisis of 2008 and, 134; establishment of, 323; *Homo economicus* ideology and, 248; nation-state formation and, 48 international relations, colonial wounds and, 10

interstate relations: Bandung Conference and, 317; de-Westernization and, 326–27; imperial and colonial differences and, 216–17; Israeli nation-state formation and, 166–69; power differentials and dependencies and, 155; racism and, 108–12

The Invention of Africa: Gnosis, Philosophy, and the Order of Knowledge (Mudimbe), 54–55

Iran: British-Soviet invasion of, 167, 588n27; de-Westernization and, 196

Iranian Revolution (1979), 167

Iraq, as nation-state, 169, 589n45

Islam: Christianity and, 101–3; de-Westernization and, 320–22; Islamization of knowledge, 327

Islam and Secularism (Al-Attas), 320

Islamic State (ISIS), 261

Islamophobia: Black Legend campaign (England *vs.* Spain) and, 106–7, 116–19; colonial origins of, 109–12; decolonization and, 125–26; historical evolution of, 122–23; origins of, 99–101

Israel: decolonization of nation-state form and, 160–64; democracy *vs.* Judaism in, 132, 155, 158–60, 174–77; formation of state of, 153; governance structure in, 157; imperialist support for founding of, 163–64; legalized land dispossession by, 172–74; Obama's visit to, 178–79; Trump's policies in, 178–79; Tutu's criticism of, 159–60; Western modernity framework for, 166–69; Zionism and nation-state of, 139–40, 155–56

ius cosmopoliticum, 205–12

ius divinus, 148

ius gentium (rights of the people), 148–52, 198, 201, 243–47

ius naturalis, 148–49, 203

Jacobins (France), 344

Japan, imperial influence in, 335–36

Jews and Jewish identity: Arendt on, 136–46; Aztec Tlatoanate linked to, 86; Christians and, 112–19; ethnicity and, 152–53; exodus from Egypt and, 164–66; expulsion from Iberian Peninsula of, 136–38, 164–66, 581n3; global population estimats for, 169; Islamophobia and, 100–101; Israel as separate from, 132, 155, 158–60, 174–77; Judeo-Christian tradition and, 101–3; in racial hierarchies, 91–93, 574n19; whiteness associated with, 171–72; Zionism and, 155–56, 158–60, 174–77

Judaism Does Not Equal Israel (Ellis), 158–60

Juicio Ético Popular a las Transnacionales (JEPT, Ethical-Popular Judgement to Transnational Corporations), 267–70, 280–83

Juntas de Buen Gobierno (Councils of Good Government) (Zapatistas), 60–61, 70, 242–43

Kant, Immanuel: on aesthetics, 55–56; cosmopolitanism of, 149, 186–89, 200, 207, 231–32, 237–40; decolonial interpretations of, 207–9; de Vitoria and, 203–4; human rights and work of, 213–14; imperialism and philosophy of, 240–43; multiculturalism and work of, 205; on nation-states, 210–12; personhood in work of, 209–10, 213; racial hierarchies in work of, 74, 113, 142, 209–12, 234–35; on religion, 91; on South/North divide in Europe, 91–93, 118–19, 246–47

Kawsay, Sumak, 197–98

Kerry, John, 132, 156

Khashoggi, Jamal, 260

Khatibi, Abdelkabir, 122

Kissinger, Henry, 315

knowledge: colonial destitution of frameworks of, 23–24; coloniality of, x–xi, 112–19, 572n1; colonial matrix of power and, 27–28, 357–58; colonial wounds and, 9–10, 31–32; defined, 11–12; de-Westernization of, 327, 333–39; *doxa vs.* episteme and, 4; hemispheric partitions and role of, 306–7; human rights and control of, xviii–xix; humans/

knowledge (*cont.*)

humanity domain of CMP amd, 39–40; non-Western knowledges, Western appropriation of, 572n1; *pacha* decolonialization of, 241–43, 598n22; racial hierarchies and, 94–98; racism and coloniality of, 112–19; theopolitics of, 112; Western totality of, 28–29

knowledge/understanding domain: colonial matrix of power and, 39; configuration of, 43; decolonialization and, 41–42; destitutions and, 51–53; enunciation and, 48–51; South American coloniality and, 41

Koonz, Claudia, 139–40

Kosovo, humanitarian intervention in, 274–75

Kuan-Hsing Chen, 352

Kurdish minority, 169

Kusch, Rodolfo, 60–61

Kymlicka, Will, 205, 592n23

labor: class structure and racism and, 109; human rights and exploitation of, 266–67; knowledge/understanding domain of CMP and, 42; partition of regions and continents and, 282–83

Lacan, Jacques, 33

la facultad, Anzaldúa's concept of, 74–75

Lakou (Haiti), 70

land dispossession: coloniality and, 119–21; legalization of, 172–74; property law and, 241; religious appropriation of conversation on, 175–77

languages: colonial matrix of power and, 47, 332–33; hemispheric partitions and, 305–6; non-Western languages, Western appropriation of, 572n1; race and ethnicity and, 109–10; racial hierarchies and role of, 94–98; religious divisions and, 101–3

Las Casas, Bartolomé de: cosmopolitanism in writings of, 188–89, 201; land dispossession critized by, 331; on racial hierarchies, 87; on rights of Indigenous

groups, 77, 205, 207; *A Short Account of the Destruction of the Indies*, 62, 114–15; on slavery and labor, 149

Latin America. *See* South America

Latinx identity, US Global South conversation on, 351–52

Lau Kin Chi, 81

law, justification of coloniality under, 120–21

Law Wing Sang, 335

Leclerc, Georges-Louis (Comte de Buffon), 113

Lectura de la Sentencia del Juicio Ético (LSJE), 281–83

Lectures on the Philosophy of History (Hegel), 117–18

Lee Kuan Yew, 17–19, 317–18

legal framework: colonial matrix of power and, 202–4; cosmopolitanism and, 204–6, 237–38, 244–47; dispossession within, 172–77; hierarchy and, 239–40; natural law and, 199–201

lesbianism, Anzaldúa on, 74–75

liberalism: colonial matrix of power and, 77–81; evolution of, 149; Gandhi's response to, 70–73

life rights: decolonial horizons of, 271–80; human rights as, 263–67, 275–80; Juicio Ético Popular a las Transnacionales on, 267–70; nature rights as, 261–67; nuclear nonproliferation and, 605n43; violations of, 258–61

linear global thinking: colonial matrix of power and, 370–73; racism and, 363–70; Schmitt's concept of, 356–57

Little Bear, Leroy, 2

Local Histories/Global Designs (Mignolo), 54–55

local history, Westernization's impact on, 13–14

Locke, John, 77, 120, 244, 259

Logical Investigations (Husserl), xv

London and the Invention of the Middle East: Money, Power, and War, 1902-1922 (Anderson), 122

Lula da Silva, Ignacio, 163, 295–96, 324

rhetoric of modernity and conversation about, 105–7

New York Times, 135

Ngũgĩ wa Thiong'o, 61

Ninety-Five Theses (Luther), 200

Nixon, Richard, 123–24

Nkrumah, Kwame, 64–65

The Nomos of the Earth (Schmitt), 151–52

Non-Aligned Movement, xix–xx; Bandung conference and, 319

noncompliant states, human rights violations and, 260–61

nongovernment organizations (NGOs), 261

nonmodernity, communal concept as, 338–39

Nova Totius Terrarum Orbis Geographica ac Hydrographica Tabula (Visscher), 362

Nueva corónica y buen gobierno (Guaman Poma de Ayala), 241–43

Obama, Barack: colonial matrix of power and, 77; Iraq policy and, 589n45; Israeli relations with, 178–79; Middle East policy and, 167; Pacific Alliance and, 297–98, 311, 322, 607n20; re-Westernization and, 340–42; Syrian invasion under, 606n13; Trans-Pacific Partnership and, 296

Occam's razor, 89, 259

oil development: British imperialism and, 167; Industrial Revolution and, 590n48

Opium Wars, 168–69, 195, 295, 316, 332, 371

Orbis Christianus: cosmopolitanism and, 185–88, 201–4, 243–47; global mapping and, 199–200; hemispheric partitions of East/West and, 308–9, 357–58

organ transplant trade, commodification of life and, 265–67

Orientalism: cartographic partitions, 290–93; colonial difference and, 246; cosmopolitanism and, 206–12; European invention of, 122–23; origins of, 109; in reverse, 287–88

The Origins of Totalitarianism (Arend), 141

Ortelius, Abraham, 367–69

Ottoman sultanate, 105, 114, 116, 122; destitutional framework and coloniality in, 206; nation-state formation and fall of, 166–69

pacha, Tawantinsuyu concept, 241–43, 598n22

Pacific Alliance, 297–98, 311, 322, 607n20

Pahlavi, Reza Shah, 167

Palau, Tomás, 268

Palestinians: Israeli nation-state and, 155–56; land dispossession for, 162; support for, 158–60

Palestine: legalized dispossession in, 172–74; partition of, 167–68; Zionism and, 175–77

Parsons, Talcott, 350

Peace of Westphalia: colonial matrix of power and, 195; cosmopolitanism and, 200, 205, 241; monarchies and church and, 154; nation-state formation and, 170; sovereignty concept and, 246

peace rhetoric, cosmopolitianism and, 225–28

Pearcy, G. Etzel, 349

Peasant Way, 81

pedagogy, decoloniality and, 358

"Pensiero Meridiano" (Cassano), 350

Pérez Esquivel, Adolfo, 267

perpetrator, human rights and role of, 259–61

Philip II (King of Spain), 105, 115

Philip III (King of Spain), 59–60

Philosophical Investigations (Wittgenstein), xv

philosophy, racial classification and, 112–19

Pizarro, Francisco, 105

Planck, Max, 359

Pletsch, Carl, 352

plurinational states: communal principles in, 337–38; decolonialization and, 161–64

pluriversality, 75–76; cosmopolitan localism and, 217–24; cosmopolitan localism and decoloniality, 250–52; de-Westernization and, xi–xii, 196–99; emergence of, 327–30 political theory: de-Westernization and, 322–27; enunciative framework for, 50–51; epistemic foundation of, 4; human rights and, 214–17; imperial foundations of, 319–20; pluriversality and, 124–26; Westernization framework of, 42–43; Western legitimization of entitlement in, 110–12

politics, of alliance, 79–81

polycentric order, pre-Renaissance structure of, 327–28

Pompidou, George, 324

Popular Education Team Pañuelos en Rebeldía, 267–70

Portugal, racism and coloniality of, 112–19

post–Cold War era: de-Westernization and, 315–16; globalism and, 247–50; international politics during, 344–45; Islamophobia and, 100–101; modern/colonial world order in, 194–95

Postcolonial Gramsci, 381, 395–96

post-colonialism, limited validity of, xi–xii

posthuman rights, 256–57

Potsdam Manifesto 2005, 271

poverty and wealth creation, 135–36; human rights and, 255–57

power: coloniality of, 5–7; Quijano's analysis of, 34–36

praxes of living: border thinking and, 246, 353; communal concepts of, 52, 240; cosmopolitan localism and, 191–92; decoloniality and, 229–30; de-Westernization and, 281–82, 327; Fanon and, 71–72; Guaman Poma on, 58; hemispheric partitions and, 312–13; *la facultad* and, 74–75; in Náhuatl philosophy, 30–31; non-Western concepts of, 354–58; organic and cultural praxes, 355–58; racial classifications and, 95; reconstitutions and, 56

Prescott, William, 116–17

Présence Africaine, 64–65

Prinz zur Lippe, Rudolf, 271–72

Prior, Michael, 157, 171

privatized healthcare, 135

psychoanalysis: aesthesic reconstitution co-existence with, 31–34; as cure, 31–32, 636n12; decoloniality and, 625n35; secularism and, 161; sociogenesis and, 449–50; unconscious and, 9–10, 463

purity of blood: Christianity and, 107; nation-state formation and, 165; race and, 74, 111, 123, 330–33

Qin Dynasty, 168–69

Quechua. *See* Tawantinsuyu (Quechua-Aymara)

Quijano, Anibal: on coloniality of power, 27–28, 79, 121; on constitution of colonial matrix of power, 34–51; decolonization and, 16–17, 65; epistemic reconstitution theory of, 4–6, 53–55; historic-structural nodes of, 24–27, 193–99; on modernity and coloniality, 7–8, 300–301, 582n11, 607n22; on racism, 89–93, 107–8, 573n6; on social classification *vs.* social class, xvii–xviii, 97–98; on Spanish colonial invasion, 134–35

race and racism: Bandung Conference discussion of, 319; capitalism and, 88–89, 108–12, 121, 573n7; coloniality of power and, 157; in colonial matrix of power, 27, 88–93, 112–19, 133–36; decoloniality and, 20–21; definitions of, 110–11, 577n17; dispensability of human beings and, 131–36, 144–46; ethno-racial pentagon (United States) and, 123–26; Fanon's analysis of, 70–73; foundational commentaries on, 107–12; geographic partitions and, 363–70; hiercharchies of colonial difference and, 87–88; Holocaust linked to, 138–39; human rights and, 258–61, 262–67, 601n12; international law and, 148; Islamophobia and, 99–101; merging of, 109–12; modern/colonial constructions of, 93–98, 574n17; nation-state formation and hierachies of, 171–72; Nazi genocide and, 146, 151–52; Quijano on, 89–93; of regions and continents, 282–83; triangles of hierarchy in, 91–93,

white homogeneity, nation-state formation and, 161–64

*Who Are We? The Challenges of America's
National Identity* (Huntington), 101

Wiener, Norbert, 136, 145–46, 599n34

Williams, Eric, 133–37

Wittgenstein, Ludwig, xv

World Bank, establishment of, 323

world cartography, evolution in European
Renaissance of, 199–204

World Economic Forum (WEF), 236

World Social Forum, 233–34

World War II, human rights history and,
213

wounds of coloniality: human rights and,
263–67; knowing and sensing of, 3–4,
9–12

The Wretched of the Earth (Fanon), 66,
70–73

Wynter, Sylvia, xx, 65; Man/Human
authority figure of, 145; on race and
racism, 107

Xi Jinping, 196–97, 235, 317, 588n30

zambos, colonial classifications of, 111–12

Zapatista movement, 60–61, 64, 81; decolonization and, 163; democracy ideology
and, 220–24; *Juntas de Buen Gobierno*
(Councils of Good Government) of,
60–61, 70, 242–43

Zhou Enlai, 316

Zionism: historical origins of, 169–72;
Islamophobia and, 100–101; Jewish
identity and, 152–53, 174–77; land dispossession and, 163–64; nation-state of
Israel and, 138–40, 155–56; opposition to,
158–60; racism and concept of, xviii